CONTEMPORARY ESOTERICISM

Gnostica: Texts and Interpretations
Series editors: Garry Trompf, Kocku von Stuckrad, Iain Gardner and Jason BeDuhn

Gnostica publishes works of scholarly interpretations on esoteric movements, including the Gnostic, Hermetic, Manichaean, Theosophical and related traditions. Contributions also include critical editions of texts, historical case studies, critical analyses, cross-cultural comparisons and state-of-the-art surveys.

Published

Contemporary Esotericism
Edited by Egil Asprem and Kennet Granholm

Angels of Desire: Esoteric Bodies, Aesthetics and Ethics
Jay Johnston

CONTEMPORARY ESOTERICISM

Edited by
EGIL ASPREM and KENNET GRANHOLM

For Peter Steele (1962–2010)
"Don't mistake lack of talent for genius"

Published by Equinox Publishing Ltd.
UK: Unit S3, Kelham House, 3 Lancaster Street, Sheffield, S3 8AF
USA: ISD, 70 Enterprise Drive, Bristol, CT 06010

www.equinoxpub.com

First published 2013

Editorial matter and selection © Egil Asprem and Kennet Granholm 2013
Individual contributions © the contributors 2013

All rights reserved. No part of this publication may be reproduced or transmitted in any form or by any means, electronic or mechanical, including photocopying, recording or any information storage or retrieval system, without prior permission in writing from the publishers.

ISBN: 978-1-908049-32-2 (hardback)

British Library Cataloguing-in-Publication Data
A catalogue record for this book is available from the British Library.

Library of Congress Cataloging-in-Publication Data
Contemporary esotericism / edited by Egil Asprem & Kennet Granholm.
       p. cm.
    Includes bibliographical references (p.) and index.
    ISBN 978-1-908049-32-2 (hardback)
  1. Occultism. I. Asprem, Egil. II. Granholm, Kennet, 1977-
    BF1411.C65 2012
    130—dc23
                                            2012019506

Typeset by JS Typesetting Ltd, Porthcawl, Mid Glamorgan.
Printed and bound in the UK by MPG Books Group.

CONTENTS

Contributors ix

1 Introduction 1
Egil Asprem and Kennet Granholm

PART I: TRADITION

2 Constructing Esotericisms: Sociological, Historical and
Critical Approaches to the Invention of Tradition 25
Egil Asprem and Kennet Granholm

3 Inventing Africa: Esotericism and the Creation of an
Afrocentric Tradition in America 49
Fredrik Gregorius

4 Secret Lineages and de Facto Satanists: Anton LaVey's Use of
Esoteric Tradition 72
Per Faxneld

5 Perennialism and Iconoclasm: Chaos Magick and the
Legitimacy of Innovation 91
Colin Duggan

PART II: POPULAR CULTURE AND NEW MEDIA

6 Occulture is Ordinary 113
Christopher Partridge

7 From Book to Bit: Enacting Satanism Online 134
Jesper Aagaard Petersen

CONTENTS

8 Accessing the Astral with a Monitor and Mouse: Esoteric Religion and the Astral Located in Three-Dimensional Virtual Realms 159
John L. Crow

9 The Secrets of Scientology: Concealment, Information Control and Esoteric Knowledge in the World's Most Controversial New Religion 181
Hugh B. Urban

10 Hidden Knowledge, Hidden Powers: Esotericism and Conspiracy Culture 200
Asbjørn Dyrendal

PART III: ESOTERIC TRANSFERS

11 Discursive Transfers and Reconfigurations: Tracing the Religious and the Esoteric in Secular Culture 226
Kocku von Stuckrad

12 Radical Politics and Political Esotericism: The Adaptation of Esoteric Discourse within the Radical Right 244
Jacob Christiansen Senholt

13 New Age Spirituality and Islamic Jihad: Paulo Coelho's *Manual of the Warrior of Light* and Shamil Basayev's *Manual of the Mujahid* 265
Eduard ten Houten

14 Deep Ecology and the Study of Western Esotericism 287
Joseph Christian Greer

PART IV: LEAVING THE MARGINS

15 The Secular, the Post-Secular and the Esoteric in the Public Sphere 309
Kennet Granholm

16 Psychic Enchantments of the Educated Classes: The Paranormal and the Ambiguities of Disenchantment 330
Egil Asprem

17 The New Kids: Indigo Children and New Age Discourse 351
Daniel Kline

18 A Small-Town Health Centre in Sweden: Perspectives on the Western Esotericism Debate 372
Liselotte Frisk

19 Entheogenic Esotericism   392
     Wouter J. Hanegraaff

20 A Deliciously Troubling Duo: Gender and Esotericism   410
     Jay Johnston

   Bibliography, Discography and Filmography   426
   Index   463

CONTRIBUTORS

Egil Asprem is research fellow at the Center for History of Hermetic Philosophy and Related Currents, University of Amsterdam, Netherlands.

John L. Crow is a graduate student at the Religion Department, Florida State University, Tallahassee, Florida, USA. He received his MA at the Center for History of Hermetic Philosophy and Related Currents, University of Amsterdam, Netherlands.

Colin Duggan is PhD research fellow in the study of religions, University College Cork, Ireland. He received his MA at the Center for History of Hermetic Philosophy and Related Currents, University of Amsterdam, Netherlands.

Asbjørn Dyrendal is professor of religious studies, Norwegian University of Science and Technology (NTNU), Trondheim, Norway.

Per Faxneld is PhD research fellow in history of religions, Stockholm University, Sweden.

Liselotte Frisk is professor of religious studies, Dalarna University, Sweden.

Kennet Granholm is assistant professor in history of religions, Stockholm University, Sweden, and docent in comparative religion, Åbo Akademi University, Finland. In 2007–8 he was visiting research fellow at the Center for History of Hermetic Philosophy and Related Currents, University of Amsterdam, Netherlands.

Joseph Christian Greer is PhD research fellow at the Center for History of Hermetic Philosophy and Related Currents, University of Amsterdam, Netherlands.

CONTRIBUTORS

Fredrik Gregorius is visiting researcher in the Department of Sociology, Pennsylvania State University, University Park, Pennsylvania, USA.

Wouter J. Hanegraaff is professor of history of hermetic philosophy and related currents, University of Amsterdam, Netherlands.

Jay Johnston is senior lecturer in the Department of Studies in Religion, University of Sydney, and in the Sherman School of Art History and Art Education, College on Fine Arts, University of New South Wales, Australia.

Daniel Kline received his MA at the Center for History of Hermetic Philosophy and Related Currents, University of Amsterdam, Netherlands. He lives in Vancouver, Canada, where he works as a clinical counsellor.

Christopher Partridge is professor of religious studies at Lancaster University, UK.

Jesper Aagaard Petersen is associate professor at the Programme for Teacher Education, NTNU, Trondheim, Norway.

Jacob Christiansen Senholt is PhD research fellow in the history of ideas, Aarhus University, Denmark. He received his MA at the Center for History of Hermetic Philosophy and Related Currents, University of Amsterdam, Netherlands.

Eduard ten Houten received his MA at the Center for History of Hermetic Philosophy and Related Currents, University of Amsterdam, Netherlands.

Hugh B. Urban is professor of religious studies, Ohio State University, Columbus, Ohio, USA.

Kocku von Stuckrad is professor of religious studies at the University of Groningen, Netherlands. In 2004–9 he was lecturer at the Center for History of Hermetic Philosophy and Related Currents, University of Amsterdam, Netherlands.

CHAPTER 1

INTRODUCTION

Egil Asprem and Kennet Granholm

The academic study of Western esotericism is well into its second decade of professionalization and institutionalization. University departments and study programmes have been established, specialist book series and journals launched, academic societies founded, and several international conferences and panels are organized every year. In addition, scholars in other subdisciplines of religious studies are starting to take notice of the scholarship produced within the field. However, the religious studies scholars who are most likely to take an interest will also notice a striking gap in scholarship on the esoteric: very little research exists on *contemporary* phenomena. Several contemporary currents that can be regarded as historically and/or typologically related to esotericism have been the focus of scholars in other branches of religious studies. For example, sociologists of new religious movements have debated "New Age spiritualities" for decades, and "pagan studies"[1] has in

---

1. So-called "pagan studies" is a problematic field, which often seems more interested in developing (neo)pagan *theology* than conducting unbiased and critical scholarly investigation (for a critical review of the state of the field, see Davidsen, "What is Wrong with Pagan Studies?"). This links to choices of terminology regarding the subject matter. Whereas "neopaganism" is more common among North American scholars, signalling that it is a new religious movement, European scholars (predominantly British) tend to prefer "paganism", often in the plural, in order to show that there are many pagan traditions, and with historical qualifiers such as "modern" or "contemporary" (see Melissa Harrington, "Paganism and the New Age", 437). In this volume we have made the editorial decision to use "neopaganism", partly in order to distance ourselves from what we consider problematic aspects of pagan studies, and partly in order to make it clear that we are dealing with modern religions with no historically valid claim to continuity with their pre-Christian namesakes. It should be noted, however, that the use of "neo" has problems of its own, as it can be taken to imply that some form of semi-uniform "pagan tradition" existed in Europe before the introduction of Christianity, with various expressions simply demonstrating external variations to an essentially similar inner core. This is not the case, of course, and therefore

1

recent years emerged as its own religious studies subfield. Meanwhile, scholars working in the field of esotericism have (with a few notable exceptions) neglected such developments.[2]

The neglect is largely due to the strong historiographical emphasis in previous research on Western esotericism. Although the professionalization of the field has largely come about within religious studies, major scholarly impulses have come from historians of ideas, historians of science, and historians of art – typically specializing in Renaissance and early modern European culture. Expertise in the field has clustered around these lines of historical inquiry, with the most influential definitions and delimitations of the field following suit with the interests of central researchers.[3] In addition, despite an often-stated embrace of interdisciplinarity, an overall reluctance to incorporate social scientific approaches has characterized the field. This has certainly had some repercussions: a fundamental challenge for the study of the esoteric in the present day is that it is not sufficient to simply transpose theories, definitions and methodologies developed for the study of, say, Renaissance magic to analyse contemporary magical practices. In short, studying contemporary phenomena poses both new problems and intriguing possibilities, the challenge to incorporate social scientific theories and methodologies being a central one. It would seem that for a proper study of contemporary esotericism to succeed, several theoretical and methodological concerns need to be addressed.

Starting from these observations, the present volume brings into attention the multifaceted status of esoteric discourse in the contemporary West. The authors combine historical awareness and findings from the historical study of esoteric currents with new theory and methodology required for contemporary issues. The chapters deal with currents and issues of particular importance for understanding the place of the esoteric in today's world, and specifically discuss theoretical and methodological implications raised by the study of contemporary esotericism.

---

we use "pre-Christian religion(s)" when discussing various religious expressions present in Europe prior to the introduction of Christianity. In a few isolated cases "pagan" or "paganism" are used and the reference is then to emic discourse, either historical Christian polemical projections of "the Other", or more current reversals of these polemics that project a non-Christian Self into the past.

2. Examples include Hanegraaff, *New Age Religion and Western Culture*, and much of the work of Olav Hammer.

3. Here we are thinking especially of Antoine Faivre's influential historical definition, which has been criticized for lack of a clear analytic rationale while being conspicuously well suited to cover Faivre's own specific areas of interest. See Faivre, *Access to Western Esotericism*, 10–15; cf. von Stuckrad, "Western Esotericism", 83.

UNRAVELLING PROBLEMS WITH THE STUDY OF ESOTERICISM

As already noted, the relative lack of research on contemporary esotericism from scholars in the field seems to be connected in part with a general reluctance to incorporate perspectives, theories, and methodology from the social sciences. In fact, it is commonplace within the field to encounter at least a mild form of hostility towards social science, although it is seldom developed into an explicit polemic. One resulting problem is that any introductory course on esotericism that aims to deal also with contemporary phenomena cannot rely solely on standard introductory volumes and reference works in the field. As none of these sufficiently address contemporary expressions and concerns, they must be complemented by scholarship from elsewhere, which most often needs to be "translated" to fit overall themes and approaches. Kocku von Stuckrad's otherwise competent *Western Esotericism: A Brief History of Secret Knowledge* (2005) is, for example, rather thin on recent and contemporary developments, although it does end with a general discussion of "Esotericism and Modernity".[4] This is a result of the lack of scholarship in the field in this subject area, and von Stuckrad makes no claim to provide a detailed account here. However, the problem is more acute in Nicholas Goodrick-Clarke's *The Western Esoteric Traditions: A Historical Introduction* (2008), where something in the way of a claim to completeness is made. The book contains a chapter entitled "Ritual Magic from 1850 to the Present",[5] but curiously "the present" seems to end in the 1950s!

The neglect of contemporary phenomena can partly be attributed to the fact that most researchers in the field identify themselves as historians, and often regard the present as outside their area of interest and expertise. This, of course, is a limited view of "history", which, after all, is constantly created. The realm of the historian thus includes the present and the recent past. Another related reason can be sought in the methodological familiarity and "comfort zone" of the strict historian. While historical material may appear "frozen in time", and thus ordered and easier to subject to meticulous scrutiny, tracing lineages, historical relations and so forth, contemporary material will seem chaotic and ever-changing, and consequently more difficult to "catch" in the way one is used to from historical records. An investigation of such material can be frustrating, and can easily appear unorganized and "unscientific".

This historical bias can be exemplified by way of an anecdote from a conference a few years back. A speaker who had presented an overview of Russian esotericism, neopaganism, secret societies, and related publications up to the mid-twentieth century was asked the question: "What about expressions of these trends in contemporary Russia?" The response was simply, "I am a

---

4. von Stuckrad, *Western Esotericism*, 133–46.
5. Goodrick-Clarke, *The Western Esoteric Traditions*, 191–209.

historian, not an anthropologist", thus positioning the question as irrelevant in the context (which, of course, it was not). Whatever the reasons for exclusions of this kind, it seems clear that historical studies from the field of Western esotericism must be combined with scholarship from studies of new religions, "pagan studies" and so on if a more comprehensive picture is sought. In order to succeed, bridges must be constructed to overcome the incongruities in method, theory and approaches that exist between the different segments of complementary scholarship.

The incongruities partly depend on differing disciplinary rationales, with most studies of contemporary "esotericism" being sociologically or sometimes anthropologically informed. The dislike of social scientific approaches in the study of esotericism was already noted. To the present authors, this aversion seems connected to similar biases in the history of religion, which followed the influence of Mircea Eliade. Eliade and the phenomenological school of "history of religion" associated with him tended to oppose sociology due to what was perceived as its inherent "reductionism".[6] In short, sociology was claimed to present the religious as not forming a phenomenon *sui generis*, but instead being an expression of broader social forces. In religious studies at large, this fear of reductionism was heavily discussed and criticized more than twenty years ago, and, despite the occasional local outbreak, aversions of this kind now seem rather dated.[7] In current scholarship on esotericism, however, this "ghost of Eliade" may still be felt – as, for example, when Goodrick-Clarke dismisses "definitions of 'the esoteric' in terms of discourse, social constructions, and legitimacy" because they "lack a hermeneutic interpretation of spirit and spirituality as an independent ontological reality" – that is, refusing to describe "it" as something *sui generis* and irreducible, indeed as "an autonomous and essential aspect of the relationship between the mind and the cosmos".[8]

There seems to be a fear that dealing with sociological issues will in some way diminish or infringe on the value of the subject. As many of the influences of Eliade have been purged – such as his problematic ahistorical approach to history – this simplistic paranoia about sociological reductionism should be discarded as well. Involving sociological perspectives, and looking at the role played by social factors in the formations of the esoteric, does *not* need to mean that one reduces one's subject to these particular social factors. Nevertheless, the accusations of sociological approaches having been reductionist to the extreme are not entirely unprovoked. Looking at sociological studies of the

---

6. See Wasserstrom, *Religion After Religion*, 6, 257n6.
7. For the "reductionism debate", see e.g. Segal, "In Defense of Reductionism"; Idinopulos & Yonan, *Religion and Reductionism*.
8. Goodrick-Clarke, *The Western Esoteric Traditions*, 12, 13. Cf. our continued discussion in Chapter 2 of the present volume.

occult/esoteric we find a strong focus on its "deviance",[9] with Marcello Truzzi even calling it "a wastebasket, for knowledge claims that are deviant in some way".[10] While the notion of deviance, so popular in sociological research of the 1970s, has been largely left aside in specialist sociology on, for example, new religious movements, associated problems remain in sociological research more broadly. Here, for example, "the occult" often stands for little more than supernatural beliefs which are difficult to place into any other category.[11] This, of course, makes "esoteric"/"occult" utterly useless in any meaningful analytical capacity. As Hanegraaff argued over a decade ago, the main problem of these sociological constructs of "the occult" is precisely their neglect, and *preclusion*, of historicity.[12] Despite these obvious prior shortcomings, we stress that the historiographic study of the esoteric could still benefit from sociological perspectives, just as sociological studies need to be informed by the conceptual frameworks and historical awareness developed by historical research.

One aspect of the historiographic study of esotericism which becomes increasingly problematic when we move to contemporary expressions is a predominant focus on elite representatives. In a Faivrean approach, the "esoteric form of thought" is primarily expressed in the intellectual philosophies and theologies of men like Ficino, Pico, Paracelsus, Bruno, Dee, Khunrath, Maier, Fludd, and so on, whereas "lowbrow" folk expressions are typically neglected.[13] This also involves the elevation of originally more popular material to "high culture" when the need arises; the origins of Rosicrucianism from a fictitious "*ludibrium*" (to paraphrase the statement of Johann Valentin Andreae, one of the masterminds behind the Rosicrucian manifestos) might already indicate this tension.[14] Partly this might be due to fewer traces of "lowbrow culture" having survived in historical records, but the overall ethos nevertheless introduces major problems when examining contemporary esotericism. Pamphlets of "New Age spirituality" will undoubtedly compare unfavourably with the philosophy of Ficino, and online message board discussions between contemporary Satanists are less impressive than an arcane letter correspondence

---

9. See e.g. Colin Campbell, "The Cult, The Cultic Milieu and Secularization"; Tiryakian, "Toward the Sociology of Esoteric Culture", 272.
10. Truzzi, "Definitions and Dimensions of the Occult", 245. See the criticism of these approaches to "the occult" in Hanegraaff, "On the Construction of 'Esoteric Traditions'", 29–42.
11. See e.g. McGuire, *Religion*, 121–2; Lynn Schofield Clark, *From Angels to Aliens*.
12. Hanegraaff, "On the Construction of 'Esoteric Traditions'", 41.
13. It is in fact quite noteworthy that there is not more collaboration and overlap between the scholarly communities studying esotericism, and those focusing on medieval and early modern magic and folk traditions – as expressed e.g. by the journal *Magic, Ritual, and Witchcraft* and the organization *Societas Magica*. While the occasional researcher would contribute to both "fields", a separation does seem to exist, and it seems to broadly follow social distinctions along the line of "elite" versus "folk"/"vernacular".
14. See Chapter 2 of this volume for more discussion on this particular theme.

between alchemists in the early modern "republic of letters".[15] This does not, however, automatically imply that such materials are any less important for academic research, and scholars should in any case avoid such biases. As we will suggest, the elite bias becomes particularly problematic when recognizing that contemporary esotericism is intimately, and increasingly, connected with popular culture and new media.

In conclusion, then, the agenda of the present volume is twofold: first, to emphasize the need for expanding the field of Western esotericism to encompass contemporary issues; and second, in so doing, to integrate the study of esotericism firmly with approaches and perspectives from the study of religion more broadly. Not only do we believe that such integration is imperative in order to sufficiently explore contemporary esotericism, but it also seems desirable in order to prevent the field from falling into professional isolation. Avoiding that fate and instead inviting a constructive and integrative dialogue between esotericism research and other subdisciplines of religious studies, especially the social scientific ones, has the promise of benefiting all parties. This volume offers an attempt to open up the field in these ways and provide mutual relevance. In so doing, it will be found to ask more new questions than it will answer.

THE STRUCTURE OF THE BOOK

The volume is divided into four parts, each with a specific focal point. These deal with issues of tradition in esotericism; with the impact of new media and popular culture on the esoteric today; with "esoteric transfers" (i.e. the influence of the esoteric on other social spheres that are traditionally thought of as "non-esoteric" and "non-religious"); and with the esoteric "leaving the margins" in a multitude of ways. While thematically separated, the sections are also tightly interwoven. As will become apparent in reading the book, chapters in one section frequently interact with the themes of other ones, and cross-references between chapters are frequent. Furthermore, there is a red thread running throughout the volume, which attempts to introduce a unity which is more common to monographs than to edited works. Thus, all chapters of the volume deal to some degree with issues of methodology and theory relevant particularly for the examination of contemporary esotericism, while at the same time engaging with associated issues in religious studies at large.

---

15. Cf. Olav Hammer's assessment of the quality of "New Age" creativity, "whereas the Romantic conception was capable of producing works of the greatest beauty, the literary, musical and artistic products of the New Age are sometimes indistinguishable from religious kitsch" (Hammer, *Claiming Knowledge*, 508). On using the new types of text emerging online in research, see Chapter 7 of this volume.

Tradition

The appeal to tradition, particularly connected to lost ancient wisdom, or perennial higher truth, is a central feature of much esoteric discourse, but so is the rhetoric of rationality and notions of progress and growth. Furthermore, claims to tradition are intrinsically linked to questions of identity and positioning in broader discursive fields, including politics and religion. The chapters of this section deal with the claims to, and constructions of, tradition in contemporary esoteric discourse, and elucidate the significance of tradition vis-à-vis conceptions of "modernity".

In Chapter 2, the first chapter of Part I, Egil Asprem and Kennet Granholm provide an introduction to the overall theme, discussing issues of general relevance to the construction of tradition and looking at these issues in the more focused context of the esoteric. Esotericism has historically been deeply connected to the concept of "tradition" in several ways, from a preoccupation with "perennial philosophy" and "ancient sages" on the emic level, to being itself often constructed as a neglected or subversive "esoteric" or "occult tradition" on the etic level. It should, however, be recognized that several different understandings of "tradition" are employed by scholars, and it is necessary to reflect on what is meant by the term before attempting an analysis. For example, anthropologically informed studies tend to use the term "traditional religion" to denote various forms of tribal religions unaffected by modernizing forces, and sociological studies similarly employ the term as a vague referent for "religion in the past". Another general use is simply "tradition" as a synonym for "religion" (e.g. "the Christian tradition" signifying "Christianity"). A common problem is that of homogenization. In anthropological understandings all "tribal religion" can easily be perceived as sharing some essential similarity, whereas in sociological understandings a unified past is projected backward in order to reflect on the fragmentation of modernity.

In their chapter, Asprem and Granholm argue that it is more fruitful to focus on the construction or *invention* of tradition. In the sense of being the creation of human activities, all tradition – in whichever sense the term is used – is of course invented. Intriguingly, instead of existing as separate, autonomous, and independent institutions which scholars may study and leave unaffected, tradition has often been the outcome of processes of invention in which scholars have played pivotal roles. This has sometimes happened actively and intentionally, as in the nationalistically and religiously informed projection of shamanism as a "universal and archaic technique of ecstasy", and at other times unwittingly, as when esotericists are informed by scholarly accounts of the esoteric and align their philosophies and practices accordingly. Today, the role of scholarship in conferring legitimacy on self-identified "esotericists" by providing frameworks for tradition is, perhaps, an inconvenient truth to many scholars in the field, but one that demands more attention. Additionally, when it comes to contemporary inventions of identity and tradition, fictitious sources and popular cultural products are becoming increasingly influential. The inclusion of popular culture in the study of contemporary esotericism, and in particular connected to notions of tradition, furthermore brings old biases of historical research in the field into question.

The creation of religious fiction in constructing ethnic and religious identity is a central theme in Chapter 3. In "Inventing Africa", Fredrik Gregorius deals with the creation of a "primordial African tradition" among African American esoteric spokespersons, a subject matter which has received very little attention from scholars of Western esotericism. Starting with Prince Hall Masonry in the late eighteenth century, Gregorius goes on to discuss Afrocentric developments in the mid-twentieth to the early twenty-first centuries. Particular attention is given to George G. M. James's *Stolen Legacy* from the mid-1950s (and its own legacy in later Afrocentric thought), Maulana Karenga's black nationalist ideas, and Molefi Kente Asante's Afrocentrism. The chapter ends with a discussion of the esoteric notion on the magical qualities of the pigment melanin, based on the ideas of Frances Cress Welsing. A running theme, all the way from Prince Hall to the present day, is the role of Egypt. Gregorius shows how "ancient Egypt" has been a hotbed of racialist polemics, with African American esotericists providing a counterpoint to the common presentations of Egypt as a "white culture". Egypt is presented as having continuity with the rest of "black Africa", and as being the source from which all subsequent "higher wisdom" has been stolen. At times, Afrocentric discussions enter similar problematic fields as white supremacist ones. This is particularly evident in Welsing's melanin theories, where the pigment not only provides superhuman powers, but also presents people of African heritage as "the master race" – infinitely superior not only to Caucasians, but all other "coloured races" as well.

As a point of comparison it is interesting to bring up the early constructions of neopaganism in Germany. Very similar racialist themes were present in the Ariosophic milieu of the early twentieth century (e.g. in the Thule society and the Guido von List-founded Hoher Armanen-Orden).[16] Racialist issues have remained a topic of heated debate in heathen milieus even to the present day.[17]

If the creation of Afrocentric tradition is marked by seriousness, Anton Szandor LaVey's creation of Satanist tradition contains a much more playful element. In "Secret Lineages and de Facto Satanists", Per Faxneld notes the importance of fiction in the Church of Satan's construction of tradition. We also find a dual, and seemingly conflicting, approach to "Satanic lineage". On the one hand, LaVey promotes the newness of his organization and philosophy, essentially claiming it to be the first of its sort, and thus the start of Satanism proper. On the other hand, he also projects a lineage of de facto Satanists back

---

16. Gardell, *Gods of the Blood*, 25–6.
17. *Ibid.* For a discussion on the debate on racialism in contemporary heathenism, see also Asprem, "Heathens up North"; Granholm, "Esoteric Currents as Discursive Complexes".

in history, with the Decadent poets of the late nineteenth century as good examples, and claims a continuity of ideology, philosophy and overall ethos. This apparent conflict is solved in LaVey's openly pragmatic approach to tradition: "you can *choose* your fiction to live by".[18] While LaVey's honesty in this regard is interesting, it would appear that many of his followers have needed a more "traditional" understanding of tradition. The case is that many later self-avowed Satanists have taken LaVey's claims as fact, either intentionally disregarding or simply being unable to grasp the "Black Pope's" sense of irony and sarcasm. This is also true of contemporary competitors in the Satanic milieu, who criticize LaVey's fictional historiography while failing to acknowledge the author's disclaimers in this regard. We also find actors in the milieu who claim to represent "traditional Satanism", which, in an ironic turn of events, is actually a more recent development that LaVey's "modern Satanism". In any case, the pragmatic approach to tradition pioneered by LaVey has also become a mainstay for many in the milieu.

While not having the same type of trickster-like quality as Satanism, the dual appeal of innovation and tradition is arguably even more pronounced in Chaos Magick. In "Perennialism and Iconoclasm" (Chapter 5), Colin Duggan provides both a general historical overview of this relatively unexplored development of occultism, and a detailed discussion of the complex interplay between two seemingly contradicting strategies of legitimacy: on the one hand, Chaos Magicians make use of a fairly standard (at least as far as esotericism goes) perennialist notion of claiming an "age-old tradition", and on the other we find a more complex idea of progress within an "age-old tradition", with new developments superseding older ones. Thus, Chaos Magick can be presented by its practitioners both as being in line with an ancient tradition – with the universalized shaman often functioning as the exemplar – and as an essentially innovative current which still exists in a lineage of ancient truth. The combination of these legitimizing strategies places Chaos Magicians in a position where they can draw on the work of earlier occultists, but at the same time also criticize them for being stagnant, outdated and conservative.

Another interesting feature of Chaos Magick, and one which marks it out as an odd bird in the otherwise often conservative realm of ceremonial magic, is its openness to popular culture as a source of inspiration and an arena for magical practice. Perhaps the most obvious example of the latter is the Scottish comic book writer Grant Morrison. A practitioner of magic, having developed his own particular approach termed "Pop Magic!",[19] Morrison has described his series *The Invisibles* as a "hypersigil".[20] That is, a grand-scale

---

18. LaVey, quoted in Barton, *The Church of Satan*, 96.
19. Morrison, "Pop Magic!". The exclamation mark is part of the name of the "school of magic" itself, with Morrison on his personal webpage (www.grantmorrison.com) spelling it "Pop Mag!c".
20. *Ibid.*, 21.

magical working that has the goal of transforming both the world and the magician. Thus, Chaos Magick already points towards the relevance of popular culture and new media for contemporary esotericism, which is the focus of the next part.

Popular culture and new media

The second part of the volume deals with how esoteric discourses and notions are created, shaped and propagated through late modern communication technologies and new media, and how they are transformed by new channels of mediation. The chapters deal with relations such as esotericism *in* new media (cyberspace), esotericists' *use of* such media, and the new conditions for interaction, innovation and practice that new forms of communication and cultural consumption (i.e. popular culture) entail.

Popular culture plays a pivotal role in religious and cultural change today. However, the ways in which the term "popular culture" is understood vary. The approach favoured by many scholars of religion and popular culture in the last five to ten years puts the focus on the *lived, everyday* experiences of ordinary people.[21] Popular culture is seen as "the shared environment, practices, and resources of everyday life in a given society".[22] The approach also has the advantage of not regarding religion and popular culture, or religion and culture for that matter, as distinct and separate phenomena. One of the major contributions of the study of religion and popular culture is that it provides perspectives on how religiosity can function outside traditional institutional settings. This also highlights problems in earlier studies of the esoteric, particularly the focus on "serious" practitioners and the apparent distinction between "real" and "simulacrum" esotericism. Approaches focusing on the intellectual dimension, on an "esoteric form of thought", automatically seem to posit the necessity of "serious conviction" and intentional agency. An example of this seems present in Henrik Bogdan's idea of the "[m]igration of esoteric ideas into non-esoteric materials", where the presence of "symbols, ideas, or techniques that traditionally are connected to a certain esoteric tradition" in fantasy literature, for example, is not *really* esoteric, as the "esoteric form of thought is not present".[23] Even more explicitly, Antoine Faivre has created a typology of the degrees and extents to which a certain fictional work and its reception should be regarded as "esoteric", based on the intentions of the author and the reader

---

21. E.g. Gordon Lynch, *Understanding Theology and Popular Culture*; Gordon Lynch, "The Role of Popular Music in the Construction of Alternative Spiritual Identities and Ideologies"; Lynn Schofield Clark, *From Angels to Aliens*; Lynn Schofield Clark, "Religion, Twice Removed".
22. Gordon Lynch, *Understanding Theology and Popular Culture*, 14.
23. Bogdan, *Western Esotericism and Rituals of Initiation*, 20.

respectively.[24] Whether or not a producer of popular culture has "authentic esoteric sentiments" is, however, largely irrelevant; the audience may still find inspiration in the material, which can have a causal influence on the development of ideas, mythologies and practices. Furthermore, the increased use of esoteric themes and elements in popular cultural products suggests an increased general interest in the esoteric. By placing the focus on communication rather than on "intent" one avoids problematic issues such as this.

The popularization of the esoteric is at the centre of Chapter 6 of this volume. Here, Christopher Partridge elaborates on the concept of "occulture", first introduced in his two-volume *The Re-enchantment of the West* (2004/5). While building on Colin Campbell's notion of "the cultic milieu", as well as later discussions on the theme by scholars such as Jeffrey Kaplan and Heléne Lööw, Partridge is critical of the focus on deviance and marginality that has been inherent in this concept. Instead, as the title of Partridge's contribution suggests, "Occulture is Ordinary". The author links this idea to late modern societal changes, such as "the turn to the self" and the rise of "post-material values", and details how this all supports the popularization, as well as the increased respectability, of the esoteric. Popular culture plays a central role here, as occulture functions as "a reservoir that is constantly feeding and being fed by popular culture". Thus, the study of the esoteric in the contemporary world must take into account popular culture, just as the study of contemporary religious change must take into account both the esoteric and popular culture. Occulture is, as Partridge suggests, fast becoming the primary mode of religiosity in the "post-Christian West". Ending his chapter with a case study of musician, artist and magician Genesis P-Orridge – who first coined the term "occulture" – Partridge comments on an intriguing feature of the occulture as such: the sites of production and networks of distribution are organized in such a way as to give otherwise "marginal" subcultural figures an unprecedented influence on culture more broadly.

As for the other (but connected) main theme of Part II – new media – it is useful to discuss the concept of mediatization. This concept, which has become central to the study of religion and media in recent years, relates to "the process through which core elements of a social or cultural activity ... assume media form".[25] This means that "the activity is, to a greater or lesser degree, performed through interaction with a medium, and the symbolic content and the structure of the social and cultural activity are influenced by media environments and media logic, upon which they gradually become more dependent".[26] Scholars have distinguished "strong" (or direct) from "weak" (or indirect) mediatization, with the former referring to a situation

---

24. Faivre, "Borrowings and Misreadings", 44–53. This article was part of a special issue of *Aries* on "Esotericism and Fiction" (vol. 7.1, 2007).
25. Hjarvard, "The Mediatization of Religion", 13.
26. *Ibid.*, 13.

where a social or cultural activity becomes so bound to media that it cannot be performed outside of this realm, and the latter to a situation where the activity is not necessarily bound to media but still strongly influenced by it.[27] An example of direct mediatization in the esoteric milieu is online initiations, where an initiate must access the Internet in order to perform the activity. As for indirect mediatization, an example is situations where interpretations of specific esoteric activities are essentially bound in popular cultural readings. While theories of mediatization contain problems, such as the common sociological overemphasis on the novelty of certain phenomena and processes, they correctly point to the need for new perspectives and approaches in studying religion in the information age. This issue is addressed in the next two chapters of the section.

In "From Book to Bit", Jesper Aagaard Petersen (Chapter 7) looks at the use of computer-relayed communication technology in the Satanic milieu, and demonstrates how one finds both continuity and innovation with regard to "offline" communication practices. Internet-based communication is in many ways a continuation of earlier esoteric networks in the forms of "books and periodicals ... suggested reading lists of occult groups; word-of-mouth and bulletin boards in occult shops; seminars, concerts, and fairs; and classified ads in magazines and newspapers". However, it also brings into play factors that are novel, such as the potential to reach larger, transnational (or translocal), audiences, as well as providing potential for new forms and functions of interaction. A major point for the scholar is the potential of online research to provide access to "the previously hard-to-get and difficult-to-see" in ways never before encountered. After all, online communication and networking leave traces of a wholly different order than offline activities do. Petersen highlights the necessity to develop new methodology and approaches when it comes to doing online research on these emerging sources. One of the avenues explored is a quantitative approach to online research, where examining the relative popularity of specific groups and tracing connections between distinct groups is made easier using Internet traffic tracking tools. In a more qualitative approach, Petersen also suggests that instead of simply looking at individual representations, researching online discussion forums provides the possibility to examine interaction in a new way, making it possible to look at how authority negotiations function both in real time and over an extended period.

Chapter 8 continues the discussion of new media and Internet-based communication technologies, but here John L. Crow ventures in a direction different from Petersen's. Starting with a historical look at the occult notion of the "astral plane", Crow moves to discuss emerging practices of "Accessing the Astral with a Monitor and a Mouse". In doing this, a qualitative method

---

27. See Hjarvard, "From Bricks to Bytes", 48–9.

along the lines of "virtual anthropology" is explored. Religion is furiously present online, and, as several scholars have noted, esotericists – particularly neopagans – "are more active on the Internet than any other religious group". Not only does online communication provide the possibility for transnational community, the development and great evolution of online virtual environments in recent times provides the possibility to recast older esoteric notions in new ways. We can observe the creation of cybercovens, but also the meeting of practitioners in virtual worlds such as Second Life. Here, many practitioners have come to describe the cyber realm as analogous to the astral plane, and some even recast their computers as sacred magical objects – with a guaranteed place on their physical altars. We can also see a convergence where vocabulary from the computer world is transposed to the magical, and computer programming comes to be regarded as a magical activity in itself. There is an obvious generational shift here, with younger, computer-literate generations increasingly diverging from older generations of occultists in their approach to magical realities.

Continuing the discussion of the impact of new media, Hugh B. Urban looks at "The Secrets of Scientology" (Chapter 9). Urban has previously made important contributions to the understanding of esotericism in terms of secrecy, particularly from a sociological perspective. In his chapter, Urban extends such analyses by taking a close look at secrecy, information control, and their wider context in social and political struggles for power, in and surrounding the Church of Scientology. In a sociologically informed historical overview, Urban shows how the new forms of communication associated with the Internet has influenced the practice of secrecy in Scientology, particularly complicating its enforcements of information control. Analysing Scientology from the 1950s to the 1980s as a "Cold War religion", preoccupied with, and implicated in, the anxieties and paranoias concerning security, surveillance, and politically motivated deception that characterized the era, Urban pays attention to the espionage war which erupted between the Church and various US government agencies, including the FBI. In contemporary times Scientology has been involved in information wars and attempts at concealment and surveillance on the web, getting increasingly complicated and difficult for the secretive organization in the time of whistle-blowing websites such as Wikileaks and "hacktivist" groups such as Anonymous. Considering these material settings together with the secretive organizational and doctrinal profile of the movement, Urban suggests that the case of Scientology gives us profound insights not just into a controversial new religion but also into questions of religious secrecy and concealment in general. Scientology illustrates that religious secrecy is rarely simply a matter of esoteric gnosis transmitted through isolated groups of initiates far removed from messy social and political contingencies. It is, on the contrary, very often intimately entwined with larger cultural and historical forces, struggles over power, and concrete material interests. Above all, argues Urban, the case of Scientology highlights what he calls (based on the sociologies of Georg Simmel and Pierre Bourdieu) "the dual nature of secrecy" – its double role as both a source of symbolic power and a potential liability for its owner.

Returning to popular culture and occulture, esoteric orders and occult currents are usual suspects in conspiracy theories, whether it be the witches' Sabbath, the Bavarian Illuminati, or secret networks of "Satanic ritual abusers". Online media outlets such as YouTube and specially created "news sites" and discussion forums are currently seething with conspiratorial ideas. In "Hidden Knowledge, Hidden Powers" (Chapter 10), Asbjørn Dyrendal considers multiple relations between esoteric discourse and conspiracy theory in contemporary occulture. While conspiracy theories *about* the esoteric are relatively well known, Dyrendal goes on to consider the considerably less researched area of conspiracy theories *in* esoteric movements, and discusses the possibility (and utility) of analysing conspiracy theory *as* esoteric discourse. The discussion follows three thematic axes, namely the role of *history*, *agency* and *knowledge* in conspiratorial and esoteric discourses. The role of *history* highlights conspiracy theories' function as apocalyptic mythologies of evil, focusing on their construction of secret societies and hidden chains of power through history. Revealing secret history leads to a focus on the nature of *knowledge*, how it is constructed and what its function is in these mythologies. Hidden knowledge about secret agents (of formidable power) furthermore brings in the question of *agency*, particularly how the possession of secretive knowledge increases power. Dyrendal proposes that these topics are good starting points not only for considering conspiracy theories *about* and *in* esoteric movements, but also suggests that they provide questions for whether, and in what sense, it may be useful to view conspiracy theory *as* esoteric discourse. These discussions are carried out on the basis of a wealth of examples from sources as varied as Rudolf Steiner (and his later interpreters), Anton LaVey, Discordianism, and the explicit conspiracy theorists Jim Marrs and David Icke.

Esoteric transfers

Part III of the volume deals with the impact and influence of esoteric discourses, currents and notions on cultural and societal fields, which are commonly regarded as "non-esoteric". One of the analytically most powerful capabilities of the concept of the esoteric is its ability to shine light on the "betwixt and between" (i.e. phenomena that transgress the seemingly impermeable border between the religious and the secular). That there has historically been a fluid area between these two fields is evident by such activities as alchemy and astrology, both of which have played important roles in religious fields as well as in "non-religious" ones such as experimental science, medicine, and politics. Isaac Newton (1643–1727), who was both an alchemist and the greatest physicist of his age, is an even more illuminating example of how these fields can interconnect without, it should be noted, internal paradox. While the hegemonic understanding is that the modern era is characterized by such a decisive divide, even if the past was not, the chapters in this section suggest that this is not necessarily the case, or at the very least that it is a truth in serious need of modification.

In "Discursive Transfers and Reconfigurations" (Chapter 11), Kocku von Stuckrad continues his project of recasting the study of the esoteric from a specialist field to dealing with the European history of religion and culture in a more general sense. From discussing the contemporary erosion of the secularization paradigm, von Stuckrad moves on to consider four central transformations, or reconfigurations, of the "religious field of discourse". These are:

- "Communitarization" – the emergence of new and diverse forms of community, and ideas of community, since the nineteenth century.
- "Scientification" – the professionalization of knowledge claims, as well as the overall hegemony of scientific (or scientificized) knowledge.
- "Aestheticization" – a redefinition of the religious in terms of, for example, emotion and experience as a response to Enlightenment rationalization, providing a new role for it.
- "Public activation" – the "emergence of a public space that is significantly different from earlier forms of public communication", and the "re-entry" of the religious in the secular public arena.

All these developments are highly visible in, and strongly affect, scholarly discourse, rather than being "objectively separated" from it. Von Stuckrad demonstrates his perspective by looking at how esoteric discourse can be found in recent (seemingly) secular discussion. The example provided is the human genome project, which has been given an esoteric dimension by several commentators and participants, discussing genes as "code", the revelation of which provides humanity with "the language of God".

The theme of politics runs as a red thread through the contributions in this section. Von Stuckrad's article deals with cultural politics reframing the societal role and location of the religious, but also with "politics of science" adapting to allow for religious vocabulary. The theme of politics is, however, more explicit in the rest of the chapters of the section.

"What do esoteric phenomena such as Chaos Magick, runic symbolism, Tantric yoga, and the mythical Atlantis have to do with radical right-wing politics?" With this question, Jacob Senholt opens Chapter 12, on "Radical Politics and Political Esotericism" (i.e. the transfers between esoteric discourse and the multifaceted milieus of contemporary right-wing ideological formations). After providing an overview of the many and well-documented historical links that exist between esotericism and right-wing politics up until the middle of the twentieth century, Senholt notes how special aesthetic and mythical connections were forged after World War II, fuelling popular culture and influencing new political and esoteric formations. While the connections between esotericism and the right are relatively well known, Senholt attempts to provide some answers to a question that has remained surprisingly little discussed: *why* do we see this overlap? In order to address this question, Senholt focuses on three ideological formations in contemporary right-wing politics: the European New Right, Radical Traditionalism, and Eurasianism. Considering recent theories that connect esotericism to polemical discourse, countercultural movements, and particularly processes of exclusion and "Othering" grounded in European cultural history, Senholt finds a tentative answer in shared polemicized constructions of history, and narratives of cultural decline and opposition. He suggests that what Wouter Hanegraaff once called the "Grand Polemical Narrative" (i.e. a process which has constructed and reified "esotericism" by a series of polemical exclusions grounded in the battle against "paganism") simultaneously gave rise to counter-narratives, questioning Christian monotheism as well as the intellectual traditions of the Enlightenment. These counter-narratives create some striking affinities between the esoteric and the radical right, which may help account for the overlaps.

Moving from one form of radical politics to another, in Chapter 13 Eduard ten Houten examines the unlikely points of connection between "New Age Spirituality and Islamic Jihad". The focus is on the curious story of how a popular "New Age" inspirational book became a handbook for revolutionary Islamists in the context of the second Chechen war. The *Manual of the Warrior of Light* (1997) was written by the bestselling author Paulo Coelho as a spiritual guide accompanying fictional works such as *The Alchemist, The Pilgrimage* and *The Valkyries*. It has been called a "key" to Coelho's "ideological world", and alleged to have "the same importance for him as the *Red Book* had for Mao or the *Green Book* for Gaddafi". In the hands of Chechen freedom-fighter (or terrorist, depending on the perspective) Shamil Basayev, Coelho's vague spiritual message to the affluent middle classes took on concrete meaning: the "New Age" manual became a call to arms against a physical oppressor – the Russians. Why would a Chechen *mujahid* be interested in the work of a Brazilian Catholic author of "spiritual" fiction? What is the link between the man best known for planning the Beslan school operation in North Ossetia in 2004 – taking 1100 hostages and ending in the deaths of 330 people, many of them children – and Coelho, who was appointed UN "Messenger of Peace" in 2007? Through comparison of the biographies of Coelho and Basayev, as well as the original *Manual* and Basayev's modified "translation" from 2004, ten Houten shows how this at first sight surprising piece of reception history reveals ironic affinities which often remain hidden, but here are brought to the light of day.

Moving to more grassroots political philosophy, Joseph Christian Greer examines "Deep Ecology and the Study of Western Esotericism" (Chapter 14). Greer criticizes earlier scholars who have uncritically connected Deep Ecology with the esoteric, as they in the process singularize the former. Instead, Deep

Ecology, just as esotericism, is a "hotly debated discursive field", in which many actors struggle to enforce their particular interpretation. In short, instead of a singular Deep Ecology we have a great number of competing, and at times contradicting, Deep Ecolog*ies*. Some of these are tied to the esoteric field of discourse more closely than others, but most engage with it in some ways due to polemics on both sides. Greer provides a detailed history of both the term and the "field", including the complexities and polemics it contains, identifying key actors. Some of these, such as "New Age" spokespersons Fritjof Capra and Ken Wilber, Joanna Macy and John Seed's Council of All Beings, and the Wiccan Gus diZerega, are intimately connected to the esoteric milieu. Furthermore, references to James Lovelock's Gaia hypothesis and the physics of David Bohm, which are also often referenced in contemporary esotericism, are commonplace. A particularly interesting example is George Sessions, who while being hostile to notions of a connection between Deep Ecology and "New Age" still draws on Aldous Huxley's *The Perennial Philosophy* and conceives of the former as "a contemporary manifestation of a primordial metaphysic". Despite these affinities, Greer maintains that equating the two fields, or firmly placing one within the other, would be erroneous. Instead, a more sound approach is to regard Deep Ecology and the esoteric as two distinct fields of discourse that sometimes converge.

Together, the chapters in this third section point to interesting future avenues to which reconceptualizing notions of the esoteric, religious, and secular can take us. Furthermore, they demonstrate the utility that the study of the esoteric can have for religious studies more broadly, and beyond, by breaking up the borders between the scientific, political, cultural and religious.

Leaving the margins

Whereas the chapters in Part III deal with esoteric transfers by discussing more marginal phenomena, the final part approaches partly the same theme by looking at something of a "de-marginalization" or "mainstreaming" of the esoteric. This undeviating of the deviant and mainstreaming of the alternative takes place in several different spheres and ways. As Christopher Partridge has noted, when considering the immense popularity of esoteric ideas, "alternative" may not be the most suitable term to describe it.[28] Furthermore, as Marion Bowman and Steven Sutcliffe note; "any talk of 'alternative' spirituality begs the question of normativity in contemporary religion".[29] This final section of the volume aims to demonstrate that the presence of the esoteric needs to be addressed in these discussions.

---

28. Partridge, *The Re-enchantment of the West*, vol. 1, 85; see also Partridge's Chapter 6 in the present volume. Cf. Znamenski, *The Beauty of the Primitive*, xi.
29. Sutcliffe & Bowman, "Introduction", 10–11.

In looking at "The Secular, the Post-Secular and the Esoteric in the Public Sphere", Kennet Granholm (Chapter 15) examines processes by which the esoteric is leaving both academic and cultural margins. The concept of the post-secular has in recent years become central to sociological theorizing about religion in modern societies. Granholm discusses and evaluates at length the meaning and importance of this concept, its relation to the secularization paradigm and its (many) theories, as well as to the place of the esoteric in contemporary culture. Taking a discursive approach to secularization theory, Granholm suggests that the notion of secularization "can be regarded a post-Enlightenment hegemonic discourse – informed by the ideology of *secularism*" – which has helped to create the situation that it tries to describe. In relation to this understanding, he argues that the "post-secular" suggests not a straightforward "return of religion", but rather an awareness of the continued relevance of religion in secular societies, as well as changing perceptions of what actually counts as religion, what functions it may have, and where it is located. Precisely with regard to these relocations and changing perceptions, as well as functions, of religion, Granholm finds that the place of the esoteric is also changing. As explored in some earlier contributions as well, the *mediatization* of the esoteric becomes particularly important as new forms of media are rapidly developed, and new uses and patterns of consumption of culture follow it. Granholm focuses on the increasing presence of the esoteric in popular culture. Analysing esoteric elements of the science fiction franchise *Stargate*, and the film *Avatar* (at the time of writing, the top-grossing movie of all time), also considering their reception, context and spread, Granholm finds there is a strong case to be made that "the esoteric has entered the mainstream, and that esoteric notions resonate with large numbers of contemporary Westerners (and beyond)". To fully appreciate this and other consequences of the post-secular condition on the esoteric might require scholars in the field to reconsider and extend their theoretical presuppositions and choice of methodology.

While paranormal beliefs are often regarded a matter for uneducated people, Egil Asprem shows in Chapter 16 that some of these are more properly characterized as the "Psychic Enchantments of the Educated Classes". Asprem demonstrates by way of statistical data that some paranormal beliefs are actually more common among those with high education, including in the natural sciences. Even the influential "new atheist" spokesperson Sam Harris is seen to entertain an ambiguity towards "psychic phenomena", suggesting that his opposition to religion rests on a very restricted understanding of that term. What is the reason for these initially surprising positive correlations between paranormal belief, high education and even claims to irreligion? Asprem seeks the answer in the emergence of modern parapsychology in the 1930s, which he links to the "intersection of two parallel processes": the disenchantment of esoteric discourse, and attempts to re-enchant science. As a prospective scientific discipline, parapsychology provided a means of "scientific sanitization" of certain occult beliefs, making them more acceptable to the educated public. The invention of new technical nomenclature to cover a number of "occult abilities" was important in this respect, even giving rise to the names of some paranormal phenomena which show up significantly in polls of beliefs: "telepathy" and "extra-sensory perception". Furthermore, Asprem shows how the presence of parapsychological beliefs in academia cannot be seen solely as an "incursion from the outside"; it is rather the result of developments occurring *within* academia itself, with relation to a broader esoteric, occultural milieu. While questioning the notion that science has enforced a "disenchantment of the world", this simultaneously suggests that occulture, which is commonly seen as spreading on a "folk" or "popular" level, has important nerve centres inside academic (presumptively secular) "elite" culture as well.

The much neglected subject of children and concepts of childhood in esoteric discourse is the focus of Daniel Kline's Chapter 17, on "The New Kids". In the wake of the "New Age movement", a peculiar discourse on gifted *Wunderkinder* with special needs and psychic powers emerged: the "Indigo children". The notion of Indigo children can be traced to the self-proclaimed "synesthete" Nancy Ann Tappe. In *Understanding Your Life Thru Color* (1986), Tappe invented a typology of personality traits corresponding to colours which, it was claimed, could be clairvoyantly seen in peoples' auras. She observed that children with previously unknown indigo auras had suddenly started to appear, "indicative of 'a new breed of children' whose 'process is to show us tomorrow'". Focusing on the Indigo Children (with mention of the "Crystalline Children", "Star Kids", "Earth Angels" and other later additions to this evolving discourse), Kline traces connections between modern esoteric thought and the history of childhood. The increased politicization of children and the commercialization of "New Age" discourse together appear as particularly important for understanding the discourse on Indigo Children. As the Indigos are usually considered a subset of the generation born in the late 1970s or later, Kline considers the notion that the Indigo discourse is "a manifestation of the failures of the 'baby boomer' countercultural generation of the 1960s and 1970s", who failed to manifest their ideological aspirations and have since projected "their hopes for saving the world upon their children". At the same time, the category of the Indigos has served a function of sacralizing "problem children" – particularly during the increase of attention deficit with hyperactivity disorder (ADHD) and attention deficit disorder (ADD) diagnoses, but also with reference to diagnoses such as autism. Getting connected to the commercial aspects of contemporary "spiritual" and "alternative" culture, the Indigo counter-diagnosis has given rise to a host of special day-care offers, training programmes, toys and games, designed to facilitate these "misunderstood" children of presumptively messianic significance.

In Chapter 18, by drawing on empirical, localized field research on "A Small-Town Health Centre in Sweden", Liselotte Frisk examines the usefulness of conceptualizations of the esoteric. Frisk pursues three main arguments in her chapter. First, while contemporary spirituality and particularly "New Age" has been conceived of as a "part of" Western esotericism (i.e. as modern or contemporary esotericism), in the *historical* sense of the word, esotericism should rather be seen as one among several other sources of *influence on* contemporary spirituality. Second, the focus on *gnosis* and experience in attaining "higher knowledge", common in some of the typological and discursive approaches to esotericism, should be linked to a broader discussion of "religious experience" and emotion, which is currently attracting new interest in the study of religion. Third, a focus on deviance, "margin–mainstream" conflicts and rejected knowledge, often discussed as a structural feature in esoteric discourse, should be brought into a broader discussion of tension between religious groups and mainstream society, and, increasingly in contemporary society, should be questioned and nuanced. The final conclusion of the chapter is that Western esotericism as a field of research could benefit from, and contribute to, ongoing discussions in religious studies by combining with select sociological research from other fields. Frisk calls for a further discussion about different kinds of criteria which could be used in this context, and welcomes a more inclusive dialogue with other approaches in religious studies.

In a programmatic article Wouter J. Hanegraaff in Chapter 19 calls for serious scholarly attention to what he calls "Entheogenic Esotericism". Noting a striking neglect of studies on the use of psychoactive substances in religious movements generally, Hanegraaff argues that an important and analytically interesting field of religious practice and innovation has been precluded by generations of scholars due to biases based largely on political circumstances as well as crypto-Protestant stereotypes of what legitimately counts as "religion". In his chapter, Hanegraaff tries to ameliorate the situation by suggesting the term "entheogenic religion", which may be subdivided into a stricter and a wider sense: in the wide sense, religious practices concerned with generating a state of ἐνθουσιασμός ("enthusiasm") are well known and common, utilizing a number of different techniques, including rhythmic drumming, ritual prayer and incantations, meditation, or breathing techniques. The ritual use of substances is only one such technique, and constitutes entheogenic religion in a stricter sense. Revising his own position on "New Age religion", and supporting with cases taken from neoshamanism, Hanegraaff argues that there is much circumstantial evidence to suggest that entheogenic practices in the strict sense have continued to influence modern and contemporary esotericism after the "war on drugs" made explicit references to such practices hazardous. The conclusion is that "specialists in the field of contemporary religion should become aware of their inherited blind spots regarding the role that entheogens have been playing in these contexts for half a century", and refine a hermeneutically suspicious attitude in order to study this much neglected aspect of the religious field.

Finally, in "A Deliciously Troubling Duo", Jay Johnston (Chapter 20) deals with an issue of acute need of treatment in the study of esotericism: gender.

Despite acquiring very little attention from scholars, discourses of gender have been of a considerable significance for esotericism in general, and surface as particularly important in relation to much of what is covered by contemporary esotericism as well. As Johnston points out, the "masculinity = culture = rationality and femininity = nature = intuition" stereotypes have been common in much of esotericism – but can also be found in the trope, often reified by scholars, of men as "occult scientists" who actively control their world by the use of magic, and women as "intuitive witches" who are passively and emotively guided by their surroundings. As such, scholarly accounts here adhere to stereotypical representations of gender and gender roles. Johnston's chapter delves into the deep (and, for many, unknown and seemingly dangerous) waters of feminist theory, dealing not only with how the approaches in question can be used to shed light on gender issues, but also how they may help in rethinking other aspects of esotericism. In terms of the field in general, Johnston notes how the common conduct of positioning the esoteric as the "other" of "the dominant discourse" both feminizes and sexualizes the discursive field of esotericism. In the end, Johnston proposes to "queer the esoteric", by applying queer theory's project of subverting problematic binary categories and dualistic logic to esotericism itself. The study of esotericism is already – at least purportedly – engaged in a project similar to queer theory, in terms of rethinking binaries in cultural and religious history. Johnston further argues that queering of the discipline might nevertheless be in order, particularly since "gender identity markers … remain resolutely normative/deviant and fixed" in most scholarship on contemporary esotericism.

Together, the chapters in this fourth and final part highlight both processes of the esoteric leaving cultural and religious margins in the West, and the benefits perspectives from the study of the esoteric could offer religious studies in general by leaving the margins of academia: Granholm suggests that the development of the study of the esoteric, as well as the growing acceptance of and interest in esotericism by the general public, is an example of "post-secular" academic and societal trends; Asprem shows that parapsychology does not simply represent an "alien incursion" into science, but instead a development in "elite" scientific discourse, and that even radical atheist spokespersons such as Sam Harris can harbour interest in phenomena which could be termed esoteric; the Indigo Child discourse discussed by Kline has breached the mainstream and connects to broader "sacralizing" discourses of childhood; Frisk's example of the health centre *Hälsogränden* shows that esoteric elements peacefully coexist with non-esoteric ones, and are growing in mainstream acceptance; Hanegraaff discusses how practices neglected by scholars have probably had an immensely larger impact on contemporary religion than acknowledged, and how scholarly perspectives need to be modified in order to address this; and Johnston proposes to interrogate the gender biases of esoteric discourse (and its attendant scholarship) to properly "queer the esoteric" and trouble the binary logic of deviancy connected to it.

CONCLUDING REMARKS

While this volume covers much ground, the theme of contemporary esotericism is too broad to be treated in any sort of comprehensive manner in a single volume. With the main criterion being an interest for theoretical and methodological innovation and reflection we have tried to include as many relevant themes as possible, but the reader will undoubtedly notice omissions. We will briefly discuss some of the most glaring ones.

First, the reader will notice that the focus is still rather heavily biased in the direction of intellectualist approaches, while those focused on practice, and particularly anthropological perspectives, are, with only a couple of exceptions, missing. Here, luckily, a lot of material continues to be produced in other subfields of religious studies (again including "pagan studies"), and within anthropology. Nevertheless, a firmer integration of anthropological studies of, and approaches to, contemporary esotericism, should certainly be embraced by a future work in this field. It should also involve a critical and careful engagement with the theoretical and conceptual work which has been made in anthropology, including cognitive anthropology (and the cognitive study of religion more broadly), which often concern issues that seem to have relevance for the esoteric. This goes for mainstay notions in anthropological research, such as "magic" (and its many differentiations), "participation", "ritual", etc.

Second, a reader familiar with the field of Western esotericism in its historiographic form might notice the general lack of discussions of lineages, currents, historical relations, continuity, and so forth, which are otherwise common in the field. While authors do deal with historical issues, we have chosen to go for a more "externalist" approach. That is, instead of meticulously investigating specific, isolated phenomena that may have some claim to consistency, continuity and autonomy over time, we have instead encouraged looking at phenomena in their particular and broader cultural and societal contexts. This is not to preclude altogether the relevance and interest of "internalist" approaches focusing on specific "traditions" or "currents". However, it seemed to us that a work of the present kind ought to be a priority, as internalist approaches to occultist, neopagan, or "spiritual" currents are hardly difficult to find elsewhere. Furthermore, our conviction is that the approach opted for will make the work – and in extension the study of Western esotericism as a field – more relevant for religious studies generally. In this way we also seek to continue the field's genuine potential for interdisciplinary research, by bringing it up to date on contemporary contexts ranging from popular culture and religion, to science and politics.

Finally, the reader will notice that the concept of esotericism/esoteric is not defined conclusively anywhere between the two covers of this book. This is no accident, but instead a conscious choice. In most recent approaches, "the esoteric" is not regarded a coherent "tradition", nor even a semi-coherent pseudo-tradition. Instead, most approaches have moved away from rigid and static definitions – such as the one introduced by Antoine Faivre, which dominated the field in the 1990s – and instead adopted more inclusive perspectives. In this book we can see the coexistence of three main theoretical approaches that have all emerged during approximately the last half decade. Together they could be considered the groundwork for something of a "new paradigm" in the study of the esoteric in Western culture. Named after their main spokespersons, these are:

1. The von Stuckrad approach. Here the esoteric is used as an analytical tool, consciously constructed by the scholar to investigate processes of identity formation on the broader European religious and cultural field. "The esoteric" becomes an instrument by which one can avoid the largely untenable focus on more or less monolithic "traditions", which seemingly overshadow smaller developments, and instead examine the inherent pluralism of European religious and cultural history. In von Stuckrad's application, the esoteric is construed to focus on discourses concerned with the "secretive dialectic of concealment and revelation" and "perfect knowledge",[30] regardless of which cultural fields these discourses might show up in.
2. The Hanegraaff approach. As above, the focus is not on the esoteric "in itself". Instead of stipulating an analytical construct, the focus is on the complex historical processes which have themselves constructed and created the notion of "the esoteric" in Western culture. Important to this "constructionist" approach are certain polemical processes grounded in the Reformation and the Enlightenment projects, whereby certain phenomena have been marginalized as "rejected knowledge", and thus become the source for later constructions of "esoteric" and "occult tradition", and later for the study of esotericism itself. As with the von Stuckrad approach, this perspective can be used to shine light on the complexities of European cultural and religious history which have typically remained veiled in earlier approaches.
3. The Partridge approach. In this approach, the focus is on contemporary processes of cultural and religious change. Designed to analyse religious expression in the present day rather than in distant historical periods, the approach looks at how previously marginalized phenomena and notions get popularized, and how the esoteric functions as part of an occultural reservoir – operating mainly through popular culture – which is used to construct beliefs, practices and identities. In this, the Partridge approach is strongly embedded in social scientific theory and method, whereas the previous ones are grounded in discourse theory and strict historiographical research respectively.

---

30. von Stuckrad, *Locations of Knowledge in Medieval and Early Modern Europe*, 67.

All three approaches derive from the mid-2000s. Von Stuckrad first presented his model in the article "Western Esotericism: Towards an Integrative Model of Interpretation" in 2005.[31] Hanegraaff presented his in the article "Forbidden Knowledge: Anti-Esoteric Polemics and Academic Research", also in 2005, which was further developed in a couple of articles[32] before finding full expression in the book *Esotericism and the Academy* (2012). Partridge's model is presented in his two-volume *The Re-enchantment of the West* in 2004/5.[33] All three explore novel theoretical and methodological avenues, opening up the study of the esoteric not only to religious studies, but also to other fields in the humanities and social sciences, thus providing, as the contributions in this volume demonstrate, broad analytical application. Furthermore, all three approaches steer away from providing a conventional substantial definition of the esoteric, instead going for more fluid and open-ended perspectives. This is also why the three approaches do not seem to clash, but rather complement one another, dealing with different areas and having different, though compatible, applications. It is in this "new paradigm", polyvalent and open-ended, as demonstrated in this volume, that the study of the esoteric has its greatest potential of contributing to and combining with other broader fields of scholarly inquiry.

---

31. See also von Stuckrad, *Locations of Knowledge in Medieval and Early Modern Europe*; von Stuckrad, *Western Esotericism*.
32. See Hanegraaff, "The Trouble with Images"; Hanegraaff, "The Birth of Esotericism from the Spirit of Protestantism".
33. See also Chapter 6 in the present volume.

CHAPTER 2

CONSTRUCTING ESOTERICISMS

SOCIOLOGICAL, HISTORICAL AND CRITICAL APPROACHES TO THE INVENTION OF TRADITION

Egil Asprem and Kennet Granholm

> [N]ovelty is no less novel for being able to dress up easily as antiquity.[1]

"Esotericism" is often linked with "tradition". References to "hidden" or "perennial" traditions abound on the emic level, and often enough esotericism has itself been conceived of as constituting a "tradition" traceable through history. These two general tendencies hide a web of interrelated questions, which can be probed from the perspectives of sociology and history. In the present chapter, we chart some of the most important of these, aiming at a comprehensive overview of the problems surrounding the notion of "tradition" in the field of esotericism and pointing at ways to deal with them.

Our approach is therefore synthetic, and ploughs through several layers of discussions. First, we discuss briefly the vague and problematic uses to which the term tradition is often put. This brings us to a discussion of attempts to operationalize the term in the context of sociology. We generally find that a lack of historical awareness is detrimental to sociological uses of "tradition"/"traditional", although the more nuanced notion of "detraditionalization" and attendant processes does have some promise. After pointing out shortcomings of these conceptualizations of tradition, we turn to a critical constructivist approach emphasizing the *inventedness* of traditions. Drawing on the approach pioneered by Eric Hobsbawm,[2] and the applications of similar approaches to religion by Olav Hammer and James Lewis,[3] and to esotericism by Hammer,[4] we recognize its strong critical potential and call for more systematic scrutiny of the social, material, contextual and situated background

---
1. Hobsbawm, "Introduction", 5.
2. Hobsbawm & Ranger, *The Invention of Tradition*.
3. Lewis & Hammer, *The Invention of Sacred Tradition*.
4. Hammer, *Claiming Knowledge*.

25

of the construction and claim of tradition in esoteric discourses. Moving then from "etic" discussions of the application of concepts to the "emic" level, we review Wouter J. Hanegraaff's recent work[5] on the formation of "esotericism" from changing discourses on knowledge and truth in European history, and draw out some implications for the study of tradition. As Hanegraaff also argues, the thesis has consequences for assessing the way scholars have construed their object of study in the twentieth century. We go on to discuss how the notion of an "esoteric/occult tradition" may in fact be seen as the result of these prior constructions of "ancient wisdom narratives" and their uses (*pro* and *contra*), sometimes with the overtones of perennialism still intact. These discussions culminate in a case study which emphasizes the *co-production* of tradition by scholars and practitioners: the construction of "shamanism" as a category by nationalistically driven folklorists, "religionist" historians of religions and anthropologists "gone native".

This is, however, not the only way in which scholars take part in construction. Focusing also on those who have had no intention or desire to found new religious trends, and even been explicitly adverse to the idea, we argue that the very existence of our field and our strategic uses of terms such as "esotericism" in particular have facilitated, through grateful reception among practitioners, a process by which "esotericism" is *becoming an object* in a sense which it arguably was not before. Finally, we round off our series of discussions by taking a final look at the role of fiction and popular culture in constructing tradition. Together, these latter points (the role of scholarship, fiction, and popular culture) mark out particularly important areas for the construction of traditions in contemporary esotericism.

THE MANY FACES OF TRADITION

The term "tradition" has been associated with a large number of different meanings in both common speech and specialist literature. A plurality of conceptualizations of tradition exists in scholarly circles, often bound up in specific disciplinary concerns and preferences. Starting with conceptualizations closest to general dictionary understandings, "tradition" can be described as:

> [A]nything which is transmitted or handed down from the past to the present ... [including] all that a society of a given time possesses and which already existed when its present possessors came upon it and which is not solely the product of physical processes in the external world or exclusively the result of ecological and physiological necessity.[6]

---

5. Hanegraaff, *Esotericism and the Academy*.
6. Shils, *Tradition*, 12.

The standard definition thus follows closely on the etymological origin of the term, with the Latin verb *tradere* meaning "to hand over" or "deliver".[7] This general understanding, however, seems hardly analytically useful.

Another common understanding, relating specifically to the field of religion, is when "tradition" functions simply as a synonym for a particular religion.[8] For example, "Islamic tradition" may simply denote the religion Islam. This use is doubly problematic, as it tends to homogenize its subject, while at the same time making a more analytically focused use of the term more difficult. Sometimes the homogenizing aspect of this use of the term is even more drastic, as when "Western religious tradition" is used to refer solely to Christianity.[9]

A third understanding, derived from the discipline of anthropology and still in use in some historiographic research informed by the discipline, is the use of "traditional religion" to denote religious expressions which are (seemingly) unaffected by (Western) modernizing influences. The goal is then to examine the particularities of pre-modern social, cultural and religious organization, often with a focus on the role played by oral transmission of knowledge and culture in non-literate societies. Sometimes the findings are then used to gain insight into what pre-modern European society might have looked like, or even getting to the "origin" of human religiosity (a kind of primitivism which connects to scholarship on "shamanism", which will be discussed in more detail later on). In part, this attempt to discard the more pejorative terms "primitive religion" and "illiterate societies" is admirable, but it is still problematic. The projection of "traditional societies", whether they be pre-modern Western or current non-Western ones, tends to say more about the scholar's perceptions of self and the society he/she comes from than accurately describing the society/religion under actual investigation. Thus, the projection of "traditional religion" is problematic both in potentially homogenizing its subject (i.e. presenting "traditional religion" as a more or less uniform category) and in being essentially bound up in colonialist discourse whereby the self is created by the construction of the Other (i.e. "modern" versus "traditional").

The sociology of religion has inherited much from the early anthropological and historical perspectives on tradition, although lacking the somewhat more complex historical model of "eras". Instead, we often deal with modernity and "that which comes before", resulting in a curiously homogeneous-looking past.[10] This is a natural result of sociology's preoccupation with the

---

7. Valliere, "Tradition", 9267.
8. *Ibid.*, 9268.
9. See e.g. Richard H. Roberts, "Body", 216–21.
10. For the simplification of "the past" in sociological theory, and in particular secularization theory, see Granholm's article in the present volume. A good example is Steve Bruce's assessment that most social scientists agree that "modern societies are less religious than traditional ones" (Bruce, *Religion in the Modern World*, 52).

present (and sometimes future), but is very problematic in containing simplified accounts of the past, which are often based on little or no empirical evidence. This, of course, is problematic for sociological accounts of modern social change as well: how are we to determine what is changing and how it is changing, if our view of the past is flawed? Consequently, it is not strange that "the notion of tradition has received little systematic attention in the literature of sociology and social theory".[11]

DETRADITIONALIZATION, DISEMBEDDING AND RE-EMBEDDING: A FURTHER NOTE ON SOCIOLOGY

While sociology is often hampered by a degree of historical naïvety, some of its perspectives can be put to good use when informed by historical awareness. In the present discussion of operationalizing concepts of tradition, this applies to the concept of *detraditionalization*, which, as most sociological terms, refers to a process of societal transformation – in this case primarily changes in perceptions of authority. One thing that the concept offers is an analytic distinction between "religion" and "tradition". Thus Paul Heelas and Linda Woodhead distinguish between *"strongly traditionalized* religion", which "involves faith in knowledge and wisdom taken to be transmitted from the transcendent and authoritative past", and *"strongly detraditionalized* religion", which "turns elsewhere for authority".[12] While commonly linked to secularization, detraditionalization is distinct in that it "has to do with the transformation not the disappearance of religion".[13] It also does not, in contrast to many secularization theories, imply a necessary decrease in the impact of religion.

In Heelas's working definition, detraditionalization "involves a shift of authority: from 'without' to 'within'", as well as "the decline of the belief in pregiven or natural orders of things".[14] This means that authority, when "detraditionalized", is rooted in individual experience and subjective validations, rather than in external standards of shared cultural custom. A problem is that Heelas's work is informed by a simplified distinction between "religions of difference", "religions of humanity" and "spiritualities of life",[15] which demonstrates obvious value judgements. Heelas clearly regards "spiritualities of life" more favourably, and as forms of religiosity which suit late modern life better, whereas "religions of difference" are deemed conservative, dogmatic and repressive.

---

11. Thompson, "Tradition and Self in a Mediated World", 91.
12. Woodhead & Heelas, "Detraditionalization", 342.
13. *Ibid.*, 346.
14. Heelas, "Introduction", 2.
15. See Heelas, "The Spiritual Revolution" for a discussion of these categories, and Heelas, *Spiritualities of Life* for a more thorough discussion of the latter.

In Heelas's view, detraditionalization is dependent on the possibility of reflection on one's situation, and is accentuated by multiculturalism and the pluralization and fragmentation of worldviews and values it brings, as well as the commodification of culture and religion in "late capitalism".[16] The multitude of possible outlooks serves to diminish the power of exclusivist and hegemonic claims to truth. This is also facilitated by previously connected spheres of life becoming increasingly differentiated and relegated to their own separate domains – with divisions between home and work, private and public, high and mass culture, as well as concepts of race and national identity, becoming influential social realities.

A pair of terms that could be linked to sociological discussions of detraditionalization, and which may even be more useful, is "disembedding" and "re-embedding". These terms refer to linked processes whereby certain cultural or religious elements are separated from their various contexts (disembedded) and situated in new ones (re-embedded). Here historiographic awareness, including from the study of the esoteric, can greatly augment sociological perspectives. Sociologists tend to regard the processes of dis- and re-embedding as in some way characteristic of modernity.[17] While this is true in the sense that the processes certainly seem to have accentuated in modernity, a look at esoteric actors demonstrates that this practice has been commonplace among so-called esotericists for a very long time, and in fact seems to be a driving dynamic in internal cultural innovation – from the translation and incorporation of the Hermetic texts, and the development of a Christian Kabbalah, to the esoteric reception of yoga and Buddhist doctrine in the late eighteenth and through the nineteenth century. Even more broadly, processes of dis- and re-embedding seem to be intrinsically linked to concepts of "syncretism".[18]

The concept of detraditionalization, particularly when coupled with the notions of dis- and re-embedding, can thus be used to make sense of the changing role of the esoteric today, and to align the study of the esoteric to sociological approaches to religious and cultural transformation. If detraditionalization is taken to imply a shift from "external" to "internal" modes of authority, and late modernity is characterized by this process, then the *popularization* of the esoteric[19] is made more understandable. With a focus on individual experience often paramount, esoteric discourse would furthermore seem to be a perfect fit with late modern individualistic sensibilities. If accentuation of the willingness to "pick and choose" elements from many different religions, as explicated by the processes of dis- and re-embedding, is part of

---

16. Heelas, "Introduction", 4–5.
17. See e.g. Giddens, *The Consequences of Modernity*, 21–9.
18. For discussions of these concepts drawing on the context of estoericism, see Asprem, "*Kabbalah Recreata*"; cf. Petersen, "'We Demand Bedrock Knowledge'", 102–9.
19. See Chapter 6 of the present volume.

this process of detraditionalization, then the inherent eclecticism of esotericism is an even better fit for the ethos of the late modern citizen. Furthermore, this eclectic function was in place long before "modernity" (as understood in a sociological sense). In fact, this may amount to a criticism of Heelas's understanding of detraditionalization, as the de facto disembedding of cultural data and their re-embedding in new contexts has very often been intrinsically linked with specific esoteric claims to *tradition* – particularly forms of perennialism, as we discuss at length later in this chapter.

While we should thus keep the above discussion in mind, the problems mentioned suggest to us that quite different analytical perspectives on "tradition" are needed for our concerns. We suggest that a fruitful way to go is to follow a critical constructivist course, focusing on the ways in which "traditions" are constructed in specific historical, social and cultural contexts, and the ways they are claimed by situated spokespersons, rather than trying to use the term as an unproblematic analytic term to be employed by the scholar for picking out features or developmental traits in a given "religion" or "culture".

INVENTING TRADITION

In a seminal collection of essays from 1983, Eric Hobsbawm and Terence Ranger launched a serious scholarly interest in the *inventedness* of tradition, and its social, historical and cultural significance.[20] The authors noticed how a large number of "traditions" in modern society (especially connected with state, government and national culture and identity, which appeared to present an aura of long-standing continuity with the past) were, upon further scrutiny, in fact constructed in the relatively recent past. The invention of traditions was seen to be intrinsically linked to nationalist projects of the eighteenth and nineteenth centuries, and as responses to the great upheavals of political and social revolutions, with Hobsbawm even pointing to a veritable "mass-production of tradition" in the period between 1870 and 1914.[21]

The notion of "invented tradition" was originally defined by Hobsbawm as "a set of practices, normally governed by overtly or tacitly accepted rules and of a ritual or symbolic nature, which seek to inculcate certain values and norms of behaviour by repetition, which automatically implies continuity with the past".[22] The focus was on the grand scale of society and on large, often "secular" institutions. Nevertheless, as a general approach to researching traditions a focus on invention has significant value for the study of religion, as

---

20. Hobsbawm & Ranger, *The Invention of Tradition*.
21. Hobsbawm, "Mass-Producing Traditions".
22. Hobsbawm, "Introduction", 2.

well as the study of esotericism.[23] As Olav Hammer and James R. Lewis note, every single known religious system cultivates invented traditions of one sort or another. Often links are created to mythic or romanticized pasts; in addition we find a strong tendency to misattribute central texts, be it through the creation of pseudepigraphic texts, the attribution of anonymous material to a founding figure (e.g. Siddhartha, L. Ron Hubbard), a revered historical authority (e.g. Aristotle), or even non-existing or mythical persons (e.g. Moses, Hermes, Zoroaster).[24] As we shall see later in this chapter, this kind of attribution has been a central part in the making of esoteric genealogies of higher knowledge, emphasizing *prisci theologi* (whether mythical or real) like Hermes and Zoroaster, or referring to entirely fictitious "secret traditions", such as in Rosicrucianism.

While Hobsbawm focused on how invented traditions "inculcate certain values and norms of behaviour by repetition", analyses of such inventions in esotericism have typically focused on the function they play in legitimating authority and establishing an aura of unique authenticity. An extensive study of "the appeal to tradition" as a rhetorical strategy in modern esoteric discourse was provided by Olav Hammer in *Claiming Knowledge*, which analysed cases from the Theosophical appeal to "ancient sages" (which in 1875 were Chaldaeans, hermeticists, and kabbalists but had morphed into Hindu yogis and secret Tibetan masters by 1888), the construction of a traditional lineage for the chakra system as used in modern occultism, and the abundant reference to "imaginary utopias" such as Egypt, India, Tibet and "primitive" societies of native Americans.[25]

At the basis of Hammer's analysis is a sharp distinction between emic and etic historiography: the "accounts of believers" about the provenance of their doctrines and rituals constitute emic historiography, and is contrasted with the "secular studies" of professional, non-confessional historians.[26] Recognizing the strong critical potential of this notion – something which often tends to be downplayed even by some of the strictest historicists in the field – Hammer makes sure to note that the emic and etic historiographies are often in direct conflict, not only over emphasis and interpretation, but about basic facts of history as well. The origin of Rosicrucianism may stand as a clear example of this from the field of esotericism: in contemporary esoteric orders which claim a Rosicrucian heritage, such as the Ancient Mystical Order Rosae Crucis (AMORC) or the Hermetic Order of the Golden Dawn, one typically

---

23. See especially Lewis & Hammer, *The Invention of Sacred Tradition*, which explicitly forms an expansion of Hobsbawm and Ranger's project – thematically to the field of religion, and historically beyond the modern period. Remarkably, it took 24 years for a volume of this kind to materialize.
24. Hammer & Lewis, "Introduction", 2–4.
25. Hammer, *Claiming Knowledge*, 85–200.
26. *Ibid.*, 86.

finds a literal belief that the Rosicrucian manifestos were in fact written by a pre-existing secret society with roots in the Middle Ages or possibly even further back.[27] In etic scholarship, however, doubts that the Rosicrucian order proclaimed by the manifestos was a fiction, which became a self-fulfilling prophecy, have long since faded. Employing the distinction between emic and etic historiography as a consistent and self-conscious methodological focus when analysing tradition and its invention thus brings us close to one of Bruce Lincoln's critical theses on method: the history of religions is, or ought to be, "a discourse that resists and reverses the orientation of that discourse with which it concerns itself":

> To practice history of religions ... is to insist on discussing the temporal, contextual, situated, interested, human, and material dimensions of those discourses, practices, and institutions that characteristically *represent themselves* as eternal, transcendent, spiritual, and divine.[28]

And, we might add, reversing the orientation of those discourses which claim a revered and exalted "tradition" or "lineage", by emphasizing their constructed nature in temporal and material contexts.

We hold that this implicitly critical edge of historical research ought to be more explicitly recognized in studies of tradition in esotericism than has usually been the case. The recent proceedings of the inaugural conference of the European Society for the Study of Western Esotericism (ESSWE), entitled *Constructing Tradition*,[29] may serve as an example. Despite its title, and with a few notable exceptions,[30] this volume focuses more on the internal (emic) conceptualizations of tradition, their related philosophies, theologies and mythologies, than on attempts to develop the critical analysis of appeals to "tradition" in esotericism vis-à-vis etic historiography. It furthermore diverges from the theme of "constructed traditions" by focusing also on actual practices of transmission of knowledge and their material and social bases, as a part of "tradition" in esoteric movements – hence, the precise analytic meaning of the concept becomes blurred.[31] Knowing more about the social and material basis for actual transmissions of knowledge is obviously of value, but the continued neglect of a clear critical stance to the invention of tradition is regrettable. This point is all the more important as long as scholarly works that lack such

---

27. See e.g. the analysis of "Rosicrucian" tradition-making in the Golden Dawn, in Asprem, *Arguing with Angels*, chapters 3 and 5.
28. Lincoln, "Theses on Method", 225 (emphasis added).
29. Kilcher, *Constructing Tradition*.
30. See especially the articles by Philipp Theisohn, Wouter Hanegraaff, Monika Neugebauer-Wölk, Henrik Bogdan, Kocku von Stuckrad and Christine Maillard.
31. See e.g. Faivre, "Note sur la transmission"; cf. Kilcher, "Introduction", xiv.

an explicit critical distance continue to be used by practitioners in attempts at *creating* and *legitimating* tradition. In a later section, we will turn to some more explicit and influential examples of this trend. First, however, we must delve deeper into the role that various (emic) concepts of tradition have played in the emergence of "esotericism".

ANCIENT WISDOM NARRATIVES AND THE HISTORICAL FORMATION OF "ESOTERICISM"

Notions of tradition have been central to many of the historical currents, movements, and discourses that are now studied in the field of Western esotericism. Historically, this is only to be expected: the cultural configurations or discursive formations which are commonly seen as being at the base of "esotericism" in the historical sense were formed in Renaissance intellectual cultures which typically went far to equate the antiquity of a doctrine with its truth. Functioning as special cases of arguments to authority, claims to "tradition" were thus a central feature of the "episteme" in which the classic esoteric discourses were formed.[32] In fact, narratives of ancient wisdom are omnipresent in esoteric discourse, whether related to Hermes Trismegistus, Zoroaster, Moses or Orpheus, or to the increasingly more exotic ancients of modern times, such as the Atlanteans, discarnate Secret Chiefs, or even space aliens from the Pleiades. As a basic scheme, such genealogies of truth even seem to have become the core foundational narrative of esotericism from the Renaissance to the present day.[33]

However, a variety of conceptions of the relation between tradition and truth existed in the Renaissance.[34] We might distinguish two concepts that are of particular importance for the history of esotericism: *prisca theologia*, and *philosophia perennis*. Although frequently used interchangeably, these in fact denote two quite different epistemic schemes, evaluating the relation between truth, history and tradition in quite different ways.[35] *Prisca theologia* refers to the notion of a "pristine theology", revealed in a distant utopian past, and since partly lost through history. This scheme, which is associated foremost with the provocative pagan philosopher Gemistos Plethon (*c.* 1355–1452) and later with the humanist programme of Marsilio Ficino (1433–99), fits basic biblical

---

32. Cf. Foucault, *The Order of Things*.
33. Hanegraaff, *Esotericism and the Academy*, chapter 1.
34. The following discussion of "ancient wisdom narratives" and their ultimate function in creating notions of "esotericism" is heavily indebted to Wouter Hanegraaff's recent study, *Esotericism and the Academy*, particularly the first two chapters. As the book is at the time of writing not yet typeset, references are unfortunately only precise to the level of chapters.
35. This operative distinction seems to have been first noted in 1970 by Carl Schmitt, "*Prisca Theologia* e *Philosophia Perennis*". Cf. the detailed discussion in Hanegraaff, *Esotericism and the Academy*, chapter 1.

narratives of the Fall and the corrupting quality of temporality. As became clear in the aftermath of the Reformation and among Catholic humanist reformers, this notion of a more authentic and authoritative past had a *radical* or even revolutionary aspect to it: it meant that the discovery and diligent study of ancient source texts had the potential of "restoring" truth and overthrowing modern and hence "illegitimate" innovations. This was the radical foundation of Ficino's translations of the Platonic and Hermetic corpora, and the currents of thought which it inspired.

The notion of *philosophia perennis* was launched by the Augustinian scholar Agostino Steuco (1497–1548) in 1540, and constitutes, when taken in a strict analytic sense, a competing type of ancient wisdom narrative.[36] Whereas the connection between tradition and truth inherent in *prisca theologia* implied a notion of decline and corruption (nostalgia concerning the loss of truth as ages pass from a distant "Golden Age" of wisdom), *philosophia perennis* presents a scheme where wisdom is *eternal*, always present underneath the surface of any historical period. Where *prisca theologia* is radical, *philosophia perennis* has a conservative tinge: contemporary traditions are authentic and ought to be preserved, since they represent a hidden but living truth. Reform is futile. In this perennialist form, the *argumentum ad antiquitatem* can even be traced back to the early Christian church fathers, and their apologetic attempts to create legitimacy for the young religion of Christianity. Since the underlying assumption in late Hellenistic culture was that nothing could be "both new *and* true",[37] church fathers like Augustine had to claim the antiquity of Christianity, even when its founders had lived only a few generations earlier and its status was that of a "new religious movement". Thus, Augustine wrote that what

> is now called the Christian religion, was with the ancients ... and it was with the human race from its beginning to the time when Christ appeared in the flesh: from when on the true religion, which already existed, began to be called the Christian.[38]

As Wouter Hanegraaff has pointed out, the revival of *philosophia perennis* as an explicit stance by Steuco in the sixteenth century must similarly be seen as a response to the calls for reform based in part on *prisca theologia*.[39] It was a way to grant the antiquity of truth, while denying the need for reform, and a legitimate basis for it could readily be found in the apologists of the early church.

---

36. It has later been reinvented by Gottfried Leibniz (1646–1716), and popularized in the twentieth century by Aldous Huxley. The relevant *locus classicus* of the concept, however, is Steuco's *De Perenni Philosophia* (1540).
37. Droge, *Homer or Moses?*, 9.
38. Augustine, quoted in Wind, *Pagan Mysteries in the Renaissance*, 21.
39. Hanegraaff, *Esotericism and the Academy*, chapter 1.

In his erudite recent study, Hanegraaff shows how the different notions of tradition implied in the ancient wisdom narratives of the Renaissance have been entirely integral to the formation and construction of "esotericism".[40] While the Renaissance intellectuals who created the "corpus of reference" for later esoteric thought (e.g. Ficino, Pico, Reuchlin, Agrippa and others) constructed their wisdom narratives to include ancient sages such as Hermes, Zoroaster, Moses, Orpheus, Pythagoras and Plato, they simultaneously played a dangerous argument into the hands of a new generation of reformers who wanted to "purify" Christianity of any form of "paganism".[41] An "anti-apologetic" discourse was born in the wake of the Reformation, with the explicit aim of combating the dangerous "hostages" that the early church had taken and kept for so long: pagan philosophy, superstition and magic. While strategies of *prisca theologia* and *philosophia perennis* had worked to legitimate the truth of doctrine with reference to antiquity or eternal truth, they now became the source for a suspicion that paganism had infiltrated Christianity. In the hands of these later Protestant reformers, the Renaissance "history of truth" was inverted to form a "history of error".[42] In their view, Zoroaster was the source of devil worship, and Plato a dangerous pagan whose ideas had infested Christian culture and especially the Roman Church. Through the application of polemical simplifications of history, all the diverse thinkers that were considered suspect of paganism, magic, or worse were lumped together and seen as representing a connected diabolical trend. With the advent of the Enlightenment, this inverted wisdom narrative was adopted by Enlightenment historians as well, now adding the many acts of treachery against reason they saw to the existing catalogue of errors. These were the first steps towards the reification of what has later become known as "esotericism". Importantly, it took shape as a category of "rejected knowledge", created in polemical battles to define correct religion, philosophy and, increasingly, science.

Despite the rejection, appeals to traditions of the sort discussed above continued throughout the early modern period and into late modernity. With the publication of the Rosicrucian manifestos in the early seventeenth century, and particularly with the creation of Rosicrucian orders about a century later and the development of esoteric Freemasonry, the notion that a higher knowledge from a mystic East and/or distant past has been handed down

---

40. Note, however, that in addition to *philosophia perennis* and *prisca theologia*, Hanegraaff identifies a third strand of *pia philosophia*; this notion is separate from the two others in that it presupposes an element of progress or evolution in truth, as, for example, in the continuation of prophecy and extended revelation.
41. When using "paganism" in this context, we refer to emic Christian polemical discourse, where fears of alien (and evil) incursions into, or corruptions of, "True Christianity" emerge.
42. See Hanegraaff, *Esotericism and the Academy*, chapter 2. These expressions are the titles of the first two chapters of the book, which deal with these developments.

through the ages found a new form in institutional settings.[43] A notion of *philosophia perennis* has indeed been kept at the base of self-mythologization in Masonic contexts, and especially in the esoteric orders that were created during the nineteenth century.[44] Furthermore, the many uses of esoteric "tradition" to provide narrative to various countercultural, anti-establishment, anti-Enlightenment, and anti-modern discourses of the nineteenth and twentieth centuries may be seen as the outcome of parallel processes of tradition building and the rejection thereof, occurring during the Reformation and the Enlightenment.[45]

"THE ESOTERIC/OCCULT TRADITION": BETWEEN PRACTICE AND SCHOLARSHIP

Representing "the esoteric" and "the occult" as something of a self-contained and coherent tradition or a cluster of such has been a standard staple of older scholarly and semi-scholarly research. Frances Yates's notion of "the Hermetic tradition" popularized such a view concerning Hermetic philosophy in the Renaissance, but it also legitimized a broader idea of a coherent oppositional intellectual and religious tradition in Europe – especially after being read and interpreted by counterculturalists of the late 1960s who used it to support their contemporary agendas.[46] The notion of an apparently stable "tradition" has also been prominent in some works by sociologists, who may additionally have been in a worse position to stay informed about the historical complexities of the matter.[47]

However, the idea of a self-contained "esoteric tradition" seems to be a special case of construction of tradition that took shape especially in the context of nineteenth-century occultism. In the wake of the Enlightenment and the French Revolution, and during the onset of industrialization, the professionalization and expansion of the modern sciences, and amidst nation building, imperial competition, and the development of new radical political programmes across Europe, yet another inversion and use of the "ancient wisdom narratives" was created. With the Enlightenment "history of error"

---

43. See e.g. McIntosh, *The Rose Cross and the Age of Reason*; Bogdan, *Western Esotericism and Rituals of Initiation*.
44. See e.g. Bogdan, "The Sociology of the Construct of Tradition and Import of Legitimacy in Freemasonry"; Asprem, *Arguing with Angels*, chapter 3; cf. von Stuckrad, "Secrecy as Social Capital".
45. Cf. Webb, *The Occult Underground*; Webb, *The Occult Establishment*. Connections between esoteric historiographies and wisdom narratives on the one side, and polemical "countercultural" constructions and rejections of modern society on the other, are explored in several chapters in the present volume (see especially Chapters 10 and 12).
46. See Frances Yates, *Giordano Bruno and The Hermetic Tradition*; cf. Hanegraaff, "Beyond the Yates Paradigm".
47. See for example the numerous mentions of "the esoteric tradition" in Tiryakian, "Preliminary Considerations".

already in place, "occultist" authors found a blueprint of rejected and oppositional knowledge dealing somehow with religion as well as philosophy and science, which provided the raw materials for inventing a new "tradition" or "lineage" from which to base one's often quite ambiguous opposition to contemporary affairs. This led to the formation of modern occultism, where one of the first and most influential tradition-builders was Eliphas Lévi (Alphonse Louis Constant, 1810–75). It is significant that it was in this context that the noun "esotericism" started to get popularized for the first time, typically referring to a perennial tradition connected with Hermeticism, alchemy, astrology, magic, and so on, but above all with the Kabbalah, conceived of as a timeless, perennial system of wisdom.[48] This notion continued to gain currency in British occultism, as it emerged in its institutionalized forms through societies such as the Hermetic Society and the Theosophical Society, and esoteric orders of initiation such as the Hermetic Order of the Golden Dawn. More influential on scholarly circles was Lévi's English translator, the occultist and autodidact scholar of magic, alchemy, Rosicrucianism, Kabbalah and mysticism, Arthur Edward Waite (1857–1942). Waite's notion of "the secret tradition" encompassed all said topics, but was above all intrinsically connected to his personal brand of Christian mysticism. The "secret tradition" was thus, for him, not necessarily constrained by any direct historical continuity of thinkers, authors, texts, or even secret societies, but rather by an "invisible community" of those who had achieved exalted mystical insights.[49]

While most current scholarship on Western esotericism strongly criticizes the idea of a coherent "esoteric tradition"[50] as being the result of emic historiography, one commonly comes across this view among non-specialists.[51] It should also be noted that it has not altogether disappeared from specialist literature either. For example, Nicholas Goodrick-Clarke's introduction to Western esotericism refers to esoteric tradition*s* in the plural, but betrays a far more essentialist position in claiming that the

---

48. See e.g. Lévi's *Dogme et Rituel de la Haute Magie* and *Histoire de la Magie*, both included in the combined edition *Secrets de la Magie*. Cf. Hanegraaff, *Esotericism and the Academy*, chapter 3. For the role of a reinterpreted Kabbalah as providing both tradition and innovation, see Asprem, "*Kabbalah Recreata*". For recent philological and genealogical studies of the term esotericism, see especially Neugebauer-Wölk, "Der Esoteriker und die Esoterik"; Hanegraaff, "The Birth of Esotericism from the Spirit of Protestantism".
49. On Waite, see Robert A. Gilbert, *A. E. Waite*. Cf. his autobiography, Waite, *Shadows of Life and Thought*.
50. See e.g. Hanegraaff, "Beyond the Yates Paradigm".
51. See e.g. the highly problematic recent work by David S. Katz, *The Occult Tradition*. Katz believes that "the occult tradition" is something really "out there", and tries to trace "it" through Western history. Defined in terms of "the readiness to relate the unrelated", and by a belief in the supernatural, his main objective is, bizarrely, to show how contemporary American Fundamentalism is connected to "the occult tradition" (which is sometimes also interchangeably denoted "esoteric" and "mystical").

perennial characteristics of *the* esoteric worldview suggest ... that this is an enduring *tradition* which, though subject to some degree of social legitimacy and cultural coloration, actually reflects an autonomous and essential aspect of the relationship between the mind and the cosmos.[52]

While (however reluctantly) accepting that socio-cultural context may have some *marginal* relevance, Goodrick-Clarke actually conceives esotericism "as such" in terms closer to the ahistorical notions of a universal *philosophia perennis*; "definitions of 'the esoteric' in terms of discourse, social constructions, and legitimacy" are all found wanting by Goodrick-Clarke because they "lack a hermeneutic interpretation of spirit and spirituality as *an independent ontological reality*".[53] Whether conceived of in perennialist form, or as a mere self-supported historical tradition (including reworked notions of *prisca theologia*), the notion of "the occult tradition" is, in fact, where emic and etic historiography often meet.[54] When recognizing that many pioneers in the field, especially among those which Hanegraaff has termed the "generalists" in the study of esotericism,[55] have had their scholarly interest sparked by personal esoteric convictions, this is perhaps not so surprising.[56] It is problematic, however, if and when religious convictions strongly inform and filter scholarship. In the following section, we shall highlight the tradition-forming functions that easily follow certain types of scholarship.

SCHOLARS INVENTING TRADITION: THE EXAMPLE OF SHAMANISM

Moving to a more focused case study of the construction of tradition, the convoluted story of shamanism is one of the more interesting ones to assess. The construction of shamanism demonstrates the influence and confluence of a multiplex of different actors – ranging from nineteenth-century national romantics, through twentieth-century scholars, to esoteric practitioners today. Naturally, then, it is impossible to provide anything in the way of a thorough discussion in this context. For this we refer to the many volumes

---

52. Goodrick-Clarke, *The Western Esoteric Traditions*, 13 (emphasis added).
53. *Ibid.*, 12. Italics added.
54. A good example of this is Holman, *The Return of the Perennial Philosophy*, which has the subtitle *The Supreme Wisdom of Western Esotericism*. The book strives to be something in the sort of a scholarly examination (but fails miserably), and the inclusion of "Western Esotericism" in the subtitle can probably be attributed to intentions of aligning it to the academic field of the same name. The impact of scholarship on esotericism is discussed further on in this chapter.
55. Hanegraaff, "Beyond the Yates Paradigm", 24–5.
56. See for example the importance of the Eranos circle on the early scholarship of Antione Faivre: Hanegraaff, *Esotericism and the Academy*, chapter 4.

that have been produced on the various topics and themes converging here.[57] Instead, we will venture on a short discussion, focused both on the role played by esoteric discourse in the construction of shamanism and the influence later asserted back on esoteric discourse – thus demonstrating how esoteric discourse is interweaved with other social and cultural factors and trends.

We will start with the fervour of national romanticism in the late nineteenth and early twentieth centuries, and turn the gaze to Finland. This particular country is a good starting point as it is here that we can discern some of the first steps in projecting shamanism as a "universal and ancient" religious technique, and where we still to this very day find scholars engaged in this project.[58] First a few words on Romanticism. This period or movement, particularly strong in its German variant from the late eighteenth century but spreading through Europe like wildfire, was in many ways a backlash to the Enlightenment and its ideals. Where the latter emphasized things like ("modern") scientific rationality, civilization and universality, Romantics instead valued the mystical, natural/organic and particular.[59] It is in this process that we see the birth of the nation state – i.e. the invention of nationalist traditions, as emphasized by Hobsbawm – with Germany again in the forefront. Here, the idea of the *Völksgeist* – a "folk spirit" uniting all people of a particular heritage and binding them together in the nation – was first articulated. In this context we also find the "first wave" of Germanic neopaganism – as a "folk-oriented" religiosity to replace universalistic Christianity – as well as examples of the racialism that would later find violent political expression in the regime of the National Socialist Party in the 1930s.[60]

This is where we turn to Finland. This country, having been a province of Sweden until 1809 when it became an autonomous Grand Duchy of Tsarist Russia, was caught up in the national romantic winds just like other European countries. In Finland, language politics were intimately tied to nationalist concerns. Swedish had been the language of the educated and the ruling class while under the governance of Sweden, and this continued to be the case under Russia. From the 1820s onwards, the Fennoman movement – with the goal of adopting Finnish as the official, main (and often only) language of Finland – was born, and it gained strength in the subsequent decades. Many in the earlier Swedish-speaking privileged classes adopted Finnish – which up

---

57. For discussions on the scholarly construction of shamanism, see e.g. Svanberg, *Schamantropologi*; von Stuckrad, *Schamanismus und Esoterik*; Znamenski, *The Beauty of the Primitive*. For the role of Eliade and the Eranos meetings, see e.g. Wasserstrom, *Religion After Religion*.
58. Notable examples are Juha Pentikäinen (1940–), emeritus professor in comparative religion at Helsinki University, and Anna-Leena Siikala (1943–), emeritus professor in folkloristics at the same university.
59. Hanegraaff, *New Age Religion and Western Culture*, 419.
60. See Gardell, *Gods of the Blood*, 20–22; Gregorius, *Modern Asatro*, 55–64; cf. Granholm, "'Sons of Northern Darkness'"; Granholm, "Esoteric Currents as Discursive Complexes".

until then had been the language of peasants – as their language of choice, and even changed their surnames to appear more Finnish, often by direct translation (e.g. Juho Kusti Paasikivi, president of Finland from 1946 to 1956, was Christened Johan Gustaf Hellstén).[61] In this process of forging a national culture and identity legitimacy was needed, and thus the study of Finnish folklore was born. Vast numbers of promising young scholars, both university educated and amateurs, ventured out to the Finnish countryside to collect folk tales – remnants of "authentic and original" Finnish culture, it was claimed. Part of this project of Finlandizing Finland was the creation of the Finnish national epic, the *Kalevala*, by Elias Lönnrot (1802–84) in the mid-1800s (the "old" *Kalevala* in 1835–6, and the extended "new" *Kalevala* in 1849); not as an authentic example of collected tales, but as a conglomerate of folk tales and the embellishments and innovations of Lönnrot, all in order to create an epic in the image of its classic Greek counterparts.[62]

Soon, Finnish folklorists ventured out to seek "the roots" of the Finnish folk, and it is here we come across some of the first (semi-)professional ethnography that would lay the foundation of the study of shamanism – as well as the creation of that particular subject. Matias Aleksanteri Castren (1813–53), who "actively moulded Finnish cultural nationalism",[63] was one of the first in this regard. He wanted to prove the antiquity of Finnish culture and find the original homeland of the Finnish folk, and for this effect he did ethnography in Siberia. His book *Vorlesungen über die Finnische Mythologie*, published in 1853, inspired later influential authors such as Mircea Eliade and Joseph Campbell. Several other Finnish ethnographers followed in Castren's footsteps in the late eighteenth and early nineteenth centuries. These included the father of Finnish comparative religion, Uno Harva-Holmberg (1882–1949), who explored "cross-culturally Eurasian shamanism as a universal Finno-Ugric-Altaic system".[64]

The popularization of shamanism in the public consciousness can be attributed to two authors in particular: Carlos Castaneda and Mircea Eliade.[65] Castaneda was studying anthropology at University of California, Los Angeles (UCLA) from 1959, and wrote a term paper focused on the use of the *Datura*

---

61. In 1906, 24,800 people were reported to have "Finlandized" their names. This paled to later developments, though, as more than 100,000 people changed their names in the years 1935–6 alone. Thilman, "Suvuista ja nimistä".
62. Similar folkloristic programmes existed all over Europe at the time, strongly connected with nationalist creations of identity. The folk tales collected by Jacob and Wilhelm Grimm in Germany, Peter Christian Asbjørnsen and Jørgen Moe's collection and publication of *Norske Folkeeventyr* (*Norwegian Fairytales*) in the 1840s can be viewed this way, as might the "Celtic revival" in Britain somewhat later, not to mention the national romantic furore over the spoof "Scots Gaelic" poems in James Macpherson's *Ossian*.
63. Znamenski, *The Beauty of the Primitive*, 28.
64. Ibid., 32.
65. Ibid., 165.

plant in Mexican indigenous religious practices,[66] later expanded into an MA thesis and published in 1968 as *The Teachings of Don Juan*. In this book, and a whole series of later ones, Castaneda expounds on his apprenticeship with the Yaqui Indian Shaman Don Juan Matus, focusing on vivid tales of "entering another reality". He was even awarded a PhD degree in 1973 for the third book in the series, *Journey to Ixtlan* (1972).[67] The books became, and still remain, hugely popular, launching (neo)shamanism[68] as a countercultural trend in the late 1960s and 1970. However, even in the 1970s critics convincingly argued that Castaneda's research was most likely to have been conducted in libraries rather than in the field, and that his "apprenticeship" with "Don Juan" was probably fictional. Still, Castaneda's books continue to be influential among religious practitioners, and even remained examples of ideal ethnography in anthropological circles for a very long time. Znamenski attributes this to a changing academic climate in the 1960s, with increasing concerns to "validate the native's point of view".[69] Interestingly, Castaneda's anthropological supporters continued to regard his work as "validating the native's point of view"[70] even though Castaneda never actually presented the views of any natives! Another interesting example is Michael Harner, who started out as an anthropologist, but moved to be a spokesperson for neoshamanism with his *The Way of the Shaman*, published in 1980. His notion of "core shamanism", the universal building blocks of shamanism worldwide, is even discussed by Michael Winkelman in his article on shamanism in the *Encyclopedia of Religion*, and included in the bibliography of Mircea Eliade in an article on the same theme in the volume.[71]

It is Mircea Eliade who is of greatest interest when it comes to esoteric influences in the invention of shamanism as an "archaic and universal tradition". Eliade is among the most influential scholars in the history of the study of religion, and "almost certainly the most familiar name in the field"[72] outside scholarly quarters. In regard to shamanism, he not only popularized it in his *Shamanism: Archaic Techniques of Ecstasy* (1964, original French edition in

---

66. For a discussion of the use of hallucinogenic substances in esoteric contexts, and the popularization of the phenomenon, see Chapter 19 of the present volume.
67. Znamenski, *The Beauty of the Primitive*, 191, 189–93.
68. The term neoshamanism is even more problematic than "paganism" or "neopaganism" (for a discussion on these terms, see footnote 1 on page 1 of the present volume). If "shamanism" is itself a construction, then the addition of "neo" to indicate modern reconstructions would seem unnecessary. However, the distinction is motivated in distinguishing scholarly constructions of pre-modern, non-Western religious "traditions" from modern Western reconstructions based on these. That is, we are dealing with second-order constructions here.
69. Znamenski, *The Beauty of the Primitive*, 195–6, 205–14.
70. Douglas Sharon, quoted in *ibid.*, 209.
71. Winkelman, "Shamanism", 8275–6; Eliade, "Shamanism", 8274.
72. Wasserstrom, *Religion After Religion*, 8.

1951), but also popularized the idea of it as a universal religious technique, cross-cultural and ahistoric, and the "original" form of religiosity.[73] However, the term "shamanism" is problematic when used to refer to religious phenomena beyond those relating to the Tungusic cultures the word originates in, and becomes increasingly problematic when considering the extremely broad application it has been put to. Already in the early 1960s the concept of shamanism had been expanded to include the Eskimos,[74] Native Americans,[75] Hungarians,[76] and even biblical stories.[77] Other locations include the Saami culture,[78] "Finno-Ugric cultures",[79] Ireland[80] and, quite recently, Africa.[81]

As is now widely recognized, Eliade's phenomenological project was intimately tied to his religionist concerns.[82] In his youth – and continuing to his death – Eliade was greatly influenced by René Guénon – author and founder of the Traditionalist school of esoteric thought.[83] The central concerns of Traditionalism were the critique of Western modernity and the pursuit of "authentic primordial tradition". For example, the term "reintegration" that was central to Eliade's work, as well as his very conception of "tradition", was most likely to have been derived from Guénon,[84] and his *Cosmos and History* – better known in English by its original subtitle, *The Myth of the Eternal Return* – can be compared with Guénon's *Crisis of the Modern World* (1927) and fellow Traditionalist Julius Evola's *Revolt Against the Modern World* (1934).[85] Eliade was an active participant, from 1949 to 1976, in the Eranos meetings arranged in Ascona, Switzerland, since 1933. There he congregated with figures such as Carl Gustav Jung, Gershom Scholem, Henry Corbin, and Joseph Campbell[86] – all respected and influential scholars in their respective fields and, even more importantly, influenced by similar esoteric–Traditionalist views, and in turn highly influential on later esotericism.

---

73. Znamenski, *The Beauty of the Primitive*, 165–80. The idea of the antiquity of shamanism has been criticized by, among others, Sidky, "On the Antiquity of Shamanism and its Role in Human Religiosity".
74. Holtved, "Eskimo Shamanism".
75. Hultkrantz, "Spirit Lodge".
76. Fazekas, "Hungarian Shamanism, Material and History of Research".
77. Kapelrud, "Shamanic Features in the Old Testament".
78. E.g. Hultkrantz, "Aspects of Saami (Lapp) Shamanism".
79. Corradi-Musi, "Supernatural Heroes in Finno-Ugric Shamanism".
80. Karjala, "Aspects of the Other World in Irish Folk Tradition".
81. See Znamenski, *The Beauty of the Primitive*, 188.
82. On the "Jung–Eliade school of thought", see Wasserstrom, *Religion After Religion*, 23.
83. On Guénon and Traditionalism, see Sedgwick, *Against the Modern World*. On later Traditionalist influences, see Granholm, "The Rune-Gild"; and Chapter 12 in the present volume.
84. Wasserstrom, *Religion After Religion*, 38, 40.
85. *Ibid.*, 46. On the influence of Traditionalism on Eliade, see Sedgwick, *Against the Modern World*, 109–16.
86. On Eranos, particularly with reference to Eliade, Corbin and Scholem, see Wasserstrom, *Religion After Religion*.

It should also be noted that the father of the modern school of the study of Western esotericism, Antoine Faivre, also participated in the Eranos meetings in the 1970s, and had particularly close relations to Henry Corbin. Together with Corbin, Faivre was even the co-founder, in 1974, of a fiercely religionist French offshoot of the Eranos meetings, called the *Université Saint Jean de Jérusalem*. Conceived of as a "counter-university", an "international center for comparative spiritual research" dedicated to reviving esoteric knowledge and fighting the evils of the modern world, the group counted a great number of early specialists of esoteric subjects among its members – including Eliade himself. As carefully documented by Hanegraaff, this platform was something of a laboratory for Faivre's ideas about esotericism in his most religionist period, which would last until approximately the end of the 1980s.[87]

Returning to shamanism, what we perceive here is a complex tangled web of inventions of tradition. Scholarly inquiry was linked to the quest for national identity and tradition, and the creation of shamanism as a "universal and archaic technique" indeed revolves around the creation of perennial tradition – at the same time influencing, and being influenced by, esoteric discourse. Furthermore, the case of Eliade makes it clear that essentially perennialist notions of tradition, similar to the idea of *philosophia perennis* discussed earlier, have asserted a strong influence on scholarly constructs such as shamanism, which in the next instance have informed actual practices and emic notions of tradition and connection with an archaic authentic past. We shall now continue to discuss aspects of this latter step in more detail.

SCHOLARS READ: ESOTERICISM BECOMES AN OBJECT

Scholars and scholarship do not exist in isolation; rather, they co-inhabit their world with their research subjects and readers. When it comes to studies of (particularly modern) esotericism, the researched and the reader are often the same person. This has major implications for scholarship in the field. Most current major scholars of esotericism stress the scholarly constructed nature of their research field,[88] asserting that "'[e]sotericism' does not exist as an object".[89] However, with esoteric actors becoming increasingly familiar with scholarship from the field of Western esotericism, esotericism is indeed *becoming* an object. It is actively created as such by esotericists who are influenced and informed by the scholarship they actively and eagerly consume. We

---

87. For the full detailed discussion of the development of Faivre's career, and the various cultural and social influences on his work, see Hanegraaff, *Esotericism and the Academy*, chapter 4.
88. See e.g. Hanegraaff, *New Age Religion and Western Culture*, 402; Hanegraaff, "The Study of Western Esotericism", 489–91; Hammer, "Esotericism in New Religious Movements", 445.
89. Von Stuckrad, "Western Esotericism", 9.

will provide a brief example of this process. In the Sweden-originated magic order Dragon Rouge, founder and head ideologist Thomas Karlsson – who is also a scholar of Western esotericism, having earned a doctorate in 2010 at Stockholm University for a thesis on the seventeenth-century rune mystic Johannes Bureus[90] – has presented an analysis of his order grounded in Antoine Faivre's conceptualization of esotericism.[91] This text, directed to practising magicians rather than to an academic audience, implies that[92] esoteric actors may easily draw on scholarship in order to align themselves to "the primordial/perennial tradition" as described by scholars – to more properly represent esotericism as "authorized" by scholarly authorities, who are much respected by many in the esoteric milieu. This invention of "esoteric tradition" is in many ways similar to the invention of "shamanistic tradition", discussed above, in the pivotal role played by academic authors. It is different, however, in that tradition is here created in *lieu* of scholarly insistence that no such tradition exists, rather than with active scholarly participation in the process of construction. In a sense, the notion of a "tradition" thus emerging is the result of a "fetishistic" reading of scholarship on esotericism.

An implication of these factors is that, when studying the esoteric in the contemporary world, we might need to expand our view to include not only "esotericists" – or only esoteric discourse, to use Kocku von Stuckrad's term – but rather the broader field of "discourse on the esoteric" (i.e. all actors who engage with the esoteric in one way or another). Thus actors "relegating" phenomena to the field of the esoteric and occult (including scholars such as Truzzi as well as non-scholarly detractors), proponents of esoteric worldviews and philosophies, as well as more neutral scholars, are all participants on this field of discourse. This approach is foreshadowed by Wouter Hanegraaff's more recent work, where he approaches the issue of how certain phenomena have been produced as "rejected knowledge" in polemical and othering discourses, and through scholarship with various types of hidden (and not so hidden) agendas.[93] However, instead of only looking at opponents and proponents, more neutral scholarly commentators should be included as well, as should the material dimensions of contemporary scholarship. The creation of specialist journals (e.g. *Esoterica*; *Aries: Journal for the Study of Western Esotericism*), specialist book series (e.g. SUNY's *Western Esoteric Traditions*), and even scholarly organizations (Association for the Study of Esotericism; ESSWE) and study programmes (the University of Amsterdam programme in "Mysticism and Western Esotericism", and Exeter University's Centre for the

---

90. Karlsson, *Götisk Kabbala och Runisk Alkemi*.
91. Karlsson, "Esoterism and the Left-Hand Path".
92. For reflections on the constructivist ontology inherent in this claim, see e.g. the many thought-provoking essays and reviews in Hacking, *Historical Ontology*.
93. Hanegraaff, "Forbidden Knowledge"; Hanegraaff, "The Trouble with Images"; Hanegraaff, *Esotericism and the Academy*.

Study of Esotericism), all using the term esotericism to signify "something" that they are "about", significantly contributes to the reification of the category for the general audience – *despite* the explicated contrary intentions of most scholars in the field.

FICTION, POPULAR CULTURE AND THE INVENTION OF TRADITION

That fiction and popular culture can play an important part in the construction of identities and traditions is something that scholars increasingly start to acknowledge.[94] Still, few scholars other than Christopher Partridge have explicitly discussed the role of popular culture in religious change, or the significance of the esoteric in this context.[95] While the importance of fiction in this regard can logically be assumed to have increased under the impact of modern entertainment media (e.g. television, movies, mass-produced music, etc.) and new interactive media (particularly the Internet and social networking sites), the phenomenon is in no way new. The example of Rosicrucianism is a good demonstration. While perhaps not being the first instance of fiction having a profound effect on the esoteric, Rosicrucianism is certainly one of the most influential examples, and one of the few that scholars of Western esotericism make regular notice of. Although the fictional background of this current is not disregarded by scholars, it is an aspect which is still seldom sufficiently acknowledged, and has yet to be treated in a theoretically interesting way. The Rosicrucian current was instigated with the publication of two spoof pamphlets, *Fama Fraternitatis* (1614) and *Confessio Fraternitatis* (1615), followed by an alchemically loaded play, the *Chymische Hochzeit Christiani Rosencreutz anno 1459* (1616). All texts were published anonymously; however, the last one has been unambiguously attributed to the (at that time very young) German theologian Johann Valentin Andreae (1586–1654), while the two earlier manifestos seem to have been collaborative efforts by Andreae and a circle of his friends and colleagues.[96]

The works presented the story of Christian Rosenkreutz, who, we are told, came in possession of significant esoteric secrets while travelling in the Middle East, and subsequently founded a fraternity in the fifteenth century. While being technically pieces of fiction, the manifestos were long taken to be genuine communications from an existing secret order dedicated to a "universal and general reformation of the whole world". They sparked a furore of debates for and against the Rosicrucians in the early to middle decades of the seventeenth century. Eventually, numerous *actual* Rosicrucian societies were

---

94. E.g. Gordon Lynch, "The Role of Popular Music in the Construction of Alternative Spiritual Identities and Ideologies"; Lynn Schofield Clark, "Religion, Twice Removed".
95. Partridge, *The Re-enchantment of the West*. See also Chapter 6 in this volume.
96. See e.g. Edighoffer, "Rosicrucianism I", 1009.

formed, all claiming to represent the "true" legacy of the fictitious Christian Rosenkreutz. Here we can also discern the role played by changing means of mediation: the impact of the Rosicrucian manifestos would never have been as immense as it was without the possibility of mass distribution offered by the invention of the printing press in the fifteenth century. Rosicrucianism has remained an influential element in the esoteric milieu, with an increased importance through its impact on Freemasonry, and through major organizations such as AMORC (founded as late as 1915) claiming its heritage. In Freemasonry, the models of Rosicrucian societies and vocational guilds fused to form an initiatory society, which in turn came to function as a model for many later magical orders, such as the Hermetic Order of the Golden Dawn (founded in 1888).

In the nineteenth century we find several more examples of fiction influencing "esoteric" currents, such as Emma Hardinge Britten's books – which further influenced the creation of later initiatory magical orders – and Edward Bulwer-Lytton's hugely influential novel *Zanoni* – which, among many other things, spread the idea of semi-immortal Rosicrucian "secret chiefs". In the twentieth century and beyond, the fiction of H. P. Lovecraft has similarly asserted an immense influence on occultism.

In more recent times, science fiction has been a significant source for religious innovations, and has often been coupled with the esoteric in these processes.[97] The most familiar example of this, and arguably one of the clearest, is Scientology.[98] The founder of Scientology, L. Ron Hubbard, was a prolific science fiction author, and many of the elements permeating his fictional work seem to have influenced the doctrines of Scientology as well. Even more recent examples are Jediism and Matrixism.[99] The former was created as a religion in religious census surveys in English-speaking countries. Pleas to write down "Jedi" as a religious orientation were posted online in advance of the census, with astounding results (in New Zealand 1.5 per cent of the population did so).[100] What started as a joke has apparently become a serious religio-philosophical conviction for many people, not in the form of fundamentalist belief in the truthfulness of the Star Wars movies but as an appreciation of the perceived spirituality and philosophy in them. In terms of the esoteric it is interesting to note that George Lucas was highly influenced by the works of Joseph Campbell when writing the movies. Campbell, as noted earlier, was a participant of the Eranos meetings, and represents the general esoteric–Traditionalist ethos of Eranos.[101] Matrixism, formed in 2004,[102] is based on the

---

97. As briefly noted by Granholm in Chapter 15 of this volume.
98. See Chapter 9 of this volume for more information on both Scientology and its esoteric/occult connections.
99. Cusack, *Invented Religions*, 120–32.
100. *Ibid.*, 125.
101. Wasserstrom, *Religion After Religion*, 85, 140, 142–3.
102. Cusack, *Invented Religions*, 113.

Wachowski brothers' Matrix trilogy, which, as several scholars have noted, in many regards represents a "neo-gnostic" philosophy influenced by individualistic interpretations of Buddhism.[103] Esoteric discourse can certainly be conceived of as playing a part, as the movies – and thus Matrixism as a religion – revolves around the idea of knowledge providing the power to shape reality.

CONCLUSION

This chapter has taken us through an admittedly large, confusing and complex array of themes and discussions. Nevertheless, certain main points may be summarized and drawn together.

First of all, we have made an argument concerning the way one should fruitfully approach the concept of "tradition" itself. Rather than operationalizing "tradition" as an analytical tool to look at, for example, means of transmission, coherence and autonomy of cultural systems, structural distinctions between "modern" and "pre-modern" societies, and so on, we have argued that a constructivist approach to the invention of tradition is a more promising path. For this kind of constructivism to succeed, one should furthermore combine historical and sociological approaches, and fully acknowledge the critical potential of the project.

Second, these discussions have consequences for the study of contemporary esotericism. We have suggested that there are especially two types of often-overlooked co-producers of tradition whose roles need to be highlighted if the broadly constructivist programme drawn up in this article is to be followed, namely: the role of scholarship, and the role of fiction and popular culture. While both of these have in fact been in operation at least since the early modern period, they have become increasingly important in the present day. Also, because of our own embeddedness in contemporary culture, they may be somewhat harder to spot; they are, so to speak, "hidden in plain sight". In the case of popular culture, the media revolutions of the late twentieth century, and the popularization of esoteric motifs that is unquestionably occurring in and through it, lead to the production of new source materials which become resources for constructions of tradition and identity. Fictitious or not, these cultural products do make an unprecedented number of historical and mythological narratives connected with the esoteric, as well as elements ripe for the construction of such, available to wide (and new) audiences. Tracing the consequences of this must be a concern of the study of contemporary esotericism.

When it comes to the role of scholarship, the question is even more complex, as we have seen. A highly significant and overlooked question at the

---

103. See e.g. Flannery-Dailey & Wagner, "Wake Up!"; Bowman, "The Gnostic Illusion".

present time is the influence that our very own research area is asserting on practices and self-conceptions "in the field". That occultists and neopagans are avid readers of works produced by scholars of esotericism is no secret, and we know historically that cultural knowledge produced or repackaged by academia, having received its official stamp of "quality goods" (with all its attendant commodity fetishism), tends to become a sought-after commodity in the more literate milieus of practitioners. In this light, some of the strategies wielded in order to claim an independent identity for "Western esotericism" as a more or less autonomous academic field may, regardless of the actual intentions and even explicit statements of some of those involved, have conferred cultural legitimacy onto practitioners who want to identify with something like a unique "esoteric tradition" as well. This calls for an increased emphasis on scholarly reflexivity in the field, particularly when questions of identity, essence, and tradition are at stake.

CHAPTER 3

INVENTING AFRICA

ESOTERICISM AND THE CREATION OF AN AFROCENTRIC TRADITION IN AMERICA

Fredrik Gregorius

Paul Gilroy's study of African Diaspora culture, *The Black Atlantic*, begins with three quotes. One of them, from Friedrich Nietzsche, reads:

> We have left the land and have embarked. We have burned our bridges behind us – indeed we have gone further and destroyed the land behind us. … Woe, when you feel homesick for the land as if it had offered more *freedom* – and there is no longer any land.[1]

The Nietzsche quote can be seen as a reflection on modernity and the futility of attempts to turn back and return to a stage that can only exist as a memory and an idealized past. In the African diaspora, not even the memory or the language remains to form an ideal of a lost homeland. Following Nietzsche's description of the state of modern man, we can claim that the African diaspora offers the most intense form of homelessness. For a long time European historical discourse construed Africa as a place without anything to offer in the way of culture or history. For those of African descent there was thus no history to claim, no cultural achievement to speak about. The culture, language and history that were available were those of Europe, representing a culture that in many ways had looked upon African people as being, at best, second-class citizens. This experience has famously been described by the early civil rights leader W. E. B. Du Bois (1868–1963) as an experience of "double consciousness":

> After the Egyptian and Indian, the Greek and Roman, the Teuton and Mongolian, the Negro is a sort of seventh son, born with a veil, and gifted with second-sight in this American world, – a world which yields him no true self-consciousness, but only lets him see

---

1. Nietzsche, quoted in Gilroy, *The Black Atlantic*, xiii.

himself through the revelation of the other world. It is a peculiar sensation, this double-consciousness, this sense of always looking at one's self through the eyes of others, of measuring one's soul by the tape of a world that looks on in amused contempt and pity. One ever feels his two-ness, – an American, a Negro; two souls, two thoughts, two unreconciled strivings; two warring ideals in one dark body, whose dogged strength alone keeps it from being torn asunder.[2]

The historiography of the experience and development of African diaspora culture in America has been filled with varied and complex responses to this experience. Some black leaders have accepted the idea of Africa as a dark continent; rather than striving to reclaim a lost cultural heritage they have regarded their role as being the leaders of an emerging African civilization based upon European values. Others have romanticized the savage Africa, construing parallels with the Germanic and Celtic tribes of pre-Christian Europe. Still others have claimed that the image of Africa presented in Western narratives is false, and that not only does Africa have a lot to offer culturally and historically, but most of what we today see as European has an African origin.[3] Rather than being clearly differentiated positions, the above approaches should be seen as ideal-types describing general trends, and often authors have based their approach, depending on context, on more than one position. The last position can be described as an *Afrocentric* one, and the purpose of this chapter is to look at how this approach has shaped and constructed ideas about Africa and its relation to modern black people in America.

More specifically, this chapter will deal with the way Afrocentric groups have tried to construct, or reconnect with, what is conceived as a "primordial African tradition" and how this relates to ideas of the existence of an "African personality". Questions about spirituality often arise in the context of this quest, and attempts have been made to find a perennial essence of African religion that is neither Christian nor Muslim, but based on indigenous African traditions. While often eclectic in their approach, Afrocentrists have become more and more focused on ancient Egypt as the primary ideal. In the development of a concept of a tradition that binds Egypt together with sub-Saharan Africa, esoteric ideas from Masonry, Jungianism, Theosophy and Rosicrucianism, among others, have been used.

In this chapter, "Afrocentricity" refers to a specific contemporary ideology that presents Africa as not only a continent of origin, but also articulates a psychological and spiritual mentality seen as essentially "African". That is, an Afrocentrist believes that there is a certain African way of looking at the world,

---

2. Du Bois, *The Souls of Black Folks*, 2.
3. Moses, *Afrotopia*.

contrasted with a European view. People will maintain this mentality regardless of where they live: Africans in the United States will have a natural inclination to look at the world from an "African point of view". Thus "Afrocentric" and "Afrocentrism" are used to refer to ideas that position Africa as a place of central and essential relevance for contemporary black people. [4]

A RACE FOR EGYPT

The debate over the racial identity of the ancient Egyptians has been central to the Afrocentric movement of the 1980s, but can be traced back to the 1800s. Just as Afrocentric writers have tried to find evidence of Egypt as a part of a larger pan-African culture, some white scholars and writers have spent as much time arguing the opposite, or at least that Egypt was a culture dominated by non-black elites.[5]

Egypt was a problem for the white establishment in the nineteenth and twentieth centuries, and while attempts were made to show that Egypt was an inferior civilization compared with ancient Greece, it was still difficult to deny the accomplishments of the ancient Egyptians. With the discovery of the Rosetta stone in 1799 (which, beside the long overdue translation of the hieroglyphs, also led to a newfound fascination with all things Egyptian) there arose a need to relate to Egypt in racial terms. In the racial discourse of the US, where slavery was not officially abolished until 1865, Egypt became a recurring battle ground for both abolitionists and white supremacists.

An example of how the racial identity of the Egyptians was used by both sides can be illustrated with an event in June 1850. American showman and Egyptologist George Robins Gliddon (1809–57), who based his understanding of history on white supremacist theories, organized a three-day event called "The Art of Mummification among the Ancient Egyptians". The highlight of the event was the unwrapping of a mummy, performed incrementally over the three days of the event in order to maximize anticipation. Gliddon let his fantasies run wild and expected the mummy to be an Egyptian princess. Connected to the event were several lectures on ancient Egypt and the racial characteristics of the ancient Egyptians. Gliddon himself would look at Egyptian skulls and proclaim: "In this man's skull we behold one of ourselves – a Caucasian, a pure white man; notwithstanding the bitumen which has blackened the skin."[6] The unwrapping of the mummy was, however, a failure for Gliddon, as it was revealed that the mummy was in fact male and not female. This led to Gliddon disappearing from the mummy scene, but also to some comments from the African American abolitionist newspaper in the article

---

4. Howe, *Afrocentrism*, 1.
5. Trafton, *Egypt Land*, 9.
6. Quoted in *Ibid.*, 44.

"Were the Thebans Negros", which concluded with a satirical comment on Gliddon's event:

> Well, the poor old mummy, was at length stripped of its swaddling clothes, and disembowled [sic], and furnished evidence of little else than that it was a veritable "he-nigger" after all. A humbling relic enough of Theban royalty, learning and renown.[7]

The ironic comments aside, we see that the idea of Egypt as a black African civilization was at least partly established as a counter-narrative in response to Gliddon and his colleagues' projection of a white Egypt.

Gliddon's display was of course not the only example where different ideas conflicted. When pictures of Ramesses II were presented, in a later book by Gliddon, some compared Ramesses's facial profile to that of Napoleon, while others, such as the former slave Frederick Douglass (1818?–95), perceived a clear resemblance to his own mother.[8] The role of the Egyptians took on clearly political dimensions in the period leading up to the US Civil War (1861–5), with the question of slavery making racial issues central in political debate. If Egypt were to become seen as an African civilization, then the argument that Africa had never created a civilization would be rendered invalid. That nineteenth-century scholars did as much as they could to promote a predominantly Middle Eastern or European image of Egypt is taken by contemporary Afrocentric writers as evidence for distortions of history in order to neglect the impact that Africa has had on European civilization, and it is hard not to agree at least in part. This was the central topic in the first part of Martin Bernal's controversial *Black Athena* (1987). Critics of Bernal claim that he paints a far too generalized picture of nineteenth-century scholarship on Egypt, and that he neglects the trend towards anti-Egyptianism among some more radical European writers. It is, however, difficult to claim that racism did not play a significant role in creating the image of the ancient world and Egypt as fair-skinned.[9] While the question of racial characteristics is generally not seen as a significant question among most Egyptologists today, it remains an issue for both Afrocentrists and white racialist groups. Arthur Kemp's *March of the Titans* (2006), for example, goes to great lengths to show that the Egyptians were descendants of white people and that black people are inferior. While the counter-narrative to white Egypt developed slowly and in different contexts, one area where it found a language to express itself was within the black Masonic movement.

---

7. *Ibid.*, 45.
8. *Ibid.*, 65–7.
9. Howe, *Afrocentrism*, 123.

PRINCE HALL MASONRY

Masonry has been an important movement in the history of the African diaspora in North America. It had a large impact on the development of the constitution of Liberia, and many early black intellectuals were Masons. Prince Hall Masonry has been particularly influential in this respect. It seems to have played an important role in creating an early black middle class by stressing the importance of culture and learning for African Americans.[10]

Prince Hall was born in 1735 and lived most of his life in Boston. While we know some details about his background, sources are scant and there is much contradiction between descriptions of his early life. One unanswered question is if he was born free or a slave. What is known is that in 1770 Hall was a free black man living in Boston. He spent a lot of energy to improve the lives of other black people in the city, by founding schools and helping to establish businesses owned and operated by African Americans, but also by working politically for the abolition of slavery.

He came into contact with Masonry during the early 1770s, and while initial attempts to join the local lodge were unsuccessful due to his race, he and fourteen other African Americans were initiated into the Grand Lodge of Ireland on 6 March 1775. Prince Hall later established the African Lodge. It was not a smooth process, as most Masons did not accept them even after their initiation, and Hall had to fight for recognition. Originally the group was only given permission to celebrate St John's day and bury their dead "in manner and form".[11] The African Lodge was not officially founded until 1776; a charter to work a lodge was granted by the Grand Lodge of England only after the American Revolution, on 29 September 1784, and it was not received until 29 April 1787. Before this, as early as 1779, the Lodge formed its own by-laws, or regulations. These regulations were fairly standard, excluding atheists and irreligious libertines, but asking no further questions regarding religious affiliation. The by-laws document is relevant not only for the history of Masonry in the US, but also as the first document to describe a form of black self-government.[12]

While the role of Masonry in facilitating black community-building seems clear, its function as transmitter of counter-narratives to mainstream white presentations of African history is more debated. According to historian Wilson Jeremia Moses, Prince Hall Masonry was a fairly standard form of Masonry based on the myth of the builders of the Temple of Solomon.[13]

---

10. Muraskin, *Middle-Class Blacks in a White Society*; Loretta J. Williams, *Black Freemasonry and Middle-Class Realities*.
11. Gray, *Inside Prince Hall*, 18.
12. *Ibid.*, 18, 34; Muraskin, *Middle-Class Blacks in a White Society*, 124.
13. Moses, *Afrotopia*, 49.

Others, like Scott Trafton and Stephen Howe, have argued that it was important in transmitting ideas about Egypt, and provided distinctly "Africanized" interpretations of Masonry.[14] The truth is probably somewhere in between. Most Prince Hall lodges seem to have been fairly traditional, but some embraced more "Egyptianized" forms. A document that gives evidence to alternative opinions of Egypt and Africa within Prince Hall Masonry is found in the writings of the black nationalist leader Martin Robison Delany (1812–85). In 1853 Delany published a short work called *The Origin and Objects of Ancient Freemasonry*. He was concerned with the creation of a strong black masculine identity and saw Masonry as a means to achieve it. But Masonry also had a deeper meaning, making Hall's efforts all the more significant for him. While steeped in biblical allegories and symbols – Delany was after all a Christian minister – the text displays a new perspective of history and Africa. What we find is one of the first examples of an Afrocentric perspective on history and tradition:

> In the earliest period of the Egyptian and Ethiopian dynasties, the institution of Masonry was first established. Discovering a defect in the government of man, first suggested an inquiry into his true state and condition. Being a people of a high order of intellect, and subject to erudite and profound thought, the Egyptians and Ethiopians were the first who came to the conclusion that man was created in the similitude of God. This, it will be remembered, was anterior to the Bible record, because Moses was the recorder of the Bible, subsequent to his exodus from Egypt, all his wisdom and ability having been acquired there; as a proof of which, the greatest recommendation to his fitness for so high and holy an office, and the best encomium which that book can possibly bestow upon him in testimony of his qualifications as its scriptor, the Bible itself tells us that "Moses was learned in all the *wisdom* of the Egyptians".[15]

Rather than breaking with biblical tradition, Delany inscribed Egypt and Ethiopia into it, giving Africa a central role as the place where Masonry was first established. The text was written during a period when conflicts with other Masonic bodies regarding the legitimacy of Prince Hall Masonry were common. One of the ways to defend the presence of black Masons was to claim an African origin for Masonry itself. In doing this, Delany reinterpreted and broke down the conventional idea of Africa as being devoid of culture. Thus, if Africans do not have the right to be Masons, then no one does:

---

14. Howe, *Afrocentrism*, 69; Trafton, *Egypt Land*, 71–3.
15. Delany, "Origin and Objects of Ancient Freemasonry", 53.

> Truly, if the African race has no legitimate claims to Masonry, then it is illegitimate to all the rest of mankind. ... [T]o Africa is the world indebted for its knowledge of the mysteries of Ancient Freemasonry. Had Moses or the Israelists never lived in Africa, the mysteries of the wise men of the East never would have been handed down to us. Was it not Africa that gave birth to Euclid, the master geomatrician [sic] of the world? and was it not in consequence of a twenty five years' residence in Africa that the great Pythagoras was enabled to discover that key problem in geometry – the forty seventh problem of Euclid – without which Masonry would be incomplete? Must I hesitate to tell the world that, as applied to Masonry, the word, *Eureka*, was first exclaimed in Africa? But – there I have revealed the Masonic *secret* and must stop![16]

Arguing that Moses had been a Mason served other functions as well. Delany argues, with Moses as a central example, that even men not born free should be able to become Masons. Here Delany unites two different strands of thought; the monumentalist notion of Egypt as the land of Africans, and the situation of Africans in the diaspora interpreted in the context of the biblical Exodus-narrative and the captivity of Moses and the Israelites in Egypt.

STOLEN LEGACY

Among the most important books in the Afrocentric paradigm is George G. M. James's (?–1954) *Stolen Legacy* (1954). Among critics, the book is usually quoted as evidence for the low academic standards of Afrocentric studies. One of the more infamous parts of the book deals with Alexander the Great sacking the library of Alexandria, an event generally seen as historically impossible.[17] What is of interest here, however, is not the factuality of James's claims but rather the history that he constructs and his use of esoteric sources. For James, the "conspiracy against the black man" is not a modern phenomenon, but one that dates back at least to Alexander the Great. Among other things, he claims that Aristotle stole all his books from the library in Alexandria and later published them under his own name. For example, Aristotle's *On the Soul* was, according to James, demonstrably plagiarized from the *Egyptian Book of the Dead*, since they both deal with the topic of the soul in some form.[18] In order to find proof for his thesis James embraced ideas found in esoteric writings, viewing Egypt as the centre of wisdom. This also led to further conspiratorial

---

16. *Ibid.*, 66–7 (emphasis original).
17. Howe, *Afrocentrism*, 128.
18. James, *Stolen Legacy*, 122–3.

ideas, such as the Masons being aware of the African origin of their teachings but hiding them.

James's book needs to be understood in the context of his time. It was written in the 1950s when the black civil rights movement was on the rise, but with accompanying feelings among many that little actual change was taking place. James's work can thus be seen as one born out of frustration and disillusionment. The perspective was no longer one of the influence of African cultural elements on Europe, but one of outright theft of African culture by Europeans. James provides a detailed description of what was stolen, and how. In the search for a chain of evidence, he turned to esoteric doctrines and views of Egypt as the centre of mysteries. For example, in the introduction of the book he writes:

> The term Greek philosophy, to begin with is a misnomer, for there is no such philosophy in existence. The ancient Egyptians had developed a very complex religious system, called the Mysteries, which was also the first system of salvation. As such, it regarded the human body as a prison house of the soul, which could be liberated from its bodily impediments, through the disciplines of the Arts and Sciences, and advanced from the level of a mortal to that of a God. This was the notion of the summum bonum or greatest good, to which all men must aspire, and it also became the basis of all ethical concepts.[19]

Not only were the Egyptian mysteries the source of all Western philosophy and ethics; James also insisted that the Egyptians had taught the mysteries in secret orders:

> The Egyptian Mystery System was also a Secret Order, and membership was gained by initiation and a pledge to secrecy. The teaching was graded and delivered orally to the Neophyte; and under these circumstances of secrecy, the Egyptians developed secret systems of writing and teaching, and forbade their Initiates from writing what they had learnt.[20]

Later, he went into more detail as to how the Egyptian mysteries operated and how people were initiated into them. Most of this is standard material from Masonic and Rosicrucian writings, and the British historian Stephen Howe has claimed that *Stolen Legacy* is as "much a mystic–ritualistic, and more specifically Masonic, work as it is an Afrocentric one".[21] Still, the specific esoteric

---

19. *Ibid.*, 1.
20. *Ibid.*
21. Howe, *Afrocentrism*, 66.

sources that James used are seldom discussed. To merely state that he is influenced by Masonic writings does little to further our understanding. Of more interest is what sort of Masonic ideas and writings were used. Despite the fact that Masonry had such an impact on the black community, there are scant indications as to James himself being a Mason. Rather, his sources seem to have been published works, often Theosophical interpretations of Masonry. Howe does, however, argue that based on James's own writings, we can infer that he was a Freemason who was "strongly influenced by the more esoteric aspects of Masonic lore".[22] While it is hardly improbable that James was a Mason, his works do not provide clear evidence for such statements. If anything, relying on the most quoted works, it would seem more likely that he was either a member of a Theosophical group or a Rosicrucian order. James refers, for example, to AMORC's magazine, *Rosicrucian Digest*.[23]

One of James's most quoted sources is a Theosophically inspired work, Charles H. Vail's *The Ancient Mysteries and Modern Masonry* from 1909. Its influence is most notable when it comes to the contents of the Egyptian mysteries and their history, and James sometimes quotes whole pages from Vail, not always with proper reference. Vail's interpretation of the origin of the mysteries differs somewhat from James's, as the former is more clearly based on Helena Blavatsky's *The Secret Doctrine* (1888). Vail was a Christian Universalist clergyman and a dedicated socialist, whose work before *The Ancient Mysteries* included titles such as *Principles of Scientific Socialism*, *The Industrial Evolution*, *Mission of the Working Class* and *Socialism and the Negro Problem*. In *The Ancient Mysteries*, however, few of his political ideas are present. According to Vail, the mysteries were first established in Atlantis, but after the fall of the civilization they survived in Egypt and Chaldea, where the mysteries had been established before Atlantis sank.[24] Considering James's strong reliance on Vail, and the latter's emphasis on Masonry, it is no surprise that the Egyptian mysteries get a Masonic flair in James's writings as well. Among other things, the mystery schools are presented as being organized in lodges, and Egypt is regarded as the home of the Grand Lodge.[25]

A central theme in James's writing is that nothing new was invented after the Egyptians, or rather that the "original version" of the mysteries was pure while later developments represented decline. The Greek versions were inferior to the Egyptian as they merely imitated the original form. One of the few Greeks that get any real recognition is Socrates, who was considered to be an initiate of the mysteries, and also a Mason.[26]

For James, philosophy is static and unchanging, and the role of the philosopher is thus to understand the mysteries, not to create new theories.

---

22. *Ibid.*, 66.
23. James, *Stolen Legacy*, 179.
24. Vail, *The Ancient Mysteries and Modern Masonry*, 14–16.
25. James, *Stolen Legacy*, 31–2.
26. *Ibid.*, 89.

James's aim is not merely to provide a mystical treatise on how to achieve esoteric goals, but rather to demonstrate how this new knowledge will serve the improvement of people of African descent in America and elsewhere. The final chapter of the book, "Social reformation through the New Philosophy of African Redemption", begins like this:

> Now that it has been shown that philosophy, and the arts and sciences were bequeathed to civilization by the people of North Africa and not by the people of Greece; the pendulum of praise and honour is due to shift from the people of Greece to the people of the African continent who are the rightful heirs of such praise and honour. This is going to mean a tremendous change in world opinion, and attitude, for all people and races who accept the new philosophy of African redemption, i.e. the truth that the Greeks were not the authors of Greek philosophy; but the people of North Africa; would change their opinion from one of disrespect to one of respect for the Black people throughout the world and treat them accordingly. It is also going to mean a most important change in the mentality of the Black people: a change from an inferiority complex, to the realization and consciousness of their equality with all the other great peoples of the world, who have built great civilizations. With this change in the mentality of the Black and White people, great changes are also expected in their respective attitudes towards each other, and in society as a whole.[27]

While James was hardly the first to perceive a need for a new attitude towards African and ancient history, as we have seen with Delany for example, he is one of the first to completely shift the focus from Europe to Africa. Other black nationalist leaders, like Marcus Garvey and W. E. B. Du Bois, usually held up European civilization as the role model for a future African culture.[28] Du Bois was particularly fond of Greek culture and made use of several classical references in his writings, even if he in later years started to be more interested in ancient Egypt and African culture.[29] James was also one of the pioneers in focusing on a spirituality that is neither Christian nor Islamic as the foundation for African people. Instead, he turned to what he considered to be "ancient mystery traditions" and esoteric paths to self-deification. For modern Afrocentrists, James's book has become a central work and is for some almost above all forms of critique. According to Wilson J. Moses, however, it has also been overemphasized by critics.[30] James's influence can even be seen

---

27. *Ibid.*, 153.
28. Austin, *Achieving Blackness*, 189–90; Moses, *Afrotopia*, 59–60.
29. *Ibid.*, 161–2.
30. *Ibid.*, 92–3.

in contemporary music: for example, the rap-artist Nas's song 'I can' (2002) ends with an appeal for young (primarily black) people to study the true history of the world. In the final verse we find how James's view of history can be used to further a moral agenda relevant for today's youth, as black youth are asked to remember their glorious past as kings and queens who ruled over vast empires, and how people from all over the world came to them to receive teaching. That is, until Asians, Arabs and Europeans conquered Africa with gold and military might. He describes how the history of Africa was destroyed by Alexander the Great, and how a "correct understanding of African history" could create a new mentality where young black people would abandon their ghetto attitude.

The idea of advanced Egyptian science and mysteries has become a recurring theme in Afrocentricity, as has the idea that Europeans stole most of it. James must be seen as an important source for this. As the use of esoteric sources has been one of the most recurring criticisms against James, some Afrocentrists like Molefi Kente Asante try to downplay the esoteric side of James's work.[31] Esoteric sources are nevertheless quite visible, and spiritual ideas about the nature of man would also become integrated in Afrocentricity. James's work did not have an immediate impact on the black nationalist movement and remained somewhat obscure for many years. During the 1970s, but especially in the 1990s, there was a revival of his ideas, and they have since then become a common theme for cultural nationalists. It is not only ideas about Egypt that have become part of the *Stolen Legacy* paradigm, but interpretations of Masonry as well. One who has developed this theme is Zachary P. Gremillion, who published *African Origins of Freemasonry* in 2005. Gremillion is clearly Afrocentric and nationalistic. He connects Masonry with the Egyptian mysteries (following Martin Delany and George James" theories), and makes connections to both Prince Hall and the Nation of Islam. He claims that Elijah Muhammad, leader of the Nation of Islam from 1934 to 1975, was a Mason and that the teachings of the movement are filled with Masonic symbolism.[32]

CULTURAL POLITICS IN THE US

In the 1960s and 1970s we find political groups with eschatological ideas based on a quest to regain a lost African tradition and mentality. One example of this is the US Organization, founded in the late 1960s by Maulana Karenga (b. 1941). US represented "us" as opposed to "them", symbolizing unity among black people against external enemies, primarily white people.[33] Originally

---

31. Asante, *An Afrocentric Manifesto*, 146.
32. Gremillion, *African Origins of Freemasonry*, 250.
33. Scot Brown, *Fighting for US*, 38.

founded by followers of Malcolm X and based on his legacy, the group soon focused increasingly on Karenga himself, who became a quasi-religious leader.[34] A priesthood was established within US to transmit and deepen the members' understanding of Karenga's teachings. Despite its focus on African culture, the movement was a part of the more political Black Power movement, and Karenga, who also pursued an academic career, wrote a dissertation on Afro-American Nationalism in 1976.[35] Still, Karenga saw the need for myths and spirituality and created a system called *Kawaida*, as a form of philosophical foundation for US. This is a form of holistic philosophy, based on his understanding of the basic principles underlying all African societies.[36] Central to *Kawaida* are seven principles, called *nguzo saba*, that became something of a creed. These are:

- *Umoja* (Unity) To strive for and to maintain unity in the family, community, nation and race.
- *Kujichagulia* (Self-Determination) To define ourselves, name ourselves, create for ourselves and speak for ourselves.
- *Ujima* (Collective Work and Responsibility) To build and maintain our community together and make our brothers' and sisters' problems our problems and to solve them together.
- *Ujamaa* (Cooperative Economics) To build and maintain our own stores, shops and other businesses and to profit from them together.
- *Nia* (Purpose) To make our collective vocation the building and developing of our community in order to restore our people to their traditional greatness.
- *Kuumba* (Creativity) To do always as much as we can, in the way we can, in order to leave our community more beautiful and beneficial than we inherited it.
- *Imani* (Faith) To believe with all our heart in our people, our parents, our teachers, our leaders and the righteousness and victory of our struggle.[37]

While "spiritual" matters were seen as important, Karenga took a rather negative view on religion and particularly what he called "spookism" (i.e. belief in the supernatural). Karenga regarded God as being within the human being itself. These ideas were probably inspired by the Nation of Islam.[38] The supernatural was an aspect of African culture which Karenga rejected as

---

34. *Ibid.*, 38–9; Austin, *Achieving Blackness*, 63.
35. Karenga, *Afro-American Nationalism*.
36. Scot Brown, *Fighting for US*, 33–6.
37. Karenga, *Kwanzaa*, 125.
38. Austin, *Achieving Blackness*, 63–4.

detrimental to the position of the black people. Still, religion was of importance as a socially unifying factor, and Karenga created his own year of celebrations, based on the Black Power struggle, to replace the Christian one. One of these celebrations, *Kwanzaa*, became rather successful even outside the black nationalist movement.[39]

After the end of the Black Power era in the 1980s, Karenga wrote more on spiritual matters. While it would take a while for the complete Egyptomania that would later define the Afrocentric movement to surface, we can see how the image of Egypt became more majestic already in Karenga's writings in the early 1980s. Still, in his *Introduction to Black Studies*, Egypt plays a prominent but hardly central role. Egyptian civilization is regarded as having its origin in Ethiopia, emphasizing the African foundation of Egypt, and there is mention of many Western ideas and religious concepts being based on Egyptian myths and concepts; the virgin birth and the Jesus figure are, for example, said to be modelled on Isis and Horus. These are, however, not Karenga's own ideas, but mainly reflections on other writers.[40] There is hardly any focus on mystical powers or deep spirituality, but rather on the political achievements of Egypt and their communal aspects. However, his second doctoral dissertation in 1994 was concerned with the moral concept of *maat* in ancient Egypt,[41] and in his later writings Egypt and its religion would figure as central components.[42]

AFROCENTRIC SPIRITUALITY

Afrocentricity can be seen as a development of the cultural nationalism of Maulana Karenga and the Black Power movement.[43] While the term itself came into popular use in the 1980s by Molefi Kente Asante (1942–), it hardly represents a clear break from older forms of black nationalism. Afrocentricity has become a controversial movement particularly in academia due to what critics consider unscientific methods and a racialized view of the world.[44] Asante answered some of these critics in one of his latest books, *An Afrocentric Manifesto* (2007), but that will hardly make the controversies go away. Asante has a tendency to dismiss all of his critics, including African-born scholars like the philosopher Kwame Anthony Appiah, as Eurocentric, thus preventing any constructive dialogue.[45] Afrocentrism is still a visible part of academic

---

39. Scot Brown, *Fighting for US*, 68–70, 161.
40. Karenga, *Introduction to Black Studies*, 55–6.
41. Karenga, *Maat, the Moral Ideal in Ancient Egypt*.
42. Karenga, *Kwanzaa*.
43. Austin, *Achieving Blackness*, 130–33.
44. For a description and analysis of the debate regarding the inclusion of Afrocentricity in schools in America, see Binder, *Contentious Curricula*. For an example of the critique levelled against Afrocentricity, see Lefkowitz, *Not Out of Africa*.
45. Asante, "A Quick Reading of Rhetorical Jingoism".

discourse on African and African American culture, but its impact is diminishing due in part to the criticism against it. What is of interest here is how Afrocentricity stands on the crossroads between academic perspectives and social ideology, which also includes spiritual values and ideas. Its aim is, after all, to shift from a European to an African mode of thinking.

As Africa is not a nation but a continent with a multitude of different traditions and peoples, defining a common African culture and mindset should be highly problematic. In order to resolve the problem, Asante creates an ideal image of African culture. Africa is first and foremost regarded as a cultural unity, a common feature of most forms of cultural nationalism. The foundation is something he calls the "African Cultural System", and, just as with the US movement, we find core values identified as African, such as "unity". Spirituality plays a central role for Asante, and like Karenga he is opposed to the idea of Africans adopting Christianity or Islam as their religion. In contrast to many other black nationalists, he spends a lot of time criticizing Islam, which he regards as a form of Arab nationalism.[46] According to Asante, a person's religion needs to be based on his/her cultural and ethnical background. For Africans, the choice should thus be some form of indigenous African spirituality rather than reinterpretations of Christianity or Islam adjusted to fit the needs of black people.

Asante's answer is an eclectic mix of religious elements, with a significant focus on ancient Egypt. He calls the basis of his worldview *Njia* – "the Way", which is similar to Karenga's *Kawaida*. *Njia* takes on ceremonial forms, is focused on ancestor worship, and furthers an Afrocentric view of the world:

> Njia is the collective expression of the Afrocentric worldview which is grounded in the historical experience of African people. … The stage was being set for Njia for over 100 years. Each level of awareness predictably leads to the manifestation of Njia. Njia represents the inspired Afrocentric spirit found in the traditions of African-Americans, and the spiritual survival of an African essence in America.[47]

While important in the early writings of Asante, *Njia* does not seem to have become as much of a living movement as Asante had hoped for. Still, the basic idea of building a spiritual tradition based upon African religion has continued to assert influence.

Concepts such as "awareness" and "spirit" are of importance in Asante's writings. It seems that Asante believes in the possibility to achieve some form of collective mindset that can be used to uplift the whole black community,

---

46. Asante, *Afrocentricity*, 5–10.
47. *Ibid.*, 30.

even those that do not adhere to Afrocentric views. To achieve this, only a small portion of the black community needs to become Afrocentrist. Rather than seeking to create a mass movement, Asante's goal is to create a form of spiritual elite who will become the spiritual leaders for the rest of the black community, echoing the ideals of Karenga's US Organization. He even mentions 250,000 Afrocentrists as the precise number necessary to achieve this transformation.[48] Asante embraces ideas about a collective unconscious that are similar to, even if not directly based upon, Jungian ideas. Conversely, Asante rejects Du Bois's theory of a double consciousness as being hostile to the interests of Africans. Du Bois's theory, in Asante's interpretation, indicated that the black person was somehow divided: he had integrated the white peoples' view of him as being inferior, and this created a mental state of victimhood that was seen as being counter to the black community's interests. Rather than focusing on the impact white culture had had on African people, the Afrocentric perspective would focus on how Africans, even in the diaspora, essentially remained "Africans" and thought in an African manner.[49] For Asante it is clear that people of African descent share a common mentality and spirit which makes it possible for them to intuitively feel and respond to African symbols and feel a connection to civilizations that have long since disappeared. This is most clearly seen in the example of Egypt.

Asante is opposed to religions that he regards as requiring submission to God. His arguments are similar to Karenga's, but rather than seeing African religions as containing "spookism", as Karenga does, Asante claims that African religions are based on the notion of God being immanent. He uses this argument in his discussions of religion among the Yoroba and the Egyptians (which he calls *Kem*).[50] In his programme to transform the situation for black people by adopting an African perspective of the world, he mentions the possibilities of a "Neo-Kemetic" outlook:

> What if African people, on the continent and in the Diaspora, looked to establish a Neo-Kemetic vision of the world? Would not the potential of this revolution be explosive in a positive way for creativity in politics, art, culture, science, philosophy, and architecture? Thus, those African leaders who speak about a renaissance of Africa must know that it is impossible without some appeal to a classical past.[51]

While Asante and his colleagues try to remain within the academic field, others position themselves more clearly as religious teachers. One example is Ra

---

48. *Ibid.*, 68.
49. Asante, *An Afrocentric Manifesto*, 157–9.
50. Asante, *Afrocentricity*, 67.
51. *Ibid.*, 11.

Un Nefer Amen (born Rogelio Alcides Straughn in Panama, in 1944) and his Ausar Auset Society, based in Brooklyn, New York, and with chapters around the world, most of which are in North America. *Ausar* and *Auset* are alternative names for Osiris and Isis, and the teachings of the society are based on a mixture of traditions that are all claimed to have their origins in Egypt. For example, the Tree of Life of the Kabbalah is seen as an Egyptian symbol. On their webpage they describe their background:

> Based on the indigenous traditional African cultures dating from the earliest documentable periods (Kamit [ancient Egypt], Indus Kush [pre-Aryan Vedantic India], Canaan [Palestine], and Kush [Ethiopia]), the classes taught revolve around the oldest religion known to mankind – the Ausarian religion of ancient Kamit. The Kamitic Tree of Life (Paut Neteru) forms the basis of the cosmogony (philosophy) of this ancient system. It reunites the traditions of the great Black founders of civilization, allowing us to weave their knowledge into a spiritually empowering way of life which aims at the awakening of the Ausar principle (the Divine Self) within each being.[52]

The proposed influence of African civilization is broadened, and even India and China are regarded as being under its influence. It is also clear that the contemporary Ausar Auset Society considers itself to be based upon the same religious beliefs found in ancient Egypt, rather than being a modern invention. The society considers man and God as being linked qualitatively but not quantitatively: a person has the potential for divine powers, but these are dormant within him until correct spiritual training awakens them. The society does not embrace the idea of salvation by faith familiar from Christianity, but rather posits that one must act in accordance with the moral laws of the universe in order to reach a happy and spiritually fulfilled life. The religious system is holistic and incorporates all aspect of life, from diet (Amen promotes vegetarianism) to relationships (guides for living in Afrocentric relationships are available). But there are also more esoteric aspects that focus on yoga and other spiritual techniques. The society adheres to the idea of sacred kingship, and the King also functions as the High Priest. Amen has been the society's leader since its foundation, and he is described as "His Excellency, Shekhem Ur Shekhem (King) and Ashem Ur Ashemu (High Priest), Ra Un Nefer Amen 1".[53] Almost all of the literature is also written by him.

Another example of Afrocentricity being used as a foundation for new religious teachings is provided by Dr Muata A. Ashby, who has published books

---

52. Ausar Auset Society, "Florida Study Group".
53. *Ibid.*

with titles such as *Egyptian Yoga* (2005), purportedly based upon ancient Egyptian teachings. Ashby's system is similar to what could be found in Germany in the 1920s when some esoteric writers created yoga systems based on the shape of the runes.[54] Ashby sees something similar in Egyptian descriptions of the gods and has created a yoga system based on the body poses of various deities in Egyptian hieroglyphs.

MAGICAL MELANIN

While many Afrocentric writers have a negative view of European civilization, it is rare to find overtly racist sentiments against white people as individuals. Still, within the Afrocentric movement we do find ideas that seem to mirror white supremacist ideologies, and, just in the same manner, we do find that these ideas sometimes interact with spiritual ones. We can find theories that explain the need to "keep the race pure", and ideas about magical possibilities related to the "blood of the race". In Afrocentricity, this is linked to ideas of the function of the pigment melanin. One of the more famous and influential examples of this idea can be found in the works of the American psychologist Frances Cress Welsing (b. 1935). In the 1970s Welsing presented what she termed "The Cress Theory of Color-Confrontation and Racism". According to Karenga, she was influenced by the radical scholar Neeley Fuller's *Textbook for Victims of White Supremacy* (1969). Karenga makes specific reference to four of Fuller's points that serve as the foundation of Welsing's theories. These are:

> 1) White supremacy was the only functional racism; 2) all Third World peoples are victims of it; 3) racism is not merely an individual or institutional phenomena [*sic*], but a universal system of domination; and 4) that European theories and systems of political and economic organization are designed to establish, insure and expand white domination.[55]

Fuller's ideas are in many ways a clear representation of ideas that were in vogue among radical groups in the 1960s and 1970s, when solidarity with the Third World and opposition to Western imperialism became a central issue for different socialist movements. Welsing develops these ideas with a focus on the colour of people.[56] According to her, white supremacy could not be explained by economic or social factors, but was rather based on an inferiority complex that white people had. White people were lacking in colour, and thus feared people of colour as their presence was a constant reminder of this

---

54. Thorson, *Rune Might*, 17–20.
55. Karenga, *Introduction to Black Studies*, 338.
56. Welsing, *The Isis Papers*, 2.

lack. As the "white gene" was regressive, it also reminded them that they eventually would become annihilated. To prevent this annihilation a system was established to keep the coloured races in place and white people dominant. Evidence of white supremacy could in Welsing's mind be seen throughout society, from pool tables – where the white ball is used to strike all the coloured ones – to candy bars that represented the genitalia of black men which white people secretly wanted to consume.[57] Most of Welsing's ideas were formulated already in the 1970s, but it was with the publication of *The Isis Papers* in 1991 that her influence became most notable.

According to Welsing, white people are the result of a mutation. Originally, existence was peaceful in an African matriarchy, but this was disrupted by the appearance of a genetic mutation: albinos. The mutants were expelled from Africa due to their inferiority. Considering the recent violence against albinos in parts of Africa, Welsing's ideas appear all the more disturbing. In an interview she explains the origin of the white race:

> Black people were the first people on the planet. ... White people ... lost the color through a genetic mutation to albinism, which genetics defines as a genetic deficiency state and they were forced out of Africa into Europe. Scientists who classify themselves as White don't want to say [this]. You can't simultaneously think White is superior and then say that White is a genetic deficiency state. I look at the system of racism having come into being consciously because the White population recognized, after they circumnavigated the globe, that they were a tiny minority, fewer that [sic] one-tenth of the people on the planet. And they were genetic-recessive compared to the genetic dominance of people who produce color. They realized that they could be genetically annihilated and White people could, as a collective of people, disappear. They worked out a system for White survival, which entails dominating all of the Black, Brown, Red and Yellow people on the planet. So racism is a behavioral system for the survival of White people.[58]

The system of white supremacy is, according to Welsing, based on controlling the coloured population by keeping them psychologically chained and unaware of their potential. One effect of this is a psychological state where people of colour feel inferior and regress to a childlike state, unaware of their inherent power. This power gives the black person almost superhuman abilities and Welsing theorizes that melanin even has magical qualities. As evidence for this, she presents the Dogon tribes and their purported knowledge of the twin

---

57. *Ibid.*
58. Welsing, "Interviews with Dr Cress Welsing".

stars Sirius and Sirius B, which would require advanced instruments not available to the Dogon to observe.[59] According to Welsing, they had this knowledge due to their higher consciousness, which was in turn a result of their high level of melanin. Furthermore, Sirius B is presented as in some way acting as a reservoir of knowledge that people with high levels of melanin can tap into, as a sort of "Akashic chronicle" available only to certain races.[60]

While all people of colour are, in Welsing's opinions, victims of white supremacy, the particular focus is on black people. They are seen as a master race among the coloured people. Welsing's work has had a larger impact than one might at first expect. Her books have sold several thousand copies and have had a minor impact in popular culture with movies like John Singleton's *Baby Boy* (2001). References to her work, without mentions of her racism, can even be found in the works of academic feminist writers such as Patricia Hill Collins, who otherwise rejects most of the ideas found in Afrocentricity.[61]

Melanin theory is a recurring black supremacy notion that can be found in the Afrocentric milieu, even if most Afrocentrists do not place any greater emphasis on Welsing's theories or similar melanin-based ideologies. Still, not only has there been a reluctance to criticize her, but it is clear that the theory does exist as a form of substratum in the milieu. Welsing is treated as an acknowledged academic in scholarly Afrocentric journals like *Journal of Black Studies* and *Journal of Black Psychology*, so she cannot be dismissed as a fringe author in the field. In 2005 she appeared in the Afrocentric documentary *500 Years Later*, written by Molefi Kete Asante Jr, the son of Molefi Kete Asante, together with other Afrocentric writers like Asante and Karenga.

If Welsing in some ways tries to downplay the magical aspect of melanin, at least in her more scholarly publications, other writers are more upfront with their ideas. In the works of another melanin theorist, Carol Barnes, we find that melanin makes a person almost divine.[62] There is also a smaller publishing industry that produces books on how to activate the power of melanin within you. These books often include health tips and different spiritual techniques like meditation by which this can be done. Particularly, there is an emphasis on maintaining a correct diet in order to awaken the melanin power within

---

59. The Sirius B controversy relates to the French anthropologist Marcel Griaule, whose descriptions of the beliefs of the Dogon people in the 1940s included interviews with Dogon elders who seemed to know that the star Sirius had a twin star next to it. As this knowledge would have been impossible without technology unavailable to the Dogon at the time, it created a debate as to how this was possible. Recent studies are critical of Griaule's descriptions, and question the supposedly isolated nature of the Dogon people. The idea of the Dogon's knowledge of Sirius B has contributed to theories on extraterrestrials and UFOs. Welsing's knowledge of the Dogon probably derived from this literature. Temple, *The Sirius Mystery*; De Montellano, "Multicultural Pseudoscience".
60. Howe, *Afrocentrism*, 269.
61. Collins, *From Black Power to Hip Hop*, 115–16.
62. Barnes, *Melanin*.

the person. Examples of such books are Deanne Meningall's *The Melanin Diet* (2009) and Llaila O. Afrika's *Nutricide: The Nutritional Destruction of the Black Race* (2001), which not only presents ways to improve health but also describes junk food as part of a white conspiracy against the black race. Afrika explains the relation between black and white people:

> We are an ancient people from an ancient civilization and we do not always use the ancient authority that melanin and our higher spiritual and mental status grants us. We are not humanistically on the same level as the Caucasian. We are biochemically and electromagnetically superior to them. Therefore, we must examine the inferior Caucasian from the superior African status. It may take some getting used to, but we are the chosen race from the spirit world and the race blessed by the Sun. We must take our position of world leadership on this planet or have no planet because the Caucasians will destroy it. I beg of you, *do not let the Caucasian junk food diet or diseases make you a prisoner in your own body*.[63]

Melanin power is of course not available to white people, who at times are not even seen as humans in this context. Welsing and other melanin theorists are fond of interpreting human as "hue-man", creating the impression that being human is to be coloured. Bernard Ortez de Montellano gives an example of this by using a quote from a speech delivered by the Afrocentric scholar Wade Nobles,[64] who said:

> CNS (central nervous system) plus EMS (essential melanic system) equals HB (human being). That the central nervous system combined with the essential melanic system is what makes you human. That in fact, to be human is to be black. To be human is to be black.[65]

The albino theory is not the only melanin-based theory of the difference between whites and blacks. Another is the ice-man theory developed by the white Canadian writer Michael Bradley in his 1991 book *Iceman Inheritance*. Bradley claims that white people are more violent and aggressive because their DNA contains elements of Neanderthal DNA, while black people are the only

---

63. Afrika, *Nutricide*, xiii (emphasis original).
64. Nobles is today professor emeritus in the Department of Africana Studies, the School of Ethnic Studies at San Francisco State University, and is the founder and Executive Director of the Institute for the Advanced Study of Black Family Life and Culture, Inc. in Oakland, California.
65. De Montellano, "Melanin, Afrocentricity and Pseudoscience", 51.

pure humans.[66] These ideas have been embraced by the Afrocentric scholar Leonard Jeffries who divides the world into black "sun people" and white "icemen".[67] Richard M. Benjamin, a senior editor of *The Journal of Blacks in Higher Education*, who followed Jeffries activities in his classroom, gave the following recapitulation of the kind of ideas presented:

> "The ecology of the cave is different than the ecology of the riverbank." Then a pause. "Cave vs. riverbank!" he (Jeffries) exclaims. People of European heritage acclimated themselves to caves and cold climates. Scavenging for food and resources to live on, they acquired their "dog-eat-dog values." Sun people, by contrast, benefited from their warm ecology. "People who live on a riverbank with an abundance of coconuts become cooperative," he says.[68]

Jeffries has been involved in several legal battles and has endangered his academic career due to his statements concerning white people and Jews. The latter, he claims, were responsible for the slave trade. Molefi Kete Asante, while generally negative to overtly racist doctrines, has also looked favourably upon the ice-man theory, though it is generally downplayed in his writings.[69]

GENERAL THEMES

Is it possible to see any general themes that can distinguish the form and role esoteric ideas have taken in African American communities when compared with other milieus? While there is a clear diversity, and we can see a shift of focus from desires to imitate Europeans to an active identification as African in the 1960s, we can also see that from the early stages of Prince Hall Masonry there has existed a focus on moral and intellectual uplifting of the black people. That there exists a moral and spiritual crisis that must be addressed has been one of the most common themes and goals for black activists since the 1700s. From black Christian to black socialist movements, there is hardly any group that has not focused especially on this. Ideas about the need for some form of enlightened elite to lead the people are also common. What esoteric orders like Masonry historically gave people was a system by which this could be accomplished.

Esoteric ideas are used in conjunction with a larger narrative explaining the current situation for black people as being due to a lack of knowledge about their glorious past, or, as in the case of melanin theories, the lack of knowledge

---

66. Howe, *Afrocentrism*, 207.
67. *Ibid.*, 270; Binder, *Contentious Curricula*, 97.
68. Benjamin, "The Bizarre Classroom of Dr Leonard Jefferies", 96.
69. Bradley, "Official Webpage".

of their potential for almost supernatural powers. In order to achieve change, the mind needs to be liberated from the mental shackles that constrain it, and black people need to be made aware of the structures that have kept them down. One central aspect of this project is to rewrite history. In this discourse it has been common to embrace conspiracy theories and ideas about a lost, secret, and/or suppressed history.[70] As we have seen with George James's seminal work, this project was sometimes based upon Masonic and Theosophical ideas. We also find ideas about a form of wisdom that is the "true foundation" of science and philosophy. While Asante claimed that there was a need for a social evolution in order for Afrocentricity to be born, the general rhetoric is based upon the idea of older and static wisdom. By understanding and adopting a new perspective based upon this knowledge the person is liberated from intellectual and spiritual bondage. As we have seen, some writers have developed techniques to enhance the powers that could purportedly be awakened by gaining knowledge. Regarding religion, we see attempts to create alternative spiritualities that are not based upon Christianity or Islam, but rather on indigenous African traditions. God is often regarded as immanent, and the human being thus has the potential to awaken the divine within him-/herself. All this is connected to larger political ambitions to change the circumstances for black people. As the sociologist Algernon Austin has argued, the development towards self-improvement, though in a highly collective form, can be seen as a means to continue after the decline of political radical groups from the 1970s.[71] This is also part of a broader shift of focus from political to moral and personal issues that can be seen as a general trend of the 1980s and 1990s, with phenomena such as the self-help book *Iron John*[72] and "New Age" therapies being prime examples. Many Afrocentric writers are focused on the importance of family and relationships and how to sustain them. Often we find conservative and predominantly heteronormative views on marriage and family.

While Afrocentricity is still a living movement in the USA, the culturally dominant role the movement had during the 1990s has declined. This has not only to do with political and social developments, but can also be attributed to Afrocentrists entering academia and establishing black studies programmes. This made them the subject of academic critique, which has grown more vocal over the years. The critique comes not only from scholars of African and ancient history, but also from academics dealing with Afro-American history and philosophy who feel that the Afrocentric paradigm is limiting, unscientific, and based on untenable essentialist notions of culture and

---

70. Such notions of history are far from uncommon in conspiracy theories generally. See Chapter 10 of this volume.
71. Austin, *Achieving Blackness*, 130.
72. Bly, *Iron John*.

race.[73] The Inclusion of black studies programmes, based on Afrocentric ideas, have also many times proved to be pyrrhic victories as the inclusions often were nothing more than symbolic.[74] What role they will play in the future is thus difficult to predict. Changing political circumstances might well prepare the way for a revival of Afrocentricity, but what form it will take is an open issue. Judging from the writings produced today, spirituality will continue to play a central role, even if the harsh critique of religions such as Christianity and Islam is being downplayed to further interreligious cooperation.

---

73. See for example Austin, *Achieving Blackness*; Appiah, "Europe Upside Down"; Moses, *Afrotopia*; Gilroy, *The Black Atlantic*.
74. Binder, *Contentious Curricula*, 13–15.

CHAPTER 4

SECRET LINEAGES AND DE FACTO SATANISTS
ANTON LAVEY'S USE OF ESOTERIC TRADITION

Per Faxneld

In this article, I will investigate how Anton Szandor LaVey (1930–97), who founded the Church of Satan in 1966, constructed a Satanic tradition in his texts, and to what use he put it.[1] James R. Lewis has discussed how Satanists in the Church of Satan, after LaVey's death, make reference to tradition.[2] In that context, tradition is basically understood as the teaching established by their founder. What I shall look at here, however, is rather how LaVey himself makes ambiguous references to a supposed pre-existing Satanic tradition. I will present an interpretation of this based on LaVey's overall ontology, and his view of religious and esoteric phenomena.

In an esoteric context, tradition will typically be invoked to provide legitimacy, and there are, as Olav Hammer has shown, several ingrained esotericist strategies for doing this.[3] Naturally, use of tradition as a means to create legitimacy is not the exclusive domain of esotericism or religion. Nations, universities, companies and so on use this strategy frequently. But several of LaVey's strategies for employing tradition harken back to approaches prevalent in Western esotericism, and are instantly recognizable to a scholar of such ideas. As will be shown, he both utilizes historical predecessors in a way that is common within Western esotericism in general, and breaks with this common usage in a way similar to what we can observe among Chaos Magicians.[4]

---

1. Satanic tradition, rather than Satanist tradition, is the more common emic term, which I shall also use here. For further discussion of themes similar to those treated in this chapter, see Petersen, "'We Demand Bedrock Knowledge'"; Petersen, "The Seeds of Satan".
2. Lewis, *Legitimating New Religions*, 103–22.
3. Hammer, *Claiming Knowledge*. On the creation of legitimacy using tradition in a Satanist group (the Denmark-based Neo-Luciferian Church), see Faxneld, "The Strange Case of Ben Kadosh", 13–21.
4. See Chapter 5 of the present volume.

LaVey discarded much of the old esoteric and Satanic material as useless and outdated, but he still emerges as dependent on it to a fairly large extent. This applies not only in the general sense that no creed is of course created *ex nihilo*, but also because LaVey explicitly calls on tradition to legitimate and, more importantly, playfully create the right atmosphere for his Satanic activities. I shall argue in this article that legitimation is not, as perhaps would be expected, the prime function of tradition for LaVey. Rather, he seems to deem tradition most useful for bringing about certain psychological effects in a framework where one practises the "willing suspension of disbelief" (to use the term coined by Coleridge) in a limited context.

I will focus almost exclusively on core movement texts, with some additional data from an interview I recently conducted with the current High Priest of the Church of Satan, Peter H. Gilmore, and occasional references to material on the Church of Satan's website. In order to get a more complete view of the theme discussed here, it would be necessary to also talk to a great number of Church of Satan members and study views concerning tradition expressed on various Satanist Internet forums. What is presented here should therefore be considered groundwork for such a larger study, which would also take more into account the enactment and actual use of tradition among Satanists.

The material for this article is primarily LaVey's two main works, *The Satanic Bible* (1969) and *The Satanic Rituals* (1972), and to some extent his two collections of essays *The Devil's Notebook* (1992) and *Satan Speaks!* (1998). The two books *The Secret Life of a Satanist: The Authorized Biography of Anton LaVey* (1990) and *The Church of Satan* (1990), both by Blanche Barton, who would later give birth to LaVey's son, will also be scrutinized to see how tradition is constructed. When it comes to some of LaVey's works, the question of authorship is not uncomplicated. As is well known, *The Satanic Bible* contains a prologue borrowed from Ragnar Redbeard.[5] Michael Aquino wrote some sections in *The Satanic Rituals*, and it has been claimed that Diane Hegarty, LaVey's partner from 1960 to 1985, also contributed to his early texts.[6] For the present article, I shall leave these questions aside and treat all LaVey's works as written solely by him. Most readers will approach them as stemming straight from his pen, and this is perhaps more important in the end. Further, even if others may have contributed, LaVey edited their contributions and fitted them into his framework, thus making the end result "his" in all relevant senses.[7]

---

5. Lewis, *Legitimating New Religions*, 112.
6. Aquino, *The Church of Satan*, 52, 691. Aquino's history of the church is a treasure trove of information, but must be read with awareness of his falling out with LaVey.
7. Concerning the composing of *The Satanic Bible* and LaVey's use of passages by other authors, see Gallagher, "Sources, Sects and Scripture".

HOW OLD IS SATANISM?

Having specialized in the early history of Satanism, I often get the question "How old is Satanism?" It seems appropriate to begin a chapter about Satanism and tradition by briefly answering this query, as it provides a necessary background for the main discussion. If we understand the question as pertaining to how long there has been an unbroken explicitly Satanic tradition, in the sense of a group of people adhering to a teaching of that type, the answer is quite simple: an enduring tradition of Satanism was initiated in 1966, when Anton LaVey founded the Church of Satan.

The answer can be problematized in various ways, of course. First off, definitions of Satanism and tradition need to be considered. In this section of the article I will use a fairly broad definition of Satanism, where the term designates any more systematic and sustained celebration of Satan, as a symbolical or actually existing figure.[8] A tradition, in turn, is here understood to be a set of more or less distinct ideas kept continuously alive by persons over a period of time spanning at least several decades.[9]

Even if no one prior to 1966 inaugurated a tradition that remains in existence to this day, there were people who nourished an intense sympathy for the Devil long before LaVey. As early as the late eighteenth century we can find purely literary Satanists, but their sympathy for the Devil seldom extended beyond occasional outbursts of lauding Lucifer in a text or two.[10] One exception is the Polish Decadent author Stanislaw Przybyszewski (1868–1927), who both openly referred to himself as a Satanist and developed a Satanic *Weltanschauung* through a series of works in different genres (novels, short stories, essays in history, art criticism). He could be said to be the first "proper" Satanist, as his literary exploration of such sympathies also resulted in a specific and lasting view of the world with Satan as its root metaphor.[11] In the context of Western esotericism, one of the first to express unequivocal praise of Satan was H. P. Blavatsky, cofounder and front figure of the Theosophical Society, in her magnum opus *The Secret Doctrine* (1888). If her system is considered as a whole, however, these ideas are peripheral.[12] The first person to build an entire esoteric system around Satan, though admittedly a rather

---

8. This is basically the same definition proposed in Faxneld, *Mörkrets Apostlar*, xiv–xvi.
9. But see the discussion by Asprem and Granholm in Chapter 2 of this volume.
10. As Peter Schock has shown, the English Romantics often labelled the "Satanic School" – Byron and Shelley – were a lot more equivocal in their praise of Satan than is sometimes assumed (and this goes for William Blake as well). Their attitude to Lucifer shifted throughout their careers, and they also employed him as a symbol of wickedness on numerous occasions (Schock, *Romantic Satanism*).
11. On Przybyszewski's Satanism, see Faxneld, "Witches, Nihilist Anarchism and Social Darwinism"; Faxneld, *Mörkrets Apostlar*, 140–49. The standard biography is Klim, *Stanislaw Przybyszewski*.
12. Faxneld, *Mörkrets Apostlar*, 108–17.

minuscule one, was the obscure Danish occultist Ben Kadosh (Carl William Hansen, 1872–1936). He did not manage to gather more than a handful of adherents to this teaching, at most, possibly none at all.[13] The next instance of esoteric Satanism is the considerably more well-populated order Fraternitas Saturni in 1920s Germany. This order had some features that can clearly be labelled Satanic, such as Luciferian masses, but whether they were pronounced enough to justify designating the entire system thus is questionable.[14] Problems of a somewhat similar type arise when trying to peg down the "Satanic" temple (this was a term she herself used) briefly operated by Maria de Naglowska in 1930s Paris, which had as its aim an integration of Satan and God.[15]

None of these groups and individuals are invoked as predecessors by LaVey, and none of them have themselves kept a tradition of Satanism alive. Though some of them, like Kadosh, have inspired present-day Satanist groups, their ideas have not been passed down in an unbroken line of transmission.[16] There is thus not a single case of an unbroken initiatory chain in the classical sense. The Theosophical Society and Fraternitas Saturni have both carried on activity to this day, but their specifically Satanic ideas have played very little or no part at all in the long run. These elements have, it seems, largely faded away with time. Hence, there is no reliably documented case of Satanic continuity, in a strict sense, earlier than the founding of the Church of Satan in 1966. The lack of evidence satisfying a scholar has not hindered some Satanists from making claims about very deep, but *secret*, historical roots for their lineages. LaVey, as we shall see, instead chose to construct tradition in a rather more inclusive and generous manner where actual continuity, or even Satanic sympathies in the supposed predecessors, are deemed to be of less importance. Had he known of the groups and individuals mentioned above (or in the case of Theosophy, that he most certainly had some familiarity with: if he had been aware of the small and seldom discussed pinch of sympathy for the Devil incorporated in it) it is quite possible he would have made reference to them.

---

13. See Faxneld, "The Strange Case of Ben Kadosh".
14. I have earlier – in Faxneld, *Mörkrets apostlar*, 177–88 – argued they should indeed be labelled Satanists, but having pondered the matter for a few years more I am no longer quite as convinced this is appropriate.
15. A good introduction to Naglowska's ideas is Hakl, "The Theory and Practice of Sexual Magic", 465–74. There are also a couple of other tiny and long-defunct Satanist groups that *may* have been founded prior to the Church of Satan – Raymond Bogart's Orthodox Temple of the Prince in Manchester, UK, and Herbert Sloane's Our Lady of Endor Coven in Toledo, Ohio – but the documentation is unreliable, and neither of them ever provided substantial evidence of having existed before 1966, despite insistent claims they had been around longer than LaVey's church. On these two groups, see Faxneld, *Mörkrets Apostlar*, 202–15. The Process Church of the Final Judgment, founded well before LaVey established the Church of Satan in 1966, seems not to have incorporated the elements of Satanism that they later became infamous for until *after* 1966 (Bainbridge, *Satan's Power*, 68–9, 87).
16. Faxneld, "The Strange Case of Ben Kadosh".

But most of them were extremely obscure, and completely unknown in the 1960s, especially in the United States.

FUNCTION OVER TRADITION

To some extent, LaVey uses references to historical Satanism to strengthen his legitimacy. More importantly, however, he utilizes (consciously constructed) tradition as a tool in the same way demons or inverted pentagrams are used – to generate certain psychological *effects*. LaVey is at most times explicitly primarily interested in what functions "traditional" Satanic symbols, rituals, and historiographic narratives have, not their pedigree or formal veracity itself.

A case in point is the Black Mass, which, according to LaVey, should be used to rid oneself of inhibitions and false ideals by blaspheming current holy cows. The point is not to please Satan or mock Christianity, as would typically be believed about this ritual, but to decondition the participant. In the 1960s, LaVey opines, it would be more useful to denigrate the widely popular psychedelic movement by trampling an LSD tablet underfoot instead of communion wafers.[17] The purpose of a ritual is to elicit a strong emotional response from the participants, which can then be used to effect healthy psychological changes.[18] For this reason, older blasphemous rituals can never be used unaltered since they cannot be expected to have the intended effect on a present-day person. LaVey dryly remarks: "one no longer reads a Victorian romance for sexual titillation".[19] Whether or not the form of the Black Mass is traditional is therefore unimportant.

LaVey's attitude when it comes to ritual magic is telling in several ways. One important feature in how he views this phenomenon is that he deems it necessary during rituals to evoke a sense of wonder and amazement, temporarily shutting down critical, intellectual thinking. This is done in order to achieve the magician's goal, "to expand his will". The room where the ritual takes place becomes an "intellectual decompression chamber".[20] The purpose is purely instrumental. It is therefore significant that a major part of LaVey's references to tradition occur in the context of descriptions of ritual practices. The tall tales being told – of Templars, secret fraternities, Middle Eastern Satanic rites, esoteric knowledge being passed from initiate to initiate, and so on – must be understood in relation to the "willing suspension of disbelief" taking place in the ritual chamber.

---

17. LaVey, *The Satanic Bible*, 101. Cf. LaVey, *The Satanic Rituals*, 34, concerning the Black Mass: "Its prime purpose is to reduce or negate stigma acquired through past indoctrination".
18. An analysis of the early Church of Satan that very much stresses this aspect is Moody, "Magical Therapy".
19. LaVey, *The Satanic Rituals*, 25.
20. LaVey, *The Satanic Bible*, 120.

In an interesting article, historian of religions Peter Jackson has discussed how such suspension can be used in a religious setting even by those who *do* believe in supernatural phenomena. By consciously setting aside critical thinking in a particular ritual situation, they can allow for mechanical devices (the shaking of metal plates to simulate sudden thunder, etc.) to amaze them and make the situation even more numinous.[21] Whereas the people in the antique examples treated by Jackson might do this in order to further heighten the impact of something they actually consider supernatural and numinous, LaVey suggests "faking" this belief too, simply to achieve the useful effects a (temporary) traditional religious/esoteric mindset can have.

LAVEY'S REJECTION OF ESOTERIC TRADITION

The attitude evinced by LaVey towards esotericism as a tradition is ambiguous. *The Satanic Bible* (1969) opens with the following diatribe: "This book was written because, with very few exceptions, every tract and paper, every 'secret' grimoire, all the 'great works' on the subject of magic, are nothing but sanctimonious fraud."[22] And on the same page, LaVey lays down that "[t]he old literature is the by-product of brains festering with fear and defeat."[23] Throughout this and other of his works, he blasts his forebears as having "lain ill with metaphysical constipation", and so on.[24] Many harsh words are uttered: "Those with the greatest degree of *natural* magical ability are often far too busy with other activities to learn the 'finer' points of the *Sephiroth, Tarot, I Ching*, etc." But then he immediately adds: "This is not intended to suggest that there is no value in arcane wisdom."[25] Its foremost value, however, appears to be as part of the content in the "storehouse of avowed fantasy gathered from all cultures and from all ages" that LaVey states a Satanist maintains. Having access to such a reservoir, a "Satanist can easily *invent* fairy tales to match anything contained in holy writ", but at the same time – unlike his Christian compatriot – admitting his invention is fictitious.[26] The first page of *The Satanic Bible* accordingly states: "Herein you will find truth – and fantasy."[27]

Given such frank admissions, how are we to read LaVey's use of the stereotypical arsenal of esoteric legitimization devices? He has, after all, practically invalidated all religious ideas as such and lowered their status to that of fairy

---

21. Jackson, "Apparitions and Apparatuses". In Jackson's discussion, belief or disbelief is held up as being an often unimportant question, and one aim of his article is to dissolve such sharp dichotomies (not only pertaining to Antiquity, but in general).
22. LaVey, *The Satanic Bible*, 21.
23. *Ibid.*, 21.
24. *Ibid.*, 155.
25. *Ibid.*, 23.
26. LaVey, *The Satanic Rituals*, 27 (emphasis added).
27. LaVey, *The Satanic Bible*, 21.

tales. Naturally, his evocation of esoteric tradition, in the specific sense of precisely a tradition being handed down, must be read with this in mind. The concept of a long and mysterious tradition informing his Satanism, an idea he does propagate, is – just like Satan, ritual robes, altars, and so on – a colourful and evocative backdrop to psychodrama of the type he prescribes.

At least this was probably his intention. However, during my fieldwork among North American Satanists (most of whom were not members of the Church of Satan, but often still very much inspired by LaVey), it has become clear to me that many read him as *literally* an inheritor of secret esoteric traditions.[28] Thus, when LaVey utilizes stereotypical esoteric markers of legitimacy and high age, such as references to the Knights Templar as predecessors, many fail to see the ironic smile and mischievous glint in his eye.[29] Irony and playfulness are significant traits of LaVey's texts which are often ignored. When he brings to the fore the Yezidi as the originators of most Satanism to come, he does this for the reason that it is evocative and sets the proper mood, regardless of if it is a historically "correct" tradition that he sketches. When he musters stalwart arguments of esoteric legitimacy, he does so because they work well to create the desired aura of tradition-based validity that help his adherents in their endeavours. Still, if the occasional "rube" was duped and figured the "traditional" elements a good reason to pay the membership fee in the Church of Satan, LaVey would probably not have minded.

LaVey was conjecturally not very serious about his claims that Satanism has deep historical esoteric roots, but intended them to be perceived by the sharp-eyed Satanist as fairy-tale fluff creating the appropriate atmosphere, rather than literal truth. Judging from what I have observed in my fieldwork, his readers are frequently not as sharp-eyed and perceptive as he had hoped, and they either misunderstand the ontological status of LaVey's claims because of lacking reading comprehension, or they project their own hopes concerning tradition into his texts. To a great extent, it would seem LaVey has suffered a fate similar to that of another great humorist and ironic, Aleister Crowley, who is also often read too literally. The English magician wrote of having celebrated child sacrifices 150 times a year between 1912 and 1928.[30] Of course, what he meant was that he had masturbated frequently in sex magical rites, thus spilling seed containing potential children. A great many people, though in this case hardly any among his actual followers, did not comprehend this obvious joke and thought Crowley a child murderer.

Though they may ultimately have a very different *raison d'être* in the Satanic context, there are several concepts in LaVey's texts that echo those well known

---

28. My fieldwork was conducted in New York City in two three-week periods in the summer of 2010 and spring of 2011. Additional fieldwork has been carried out continuously in Sweden 2007–11.
29. LaVey, *The Satanic Rituals*, 54–5.
30. Crowley, *Magick in Theory and Practice*, 95.

from esotericism. For example, LaVey's dividing of history into different eras and ages, where the latter bear the mark of either Fire or Ice (symbolizing different religious/moral ideals), is very similar to concepts familiar from Theosophy and Thelema.[31] LaVey, who was reasonably familiar with esoteric source material, developed his own creed in dialogue with it, discarding most of its intricate metaphysics with a happy grin, but always keeping that which was useful for his goals. Some esoteric notions and trappings are, simply put, nice-looking frosting on an otherwise perhaps somewhat bland-looking ideological cake. Such use of it is entirely in accordance with a characteristically LaVeyan statement in *The Satanic Bible*: "Man needs ceremony and ritual, fantasy and enchantment."[32]

By fiercely attacking the esotericists of old, and then still making ample use of their material, for example John Dee's Enochian language (almost half of *The Satanic Bible* consists of a reworking of Dee's material),[33] LaVey can both have his cake and throw it in the garbage can. The esoteric tradition is fraudulent, an old worm-stung idol that needs to be smashed. But if one has the right understanding of it, LaVey seems to say, much that is useful can be salvaged and incorporated into a new and entirely rational tradition – that still has continuity with the past. LaVey, in short, is not blind to how attractive high age is to many when it comes to ideas, but pairs the appeal of tradition with rational, materialistic interpretations more in unison with his time.

ESOTERIC GENEALOGIES

Constructing historical lineages was once very important among most esotericists. Theosophist Henry Olcott, for instance, held up his society as the inheritors of a tradition encompassing Albertus Magnus, Cagliostro, Pico della Mirandola, Paracelsus, Cornelius Agrippa, alchemists, Rosicrucians, and many others. In more recent times, there has been a decreasing tendency to explicitly view older generations of esoteric writers as spiritual forebears. The more or less tangible initiatory chain Antoine Faivre has written of is no longer quite as essential to all practitioners.[34]

LaVey is not, as perhaps would have been expected, disinterested in esoteric genealogies. In fact, he spends quite a few pages on delineating them. For instance, he details how rites of the Illuminati influenced Ordo Templi Orientis

---

31. LaVey, *The Satanic Rituals*, 219–20. LaVey's description of epochs seems to be derived from Hans Hörbiger's World Ice Theory.
32. LaVey, *The Satanic Rituals*, 53.
33. For Satanic uses of Enochian, see Asprem, *Arguing with Angels*, chapter 6.
34. Faivre, *Access to Western Esotericism*, 14–15; Hammer, *Claiming Knowledge*, 86–7. It is worth noting that the Theosophical Society later moved away from the heavy emphasis on being inheritors of the *Western* esoteric tradition.

and the Order of the Golden Dawn. The ideas of the Illuminati are described as being in fairly good accordance with his own.[35] Ordo Templi Orientis, LaVey states in *The Satanic Bible*, were "practicing some of the principles set forth in this volume".[36] Various inter-war German groups are also said to be derived from the Illuminati to some extent. Practices within these groups, LaVey claims, form the basis for his ritual "Die Elektrischen Vorspiele".[37] The main symbol of the Church of Satan, the Sigil of Baphomet, was according to LaVey "used by the Knights Templar to represent Satan".[38] The symbol has survived through the ages, and has been known by many names, he explains. In one of his more bombastic essays, first published in 1970, LaVey writes of forebears who were "tortured as agents of Satan", and pours scorn on those dabblers in the occult today who refuse to accept the label of Satanist, the label which "killed their brothers and sisters of the past".[39] Their refusal to do so besmirches "the names of those who bore the mark of brand and tongs and gazed upon their dead and dying with curses softly spoken". Toward the end of the essay the Templars are mentioned, giving them the position of Satanic pioneers.[40] Making this group part of one's own genealogy is of course among the most common devices of esoteric legitimation.

Occasionally LaVey also makes claims to possess esoteric knowledge, in the sense of something truly secret, passed down between initiates only. For example, he states concerning a supposedly Russian ritual: "Oral communication and fraternal legacy have made the following rite available."[41] Using a familiar line of argument, he also makes himself out to be the custodian of a higher wisdom than that of older esotericists, incorporating their systems but surpassing them. For example, "L'Air epais", a putatively Templar-constructed rite that LaVey presents, is according to him an expression of an insight supreme to that disseminated in Freemasonry, and could be called a thirty-fourth degree, above the thirty-three in Masonic systems.[42] His Satanic system thus supplants the limited understanding of esotericists that came before. Clearly, tradition is not unimportant to this writer, even if he may often be cheerfully disrespectful towards it.

---

35. LaVey, *The Satanic Rituals*, 78.
36. LaVey, *The Satanic Bible*, 103.
37. LaVey, *The Satanic Rituals*, 106. It is obvious that the ritual did not originate in inter-war Germany, but was written much later, since it contains references to Lovecraft's mythos (for example on pp. 120–21). LaVey's bringing together of these groups under the heading *Schwarze Orden* is further undoubtedly somewhat arbitrary.
38. LaVey, *The Satanic Bible*, 136.
39. LaVey, *The Devil's Notebook*, 33. Originally published in *Cloven Hoof*, March 1970. Also reprinted in a 1986 issue of the same newsletter.
40. Ibid., 34.
41. LaVey, *The Satanic Rituals*, 136.
42. Ibid., 55.

LaVey was well read in the literature concerning older Satanism that was available in the late 1960s, and fairly faithfully reproduces its accounts of the phenomenon.[43] He is sharply critical of some examples of historical Satanism, and for instance labels La Voisin's activities in seventeenth century France "organized fraud" and "degraded".[44] Some other predecessors fare better, notably Sir Francis Dashwood and his eighteenth-century Hell-Fire Club.

This group has emerged as one of the most important sources of historical inspiration for the Church of Satan. They are mentioned in several texts by LaVey and in interviews with him in Barton's books. More recently, attesting to their significance, the current High Priest of the church celebrated a ritual in caves on Dashwood's former estate.[45] Dashwood, according to LaVey, "managed to conduct rituals replete with good dirty fun, and certainly provided a colorful and harmless form of psychodrama"[46] – much like LaVey himself, one suspects the intended subtext is. In *The Secret Life of a Satanist*, LaVey's biographer Blanche Barton writes: "There had always been a Satanic underground, centuries old, but there had never been an organized Satanic religion, practicing openly."[47] Yet, even though "there has never been a Church of Satan before, there have been groups dedicated to similar principles", and here the Hell-Fire Club is given pride of place.[48] Barton quotes LaVey concerning Benjamin Franklin's involvement with this clique of influential men: "If people knew of the role the Hell Fire Club played in Benjamin Franklin's structuring of America, it could suggest changes like: 'One nation, under Satan,' or 'United Satanic America.'"[49] Setting the club in such a historical frame has some similarity to conspiracy theory – though one which celebrates the machinations of the secret cabal instead of worrying about it.[50] When LaVey hints that a founding father of the United States may have been a Satanist, he makes Satanism a crucial part of the perhaps most important grand narrative for Americans (the creation of the Constitution and the founding of the nation). This construction of tradition may be done tongue in cheek, but even half-jokes will have an effect when told many times.

There is a tension in LaVey's texts between wanting to be the founder of the first real Satanic society, and referring to (often prestigious, like Franklin) historical figures and groups as predecessors. In the collection of LaVey aphorisms that conclude his last book, *Satan Speaks!*, one of them lays down: "The

---

43. LaVey mentions books like Elliot Rose's *A Razor for a Goat* (1962) and H. T. F. Rhodes's *The Satanic Mass* (1954), which were standard works on the subject at the time (*ibid.*, 21).
44. LaVey, *The Satanic Bible*, 102. On La Voisin, see Mollenauer, *Strange Relevations*.
45. Peter H. Gilmore, interview by author, New York, 6 April 2011.
46. LaVey, *The Satanic Bible*, 102.
47. Barton, *The Secret Life of a Satanist*, 81.
48. *Ibid.*, 81.
49. *Ibid.*, 81–82.
50. On LaVey and conspiracy theory, see Dyrendal, "Hidden Persuaders and Invisible Wars", and Chapter 10 of the present volume.

only person in recorded history to codify Satanism into an applicable religion is Anton Szandor LaVey."[51] In one of Barton's books, LaVey is said to be "the first man ever to found an above-ground organization dedicated to Satan and the delights of the flesh".[52] These are rather guarded phrasings. Since "an applicable religion" is a subjective assessment, and how to define "organization" and "above-ground" is not self-evident either, it is hard to argue against LaVey being first.

If the Church of Satan was according to its own historical narrative the first Satanic *organization* of note (and most scholars would agree), Anton LaVey certainly never tried to lay claim to being the first Satanist. He considered, as we shall see, some highly unexpected persons in history to be worthy of this epithet. In Barton's discussion of predecessors, she also mentions other earlier "enclaves of Satanism": Rabelais's Abbey of Thelema, a circle of 1930s Hollywood actors and Charles Fort's Fortean Society.[53] Most of these were decidedly not Satanists in the sense that they used Satanic symbolism, but can still be labelled thus if one employs the rather inclusive criteria suggested by LaVey under the heading de facto Satanists.

DE FACTO SATANISTS

What constitutes a de facto Satanist, then? In an interview in Blanche Barton's *The Church of Satan*, LaVey talks of figures, "sometimes historical, sometimes contemporary", who he "would identify as de facto Satanists, even though they might not have called themselves that because of the times they lived in. But by their actions, their writings, their attitudes, you can see that they were Satanists through and through."[54]

Even though the actual term is not used early on, the concept of de facto Satanists crops up on numerous occasions throughout LaVey's first publications as well. He writes of Galileo and Leonardo da Vinci that they "most certainly were Satanic in the sense that they expressed ideas and theories destined to break down the status quo".[55] Erotic sects in Russia were led by men "whose visionary abilities, practices, and goals revealed them as Satanists of the first order".[56]

LaVey presents what can best be described as an esoteric (in the sense that it is only visible to those with the correct understanding) history of Satanism:

---

51. LaVey, *Satan Speaks!*, 169.
52. Barton, *The Church of Satan*, 116.
53. Barton, *The Secret Life of a Satanist*, 82. A nearly identical passage is found in Barton, *The Church of Satan*, 10–11.
54. LaVey, quoted in *Ibid.*, 70.
55. LaVey, *The Satanic Rituals*, 32.
56. *Ibid.*, 133.

"The pseudo-Satanist has always managed to appear throughout modern history, with his black masses of varying degrees of blasphemy; but the *real* Satanist is not quite so easily recognized as such."[57] The real Satanists are simply the most successful individuals in any given time, and not the people who celebrate Satan.[58] Since Satan to LaVey is a thing of fairy tale, a pure construct and useful symbolic tool, it would be absurd to make him the focal point in the same way God is for a Jew. Celebrating Satan is thus not necessary in order to be a (de facto) Satanist. However, LaVey holds up men like Rasputin and Cagliostro as examples of successful persons who, he claims, incidentally also dabbled in the black arts.[59] Their names are "links – clues so to speak, of the true legacy of Satan". Even if the esoteric is explicitly said not to be a necessary ingredient in the making of a real Satanist, many of the actual examples provided have allegedly been involved with at least some form of esoteric practices. Hence, a tradition is constructed that *does* overlap with older esoteric historiography.

LaVey balances, especially later in his career, these esoteric forebears with references to a different type of lineage. Satanism, he says, has its roots in figures that "are all Satanic, always have been, but just might not have been labeled that yet. There has always been a *genetic strain* of Satanists, but it's just now getting to the point where we can stand up to identify ourselves and our forebears."[60] The idea of de facto Satanists – though later vaguely clothed in "scientific" garb by introducing the idea of Satanists as a special genetic strain – can be viewed as a form of Satanist perennialism: there is a worldview which has always existed, in all cultures and times, but has not been known under a single name. But now someone has come forward to proclaim what this ancient wisdom (or ancient street-smart egocentric cynicism, as it were, in this specific case) is, to give it a name, and point out who the long series of respected predecessors were, who all swore by this creed without using a specific word for it. It is interesting to note that this perennialist approach to Satanism is not entirely novel. Already Stanislaw Przybyszewski, mentioned earlier in this chapter, had practically the same view.[61] LaVey, however, did not derive this idea from the Pole, but from a less specific reservoir of esotericist concepts.

---

57. LaVey, *The Satanic Bible*, 104.
58. *Ibid.*, 104. LaVey qualifies this notion by writing: "It would be an over-simplification to say that every successful man and woman on earth is, without knowing it, a practicing Satanist; but the thirst for earthly success and its ensuing realization are certainly grounds for Saint Peter turning thumbs down." Exactly what then keeps all these people from being de facto Satanists is not entirely clear. What LaVey three years later writes of Galileo and others in *The Satanic Rituals*, as quoted above, could be the answer: the term is meant to encompass persons who were successful and at the same time challenged the status quo.
59. *Ibid.*, 104.
60. Barton, *The Church of Satan*, 59 (emphasis added).
61. Faxneld, "Witches, Nihilist Anarchism and Social Darwinism". Przybyszewski's concept of what the transhistorical Satanism entails was radically different on many levels, though.

The fact that LaVey's previously hidden "tradition" is described as transcultural – he writes that it "transcends ethnic, racial and economic differences and temporal ideologies"[62] – brings to mind the analogues between Eastern and Western traditions that are typical of esoteric perennialism, a theme to which we shall now turn.

LEFT HAND AND RIGHT HAND, EAST AND WEST

The notion of unity of all religious faiths, a prevalent legend among esotericists, is given a different spin by LaVey.[63] Where Theosophists and many New Agers would claim all religions are basically the same at their core, for example, LaVey divides them into Right-Hand and Left-Hand Path varieties that stand in opposition to one another. But within each of these distinct categories, different creeds are pretty much alike: the left liberates and the right represses.[64] To LaVey, allegedly Left-Hand Path groups like the Yezidi in the Middle East are in essence very similar to the medieval Templars, erotic sects in eighteenth- and nineteenth-century Russia and Satanists in 1960s California.

Supposedly, there are also historical connections. According to LaVey, the Templars encountered the Yezidi during their journeys and as a result later developed "one of the most significant rites of Satanism".[65] Through this meeting of Yezidi and Templars, Eastern "prideful, life-adoring principles joined with Western goal-oriented materialism", and these ideas lived on in various later fraternal orders.[66] The Yezidi themselves were, he claims, "a link between Egypt, Eastern Europe, and Tibet".[67] Their influence, he says, made itself known in most of the underground Satanism that preceded the Church of Satan.[68] In Blanche Barton's biography of LaVey, we find a description of how LaVey ritually shaved his head when he founded the Church of Satan, something that is "[t]raditional to the Yezidi devil worshippers" as a rite of passage.[69]

In his appropriation of various exotic elements, LaVey utilizes the esotericist strategy described by Olav Hammer where the use of correspondences hides

---

62. LaVey, *The Satanic Bible*, 104.
63. On this notion, see Hammer, *Claiming Knowledge*, 155, 161.
64. On the history of these originally Indian terms in the context of Western esotericism, and how the Left-Hand Path can be defined, see Granholm, "Embracing Others Than Satan"; for an update, see Granholm, "Esoteric Currents as Discursive Complexes".
65. LaVey, *The Satanic Rituals*, 55. The Yezidi are mentioned also in LaVey, *The Satanic Bible*, 43, 59, but are given a much less prominent place there. That the Templars were Satanists – in the sense that they revered Satan – is decidedly emic historiography, as scholarly experts on them agree they were certainly nothing of the sort. See for instance Partner, *The Murdered Magicians*; Barber, *The New Knighthood*.
66. LaVey, *The Satanic Rituals*, 55.
67. Ibid., 152.
68. Ibid., 155.
69. Barton, *The Secret Life of a Satanist*, 82.

cultural differences. For example, Russian symbols and deities are equalled with items of Yezidi and Graeco-Roman origin.[70] He repeatedly declares his work to be transcultural, incorporating elements from many types of esotericism. "Satanic Ritual", he explains, "is a blend of Gnostic, cabbalistic, Hermetic, and masonic elements" and even if he freely mixes practices from a variety of different countries and times "it will be easy to perceive a basic undercurrent through the central variants".[71] Perhaps this undercurrent is easy to perceive because many of the rituals have been constructed by LaVey himself, and do not have the origin in distant places and times he claims. This does not mean LaVey is a liar, any more than is the case with an author of fiction employing his inventiveness and poetic licence. Incensed reactions accusing him of forgery, as I have frequently encountered among Satanists not belonging to the Church of Satan, simply miss the point. The Satanic "tradition", ritual texts, even Satan himself, are all fiction to LaVey. They are consciously constructed by him to be used with certain purposes, not as something to believe in the same way a Mormon clings to the veracity of Joseph Smith's texts or a devout Pentecostal views God.

The figure used as the Church of Satan's prime symbol is explained to be a transcultural, timeless one: "We are not limited to one deity, but encompass all the expressions of the accuser or the one who advocates free thought and rational alternatives by whatever name he is called in a particular time and land. It so happens that we are living in a culture that is predominantly Judeo-Christian, so we emphasize Satan".[72] But the reasons why LaVey advocates transcultural *bricolage* are quite different from those of Blavatsky or New Age writers. When he boldly proclaims "You aren't limited to Judeo-Christian myths", the motivation has nothing to do with a supposed unity of figures – taken from different contexts – on a level of true esoteric understanding, but is based on his view of religious ideas as simply colourful fiction: "Unlike those who depend on dogma and blind faith, you can *choose* your fictions to live by".[73] His perennialism and use of material from other cultures thus has highly pragmatic rationalist underpinnings, instead of being grounded in mystical insights. Interestingly, he still often ends up handling his material in much the same way esotericists in general do.

---

70. LaVey, *The Satanic Rituals*, 132; Hammer, *Claiming Knowledge*, 160–61.
71. LaVey, *The Satanic Rituals*, 21. A variation on this theme can also be found further on in the same book, where LaVey states: "The guiding thoughts behind Satanic rituals past and present have emanated from diverse minds and places, yet all operate on much the same 'frequency'" (*Ibid.*, 26).
72. LaVey, quoted in Barton, *The Church of Satan*, 71. Cf. Granholm, "Embracing Others Than Satan". He does not mention this statement from LaVey, but this is only natural since the article focuses on the Temple of Set, Rune-Gild and Dragon Rouge.
73. LaVey, quoted in Barton, *The Church of Satan*, 96.

LITERARY SATANISM AS "TRADITION" AND HIGHBROW CULTURAL CAPITAL

Regarding the Black Mass presented in *The Satanic Rituals*, LaVey mentions that the text draws on sources such as Baudelaire and Huysmans. Indeed, the latter's description in his novel *Là-Bas* ("Down There", 1891; published in English as *The Damned*) seems to be the main source of inspiration, and thus LaVey's claim that his ritual "is the version performed by the *Societé des Luciferiens* in late nineteenth and early twentieth century France" needs to be taken with a grain of salt.[74] The fictional basis is highlighted by his biographer Barton as well, who writes: "In Anton's church all the Satanic fantasies became realities."[75] These are not the words of a representative of a group that considers itself steeped in ancient tradition, but of a group whose founder fully admits to having constructed its rituals based on fiction. In *The Satanic Bible*, LaVey explains: "Your ritual chamber is your fantasy world."[76] A fantasy world, one might add, that draws heavily on nineteenth-century literary fantasies.

Literary tradition seems to serve a more conventional legitimating function than esoteric tradition. The Church of Satan obviously enjoys the cultural capital and historical legitimacy Satanism gains from old literary panegyrics to Lucifer. For instance, contemporary Satanist hearts swell with pride at the fact that Nobel prize-winner Giosuè Carducci wrote "Inno a Satana" (1863), a long poem celebrating Satan. In an essay about the poet on the church's homepage, "R. Merciless" states: "Carducci's credentials as a Satanist include not only his worldly successes and overt opposition to Christianity but his writing of the highly controversial poem, *Inno a Satana*". In other words, Carducci is hailed both as a de facto Satanist, and as an explicit one. It appears important to "Merciless" to emphasize (quite correctly, it is worth noting) the fact that Carducci "stepped firmly beyond his paganism and even his anti-clericalism into the realm of modern Satanism by embracing the mythic character of Satan as an exemplary role model and heroic archetypal symbol", something that to "Merciless" is in fact "the defining characteristic of the Modern Satanist".[77] Even if Carducci would not have used the term Satanist about himself, he all the same, "Merciless" proudly proclaims, belongs "firmly within the Satanic tradition".[78] This is in line with LaVey's description of Carducci's poem as a precursor of contemporary Satanism in *The Satanic Rituals*.[79]

LaVey himself frequently connects his rituals to literature. His Black Mass is, he admits, inspired by Huysman's *Là-Bas*, and his "Tierdrama" ritual is, he states, based on an Illuminati ritual that influenced writers (who, according to

---

74. LaVey, *The Satanic Rituals*, 34 (cf. 37–53); Huysmans, *The Damned (Là-Bas)*, 222–7.
75. Barton, *The Secret Life of a Satanist*, 88.
76. LaVey, quoted in Barton, *The Church of Satan*, 96.
77. Merciless, "Giosuè Carducci".
78. *Ibid.*
79. LaVey, *The Satanic Rituals*, 77.

LaVey, were members of Illuminati-derived orders) like W. B. Yeats and Robert W. Chambers. This ritual is also supposedly reflected in the work of George Orwell, H. G. Wells and Aldous Huxley.[80] Embedding his rituals in a literary tradition, LaVey creates cultural legitimacy for them. They are not invented on the spot, but have the dignity of the literary canon to support them. This is thus an instance of LaVey using (literary) tradition as a legitimating device.

LaVey may have lambasted the esotericists of old, but as demonstrated this does not mean he was blind to the effectiveness of tradition as a powerful tool for creating the right mysterious atmosphere to surround rituals, and to some extent for general legitimation. This could potentially be viewed in the light of how one of his heroes, horror author H. P. Lovecraft, created elaborate pseudo-history concerning his fictitious tome of esoteric lore, *The Necronomicon*, in order to generate the right mood (Lovecraft, it is stated in *The Satanic Rituals*, was the author of tales "uniquely embellished with painstaking *pseudo-documentation*").[81] It is in this Lovecraftian spirit we should understand LaVey's claim about a certain ritual described by him that it was first performed "in Munich, 31 July 1781; the present manuscript dates from 1887".[82] Likewise, his assertion about the mysterious language used in Satanic ritual, Enochian, that it is "thought to be older than Sanskrit" is comparable to how Lovecraft built up his fictional universe.[83] The fact that LaVey also provides rituals based directly on Lovecraft's fiction should be enough for anyone to see that he does not make a clear distinction between evocative fiction and actual historical tradition. In this he is close to Chaos Magicians, who are (almost) as prone to summon up Donald Duck as a goetic demon.

Current High Priest Peter H. Gilmore has an unsentimental and detached view of the historical roots of Satanism. Regarding LaVey's take on older tradition, he explains how his mentor would talk of it: "The Doctor [the honorary title his adherents use when speaking of him] would say: 'None of it is authentic, but we'll use whatever props work best.' ... Authenticity was not an issue for him. He was a showman, he was a practical person".[84] As Gilmore testifies, tradition was not unimportant for LaVey. On the contrary, it was quite significant – as an excellent prop.

---

80. *Ibid.*, 78–9. That Yeats was deeply involved in esotericism is well known, but that the orders he was a member of were derived from the Illuminati is, to say the least, doubtful.
81. *Ibid.*, 175 (emphasis added). This passage in the book was written by Michael Aquino, *The Church of Satan*, 691.
82. LaVey, *The Satanic Rituals*, 78.
83. LaVey, *The Satanic Bible*, 155. Enochian was first presented to the world by Elizabethan scholar John Dee, who claimed to have received it in revelations from angels. According to Dee, this was the angels' own language. On Dee, see Håkansson, *Seeing the World*. LaVey's "Enochian Keys" are based on Aleister Crowley's reworking of the material. For a full-length study of the reception of Dee's work in modern occultism – including Satanism – see Asprem, *Arguing with Angels*.
84. Peter H. Gilmore, interview by author, New York, 6 April 2011.

MORE TRADITIONAL THAN THOU

LaVey's often breezy attitude towards tradition prompted many of his later competitors in the Satanic milieu to contrast themselves with him by making stronger appeals to tradition. On the one hand, several Lucifer-loving persons reading LaVey were probably genuinely incensed by his cheerful impudence when handling the esoteric tradition, and perhaps felt a longing for something more "genuine", "mysterious" and "classic". On the other hand, their appeals to ancient arcane wisdom and secret lineages are quite possibly also a conscious strategy to build legitimacy in a way differing from LaVey's successful methods (appeals to rationality/science, personal charisma, and only to a lesser extent tradition).[85] This can be seen in groups like the Order of the Nine Angles, probably founded in the late 1960s, who designate themselves practitioners of "Traditional Satanism", a self-description also used by several later theistic Satanist groups like The Brotherhood of Satan.[86]

LaVey has described how he looked for Satanists before founding the Church of Satan, but did not find any.[87] This is similar to how Graham Harvey speculates that Gerald Gardner searched for "traditional Witches", but without much success. Eventually, after the founding of Wicca, others stepped forward and proclaimed they, unlike Gardner, were in fact truly traditional Witches.[88] Exactly the same thing happened in the case of Satanism.

It is worth noting that Satanism shares many traits with Wicca and the wider milieu of neopaganism when it comes to handling tradition. As Harvey has pointed out, neopagans "are usually fully aware of the disjunctions between the past and the present", and know very well that they are making a reconstruction based on scanty sources.[89] Harvey also mentions neopagans who construct rituals based on *Star Trek*, something that can be considered analogous to LaVey's Lovecraft rituals.[90] The very fact that neopaganism is an invented tradition can also be considered part of its appeal, since people can then freely continue inventing.[91] This can potentially apply to Satanism too.

It cannot be ignored that many Satanists, in spite of being aware that LaVey assembled rituals from a hodgepodge of historical sources, literary as well as esoteric, but non-Satanic, just like the neopagans discussed by Harvey, seem

---

85. On LaVey's legitimation strategies, see Lewis, *Legitimating New Religions*.
86. On the Order of the Nine Angles, see Senholt, "Secret Identities in the Sinister Tradition".
87. Barton, *The Secret Life of a Satanist*, 61.
88. Harvey, "Inventing Paganisms", 282.
89. *Ibid.*, 279.
90. *Ibid.*, 289. There is of course still a noticeable difference between the *completely* open admission of invention in *Star Trek*-based neopaganism, or for that matter Chaos Magick astral journeys to Narnia, and the way tradition and popular culture is used in the Church of Satan.
91. *Ibid.*, 281.

"to find authenticity in alleged historicity". To Harvey, there is an inherent paradox in consciously creating rituals "to provide a semblance of antiquity".[92] If neopagans have similar ideas as LaVey, as I suspect at least some of them do, the paradox is dissolved. The "willing suspension of disbelief" in the ritual context then becomes an instrument to make the rituals more effective, even if the participant in some other contexts may be a conscientious philological scholar of his own religion (something not uncommon among neopagans, but less so in the Church of Satan). Harvey suggests we must consider "role-play, play-acting, active imagination, and creativity" important processes in neo-paganism.[93] This no doubt holds true for the Church of Satan and its approach to tradition as well.

Seldom will you hear a founder in a (more or less) religious context state frankly "I simply made this stuff up just now". LaVey does not say so either, though he not-so-tacitly admits to freely picking and choosing whatever is fun and colourful from older tradition, without any pretence at mystical insight concerning the material. In a more classically esoteric context, this would never be the case. Still, tradition is something constantly being renegotiated in a world such as the present one, even among those esotericists that may appear to be of a slightly more traditional bent. When I interviewed prominent Left-Hand Path adherents Zeena (estranged daughter of Anton LaVey) and Nikolas Schreck in 2005, they were very clear that they would happily modify their beliefs and practices in accordance with any new convincing scholarly findings pertaining to the Egyptian god Set, the main focus of their spirituality.[94] Their emphasis on "correct" tradition therefore leads to their own worldview being open to shifts in academic opinions concerning the ancient religious material they are employing to construct "tradition".

LaVey would never have felt any need to make changes in his system to harmonize it with the latest word from academia. This holds equally true for many old-fashioned esotericists as well. Since Rudolf Steiner was able to gain mystical insights about the Guardian of the Threshold, research demonstrating the fact that this concept was derived from the fiction of Edward Bulwer-Lytton would to an Anthroposophist simply be a reflection of the scholar's lacking mystical abilities that hinder a higher understanding of esoteric tradition. LaVey's reasons for being able to stay aloof are different. Bluntly put, esoteric tradition is simply fun fluff to him, helping to create an appropriate atmosphere for his activities, just like plastic devil-horns, fake skulls, and arcane symbols. The potential psychological *effects* of silly costumes and playful constructions of tradition are, however, anything but a joke to LaVey.

---

92. *Ibid.*, 288.
93. *Ibid.*, 289.
94. Nikolas and Zeena Schreck, interview by author, Berlin, Germany, 28 April 2005.

CONCLUSION

Though Anton LaVey may be sceptical of esotericism as a "religious" belief, and frequently mocks esoteric systems as old-fashioned rubbish, he nevertheless makes much use of its tropes. But for what purpose, exactly? LaVey seems to say: we are now going to enact a psychodrama, to achieve specific goals, not only in the ritual chamber. I shall assume the role of high priest. In order for this exercise to work properly, we will build up the appropriate atmosphere with much reference to tradition and esoteric tropes.

The most common reason for inventing a religious tradition and creating an emic historiography is, as Hammer and Lewis put it, that this "confers legitimacy to religious claims and practices".[95] On a more detailed level, tradition typically strengthens group cohesion by letting adherents identify with a common history, gives plausibility to doctrines and practices, and provides leaders with opportunity to give legitimacy to new ideas they may come up with along the way by ascribing them to ancient figures.[96] At least the first two are clearly observable in the Church of Satan. But more important, I contend, are the openly displayed and consciously utilized mechanics of tradition as mood-creating spectacle for purely instrumental purposes.

Hence, Anton LaVey should not be considered a counterfeiter of tradition, but a person quite openly playing with the psychological effects of tradition, and inviting others to take part in this game. LaVey cynically suggests always asking the question "Who gains?".[97] In the case of belief, half-playful or temporary, in a Satanic tradition with deep roots, who gains? The answer is probably not – as some might suggest – only Anton LaVey and his church's bank account, but the individual member as well, who gains psychological benefits both in and outside of the ritual chamber. My impression is that most members of the Church of Satan will assume the position Hammer and Lewis describe among reiki and reflexology healers, reproducing semi-mythical historical narratives, but in the end insisting that historical background is irrelevant as long as the system works.[98] Satanism and its rituals, it seems, "work" for many adherents, thus leaving them quite happy to have a tradition that is fictitious to some extent.

---

95. Hammer & Lewis, "Introduction", 4.
96. *Ibid.*, 6.
97. Barton, *The Secret Life of a Satanist*, 229.
98. Hammer & Lewis, "Introduction", 15. My statement concerning the view of tradition among "most" Church of Satan members is quite impressionistic, and is based on very limited fieldwork in combination with regular reading of various Internet forums for Satanists during the last decade. Admittedly, the analysis is hence very preliminary, and needs more substantiation.

CHAPTER 5

PERENNIALISM AND ICONOCLASM

CHAOS MAGICK AND THE LEGITIMACY OF INNOVATION

Colin Duggan

Chaos Magick[1] is an innovation of twentieth-century occultism that draws influence from a variety of sources, including occultists such as Aleister Crowley and Austin Osman Spare. It began in the late 1970s with the publication of Peter Carroll's *Liber Null* and Ray Sherwin's *The Book of Results* in 1978. These seminal texts would form the theoretical and practical underpinnings for a second wave of authors in the mid-1980s. Some of these later texts provided a critical evaluation of the development of Chaos Magick and firmly established it within the discourse on twentieth-century occultism. There have been very few scholarly commentaries on Chaos Magick, and most of those that have been produced lack the methodological and theoretical components required to build common terminology and further understanding. Of the scholars who have commented on Chaos Magick, Dave Evans has proved to be the most thorough with the historical analysis he offers in *The History of British Magick After Crowley*, despite his claim that an accurate overall history of Chaos Magick "may not yet be possible".[2] Richard Sutcliffe's article "Left-Hand Path Ritual Magick: An Historical and Philosophical Overview" gives a description of Chaos Magick as one of the currents of Left-Hand Path Magick, but does not focus on it specifically.[3] This shortfall of scholarly

---

1. Chaos Magick is capitalized and spelled with a "k" in this chapter as this is how it most often appears in the primary sources. The addition of the "k" is due to the influence of the British occultist Aleister Crowley, who introduced this convention. See Crowley, "Magick in Theory and Practice", 123–35.
2. Evans, *History of British Magick*, 351. See also Versluis, *Magic and Mysticism*, 139–42; Barrett, "Chaos Magick", 105–6; Houston, "Chaos Magic", 55–9; Urban, *Magia Sexualis*, 222–54.
3. For discussion of Left-Hand Path Magic, see Evans, *History of British Magick*, 177–228; Granholm, "'The Prince of Darkness on the Move'"; Granholm, "Dragon Rouge"; Granholm, "The Left-Hand Path and Post-Satanism".

attention, particularly from within the field of Western esotericism, prompted the research on which this chapter is based.

This chapter will take Chaos Magick as its example and investigate how tradition and perennialism are used to legitimize innovation among its practitioners. There will be a brief discussion of contemporary occultism and magic, as they are understood here, as well as an outline of the relevant Chaos Magick texts and authors. The appeal to tradition is a common strategy used by a broad range of groups and individuals to seek legitimacy for the claims they make. This strategy has been examined closely by Olav Hammer[4] and will be discussed in relation to Chaos Magick before finally embarking on the discussion of the legitimizing of innovation through ambivalent appeal to tradition.

CONTEMPORARY OCCULTISM

In order to discuss Chaos Magick and its subsequent reinterpretations in terms of contemporary occultism, a clarification of the term "occultism" itself, as it is deployed in the field of Western esotericism, is required. Wouter Hanegraaff's analysis describes occultism as:

> [a] category in the study of religions, which comprises *all attempts by esotericists to come to terms with a disenchanted world or, alternatively, by people in general to make sense of esotericism from the perspective of a disenchanted secular world.*[5]

This definition serves to delineate post-Enlightenment esotericism and highlight the subsequent reinterpretation of esoteric ideas. The definition has, however, been problematized by Marco Pasi, who outlines the different uses of the term and suggests more specific characterizations than Hanegraaff.[6] Pasi also takes into account the differences between many of the groups that constitute occultism for Hanegraaff.[7] Agreeing with Hanegraaff, he notes that "[o]ccultism presents … clear signs of the impact that secularization was

---

4. Hammer, *Claiming Knowledge*, 85–200.
5. Hanegraaff, *New Age Religion and Western Culture*, 422. Christopher Partridge has argued against Hanegraaff's usage of the term secularization and suggests that "[i]f a society as a whole is undergoing a process which does not involve anything like 'a disappearance or marginalization of religion', it has to be described in terms other than 'secularization'. If it is not, one is led into a thicket of terminological and theological problems". Partridge, *The Re-enchantment of the West*, vol. 1, 40.
6. Pasi, "Occultism".
7. A good example of this occurs when considering the fact that those engaged in spiritualism are communicating with the souls of the dead and trying to present their practice as scientific while those who proclaim themselves to be occultists (an emic distinction) are communicating with non-human discarnate entities and claim to be heirs to a long line of initiatic wisdom (*ibid.*, 1367).

having … on the most heterodox fringes of European culture and represents an important development in the history of Western Esotericism."[8] However, he insists that "the spiritual realisation of the individual" and the role of the traditional "occult sciences" are vital to any thorough understanding of the term.[9] Both the general definition and the specific characterization given above place occultism in a post-Enlightenment context. However, the former refers to all post-Enlightenment esotericism whereas the latter describes a specific current within Western esotericism. Pasi's characterization is relevant when considering late twentieth-century developments where the focus shifts from the institutional occultism of groups like the Hermetic Order of the Golden Dawn to the radical subjectivity of developments like Chaos Magick. The individualist aspect has its roots in the occultism of the late nineteenth century and is paramount to understanding late twentieth-century occultism. Ray Sherwin's *The Book of Results* states the importance of individualism in Chaos Magick as follows: "Since magick is an individualist pursuit the individual must always be of paramount importance and anyone who denies this is looking for profit or power or does not know any better."[10] In this chapter, occultism will be referred to as either early or late twentieth-century occultism, both of which are concerned with magical practice and "the spiritual realisation of the individual". Late twentieth-century occultism takes into account factors such as increasing access to a large amount of information and the increasing democratization of text production.

It is also necessary at this stage briefly to review usage of the term "magic", particularly as it has many diverse definitions and remains problematic. The early history of the term is encapsulated by Marco Pasi in the entry "Magic" in *The Brill Dictionary of Religion* where he states:

> The ancient Greek term *mageía*, which is at the origin of all modern words related to "magic", had a Persian origin, and served to indicate, since its adoption by Greek culture, religious activities considered to be exotic, unsanctioned, or forbidden. The term kept these mostly negative connotations in Roman culture, where it was translated as *magia*.[11]

Pasi also notes the role played by late nineteenth-century scholars, working in the social sciences, in universalizing the category of "magic" and the strong tendency to cast magic as a primitive form of religion.[12] The negative and positive connotations of the term "magic" are a central issue in the

---

8. *Ibid.*, 1366.
9. *Ibid.*
10. Sherwin, *The Book of Results*, 7.
11. Pasi, "Magic", 1134.
12. *Ibid.*, 1134–5. For a review of the history of "magic" see also Lehrich, *The Language of Demons and Angels*, 2–11.

history of how the term has been deployed. In his article "Sympathy or the Devil", Hanegraaff analyses the way theories of magic were presented in the Renaissance.[13] These were typically based on the inherent harmony in the cosmos as created by a loving God. However, there were also contemporaneous accusations that any effects observed in magic were actually being carried out by some kind of intermediary demon associated with the Christian devil. In post-Enlightenment occultism, there is a shift to a psychologized conception of magic. An outstanding example of this shift is the early twentieth-century British occultist Austin Osman Spare who claimed a wholly psychologized system of magic. Aleister Crowley also played a major role in this shift, but displayed ambivalence on the issue of magical efficacy on more than one occasion. Although Chaos Magick is in many senses an extension of this psychological model, given its emphasis on subjectivity,[14] Chaos Magicians are also quick to claim the influence of chaos theory and the modern proliferation of information on their conception of magic. In the psychologized vein, Ray Sherwin, in *The Theatre of Magick* claims that

> [m]agick has always been a study of the mind and how to make use of its latent powers. Some of these powers are still considered by most people to be supernormal. It also sought to use the powers the people saw in nature.[15]

The key idea here is the belief that humans can develop and improve themselves through the use of some system of magical practices. The importance of the individual aspect of Chaos Magick is commented on by Versluis in his *Magic and Mysticism*:

> One is struck by the individualism that resonates throughout the chaos magical movement to such a degree that one can hardly speak of a chaos magical tradition even if there is an order of "Magical Pact of the Illuminates of Thanateros".[16]

The strategies employed in the texts of Chaos Magick demonstrate that there is no self-contained "chaos magical tradition" but that Chaos Magick is an innovation of twentieth-century occultism. It makes a set of claims about a constructed tradition of magic which are then modified by individuals to suit

---

13. Hanegraaff, "Sympathy or the Devil".
14. The Crowleyan idea of magic as a lifelong commitment to better the self is certainly a part of Chaos Magick and is just one of the indicators of Crowley's influence.
15. Sherwin, *The Theatre of Magick*, 7.
16. Versluis, *Magic and Mysticism*, 142. Founded by Peter Carroll, the Illuminates of Thanateros (IOT) is the most prominent Chaos Magick organization. The word "Thanateros" comes from the Greek terms for death and love combined.

their own purposes. These purposes are often attempts at gaining legitimacy for their own versions of Chaos Magick or any changes they are making to some of the more established ideas that preceded them.

THE TEXTS OF CHAOS MAGICK

There are quite a number of primary texts on Chaos Magick currently in print. Many of the texts have been reproduced in electronic versions and are readily available online, and while some of these have been illegally distributed, others are self-published e-books allowing the author access to a broad audience. The e-books often contain instructions to copy the book and pass it on to as many people as possible. This is not surprising, as early adoption of online communication and distribution is very common among religious innovators of the 1980s and 1990s. This study will restrict itself to the primary texts by a number of authors associated with the emergence and development of Chaos Magick. Due to limited space a number of other authors are not included. The literature presented serves the overall thesis well and represents the more popular and pervasive texts. Peter Carroll and Ray Sherwin will constitute the bulk of the representative literature. The second wave of authors on Chaos Magick began in the mid-1980s, and contributions by Phil Hine, Julian Wilde and Joel Biroco will form the representative literature for this later period.

There are two other related developments that run parallel with Chaos Magick as it is described in this chapter: Thee Temple ov Psychick Youth and Discordianism. Limited space allows for only a brief description of these and a word on how all three are related. The first of these, Thee Temple ov Psychick Youth (TOPY), was formed in 1981 and is most often associated with Genesis P-Orridge.[17] It is described by Partridge as "arguably the most significant organized, online occult community",[18] and it was instrumental in the spread of Chaos Magick-related ideas and resources. TOPY was a loose (but highly effective) network of artists and magicians who were, like the magicians discussed in this chapter, influenced by occultists Aleister Crowley and Austin Osman Spare, and used sigil magic as a core element of their practice. This is most evident in the two main texts: *Thee Grey Book* and *Thee Sigil Book*.[19] However, TOPY was also strongly influenced by the writer William S. Burroughs and the artist Brion Gysin. The performance art aspect of TOPY expressed itself in many ways, most notably through the band Psychic TV, and their interaction with the art scene throughout the 1980s is just one reason

---

17. For discussion on these subjects, see Chapter 6 of this volume.
18. Partridge, *The Re-enchantment of the West*, vol. 2, 159.
19. *Thee Grey Book* was first published in 1982 and *Thee Sigil Book* (aka *Thee Black Book*) was first published in 1983. Versions of both of these texts were republished in P-Orridge, *Thee Psychick Bible*, 35–57 and 83–99, respectively.

why it deserves to be treated as a parallel development rather than subsumed into a general discussion on Chaos Magick. The second of these parallel developments is Discordianism. Kerry Thornley and Gregory Hill claim to have founded Discordianism in 1958 or 1959 after a revelatory experience at a bowling alley in a Los Angeles suburb. According to their text, the *Principia Discordia*, "Both order and disorder are manmade concepts and are artificial divisions of PURE CHAOS, which is a level deeper than the level of distinction making."[20] This engagement with the concept of chaos is similar to that of Chaos Magick and is reminiscent of the occultism of Crowley and Spare. Discordianism places a lot of emphasis on humour; the *Principia Discordia* states that "occultists have been blinded to what is [sic] perhaps the two most important pairs of apparent or earth-plane opposites: ORDER/DISORDER and SERIOUS/HUMOROUS".[21] There are clear relationships and similarities between the three developments mentioned here and the division is largely an artificial one. A longer discussion on Chaos Magick would certainly include both of the developments that were left out and could properly trace the connections between the groups and figures involved.

As previously observed, Chaos Magick emerged with the publications of Carroll and Sherwin in 1978. From 1976, both of these authors were publishing articles in Sherwin's own magazine *The New Equinox*, and it was this medium that was used to announce the formation of the Illuminates of Thanateros (IOT), one of Chaos Magick's most notable groups. 1981 saw the publication of Carroll's second book, *Psychonaut*, while Sherwin's second publication, *The Theatre of Magick*, followed in 1982. Other texts used here are Phil Hine's three-volume work *Techniques of Modern Shamanism* (published in 1989–90[22] and sometimes called the *Urban Shaman Trilogy*) and *Condensed Chaos*, first published in 1992 and now available online as *Oven-Ready Chaos*. Julian Wilde's *Grimoire of Chaos Magick* represents a slightly different take on Chaos Magick, particularly in terms of the tradition he constructs. Finally, Joel Biroco's 2002 publication of *KAOS 14*, the fourteenth issue of his Chaos Magick magazine, will be discussed in relation to the legitimizing of innovation.

There were many other authors writing about Chaos Magick in the magazines that were published during the height of its popularity. Through the

---

20. Hill & Thornley, *Principia Discordia*, 49.
21. *Ibid.*, 61.
22. There is some confusion over the exact publication dates for these volumes and it arises out of a problem that is being faced more often. The electronic editions (available as PDF files on the author's website) of volume II and III claim that the original paper versions were published in 1989, whereas volume I claims a copyright from 1986. However, the author's website lists volume I and II as being published in 1989 and volume III in 1990. 1986 is a little early for the first volume to have been produced, so it seems to be a mistake in the electronic version. This chapter will take 1989–90 as the years of original publication for the three volumes.

1980s and 1990s, publications[23] like *Chaos International*, *The Lamp of Thoth* and *NOX* were some of the main vehicles for debates between practitioners. Articles in these publications addressed a wide range of subjects. For example, the first issue of *Chaos International* contains some descriptions of rituals, articles about the theory of magic, a piece on the role of women in magic, and three computer programs designed for gematria.[24] Joel Biroco's *KAOS* magazine[25] was also a major vehicle for debates on Chaos Magick and this will be considered below. A major problem in researching these publications is access, particularly to those that were published in pamphlet form, as they are generally in the hands of private collectors. Another issue is bibliographic detail. Some of these publications were republished at different times and given new publication dates. Others were published with issue numbers to give the impression that the publication had been in print for longer than it actually had. For this reason, this chapter will be using sources that are accessible to and verifiable by any interested party. That is to say, the texts used here are representative simply because they have been the most pervasive, successful texts, and therefore have been the first texts encountered by interested parties seeking to learn about Chaos Magick. This does not mean that the other kinds of texts mentioned earlier are not important. Any future detailed historical analysis of Chaos Magick will need to have access to them, but for the purposes of this chapter the sources available are sufficient.

THE APPEAL TO TRADITION

In *Claiming Knowledge*, Olav Hammer devotes a substantial section to the legitimizing strategy of the appeal to tradition in post-Enlightenment esotericism. Some of his ideas will prove useful when talking about strategies of legitimacy for Chaos Magick. In his section on "source amnesia", he states that "[t]he latest innovation and the ageless tradition are perceived to be essentially the same."[26] This is in reference to strategies used for the construction of tradition in various forms of Theosophical and post-Theosophical esotericism (including twentieth-century occultism) or what he terms the "Modern Esoteric Tradition". However, it will be shown in the following sections that different appeals to tradition emphasize one or other of these two aspects of tradition. Emphasizing either the latest innovation or the ageless tradition is used as a strategy to legitimize individual reinterpretations in Chaos Magick.

---

23. Many of these publications started life as "zines". These are usually A5 homemade pamphlets and have been used by many groups as a cheap and effective way to communicate.
24. Published in 1986. Gematria is a system of assigning numerical value to letters and words.
25. This publication was originally called *CHAOS* and later changed to *KAOS*. It is not to be confused with *Kaos Magick Journal*.
26. Hammer, *Claiming Knowledge*, 181.

The ambivalent appeal to tradition is used to distinguish one's self and one's innovations from those of one's predecessors. Hammer also comments that "[w]riters will attempt to stress continuity and disregard change, a legitimizing process that has its typical elements."[27] In the case of Chaos Magick, it will be shown that although continuity is stressed when legitimizing the tradition, legitimacy for innovations can be sought through emphasizing change and showing that innovation is itself a part of Chaos Magick. This will be explained through an analysis of iconoclasm and perennialism.

Iconoclasm is used figuratively by Chaos Magicians to signify an irreverent act of tearing down and deriding the established, the dogmatic, or the conventional. This meaning is derived from iconoclasm as literally destroying images, icons and idols of a culture, particularly divine images. The word iconoclast has been appropriated figuratively to mean a person disregarding the established ideas of a culture or field which the iconoclast disagrees with and wishes to disparage in some way. The figurative use of iconoclasm is meant to refer to the act or process of attacking or destroying conventions in order to bring about a (need for) change. For the purposes of this chapter, the term should be understood as a strategy of completely disregarding the established ideas of one's predecessors in favour of one's own ideas. This is how the word is used by Chaos Magicians. In *Liber Null*, Carroll states the importance of iconoclasm for Chaos Magick as follows: "Chief among the techniques of liberation are those which weaken the hold of society, convention, and habit over the initiate, and those which lead to a more expansive outlook. They are sacrilege, heresy, iconoclasm, bioaestheticism [sic], and anathe-mism [sic]."[28] This conception of iconoclasm will be problematized and further clarified in the larger discussion on perennialism.

The terms *prisca theologia* and *philosophia perennis* are familiar in the field of Western esotericism and are just two of

> a wide range of terms [that] have been used to refer to the idea that there exists an enduring tradition of superior spiritual wisdom, available to humanity since the earliest periods of history and kept alive through the ages, perhaps by a chain of divinely inspired sages or initiatory groups.[29]

Antoine Faivre explains these terms in his work with regard to Renaissance esotericism and the Christian context, including precursors to Christianity.[30]

---

27. *Ibid.*, 159.
28. Carroll, *Liber Null and Psychonaut*, 45–7.
29. Hanegraaff, "Tradition", 1125. For a discussion, see Asprem and Granholm's chapter on tradition above.
30. For Faivre's review of these concepts, see Faivre, *Access to Western Esotericism*; Faivre, *The Eternal Hermes*.

The specifics of this historical overview are not required for the following discussion, but it is necessary to distinguish between the perennialism described in this chapter and the notions described in Faivre's work. These concepts (*prisca theologia* and *philosophia perennis*) assume that an eternal, primordial truth is handed down by extraordinary teachers through the ages. However, *prisca theologia* "emphasized the idea of a wisdom that has been lost, forgotten, overlooked or neglected, and should now be recovered".[31] This implies a certain degradation of the wisdom over time and superiority over current wisdom. *Philosophia perennis*, on the other hand, "emphasized the continuity of true wisdom through the ages"[32]. The latter of these is more important for the discussion of Chaos Magick. One further note on the usage of these terms in the field of esotericism concerns their deployment by René Guénon, the French Traditionalist author. Guénon's usage of the terms "perennial philosophy" and "perennialism" is derived from the preceding Renaissance usage, and is described by Mark Sedgwick as follows:

> For a century and a half after Ficino, the idea that there was a Perennial Philosophy became increasingly widely accepted. Perennialism was, however, discredited in the early seventeenth century and thereafter survived only at the edges of Western intellectual life. Then, in the nineteenth century, Perennialism was revived in a slightly modified form, with the newly discovered Vedas being taken as its surviving textual expression.[33]

There is also a more general idea of perennialism arising out of twentieth-century sources such as Aldous Huxley's *The Perennial Philosophy*. Hanegraaff comments that "a vague notion of a 'perennial philosophy' has come to enjoy a certain vogue in the domains of alternative spirituality and the New Age movement".[34] Deriving from this brief history of the concept, "perennialism", as it is understood here, is the notion that there *is* an eternal truth or wisdom which *can* be accessed and has been expressed in the world by various elements down through the ages. It is a useful idea in this form as it can be used to analyse the discourse on late twentieth-century occultism as having incorporated a large degree of subjectivization and democratization. Radical subjectivity, combined with increasing access to information relating to the many different aspects of Western esotericism, forced a perennialized perspective into the discourse. For Chaos Magicians, the processes of individualization and democratization are expressed through the discourse on perennialism and iconoclasm. Perennialism becomes a democratic framework that includes

---

31. Hanegraaff, "Tradition", 1126. Cf. Chapter 2 of this volume.
32. *Ibid.*
33. Sedgwick, *Against the Modern World*, 24.
34. Hanegraaff, "Tradition", 1134.

a vast array of historicized occultural elements in which the current or latest instance of knowledge or wisdom is just as valid as the oldest instance. There is an expectation that the *philosophia perennis* extends into the future as well as the past. In this way, iconoclasm is a valid interpretation of perennialism because *all* instances of the tradition, in whatever form they may appear, are valid. This not only validates the act of iconoclasm in the discourse on perennialism but encourages it as reinterpretation of constructed traditions. Iconoclasm is the driving principle of this perennialism since the established, conventional, or dogmatic must be challenged or even destroyed to produce the next instance of knowledge or wisdom. This important point will be returned to below.

The perennialist impulse is demonstrated in a number of different ways in the following examples from Chaos Magick. There is an affirmation of the core similarities of magic across history and across cultures. References to the figure of the shaman abound in these texts and are almost always made in a transcultural and transhistorical sense.[35] In *Psychonaut*, Carroll states that "despite the enormous geographical separation between shamanic cultures, they share almost identical methods".[36] Shamanism, understood as the origin of magic, is an important part of the constructed tradition in the latter half of the twentieth century. Kocku von Stuckrad has argued that the emergence of the Western discourse of shamanism as a transcultural feature of religion at this time has its roots in the late nineteenth century.[37] However, the uses of the shaman as a referent in the texts of Chaos Magick are not an appeal for a return to nature but function almost solely for the purposes of garnering legitimacy by appealing to the ancient origin of magic. Versluis comments briefly on this relation between tradition and shamanism in Chaos Magick.

> In this movement, the term *initiation* takes on the neoshamanic meaning of a period of trial and growth rather than an institutionalised series of hierarchic degrees ... Chaos magic represents an anarchic and radical individualist mystico-magical movement that is by self-definition antitraditional, but that nonetheless draws from religious traditions and emphasizes transformations of consciousness.[38]

---

35. For a thorough investigation of the universalized concept of the shaman see Znamenski, *The Beauty of the Primitive*.
36. Carroll, *Liber Null and Psychonaut*, 169.
37. Von Stuckrad, "Reenchanting Nature"; cf. the discussion in Chapter 2 of this volume. For a critical review of literature on modern shamanism see von Stuckrad, "Constructions, Normativities, Identities", and for investigation into the Western construction of the shaman see Znamenski, *The Beauty of the Primitive*.
38. Versluis, *Magic and Mysticism*, 142.

One final point to make before discussing how ambivalent appeals to tradition can legitimize innovation concerns the audience to whom these claims are directed. In the first instance, are these appeals meant to confer legitimacy in the eyes of the wider world and mainstream culture? Or are they designed to grant legitimacy within a particular, specialized audience? Kennet Granholm argues that:

> A distinctive trait of esotericism is that of imagined community. As per the non-intrinsic characteristic of concordance ... an esoteric history of humanity is constructed, and through this imagined history a cross-cultural and cross-historical community of esotericists is created. This imagined community grants the esotericist a feeling of belonging, even though he or she might be the only esotericist in his or her community, lacking any contacts with other living practitioners.[39]

It is necessary to grasp this idea of "an imagined community of esotericists"[40] in order to understand how the appeals to tradition change after the emergence of Chaos Magick. In effect, the idea of tradition is constrained by the existence of a community that is familiar with appealing to tradition in the manner outlined in this chapter. Hanegraaff also points to the importance of this idea in his entry "Tradition" in the *Dictionary of Gnosis and Western Esotericism*, where he states:

> What characterizes the currents and authors treated here, however, is precisely this sense of being part of a trans-historical "community", of which it is believed that all members would basically have agreed among one another, had they been able to meet.[41]

This consenting hegemony of perennialism among the community provides the framework in which the appeals to tradition are made. One way of thinking about this audience is Christopher Partridge's idea of "occulture":

> Very briefly, occulture includes those often hidden, rejected and oppositional beliefs and practices associated with esotericism, theosophy, mysticism, New Age, Paganism, and a range of other

---

39. Granholm, "The Sociology of Esotericism", 791.
40. It should also be noted here that the "imagined community of esotericists" is not now so imaginary, geographically speaking, as it would have been when considering the capacity for networking available to contemporary occultists. For a thorough treatment of online communities in this regard see Partridge, *The Re-enchantment of the West*, vol. 2, chapter 4, entitled "CyberSpirituality", 135–64.
41. Hanegraaff, "Tradition", 1126.

subcultural beliefs and practices, many of which are identified by Campbell as belonging to the cultic/mystical milieu and by Stark and Bainbridge as belonging to the occult subculture.[42]

The audience to which appeals for legitimacy are made will be constituted by people who are interested in any or all of the elements outlined by Partridge. This occultural audience engages in a consenting perennialism with respect to constructed traditions. However, given the importance of subjectivity, individuals legitimize their own reinterpretations of these traditions through the iconoclastic impulse. Iconoclasm is seen as a valid interpretation of perennialism because all instances of the constructed tradition are valid. The next instance will share the core features of the tradition no matter what form the new instance takes. In this way, iconoclasm is the driving force of perennialism in Chaos Magick, permitting radical subjectivity.

THE LEGITIMACY OF INNOVATION

There are two strategies involved in the legitimization of Chaos Magick through an appeal to tradition. The first strategy is one where an appeal is made to "the age of the tradition" with an emphasis on continuity. The second strategy is an appeal to the most recent instance of a constructed tradition. This involves claiming to be the next in a natural progression of innovations that supersedes the previous one. With regard to the seminal authors, Carroll and Sherwin, both strategies are used together. This serves as an establishing, legitimizing act for Chaos Magick in general, positing it as the natural successor in an age-old tradition of magic. The later author Phil Hine will be included in the discussion as he shares Carroll and Sherwin's position with regard to these strategies. Authors who have sought to reinterpret Chaos Magick and legitimize their own innovations have tended to opt for one or other of the two strategies. Examples are Julian Wilde, who employs the first of the strategies mentioned above, and Joel Biroco, who employs the second. Wilde seeks to delegitimize, through iconoclasm, that which is seen to be the predecessor of Chaos Magick (i.e. early twentieth-century occultism) and to re-emphasize the importance of a transhistorical and transcultural tradition of magic by referring to shamanism. Biroco seeks to delegitimize the Chaos Magick of others through iconoclasm and to re-emphasize the place of his own version of Chaos Magick as the natural successor to Crowley's occultism. A sense of the way perennialism and iconoclasm interact in relation to a constructed tradition is central to the deployment of these strategies of legitimacy. The three positions outlined here will now be discussed in detail.

---

42. Partridge, *The Re-enchantment of the West*, vol. 1, 68. See also Chapter 6 of this volume.

Carroll, Sherwin and Hine

As mentioned earlier, Carroll and Sherwin drew on both of the legitimizing strategies discussed by appealing to a long-established tradition of magic *and* by claiming to be the next instance in a natural progression of this tradition. These strong claims serve as an appeal for legitimacy to a wide audience, namely the occultural milieu. Carroll's first book, *Liber Null*, is one of the most widely read and recommended texts on Chaos Magick. In the introduction, Carroll states that "The Illuminates of Thanateros are the magical heirs to the Zos Kia Cultus and the A∴A∴."[43] Sherwin confirms this claim of affiliation with early twentieth-century occultism in general, and with Austin Osman Spare in particular. He states that Spare was "emphatic about the workability of sigils" and that his own (Sherwin's) "experiments over the last fifteen years confirm his confidence in the technique as do the experiments I have persuaded other people to do".[44] This claim fits with the second type of strategy. The affiliation with both Austin Osman Spare and Aleister Crowley serves to place Chaos Magick as the next instance of the magical tradition in a natural progression. It appeals to the wide occultural audience with an interest in early twentieth-century occultism as it seeks to be *the* magical movement of the late twentieth century. Carroll also provides a diagram, a kind of flowchart, on the page following the introduction. It is called "The survival of the magical tradition" and it includes shamanism as the origin and precursor of the beliefs and practices of a whole host of other people, groups and movements. The idea of the shaman as the origin of magic or as the first magician is prominent throughout many Chaos Magick texts. Carroll's *Psychonaut* describes it as "our oldest magical and mystical tradition. It is from shamanism that all religious arts and magical sciences originate".[45] Sherwin also refers to the activities of the shaman in *The Book of Results* and *The Theatre of Magick*. In the former, Sherwin claims that

> It is absurd that sophisticated magicians spend so much of their energy in keeping out impressions from the chaos or weird side of consciousness when shamans the world over go to extreme lengths to open themselves up to those impressions and energies.[46]

---

43. Carroll, *Liber Null and Psychonaut*, 7. The Zos Kia Cultus is a magical order occultist Kenneth Grant claimed to have founded with Austin Osman Spare. Some of Grant's reports about Spare have been found to be less than accurate. The reference to the Zos Kia Cultus is undoubtedly a reference to Spare. The A∴A∴ is the magical order Crowley founded in 1909. Grant played an important part in the popularization of Crowley and Spare.
44. Sherwin, *The Book of Results*, 31. A sigil is a glyph used in magical ritual. At its simplest, it is created by rearranging the letters in a given phrase to form a pictogram or subjective symbol.
45. Carroll, *Liber Null and Psychonaut*, 169.
46. Sherwin, *The Book of Results*, 24.

Here again, the constructed transcultural shaman is held up to have always been involved in practices concerned with chaos, and shamanism is held to share some core principle with Chaos Magick. It is no surprise then that the diagram in *Liber Null* includes Tantra, Taoism, Sufism, Gnosticism, the Knights Templar, Hermeticism and alchemy, medieval goetia, Rosicrucianism, Freemasonry, John Dee, the Bavarian Illuminati, Ordo Temple Orientis, the Hermetic Order of the Golden Dawn, Aleister Crowley, Austin Osman Spare and the Zos Kia Cultus, witchcraft and sorcery, and finally ends in the Illuminates of Thanateros (IOT). This is the kind of list that scholars of Western esotericism will be familiar with as it includes much of the subject matter that constitutes the field. Not only that, it is a perfect example of the kind of perennialism prevalent in the late twentieth century. Overall, it is a syncretistic yet selective rendering of a constructed history of magic and fits well with the first strategy outlined above. This appeal to age-old tradition claims an ancient origin for, and the continuous transmission of, the core ideas of magic that are, by the end of the diagram, preserved in the IOT. Carroll goes on to state that:

> The secrets of magic are universal and of such a practical physical nature as to defy simple explanation. Those beings who realize and practice such secrets are said to have achieved mastership. Masters will, at various points in history, inspire adepts to create magic, mystic, religious, or even secular orders to bring others to mastership. Such orders have at certain times openly called themselves the Illuminati; at other times secrecy has seemed more prudent. The mysteries can only be preserved by constant revelation. In this, the I.O.T. continues a tradition perhaps seven thousand years old, yet the Order in the outer has no history, although it is constituted as a satrap of the Illuminati.[47]

This affirmation of the IOT as the Illuminati of the late twentieth century while attesting to a tradition that is "perhaps seven thousand years old" reiterates the employment of both strategies discussed in this chapter. As an establishing act and an appeal to the community of esotericists, a strong and encompassing appeal to tradition is offered.

Before moving on to the discussion of Wilde and Biroco, some of the work by Phil Hine will be discussed. His work was published later than Carroll and Sherwin's, but he is supportive of their position of an ambivalent appeal to tradition as I have outlined it here. That is to say, he employs both strategies of legitimization and seeks to add to the work of his predecessors by developing and strengthening this double appeal. His three-volume work *Techniques*

---

47. Carroll, *Liber Null and Psychonaut*, 9.

of Modern Shamanism is a strong reiteration of the importance of the shaman in Chaos Magick. In the first volume, *Walking Between the Worlds*, he echoes Carroll's claim that the shaman is the original magician: "The Shaman is one of the most ancient and one of the most enduring figures in human evolution. Shamanism is the source of both Magic and Religion, and as Mircea Eliade put it, is 'an archaic technique of ecstasy'."[48] The reference to Eliade's 1951 work (trans. 1964), *Shamanism: Archaic Techniques of Ecstasy*, perhaps reveals the source of the notion of a transcultural shaman, referred to in this and many other of the Chaos Magick texts. This provides a good example of the difficulties that arise when scholarship begins to shape the discourse on religion or magic.[49] Though Eliade is still an important figure in religious studies, the difficulty in ascribing religious or non-religious positions to him compounds these difficulties. As Bryan Rennie states: "Despite the fact that he did not practice any religious tradition and despite the complexity of argument needed to describe him as religious, Eliade was often apprehended as profoundly religious."[50] This also makes his work very appealing to anyone involved in religious innovation in the late twentieth century. Hine goes on to state that:

> Its [shamanism's] structural elements can be traced well back into the Upper Palaeolithic era, and these elements are essentially similar throughout many different cultures, in different frames of time. Even though the surface details of the shamanic world-view tends to differ even within particular cultures, the underlying principles remain similar, supplying some elemental requirement of the human psyche which has remained constant over a period of hundreds of thousands of years.[51]

Here we see the confirmation of the idea of the shaman as an age-old transcultural entity, but, taken together, these quotes introduce the language of scholarship. With references to Eliade and the "Upper Palaeolithic era", there is an effort here to gain legitimacy through an appeal to academia. Of course, Chaos Magick appeals to science in many ways but these are beyond the scope of this paper. Hine's use of scholarly and scientific language aids him in his description of the history of magical models:

> Until fairly recently (in a broad historical sense), practitioners of magick subscribed to the "Spirit" Model of Magick, which basically

---

48. Hine, *Techniques of Modern Shamanism*, vol. 1, 5.
49. For the role played by academics in shaping discourses on shamanism, see Znamenski, *The Beauty of the Primitive*. For an example of how similar processes affect discourses on Tantra, see Urban, *Tantra*. See also Chapter 2 of this volume.
50. Rennie, "Eliade", 576.
51. Hine, *Techniques of Modern Shamanism*, vol. 1, 5.

> states that the Otherworlds are real, and inhabited by various pantheons of discrete entities – elementals, demons, angels, goddesses, gods, etc.[52]

This "Spirit" model corresponds generally to the scholarly descriptions of pre-Enlightenment magic where the existence of discarnate intelligences informs theory and practice. Hine continues to demonstrate a systematic view of the history of magical models. The next model outlined is the "Energy" model:

> By the Eighteenth Century, and the rise of Science, the idea of "Animal Magnetism" arose in the West, being the first manifestation of the "Energy" Model of magick. This model places emphasis on the presence of "subtle energies" which can be manipulated via a number of techniques. Along came Bulwer Lytton and his idea of "Vril" energy, Eliphas Levi and the Astral Light, Mediums & ectoplasm, Westernised "popular" accounts of Prana, Chakras, and Kundalini, and eventually, Wilhelm Reich's Orgone energy.[53]

This model shows the perceived shift from a view of magic that was "supernatural" to a model where explanation was sought and offered based on the existence of invisible forces. Hine continues by describing the psychologization of magic:

> The next development came with the popularisation of Psychology, mainly due to the Psychoanalytic fads of Freud, Jung & co. During this phase, the Otherworlds became the Innerworlds, demons were rehoused into the Unconscious Mind, and Hidden Masters revealed as manifestations of the "Higher Self".[54]

This model is strongly associated with early twentieth-century occultism, particularly Crowley and Spare. The systematic manner in which Hine historicizes magical models serves not only as an implicit appeal to tradition but also displays the appeal to academia and science mentioned earlier. These models, though historicized, are not abrogated. The Chaos Magician is free to choose from any one of them or a combination of them all. Hine goes on to describe the latest model of magic:

> The current up-and-coming paradigm is the "Cybernetic" model, as we swing into being an information-based culture. This model

---

52. Hine, *Oven-Ready Chaos*, 19–20.
53. *Ibid.*, 20.
54. *Ibid.*, 20–21.

says that the Universe, despite appearences [sic], is stochastic in nature. Magick is a set of techniques for rousing a neurological storm in the brain which brings about microscopic fluctuations in the Universe, which lead eventually to macroscopic changes – in accordance with the magician's intent.[55]

This model differs from the previous one by placing the emphasis on neurology rather than psychology. A reinterpretation of the macrocosm/microcosm dynamic, this distinction serves to emphasize the connection between biological activity in the brain and the universe. The significant increase in ability to access and share information about occultism, esotericism, and new religions at this time informs this model of magic. This ability was further increased as Internet communities developed and expanded. However, despite the insistence on the importance of information, the reliance of most instructional manuals on techniques such as sigilization[56] suggests that a strong psychological element remained prominent in Chaos Magick.

There is one final point to note about Hine's description of magical models and it demonstrates a real awareness of how appeals for legitimacy function:

> It is also worth noting that should you ever find yourself in the position of having to "explain" all this weird stuff to an non-afficiando [sic] or skeptic, then the Psychological model is probably your best bet. These days, people who ascribe to the Spirit model, if they are not of a Pagan or Occult persuasion themselves, tend to think that they have an exclusive copyright over the use of Spirits! If the person is a computer buff or Fractal phreak, then by all means go for the "cyberpunk" paradigm. Scientists only tend to accept something if a scientific "rationale" can be wheeled up to slot it into.[57]

Hine advises that one's explanation of magic should be altered according to the type of person to whom the explanation is being made. Awareness of how and when to use different appeals for legitimacy is an important feature of Chaos Magick, and twentieth-century occultism as a whole, and is a result of the significant increase in access to information occurring in the 1970s and 1980s.

---

55. Hine, *Oven-Ready Chaos*, 21. By "stochastic" he means non-deterministic: a system in which its current state does not determine its next state.
56. This technique is most often attributed to Austin Osman Spare by Chaos Magicians. Spare's ideas of magic were wholly psychologized.
57. Hine, *Oven-Ready Chaos*, 21.

Wilde

In the *Grimoire of Chaos Magick*, published in 1986, Julian Wilde seeks to legitimize his innovations of the established Chaos Magick of the authors mentioned above. By this time, there are already ongoing debates about theory and practice within the community of Chaos Magicians and Wilde will serve as just one example. He engages in an appeal to tradition of the first type only by emphasizing the place of the shaman as the original magician. He asserts shamanism as ancient and primitive, a precursor to organized religion:

> The collection/accumulation of techniques and beliefs known as shamanism pre-dates all organised religion. The witch-doctor, the medicine man, the primitive sorcerer of the hunt, all have much in common and would have little difficulty in relating to each others [sic] practices – and yet shamanism remains an intensely *personal* and relevant system of application – each "wise man" (or woman), through a result of his own cultural heritage, retains and enjoys a fresh inter-relationship with those spirits, ancestors, animal-allies and supernatural beings that probe [sic] beneficial to him and his work – all progress is made through a fresh personal application of the inherited world-view. It is interesting (and perhaps reassuring to some of you/us) to note that from Eskimo to aborigine, in many cases the shaman is a misfit, sickly, reclusive and temperamental.[58]

Here, the shaman is constructed as a universal figure who shares core features transculturally. However, in this case there is an inherent ability to renew the relationship between the shamans and the culturally specific entities with which they traffic. This characterization of the shaman as a natural innovator creates the space for Wilde to legitimize his own innovations. He emphasizes the personal aspect of his constructed shaman and this also lends itself to the legitimization of personal innovation while simultaneously placing the shaman within the individualized framework of twentieth-century occultism. As stated, Wilde uses the first strategy of legitimacy only and does not seek to place himself as the next instance in a natural progression of "the magical tradition". He engages in iconoclasm with respect to early twentieth-century occultism and states very clearly those with whom he does not agree:

> I grow wary/weary and increasingly intolerant of those organisations/movements (the IOT and a few other notables excepted) that seek to codify and delineate every tiresome aspect of an increasingly over-blown and irrelevant world-view. Theosophic/

---

58. Wilde, *The Grimoire of Chaos Magick*, 14.

> Kabalistic/Monotheistic lore is/should be dead, further, is evil, is rigid, is sexist, is status-ridden, is of a past we should have outgrown/disowned. It is time for new god/esse/s/daemons – learn to call them – they will always answer.[59]

The reference here to the "Theosophic/Kabalistic/Monotheistic" includes much of the institutionalized occultism of the early twentieth century and organized religions such as Christianity, Judaism and Islam, if "Monotheistic" is taken as a catch-all term. This acknowledging and turning away from the most recent predecessor in the perennialized tradition of magic is reiterated with direct reference to the most recognizable and important magical order of the late nineteenth and early twentieth centuries:

> I find it inconceivable that so many talented occultists still cling to a perverted, post-victorian [sic] perspective of reality. The Golden Dawn and other movements of that ilk bestowed upon the world great pioneers/warriors (and I here acknowledge my debt and gratitude to them) but one can no longer trudge drearily in their well-worn footsteps, hoping that (by some process of sympathetic magic?) some of their accomplishments/abilities will rub off – if you pursue dinosaur tracks all you are likely to acquire are dinosaur droppings and a few bones – small reward for a life-time's work. A fossil is not a living creature – discovering someone else's reality and making it your own may be convenient and gratificatory [sic], but it is also second-rate.[60]

Wilde employs the first strategy but not the second. He seeks to affiliate with an age-old and authentic tradition of magic originating with the shaman while rejecting the systematization and organization of the Hermetic Order of the Golden Dawn and the Theosophical Society. In this way he is trying to legitimize his own innovations on Chaos Magick and delegitimize the parts of Chaos Magick from which he distances himself. These appeals are made to the community of Chaos Magicians and are part of the debate on the theory and practice of Chaos Magick. One of the main reasons for Wilde's rejection of the most recent predecessors can be seen from this section of his text:

> My greetings to you, fellow-seekers/warriors of the/your new aeon! ... those who have recognised/wished to actualise more pertinence in the writings of Moorcock, Brady, Tolkien and Castenada [sic] than in Regardie, Fortune or even Crowley, those who have

---

59. *Ibid.*, 12.
60. *Ibid.*, 26.

turned their back on a golden dawn and have flown instead to the rainbow-jagged darkness of Vajrana (the tantric-gnostic Shambala), those with jaded magickal appetites, those who wish to live in their own universe and not in someone else's – this is for you in the fond hope that it will inspire/encourage you enough to sweetly/awe-fully disturb your magic and your life.[61]

Wilde is attempting to gain legitimacy for his emphasis on the importance of fictional works in Chaos Magick. He wants innovation itself to become an inherent part of what Chaos Magicians do. Liberating Chaos Magick from the organizing forces of early twentieth-century occultism and focusing on the inherently innovative and free shaman of his construction are the changes Wilde makes with regard to the perceived tradition of magic.

Biroco

Joel Biroco was heavily involved in the debates about theory and practice in Chaos Magick through the pages of *CHAOS* (later *KAOS*) magazine. He uses the second strategy only by placing himself and his version of Chaos Magick as the next instance in the natural progression of "the magical tradition". There are practically no references to an ancient tradition of magic and no emphasis on the shaman as the origin of this tradition. He appeals only to the most recent predecessor of Chaos Magick in the perennialized tradition, Thelema. He seeks to legitimize his innovation which he calls the "156 current" and delegitimize all other types of Chaos Magick. Even though his appeal for legitimacy is based on being the next instance of the magical tradition and is directly linked with Thelema, he makes sure that Thelema is also delegitimized by referring to it and Chaos Magick as "nostalgia currents":

> I regard the 156 current as an essentially underground current of frontline occultism and the true successor to what was the 93 current of Thelema (now another nostalgia current) and also the Chaos current, both outmoded by KAOS-BABALON yet foreshadowed in both.[62]

KAOS-BABALON is another name for the "156 current" and is so named to mark this type of Chaos Magick as his interpretation. The significance of the numbers comes from employing gematria, a system of assigning numerical values to letters and words widely used by Aleister Crowley. In this case 93 is

---

61. *Ibid.*, 10.
62. Biroco, *KAOS 14*, 11.

equivalent to Thelema and 156 is equivalent to KAOS-BABALON. Biroco is drawing a direct line from Crowley's Thelema to his version of Chaos Magick and disregarding other types of Chaos Magick almost entirely. Biroco uses another strategy to seek legitimacy for his version of Chaos Magick from the community of interested parties:

> I instigated KAOS-BABALON or "156 current", which I had been working on in the background as a truly "occult" (hidden) current, regarding Babalon as having occult identity with Chaos, essentially being female and male counterparts. It turned the Chaos current into a hard-edged and dark sex magick current.[63]

Here, he is claiming his innovation to be authentic and legitimate because it is hidden, and in the previous quote it is described as underground. The operative ideas here are secrecy and popularization. Biroco's claim that his "156 current" has been hidden is to allude to its being secret and therefore authentic. As von Stuckrad states:

> The idea of higher knowledge is closely linked to a discourse of secrecy, albeit not because esoteric truths are restricted to an "inner circle" of specialists or initiates but because the dialectic of concealment and revelation is a structural element of secretive discourses. Esoteric knowledge is not so much elitist as hidden.[64]

Biroco's emphasis on the hidden, underground nature of his innovation also functions as a rejection of the popularization of Chaos Magick. Biroco sees popularization as a dilution of Chaos Magick. His reference to "frontline occultism" suggests that other versions of Chaos Magick are distracted from the primary goal of occultism. This emphasis on complete commitment to magic is another example of the influence of Crowley on Biroco's ideas.

CONCLUSION

Through ambivalent appeals to tradition, Chaos Magicians have legitimized their own innovations of the already-established types of Chaos Magick. Chaos Magicians are not attempting to convince a wide audience of the legitimacy of their claims. However, they knowingly engage in creation and innovation while directing their appeals for legitimacy at a select audience who share perennialism about traditions of magic. There is an acceptance among

---

63. *Ibid.*, 10. See Crowley, "The Vision and the Voice" for the source of Biroco's KAOS-BABALON.
64. Von Stuckrad, "Western Esotericism", 88–9.

this occultural audience that construction of tradition and appealing to that tradition for legitimacy are constituents of late twentieth-century occultism. Chaos Magicians do not have to claim to have found an unpublished text by a revered author. They have no single religious leader. They are fully aware of the plurality of individualisms that make up Chaos Magick. Innovation and creativity are encouraged as products of the dynamic that exists between conceptions of perennialized, constructed traditions of magic and the call to iconoclasm. In the knowledge that traditions are constructed and can be appealed to in different ways at different times, iconoclasm acts as a valid interpretation of perennialism. This creates a space within which the individualism of twentieth-century occultism coincides with the perennialism of the occultural audience. The appeal to tradition is only one of the ways Chaos Magicians seek legitimacy. There is plenty of scope for a proper exploration of the way science is used to describe and legitimize how Chaos Magick works. The theory behind Chaos Magick is another point of contention for practitioners. Appeals to the science of chaos theory for legitimacy form a major part of the writings on Chaos Magick, and offer an interesting and complex focus for future research.

CHAPTER 6

OCCULTURE IS ORDINARY

Christopher Partridge

While Western esotericism has its roots in the Hellenistic world of the first few centuries of the Common Era, and while much contemporary esoteric thought can be traced back to the rediscovery of early texts during the Renaissance (and, particularly, to the modern occult revival of the nineteenth century), the late modern period since the 1960s has witnessed the emergence of a political and cultural context that has proved particularly conducive to the proliferation of broadly esoteric ideas. Indeed, no longer can such thought be considered occulted or esoteric, in the sense of being recondite and secretive. While there are, of course, occult traditions and organizations that are styled as such, concerned with the cultivation of a sense of gnostic privilege, the culture in which they are embedded is no longer hidden or unfamiliar. It is ordinary and everyday.

The well-documented shift from "religion" to "spirituality",[1] the turn to the self, the change of focus from external authority to inner experience has significantly increased the appeal and respectability of esotericism. Indeed, such has been the change in the oc/cultural climate that, not only is there widespread popular interest in magic and occultism, but students can now study for degrees in esotericism at some European universities.[2] This chapter is

---

1. See Woodhead & Heelas, *The Spiritual Revolution*; Heelas, *Spiritualities of Life*; Partridge, *Re-enchantment of the West*, vol. 1.
2. For example, there is a "Center for History of Hermetic Philosophy and Related Currents" at the University of Amsterdam, and Exeter University has established the "Exeter Centre for the Study of Esotericism". There are also several learned societies, notably, the "European Society for the Study of Western Esotericism", the "Association for the Study of Esotericism", the "Society for the History of Alchemy and Chemistry", and "Societas Magica". There are also a number of academic journals devoted to the study of the subject: *Aries: Journal for the Study of Western Esotericism*; *Esoterica*; *Gnostika*; *Ambix*; and *Magic, Ritual and Witchcraft*.

about this new climate. That is to say, rather than providing an analysis of, for example, particular esoteric traditions or organizations, the following discussion is primarily concerned with exploring the social and cultural conditions, the occultural context within which contemporary esotericism thrives.

OCCULTURE IN LATE MODERN SOCIETIES

The winds that ushered in this more temperate climate within which esotericism has flourished have been guided by the broad contours of modernization and related cultural influences, from Romanticism to Easternization.[3] We might, for example, consider the ways in which modern societies and political systems have witnessed a shift towards individualization, the result of which has been a turn away from deference to traditional sources of authority, and a turn towards personal experience and freedom of choice. It is also worth noting that Western modernity has been shaped by colonialism, in that not only has there arguably been significant Easternization,[4] particularly evident in Theosophical currents, but that this has included a conspicuous orientalism,[5] which has, in turn, significantly supported the turn to the self. This, again, has all provided a climate favourable to the growth of esotericism. Furthermore, late modern capitalist societies, characterized by unprecedented levels of affluence, have become sites of conspicuous consumption within which spirituality, therapy and the pursuit of wellbeing have become commodified, marketed, branded and invested with economic value.[6] Of course, for many Westerners born since 1960, this is not an odd state of affairs. Because they have been shaped by a culture of consumption, they have, as Wade Clark Roof has commented, "looked on [spirituality] in much the same way as other purchasable goods".[7] While this does not necessarily reduce esotericism and the pursuit of spirituality to the profit motive, it does link it, along with other lifestyle acquisitions, to identity and the construction of the self. Added to this, globalization and technological advance have led to rapid recent changes in people's lifestyles, the corresponding result of which has been ever more complex changes to our self-identities.[8] Indeed, in the 1970s, Ronald Inglehart persuasively argued that the affluence of post-industrial societies had created a situation in which individual values were being transformed from materialist values,

---

3. See Partridge, *Re-enchantment of the West*, vol. 1; Woodhead & Heelas, *Religion in Modern Times*; Heelas, *Spiritualities of Life*; Colin Campbell, *The Easternization of the West*.
4. See Partridge, *Re-enchantment of the West*, vol. 1, 87–118; Colin Campbell, *The Easternization of the West*.
5. See Partridge, "Lost Horizon".
6. See Einstein, *Brands of Faith*.
7. Roof, *A Generation of Seekers*, 195.
8. See Robertson, *Globalization*; Clarke, *New Religions in Global Perspective*.

which focused on the securing of life's basic necessities, to post-materialist values, which emphasized self-expression, subjectivization, and experience.[9] However, the point is that such post-materialist values provide fertile ground for contemporary esotericism, the claimed effect of much of which is, generally speaking, personal empowerment, metamorphosis, and liberation through the acquisition of illuminated knowledge (gnosis) and, as such, the developing of one's potential as a human being in relation to the cosmos. In other words, in affluent, information-rich, self-oriented societies, in which our basic needs are catered for, we have the time to seek and the money to purchase experiences and lifestyles.

Finally, in recent years, it is difficult to ignore the findings of studies which suggest that generational repositioning has contributed to subjectivization, post-materialism, and a culture within which esotericism flourishes. For example, in their study of post-Christian spirituality, Stef Aupers and Dick Houtman argue that this is largely driven by cohort replacement, in that younger generations with stronger affinities to, and a greater penchant for, post-Christian spirituality have simply replaced an older generation for whom this was not the case.[10] This concurs with other research indicating a shift from the religious patterns of pre-baby-boomers (who came of age in the 1960s) to the largely self-oriented spirituality of Generation X (born between 1961 and 1981). Key to this shift, of course, was the rise of youth culture and the increased influence of popular culture, both of which have contributed to an independence from the values of the previous generation. Moreover, this was a generation born into an affluent society that enabled the exercise of that independence and to challenge, what appeared to be, the flawed values of the previous generation – values which had walked them into Vietnam, the Cuban Missile Crisis, Watergate, and much more. Generation Y (born between 1982 and 2000) have, as well as continuing to benefit from higher rates of education and affluence, not to mention the growth of information technologies ("the Internet is one of the most important places where Witches meet"[11]), become increasingly alienated from traditional religiosity.[12] As Peter Brierley has shown of church attendance in the UK, "undoubtedly the biggest shift age-wise in the church in recent years was the huge decline in numbers of young people in the 1990s".[13] Influenced far more by popular culture and subcultural peer

---

9. See Inglehart, *Culture Shift in Advanced Industrial Society*; Inglehart & Abramson, "Measuring Postmaterialism". Interestingly, from a different perspective, Frank Furedi has made a similar point concerning the new highly individualized and emotivist therapeutic culture in which the self is perceived to be diminished and vulnerable and in which "virtually every challenge or misfortune that confronts people is represented as a direct threat to their emotional well-being" (Furedi, *Therapy Culture*, 1).
10. Houtman & Aupers, "The Spiritual Turn and the Decline of Tradition".
11. Berger & Ezzy, *Teenage Witches*, 139. See also Cowan, *Cyberhenge*; Erik Davis, *Techgnosis*.
12. See Tomasi, *Alternative Religions Among European Youth*.
13. Brierley, *Pulling Out of the Nosedive*, 112.

pressure, there has, again, been a shift away from the authoritarian aspects of religion and toward the creation of personal spiritual paths. As Helen Berger and Douglas Ezzy comment of contemporary Wicca in their study of teenage witchcraft, "the emphasis in ritual and in all self-transformation techniques is individual discovery and self-development. There is no clear list of behaviours, such as those that exist in Islam, Judaism, or Christianity, that adherents are expected to change or adopt."[14]

The evidence, therefore, would seem to suggest that Western culture is not becoming *less* religious, but rather that it is, for a variety of reasons, becoming *differently* religious. Rather than becoming secularized it is, as I have argued elsewhere, witnessing a confluence of secularization and sacralization, at the heart of which is a deceptively powerful "occulture".[15] Even if individuals are not convinced of all the claims made by particular spiritualities, philosophies or esoteric systems, there is, nevertheless, a conspicuous interest in them and a growing credulity concerning their plausibility. Indeed, there appears to be a constantly replenished reservoir of beliefs and practices associated with esotericism, Theosophy, mysticism, neopaganism, the paranormal, and a range of other ideas from the bizarre to the familiar, a reservoir that is constantly feeding and being fed by popular culture.[16] In order to adequately theorize and organize these processes, I introduced the category of occulture. Just as, arguably, occult and magical thought was once a widespread familiar feature of Western societies, in the sense that their members possessed a consciousness that genuinely participated in an enchanted world,[17] so today, particularly since the 1960s, we are witnessing the increasing ordinariness of occulture.

Occulture, as a sociological term, refers to the environment within which, and the social processes by which particular meanings relating, typically, to spiritual, esoteric, paranormal and conspiratorial ideas emerge, are disseminated, and become influential in societies and in the lives of individuals. Central to these processes is popular culture, in that it disseminates and remixes occultural ideas, thereby incubating new spores of occultural thought. For example, whether one considers the ideas articulated in television series such as *Dark Skies*, *The X-Files* and *Supernatural*, films such as *Rosemary's Baby* (1968), *The Wicker Man* (1973), *Angel Heart* (1987), *Contact* (1997), *The Sixth Sense* (1999) and *Paranormal Activity* (2007), the claims made for the phenomena captured in reality television programmes such as *Ghost Hunters* and *Most Haunted*, the conspiratorial ideas developed in books such as *The*

---

14. Berger & Ezzy, *Teenage Witches*, 34.
15. Partridge, *The Re-enchantment of the West*; Partridge, "Alternative Spiritualities, New Religions, and the Reenchantment of the West".
16. Partridge, *The Re-enchantment of the West*, vol. 1, 65. See also Kripal, *Authors of the Impossible*.
17. See Frances Yates, *The Occult Philosophy in the Elizabethan Age*; Berman, *The Reenchantment of the World*.

Stargate Conspiracy, *Holy Blood, Holy Grail* and *The Da Vinci Code*,[18] or the ideological themes and styles disseminated within popular music and acted out within their attendant subcultures,[19] popular (oc)culture provides a space within which there is an openness to the possibility of metaphysical interpretation. For the scholar of religion this is, of course, important, in that popular culture becomes a significant area of inquiry as an agent of contemporary re-enchantment.[20] However, it is no easy task mapping the flow of ideas and the creation and dissolution of synergies, whether in popular culture or elsewhere. So rapid is the flow that once mapped, occultural content quickly becomes passé.

OCCULTURE, THE OCCULT AND THE CULTIC MILIEU

In the early 1970s, the British sociologist Colin Campbell observed that cultic organizations seem to arise out of a general cultural ethos, a cultic milieu, which, he argued,

> can be regarded as the cultural underground of society. Much broader, deeper and historically based than the contemporary movement known as *the* underground, it includes all deviant belief systems and their associated practices. Unorthodox science, alien and heretical religion, deviant medicine, all comprise elements of such an underground.[21]

The cultic milieu described by Campbell included networks and seedbeds of ideas, as well as various authoritative sources and particular groups. Indeed, the cultic milieu, as understood by Campbell, was essentially "occult culture". That is to say, its centre of gravity is modern occultism, magic, and certain ideas and Easternized themes developed within 1960s countercultural movements. More recently, Jeffrey Kaplan and Heléne Lööw have revisited the theory, identifying the cultic milieu as a "zone in which proscribed and/or forbidden knowledge is the coin of the realm, a place in which ideas, theories and speculations are to be found, exchanged, modified and, eventually, adopted or rejected by adherents of countless, primarily ephemeral groups".[22] However, while Kaplan and Lööw have made creative use of Campbell's theory and highlighted its value, they have not, it seems to me, been wholly successful

---

18. See, for example, Partridge, "The Occultural Significance of *The Da Vinci Code*".
19. See Partridge & Christianson, *The Lure of the Dark Side*; Granholm, "'Sons of Northern Darkness'".
20. See Partridge, *The Re-enchantment of the West*; Partridge, "Religion and Popular Culture".
21. Colin Campbell, "The Cult, the Cultic Milieu and Secularization", 122 (emphasis original).
22. Kaplan & Lööw, *The Cultic Milieu*, 3.

in applying it to the contemporary world. Their attempt to develop the cultic milieu model is essentially Procrustean. Indeed, they themselves seem to recognize this, in that, in seeking to account for a relatively wide spectrum of ideas from nature mysticism to spiritual articulations of the gothic, and from Charles Manson to National Socialism, the theory is being stretched so far that it is beginning to show cracks:

> Adherents ... are not easily diffused through the cultic milieu. Racists and neo-Nazis do not easily mix with adherents of radical environmental subculture, although the same could be said for Black Bloc anarchists and members of mainstream labor unions or adherents of the Catholic Church ... This observation ... points to a more complex picture than Campbell envisioned ... As those of us who have studied the more esoteric reaches of the cultic milieu would attest, the milieu is vast.[23]

However, the picture is, in fact, not only rather more complex than Campbell realized, but also, I would argue, far vaster and more ubiquitous than that painted by Kaplan and Lööw. While there is, in the book they edited, a broad range of ideologies and spiritualities discussed, from the far right to the far left, they are all "oppositional by nature"[24] and, together, constitute a counterculture concerned with hidden and rejected knowledge. Indeed, although seeking to account for a vast range of ideas that converge and mutate at speed, Kaplan and Lööw still want to retain a sociological model that theorizes this enormous diversity as "a single entity".[25] This is, to say the least, problematic. Although attempting to rethink the milieu in terms of a "vast imaginary landscape inhabited by many neighbourhoods",[26] it is clearly being stretched too far. The cultic milieu theory is currently not fit for purpose.

Having said that, even if Kaplan and Lööw were able to revise Campbell's theory in order to account for the plethora of ideas they have identified, it would still fail to make sense of the processes of re-enchantment. This is why we need to think in terms of "occulture" rather than "the cultic milieu". While including the oppositional and "heterogeneous assortment" of the cultic milieu, occulture is less concerned with particular groups, systems of belief and spiritual practices – although these are important – and much more concerned with the conditions within which particular "lifeworlds"[27] are formed

---

23. *Ibid.*, 5.
24. *Ibid*, 3.
25. Colin Campbell, "The Cult, the Cultic Milieu and Secularization", 122.
26. Kaplan & Lööw, *The Cultic Milieu*, 6.
27. I am following Jürgen Habermas in my use of the term "lifeworld". This is important, in that it refers to the latent, taken-for-granted core values, beliefs, and understandings about who we are, how we relate to others, what the world is like, and how we fit into it. See Habermas, *Theory of Communicative Action*, vol. 2, 113–98.

and within which plausibility structures[28] are shaped. Indeed, we will see that, from an occultural perspective, there are questions to be asked as to the extent to which we can speak of an "oppositional counterculture".[29] Hence, while there are conspicuous areas of continuity between the two theories,[30] and while I am myself indebted to the cultic milieu theory, I am suggesting that something more ubiquitous, ordinary, and less oppositional is happening. For this reason, the introduction of the term "culture" is important.

Of course, while "culture" might be interpreted in any number of ways, as a composite part of the compound "occulture", it broadly follows Raymond Williams's thesis that "culture is ordinary".[31] Hence, while the use of the term "occult" in "occulture" suggests the hidden, the exotic and the elite (which, of course, is a large part of the bookish, secretive, gnostic appeal of much Western esotericism), the addition of the term "culture" opens up a very different perspective, signifying that which is everyday. It is this latter cultural dimension that is the key to understanding contemporary occulture. This is, again, not to deny that there is, within occulture, that which is occult, esoteric, oppositional, or countercultural, but rather that occulture *per se* is largely ordinary and everyday. Again, within the idea of "occulture", the "occult" is radically modified by the word "culture". As a compound, "occulture" suggests a democratized occult, an open esotericism – "occulture is ordinary". Again, it is this very ordinariness of occulture that is not at all clear in discussions of the cultic milieu, which, we have seen, is described as being "an underground", a "zone in which proscribed and/or forbidden knowledge is the coin of the realm".[32]

Occulture describes certain shared attitudes, values, and practices that characterize society. While we might think of periods when occultural lifeworlds become particularly conspicuous and influential in terms of re-enchantment, actually, occulture is never absent. It is, historically, a feature of all societies. As Kaplan and Lööw have commented of the cultic milieu, the phenomenon is hardly new:

> That there exists within every society a small but dedicated underground of true seekers of esoteric and, very often, forbidden knowledge, is well known. The Middle Ages had its heretics, magicians and alchemists whose quests were not unlike those of the seekers described by Campbell as inhabiting the cultic milieu.[33]

---

28. On plausibility structures, see Berger, *The Sacred Canopy*.
29. Kaplan & Lööw, *The Cultic Milieu*, 1.
30. See Partridge, *The Re-enchantment of the West*, vol. 1, 24–9.
31. Raymond Williams, "Culture is Ordinary".
32. Kaplan & Lööw, *The Cultic Milieu*, 3.
33. *Ibid.*, 1.

Therefore, they argue, "the cultic milieu is not a product of the 1960s. Rather, it is a permanent feature of society – not just this society, but of every society for which we have historical records".[34] My point is that, while this is true, the theory of occulture requires that we consider not simply elite, underground communities with a penchant for the occult and the forbidden, but society as a whole. For example, not only did the religious values of the Church have a shaping effect on medieval society and culture, in that, as A. D. Gilbert has commented, "at all levels of social life and human need the Christian religion acquired immense and ubiquitous *utility* in the minds of medieval men", but also, at the level of popular consciousness, it actually functioned as "a vast reservoir of magical power, capable of being deployed for a variety of secular purposes".[35] This largely Christianized occulture, these synergies of Christian theology and indigenous folk beliefs, permeated all levels of medieval society. Again, evidence for such medieval Christian occulture is clearly evident in Karen Jolly's study of elf charms and popular religion in England:

> [I]nvisible powers associated with the Devil afflicted people with physical as well as spiritual ailments; hence Christian words of power made herbal medicine handed down through classical and Germanic lore efficacious against these forces … All of the remedies show the conjunction of good forces against evil forces without a necessary distinction between physical and spiritual, natural and supernatural … Any material phenomenon had a potential spiritual meaning, whether it be a demonic illness or temptation testing the resistance of a Christian or a weakness of body designed to demonstrate God's miraculous power.[36]

Keith Thomas likewise provides evidence for the widespread popular supernaturalism of the medieval period:

> The medieval Church … found itself saddled with the tradition that the working of miracles was the most efficacious means of demonstrating its monopoly of the truth. By the twelfth and thirteenth centuries the *Lives* of the Saints had assumed a stereotyped pattern. They related the miraculous achievements of holy men, and stressed how they could prophesy the future, control the weather, provide protection against fire and flood, magically transport heavy objects, and bring relief to the sick.[37]

---

34. *Ibid.*, 4.
35. Alan D. Gilbert, *The Making of Post-Christian Britain*, 19.
36. Jolly, *Popular Religion in Late Saxon England*, 170–71. See also Kieckhefer, *Magic in the Middle Ages*.
37. Thomas, *Religion and the Decline of Magic*, 28. See also Jones & Pennick, *History of Pagan Europe*.

Again, as Nicholas Goodrick-Clarke has noted, D. P. Walker's landmark 1958 study, *Spiritual and Demonic Magic from Ficino to Campanella*, demonstrated that "magic was part of the mainstream in the late fifteenth and sixteenth centuries, closely connected with religion, music, mathematics, and medicine".[38] Likewise, B. J. Gibbons has shown that Western esotericism played a significant cultural role in the emergence of the modern period.[39] Indeed, whether we explore, for example, Romanticism or the cult of the Gothic, during the Enlightenment period there emerged, as Roy Porter has argued, a common trade in stock elements:

> ... the mist-shrouded castle, the villain sworn to the Devil, ghosts, spectres, sorcerers and witches, a flirting with the weird, the uncanny, the bizarre, with sado-masochistic sexuality – and, underpinning all, the Burkeian obsession with dread and the infinite unknown. Supernatural elements like spectralization triggered new sexual frissons; the old demonological themes of possession, incubi and succubi were eroticized ... Such disciplines as alchemy, astrology and animal magnetism, and the fringes of physiognomy and phrenology evidently enjoyed a certain vogue.[40]

While many other studies might be cited, the point is that it is hardly a new state of affairs that occulture is everyday, rather than the sole preserve of some underground cultic milieu. While continuously flowing and changing in content, breadth and intensity, it is not primarily a subterranean phenomenon, the ideas of which periodically emerge, filtered and proscribed, into the mainstream. Of course, the notion of a cultic milieu does not necessarily contradict occulture, in that occulture would help to account for the progress of the cultic milieu and the mainstreaming of its ideas. Understood in this way, the cultic milieu becomes just such an underground site of occultural coalescence, a space in which esoteric and exotic ideas can be incubated. But that is only one aspect of occulture.

In order to unpack further the notion that occulture is ordinary, it is worth quoting Williams at length, for the points he makes about *culture* can easily be applied, with a little imagination and contextualization, to *occulture*:

> The making of a society is the finding of common meanings and directions, and its growth is an active debate and amendment under the pressures of experience, contact, and discovery, writing themselves into the land. The growing society is there, yet is

---

38. Goodrick-Clarke, *The Western Esoteric Traditions*, 5.
39. Gibbons, *Spirituality and the Occult*.
40. Roy Porter, "Witchcraft and Magic in Enlightenment, Romantic and Liberal Thought", 249–50.

> also remade in every individual mind. The making of a mind is, first, the slow learning of shapes, purposes, and meanings, so that work, observation and communication are possible. Then, second, but equal in importance, is the testing of these in experience, the making of new observations, comparisons and meanings. A culture has two aspects: the known meanings and directions, which its members are trained to; the new observations and meanings, which are offered and tested. These are the ordinary processes of human societies and human minds, and we see through them the nature of a culture; that it is always both traditional and creative; that it is both the most ordinary common meanings and the finest individual meanings. We use the word culture in these two senses: to mean a whole way of life – the common meanings; to mean the arts and learning – the special processes of discovery and creative effort. Some writers reserve the word for one or other of these senses; I insist on both, and on the significance of their conjunction. The questions I ask about culture are questions about our general and common purposes, yet also questions about deep personal meanings. Culture is ordinary, in every society and in every mind.[41]

Occulture is likewise used to mean *both* a whole way of life *and* the special processes of discovery and creative effort. Like Williams, I insist on both and on the significance of their conjunction. The questions I ask about occulture are questions about our general and common purposes, yet also questions about deep personal meanings. Occulturally, special processes of discovery and creative effort might include the ideas, practices and movements identified by Campbell, Kaplan and Lööw as belonging to the cultic milieu. However, while occulture *per se* includes these, it is also "a whole way of life – the common meanings".

We have seen that, in contemporary civil societies in the post-industrial West, there has been a decline of Christian hegemony, a distaste for deference to traditional authorities, such as the Church, and a turn within to the subjective life. Since the 1960s this has been supported by growing affluence, increased leisure time, the emergence and expansion of youth culture, and the triumph of both democracy and capitalism. Moreover, if the making of a society is, as Williams claims, "the finding of common meanings and directions, and its growth is an active debate and amendment under the pressures of experience, contact, and discovery", then it is also difficult to ignore the roles of media and popular culture. That is to say, not only is popular culture increasingly important for the establishment of common meanings and

---

41. Raymond Williams, "Culture is Ordinary", 6.

directions, but, in so doing, it has significantly contributed to the growth and significance of contemporary occulture. From the relatively mundane to the bizarrely esoteric, from approaches to health and wellbeing to conspiracies relating world domination and apocalypse, popular culture disseminates occultural content, creates synergies and encourages new spores of occultural thought to emerge. These "new observations and meanings" are then incorporated into lifeworlds simply as presuppositions or as elements within particular systems of belief. To paraphrase Williams again, these are the ordinary processes of human societies and human minds, and we see through them the nature of occulture, both the most ordinary common meanings and the finest individual meanings.

Particularly interesting are the successes of conspicuously occultural books and films such as Dan Brown's *The Da Vinci Code* and *Angels and Demons*, and films such as Roman Polanski's *The Ninth Gate*.[42] *The Da Vinci Code*, for example, won "best book" in the 2005 British Book Awards;[43] it has sold more than 30 million copies in 40 languages, and Penguin Books have even produced a guide to what I would describe as the occultural context of the novel in its Rough Guides series.[44] Indeed, as Stig Hjarvard has shown, *The Da Vinci Code*, as mediatized spirituality, not only reflects, but stimulates alternative religious interest. In a Danish survey, "more than half of the respondents report an increased interest in religious issues" after reading *The Da Vinci Code* and *Angels and Demons*.[45] As to the book's occultural content, not only is, for example, Wicca explicitly mentioned, but key neopagan themes, such as Goddess Worship, are prominent, as are discussions of popular and subculturally trendy symbols, such as the pentacle, practices such as the Tarot, and romanticized rituals such as the *hieros gamos*.[46] This contemporary everyday interest in popular occultism, reflected in *The Da Vinci Code*'s enormous success, is, again, not simply reserved for fiction, but is also evident in the fact that the percentage of esoteric books published since 1930 has more than doubled: in 1930 occult books constituted 7 per cent of religious books published. This gradually rose to 17 per cent in 1990, dipped to 11 per cent in 1995 and rose again to 15 per cent in 2000.[47] Again, Elizabeth Puttick has recently observed that there has been

> an explosion of holistic ideas and practices into the mainstream … Mind-body-spirit publishing has expanded from a specialist niche to the fastest growing non-fiction genre in a multinational,

---

42. See Partridge, "The Occultural Significance of *The Da Vinci Code*".
43. BBC, "*Da Vinci Code* Wins Top Book Award".
44. Haag & Haag, *Rough Guide to The Da Vinci Code*.
45. Hjarvard, "The Mediatization of Religion", 22.
46. Dan Brown, *Da Vinci Code*, 42, 43, 59–62, 129, 172, 409–10.
47. Brierley, "Religion", 666–7.

multimedia industry. This growth contrasts with traditional religious publishing, which is in decline. In the process, the most successful spiritual authors have become both gurus and global brands.[48]

While this shift towards an increasing occultural hegemony is relatively well documented, from both emic and etic perspectives,[49] the point here is, again, simply that occulture is ordinary.

ESOTERRORISM AND THE GENESIS OF OCCULTURE

Having discussed the theory of occulture and its relationship to the cultic milieu hypothesis, I want to return to the beginning, as it were, and briefly explore the context within which the term "occulture" arose, because, to my mind, there are few better examples of contemporary esotericism, the significance of occulture, and the power of popular culture.

Going back over a decade now, my use of the term "occulture" can be traced back to attempts to make sense of what I understood to be an ambient supernaturalism, a spiritual environment, a culture of the occult broadly conceived. At the same time, I became aware of the term "occulture" within a particular esoteric subculture oriented around industrial music and performance art. The neologism, I discovered, was probably coined by the esotericist, musician, artist and self-styled "cultural engineer" Genesis P-Orridge (Neil Andrew Megson, 1950–), whose work with the performance art group COUM Transmissions, the bands Throbbing Gristle and Psychic TV, and the spoken word project Thee Majesty developed a particular brand of transgressive, experimental, sonic and visual art. A confluence of esotericism, pornographic eroticism, violence, death, degradation, confrontation of taboo subjects and noise, his work is rarely less than confrontational. As Paul Hegarty comments of Throbbing Gristle's work, it offered "a thoroughgoing critique or even attack on conventional, modern, Christian, artistic, moral, capitalist thought and living", much of which could be understood in terms of "transgression and perversion".[50] While much of this transgression can perhaps be understood in terms of a juvenile delight gained from extreme behaviour and the offence caused by challenging taboos,[51] one also needs to understand that, certainly

---

48. Puttick, "Rise of Mind–Body–Spirit Publishing", 129.
49. For an interesting emic insight into contemporary occultism and youth culture, see Louv, *Generation Hex*.
50. Hegarty, *Noise/Music*, 107.
51. They will have been pleased, no doubt, when, in 1976, the Conservative MP Nicholas Fairbairn declared in the *Daily Mail*, "these people are the wreckers of civilisation" (Ford, *The Wreckers of Civilisation*, 0.12).

in the case of P-Orridge, there was, as Don Watson argues, "a deeply rooted desire to expose and challenge the hidden mechanisms of social control".[52] It is this latter underlying motivation, influenced, we will see, very much by William S. Burroughs, that opens up some interesting analysis.

During the late 1970s P-Orridge became interested in "how a small number of fanatical individuals could have a disproportionate impact on culture"[53] – a process that became key to the sociological understanding of occulture that I was beginning to construct: micro-ideas with macro-effects. Occultural ideas articulated and developed in films, in literature, in music or on the Internet are able to have, through synergies and networks, a disproportionate influence on large numbers of people and, consequently, on institutions and societies.[54] From a sociological perspective, because occulture is ordinary, taken for granted, embedded in the everyday, its viral potential is enormous. This is a significant point, which is not lost on P-Orridge, whose interest in the influence and dissemination of esotericism is long-standing. Indeed, although it is not fully articulated in his work, it would appear that, for P-Orridge, the disproportionate influence of the esoteric ideas of a minority could have "eso-terrorist" potential, if engineered carefully. Likewise, he insisted that music is "a platform for propaganda",[55] in that an individual musician or a band is able to disseminate selective information which will, not only significantly emotively influence the thinking of a particular group of people, but, by means of that affective manipulation, also subvert mainstream thinking and challenge established authorities.[56] When such activities are coupled with the energies available in magick, however these might be understood, it becomes esoterrorism. Hence, for P-Orridge, music is a particularly powerful weapon in the arsenal of the esoterrorist, for not only is it propaganda, but, he insists, "music is magick", and, as such, key to the creation of "occult culture":

> We live in limbo and thirst for freedom ... Vested interests of every kind want us lazy and atrophied ... Man's fall from grace is his fall from inner security. His defeat is his surrender to conditioned boundaries imposed by the strict regime of acceptability instead of the natural honesty of his individual instinct that recognises all things to be in a state of flux ... We are trained to not even *want* to

---

52. Watson, "Beyond Evil", 30.
53. Ford, *The Wreckers of Civilisation*, 10.29. See also Vale, *RE/Search 4/5*, 62–77; P-Orridge, *Painful but Fabulous*.
54. Of particular interest is *In the Shadow of the Sun*, an occult film by Derek Jarman for which Throbbing Gristle produced a particularly menacing soundtrack.
55. Vale, *RE/Search 4/5*, 87 (see also 64–5).
56. Here, we might again mention the influence of Burroughs, who warned of the "Control Machine", by which he referred to the forces of conformity that would destroy the unique qualities of the individual.

think. Decondition the condition. Conditioning is control. Control is stability. Stability is safety for those with a vested interest in control. Let's go out of control. What breaks this cycle is a psychic jolt. Music is magick, a religious phenomena that short circuits control through human response. The moment we forget ourselves and end the limbo-dance we enter a world of struggle, joy and clarity. A tragic, but magickal world where it is possible to accept mortality and thereby deny death. Experience without dogma, anguish without shame or sham. A morality of anti-cult. Occult culture. Its rituals collective, yet private, performed in public, but invisible … The rites of youth. Our alchemical human heritage, encased like a cadaver in a black suit.[57]

This, of course, is a relatively idiosyncratic and convoluted understanding of magick and the occult. Having said that, it is intended to be a practical, protest esotericism for a disillusioned, unemployed "blank generation".[58] Rather than

> the magick of the Golden Dawn, designed for the stately Victorian manor … it was magick designed for the blank-eyed, TV-flattened, prematurely abyss-dwelling youth of the late Twentieth Century – like the punk kids in Derek Jarman's *Jubilee*, who have never ventured out of the council flats they were born in. Rather than high ceremony, drawing-room intrigue and exalted initiatory ritual, the focus more often than not became simple survival, and defense of individual vision from a malevolently dehumanizing culture that the Victorians and Modernists, even in their most racist and reactionary moments, could never have foreseen.[59]

Similarly, Thee Temple ov Psychick Youth (TOPY), in *Thee Grey Book*, states that it

> requires an active individual, dedicated towards thee establishment ov a functional system ov magick and a modern pagan philosophy without recourse to mystification, gods or demons; but recognising thee implicit powers ov thee human brain (neuromancy) linked with guiltless sexuality focused through Will Structure (Sigils). Magick empowers thee individual to embrace and realise their

---

57. Vale, *RE/Search 4/5*, 87.
58. *Blank Generation* is the title of the 1977 debut album from Richard Hell and the Voidoids. The title song reflects the despair and nihilism of the generation (see McNeil & McCain, *Please Kill Me*, 282–283). It is this despair and nihilism that lies at the heart of P-Orridge's analysis of society in the 1970s and 1980s.
59. Louv, in P-Orridge, *Thee Psychick Bible*, 18.

dreams and maximise their natural potential. It is for those with thee courage to touch themselves. It integrates all levels ov thought in thee first steps towards final negation ov control and fear.[60]

While clearly idiosyncratic, this functional, anti-mystical "system ov magick" indicates the breadth of interpretation of esotericism in the contemporary world. However, to understand this particular interpretation more fully, something needs to be said about the occulture of Genesis P-Orridge, about the various occultural streams that met in his life and work.

A friend of Burroughs (whom he had known since 1971), P-Orridge had, for several years, requested an introduction to Brion Gysin, the principal architect of the cut-up method, developed in 1959 and used to great effect by Burroughs. Eventually, Burroughs wrote him a letter of introduction and he met Gysin in Paris in the late 1970s, probably 1978,[61] and quickly established a close master–disciple relationship.[62] While P-Orridge was enormously influenced by Gysin, it was the cut-up method, as discussed in *The Third Mind* (a book-length collage manifesto on the method and its uses), that became central to his thought.[63] Put simply, cut-up involves cutting a text into pieces, which are then rearranged into a new text. "Whatever you do in your head", insisted Gysin, "bears the prerecorded pattern of your head. Cut through that pattern and all patterns if you want something new … Cut through the word lines to hear a new voice off the page."[64] This method of progressing beyond current patterns of thought and belief was, for P-Orridge, revolutionary. Gysin, he argued,

> understood more than anyone else at that point in culture that, just as we can take apart particles until there's a mystery, so we can do the same with culture, with words, language and image. *Everything can be sliced and diced and reassembled, with no limit to the possible combinations.*[65]

There could hardly be a better summary of occultural processes than the sentence italicized above.

---

60. TOPY, *Thee Grey Book*.
61. See Vale, *RE/Search 4/5*, 71.
62. See P-Orridge, *Esoterrorist*, 34–7.
63. The cut-up method was also used by other artists, notably David Bowie and Patti Smith. "'I use Burroughs' cut up technique', Bowie explained in the BBC documentary, *Cracked Actor*. The camera panned in to show Bowie tearing sheets of lyrics down the middle and moving the edges against each other to find new lines created in the process" (Sandford, *Bowie*, 120).
64. Burroughs & Gysin, *The Third Mind*, 44.
65. P-Orridge, "Eyes Wide Shut" (emphasis added).

If one didn't look at the very nature of how we build and describe our world, [Gysin] thought, we get into very dangerous places. Once you believe things are permanent, you're trapped in a world without doors. Gysin constructed a room with infinite doors for us to walk through. What amazed me about Gysin's work was how it could be applied to behaviour: there were techniques to free oneself through the equivalent of cutting up and reassembling words. If we confound and break up the proposed unfolding the world impresses upon us, we can give ourselves the space to consider what we want to be as a species ... He would take words, break them down into hieroglyphics, then turn the paper and do it again and again until the magical square was filled with words. Gysin worked with the idea of painting as magic, to change the perception of people and to reprogramme the human nervous system ... I made an agreement with Gysin before his death that I would try to champion and vindicate his work and legacy.[66]

It is difficult to imagine anyone championing his work and legacy more enthusiastically than P-Orridge. Indeed, not only did he use the cut-up method to produce new ideas, but he applied it, quite literally, to his own body in an attempt to recreate himself. He and his late partner, Jacqueline Breyer ("Lady Jaye"), following their marriage in 1993, embarked on what he termed the "Pandrogeny Project",[67] which, informed by the cut-up technique, embraced the aesthetics of body modification as the first step towards becoming a single "pandrogynous" being. Indeed, it is important to understand that, speaking in terms of a "genderless state", for P-Orridge, who now has breast implants and looks feminine, the surgery was not motivated by transsexual concerns. That is to say, he was not struggling to be female while trapped in a male body. The surgery was not even, primarily, about the construction of a post-human, post-gendered self, such as Marilyn Manson sought to explore on *Mechanical Animals* (1998).[68] Rather, this was far more of an esoteric project, in that it was an expression of his belief that the self is pure consciousness trapped in flesh and controlled by DNA. Humans are, he believes, at an early stage in their psychic evolution towards fleshless consciousness; the Pandrogeny Project is a step towards that evolutionary goal; a step away from the "control" of the DNA. He and Lady Jaye, therefore, sought to become one, in the sense

---

66. *Ibid.*
67. He was able to do this when, in 1998, he was awarded $1.5 million when he sued the producer Rick Rubin, following serious injuries, including nearly losing his left arm, when escaping a fire at Rubin's Los Angeles home.
68. For a good discussion of the post-human in relation to Marilyn Manson, see Toffoletti, *Cyborgs and Barbie Dolls*, 81–105.

of becoming a "third being", Breyer P-Orridge.[69] That is to say, they referred to themselves *together*, in the singular, as Breyer P-Orridge. The Pandrogyny Project, therefore, was an empirical reflection of that singularity. However, as with much of P-Orridge's thought, it is typically occultural, in that pandrogyny is a synergy of ideas, the principal thesis drawing on a common stock of esoteric and transpersonal theories of consciousness and "Mind".[70] In other words, in a typically occultural manner, P-Orridge, wittingly or unwittingly, remixes a range of ideas with theories learned from Gysin and Burroughs, as well as his own long-standing interest in body modification.

For the esoterrorist, cut-up and the cultivation of occult culture are central to the subversion of social control, just as pandrogyny is an act of resistance to the control of the DNA. All forms of control must be disrupted and subverted. Using cut-up as an occult technique, a form of magick, he argued that a small group of esoterrorists could "have a disproportionate impact on culture",[71] disrupt social programming and consensus solipsism.

> Control. Control needs Time (like a junkie needs junk). Time appears linear. Cut-ups make time arbitrary, non-linear. They reveal, locate and negate Control. Control hides in social structures like Politics, Religion, Education, Mass Media. Control exists like a virus for its own sake. Cut-ups loosen rational order, break preconceptions and expected response. They retrain our perception and acceptance of what we are told is thee nature of reality. They confound and short-circuit Control. All Control ultimately relies upon manipulation of behaviour. In culture thee Cut-up is still a modification of, or alternate, language. It can reveal, describe and measure Control ... Magick as a method is a Cut-up Process that goes further than description. It is infused with emotion, intuition, instinct and impulse, and includes emotions and feelings ... Control Disintegrates. Magick integrates. Thee idea is to apply thee cut-up principle of behaviour. Thee method is a contemporary, non-mystical interpretation of "Magick." Thee aim is reclamation of self-determination, conscious and unconscious, to the Individual. Thee result is to neutralise and challenge thee essence of social control.[72]

---

69. "Third being" is a reference to the "third mind", created by cut-up, as discussed in Burroughs & Gysin, *The Third Mind*.
70. See, for example, Capra, *The Turning Point*, 410; Castaneda, *Tales of Power*, 100; Ferguson, *The Aquarian Conspiracy*, 73–5; Hanegraaff, *New Age Religion and Western Culture*, 245–55; Wilber, "The Atman Project".
71. Ford, *Wreckers of Civilisation*, 10.29. See also Vale, *RE/Search 4/5*, 62–77; P-Orridge, *Painful but Fabulous*.
72. P-Orridge, *Esoterrorist*, 18.

It's worth noting that the spelling and grammar are important. Whereas the spelling of "magick" is simply taken from Aleister Crowley's spelling convention (originally designed to distinguish his theories of magic from other interpretations he considered superstitious or misguided), the other odd spellings and grammatical constructions are intended to challenge thought and ways of reading; our angle of vision is bent during the process of reading.

Concerning cut-up, this is in many ways an essentially occultural process. Indeed, it can be seen as a form of remix, as utilized in contemporary electronic music. With roots in Jamaican reggae culture, which was itself embedded in a particular occulture, remixes are often radical deconstructions of recordings.[73] The point is that cut-up or remix is central to occulture. It is not simply that particular ideas and signifiers are disseminated within an occultural environment, but rather that in the process they are cut-up, remixed, deconstructed and reconstructed. New synergies are formed, which are then, in a dialectic process, cut-up and remixed, the results of which then attach to other ideas and signifiers and so on. P-Orridge, therefore, did not simply coin the term, but he is himself an excellent example of the subsequent sociological theory. Central to P-Orridge's esoterrorist use of magick was his band Psychic TV and the related esoteric organization TOPY, founded with members from Current 93 (notably David Tibet)[74] and also, significantly, The Process Church of the Final Judgment,[75] the latter having had a formative influence on the development of his occult thought.[76] This is, again, a helpful illustration of the social processes involved. That is to say, if one considers the numerous small occultural organizations that coalesced as concrete social forms, such as those within the vampire community (e.g. the House of Kheperu and the Order of the Vampyre, the latter being a part of the Temple of Set)[77] or the UFO subculture (e.g. the Aetherius Society, Unarius, and the Raelian Movement)[78] or the numerous other occulturally informed subcultures, often there is a confluence of esoteric ideas, popular culture, and traditional supernaturalism. In other words, as with TOPY, common interests and convictions lead to the formation of concrete communities or organizations, whether virtually or in the flesh.[79]

---

73. See Partridge, *Dub in Babylon*; Partridge, "King Tubby Meets the Upsetter".
74. See Keenan, "Childhood's End". On Tibet and Current 93, see Fava, "When Rome Falls, Falls the World"; Moliné, "Road to Salvation".
75. On The Process Church of the Final Judgment, see Bainbridge, *Satan's Power*; Wyllie, *Love, Sex, Fear, Death*.
76. See P-Orridge, "The Process is the Product".
77. Keyworth, "Occultism and the Contemporary Vampire Subculture"; Keyworth, "The Socio-Religious Beliefs and Nature of the Contemporary Vampire Subculture"; Laycock, *Vampires Today*; Partridge, *The Re-enchantment of the West*, vol. 2, 230–38.
78. See Partridge, *UFO Religions*; Partridge, *The Re-enchantment of the West*, vol. 2, 165–206; Lewis, *Encyclopedic Sourcebook of UFO Religions*.
79. See Cowan, *Cyberhenge*; Partridge, *The Re-enchantment of the West*, vol. 2, 135–64.

The idea of a "psychic television" is, again, significant. Although highly critical of television as a tool of mind control and mass indoctrination, it might also, as indicated above, be used by an esoterrorist as a form of magick to combat "Control" – "a modern alchemical weapon":

> [Psychic TV] are attempting to knit together thee fine lines ov shamanic initiation and voodoo invokation allegorically coded into western X-tian myth. TV itself becoums thee ceremony, thee language ov thee tribe. It becoums apparent that, cloaked in spurious messianic trivia, are ancient tantric rituals involving small death, limbo and resurrection that have now been literalised and usurped by a base language system named religion. Just as religion cloaks ancient knowledge and techniques, so Television cloaks its power to invoke thee lowest coumon denominator ov revelation ... We intend to reinstate thee ability ov TV to empower and entrance thee viewer. To remove thee window and passibity, and re-enter thee world ov dreams beyond. We believe TV is a Modern alchemical weapon that can have a positive and cumulative effect upon Intuition.[80]

Understanding TOPY to be the natural successor to the early Ordo Templi Orientis (OTO), particularly under Crowley's leadership, it was established to be "a secret society created as an access point into the world of magick".[81] As Jason Louv comments in P-Orridge's *Thee Psychick Bible*:

> Neither the OTO nor TOPY were teaching orders, existing instead to foster socialization around occult ideas – halfway points for those interested in the hidden undercurrents of reality, training wheels that, when eventually discarded, would lead the individual either towards more abstruse orders of robed ritualists or, preferably, onto their own two feet and their own personal apotheosis.[82]

Concerning "occulture" *per se*, while it is not widely used in P-Orridge's writings and never fully theorized, it is important, particularly to TOPY. As Carl Abrahamsson writes in his Foreword to *Thee Psychick Bible*:

> Probably no word does better justice to the TOPY phenomenon than "Occulture." Meshing "Occult" with "Culture," there's also

---

80. P-Orridge, *Esoterrorist*, 18–19.
81. Louv, in P-Orridge, *Thee Psychick Bible*, 25.
82. *Ibid.*, 25.

a prefixed trace of "Occident" if you will. The defined concept as such was integrated in the inter-TOPY-"lingo" in the late 80s, and then grew to become a readily accepted general term for anything cultural yet decidedly occult/spiritual. As a more or less unnamed concept, Occulture had already been active in TOPY since day one. The field of research was never ever occultism *per se* or culture *per se*, but always consisted of interchangeability where eventually the clear-cut borders were gently erased. Books, pamphlets, newsletters, film and video screenings, record and cassette releases and other manifestations could certainly contain more or less blatant esoteric form or content, but it was in no way a prerequisite. The literal meaning of "occult" (as in "hidden") was given a wider perspective than the merely "magical" one.[83]

This, then, is the original context within which the term "occulture" emerged. Although there is much about P-Orridge's work with which one might take issue, such as its articulation of oppression, suffering and abuse, occasionally defended with what appears to be a veneer of unreflective or uncaring faux morality,[84] for several reasons "occulture" has proved to be a pregnant and useful term, as we have seen. Moreover, key aspects of occult culture, as understood by P-Orridge and TOPY, are useful in understanding occulture *per se*, as well as being themselves good examples of the novel ways in which esotericism is evolving in late modernity.

CONCLUDING COMMENTS

The aim of this chapter has been to develop further the theory of occulture that I posited some years ago. In order to articulate the important distinction between *occulture* and *occult culture*, this has been done with reference to Campbell's theory of the cultic milieu, the esoteric ideas of P-Orridge and TOPY, and Williams's theory of culture as ordinary. Occulture is not occult culture, in the sense that it is not a milieu of the esoteric and the hidden (although it certainly includes that which is esoteric and hidden); nor is it a site of the exotic and the forbidden (although it certainly includes the exotic and the forbidden). Rather, like culture – which, of course, it is – it is ordinary and everyday. As such, occulture, as culture, is an explanans for Western re-enchantment rather than jargon for occult culture. Indeed, it is the reason why occult culture *per se* often seems, at some level, plausible and attractive to so many people.

---

83. Abrahamson, in P-Orridge, *Thee Psychick Bible*, 11.
84. Stubbs, "Clearing the Wreckage"; Reynolds, *Rip It Up*, 224–44.

Not only is there good evidence for occulture, but there is evidence that it is both generational to some extent and that popular culture is key to its efficacy. Indeed, although there are obviously exceptions and confounding variables, occulture's *current* persuasive power has a generational specificity. Again, this is perhaps saying little more than occulture moves with the times; occulture is ordinary; occulture is in accord with the *zeitgeist*. However, because occulture is ordinary, as we have seen with P-Orridge and TOPY, largely by means of popular culture and new media, individuals and small groups are able to have a disproportionate impact on the *zeitgeist*. Again, because occulture is ordinary, and because, therefore, occult culture has a certain cogency and plausibility, subversive ripples caused by minority esoteric ideas can travel a long way in society. This, of course, makes esoterrorism and theories of occultural propaganda a particularly rich area for future research.

Finally, we have seen that P-Orridge, who coined the term "occulture", is himself an interesting occultural case study. His use of the cut-up method, his founding of TOPY as an occultural offshoot of the esoteric outfit Psychic TV (through which he sought to disseminate politically subversive and occult ideas), his occultural eclecticism, his related understanding of popular music as propaganda and his esoterrorist agenda, all suggest avenues of thought that are helpful to the construction of a more developed theory of occulture.

CHAPTER 7

FROM BOOK TO BIT

ENACTING SATANISM ONLINE

Jesper Aagaard Petersen

Although overshadowed by pornography and file sharing, religion is a popular topic online, and increasingly so.[1] As a consequence, the previously hard-to-get and difficult-to-see has blossomed as the virtual environment supports the easy transmission, archiving and recontextualization of texts and imagery. Even if the adoption of new technologies has not been even, all kinds of esotericism, occultism and alternative religiosity previously relegated to the margins as fringe pursuits are now exhibited and easily found alongside established offline religions through hyperlinks and search engines. With this propagation of information we lose a sense of relative comprehension, but we gain something else. In her research, Annette Markham has proposed two important ways in which the Internet and related computer-mediated communication technologies are viewed and used: as a tool for communication and as a virtual social space.[2] Extending that notion and drawing on examples from contemporary religious Satanism, this chapter provides a discussion of new *contexts* for source material as well as new *types* of material on the Internet, both of which are highly relevant in the study of modern esotericism.

As a context, the new virtual space magnifies something that has been very difficult to see, let alone study, namely the fluid relations between free-floating material and the audiences and practitioners using it. The cacophony of online meaning-making actually supports established sociological models of occult affiliations and "rejected knowledge" as transmitted through a *cultic milieu* between *seekers*, originally formulated by Colin Campbell in the early 1970s.[3]

---

1. See Højsgaard & Warburg, "Introduction", 2–3.
2. Cf. Markham, "The Internet as a Research Context", 360–63. Markham includes a third view: Internet as a "way of being" which extends the second category of Internet as "place" through internalization.
3. Colin Campbell, "The Cult, the Cultic Milieu and Secularization". For elaborations with relevance to the study of modern esotericism see e.g. Barkun, *A Culture of Conspiracy*;

Traditionally, this milieu was "located" in informal networks and flows that were in place long before the Internet, especially via books and periodicals, but also more broadly disseminated through suggested reading lists of occult groups, word-of-mouth and bulletin boards in occult shops, seminars, concerts and fairs, and classified ads in magazines and newspapers. So, in a sense, the cultic milieu has always been mediatized and thus "deterritorialized".[4] What the Internet offers is a new access point. Thus, the virtual realm has a potential to reterritorialize research aiming at "thick description", just as it has affected the development of and recruitment to decentralized religious movements by providing new gateways.[5]

Turning to new types of material, the actual propagation of places of "online-religion" (new interactive environments) and tools of "religion-online" (traditional top-down communication) has to be seen in relation to specific offline interests, rhetorics of tradition, authority and legitimacy, and the real or imagined fears of pollution and dilution.[6] This is a sound approach, and not new. What is new are the *hybrid* texts we find online, situated between text and speech, displaying interpretative practices which on the one hand construct a meaningful social order and on the other are conditioned by the same order – ideally in the form of "virtual community". As the speech situation is embedded in these sources in a unique way through the medium, it should be possible to see the negotiations, conflicts and tactics that encircle any text concretely *expressed* in these texts. In order to assess such community and authority building in a virtual environment, I will argue for a discursive approach as a conduit between the traditional methodologies of the

---

Hammer, *Claiming Knowledge*; Hanegraaff, *New Age Religion and Western Culture*; Jorgensen, *The Esoteric Scene*; Partridge, *The Re-enchantment of the West*, vol. 1.

4. This understanding of "territory" is anthropological and tied to issues of "glocalization"; see Appadurai, *Modernity at Large*; Lyon, *Jesus in Disneyland*. On market models and commodity networks, see e.g. Ezzy, "The Commodification of Witchcraft"; Ezzy, "White Witches and Black Magic"; Heelas, *Spiritualities of Life*; Redden, "The New Age". On the importance of books, journals, and the media, see e.g. Aloi, "Rooted in the Occult Revival"; Ezzy, "New Age Witchcraft?". On older "networks" of books, see Owen Davies, *Grimoires*, chapters 5–8.
5. Much has been done on cyber-paganism, see e.g. Cowan, *Cyberhenge*; Ezzy, "The Commodification of Witchcraft". On the "technopagan" avant-garde, see e.g. Hadden & Cowan, "Virtually Religious"; Erik Davis, *Techgnosis*, especially 190–225.
6. For a good summary of the state of affairs in researching these matters, see Dawson, "Religion and the Internet". The very useful distinction between "online-religion" and "religion-online" is proposed in Helland, "Online-Religion/Religion-Online and Virtual Communitas"; Helland, "Surfing for Salvation". For recent studies with special relevance to Religious Studies, I suggest Heidi Campbell, *Exploring Religious Community Online*; Dawson & Cowan, *Religion Online*; Højsgaard & Warburg, *Religion and Cyberspace*; and Karaflogka, *E-religion*.

history of religions and the various methodologies of "cyber-anthropology".[7] This alternative should facilitate virtual fieldwork by softening the textual bias of historiography and the actor bias of participant observation.

NEW CONTEXTS, NEW BOUNDARIES: CHARTING THE SATANIC MILIEU

A standard web search for "Satan", "Satanic" and "Satanism" produce hits in the millions, offering anything from *Satan's Cheerleaders* to film clips outing President Obama's "satanic agenda". Broadly speaking, there are two main discourses on the satanic today, both of which can be located online. On the one hand, we have the various cultural narratives on Satan and Satanism, which form part of the "occultural" landscape of Western societies and are recycled in popular culture by moral entrepreneurs such as media commentators, conspiracy bloggers and cult watch groups, and occasionally by adolescents and provocateurs.[8] On the other hand, there are the satanic discourses among self-declared Satanists within a "satanic milieu", appropriating the figure of Satan into identity work.[9] This is a discursive subgroup within the cultic milieu comprised of self-identified satanic "belief systems and their associated practices", and includes "the collectivities, institutions, individuals, and media of communication associated with these beliefs".[10] It is the basic constituency and character of this milieu that is our first concern.

Rising out of the cultic milieu of 1960s California, Anton LaVey established the Church of Satan in 1966. In the "golden age" from 1966 to 1972, the High Priest and his church enjoyed a strong media presence, fully in tune with the general upsurge of interest in the occult and witchcraft, which stimulated the condensation of an autonomous *satanic* milieu out of the heterodox discourses at the time.[11] However, as illustrated by even a cursory reading of biographic material, the church was never alone.[12] As the Internet opened the floodgates in the 1990s, the quantity and visibility of material produced and distributed by alternatives to the Church of Satan underwent a drastic surge, transforming the satanic milieu itself into a more polyvocal entity through feedback loops.

---

7. As a young discipline, nomenclature is still under negotiation (cyber-anthropology, webnography, netnography, virtual ethnography); a good overview, with an extensive bibliography, is provided by Markham & Baym, *Internet Inquiry*.
8. Petersen, "The Seeds of Satan", 92. Cf. Partridge, *The Re-enchantment of the West*, vol. 2, 207–55; Petersen, "Smite Him Hip and Thigh".
9. Petersen, "Introduction", 3–6; Petersen, "The Seeds of Satan", 92–3.
10. Colin Campbell, "The Cult", 122. I understand "belief" as a dynamic, practised concept rather than static substance; Petersen, "Introduction", 3.
11. Petersen, "Satanists and Nuts"; Petersen, "The Seeds of Satan", 94–101. Cf. Barton, *The Church of Satan*.
12. For examples, see Aquino, *The Church of Satan*; Baddeley, *Lucifer Rising*, 100–113; Barton, *The Church of Satan*, chapters 2 and 4; Mathews, *Modern Satanism*, chapter 5.

In consequence, Satanism has become both a global deterritorialized phenomenon and reterritorialized in local contexts outside the United States and LaVey's original church. First of all, clashes over the definition of Satanism itself have produced numerous small networks, communities, and organizations, first through email discussion groups and Usenet (e.g. alt.satanism), and later through community groups (such as Yahoo and Google) and social network sites (especially Myspace and Facebook). Many have a website of their own and participate in the frequent "flame wars" that are so prevalent online. Second, even though LaVey's *Satanic Bible* (1969) has stayed atop the status pile, it now has serious competition from Internet-based material and material *promoted* through the Web.[13]

To take the second issue first, the print-on-demand site Lulu.com offers a variety of Satanic material, such as Michael Ford's *Luciferian Witchcraft* and Tsirk Susej's *The Demonic Bible*, alongside Church of Satan-"approved" essay collections like James D. Sass's *Essays in Satanism*. Books can of course also be bought through Amazon or independent publishers such as Stephen E. Flowers's Rûna Raven. In the same vein, Michael Aquino's massive e-books on the Church of Satan and the Temple of Set can be downloaded for free from the Temple website.[14] Finally, some websites actually function as archives with material of both introductory and advanced nature, superseding any engagement with printed books.[15]

The uneasy connections between these examples point to the difficulty of establishing the *boundaries* of the satanic milieu and satanic discourse from both an insider and outsider perspective. Subjects such as witchcraft, demonology and Chaos Magick are discussed by many of these writers, and both Diane Vera and Joy of Satan link to a variety of neopagan, esoteric, and occult websites. In contrast, the Church of Satan's disdain towards devil worshippers, neopagans and occultists is widely documented, even though LaVey frequently borrowed from them all.[16] Thus the discourse of individual Satanists and even

---

13. See Lewis, "Infernal Legitimacy", 42, 44. Studies focusing on "cyber-Satanism" have been few, arguably beginning with Roald E. Kristiansen's now dated "Satan in Cyberspace" (1995, updated 2001). Important sociological work has been done by James R. Lewis, especially on the basic demographics of Satanism today (e.g. "Who serves Satan?", "Infernal Legitimacy", "Fit for the Devil"). Finally, there are a handful of local case studies making use of Internet material and shorter, exploratory essays on Internet-Satanism, usually based on a period of "surfing" and snowball-sampling sites, texts and images (e.g. Alisauskiene, "The Peculiarities of Lithuanian Satanism"; Dyrendal, "Devilish Consumption"; Petersen, "Binary Satanism"; Petersen, "The Seeds of Satan"; Ringvee, "Satanism in Estonia"; Sieg, "Angular Momentum"; Smoczynski, "Cyber-Satanism and Imagined Satanism").
14. See ToS, "Temple of Set".
15. See e.g. JoS, "Joy of Satan"; Crabtree, "The Descriptions, Philosophies and Justification of Satanism"; Vera, "Theistic Satanism".
16. Cf. Petersen, "Satanists and Nuts", 226–32; Petersen, "'We Demand Bedrock Knowledge'"; Petersen, "The Seeds of Satan". Cf. Chapter 4 of the present volume.

identifiable groups often transcend any easy categorization as "satanic", blending with other discernible clusters such as the "neopagan" and "Left-Hand Path" milieus. Neither field is completely congruent with each other, but they do share a lot of discursive ground, most notably the focus on expressing or transforming the self and the eclectic use of ritualized practices such as magical work, art, music, poetry, or any combination of these. More specifically, what Nevill Drury has dubbed the "cthonian" orientation towards the carnal, the transgressive, and the subconscious, as well as the choice of darker gods such as Satan, Set and Kali, makes associations between "satanic" and "Left-Hand Path" groups especially salient and solid boundaries between their respective discourse and practices particularly difficult to trace.[17]

In an attempt to manage this complexity, we can approach modern Satanism as related to esoteric discourse in general through two complementary strategies of appropriation, namely "secularizing" the esoteric and "esotericizing" the secular.[18] By combining concrete "boundary-work" with strategies of legitimation in the satanic milieu, we can see how particular understandings of Satanism are actively built by engaging with a wide variety of cultural material, simultaneously constructing a positive self-religion and distancing oneself from other, competing articulations. Hence rationalist Satanism(s) in the tradition of LaVey (including groups outside the church but sympathetic to the ideology of the founder) are foregrounding natural and pragmatic elements, but infusing the secular narrative with esoteric modes of legitimacy, while esoteric Satanism(s) are suffusing the esoteric structure of the "cthonian" with secular modes of legitimacy. In contrast to the systematic discourse of these two types, reactive Satanism(s) are appropriating cultural narratives and stereotypes of Satanism as a strategy of resistance-through-inversion, making it a category on the border between the satanic milieu and generalized rebellion.[19] In general, the "cthonian" style has had a lot of success in horror movies, avant-garde art, and "deviant" subculture: vampire groups, modern primitives and Goths listening to post-punk, industrial and metal, to name a few "scenes", regularly tap into material provided by Satanism and the Left-Hand Path.[20] Conversely, formal groups in both milieus are trying to control the socialization of subcultural "tourists", dedicated "seekers", and devoted "members" in

---

17. See Drury, *Rosaleen Norton's Contribution to the Western Esoteric Tradition*, chapter 3; Granholm, "Embracing Others Than Satan"; Partridge, *The Re-enchantment of the West*, vol. 1, 78–84; vol. 2, 207–55; Petersen, "Introduction"; Petersen, "The Seeds of Satan" for academic discussions.
18. This understanding of Satanism and its relation to esotericism is indebted to Kocku von Stuckrad, Olav Hammer and Wouter Hanegraaff; on this, see Petersen, "'We Demand Bedrock Knowledge'", especially 69–73, 103–9; Petersen, "The Seeds of Satan", 94–101, 107–9.
19. On my typology, see especially Petersen, "Introduction", 6–7; Petersen, "Smite Him".
20. For examples, see Baddeley, *Lucifer Rising*; Laycock, *Vampires Today*; Nocturnum, *Embracing the Darkness*; Petros, *Art that Kills*.

terms of guided consumption, but to various effects. Outside formal groups the control is entirely individual. In this sense, popular culture and "occulture" are pathways to and from the satanic milieu, blurring core and peripheries considerably.[21]

Returning to clashes and "flame wars", the conflict over the nature of modern Satanism and LaVey's heritage in particular intensified after his death in 1997, culminating in a gradual exodus of disgruntled members from the Church of Satan in the early 2000s as the leadership changed.[22] Many of these ex-members created websites and local networks, which in turn has forced the Church of Satan to step up its Internet presence while still repeating the trivializing rhetoric on cyberspace.[23] The present constitution of the satanic milieu seems to stimulate two distinct reactions to online community building and Internet Satanism, an inclusive/tolerant and an exclusive/dismissive, based on the strength of offline presence as well as organizational integration. This mirrors the activities of many other esoteric "subcultures" online.

The first can be exemplified by Venus Satanas, author of a large amount of YouTube clips and the hostess of the website *Spiritual Satanist*, an associated blog, online store, Facebook page, and live video feed of exotic pole dancing.[24] On her website, she states:

> Since there are many methods of expressing Satanism, you have to find the one that suits you the best. Only you can know what is right for you in the end. Your choice should be a spiritual or philosophical commitment that is based on an informed decision. In my opinion, there is no one right way to be a Satanist; they are all forms of Satanic expression. But, no matter what the origin of our beliefs, as Satanists, we are all a part of the current of Satanism.[25]

As a consequence, she formed the Horde of Independent SatanistS (HISS) in 2008 with another Satanist, Nagasiva Yronwode (aka NocTifer), to provide apprenticeship and correspondence for Satanists of a more theistic and esoteric bent. Both are quite prolific writers and networkers on the Internet outside the auspices of the Church of Satan, and as such, they blend into the wider assemblage of Thelemites, Chaos Magicians, and followers of the Left-Hand Path that are active online. This feeling of connection and "movement" is confirmed by Corvis Nocturnum – reiki practitioner, psychometrist, Warlock in the Church of Satan and author of *Embracing the Darkness*:

---

21. On pathways, see e.g. Campbell & McIver, "Cultural Sources of Support"; Dyrendal, "Devilish Consumption".
22. I discuss this briefly in Petersen, "Satanists and Nuts", 242–3.
23. See e.g. Paradise, *Bearing the Devil's Mark*, 60–66.
24. For links to all these sites see Satanas, "Spiritualsatanist.com".
25. Satanas, "Foundations of Satanism".

> What becomes clear is that most, if not all of the subcultures covered in this book overlap, having been shaped by the effects of shared philosophies. In doing so, individuals within these subcultures come to share an appreciation for similar ideals, and eventually form larger communities. ... The answer lies in not focusing on the lines of the picture, but in stepping back and letting these lines blur until all you see is that one image that we've become.[26]

In Nocturnum's vision, Goth, dark spirituality, Satanism, Vampirism and BDSM are "dark subcultures" which cohere in shared ideals, philosophies and values.

Of course, not all Satanists agree with this "letting the lines blur" or "many-in-one image" of Satanism. Peter H. Gilmore, current high priest of the Church of Satan, represents the second position based on exclusivity ("the alien elite" in church parlance). Interviewed in Nocturnum's book about adolescents and "pseudo-Satanism", Gilmore remarks:

> There are definitely some pathetic web sites and hilariously goofy "organizations," which are usually some disturbed fellow with a web site and his equally naive online pals pretending to be "evil". That sort of rebellion, using pre-packaged "dark" imagery, usually is short-lived. The only folks who regularly see these antics are people who take a good deal of time to search them out, as the sites and chat rooms that these wannabes frequent receive little traffic.[27]

Like Satanas and HISS, the Church of Satan has an active presence on the Internet – an official website established in 1997, several semi-official community sites, and a host of affiliated sites like the CoS Emporium (shopping) and Radio Free Satan (media). Nevertheless, it is quite clear that most of the offerings online are viewed as misguided at best; Satanism needs to be lived in the *real* world, through concrete accomplishments based on a thorough understanding of Anton LaVey's books. Gilmore has a quite conscious "tunnel vision", viewing all non-aligned Satanists online and offline as losers, devil worshippers, or rebel poseurs. By contrasting "we Satanists" with the "ghetto of online Satanism", the high priest simultaneously downplays the numbers, coherence, and influence of social contenders and monopolizes satanic discourse as "LaVeyan".[28]

---

26. Nocturnum, *Embracing the Darkness*, 233. Nocturnum's bioblurb can be found on page 235.
27. Gilmore, in *ibid.*, 139.
28. See for example Gilmore, "A Map for the Misdirected"; Gilmore, *The Satanic Scriptures*, 170–86; and many interviews available online such as Shankbone, "Satanism". This position is frequently and forcefully asserted on affiliated community sites as well. See also the

While the reactions of Gilmore or some Church of Satan zealots are not surprising, the reciprocal "defrocking" of the "Black Pope", his successor Gilmore, and the institution itself by ex-members and non-joiners are even less unexpected. Thus the Internet is overflowing with Church of Satan "rap sheets", LaVey biographies and "anti-LaVey" statements. Such dismissiveness is not rare in cultic circles, but it has a certain edge in the case of the Church of Satan because of its age, founder and status.

VIRTUAL MILIEUS, IMAGINED COMMUNITIES: MODELLING THE SATANIC MILIEU ONLINE

How, then, are we to grasp this proliferation of antagonistic inclusions and exclusions of Satanism online? Specifically, is there any validity to the unsubstantiated "large, heterogeneous online community" postulated by Chris Mathews, echoing the inclusivist assertions of Venus Satanas and Corvis Nocturnum above?[29] The temptation to appropriate an emic term and talk about a "satanic community" or "movement", understood as a broad heterogeneous social trajectory much like the "black" or "gay" community, should be anchored in empirical fact, as shown by the conflict between inclusive and exclusive viewpoints.

A starting point for analysis could be a representative list, which in essence charts a selection of observable groups and sites. What is possible online, though, is to utilize various free "webometric" meta-tools to expand the basic list with additional information. The very idea of a milieu is show-casing the interplay between abstract deterritorialized spaces within global flows of occulture, and local reterritorializations of the milieu, fixing flows in intelligible localities. The Internet has much value in mapping both, and I have used three meta-communicative tools to answer three relevant questions:

- Who was responsible and when was the site established?
- How popular is the site and what is its reputation in the milieu?
- Who is connected to whom?

The first list (see Table 7.1) provides basic registration data (date, registrant, and/or domain) for some well-known groups as well as relative newcomers and obscure sites. While I have tried to be representative, the countless offerings necessitate a selection based on more impressionistic criteria. After compiling the list, I have used the website Europe Registry's WHOIS domain

---

pre-Internet "Satanic Bunco Sheet" in Barton, *The Church of Satan*, 125–8. For an updated form, see Church of Satan, "Satanic Bunco Sheet" (briefly analysed in Petersen, "Binary Satanism", 600–601).
29. Mathews, *Modern Satanism*, 91.

Table 7.1 Registration data for a selection of satanic/Left-Hand Path websites.

Domain name	Registration date	Registrant (if applicable) and/or domain server (if relevant)
The Undercroft and Letters to the Devil – both hosted by www.satannet.com	1996	L. Ventrue/ NS3.ninethirteen.com NS1.ninethirteen.com
Church of Satan (Anton S. LaVey) – www.churchofsatan.com	1997	Peter H. Gilmore/ Central9.ninethirteen.com NS9.ninethirteen.com
Temple of Set (Michael Aquino) – www.xeper.org and www.templeofset.org	1997	Robert Menschel/ NS1.Xeper.org + NS2.Xeper.org
First Satanic Church (Karla LaVey) – www.satanicchurch.com	1998	None* (FSC International)
First Church of Satan (John Allee) – www.churchofsatan.org	1998	John Allee
The 600 Club – www.the600club.com	1998	None* (The 600 Club)
Purging Talon – www.purgingtalon.com	1999	Matt Paradise
NocTifer's Real Satanism site – www.satanservice.org	1999	Nagasiva Yronwode
Radio Free Satan – www.radiofreesatan.com	2000	Shane Bugbee
Temple of the Vampire – www.vampiretemple.com	2000	None* (TOTV)/ Central9.ninethirteen.com NS9.ninethirteen.com
Vexen Crabtree's Description, Philosophies and Justification of Satanism site – www.dpjs.co.uk	2001	Simon Crabtree
Satanisk Forum – www.sataniskforum.dk	2001	A. O. Lap
Diane Vera's Theistic Satanism site – www.theisticsatanism.com	2005	Diane Vera (Church of Azazel)
Joy of Satan – www.joyofsatan.org (also hosted on www.angelfire.com/empire/serpentis666)	2005 (2003)†	Andrea Dietrich (Maxine Dietrich)/ NS1.joyofsatan.org NS2.joyofsatan.org
Modern Church of Satan – www.modernchurchofsatan.com	2006	None*

Domain name	Registration date	Registrant (if applicable) and/or domain server (if relevant)
Stephen E. Flowers's Rûna Raven newsletter and community – www.edred.net	2006	Stephen E. Flowers
Temple of the Black Light – www.templeoftheblacklight.net/main.html	2007	None*
Venus Satanas's Theistic Satanism and Magick site – www.spiritualsatanist.com	2007	Venus Satanas
Satanic Reds (Tani Jantsang) – www.satanicreds.org	2009‡	Johnni Pedersen (J. Nymann)

* "None" refers to registrants with high privacy settings, which affect searches.
† www.joyofsatan.com links directly to the angelfire website, as does most of the material on the joyofsatan.org site.
‡ Satanic Reds recently moved from a geocities address – the group's online birth is around 1997 (see Satanic Reds, "The Roots of the Satanic Reds"; Lap and Wolf, "Satanismens Danske Rødder", 14).
Source: based on information collected from http://whois.europeregistry.com/displayWhois.php on 15 November 2010.

search to access domain registrars for information.[30] Although the results are unsurprising, this method fixes the sites in time and place, something seldom given in the "here and now" of online production.

What do we learn? First, Internet Satanism predates 1996, but mainly as a text-based phenomenon. With the World Wide Web and the graphics-based web browsers introduced around 1993, usage gradually shifted from text to hypertext and image. We can see how the Church of Satan and the Temple of Set, as well as offshoots and affiliates, purchased domain names from the mid-1990s to establish a graphics-based online presence. The earliest community sites and message boards, satannet.com and the 600 club, were in place before 1998 as well. Of course, a given start date does not guarantee activity, just as a given registration date is not an absolute start date; for example, the Church of Satan existed on www.coscentral.net/cos for at least two years before actually launching the present address. Conversely, the Satanic Reds had a geocities address for a decade before "upgrading".

Second, turning to registrants, the geographical distribution is predominantly American, but this is an artefact of both the Californian birthplace of modern Satanism and my sampling bias. Most names are well known in the milieu. Apart from providing email addresses and even offline addresses in some cases, a registrant search is helpful when following linkages between

---

30. See http://whois.europeregistry.com/displayWhois.php. In some cases I have cross-checked with www.betterwhois.com and www.whois.com, but neither work on non-American sites.

143

groups by biography, although, again, a given registrant is no guarantee for continued affiliation or the presence of large numbers. In the case of domain servers, many different websites are hosted on individual servers. Nevertheless, the Church of Satan, the Temple of Set and the Joy of Satan operate with name-specific domain servers; we can use this to see, for example, that the Church of Satan actually hosts the Undercroft, Letters to the Devil and the Temple of the Vampire, reinforcing the feeling of connection between these sites.[31]

Next, to gauge the respectability and popularity both within the milieu and in general, I have entered the same domains into Alexa's Web information database.[32] The list (Table 7.2) is sorted by *traffic rank*, a number "based on three months of aggregated historical traffic data from millions of Alexa Toolbar users and data obtained from other, diverse traffic data sources".[33] By combining daily visitors and quarterly page views, the number gives us a clue to the relative popularity of the site over time compared to simple lists of unique page views. Nevertheless, data on sites with a traffic rank over 100,000 are not entirely trustworthy, which applies to all the satanic and Left-Hand Path sites measured here. The only sites with some popularity are the Church of Satan and (somewhat paradoxically) Joy of Satan's page base on the angelfire network, and they are still very far from Scientology or YouTube. Most of these sites are decidedly "fringe".

Similarly, the number of *links to sites* is wildly imprecise, as Alexa only counts links "from sites visited by users in the Alexa traffic panel. Links that were not seen by users in the Alexa traffic panel are not counted".[34] Accordingly, the numbers seem quite low. For this reason I have done another search on Yahoo's site explorer, providing "inlink" data that seems intuitively more correct. Both these inlinks and Alexa's link numbers are from diverse sources, from Wikipedia and Facebook to other satanic sites, making the data somewhat complicated to use uncritically. Nonetheless, used heuristically the relations between the sites do say something significant about relative strength, network building, and authority whether we are working with one or the other data set. We could call it a *reputation* or *saturation* indicator. The Church of Satan scores high on both searches, indicating a stable network *to* this site. Anomalies include Vexen Crabtree's site, The Joy of Satan, the Temple of the

---

31. Additional information on the issue of servers can be found on RobTex's *Domain Name System search* at www.robtex.com/dns.
32. www.alexa.com.
33. Alexa, "About the Alexa Traffic Rankings". I have chosen traffic rank over the more intuitively understandable "unique visitors" and "site views" stats from e.g. www.siteanalytics.com because of this aggregate nature – by combining quarterly and daily activity, a relatively stable number or rank is reached, which is all I need for comparison between my chosen sites.
34. I quote from the small drop-down explanation window next to the number. See also Alexa, "Sites Linking In".

Vampire, the Temple of Set, and NocTifer's satanservice.org; otherwise, most sites are in the tens or hundreds, indicating a small integration both in the milieu and outside. Concluding on the basis of traffic rank and links we can say that most satanic and Left-Hand Path sites live in obscurity.

In an attempt to answer the final set of questions about connectivity, I used a third meta-communicative tool called *Issue Crawler* to perform "snowball" and "co-link" analyses on the sample which could be translated into a visible representation called a "cluster map".[35] Basically, a snowball analysis crawls a given set of sites for links and retains them; this can be done in up to three degrees of separation, resulting in enormous clusters of equivocal links and nodes. In contrast, a co-link analysis only retains outlinks that at least two starting points have in common, restricting the model to confirmed relations. The results are by far the most provisional, as I have yet to strike a balance of starting points in either mode to get a manageable model. The problem lies in the nature of Internet linking itself – all of my data sets were either too large and inclusive or too exclusive and limited, resulting in misleading charts. If too inclusive, as most snowball searches were, the data included irrelevant Facebook pages, porn sites, and other inappropriate links in unmanageable files of 60 or more megabytes (that is 40,000+ links and nodes, too large for modelling). If too exclusive, many interesting relations disappear because of the specificity of co-link measurement. Nevertheless, a more restricted map based on a co-link analysis of fourteen starting points is very useful, as it only charts *significant* links that are mutually supported, indicating a certain amount of commonality.

Although a model created with *Issue Crawler* looks confusing at first glance, some of the nodes are recognizable sites from the previous lists. Other sites are expected, like the Ontario Consultants on Religious Tolerance (www.religioustolerance.org) who have written extensively and fairly about Satanism, and the Feral House–Coopstuff connection to the Church of Satan (via publisher Adam Parfrey and the artist Coop, both affiliated with the Church of Satan). In addition, when perusing the "extract URLs" result file behind the model, we find that angelfire.com covers Diane Vera and Joy of Satan, geocities.com covers the old Satanic Reds site, and so on. All the same, many of my starting points are absent, which is surprising when taking the inlinks provided in Table 7.2 into account. A high number of links to the site does not guarantee a central place or even a node in the cluster map, indicating that sites such as Vexen Crabtree's or Venus Satanas's have a reputation (i.e. inlinks) *outside* the satanic milieu in a narrow sense. Looked at in another way by correlating with Table 7.1, of the websites established before 2000, only the First Satanic Church, First Church of Satan and the 600 club are *absent*; after 2001, only Diane Vera, Joy of Satan and Satanic Reds are *present*, and only

---

35. The program can be found at www.issuecrawler.net. The following description is based on the website's instructions and Bainbridge, "Expanding the Use of the Internet".

Table 7.2 Traffic ranking data on a small selection of satanic/Left-Hand Path websites.

Domain name	Type	Traffic rank – Alexa	Links *to* the site – Alexa	Inlinks – Yahoo
Church of Satan www.churchofsatan.com	Website	189,260	585	33,053
Vexen Crabtree www.dpjs.co.uk/index.html	Archive	638,054	94	572
Venus Satanas www.spiritualsatanist.com	Website with blog	823,751	29	640
Modern Church of Satan www.modernchurchofsatan.com	Website with message board	890,559	3	115
Purging Talon www.purgingtalon.com	Media website with blog	1,042,576	98	972
Joy of Satan www.joyofsatan.org	Website with community sites	1,043,688	28	1505
www.angelfire.com/empire/serpentis666		230,947	(0)	49
Temple of the Vampire www.vampiretemple.com	Website with community	1,254,593	(65)	4961
First Church of Satan www.churchofsatan.org	Archive	1,280,688	84	768
Temple of Set www.xeper.org	Website, archive	1,298,692	(100)	9469
Diane Vera www.theisticsatanism.com	Website	1,490,341	46	422
Undercroft, Letters to the Devil www.satannet.com	Community sites (closed and open)	1,526,325	52	569

The 600 Club www.the600club.com	Community site	1,633,231	(26)	285
Temple of the Black Light www.templeoftheblacklight.net/main.html	Website, archive	1,889,509	(27)	299
NocTifer www.satanservice.org	Website	2,198,730	71	10,448
First Satanic Church www.satanicchurch.com	Website, links to the600club.com as community	2,689,478	32	180
Stephen E. Flowers www.edred.net	Community and archive	5,695,414	20	115
Radio Free Satan www.radiofreesatan.com	Radio station	6,636,606	36	766
Satanisk Forum www.sataniskforum.dk	Website with message board	8,186,840	9	77
Satanic Reds www.satanicreds.org	Website, archive	No data	1	6
Scientology International www.scientology.org	For comparison – website and forum	32,760	1228	34,432
YouTube www.youtube.com	For comparison – video sharing	3	686,159	8,546,000,000

Sources: traffic rank (measuring aggregate traffic based on average daily visitors and average quarterly page views) and the number of links *to* the site are both based on information gained from www.alexa.com on 18 November 2010. Note that lower traffic rank indicates higher activity. For comparison, I have provided inlink numbers from Yahoo's site explorer at www.siteexplorer.search.yahoo.com for the same date.

by proxy (through host domains and not their individual sites). So duration seems to play a role. On the other hand, many of the nodes are not associated directly with Satanism (like otohq.org, Ordo Templi Orientis's now-defunct directory) or not operational, limiting the explanatory power if relying too heavily on the map alone.

Is there a "large, heterogeneous online community" of Satanists, as Chris Mathews, Venus Satanas and Corvis Nocturnum claim, or is there rather a bunch of loose networks with one dominant community, as Peter Gilmore asserts? The cluster map indicates that relations and networks of communication do exist. Correlated with Tables 7.1 and 7.2, we do see actual community *sites*, but little to confirm any community in the singular. Combined with a little surfing on these sites, it is obvious that networks are established by linkage; for example, Diane Vera links to blog and forum networks, and Satanic Reds lists "members" and affiliates.[36] But little *interlinkage* is done. Twelve of the nineteen sites I have analysed do not even show up on a co-link analysis, indicating that little is done to build or strengthen the network into a mutual practised community or movement of interest. In fact, using "community" in the singular glosses over (or completely ignores) the struggles and conflicts inherent in actual delimitations of "community" between the various groups and actors. It would seem that heterogeneous communities in the plural do develop both online and offline, but mostly around relatively homogeneous social entities, such as the ideologies, worldviews, and practices of *organized* satanic groups with specific texts, spokespersons and interpretations. This is visible in the cluster map confirming the gist, if not the conclusion, of Gilmore's argument discussed earlier. For the wider cultural context and the ephemeral networks within, "milieu" is in fact a much better term.

This substitution is not done to criticize the veracity of perceived feelings of togetherness or the authenticity of emotional, ethical, and aesthetic communion between satanic seekers. Rather, it is to emphasize the discursive nature of these emotions and cognitions, and the basic imaginary nature of communities and currents. Thus I do not reject the basic understanding of modern Satanism as a cohesive current, but I do claim that this cohesion is of a second order far less communitarian and far more fuzzy than implied in terms like "community" and "movement" in the singular.[37] In contrast, "milieu" acts as an aggregate noun demarcating certain ideological and symbolic interests and shared patterns of consumption, and it should be understood as a mid-level analytical concept between the general "occulture", or boundary culture between margin and mainstream, and distinct communities, groups and organizations within it.

---

36. On Vera's networking, see Vera, "Theistic Satanism". On Satanic Reds, see Satanic Reds, "Member Sites". Most of the 19 member sites are defunct or have not been updated for three or more years.
37. See Petersen, "Introduction", 4–6.

Based on Benedict Anderson's influential idea of *imagined communities*, Derek Foster proposes that all communities larger than face-to-face networks must be imagined.[38] Hence it is complicated navigations of recognition between the public and the private, the subjective and the collective, that creates (produces) the community: "That which holds a virtual community intact is the subjective criterion of togetherness, a feeling of connectedness that confers a sense of belonging. Virtual communities require much more than the mere act of connection itself."[39] The "more" hinted at is of course *intentional* communication and *interpretative* practice.[40] While there may be an imagined "Satanic community" which has a social reality for some inclusive-minded Satanists, the model shows little performance of this community outside a narrowly defined "we" and a lot of resistance from other sectors of the milieu. Accordingly, we should be very careful not to homogenize and simplify the Internet or milieu as singular entities as "a multiplicity of cultural phenomena" is contained within these concepts.[41]

People tend to cluster in networks around discourses and practices sharing specific themes, even if they move from one to the next in their search for knowledge and experiences. There are thus various levels of "we-information" and a choice of avenues of "togetherness" and "antipathy" from which to build communities in the plural, all of which are distributed and amplified by the virtual realm. The early "frontier" of deterritorialized online Satanism has been both strengthened and weakened by the gradual reterritorialization of Satanisms online in the past decade, limiting heterodoxy and constructing boundaries to establish a semblance of dominance. All the websites discussed have "border zones", whether it is a guestbook, a forum, or user-generated content, stimulating conflict within and between local domains. To understand such communities and authorities online, we have to understand the "morphology" of discourse online, something enacted in speech – or writing. This brings us back to the doorstep of the text. We will now turn to some interesting ways of re-assessing the text-centric methodology of historiography in light of these "webnographic" reflections.

---

38. Foster, "Community and Identity".
39. *Ibid.*, 29. See also Appadurai, *Modernity at Large*, 178–9, whose notion of "locality" as a phenomenological concept is tied to the concept of "neighborhood" (both virtual and spatial) as "situated communities".
40. Foster, "Community and Identity", 34–35. Forster refers to Jürgen Habermas's central positioning of the *speech act* and concludes the article with the comment: "Perhaps then, the fullest understanding of the term [virtual community] is gained by grounding it in the communicative act itself".
41. Markham, "The Internet as a Research Context", 360. See also Kendall, "Recontextualizing 'Cyberspace'", who suggests four research contexts eminently applicable to the study of milieus.

FROM BOOK TO BIT: A BRIEF ASIDE ON TEXTUAL GENETICS

To assess textual practice online we must revisit the issue of inferences from oral, written, ritual, or pictorial *expressions* to individual or collective *systems of belief*. Tord Olsson convincingly argues that we have to be extremely careful when analysing utterances as representations, as the adherents of a given religion do not necessarily *believe* what they are saying and doing, because what they are saying and doing is context-dependent. In other words, we cannot expect the multitude of divergent expressions of a religion to be systematically connected in an isolate, coherent system implanted in people's heads or in the culture shared by them. This is especially clear with representations of gods which "are conditioned by genre and speech situation"[42] and may appear radically different in different contexts: anthropomorphic and concrete in myths associated with a narrative situation, and pantheistic and abstract in hymns related to a situation of praise. "[D]ifferent understandings dominate in different speech contexts; ... given conceptions find expression in given genres".[43] Accordingly, it is prudent to include reflections of the formal traits of aesthetic and communicative genres in the analysis of religious expressions.

These constructivist rules of thumb do not become any less relevant when we address sources found on the Internet. I see at least two avenues of application in the present context. First, we can apply genre dependency of gods directly, noting that *how* Satan (and other sinister beings) is understood must be related to genre and speech context. Whether Satan is a metaphor, a symbol or a real entity is partly dependent upon the dogmatic stance of the group or person in question, but also upon the conduit in which this "belief system" is communicated – reflexive essays, mythical narratives and (especially) hymns, prayer and ritual texts such as invocations.

Secondly, and more importantly here, genre-dependency and speech contexts can be applied more broadly as a theoretical reorientation of *how we view* texts. This is not so much about the nature of gods as about how Olsson's insights on oral literature can be applied to "hypertext" and new media practices. Basically, online texts constitute a new genre. I will focus on a particularly interesting example, namely the "posts" and "threads" on message or discussion boards, which is both a common form of community software and an accessible field for research. Here we move from fixed text consumption to fluid text production and to the discursive negotiations of ideology, identity, and community in hybrid texts. An analysis of these floating hybrids *between* text and speech should be mindful of the hybridity of both the isolate post and the thread as a whole, as well as the relation between threads and other types of text and performance. The specific boundaries must be placed pragmatically

---

42. Olsson, "Verbal Representation of Religious Beliefs", 91.
43. *Ibid.*, 82–83.

in relation to the concrete research programme; it is the dialogical aspect which is of interest here – it is never sufficient to analyse a single post.

"Texts" are not only referential, content-oriented and fixed, and "speech" is not only performance. However, thought of as generic extremes on a continuum, these types could illustrate different aspects of the functionality of communication – primarily the *asynchronous* and the *synchronous* on one hand and the *mediate* and the *immediate* on the other.[44] "Posts" and "threads" could be placed on this continuum as expressions between "chat" and "email", on a scale going from text to speech. In his analysis of "cybertalk", Norman Denzin makes similar connections through his concept of "performance speech" – a text which, when in the form of a thread, is messy, dialogical, immediate, situated, and constantly reinterpreted, as speech; but which is precisely *also* a text because it is written and therefore more unambiguous, proofread and thought through beforehand.[45] As such, "performance speech" is an enacted, hybrid text revealing the immediacy of speech and the "mediacy" or fixation of writing, and thus the provisional and intermittent character of communication. The written dialogue is in other words "betwixt and between", at once producing community and fixating meaning, including and excluding, which is especially useful in an analysis attempting to correlate structure and actor, system and practice, or speech situation and expression. Let us have a look at a specific example.

AUTHORITY AND HYBRID TEXTS: DISCUSSING "RITUAL" ON SATANIC FORUM'S MESSAGE BOARD

> [Sp34k:] *makes a lovely curtsy* A-hoy out there land crabs ... I have been thinking "Many Satanists say that they go through different rituals and achieve a greater power/force within themselves when they perform it/When it is performed" Well, I am curious and want to know how the rituals YOU perform are done "if you perform rituals" And how does one achieve this "strength"?[46]

This is the first post in a thread on the Danish *Satanisk Forum Message Board*, an official public discussion board established in 2002 by the organization Satanisk Forum (Satanic Forum) to facilitate interaction between members and accommodate guests.[47] "Sp34k" asks the other participants about their

---

44. See e.g. Simeon J. Yates, "Researching Internet Interaction", 96–7.
45. Denzin, "Cybertalk and the Method of Instances", 111–112.
46. SFO, "Ritual=Styrke". Posted 25 October 2005. All posts are translated by the present author. I have tried to convey the free style of grammar and punctuation.
47. I have previously discussed Satanisk Forum in Petersen, "Binary", 600–606; and Petersen, "'We Demand Bedrock Knowledge'", 99–102.

take on the significance and interpretation of ritual in a satanic context. As we can see from Table 7.2, Satanisk Forum is a small fish in the global satanic milieu, ranking low in both traffic rank and inlinks. This is probably due to the language barrier, as well as the quite explicit and enforced rationalist take on Satanism, which prohibits any large-scale networking with esoteric Satanists, talk of "Satanic community" and "Satanic 'subculture'" notwithstanding.[48]

Satanisk Forum itself developed from a small group of individuals associated with the Church of Satan-affiliated organization Prometheus Grotten (the Prometheus Grotto, briefly named COS DK) in the late 1990s. In the aftermath of LaVey's death, they reorganized first as an independent group and later after internal disagreement, split the organization into two separate entities in 2001, of which Satanisk Forum was the largest and most successful in terms of media penetration and subcultural support. Today, although the activity has declined due to further schism and general fatigue, Satanisk Forum is the most visible and accessible association of rationalist Satanists in Denmark with about 200 members and 555 participants on their message board. I have chosen this particular thread because it reflects the character of the board in the heyday of the group, even though it is now certainly a thing of the past.

Sp34k's post is characterized by an immediate and speech-oriented form. It is filled with language markers of an oral nature and the sentence construction is typical of speech, not writing. In addition, one finds a lot of grammatical and spelling errors, expressive use of quotation marks signifying reservation or addition, and the use of the slash to vary or optimize information. Notice also the common paralinguistic use of asterisks to perform an action in writing: "*makes a lovely curtsy*". This is typical of chat and SMS-language, and is a written contextual event – a stage management of sorts. The many speech codes soften the written form and set an informal tone, but the post is in effect a written text using oral codes and is as such asynchronous and mediate in spite of the form. The post gives the impression of an inquirer who is of minor importance on the specific message board, in the offline group behind it, and in the amorphous milieu of Satanists online.

Sp34k is asking two questions: how other Satanists perform rituals, and how he (or one) achieves strength through them. The same day, "Amina" answers:

> There aren't many users of ritual on the board (in particular) judging by earlier threads. As a replacement I would recommend the section on rituals in "Gud er (stadig) blå" which gives some theoretical background. Otherwise you might relate to peoples experiences with certain types of rituals by thinking of some piece of

---

48. See SFO, "Vedtægter for Satanisk Forum", article 2 (my translation).

music that has affected you strongly. The special thing about rituals is that they speak directly to our feelings in the same way music can do. The best known satanic rituals are those mentioned in "The Satanic Bible" and "The Satanic Rituals". In my opinion these rituals are not practised by many, however.[49]

This post is much more text-oriented and distanced than Sp34k's: notice the construction of sentences and the informational "flow" in the text. It seems proofread and professional. Amina refers to previous threads on the board, academic literature (*Gud er (stadig) blå* by Michael Rothstein), personal experience (articulated through a "we"), LaVey's books, and personal assessments in the beginning and end. Without rejecting the question outright, the answer nevertheless communicates that practising rituals is something marginal in satanic circles (not many users [in particular], not practised by many), something natural (equal to strong emotions), and something that can be studied in both academic and satanic literature (Rothstein and LaVey).[50] An interpretation of ritual is thus articulated that is not only substantiated by the content of the text, its "what", but also its form, the "how", for example through the references to real texts offline and the textual essayistic appearance of the post itself.

After the initial encounter the thread develops into a pseudo-conversation where Sp34k is lectured by Amina and "Wolf" on such subjects as dream travel, New Age, nihilism, and religious education in primary school.[51] The characteristics found in the two posts analysed above is consistent with these; Sp34k is using a lot of emoticons and codes from speech, while Amina is writing longer and more essayistic posts. Wolf is interjecting brief comments (more like corrections) twice, in both instances referring to written materials found online, namely Wikipedia and the FAQ on Satanic Forum's website. One gets the sense that Amina and Wolf are playing "good cop – bad cop" with Sp34k, gently correcting his mistakes (such as mentioning out-of-body experiences in the same breath as satanic rituals or claiming to have read New Age's website in the singular). It is here important to understand that different message boards and discussion groups provide different degrees of freedom – they produce different types of hybrid text, depending on such matters as *moderation* and *tacit rules* within the group. A heavily moderated site results in spellchecked and corrected posts similar to essays, while a less moderated site results in messy posts filled with errors in grammar and spelling, emoticons, and chat-style abbreviations similar to the immediacy of speech.[52]

---

49. SFO, "Ritual=Styrke". Posted 25 October 2005. My translation.
50. The other answer on the same day, by "Zigma", refers to a text from the group's own magazine, *Satanic Bulletin*. The article in question is written by Amina.
51. See the following eight posts, all from 26 October 2005, at SFO, "Ritual=Styrke".
52. See e.g. Connery, "IMHO"; Denzin, "Cybertalk".

This relates to a core problem: whether traditional or virtual, both community and communication *implies power*, setting the issues of authority and authenticity in the foreground of all engagements with virtual texts and virtual populations. In her study of religious authority online, Heidi Campbell discusses the necessity of understanding the asymmetric relations between actors and religious hierarchy, structure, ideology and text when analysing authority at play.[53] Her empirical research indicates that "multiple layers or perceptions of authority" have to be discerned, yet her understanding of authority itself is curiously old-fashioned. For online hybrids and discursive constructions of togetherness, Bruce Lincoln's definition of authority as the right to speak explicitly ties its presence to a dynamic and concrete instance of authorization and trust.[54] Thus, the right to speak is a structural process in a symmetrical relation with persuasion and force and not an essential "thing", a process which merges the concepts of "power" and "community" as relational authorization.[55] A lot of elements indicate that Amina and Wolf's posts have hegemonic or authoritative status, both when considering the formal characteristics and the content. In addition, when moving beyond the posts themselves, the fact that they are both site administrators and moderators on the board, both are members of Satanisk Forum (which is indicated by a banner below the avatar) and both have posted extensively (2460 and 1117 posts for Amina and Wolf, respectively, at the time of writing – that is about 30 per cent of *all posts* on the board when combined) contribute to this conclusion. On the other hand, Sp34k has joined the message board five days before his inquiry, is not a member of the parent group, and has posted 102 times (about 1 per cent of all posts, which makes him an active member on the board – but I will return to that below).

This asymmetry of authority is further expressed in the marked difference between the "old guard" and new members. If we compare with other threads on the message board such as "A Request to the Users" and "LaVey's 'The Satanic Rituals'",[56] we can categorize posters within diminishing roles of status and power: administrators, active members of Satanisk Forum, active non-members, inactive members, infrequent posters, "I have been issued a warning"-debaters (indicated by another banner on the profile), and the banned and expelled. But aside from the date of registration and membership of the parent body all of these roles and positions of power are constituted communicatively – they exist locally by the very fact that there is intentional communication.

---

53. Heidi Campbell, "Who's Got the Power?". See also the introduction to Dawson & Cowan, *Religion Online*, and Dawson, "Religion and the Quest for Virtual Community", for more on virtual community and power.
54. Lincoln, *Authority*, 10–11.
55. *Ibid.*, 4–6, 11. See also the distinctions presented in Lincoln, *Discourse and the Construction of Society*.
56. See SFO, "En Anmodning til Brugerne"; SFO, "LaVey's Sataniske Ritualer".

Hence we can follow the discursive construction of conceptual meaning and online community through individual posts and threads. Core members are articulating one discourse and marginalizing others, so that some posts have more meaning than others even though there are several interpretations present within one thread. This is in fact a virtual community with an inside and an outside. This becomes evident about a year later when the hegemonic interpretation of rituals is challenged by "Satani", who writes:

> It is different how one has one's rituals, some has them to prove to themselves that they are worth more and actually mean something. I hold (perform) rituals to support my faith, not to prove anything. I believe in myself and really don't care what everybody else is saying and think of me. I trust only myself and my god satan. I am the inverse of what the Christians. A real God fulfils one's wishes, that never happened when I was a Christian, never. I know that the Christian's God take care of light and dry weather. In that case I do the opposite. I listen to satan. Have been to some ritual meetings, one feels valuable and is a servant of Satan. Sometimes I lie outside at midnight, full moon and rain. And feel satan's power. He is the one that is the creator, him that should be respected. Does someone have other rituals? – I would like very much to hear about it.[57]

This post is different from the previous ones both in form and content. To take the last aspect first, Satani is more in sync with the spirit of Sp34k's initial inquiry than Amina or Wolf. The post provides answers to both what rituals are performed and what strength or power one gains from it. This is an interpretation of rituals that is radically different from Amina and Wolf's, whose understanding corresponds to the official, rationalist and psychologizing discourse of Satanisk Forum as articulated through the FAQ, the official magazine, and so on. Satani, on the other hand, is referring explicitly to Christianity in an anti-Christian, theistic and deeply metaphysical discourse; rituals work because God and Satan exist – God provides us with light and dry weather, Satan fulfils one's wishes. Formally, the post has traits of both speech and text, although the oral and immediate nature is predominant. This is expressed in amplifying adverbs, repetitions, syntax and spelling, the absent subject in several sentences, and finally the double question in the end. The text-oriented and mediate can be seen in the overall coherence and flow of the post.

Satani does not stand a chance. On the same day Wolf quotes the passage about light and dry weather, and dryly remarks that the answer to that rather should be found in meteorology,[58] while Amina the next day asks where

---

57. SFO, "Ritual=Styrke", posted 18 November 2006. This post has so many errors I have omitted the use of [sic]; thus all errors in the translation are intentional.
58. Ibid.

Satani gets his ideas from, as "your description of your faith on the face of it seems very different than what most other Satanists express".[59] Even though Satani dutifully answers that the meetings take place in cemeteries at midnight with "a lot of Satanists" and are called "The Holy Sign", and that we can read about them "in the Satanic books",[60] Amina is not convinced. She effectively ends the "discussion" by first referring to "the many books and articles I have read together with about ten years in the milieu", and secondly through a total deconstruction of Satani's post by embedding it in an academic discourse – she demands explicit references and calls his interpretation of rituals "ostensive acting", an emulation of popular Western demonology by living out a mythical frame. Satani has not written a post since.

In conclusion, the thread as a whole is also an example of a hybrid text. We can see that there is a hegemonic discourse of ritual, but that it has to be articulated, indeed activated and reconstructed constantly. In this case powerful resources like brutal moderation or banning does not appear, but it is obvious that there are more open and more closed posts which in themselves are playing up against group values as formulated in other threads, in the FAQ and on the group's website. Sp34k ends on the inside of this community while Satani ends on the outside, and it is to a large degree a matter of "walking the walk and talking the talk" (or perhaps "when in Rome ..."). Perhaps Sp34k *cannot* write in another way, but through the oral codes and traits his inquiry exhibits an imprint of genuine interest in knowledge as well as community. Amina and Wolf are accommodating and enter into cautious dialogue with him, whereas they cut off Satani completely because he *challenges* the boundaries of the established discourse.

There are many paths to follow from this example. One course is to focus on how socialization works as a unification or regimentation under the hegemonic discourse of Satanism on the site. Substantially, contributors have to read the FAQ before posting;[61] formally, they have to conform to certain stylistic rules (understood both orthographically and rhetorically).[62] Posters such as Sp34k and "The ONE" are examples of users who are socialized successfully – they write a large number of posts and adopt Amina's, Wolf's and, therefore, Satanisk Forum's discourse – while Satani and Woland are users who, though expressing very different interpretations of Satanism and huge differences in communicative skill, nevertheless are not successfully socialized; they write a small number of posts and disappear rather than adopting anything. Two other interesting types are exemplified by "Einstürzende", who produces a lot,

---

59. *Ibid.*, posted 19 November 2006.
60. *Ibid.*
61. This is a classic response to many inquiries especially from pupils and students. See e.g. SFO, "Hvad Indenbære Satanismen ...".
62. See Wolf's posts: Wolf, "Nye retningslinjer"; Wolf, "Danskproblemer", both posted as moderator of the board.

but does not adopt the discourse (but his posts gradually become friendlier towards Amina and Wolf; they simply avoid contentious issues), and "Serdan" and "Ko18", who post a lot of mainly divisive writings and are eventually banned by the moderator (Wolf).[63] On a formal level, contributors who are inside the virtual community become more text-oriented, even though literacy is not a guarantee of affiliation. Nevertheless, when compared with other forums there seems to be an overabundance of academics, and thus a clear tendency towards intellectualization and an academic orthographical norm, and this is of course related to such offline contexts as the membership base of the parent body and the extant values there.

CONCLUDING REMARKS

The hybrid texts of a discussion forum can be utilized to isolate and analyse themes (as "ordinary" texts), but they are even more useful when used to take a closer look at the creation of discourse, closure and conflict. The virtual community is *both* creator of the text *and* created with it, because the text contains both the pros and contras to the discourse itself. This presents the opportunity to track both the formal and substantial constitutive traits of the interpretative practice inherent in the hybrid text. We can look at the "careers" of individual debaters in a formal and/or substantial sense, take a closer look at thematic *leitmotif*, or stratify the nuances between the different articulations and degrees of engagement, status and activity.

Hence I agree with Mark MacWilliams that virtual communities are *at least* "symbolically real heteroglossic spaces", constituting a "diverse mixture of voices" that creates places in which to include or exclude others.[64] Naturally, not all communication, nor communication in itself, creates community, but it is difficult to imagine a community both off- and online *without* communication.[65] In a sense, the tool and the place align themselves. As a consequence, I have focused on the meso-level of discourse, a middle-ground between actor and structure and thus an entity that can be found both *in* the singular utterance, expression, or text, as well as *between* utterances without being *above* them. The concept of "discourse" marks an attention towards exactly the constructive and dialectical aspects, that is an integration of the structurally conditioned ("what") and the conditioning in practice ("how").

Sociologically, the use of new media entails new opportunities for transformation and interaction, but also old problems. Satanisk Forum and the Church of Satan are not that far apart in organizational ethos oriented

---

63. For a discussion of similar dynamics on Baha'i message boards see e.g. Piff & Warburg, "Seeking for Truth".
64. MacWilliams, "Digital Waco", 180–82.
65. Foster, "Community and Identity", 24, 30.

towards the real world, and they do share strategies of in-group cleansing and out-group marginalizing, especially when compared to other, more esoteric groups less socially embedded offline such as Venus Satanas and HISS. In contrast to individual networks, organizational relations need to be regulated or the boundaries between group and wider setting become unstable. In a wider picture, whether the tool of communication is used honestly or deceptively, and whether the virtual place itself is viewed as a goldmine or a rubbish heap, depends on the identity of the group in question, the relations of participants, and a host of other aspects tied to global and local factors. The Internet is heterogeneous and constantly negotiated to different extents depending on situation, individual interests, and collective decisions.

The basic analysis presented here can be extended to other comparable religious milieus exhibiting a decentralized and fragmented nature offline and online, such as the "Thelemic milieu", which resembles the satanic one studied in the present context. The proliferation of accessible sites makes it possible to follow currents, groups and individuals from a variety of perspectives, and the webometric meta-tools provide both data and visual aid when charting these milieus from the ground up. We can study official organizational websites, compare them with regional or individual sites, and thus facilitate a geographical comparison of distinctive styles and common iconography, parlance and identity. Or we can focus on the milieu itself, through Facebook fan pages, detractors and even concepts; online literature archives; relevant studies available from private sites; and Wikipedia or one of the increasingly specialized Wikis. Finally, when combined with the reflections on virtuality and power, we can use this methodological apparatus on a micro level as well, and be attentive to the small-scale interventions and their ideological and performative dimensions. The discussions on message boards as hybrid texts are an obvious source for these investigations; indeed, the hybrid text is a new genre with direct access to plays of power and discourse.

ACKNOWLEDGEMENTS

This chapter is based on the paper "Enacted Satanism: Religion in Hybrid Texts" presented at the EASR/DVRW conference *Plurality and Representation: Religion in Education, Culture and Society*, University of Bremen, 23–27 September 2007. I would like to thank Asbjørn Dyrendal, Olav Hammer and the editors for valuable comments on earlier versions of the chapter.

CHAPTER 8

ACCESSING THE ASTRAL WITH A MONITOR AND MOUSE

ESOTERIC RELIGION AND THE ASTRAL LOCATED IN THREE-DIMENSIONAL VIRTUAL REALMS

John L. Crow

During the new moon every month, at a predetermined time, a worldwide group of occultists astrally meet at Moonbase Temple located under the surface at the centre of the visible part of the moon. Here each participant performs individual rituals in the astral temple, while working with the agreed-upon word of power and sigil. After the ceremony, each participant records his or her experiences, and these are distributed among the group for comparison.[1] According to Margaret Ingalls, who uses the pseudonym of Soror Nema and coordinates these ceremonies, there is a reflecting pool at the centre of the temple with the Earth centred in it sending all positive energy from the rites back to the planet. When asked if she could see others in the temple when present, she said she could not distinguish individuals but often could feel their presence.[2]

Ingalls's description of astral travel is typical within occultism and can be traced back to the techniques and experiences recorded by individuals in such nineteenth-century groups as the Hermetic Order of the Golden Dawn and the Theosophical Society. During these astral travel episodes, the individual imaginatively leaves her or his physical body and travels to places in this world or another dimension. The travellers claim that their inner selves travel into an imaginative environment generally accessible only to themselves. Here they encounter various entities, objects and structures with which they can interact. In 1895, prominent Theosophist and clairvoyant, Charles Webster Leadbeater (1854–1934) published *The Astral Plane*, which described the various sceneries, phenomena, and human and non-human inhabitants one might encounter in the astral environment.[3] Within the Hermetic Order of

---

1. Ingalls, "The Evolution of Maat Magick", 181.
2. Telephone interview by author, 22 September 2006.
3. Leadbeater, *The Astral Plane*.

the Golden Dawn, a nineteenth-century initiatory occult organization, travelling or "descrying" on the astral plane was an important activity an initiate was required to master in order to "obtain a clear idea of the relation of Man to the Universe, and to the spiritual planes".[4] These notions of the astral and the abilities and techniques to travel in it were adopted by many occultists, such as Aleister Crowley (1875–1947) and Edgar Cayce (1877–1945), and transmitted into the twentieth century. By the mid- to late twentieth century these ideas and techniques were diffused and incorporated into numerous groups and esoteric religions, the most prominent being New Age and neopaganism.

With the emergence of computer technology, and the Internet specifically, various groups of people began to transfer the imaginative quality of the astral environment to cyberspace, and language that was previously used to refer to the astral was now used to describe cyber realms. Some of the earliest references to the Internet as the astral plane can be found in the work of Erik Davis, a self-described culture critic. In "Technopagans", published in *Wired* in 1995, Davis interviewed Mark Pesce, a computer programmer and neopagan, about his understanding of the Internet. Pesce notes that "Both cyberspace and magical space are purely manifest in the imagination. ... Both spaces are entirely constructed by your thoughts and beliefs."[5] Indeed, even the essay's subtitle, "May the Astral be Reborn in Cyberspace", denoted the ideological transference of occultism's astral plane to cyberspace. Yet there were still significant impediments to cyberspace becoming just like the astral plane as described by nineteenth- and twentieth-century occultists. One was that text and static images on webpages still required the individual to look at the content and then imaginatively construct the "cyberastral" with their imaginations. The Internet was simply a way to deliver the content, but the person still had to imaginatively assemble it to bring the cyberastral realm alive. This process significantly changed with the emergence of three-dimensional graphical representation on the Internet. Another problem was the physical body. What happened to one's body while in the astral? This question similarly occupied nineteenth-century occultists. Yet contemporary practitioners in the cyberastral have found new ways to deal with this question, or significantly adapted older solutions.

The newest three-dimensional virtual worlds do provide the possibility to convincingly represent a cyberastral world, and some esoteric religious practitioners are using these worlds as places to practise their religion. One of these virtual environments is a computer system called Second Life. More than just seeing Second Life as an alternative place for communicating with others in virtual reality, some esoteric religious practitioners understand it to actually be the astral world. That is, they see no substantive difference between an

---

4. King, *Astral Projections, Ritual Magic, and Alchemy*, 75.
5. Erik Davis, "Technopagans".

imaginary astral plane described by the early occultists and the Second Life computer system itself. Moreover, this cyberastral environment has an added benefit that the astral environments visited by nineteenth-century occultists lacked: one can travel to the cyberastral and communicate with others while doing so. Thus the transfer of ideas about the astral plane to cyberspace and the development of sophisticated three-dimensional virtual worlds has led to the emergence of a particularly new type of astral plane, one that is imaginative, embodied, computer generated, and most importantly, social.

THE EMERGENCE OF THE ASTRAL PLANE AND NOTIONS OF THE SELF WITHIN IT

To understand why these changes in the perception of the astral are significant, it is useful to briefly trace the philosophical and practical history of the astral and its connection to evolving notions of the self. The idea of an astral plane as a distinct realm emerged during the late nineteenth century. It was made possible by a convergence of concepts about the cosmos and notions of the self and its relationship to the body. In particular it was the closing of the divide between this world and the next, and the emergence of the bifurcated self, a notion of the self understood as being separable from the body. Notions of other worlds have existed from ancient times. Platonic and Neoplatonic ideas posited various dualistic cosmologies where the material body was a lesser copy or emanation of the soul just as the material world was a lesser version of the transcendent. A recurring concern of these thinkers was that the body could somehow injure the soul. In turn, salvation depended on disciplining and refining the body, making it a proper vehicle for the soul.[6] Underlying all these cosmologies was the notion that there was a distant source, the place where the soul originated, that was separate, different, and generally superior to the material world. With the emergence of Christianity, a new understanding of the relationship between the body and soul developed as did man's relationship to the transcendent. A "productive tension between immanence and transcendence" arose where various communities manifested this tension in their personal and communal practices.[7] Christianity's history includes a number of theologians, such as Augustine and Paul, who wrestled with the way the soul related to the body, building on the previous Graeco-Roman ideas and incorporating new understandings of the soul–body relationship. Implicit in these debates was the relationship of this world with the next. What was the

---

6. Vásquez, *More than Belief*, 24. Modern, usually psychological notions of the self as being distinct from the soul, which is associated with theological claims, are not reflected in the distant past. Thus in this section there is a necessary ambiguity and interchangeability between the terms "soul" and "self".
7. *Ibid.*, 29.

role of Christ? How was salvation attained? What part of the self was immortal and what was not? Where did the immortal part of the person go when it left this world?

During the Middle Ages the soul was fully integrated with the body, "bound to sensations, emotions, reasoning and identity".[8] Not surprisingly, it was at this time that the supernatural was often claimed to be penetrating this world, manifesting angels, miracles, demons and devils. As Europe emerged out of the Middle Ages, philosophical and theological distinctions binding the soul to the body were weakened. Concordant with this separating of the body and soul was the view that the natural world allowed direct access to the transcendent. By the sixteenth century figures such as John Dee (1527–c. 1609) and Edward Kelly (1555–97) used a crystal ball, prayers and magic to contact angels in higher realms, bridging the divide between this world and the other, and making it experienceable, in part, while remaining physically embodied.[9] In the eighteenth century, Emmanuel Swedenborg (1688–1772) claimed to have repeatedly travelled to other worlds through visions, and described the inhabitants and scenery in naturalistic language. Connected to Swedenborgianism,[10] modern Spiritualism emerged in the mid-nineteenth century, in which mediums claimed the ability to contact the dead lingering on "the other side". The barriers and distance between the other world and this world had minimized so much that the two were nearly identical. According to the mediums, the self on the other side looked exactly like the physical body, often carrying with it race, gender and age.[11] Whereas in Graeco-Roman cosmologies the body was a lesser copy of the soul, by the nineteenth century this had become inverted and the soul in the next world resembled its body in this world.

Despite the brevity of the previous chronology, the most important aspect to the history of the astral plane is how, over time, otherworldliness became completely accessible while embodied and how its nature changed to resemble the material world. By the end of the nineteenth century, occultists like Leadbeater could assert that the astral plane is an "absolute reality" and that "the objects and inhabitants of the astral plane are real in exactly the same way as our bodies".[12] However, this was not the only way the astral plane was understood. For members of the Golden Dawn, for example, it existed symbolically, structured according to elaborate systems of correspondences.

---

8. *Ibid.*, 31.
9. For an overview of the activity of John Dee and Edward Kelley, see Harkness, *John Dee's Conversations with Angels*.
10. J. Arthur Hill, *Spiritualism*, 228.
11. McGarry, *Ghosts of Futures Past*, 66–93. McGarry documents how Spiritualist mediums saw Native Americans in the other world as retaining their race and cultural roles, to the point where they described the hunting and gathering practices of Indians in the other world, and the need to convert them and civilize them, also projecting Euro-American colonial aspirations.
12. Leadbeater, *The Astral Plane*, 3.

Nevertheless, they, like the clairvoyants in the Theosophical Society and the Spiritualist mediums, all saw the astral as closely connected to the material word; a place that could be entered through a variety of techniques whereby they would individually leave this world, temporarily leaving behind materiality and their bodies.

To leave the physical body behind and enter another world required a certain conceptual understanding of the self. Throughout history humanity has come to understand the self in a variety of ways. Significant for our understanding of the astral plane was the sense of self that emerged from Cartesian dualism. The sense of self coming out of Christianity, especially Pauline Christianity, is one in which the self is internal and personal. This changed with the philosophy of René Descartes (1596–1650), which identified the mind with consciousness and self-awareness. Mind was then placed in contradistinction to the body (and, in particular, to the brain). Manuel Vásquez writes that Paul's

> elevation of inner faith and spirituality as signs of the authentic selfhood will interact with Greco-Roman anti-materialist tendencies, feeding into Western thought via Agustine, who, in turn, inspired Descartes's less ambivalent mind-versus-body and spirit-versus-matter dualisms.[13]

This resulted in a dualism whereby the individual's sense of self, one's "consciousness", was understood to be distinctly separate from the body in which it resided. "That the thinking thing is not only different from the extra-world and the body, but that it is autonomous, that it does not need material reality to exist."[14] Within esoteric traditions, Cartesianism combined with already existing esoteric models of the self. As mentioned before, Neoplatonic ideas understood the physical body as separate from the soul. Bridging this divide is what Wouter Hanegraaff describes as "subtle bodies".[15] These subtle bodies, their divisions, enumeration and constitution differ from tradition to tradition, but are often found mediating or constituting parts of a person. For instance many Jewish Kabbalists understood the soul to be divided into four parts that, when combined, formed the whole person. Historian Julie Hall traces numerous threads, including Neoplatonism, Egyptian cosmologies, Kabbalah, Paracelsianism, Spiritualism, and more that contributed to the synthesis which manifested in Theosophical understandings of the self and world.[16] This evocative amalgam of esoteric representation of the self and its relationship to the body and the world combined with nineteenth-century notions of the

---

13. Vásquez, *More than Belief*, 29.
14. *Ibid.*, 38.
15. Hanegraaff, *New Age Religion and Western Culture*, 221–3.
16. Hall, "The Saptaparna", 11–24.

self which was connected to the spiritual and emotional, creating a "true" or "authentic" self.[17] This spiritual self was seen as able to directly connect with the transcendent. The result was the creation of a double-self, or simply "the double" as it was frequently called in Theosophical circles, which caused individuals to identify the self as both mind (subject) and body (object) simultaneously. As John Corrigan notes, "[t]he irresistible logic of each of the two compelling views of the self – a spiritual and emotional subject as opposed to embodied, mechanical object – in the end required that the self be both".[18] Thus the notion of the double-self combined with a view of the other world as accessible in this world while still possessing a body allowed occultists of the nineteenth century to imaginatively leave their physical bodies behind. In this way they could travel in an astral environment that was similar to the material world, but also transcend the limits imposed by materiality and the body.

THE TECHNIQUES, EMBODIMENT AND PHYSICAL STATES OF ASTRAL TRAVEL

In general, there were two types of astral travel in the nineteenth and early twentieth centuries. The first was when the individual left his or her body and travelled in the astral level of the material world, either in terms of the present, but also in the past and future. For the purposes of this chapter, I shall label this type of astral travel "geo-temporal astral travel". The other kind is where the individual travelled in a world very different from the material one; an environment controlled by symbols and symbolic correspondences rather than natural laws. I label this type of astral travel "symbolic astral travel". Two examples of these kinds of astral travel can be found in the Theosophical Society and the Hermetic Order of the Golden Dawn respectively. While both groups engaged in each type of astral travel, the members of the Theosophical Society were more concerned with issues regarding the astral and its relation to the material world. In contrast, the members of the Golden Dawn understood their astral travel experiences as part of a magical and initiatory context where travelling on the astral plane helped develop a deeper understanding of the self and the universe.

While Theosophical literature has many examples of astral travel, the recorded experiences of two prominent members are illustrative. First, William Quan Judge (1851–96) headed the US branch of the society until his death in 1896. The other is Charles Webster Leadbeater (1854–1934), who, next to the co-founder of the society, Helena Petrovna Blavatsky (1831–91), was one of the most prolific occultists to develop Theosophical doctrine. Within the Theosophical conception of the world, the astral plane was simply another

---

17. Corrigan, *Business of the Heart*, 3; Russett, *Sexual Science*, 197.
18. Corrigan, *Business of the Heart*, 3.

dimension of the physical world, but one not controlled by the ordinary laws of physics. When the double travelled, it travelled in the astral dimension of the physical world. Yet the two were so close that when the double left the physical body it could see the material world as if it was looking at it while embodied. Those in the material world could also see the double, which generally looked like the physical body, including clothing. Moreover, in the early years of the society, astral travelling (or "liberating the double", as it was called) was seen as the highest possible achievement in magic.[19]

When Judge gave a lecture in 1876 about his experiments with astral projection, published in the May 1877 issue of *Psychische Studien*, it was given within this context.[20] He describes the experiments he had performed up until that time, and in each of these Judge's body is left behind, usually sleeping, but his double roams freely. He describes one instance as follows:

> One evening I lay down in Madame Blavatsky's, intending to try to see if I could get out of my body. The bystanders said that in a few minutes I snored very loudly, but with me it was totally different. I could notice no break of unconsciousness, nor a moment of sleepiness. It seemed to me as though I was awake and standing up to go out into the hall, and that a handkerchief lay over my eyes just as I had placed it when lying down. An effort to throw off the obstacle was unsuccessful, and so I went out into the hall down which I thought to go to see my body in the kitchen, and there I threw off the handkerchief through a mighty effort – whereupon I immediately again found myself where I had laid myself down, in the laughter of those watching who had heard my unmusical snoring.[21]

In another example Judge not only roams free from his body but his double can be seen by others. He states "that while my body was snoring, my double, or simulacrum, *scin lecca*, or whatever you might call it, which is a visible exact replica of me, could be seen as it went down the way to the kitchen".[22] In both examples his body slept, unconscious of his surroundings, while his double roamed the halls freely.

Judge's descriptions of his geo-temporal astral travel are similar to those attributed to Leadbeater. In 1909 Leadbeater met Jiddu Krishnamurti (1895–1986), and claimed that through his clairvoyance he could see that one day Krishnamurti would be the next world teacher.[23] Leadbeater claimed to have astrally travelled back in time to view the past lives of Krishnamurti, and these

---

19. Deveney, *Astral Projection or Liberation of the Double*, 17.
20. For the text of the lecture, see Deveney, "An Unpublished Lecture by W. Q. Judge".
21. *Ibid.*, 15.
22. *Ibid.*
23. See Jayakar, *Krishnamurti*, particularly chapter 2.

accounts were subsequently published as *The Lives of Alcyone* in the society's journal, *The Theosophist*, beginning in 1910. In 1947, Earnest Wood (1883–1965), Leadbeater's assistant, published a small pamphlet which described the ways in which Leadbeater travelled astrally. Wood's first example describes Leadbeater as being suddenly contacted on the astral regarding an emergency. In response Leadbeater told Wood, "[c]all me if I am not back in ten minutes". He then went to sleep. Upon awakening Leadbeater described how he had assisted some astral "boys" preventing a person from committing suicide.[24] Another time Wood was assisting Leadbeater with a project when the latter suddenly "slip[ped] out of his body apparently unintentionally" and seemed "fast asleep with his eyes closed". However, within minutes Leadbeater awoke, claiming that while he seemed asleep he was still dictating to Wood. Thus Leadbeater was forced to "go over the missing portion again".[25]

These examples of geo-temporal astral travel demonstrate that, according to the Theosophists involved, it was an activity the double partook in while the physical body was asleep. Moreover, the double could travel in this world, being visible or invisible, and in the present as well as forward and backward in time.[26] Geo-temporal astral travel also allowed the astral traveller to see others and at times interact with them in limited ways. This form of astral travel differed significantly from the symbolic astral travel undertaken by members of the Hermetic Order of the Golden Dawn.

Unlike the Theosophists mentioned above, the symbolic astral travel was experienced while awake. The Golden Dawn's internal organizational instructions, called "Flying Rolls", give detailed instructions as to how to interact with the astral as well as examples of what one should experience. The Golden Dawn divided their astral work into three types: Descrying in the Spirit Vision, Astral Projection, and Rising on the Planes.[27] This section will briefly focus on one example where a member entered a symbolic astral environment using a tarot card as a portal.

The narrative of this astral experience, an example of Descrying in the Spirit Vision, was given in Flying Roll No. IV. In it two female Golden Dawn initiates, Soror SSDD (Florence Farr Emery, 1860–1917) and Soror Fidelis (Elaine Simpson), describe the process of entering the astral plane. First, the traveller is to enter a room and sit still meditating for a period of time. Then preliminary magical rituals are performed, a tarot trump to astrally explore is chosen, and then the card is studied. After a while this studying can be continued with

---

24. Wood, *Clairvoyant Investigations*, 8.
25. *Ibid.*, 11.
26. Wood also describes the events in which Leadbeater travelled forward in time describing the upcoming sixth root-race in which humans had evolved to be very different creatures than they are today. These results were published as Leadbeater & Besant, *The Beginnings of the Sixth Root Race* (1931).
27. King, *Astral Projections, Ritual Magic, and Alchemy*, 76

the eyes closed. At the point where the member feels "a state of reverie" she imaginatively steps into the tarot card and begins symbolic astral travel. The initial part of an example is as follows:

> The Tarot Trump, the Empress was taken; placed before the persons and contemplated upon, spiritualized, heightened in coloring, purified in design and idealized. In vibratory manner pronounced Daleth. Then, in spirit, saw a greenish blue distant landscape, suggestive of the mediaeval tapestry. Effort to ascend was then made; rising on the planes seemed to pass up through clouds and then appeared a pale green landscape and in its midst a gothic temple of ghostly outlines marked with light. Approached it and found the temple gained in definiteness and was concrete, and seemed a solid structure. ... Opposite the entrance perceived a cross with three bars and a dove upon it; and beside this, were steps leading forwards into the dark, by a dark passage. Here was met a beautiful green dragon, who moved aside, meaning no harm, and the spirit vision passed on. Turning a corner ... there appeared a woman of heroic proportions, clothed in green with a jewelled girdle, crown of stars on her head, in her hand a sceptre of gold, having at one apex a lustrously white closed lotus flower; in her left hand an orb bearing a cross. She also had a shield with a dove upon it. She smiled proudly, and as the human spirit sought her name, replied: I am the mighty Mother Isis; most powerful of all the worlds, I am she who fights not, but is always victorious.[28]

The vision continues for some time, ending with a message of universal love, a theme attributed to the Empress Tarot card. With the presence of a dragon and the Egyptian goddess Isis, symbolic astral travel operates in an environment not connected directly with the physical world but rather in a fantastic or mythical one. It is an imaginary world where individuals can fly and encounter myriad entities, including angels, monsters, gods and goddesses. While the realm may seem completely dreamlike and plastic, this was not how it was understood by occultists. These symbolic astral realms have rules and laws. Certain actions, rituals and words brought from the physical world obtain great effects in the astral. Moreover, these realms are bounded by a complex set of symbolic correspondences. These limits predetermined the experience of the astral. Nevertheless, symbolic astral travel was generally practised individually with results frequently being recorded afterwards.

---

28. *Ibid.*, 72.

RELIGIOSITY IN THE ASTRAL AND THE INTERNET

Before continuing the examination of the cyberastral plane, it is necessary to take a moment to follow the trajectory of religious development in the late twentieth century. Two important factors need to be explicated. The first is the transference of astral travel to a larger cultural and religious context. The second is the emergence of religious activity online. Much has been written about the 1960s and the occult revival, where nineteenth-century occultism was combined with an emergence of neopaganism and the incorporation of Eastern religions such as Zen Buddhism. Notions of the astral were part of this cluster of ideas and were gradually diffused into a larger religious context.

Within neopaganism, the astral plane became fused with traditions claimed to trace back to ancient times. One of the most important figures for modern neopaganism is the British civil servant Gerald B. Gardner (1884–1964). Prior to founding Wicca in the 1950s, Gardner was involved with individuals who traced their occult and religious practices back to the Theosophical Society, the Hermetic Order of the Golden Dawn, Ordo Templi Orientis, Aleister Crowley and older occult or esoteric traditions.[29] It was through these channels that we find Gardner incorporating numerous occult doctrines into Wicca, which subsequently disseminated into the larger neopagan milieu. One example can be found in *A Witches' Bible Complete*, written by Janet and Stewart Farrar, influential figures in modern neopaganism and Wicca. Quoting from Gardner's *Book of Shadows*, his magical ritual book, the Farrars detail Gardner's instructions "To Leave the Body". They write that the purpose of this practice is "to help bring about what may variously be called clairvoyance, expansion of consciousness, opening up the levels, opening the Third Eye, or communication with the Goddess; and, at a more advanced stage, astral projection".[30]

Neopaganism was not the only tradition to absorb notions of the astral. As Hanegraaff observes, a central aspect of New Age religion is the belief in "other realities" which can be accessed freely by human beings. This he notes can be accomplished through what he labels "Altered States of Consciousness" (ASC).[31] In these altered states of consciousness, New Age practitioners experience other realities, frequently similar to experiences described above in both symbolic and geo-temporal astral travel. Throughout the twentieth century, occult practices and worldviews diffused and were adopted and incorporated into a variety of New Age religions.[32] As Hanegraaff notes, the complex

---

29. See Philip G. Davis, *Goddess Unmasked*, chapter 14. See also Kaczynski, *Perdurabo*, chapter 22, for Gardner's relationship with Crowley.
30. Farrar & Farrar, *A Witches' Bible*, II: 60.
31. Hanegraaff, *New Age Religion and Western Culture*, 259–62. See also Chapter 19 of the present volume.
32. See Pike, *New Age and Neopagan Religions in America*, chapter 3, where she meticulously traces New Age and neopagan practices back through nineteenth-century America and Europe.

hierarchy of worlds developed by the Theosophical Society compare to the view found in New Age religion.[33] Various aspects of the astral have also been incorporated into New Age channelling practices where, as Michael F. Brown describes, "practitioners believe that they can use altered states of consciousness to connect to wisdom emanating from the collective unconsciousness or even from other planets, dimensions, or historical eras".[34] Brown traces New Age channelling back to Spiritualist mediums who also communicated with those on the other side.

Christopher Partridge has traced notions of the astral in mid-twentieth-century UFO-related religions back to Theosophy.[35] He also sees numerous similarities with New Age and Theosophy including ideas of "reincarnation, chakras, past lives, future lives, psychic therapy, oneness with the Earth, channelling, astral travel and so on".[36] Also, "churches of magic" have retained similar astral practices throughout the twentieth century. One example is the Church of the Sun, which operated in the 1960s and 1970s. As Frederick R. Lynch documents, the organization incorporated astral cosmologies and travel as part of its doctrine.[37] Similarly, during the same time period, a different church of magic, the Solar Lodge, incorporated various astral occult practices into its organization.[38] Lastly, Ordo Templi Orientis, still active today with international headquarters in the United States, United Kingdom and Australia, traces its origin, ideas, and practices back to a number of organizations including esoteric Freemasonry and, through Crowley, the Golden Dawn. Crowley incorporated astral travel into his magical curricula and this is still promoted by the group.[39] Thus it becomes evident quickly that the various concepts and practices regarding the astral that were practised by the Theosophical Society and the Hermetic Order of the Golden Dawn, found their way into a wide spectrum of alternative religious practice throughout the Western world. However, these practitioners did not just practise their esoteric religions in their communities. Beginning in the mid-1990s the Internet became a central place for the dissemination of religious information, communication and community. Indeed, the Internet became a central place for all of these traditions to meet and communicate.

---

33. Hanegraaff, *New Age Religion and Western Culture*, 260.
34. Michael F. Brown, *The Channeling Zone*, 6.
35. Partridge, *The Re-enchantment of the West*, vol. 2, 177.
36. *Ibid.*, 196.
37. See Frederick R. Lynch, "'Occult Establishment' or 'Deviant Religion'?".
38. Solar Lodge traces its origins through figures like Aleister Crowley and organizations like Ordo Templi Orientis. Little scholarship discusses the Solar Lodge except Starr, "Chaos from Order". A former Solar Lodge member published an account of the group which, in part, discusses the group's astral travel teachings and practices. See Frater Shiva, *Inside Solar Lodge/Outside the Law*.
39. The website of the US branch of the Ordo Templi Orientis explicitly recommends Crowley's *Magick in Theory and Practice* which contains extensive instructions as to the use of the astral. See OTO, "Library".

Since its emergence, the Internet has been used for religious purposes. The Pew Internet and American Life report for 2001 states that a quarter of the Americans who had access to the Internet used it for religious purposes, often information searching, accessing religious material or connecting to others of the same faith.[40] In a similar report in 2004 this number had increased to 64 per cent.[41] There can be no doubt that for many, the Internet is a place where religion is alive and flourishing. Indeed, as Lorne L. Dawson notes, "Religion of every kind, big and small, old and new, mainstream and more exotic, is present online, and in great abundance."[42] Not surprisingly, this includes those who practise esoteric religions. In fact, as Stef Aupers remarks, recent studies have found that neopagans are more active on the Internet than any other religious group.[43] Yet, being so active on the Internet has its challenges. Coming from a relatively new and individualistic religion, neopagans are not averse to religious experimentation and change. Indeed, they are willing to take traditional forms of practice and adapt them for online use. As Dawson and Douglas Cowan note, "when covens go online – when they become 'cybercovens' … the notion of a coven [becomes] considerably more elastic".[44] Nonetheless, having the coven online is central to the religious practice of many neopagans. Community is the focus of many people who use the Internet for religious purposes. This communal orientation derives from the social networking aspect where the members do not just create individual social connections, but large social webs of interaction.[45] Within the neopagan community, these cybercovens act as places where large social networks emerge, but still within boundaries. It is this boundary that psychologically contributes to the participants understanding of the cybercoven as a sacred space, even if the interaction is through a website or online message boards.[46] It is not only neopagans that view online community as fitting into their esoteric religious worldview. As Brown writes about the New Age channelling community:

> The problem of Internet-based community, however, is that it is both specialized and diluted. "Probably the first thing anybody notices when they go online," writes another believer in the Net's social magic, "is the community-building taking place all through cyberspace".[47]

---

40. Larsen, *CyberFaith*. For more discussion on this, see Chapter 7 of the present volume.
41. Clark *et al.*, *Faith Online*.
42. Dawson, "The Mediation of Religious Experience in Cyberspace", 15.
43. Aupers, "'Where the Zeros Meet the Ones'", 221.
44. Dawson & Cowan, *Religion Online*, 2. See also Cowan, *Cyberhenge*, chapter 4, where he discusses cybercovens in depth.
45. Heidi Campbell, *Exploring Religious Community Online*, 41.
46. Cowan, *Cyberhenge*, 144.
47. Michael F. Brown, *The Channeling Zone*, 125.

Brown continues by mentioning the way the community "consists of a shared identity rather than an enduring commitment to a circle of neighbors and kin".[48] This is central to social networking with groups that practice esoteric religion. Because their numbers are few and they are geographically scattered, the Internet acts as a way for individuals to create affinity communities with others who share the same interests and beliefs. Indeed, this is one of the primary reasons why many cybercovens were created, to overcome geographic isolation of many solitary neopagans.[49] Nevertheless, there are still significant barriers to creating a community through text and static images. While one may feel an affinity with those who share the same chat group or discussion board, the episodic interaction requires one to revisit frequently to see replies. While one may feel a sort of presence from the website that feeling can only get members so close. This is a barrier some have tried to overcome.

ADDING THREE DIMENSIONS AND EMBODIMENT TO VIRTUAL ENVIRONMENTS AND WORLDS

As mentioned previously, Erik Davis's "Technopagans" essay frequently refers to cyberspace in terms similar to the astral plane. This is also the case of many others in the neopagan community. Cowan quotes Lisa McSherry as writing that cyberspace is "a technological doorway to the astral plane".[50] Yet, as he continues:

> The hyperbole and exaggerated rhetoric in which so many claims for the power of the Internet seem to come cloaked is met by the reality that we are all ineluctably embodied, subject to the constraints of time and space, and that our ability to interact online is hardly a global phenomenon.[51]

This embodied state is a challenge to all those who wish to create community in cyberspace. The difficulty is that the medium of text and static graphics does not create an immersive experience. To meet this need, many have turned to three-dimensional virtual environments. One of the technopagans Davis interviewed, Mark Pesce, was on the forefront of meeting this challenge as he helped develop one of the first three-dimensional modelling languages used on the Internet. Called VRML (Virtual Reality Modeling Language), this language, developed in the mid-1990s, was one of the attempts to move beyond text and static images towards three-dimensional realms. However, the results

---

48. *Ibid.*
49. Cowan, *Cyberhenge*, 83–90.
50. *Ibid.*, 1.
51. *Ibid.*, 3.

were very rudimentary and it has taken many years before computer graphics and computational abilities have allowed wide adoption of convincing three-dimensional realms. Gordon Calleja traces the evolution of virtual worlds and environments leading to modern, sophisticated systems.[52] Building on the graduate work of Lisbeth Klastrup, he makes the important distinction between a virtual world and a virtual environment: "Virtual environments are computer generated domains which create a perception of space and permit modification through the exertion of agency."[53] These environments are then encapsulated in virtual worlds, which are "composite assemblages of persistent, multi-user virtual environments extending over a vast geographical expanse".[54] The distinction becomes one of agency. In virtual environments, the individual can exert agency to manipulate the environment, whereas on websites and discussion boards this type of manipulation is precluded. Secondly, the virtual world is a persistent, multi-user collection where virtual environments overlap creating a polyvalent system of interaction where each individual's action becomes part of the environment for others.

Moving beyond websites with virtual reality dimensions as originally created by Pesce and others utilizing VRML technologies, Calleja traces the evolution of three-dimensional multi-user environments and worlds through text-based MUDs (multi-user domains/dimensions/dungeons) to sophisticated three-dimensional graphic realms. Beginning with MUDs, text-only environments with lists indicated the presence of others, and then moving towards more sophisticated systems with graphics and the ability to interact with others simultaneously, Calleja discusses MMOGs (massively multiplayer online games). These online games, accessed through commercial software, evolved on the Internet and attracted millions of players worldwide. While these virtual worlds were designed with episodic goals requiring collaboration, many players found other uses for the system. In MMOGs and MMORPGs (massively multiplayer online role-playing games), like *World of Warcraft*, participants look for information, help each other, or socialize via text and voice chat.[55] In this way they often foster small communities. However, these virtual worlds impose teleology; one generally plays to win the game.

One example of a virtual world without teleology is Second Life. This is a three-dimensional virtual world where individuals are free to purchase digital property and supplies, build whatever they want, and travel wherever they like. The virtual world embodies participants with customizable avatars that allow changing of the skin, hair and eye colours, gender, clothes, and more. This ability to alter the appearance of the avatar is significant since, Craig D. Murray and Judith Sixsmith argue, participants in virtual worlds bring their

---

52. Calleja, "Virtual Worlds Today".
53. *Ibid.*, 14.
54. *Ibid.*, 15.
55. Subrahmanyam & Greenfield, "Online Communication and Adolescent Relationships", 122.

notions of race, gender, ethnicity and culture into the virtual.[56] Moreover, participants understand the virtual environment from their own embodied perspective.

> By drawing on our evolutionary history, VR [virtual reality] has allowed our embodied reality to map onto our embodied experiences in cyberspace. ... the point of projection is at standing height. The perspective offered to viewers mimics their experience in the world, and viewers measure objects in the virtual environments as they do in reality – that is, against their own bodies.[57]

This naturalized representation of the virtual environment allows for a more convincing experience. Second Life also allows two views – one of the body of the avatar and the other through the eyes of the avatar. This reinforces a perception of physical presence in the virtual. However, in contradistinction to the earlier nineteenth-century understanding of the self, Murray and Sixsmith argue that what virtual reality users experience is not a projection of the subjective self into the virtual world as the nineteenth-century occultists did. Instead, a model is offered where the subjective understanding of the body's boundaries become malleable and ambiguous. They use a phenomenological model because "it is concerned with perception and bodily activity, enabling the exploration of phenomena as they are lived and experienced".[58] With this understanding of the body, and building on research in which users of prosthetic devices come to see the mechanical limb as part of their body, Murray and Sixsmith argue that a phenomenological polymorphic understanding of the body is necessary because it "reveals that the body in the world is both foreground and background. It constitutes our locus, so that we are 'here', rather than 'there'. Yet, at the same time, the body recedes from conscious reflection."[59] This means that the body is both present and distant, allowing the participant in the virtual environment to use their body, for instance to view the screen and use a mouse, but also to be distanced from it and present in the virtual world, interacting with others. As they note, "[a] sense of presence, of *being there* in virtual environments ... calls for a dampening of awareness in reality and a heightening acceptance of the surrounding virtuality".[60] This distancing process becomes easier as the individual becomes more comfortable with technology.

This comfort level is most evident in the generations growing up with digital technology. Being a significant issue for educators, cognitive scientists

---

56. Murray & Sixsmith, "The Corporeal Body in Virtual Reality", 320–22.
57. *Ibid.*, 320.
58. *Ibid.*, 322.
59. *Ibid.*, 323.
60. *Ibid.*, 324.

have been examining the ways digital technologies affect children in regard to learning. They have found that not only does immersion in digital technological environments stress some skills over others, it *physiologically* changes the brain. There is an increase in the density of neurological connections in the areas of the brain used for experiencing virtual environments. However, as Marc Prensky, a specialist in digital learning, writes, "these differences ... are less a matter of kind than a difference of degree".[61] Nevertheless, these changes are significant because the exposure to digital environments improve the very mental skills needed to traverse virtual worlds. The thinking skills enhanced by repeated exposure to computer games and other digital media include:

> reading visual images as representations of three-dimensional space (representational competence), multidimensional visual-spatial skills, mental maps, "mental paper folding" (i.e. picturing the results of various origami-like folds in your mind without actually doing them), "inductive discovery" (i.e. making observations, formulating hypotheses and figuring out the rules governing the behavior of a dynamic representation), "attentional deployment" (such as monitoring multiple locations simultaneously), and responding faster to expected and unexpected stimuli.[62]

Moreover, events experienced while immersed in the digital environment can have direct psychological and physiological feedback within the body. This kind of feedback from the virtual is noted by Chris Dede in *Science*:

> Inducing a participant's symbolic immersion involves triggering powerful semantic, psychological associations by means of the content of an experience. As an illustration, digitally fighting a terrifying, horrible virtual monster can build a mounting sense of fear, even though one's physical context is unchanging and rationally safe.[63]

In many examples, Dede points to highly immersive three-dimensional environments, such as using headsets or panoramic displays. However, as Ciaran Scott Hill of the Institute of Neurology, University College London, replied, children already have these kinds of immersive environments with commercially available game consoles. He writes:

> the opportunity for motor skill development by immersive interfaces is not limited to specialist training – the Nintendo Wii console is one example of a commercially available games system that

---

61. Prensky, "Digital Natives, Digital Immigrants, Part II".
62. *Ibid.*
63. Dede, "Immersive Interfaces for Engagement and Learning", 66.

integrates hand and, in some cases, whole body movements in a range of simulated environments.[64]

Indeed, the view that the whole environment needs to be simulated ignores the fact that a focus can be centred on a set of stimuli with the exclusion of the surrounding environment. It is no different than being absorbed in a book, movie, or television show to the point that one's surroundings are temporarily forgotten. Thus, while the three-dimensional virtual immersion experience was rudimentary initially, its sophistication, matched with the heightened skills and familiarity with technology by the last couple of digital generations, have acculturated many to allow their sense of self to become malleable and to be able to operate in the physical world while simultaneously existing subjectively embodied to varying degrees in a virtual environment interacting with others in a virtual world creating community.

VIRTUAL RELIGION, RITUAL AND ASTRAL TRAVEL IN SECOND LIFE

As noted earlier, the Internet was used for religious purposes right from its inception and this trend has increased since. Thus it is not surprising to find myriad religious traditions and communities bringing their practices and beliefs into the virtual world of Second Life. Kerstin Radde-Antweiler and Simon Jenkins, both scholars publishing in *Online: Heidelberg Journal of Religions on the Internet*, have made extensive studies of religion and ritual in three-dimensional virtual worlds, with Radde-Antweiler specifically focusing on Second Life. What they found was that, indeed, numerous people have participated in online religious rituals and have had, to some degree, satisfying experiences. Jenkins notes comments from participants, such as "I was touched by how everyone 'fell silent' for the duration of the service" and that many felt a "reverence in the services".[65] He continued to note how the textual input of the Lord's Prayer allowed the participants to bond and form community:

> The experience of praying the Lord's Prayer together focused attention on our togetherness in prayer and worship, despite our distance in terms of geography, culture, language and faith expression. The people sitting on either side of you in a Church of Fools pew could be from Melbourne and Kansas City, and yet here you were, sitting in the same imaginative space, and being able to talk and pray together, even though you would probably never meet each other face to face in the physical world.[66]

---

64. Ciaran Scott Hill, "Developing Psychomotor Skills the Wii Way".
65. Jenkins, "Rituals and Pixels", 108.
66. *Ibid.*, 109.

Similar to Jenkins, Radde-Antweiler notes that there have been numerous "clusters" of religiosity in Second Life. She documents the Jewish, Christian, Muslim, New Age, Buddhist and Hindu clusters, which offer information and a variety of services.[67] For instance, in one virtual temple the participant can have his/her avatar meditate in front of the digital representation of the Hindu God Ganesh. Radde-Antweiler also notes how the Second Temple in Jerusalem, destroyed by the Romans in 70 CE, has been rebuilt. When entering the temple a digital note greets the visitor:

> Welcome to our Holy City. Outside you will see the walls of a full-scale reconstruction of the Second Temple that stood in Jerusalem until the year 70. To experience the size of the building move around in mouse-mode: it will be you walking through the gates.[68]

As is evident by the greeting, the makers of the temple equate the viewing of the virtual temple as equivalent to seeing the temple in the physical world, at least to some degree.

Not surprisingly, neopagans, New Age practitioners and occultists have also established presences in Second Life. Following the pattern of earlier formats, cybercovens have been established, but unlike previous versions this technology allows a full manifestation of the romantic imagery associated with neopaganism. One cybercoven, called Covenstead, consists of a massive digital campus with multiple parts, including a pub for drinking cyber-mead, dancing and playing trivia, a library with digital versions of magical and neopagan texts, a marketplace to purchase various virtual clothes and objects for use by the avatar, a large field for group meditation, a Stonehenge setting used for community ritual (complete with altar and central bonfire), and more. There is also a digital carriage ride so one's avatar can tour the campus, as well as multiple teleports that can whisk one's avatar to different places on the campus without the need to walk or fly there.

However, for many Covenstead members, Second Life is not just a place for community. They view their participation in it, especially during ritual, as a form of astral travel. Unlike Ingalls and her group of occultists who travel to a distant temple and perform their rituals separately, these neopagans, who are spread throughout the world, come together in their cyberastral Stonehenge temple to celebrate neopagan religious events. In June of 2009, I interviewed some members of Covenstead and observed the celebration of one of their online sabbaths. The cybercoven was created by Ainsley Weatherwax[69] and is

---

67. Radde-Antweiler, "'Virtual Religion'".
68. *Ibid.*, 177.
69. All names given for participants are avatar pseudonyms. In some cases the participants gave their real names and personal details, but in most cases they preferred to simply use their avatar's identity for the interview. Those who did give their physical world location

operated by her and a number of volunteers who contribute time and money for the continuation and maintenance of the cybercoven. When discussing the community with Weatherwax, she noted that as a cybercoven "the community expects to be able to be themselves among other Pagans and to have classes, rituals and events offered".[70] One of the ways they coordinate their schedule is by using an online calendaring system where event titles, descriptions, and times are posted. As individuals from around the world participate, all the times are standardized on Pacific Standard Time. She also noted that most of the participants were from North America and Europe, and that the events were generally conducted in English.

When our discussion turned to cyber-ritual, she noted that there were positive and negative aspects regarding its performance in Second Life. She mentioned that some of the technical limitations for Second Life hampered the performance of ritual. With more participants, there is a greater lag time for the animation and this disturbed the semblance of the ritual. She also said that there were conceptual difficulties with cyber-rituals. Mirroring the cultural transference noted by Murray and Sixsmith, Weatherwax stated that many participants bring their experiences with ritual in the physical world into Second Life. Moreover, she said that the negotiation of ritual in Second Life is ongoing: "I see ritual in Cyberspace as a work in progress. No one seems to really know what works best yet." She continued:

> We need to experiment to find out what works in Cyberspace best. And a lot of people seem so mired in the trappings of RL [real life] traditions in ritual they aren't willing to let go of them to discover what really works. I see cyberspace as an amazing vehicle for magic. SL [Second Life] could be even more so with its amazing graphic creation capabilities. ... These could add amazing dimension to [what] was once just "chatroom" ritual. And if you have a totally hearing crowd, the ability to add voice and sound to the imagery is wonderful. ... The ritual should fit what is available. Imagination plays [a part in] all of it. So why should we force our avatars into human shapes to do human gestures for ritual when this is obviously not a necessity in cyberspace? We could do the whole ritual in colour and light and pure visual effect. [This] might work much better. The environs always dictated ritual in RL, so perhaps different environs should dictate different ritual technique

---

were located in the United States and Canada. No formal questions were prearranged but the general nature of the discussion, goals for the interview and the physical world identity of the interviewer was given to the participant prior to their agreeing to be interviewed. Thus each interview began at a similar starting point but went in the direction generally determined by the interviewee. For issues regarding virtual ethnography see Christine Hine, *Virtual Ethnography*; Hine, *Virtual Methods*.

70. Interview by author, 13 June 2009.

> ... I think imagination can get around mostly anything and electricity has always been an amazing channel for spiritual energy. We might actually find a way to use it [Second Life] that will exceed our results in RL.[71]

Clearly Weatherwax notes the limitations of cyber-ritual. Not surprisingly, she is not one who sees Second Life as synonymous with the astral. She also mentions the limits the physical body introduces to the performance of the cyber-ritual. In general the cybercoven desires to be inclusive during its ritual and thus does not use voice but instead uses text to deliver speech as it is inclusive of the hearing impaired. Although it is not the case for all the participants, this limits the ability for some to feel completely immersed in cyber-ritual.

One participant, Tamaya Rayna, claimed that she did understand her participation in Second Life as being like the astral plane: "My thought on that is, if I am actually a spirit being, then my 'physical' body is a form of an avatar. If we are doing energy work on the astral or other planes, I am just using a different kind of avatar to identify with."[72] Cartesian dualism underlies Rayna's language, mirroring the language used by nineteenth-century occultists. Later in the conversation she added that "Part of magical training and practice is learning to focus and feel the energies. ... I can get that sense either in SL or RL. My theory is that whether I am in physical proximity to a person or not, I can still sense their energy." Rayna's language here parallels Ingall's and her astral ritual on Moonbase Temple. Another participant who saw Second Life as a form of the astral was Jimmy Orsini. He also claimed to feel the energies of others while in ritual,[73] and, moreover, saw his laptop as a ritual object to enter the cyberastral, much like nineteenth-century occultists used magic mirrors and crystal balls. While participating in cyber-ritual, Orsini, who is a solitary pagan, places his laptop on his altar with other ritual objects. "I usually sit in front of my altar and light a candle during the rituals",[74] Orsini says. He also notes that he uses the scripts and chants of others during the ritual to build energies to connect with other participants. The use of the computer as a ritual object is becoming more common with neopagans. As the complexity of the device exceeds the knowledge of the user, the device becomes opaque and unpredictable. This opacity opens up the opportunity for enchantment whereby the laptop becomes an object for ritual.[75] As Aupers comments, "Magic and (computer) technology are not mutually exclusive and, more than that, technological progress may paradoxically be responsible for the growth and flowering of mystery and magic in the late modern world."[76]

---

71. *Ibid.*
72. Interview by author, 15 June 2009.
73. Interview by author, 12 June 2009.
74. *Ibid.*
75. Aupers, "'Where the Zeros Meet the Ones'", 234–5.
76. *Ibid.* 237.

Aupers also remarks that those who can master computer technology, particularly the computer programmers, are seen as magicians.[77] As one programmer said, "we put these words together, these little characters together, and create these magical things".[78] This perception of being a magician due to creative programming was found in one of the Second Life interviewees. His avatar name is Thaleenin Sydney, and in the physical world he is a ceremonial magician and works as a programmer. He claimed that his programming skills were part of his magical practice, which included creating scripts for avatars in Second Life to use in ritual. His scripts included ones used in ritual at Covenstead. These scripts, when run on an avatar, make them mimic specific ritualistic actions. For neopagans these include motions for invoking and banishing pentagrams, and the fivefold kiss. During our conversation, he stated that scripting avatars was not always easy: "we have some of the sounds done and I'm in the middle of scripting them so the timing is right, which is turning out to be the hardest part".[79] Nevertheless, Sydney saw the incorporation of Second Life into his magical and astral work as natural. In fact, he claimed that Second Life was so much like the astral that he used it to help his magical students with initial astral experiences:

> For someone advanced SL is just another aspect of the astral depending on what they want to do. For a beginner SL is best. People can get here in 5 min of downloading the program as opposed to whatever it may take to get on the astral.[80]

Throughout the interview Sydney continued to mix his discussion of scripting Second Life avatars and working on the astral. It seemed, from his point of view, there really was little difference, or, as he noted, it was an educational tool where students learn their magical practices and obtain access to the astral in both types of embodiment, digital and physical.[81] This kind of ambiguous embodiment supports the model of Murray and Sixsmith. In each of the cases where the participant saw Second Life as some form of astral, there was a mixing of the self, the body, the technology, the imagination, and community where all of these come together to blend the physical world with the virtual. Moreover, the ways the participants discussed the cyberastral showed a blending of geo-temporal and symbolic astral travel. The virtual world is flexible like the symbolic, but with the ability to interact with others, it also had aspects of geo-temporal thus creating the cyberastral as its own category of astral travel. The participants would generally eschew these categories, instead substituting

---

77. *Ibid.*, 230–31.
78. *Ibid.*, 231.
79. Interview by author, 16 June 2009.
80. *Ibid.*
81. *Ibid.*

traditional terminology and adapting it to their circumstances. Nevertheless, these categories allow the scholar to historicize and contextualize the types of astral travel experienced. This, in turn, could help to include these kinds of phenomena into the larger discourse of religious practice and embodiment.

CONCLUSION

This chapter has traced the continuities regarding the astral from nineteenth-century occultism to modern three-dimensional virtual communities embodied in Second Life. Because of the diffusion of occult ideas and their combination with notions of cyberspace and virtual reality, the emergence of a cyberastral has taken place for some who practise esoteric religion. Extending notions of the self to include the physical body and the digital, users create subjective selves which navigate virtual worlds. These virtual embodied selves, or avatars, can represent the gender, race and culture embodied in the physical or they can embrace a polymorphic identity taking on the form of the creatures listed in Leadbeater's *The Astral Plane*, or assuming alternative genders and bodily characteristics. Indeed, many avatars have wings, fly, wear clothing the person is unlikely to don in the physical world, or are have the appearance of a gender different from the normative gender performed by the participant. Thus the virtual world is not only a place where the astral manifests, but forms a larger context for identity exploration.

Does this mean that everyone who participates in Second Life views it as the astral plane? No; this is hardly the case, and I located only a small number of participants who made such a claim. Nevertheless, this should cause scholars to pause and think more about the role of digital technologies when it comes to the practice of religion as well as pay attention to notions of self and identity when it comes to religious embodiment, virtual and physical. The Internet and virtual reality technology are adding a significant dimension to religious practice and this does not only apply to esoteric religion.

In 1995 Erik Davis hoped that the astral would be reborn in cyberspace. With Second Life one might ask if it finally has been. With the way digital technology and three-dimensional reality is progressing, it might not be long before more people develop an expansive embodiment, and perhaps, for them at least, the astral may actually be reborn in cyberspace.

CHAPTER 9

THE SECRETS OF SCIENTOLOGY

CONCEALMENT, INFORMATION CONTROL AND ESOTERIC KNOWLEDGE IN THE WORLD'S MOST CONTROVERSIAL NEW RELIGION

Hugh B. Urban

> Secrets, secrets SECRETS! Ah, the endless quest, the far, far search, the codes, the vias, the symbols, the complications, the compilations, the mathematicity and abstracticity of secrets, secrets, SECRETS![1]

> The secret operates as an adorning possession ... This involves the contradiction that what recedes before the consciousness of others and is hidden from them is emphasized in their consciousness; that one should appear as a noteworthy person through what one conceals.[2]

From its origins in the 1950s, the Church of Scientology has been one of the most controversial, contested, and yet also poorly understood new religions in the world. Best known for its cast of high-profile celebrity spokespersons, such as John Travolta, Tom Cruise and Kirstie Alley, the Church has also been widely attacked by the media, anti-cult groups and various government agencies as a rapacious business and a dangerous "cult of greed".[3] And yet despite its infamous reputation in popular culture, Scientology has – with a few notable exceptions[4] – rarely been subjected to serious critical analysis by historians of religions.

The reasons for this neglect are not far to seek. From its first incorporation in 1953, the Church of Scientology has been not only one of the most lucrative

---
1. L. Ron Hubbard, *Dianetics 55*, 3.
2. Georg Simmel, "The Secret and the Secret Society", 377.
3. See, among many other articles, Behar, "The Thriving Cult of Greed"; Childs & Tobin, "Scientology".
4. The few scholarly discussions of Scientology in English include Wallis, *The Road to Total Freedom*; Lewis, *Scientology*; Kent, "Scientology"; Whitehead, *Renunciation and Reformulation*; Christensen, "Inventing L. Ron Hubbard"; Urban, "Fair Game"; Urban, *The Church of Scientology*.

but also arguably the most secretive (and litigious) new religion in the world, maintaining very tight control over the flow of information both within and outside the organization. Not only did the Church develop a complex esoteric series of training levels or "advanced technology", but it has also been extremely aggressive in enforcing its rights to the information contained in these higher grades.[5] By the late 1960s, moreover, Scientology had also created elaborate mechanisms of surveillance to monitor both its own members and its critics in the surrounding society, including its own intelligence agency, which many have likened to the FBI and the CIA. As Ann Brill and Ashley Packard observe in their study of Scientology's war of information on the Internet, "What makes the Church of Scientology controversial is not so much Hubbard's teachings, but the Church's tenacious secrecy and the extremes to which it is willing to go to protect itself."[6]

This chapter will critically examine the role of secrecy in the Church of Scientology, placing it within the historical and sociological context of the United States during the last six decades. Specifically, it will explore three periods in the development of Scientology from the late 1940s to the present:

- the early life and biographical narrative of Scientology's founder, L. Ron Hubbard, particularly his involvement in occultism and ritual magic in the late 1940s;
- the origins of the Church of Scientology in the context of Cold War America, where it reflected (and indeed epitomized) the obsession with secrecy and information control that characterized this period; and
- the ongoing wars of information currently being fought in cyberspace, as ever more of Scientology's esoteric knowledge is leaked online, and the Church wages massive legal battles over copyrights and trade secrets in the digital realm.

From the outset, we should note that Scientology is not exactly an esoteric organization in the traditional sense, comparable with fraternal orders such as Freemasonry or magical groups such as the Golden Dawn. Many of Scientology's secrets, we will see, have had less to do with transmitting esoteric gnosis than with preserving the Church, its wealth and its power, often in hostile social and political contexts. However, Scientology did develop an elaborate esoteric hierarchy of training levels, a complex esoteric cosmology and a very tight system of information control that rivals (if not surpasses) that of any other Western esoteric tradition.

As such, I will argue, the Church of Scientology is a striking example of the fact that religious secrecy is typically not just a matter of esoteric gnosis with

---

5. See Urban, "Fair Game"; Cowan, "Researching Scientology".
6. Brill & Packard, "Silencing Scientology's Critics on the Internet", 5–8. See Urban, "Fair Game"; Raine, "Surveillance in a New Religious Movement".

no connection to the broader social and political domain. On the contrary, it is often intimately entwined with politics, power, social struggle, and historical change. Perhaps most important, Scientology offers profound insight into what I call the dual nature of secrecy – its role both as a source of symbolic power and a potential *liability* for its owner. As the sociologist Georg Simmel famously observed, secrecy can serve as a kind of "adorning possession" for its owner;[7] like fine clothing or jewellery, esoteric knowledge can ironically enhance the status of its owner precisely by virtue of what it conceals. Yet, at the same time, secrecy can also bring even more suspicion, scrutiny and attack from critics, opponents and government agencies who see such concealment as a potential threat; and, in turn, increasing government scrutiny tends to foster even more elaborate tactics of concealment, obfuscation and dissimulation on the part of the religious organization.[8] It is just this sort of spiralling feedback loop of secrecy, surveillance, government scrutiny and increasing dissimulation that we see in the tangled history of the Church of Scientology over the last sixty years. As such, it offers some profound insights into the role of secrecy, surveillance and information control in the twenty-first century.

THE OCCULT ROOTS OF SCIENTOLOGY? ESOTERIC THEMES IN HUBBARD'S EARLY LIFE AND WRITINGS

Secrecy surrounds many aspects of the Church of Scientology, beginning with the biography of its founder, L. Ron Hubbard himself. According to official narratives promoted by the Church to this day, Hubbard was a unique combination of rugged explorer, world traveller and engineer, equally accomplished as "a daredevil barnstormer, a master mariner, [and] a Far East explorer", as well as the founder of a revolutionary new religious philosophy.[9] Born in Nebraska in 1911, Hubbard claims to have been initiated by Blackfoot shamans in Montana, then to have travelled widely in Asia and learned the secrets of Eastern sages, Buddhist priests and "the last remaining magician from the line of Kublai Khan's court".[10] Back in the United States, he pursued the sciences, studying engineering and atomic physics at George Washington University, before enjoying a decorated naval career during World War II.

Virtually every detail of Hubbard's life narrative, however, has been the subject of debate, and many critics have argued that most, if not all, of his official biography is a fabrication. Indeed, after reviewing the large body of biographical materials produced in the lawsuit of *The Church of Scientology*

---

7. Simmel, "The Secret and the Secret Society", 337.
8. See Simmel, "The Secret and the Secret Society"; Urban, "Secrecy in New Religious Movements"; Tefft, *The Dialectics of Secret Society Power*.
9. Friends of Ron, *L. Ron Hubbard*, 102.
10. Scientology.org, "L. Ron Hubbard".

of California v. Gerald Armstrong in 1984, Judge Paul Breckenridge was led to conclude that "the evidence portrays a man who has been virtually a pathological liar when it comes to his history, background, and achievements".[11] As Dorthe Refslund Christensen suggests, however, Hubbard's biography is perhaps best understood not as a factual account at all, but rather as a kind of "hagiographic mythology";[12] as such, it is not dissimilar to the hagiographic biographies of founders of other esoteric traditions and new religions, such as Madame Blavatsky or Joseph Smith.

Perhaps the most controversial chapter in Hubbard's biography was his involvement in occultism and ritual magic in California during the late 1940s. This rather bizarre story is far too complex to do justice in a short article, so interested readers may look at some of my and others' works where this curious tale is related in more detail.[13]

After leaving the Navy following World War II, Hubbard moved to Pasadena, California, where he befriended one of the most enigmatic occultists of twentieth-century America, John (Jack) Whiteside Parsons. In addition to being one of the most prominent rocket scientists of his day (with a crater on the moon named after him), Parsons was also an avid disciple of the infamous British magus, Aleister Crowley (1875–1947) – the self-styled "Great Beast 666" – who is arguably the most important figure in the revival of magic, neopaganism and occultism in the twentieth century. Parsons was an initiate in Crowley's highly esoteric group, the Ordo Templi Orientis, and immersed in its most secret and dangerous rituals. Sharing his interest in science fiction and magic, Hubbard became Parsons's close friend and a partner in his esoteric magical rites.[14]

According to Parsons's detailed record of this period, entitled "The Book of Babalon", he was engaged in a series of esoteric rituals based on Crowley's magic and the concept of the "moonchild". The aim of Parsons's "Babalon Working" was first to identify a female partner who would serve as his partner in sexual rituals; the partner would then become the vessel for the "magickal child" or "moonchild", a supernatural offspring that would be the embodiment of ultimate power: indeed, this child would be "mightier than all the kings of the Earth".[15] Impressed by Hubbard's natural magical abilities, despite his lack of any formal training, Parsons made Hubbard an intimate participant in the Babalon Working, and even his "Scribe", who served as the voice for Babalon herself during the rites. According to Parsons's account of 2–3 March 1946, Hubbard channelled the voice of Babalon, speaking as the beautiful but terrible lady who is "flame of life, power of darkness, she

---

11. Breckenridge, "Decision".
12. Christensen, "Inventing L. Ron Hubbard", 227–58.
13. Urban, "The Occult Roots of Scientology?"; Pendle, *Strange Angel*; Carter, *Sex and Rockets*.
14. Carter, *Sex and Rockets*, 150.
15. *Ibid.*, 150.

destroys with a glance, she may take thy soul. She feeds upon the death of men. Beautiful–Horrible."[16]

Apparently, Parsons believed that the rituals had been successful. Thus, on 6 March, he wrote excitedly to Crowley:

> I have been in direct touch with One who is most Holy and Beautiful ... First, instructions were received direct through Ron, the seer ... I am to act as instructor guardian guide for nine months; then it will be loosed on the world.[17]

In short, Parsons believed that he had successfully "conceived" a supernatural being, who would then gestate for nine months before being born into the world. Ironically, however, Crowley himself was by no means approving when he learned of the ritual activities of Parsons and Hubbard. On the contrary, he seems to have been quite upset, writing in April 1946: "Apparently Parsons or Hubbard or somebody is producing a Moonchild. I get fairly frantic when I contemplate the idiocy of these goats."[18]

The magical collaboration between Parsons and Hubbard was short-lived, however, and Parsons would never see his dream of the moonchild fulfilled. In 1946, Hubbard, Parsons and Parsons's former girlfriend, Betty, formed a partnership called Allied Enterprises. Their scheme was to purchase yachts on the US East Coast, sail them to California and then sell them for a profit. Parsons put up $20,970.80, almost the entirety of his life's savings, while Hubbard put up a mere $1,183.91. Upon hearing of the scheme, Crowley himself suspected that Hubbard was playing Parsons for a fool and planning to betray him. In a cable he wrote: "Suspect Ron playing confidence trick – Jack Parsons weak fool – obvious victim prowling swindlers."[19] Finally, Parsons concluded that Hubbard had stolen not just his girlfriend but all his money and so chased him down in Miami. As Hubbard and Betty attempted to flee on one of the yachts, Parsons performed a ritual curse involving the "invocation of Bartzabel", the spirit of Mars. Curiously enough, a sudden squall came up and forced Hubbard's ship back to port.[20]

Perhaps the most remarkable part of this whole story about Hubbard, Parsons and secret sexual rites is that the Church of Scientology *admits that all of this did happen*. In October 1969, the *Sunday Times* in London published an article that documented Hubbard's links to Parsons and Crowley; the Church promptly threatened legal action and forced the *Times* to pay an out-of-court settlement. Scientology then published a statement in the *Times*

---

16. Parsons, *The Book of BABALON*, 2 March 1946.
17. Parsons, letter to Crowley, 6 March 1946, in Symonds, *King of the Shadow Realm*, 564.
18. Crowley, letter of 19 April 1946, in Sutin, *Do What Thou Wilt*, 414.
19. Crowley, letter of 22 May 1946, in Sutin, *Do What Thou Wilt*, 414–15.
20. Mitchell, "Scientology". See Symonds, *King of the Shadow Realm*, 564.

in December 1969, asserting that these rites *did* indeed take place but that Hubbard was sent in on a special military mission to "handle the situation". This he successfully did, the Church claimed, rescuing the girl (Betty) and shutting down the occult operation:

> Hubbard broke up black magic in America ... [H]e was sent in to handle the situation. He went to live at the house and investigated the black magic rites and the general situation and found them very bad ... Hubbard's mission was successful far beyond anyone's expectations ... Hubbard rescued a girl they were using. The black magic group was dispersed and destroyed.[21]

It is worth noting, however, that neither the Church of Scientology nor any independent researcher has ever produced any evidence for this claim.

Not surprisingly, there has been tremendous debate over Hubbard's involvement with Parsons and the influence of Crowley on later Scientology. While Hubbard only refers to Crowley by name in one series of lectures from 1952 – calling him "my very good friend" – there has been much speculation as to whether any occult or magical ideas carried over into the early Scientology movement.[22] On one side, critics of the Church (such as Hubbard's own son, L. Ron Jr) have suggested that Hubbard was "deeply involved in the occult" and that he even saw himself as the modern successor to the Great Beast.[23] Other ex-members and critics of the Church such as Jon Atack have alleged that Crowley's magic lies at the inner core of Scientology.[24] On the other side, the Church of Scientology itself has adamantly denied any connection between Crowley's magic and Hubbard's religious ideas; indeed, it forced the *Sunday Times* to pay a settlement for suggesting that there might be such a connection.[25] Meanwhile, many scholars such as Roy Wallis and J. Gordon Melton have largely dismissed Hubbard's connection to Crowley, arguing that "there is no evidence that Hubbard's system of Scientology owes any great debt to that of Crowley".[26]

Here I will not attempt to resolve this complex debate, which has been argued fiercely by scholars, Scientologists and ex-Scientologists alike (and elsewhere I have outlined the possible links between Crowley's magic and early Scientology[27]). Instead, I would suggest that Hubbard's early involvement

---

21. Church of Scientology, "Letter".
22. Hubbard, *Philadelphia Doctorate Course*, 185–8. See Urban, "The Occult Roots of Scientology?".
23. Hubbard, Jr, "Penthouse Interview", 113.
24. Atack, *A Piece of Blue Sky*, 9–93.
25. Wallis, *The Road to Total Freedom*, 111–12.
26. *Ibid.*, 111; Melton, *The Church of Scientology*, 8.
27. Urban, "The Occult Roots of Scientology?" Direct and indirect links include the following: (i) Hubbard himself in the *Philadelphia Doctorate Course* compares the practice of

in occultism and the Church's attempts to deny the connection reflect a much deeper concern with secrecy, information control and concealment that surrounds Hubbard's entire biography. Indeed, Hubbard would spend much of his life dodging investigations by various government agencies, and finally spent the last years of his life in hiding in the California desert. Regardless of the exact nature of his involvement in occultism, the theme of *occultation* is one that runs throughout his entire life and hagiographic mythology.

A COLD WAR RELIGION: SECRECY, SURVEILLANCE AND SECURITY

The period during which the Church of Scientology was founded and experienced its most rapid growth – from the early 1950s to the late 1980s – almost exactly corresponded to the decades of the Cold War. Just four years after parting company with Parsons, Hubbard published his bestselling new science of human mind called "Dianetics" – first in a science fiction magazine called *Astounding Science Fiction* in May 1950, and then in book form later that same year.[28] His new science of the mind was soon followed by the birth of a new self-described religion called the Church of Scientology, first incorporated in 1953. From its origins until the death of its founder in 1986, Scientology was very much a Cold War religion, deeply influenced by and preoccupied with the central anxieties of these decades – and perhaps above all by the Cold War obsession with secrecy, surveillance and information control.

From the very outset, Hubbard himself presented Scientology as a kind of Cold War religion and as the ultimate solution to the threat of nuclear war. Now that human beings possessed the technology of weapons that can destroy the entire planet, we needed a new technology that can control man:

> With man now equipped with weapons sufficient to destroy all mankind on earth, the emergence of a new science capable of handling man is vital. Scientology is such a science. It was born in the same crucible as the atomic bomb.[29]

Scientology with Crowley's magic (185–8), and the eight-pointed Scientology cross bears a very close resemblance to the Rose-Cross lamen that adorns the cards in Crowley's famous Thoth tarot deck; (ii) Hubbard's key symbol for the Thetan or spiritual self (Θ) is identical to the central symbol of Crowley's Sigil of Babalon; (iii) Hubbard's early Scientology lectures focus heavily on the idea of "exteriorizing" the Thetan from the body, which bears a close resemblance to the exteriorization of the astral body or body of light, a key theme in Crowley's *Magick in Theory and Practice*; and (iv) Hubbard's early lectures assert that the liberated Thetan has full self-determinism and can essentially do anything it chooses, a goal reminiscent of Crowley's ideal of the fully realized magus and his dictum of "do what thou wilt".

28. Hubbard, "Dianetics"; Hubbard, *Dianetics*.
29. Hubbard, *Scientology*, 163.

At the same time, however, Hubbard was also quite preoccupied – if not obsessed – with Communism, writing numerous letters to J. Edgar Hoover and the FBI. Not only did he identify various individuals (including his own ex-wife) as Communist sympathizers, but he also offered his techniques as a means to combat the Soviet menace.[30]

But perhaps nowhere was Hubbard's Church more a "Cold War religion" than in its intense focus on secrecy, surveillance and information control. As Angus MacKenzie notes in his study of secrecy in the post-World War II decades:

> The US government has always danced with the devil of secrecy during wartime ... the cold war provided the foreign threat to justify the pervasive Washington belief that secrecy should have the greatest possible latitude and openness should be restricted as much as possible – constitutional liberties be damned.[31]

Hubbard's early Dianetics movement had focused on the goal of achieving the state of "Clear" – a kind of optimal mental and physical wellbeing; yet, by the late 1960s, Hubbard added a series of increasingly esoteric levels beyond the Clear state called Operating Thetan (OT), in which one gains deeper knowledge about one's true spiritual nature (Thetan) and the history of the universe. As Wallis notes, "[t]he belief system of the movement became increasingly esoteric, and a 'hierarchy of sanctification' emerged. Members could locate themselves on levels of initiation into the movement's mysteries".[32] While the grades leading up to the Clear state are fairly "exoteric", the higher levels beyond Clear are quite secret and of highly restricted access. Harriet Whitehead explains in her study of the Church,

> After the Grades ... matters become more complicated because the pre-clear proceeds to the Confidential levels of auditing ... Hubbard decided to cordon off all processes and techniques beyond Grade IV so that the uninitiated would have no prior knowledge ... of the special theories explaining the significance of each level.[33]

More than one observer has thus compared Scientology to a modern version of a "mystery religion", not unlike the Greek mysteries or various other secret societies and esoteric orders (including modern esoteric orders, such as Parsons's and Crowley's OTO).[34] Although the Church's official map of the

---

30. See Urban, "Fair Game".
31. MacKenzie, *Secrets*, 201; see also Curry, *Freedom at Risk*, 8.
32. Wallis, *The Road to Total Freedom*, 125.
33. Whitehead, *Renunciation and Reformulation*, 130.
34. Barrett, *Sects, "Cults" and Alternative Religions*, 255.

Scientologists' progress, the "Bridge to Total Freedom", lists fifteen OT levels, only seven or eight of these appear to have been completed before Hubbard's death, or at least are currently available to Church members.

Since they were first released in the late 1960s and early 1970s, the OT levels have been surrounded by an intense and tantalizing aura of secrecy. Those moving through the OT levels must carry the materials in locked briefcases and are instructed to keep them in secure locations. They are forbidden to discuss any aspect of the materials with anyone, including family members.[35] As the Church's official website explains, the advanced technology of the OT levels must be "strictly confidential"; because the individual must "meet the highest ethical standards and have completed earlier levels of spiritual release" before even being allowed to see them.[36] However, it also seems clear that the advanced technology materials of the OT grades also play the role of "adorning possessions" in Simmel's sense – that is, as sources of prestige and honour that enhance the individual's status precisely by virtue of what they conceal.

The most infamous of the OT materials is the narrative revealed at OT level III, which explains the past history of the physical universe and the source of human suffering in this life (this was the narrative that was also viciously ridiculed in an episode of the cartoon *South Park* in 2005[37]). The contents of OT III are surrounded with a profound aura of mystery and power. According to Hubbard's audio journal of 1967, this level is "so occluded that if anyone tried to penetrate it … they have died".[38] Yet Hubbard risked his own life and health in order to achieve the dramatic breakthrough to OT III, passing through the "Wall of Fire" to uncover the secret history of our galaxy and the means to recover our ultimate potential as spiritual beings:

> Here are contained the secrets of a disaster which resulted in the decay of life as we know it in this sector of the galaxy. The end result of OT III is truly the stuff of which dreams are spun: The return of full self-determinism and complete freedom.[39]

Although the details of OT III are only available to qualified Scientologists, the text of these materials was made public through two court cases and has since circulated widely in print and online. Essentially, this complex narrative tells the story of the intergalactic Emperor Xenu (or Xemu in some versions) who ruled 75 million years ago and tried to solve the problem of over-population by gathering individuals onto planet Earth (then called Teegeeack) and planting

---

35. Reitman, "Inside Scientology".
36. Religious Technology Center, "Protecting the Advanced Technology".
37. *South Park*, "Trapped in the Closet".
38. Hubbard, *Ron's Journal 67*, 2.
39. Hubbard, *Have You Lived Before This Life?*, 307.

hydrogen bombs in the Earth's volcanoes. The beings were blown up, but their thetans or spirits survived in a confused state and eventually adhered to modern humans like spiritual barnacles. These "extra-body thetans" that adhere to each one of us are a chief cause of the ignorance and suffering that we experience in this life. Advanced auditing therefore requires clearing and removing these extra-body thetans.[40]

But beyond their secrecy and complex metaphysical content – which really is not particularly remarkable when compared with other esoteric traditions – perhaps the most controversial aspect of the OT levels is simply their cost. According to price lists from 2009, the OT levels range from $2800 to $8400, which is on top of the thousands of dollars required to reach the preliminary state of Clear and the preparatory training required to begin the OT levels, not to mention the various additional costs such as books, videos, the latest E-meter[41] ($4600) and the cost of staying at facilities offering the OT courses, such as the Fort Harrison Hotel in Clearwater, Florida (rooms ranging from $150 to $15,000 a night). As such, conservative estimates suggest that a Scientologist hoping to reach Clear would spend a minimum of $128,000, while those attaining level OT VIII would invest a minimum of somewhere between $300,000 and $400,000 in the Church of Scientology.[42]

In part because of its growing wealth and influence, Scientology came under increasing (and often aggressive) scrutiny by various branches of the US government in the 1960s and 1970s. As early as 1963, the Food and Drug Administration (FDA) had begun to investigate the Church of Scientology, and finally raided its centre in Washington, DC, on the grounds that Scientology was making false claims about the benefits of its counselling device, the E-meter. Moving in with unmarked vans, a squad of FDA agents and US marshals confiscated more than three tonnes of materials, books, paper and E-meters.[43] In 1967, the IRS also began to investigate Scientology, stripping it of its tax-exempt status and claiming that it owed several million dollars in unpaid taxes. This in turn launched a massive legal war between the IRS and the Church that involved literally thousands of lawsuits and dragged on until the Church's victory in 1993.[44]

In response to this increasingly aggressive government surveillance, Scientology began to undertake its own elaborate tactics of counter-espionage and covert operations that almost rivalled those of the FBI. Indeed, in its obsession with secrecy and information control, Scientology was almost a kind of

---

40. See Urban, *The Church of Scientology*, chapter 3; Rothstein, "'His name was Xenu. He Used Renegades ...'".
41. The E-meter (or Electro-psychometer) is a kind of skin galvanometer that operates somewhat like a lie-detector.
42. Behar, "The Thriving Cult of Greed"; Urban, *The Church of Scientology*, chapter 4.
43. Miller, *Bare-Faced Messiah*, 247.
44. See Urban, "Fair Game".

strange mirror image of the FBI itself. More than one critic has noted that "the FBI was quite as paranoid about Hubbard as Hubbard was about the FBI".[45] Or as Ted Gunderson, the former head of the FBI's Los Angeles office, put it, "the Church has one of the most effective intelligence agencies in the US, rivalling even that of the FBI".[46] Formed in 1966 under the directorship of Hubbard's wife, Mary Sue, this agency became known as the Guardian's Office (GO) and operated in a variety of intelligence capacities until 1983 (currently, a new agency operates under the title of the Office of Special Affairs).

In the late 1960s, in order to respond in kind to his political and journalistic enemies, Hubbard also introduced an aggressive principle known as "fair game". Someone who was labelled fair game was an individual identified as a threat to the Church of Scientology, and who could therefore be harassed, threatened or punished using any and all means possible – indeed, "tricked, sued or lied to or destroyed".[47] At the same time, Hubbard also began using a process known as "Security Checks" on members of the Church itself in order to weed out any potential subversives within the organization. Members were hooked up to the E-meter and asked a series of sensitive questions about their loyalty to the Church, any secrets they might be keeping, and any possible connections they might have to Communism:

> Are you a pervert?
> Are you guilty of any major crimes in this lifetime?
> Are you or have you ever been a Communist?[48]

> Do you have a secret you are afraid I'll find out?
> Do you collect sexual objects? ...
> Have you ever had any unkind thoughts about L. Ron Hubbard or Scientology? ...
> Are you upset by this security check? [49]

> Do you hope you won't be found out?
> Do you think there is anything wrong with having your own privacy invaded?[50]

---

45. Miller, *Bare-Faced Messiah*, 198. See also Raine, "Surveillance in a New Religious Movement", 63–94.
46. Behar, "The Thriving Cult of Greed". It is worth noting that Gunderson gained a reputation as something of an occult conspiracy theorist in the years after he retired from the FBI. He publicly claimed that several high-profile deaths were caused by satanic cults, often alleging that high-level government officials were involved.
47. Hubbard, "Penalties for Lower Conditions".
48. Hubbard, "HGC Pre-Processing Security Check".
49. Hubbard, "The Only Valid Security Check".
50. Hubbard, "Auditor's Security Check". See Wallis, *The Road to Total Freedom*, 149; Urban, "Fair Game"; Raine, "Surveillance in a New Religious Movement".

Finally, and perhaps most audaciously, the Church of Scientology undertook efforts to infiltrate government agencies themselves in order to engage in covert operations. The most remarkable of these began in 1975, when the GO planted hidden microphones and undercover agents within the offices of the IRS itself in order to obtain and photocopy all of the service's vast files on Scientology. This was soon followed by a massive FBI raid – one of the largest in the Bureau's history – on the Scientology offices in Los Angeles and Washington, DC. Some 134 agents were involved in the raids, armed with crowbars, sledgehammers and battering rams. In July 1977, the FBI confiscated as many as 200,000 documents, along with eavesdropping equipment and burglary tools – so much material that it took a truck to haul it away.[51] Eleven Scientologists, including the GO head Jane Kember and Mary Sue Hubbard, were apprehended, tried, convicted and imprisoned; L. Ron himself was named as an unindicted co-conspirator, and then spent most of his remaining years in hiding until his death in 1986.[52]

In summary, the Church of Scientology not only developed a complex esoteric hierarchy of secret knowledge transmitted through the confidential OT levels, but, at the same time, the Church and the US government also became entangled in an extremely complex, often quite bizarre game of secrecy, surveillance, paranoia and counter-espionage that is in many ways the epitome of the larger obsession with secrecy in Cold War America.

SECRETS, SECURITY AND CYBERSPACE: BATTLES OVER ESOTERIC KNOWLEDGE IN A NEW AGE OF INFORMATION

Scientology's preoccupation with secrecy is by no means simply a relic of the Cold War era, however. Indeed, its concern with esoteric knowledge and control of information became in many ways even more intense in the 1990s amid the rise of new information technologies such as the Internet. Not long after the birth of the World Wide Web itself, the Church's most confidential Operating Thetan materials were leaked and soon began to circulate wildly in cyberspace, leading to a series of complex lawsuits and an array of aggressive measures designed to staunch the flow of esoteric information online. The backbone of the Church's war in cyberspace has been its Religious Technology Center (RTC), which describes itself as "the ultimate ecclesiastical authority regarding the standard and pure application of L. Ron Hubbard's religious technologies".[53] Since the 1990s, the RTC has been increasingly focused on policing the flow of information on the Internet, which has become one

---

51. Robinson, "Scientology Raid Yielded Alleged Burglary Tools", A13.
52. Sentencing Memorandum, *United States of America v. Jane Kember*, 20–21.
53. Religious Technology Center, "Mr David Miscavige".

of the most complex and apparently frustrating new challenges faced by the Church.[54]

At the same time, Scientology's wars of information in cyberspace have also raised a series of profound legal and ethical questions. On the one side, the Church has argued that its advanced tech materials are not only copyrighted and trade secrets but also confidential religious texts; disseminating these texts without permission, the Church has argued, is as offensive as stealing the esoteric teachings of Australian aboriginal cultures or other religious traditions.[55] On the other side, however, critics of the Church have argued that their right to disseminate these materials is *also* protected as free speech, and that revealing these materials is not only justifiable but a moral obligation so that the public can see what lies at the heart of this dangerous organization.[56]

Scientology's war in cyberspace is vast and complex, but for the sake of simplicity here I will mention just two of the more important cases, which developed around ex-Scientologists Larry Wollersheim and Stephen Fishman. Confidential OT materials were first introduced as evidence in court in November 1985 as part of a civil case brought against Wollersheim by the Church. A remarkably long and drawn-out ordeal, the Wollersheim suit had begun in 1980, and OT documents, including the confidential Xenu story, were eventually introduced as exhibits in the proceedings. Despite the fact that Scientology's attorneys argued that "disclosure of the materials is a violation of the group's religious freedom", the Los Angeles Superior Court judge ordered the documents to be made public at the clerk's office.[57] In response, some 1500 Scientologists crammed into the court buildings, swamping workers with hundreds of requests to photocopy the documents in an attempt to ensure that the materials were not made public. In spite of these remarkable efforts, however, the *Los Angeles Times* obtained copies of the OT materials and revealed them in an article in 1985.

In 1994 Wollersheim founded the website "Fight Against Coerce Tactics Network" (FACTNet), designed to expose Scientology's activities and provide support for ex-members. Having amassed some twenty-seven gigabytes of materials on Scientology, FACTNet was, not surprisingly, hit with intense legal threats. The Church's argument was that the confidential OT materials were both copyrighted and trade secrets, the disclosure of which could cause "irreparable spiritual injury if a rival church were allowed to disseminate them". In August 1995, a federal court ordered a raid on the homes of Wollersheim and another ex-Scientologist, led by two US Marshals and RTC representatives. This resulted in a the confiscation of all their computers and software,

---

54. Scientology.org, "What has been the Church's Role in Protecting Free Speech?".
55. Rothstein, "'His Name was Xenu. He Used Renegades ...'", 368.
56. Heldal-Lund, "What is Scientology?"
57. Sappel & Welkos, "Scientologists Block Access".

and dozens of boxes of files – and in turn sparked an intense debate on the Internet about copyright protections, trade secrets and free speech.[58] After intense legal debate, a settlement was reached in 1999, according to which FACTNet agreed to pay the Church $1 million if it was ever found guilty of violating Church copyrights.

A second major war online began at roughly the same time as the Wollersheim ordeal, as a result of the trial of another former Scientologist, Stephen Fishman. In 1990, Fishman was convicted of mail fraud, a crime that he claimed he had been brainwashed into committing in order to pay for his Scientology auditing. The Church sued Fishman for libel, and in the course of the trial Fishman submitted sixty-nine pages of confidential OT materials, including the Xenu story and secret documents all the way up to OT VIII.

The materials presented in the Fishman case are even more problematic than those from the Wollersheim suit. Among them is a text alleged to be one of Hubbard's own Church bulletins from 1980, and a key part of the topmost OT VIII materials. Labelled "confidential", the text makes a number of astonishing statements. Among others, it dismisses Jesus as a "lover of young boys" who was "given to uncontrollable bursts of temper and hatred"; more surprising still, it identifies Hubbard *both* as the future Buddha Maitreya *and* as Lucifer, the light-bringer and anti-Christ:

> The anti-Christ represents the forces of Lucifer (literally, the "light-bearer" or "light bringer"). My mission could be said to fulfill the Biblical promise represented by this brief Anti-Christ period. During this period there is a fleeting opportunity for the whole scenario to be effectively derailed, which would make it possible for the mass Marcabian landing (Second Coming) to take place.[59]

Interestingly enough, the RTC initially claimed copyright of all the OT materials in the affidavit – including this OT VIII text – but later amended its claim to exclude the OT materials, now arguing they are a forgery. At present the authenticity of the OT documents remains unclear. Regardless of their authenticity, however, the presence of these documents in cyberspace has encouraged the belief among many critics that Hubbard was in fact still immersed in the works of Aleister Crowley and continued to see himself in the lineage of the "Great Beast 666".

Copies of these materials were placed in a Los Angeles court file that was to be publicly available for two years. Again, Church members undertook a remarkable effort to maintain the documents' secrecy throughout this period by consistently checking out the files and keeping them until the clerk's office

---

58. See Prendergast, "Stalking the Net".
59. *Church of Scientology International v. Fishman.* No. CV. 91–6426. (C.D. Cal. 1994). Reproduced online at Spaink, "The Fishman Affidavit".

closed each day.⁶⁰ Even with these intensive measures, however, copies of the documents were made and soon found their way onto the Internet. In October 1994, they appeared on the newsgroup alt-religion.scientology, formed three years earlier in order to facilitate critical discussion of the Church. The real battle started, however, when a former high-ranking Scientologist named Dennis Erlich began to comment regularly on the site. In January 1995, attorneys from the RTC attempted to have alt-religion.scientology removed from the Internet, and then filed a massive lawsuit against Erlich for copyright violations.

Despite the Church's legal efforts, however, the Fishman affidavit along with all of the confidential OT materials reappeared on alt-religion.scientology in July 1995, and have since been reproduced and disseminated in multiple languages across the World Wide Web. Today, ironically, the Fishman papers are among the first things one encounters when beginning to explore information about Scientology online. As Wollersheim observes, the Fishman papers have now been "translated, encrypted, and hid just about anywhere you can imagine around the world ... [Scientology] tried to put out a fire with matches and gasoline".⁶¹

Moreover, the Church's legal and extra-legal wars in cyberspace have also continued into the twenty-first century. In 2002, lawyers representing the Church targeted Google, the web's most powerful search engine, demanding the removal of confidential Scientology materials – most notably, the secret OT materials – along with a list of allegedly infringing URLs (these demands have been only minimally successful).⁶² Far more audacious, however, was the Church's war against Wikipedia. In May 2009 Wikipedia's arbitration council voted 10–0 to ban any users coming from any IP addresses owned by the Church of Scientology or its associates. The landmark action was taken because the Church was found to have repeatedly and deceptively edited hundreds of articles related to the controversial religion, thus damaging Wikipedia's reputation for neutrality.⁶³

Finally, perhaps the Church's most formidable opponent in cyberspace has come from an unexpected source: the loose, decentralized network of Internet users known as "Anonymous". Less a coherent movement than a sort of complex, shifting and anarchic collective, Anonymous first began to target the Church of Scientology in January 2008 after the leak of a confidential video featuring Tom Cruise. The video in question is a nine-minute promotional interview, with Cruise talking about his intense commitment to Scientology and urging other Church members to commit themselves just as intensely.

---

60. Brill & Packard, "Silencing Scientology's Critics on the Internet", 9–10.
61. Prendergast, "Stalking the Net".
62. Sherman, "Google Airs Scientology Infringement Demand".
63. Singel, "Wikipedia Bans Church of Scientology".

The video was leaked to YouTube on 15 January 2008 – the same day that Andrew Morton's highly critical *Tom Cruise: An Unauthorized Biography* was released in bookstores worldwide. The video was viewed millions of times, and was apparently considered so embarrassing and so damaging that lawyers representing the Church and Cruise immediately demanded that it be removed. And so it was, but not before it had already spread virally to numerous sites throughout the Internet. Scientology's threats against YouTube became a powerful catalyst for the Anonymous collective, which saw this as a dangerous attack on free speech and the open flow of information online. Dubbed "Project Chanology" (from chan message boards), the new Anonymous initiative was aimed at fighting Scientology's intense information control with the anarchic powers of the Internet. Indeed, as one member of Anonymous put it, "The Internet is Serious Business", and Scientology immediately became a kind of icon for all the bullying corporate powers that try to squelch the free circulation of knowledge in cyberspace.[64] According to its own video "Message to Scientology" released in January 2008, Anonymous has determined that this organization

> should be destroyed. For the good of your followers, for the good of mankind, and for our own enjoyment, we shall proceed to expel you from the internet and systematically dismantle the Church of Scientology in its present form.[65]

Today, Anonymous makes sophisticated use of both virtual and physical tactics in its war against Scientology. Shortly after the conflict began in 2008, a distributed denial of service (DDOS) attack was launched against Scientology websites, temporarily shutting them down with high volumes of traffic.[66] A year later, in May 2009, a 19-year old New Jersey man pleaded guilty for his role in the attacks, identifying himself as a member of Anonymous.[67] More commonly, however, the Anonymous collective has relied on legal and (arguably more effective) cyber tactics. They make use of a wide array of websites to share guerrilla tactics and coordinate protests, including Encyclopedia Dramatica and Facebook, where their page had over 11,000 fans as of October 2010.

Anonymous's protests, however, have not been limited to cyber-attacks. The movement has been active worldwide, protesting physically outside Scientology churches across the globe, from Copenhagen to Clearwater, Florida and Columbus, Ohio. Members usually mask themselves, either with bandanas or, more often, with Guy Fawkes masks modelled on those in the

---

64. Landers, "Serious Business".
65. "Anonymous", "Message to Scientology".
66. In a DDOS attack, hackers use so many zombie computers to visit a site that the server overload becomes crippling and the site crashes.
67. Sarno, "Anonymous Hacker Pleads Guilty".

film *V for Vendetta*. Anonymous protestors typically carry an array of signs bearing slogans such as "Religion is free: Scientology is neither", "$cientology kills" and "Google 'Fair Game'". One of the more colourful protests even had a pirate theme and was an event called "Operation Sea Arrrgh" (a play on Scientology's elite inner group, the "Sea Org" or Sea Organization), highlighting their keen sense of irony and satire.[68]

Perhaps the most damaging aspect of Anonymous's war on Scientology, however, has simply been its decentralized but utterly pervasive ability to disseminate information – including the most esoteric OT materials and other confidential Church documents – wildly (and indeed infinitely) in cyberspace.[69] Despite the Church's myriad lawsuits and its ongoing wars with Anonymous and other enemies online, Scientology's most esoteric advanced technology continues to proliferate endlessly in the digital realm. As of December 2010, a simple Google search on "OT III" produced over 44,000 hits, while a search on "Xenu" produced over 700,000. Clearly, the Church is not winning its war of secrecy and knowledge control in cyberspace. Indeed, various observers have noted that the Internet may well prove to be "Scientology's Waterloo" – that is, a battle of information that it cannot realistically win.[70] As such, some critics are quite pessimistic about Scientology's ability to survive its new wars in the information age. As ex-Scientologist Gerry Armstrong commented in an interview with me in August 2009, he believes that this could well be "the last generation of Scientologists", since young people today grow up on the Internet, live increasingly in cyberspace and get all of their information online.[71] It is difficult, he thinks, to foresee great numbers of converts coming from a generation that has ready access not just to the secret OT levels on hundreds of websites, but also to countless YouTube videos and *South Park* clips that ridicule the beliefs and practices of Scientology.

As author and former Scientologist William S. Burroughs noted in 1978, well before the dawn of the Internet, "if the Scientologists persist in self-imposed isolation and in withholding their materials from those best qualified

---

68. McKee, "Taking it to the Streets".
69. It is worth noting that the Anonymous collective became involved in another major war over information control and free speech on the Internet in late 2010, this time inspired by the controversy surrounding the whistleblower website, Wikileaks. After its release of numerous US State Department diplomatic cables in November 2010, Wikileaks was widely criticized by various governments, and several financial corporations, including Visa, MasterCard and PayPal, suspended transactions with the organization. Seeing this as another profound threat to free speech and the flow of information online, members of Anonymous launched DDOS attacks on Visa, MasterCard, PayPal and, for good measure, Sarah Palin, temporarily shutting down their websites. As such, the Anonymous group continues to raise profound questions about the very nature of secrecy, knowledge and information control in the new public sphere of the Internet. See BBC, "Anonymous Hacktivists Say Wikileaks War to Continue".
70. Cook, "Cult Friction".
71. Telephone interview by author, 10 August 2009.

to evaluate ... them, they may well find themselves bypassed".[72] In the digital age, when even the most intense efforts of the RTC appear to be largely unsuccessful at staunching the relentless flow of information in cyberspace, Burroughs may well prove to be correct. As Hubbard himself remarked in 1954, "you cannot unveil the SECRET and have it ever be quite so secret again".[73]

CONCLUSIONS: THE DUAL NATURE OF SECRECY – ESOTERIC RELIGIONS IN AN AGE OF INFORMATION, SURVEILLANCE AND TERRORISM

Obviously, the role of secrecy and esoteric knowledge in the Church of Scientology is far too complex to cover in a whole book, much less a chapter. However, I have tried in these pages to highlight just a few of the more important examples of secrecy and information control in the Church over the last six decades, beginning with Hubbard's hagiographic mythology and continuing into twenty-first-century cyberspace. To conclude, I would like to suggest that the case of Scientology gives us profound insights not just into a controversial new religion, but also into much larger questions of religious secrecy and concealment over the last sixty years. Scientology is a particularly striking example of the fact that religious secrecy is rarely simply a matter of esoteric gnosis transmitted through isolated groups of initiates far removed from the messy social and political realm; on the contrary, religious secrecy is very often intimately entwined with larger cultural and historical forces, with struggles over power, and with very real material (as well as spiritual) interests. Above all, the case of Scientology highlights in excruciating detail what I call the dual nature of secrecy – its double role as both a source of symbolic power and a potential liability for its owner.

On the one hand, the increasingly esoteric levels of Hubbard's OT "advanced tech" clearly served as a kind of "adorning possession", in Simmel's sense – that is, a source of status, prestige and power that enhances one's character precisely by virtue of what it conceals. Or, to borrow a phrase from sociologist Pierre Bourdieu, secrecy can also serve as a form of "symbolic capital"; that is, a symbolic resource of distinction, honour and status that comes from possession of rare, highly valued esoteric knowledge.[74] Yet, on the other hand, secrecy can also be a profound liability for a religious group. By its very exclusivist nature, the practice of secrecy tends to arouse suspicion among dominant social and political powers, giving rise to all manner of fears: "Freemasons are running the country", "the Mau Mau are ready to revolt", and

---

72. Burroughs, *Ali's Smile*, 87.
73. Hubbard, *Dianetics 55*, 7.
74. See Urban, "Fair Game"; Bourdieu, "The Forms of Capital", 241–58.

so on. And this in turn brings new forms of government surveillance of groups who choose to keep aspects of their beliefs and practices secret.[75]

Scientology is a striking embodiment of both these aspects of secrecy – its power and its liability. Indeed, the Church soon found itself not just generating large amounts of income through its confidential advanced tech, but also quickly enmeshed in a complex war of surveillance, information control and espionage, both within its own ranks and with numerous government agencies, media outlets and online critics. The result has been an escalating, spiralling feedback loop of secrecy, esoteric knowledge, government scrutiny, media exposés, counter-espionage, and now all-out information warfare in the cyber-domain.

As such, the example of Scientology also has profound implications for the study of religions today, particularly in our own new age of religious secrecy, terrorism and government surveillance. As Michael Barkun notes in his study of secrecy and privacy after 9/11:

> [D]uring periods of social or political tension, religious secrets, real or imagined, take on a broader and more sinister importance, for they may be seen as evidence that a religious community has unsavory beliefs or behaviors that it must hide ... We entered such a period after the September 11, 2001, attacks.[76]

Today, we face a host of complex questions as to how to deal with secretive religious groups that might be engaged in subversive, dangerous and/or illegal activities. Do government agencies have a responsibility to use virtually any and all means at their disposal to monitor secretive groups and protect the public – including warrantless wiretapping, "sneak and peak searches", "enhanced interrogation" techniques, and other aggressive methods that were previously considered illegal? Or, conversely, are these highly invasive new measures in fact dangerous erosions of basic civil liberties and rights to privacy, reflecting what legal scholars David Cole and James Dempsey call a new "McCarthy-era philosophy"?[77] As Barkun asks, moreover, are such new forms of government surveillance ultimately counter productive, generating more fear and paranoia, and a "siege mentality", which leads to even more secrecy among marginalized religious groups?[78]

As such, the critical, historical study of religion and esotericism will probably have an increasingly vital role to play in the years to come.

---

75. Simmel, "The Secret and the Secret Society", 375; Tefft, *The Dialectics of Secret Society Power in States*. Cf. Chapter 10 of this volume for a discussion of conspiracy theories, in, about and *as* esoteric discourse.
76. Barkun, "Religion and Secrecy after September 11", 276.
77. Cole & Dempsey, *Terrorism and the Constitution*, 153.
78. Barkun, "Religion and Secrecy after September 11", 296.

CHAPTER 10

HIDDEN KNOWLEDGE, HIDDEN POWERS
ESOTERICISM AND CONSPIRACY CULTURE

Asbjørn Dyrendal

The relation between esotericism and conspiracy theory takes many forms. However, the scholarly literature has focused mainly on conspiracy theories *about* esoteric societies. This is understandable. Leafing through the literature of conspiracy culture one may often be struck by the prominence given to esoteric societies in these alternative versions of history. Many websites of conspiracy theory pay an enormous amount of attention to "occult" groups, some imaginary, others well known. Seemingly small and powerless societies like the Ordo Templi Orientis may be presented as the polar opposite. Societies long defunct according to academic historiography may be presented as driving forces in history, the crowning example being the Bavarian secret society Illuminati, theories about which have grown only more expansive since the order's demise in the 1780s.[1]

Such theories are often viewed as quaint expressions of fundamentalist outrage against unorthodox and largely unknown expressions of religion. They may, however, be related to more than fundamentalisms and become anything but quaint. Both recently, such as during the Satanism scare, and more distantly, in the aftermath of the French Revolution,[2] conspiratorial versions of history and society have acquired prominence. In such cases fear and outrage may reach the level of moral panic. These occasions of collective action have "mainstreamed" certain theories for a limited period of time, and have sparked both public and academic interest in conspiracy theories about esoteric societies. This is why we know so much, relatively speaking, about them.

Collective action and mainstreaming have been less prominent in a correspondingly less researched phenomenon: varieties of belief in, and use of, conspiracy theories *in* esoteric movements. But if "esotericism" is the construct of

---

1. See e.g. Sørensen, *Den Store Sammensvergelsen*.
2. E.g. John M. Roberts, *The Mythology of the Secret Societies*.

a "Grand Polemical Narrative"[3] we should, perhaps, consider that the polemical construction of otherness might be reciprocal.[4] Their common rejection by the mainstream may lead those defined as Other by a self-proclaimed orthodoxy to define their ties to each other and their emically constructed historical forebears as close.[5] They may also project a similar kind of otherness onto *their* preferred opponents, effectively demonizing the mainstream as much as any discourse of the more powerful.

That such polemical narratives may take the form of conspiracy theory has already been considered with regard to *some* examples from esoteric groups. The presence of anti-Semitic conspiracy theories in far-right esoteric movements is, for instance, well known.[6] Here, however, I will show further examples of conspiracy theory *in* esoteric societies, with three largely different usages; in anthroposophy, Satanism and Discordianism. As we shall see in these examples, conspiracy theories *about* secret, esoteric societies crop up even within the esoteric discourse on conspiracy.

It should come as no surprise that some "esotericists", when believing in conspiracies, may *also* ground them in esoteric discourse. We should perhaps try to delve deeper, into the less easily seen. So in order to assuage the thirst for esoteric knowledge, I shall attempt a tentative answer to a discussion I have had with one of the editors of the present volume: may conspiracy theories in themselves qualify for membership in contemporary esoteric discourse in any useful manner? Does relating them to each other help us understand anything better?

In order to delve into this issue, I look next at two examples of conspiracy discourse written by recognized spokespersons within conspiracy culture. To assist in the venture of examining whether conspiracy discourse itself is also usefully considered *as* esoteric discourse, I will look at the examples through the lens of three interrelated topics that follow closely on my chosen definitions of conspiracy theory and esoteric discourse (below): notions of *history, agency* and *knowledge*. The first topic raises questions related to conspiracy theories as apocalyptic mythologies of evil, and their construction of secret societies in history. Revealing secret history brings us to the nature of knowledge, how it is constructed and what its function is in these mythologies. Hidden knowledge about secret agents who are more effective than those seen, also brings in the question of agency, and how secret knowledge may make it more powerful. These topics should, hopefully, be a good starting point for considering conspiracy theories both *about* esoteric movements and *in* esoteric discourse, and

---

3. Hanegraaf, "Forbidden Knowledge".
4. E.g. Hammer, "Contested Diviners". This reciprocity is implied by Hanegraaff and others as well, but it is rarely explicitly addressed.
5. Cf. Barkun, *A Culture of Conspiracy*.
6. E.g. Goodrick-Clarke, *Black Sun*; Barkun, *Religion and the Racist Right*; Barkun, *A Culture of Conspiracy*.

a promising set of questions for reflecting on whether considering conspiracy theory *as* esoteric discourse is useful.

CONSPIRACY THEORY, CONSPIRACY CULTURE AND ESOTERICISM

Conspiracy theory is, in common parlance, a denigratory label indicating that a theory about the causes of an event or phenomenon, among other things, (i) involves a deliberate conspiracy, (ii) is fanciful and (iii) commits glaring errors of fact and/or reasoning. These connotations are so pervasive that they cannot be overlooked, so I shall instead make use of them. In this context, "conspiracy theory" is taken to mean theories involving consciously plotting cabals, theories that are, in regard to extant knowledge, fanciful, and which make use of what is, from an academic perspective, specious reasoning, factually unlikely, or simply wrong. The latter is also an implication of Michael Barkun's scheme of classifying conspiracy theories as "stigmatized knowledge".[7] Taken together, these elements focus on the notion of explicitly *intentional* agency in conspiracy theory, and on the importance of claims to hidden, "esoteric" knowledge stigmatized by mainstream society's "Grand Polemical Narratives" to hide the truth.

The consciously plotting cabal mark out what constitutes "conspiracy theory" from a broader family of narratives about hidden forces limiting human agency and subverting our quest for knowledge. This broader family is what is usually meant by "conspiracy culture".[8] In this article I subscribe to a narrower understanding of conspiracy culture to delimit the milieu and discourses surrounding conspiracy theorists understood as "spokespersons". I only rarely draw on narratives not involving deliberate conspiracy, and then only as background or comparison.

With regard to what may count as esoteric, I take a broad stance influenced by, among others, Kocku von Stuckrad's focus on "the esoteric" as discursive strategy[9] and Christopher Partridge's concept of occulture.[10] For the purposes here, I follow von Stuckrad's delimitation of esoteric discourse:

> What makes a discourse esoteric is the rhetoric of hidden truth, which can be unveiled in a specific way and established contrary to other interpretations of the universe and history – often that of the institutionalised majority.[11]

---

7. Barkun, *A Culture of Conspiracy*.
8. E.g. Knight, *Conspiracy Culture*; Knight, *Conspiracy Nation*.
9. E.g. von Stuckrad, *Western Esotericism*.
10. Partridge, *The Re-enchantment of the West*. See also Chapter 6 of this volume.
11. Von Stuckrad, *Western Esotericism*, 10.

We may note that by including opposition to "the institutionalised majority", this way of viewing esoteric discourse foreshadows the possibility that *reflected* polemical narratives may be used by those forced into the domain of rejected knowledge. As Wouter Hanegraaff notes with regard to the mainstream, identity construction depends on "simultaneously constructing an 'other' who represents whatever we do *not* want to be".[12] This works the other way around as well, and demonizing the "other" can strengthen identity when social bonds are loose.[13] When interest in content also overlaps, we may find a broader occulture in a more sociological sense of "amorphous networks"[14] clustering – at least for a while – around certain ideas. The ideas circulating in, from and to a broader "alternative" mainstream is what Partridge terms occulture: a "reservoir of ideas, beliefs, practices, and symbols"[15] related to "arcane and restricted knowledge"[16] from a broad spectrum of sources. Unlike Campbell's focus on a monist nature of the mystical religion he termed *the cultic milieu*, Partridge's occulture includes the dualist. The ideas constituting *dark* occulture, to which conspiracy theory belongs, are thus a phase of, or subscene within, the broader "occultic" milieu. As we shall see next, conspiracy thinking is also a far from uncommon element in esoteric discourse.

CONSPIRACY THEORY AMONG ESOTERIC SPOKESPERSONS

The examples below are drawn from three fairly different representatives of esoteric discourse, all of which are at least at one order removed from the right-wing esotericism most often tied to conspiracism: Rudolf Steiner and anthroposophy; Anton LaVey, founder of the Church of Satan; and the Discordian movement represented by *Principia Discordia* and the *Illuminatus!* trilogy. They differ: Steiner is an important and recognized representative of esoteric discourse; LaVey combines "secularized esotericism" with a less recognized "esotericized secularism";[17] and the Discordian movement is least easily placed, being perhaps the most unorganized representative of a "chaotic" stream within neopaganism. Discordianism started as a mock religion, and became more of a serious joke as it developed in many different directions.[18] It is the branch of chaotic thought where conspiracy theory is most prominent, albeit in a surprising manner resonating with several others.[19]

---

12. Hanegraaff, "Trouble with Images", 109.
13. See e.g. Dyrendal, "Sykdomsindustrien".
14. Partridge, *The Re-enchantment of the West*, vol. 1, 66.
15. *Ibid.*, 84.
16. *Ibid.*, 69.
17. See Petersen, "'We Demand Bedrock Knowledge'".
18. For a good introduction, see Cusack, *Invented Religions*.
19. Partridge's chapter in this volume shows that "esoterrorism" and related conceptualizations of art closely parallel ideas about agency and the use of conspiracy theory in Discordianism.

Rudolf Steiner and the materialist "vaccine conspiracy"

Like their forebears,[20] modern-day disciples of Rudolf Steiner vary widely in their opinions on a multitude of topics. This includes vaccination: While many anthroposophists follow ordinary vaccine programmes, others clearly do not, and Waldorf schools seem to have been the fulcrum of vaccine-preventable diseases more often than should be their due.[21] Some are generally negative towards vaccines and vaccine programmes. This seems to have been the case with anthroposophical doctor Philip Incao, a prominent promoter of alternative medicine and the author of a number of articles on vaccines. Writing for the anthroposophical journal *Gateways* in support of the anti-vaccine organization *National Vaccine Information Center*, he places his remarks within a generally vaccine-critical position, and posits a conspiracy theory he grounds in Steiner and anthroposophical cosmology: "Rudolf Steiner's comments ... leave no doubt about the 'hidden agenda' behind the plan to vaccinate all the world's children with as many vaccines as possible, thus devastating their spiritual development."[22]

There is a plan. It is secretive, destructive and directed against human agency by blocking children's spiritual development, thus barring them from freedom. Incao builds his theory by first finding fault with the scientific backing behind vaccines, misrepresenting along the way the state of research in standard conspiracist manner. Since he finds no good medical rationale behind vaccines, there must be another explanation for the implementation of vaccination programmes. This he finds by going to Steiner, which reveals to him a more sinister "hidden agenda" behind vaccines. Clearly disappointed in his fellow anthroposophists for their lack of interest or zeal with regard to anti-vaccination, he brings forward the appeal to what "der Doktor hat gesagt". What Steiner *did* have to say on the issue is more complicated. It is far from clear that it must be read as Incao does (indeed, it seems overly narrow), but we do see several instances where Steiner put forward varieties of the statement Incao quoted, and which puts the statement in context. In a Dornach lecture of October 1917, Steiner stated that:

> [W]hile human bodies will develop in such a way that certain spiritualities can find room in them, the materialistic bent, which will spread more and more under the guidance of the spirits of darkness, will work against this and combat it by physical means. I have told you that the spirits of darkness are going to inspire their human hosts, in whom they will be dwelling, to find a vaccine that

---

20. E.g. Zander, *Anthroposophie in Deutschland*.
21. Hoggendorf *et al.*, "Spotlight on Measles"; cf. Ernst, "Anthroposophy".
22. Incao, "Report on Vaccination".

will drive all inclination towards spirituality out of people's souls when they are still very young.[23]

This is an important attack on and threat towards human freedom and agency as understood by Steiner: to become a free and complete individual capable of moral imagination, humanity needs spirituality. What his esoteric vision tells him, is that the evil spiritual forces of different ages will by necessity work for a "vaccine" *against* the spiritual development of the age, and *for* a soul-killing materialism. Materialism as a cultural force may thus seem to be the central enemy, but through application of esoteric insight, it is revealed that it reflects deeper forces, and that a "vaccine" against spirituality will be the tool of evil (materialistic) spirits. They are just waiting for the right time and knowledge to put this plan into action. If we take Incao literally, he claims that mankind has now reached that stage and vaccines as a whole have become such a tool where, to use his own Steiner quotation, "Materialistic doctors will be entrusted with the task of driving souls out of human beings."[24]

How does Steiner know? He knows, of course, through his special, spiritual insight, which leaves him able to experience higher knowledge directly. To all of lesser abilities, it works as *declaration* about esoteric knowledge. This knowledge concerns power and agency, revealing a conspiracy against human freedom by evil spiritual forces that work through human beings, some of whom are organized in "secret brotherhoods".

In lecture three of the compilation *Secret Brotherhoods and the Mystery of the Human Double*, composed of seven lectures from 1917, Steiner recapitulates what is going on "behind the scenes of external events". He starts with a mystery: the "incomprehensible" murder of what he calls a noble woman. More accurately, although Steiner does not say so explicitly, it is about the murder of Empress Elisabeth of Bavaria (1837–98) by the anarchist Luigi Lucheni. In the materialist world, the murder may look "incomprehensible", as it did to people such as the theatre critic who was Steiner's interlocutor in the text.[25] Once seen through the lens of esoteric insight, however, it is all made sensible: spiritually inclined people, Steiner reveals, will now develop towards something belonging to the "sixth post-Atlantean age". These will be less interested in "matters of the physical plane", leaving more earthly power to those less spiritually inclined.[26] Put another way, the very vision of human development towards freedom by spiritual development, is threatened because spiritual development leaves those of higher knowledge less interested in material, political agency. By default, this leaves influence in earthly affairs, including the power to hinder spirituality (thus freedom and agency), vulnerable for

---

23. Steiner, "Fall of the Spirits of Darkness, Lecture 13".
24. Steiner, quoted in Incao, "Report on Vaccination".
25. Steiner, *Secret Brotherhoods*, 77.
26. *Ibid.*, 81.

appropriation by powers of evil. "Secret brotherhoods" of occultists are of the latter kind. Since they are probably possessed and greedy for knowledge and power, they have been killing people, seemingly wantonly. Why? Because, Steiner tells us, the souls of those killed may be used to gather knowledge and power, and transmitted from the dead through trained mediums.[27]

What relates this theory of assassination by occultists for evil, esoteric purposes to vaccination? Both are related through the underlying forces at work in time: "During the fifth post-Atlantean epoch the human being's physical apparatus for thinking will become mature enough to comprehend fully certain elements of disease, certain processes of healing, and connections between natural processes and diseases."[28] This knowledge may be used for good or for ill, and must be brought about in its right time. The purposes of the conspiracy are of course other; "to get those secrets into one's clutches for the purposes of turning in a certain direction that have to do with processes of disease, and also of procreation".[29] The secret knowledge of a "vaccine" against spirituality thus seems one of the goals of assassinations, and the secret societies seek it to promote their goal of power. Materialism is one part of a ploy for power, and it will express itself as a determined attempt at rooting out spiritual inclination. It will do so in a fairly radical manner,

> by bringing out remedies to be administered by inoculation, just as inoculations have been developed as a protection against diseases, only these inoculations will influence the human body in a way that will make it refuse to give a home to the spiritual inclinations of the soul.[30]

Thus the apparently random is made to make sense: secret ways of knowledge reveal the secret brotherhoods, the evil spirits influencing them, the deeper tendencies of the time, and their connection to minute details of history. The topic of threats towards spiritual agency and human freedom, framed in Steiner's anthroposophy, is an undercurrent through it all. But we may note that although "inoculations" are mentioned as part of the materialist conspiracy of evil powers, Steiner clearly differentiates between existing vaccines against diseases, and those to come, which will be against the spirit. The conflation made by Incao is easily understandable from many other uses Steiner made of the same trope, but it is produced by later interpretation. That is not the case with our next example.

---

27. Ibid., 85–89.
28. Ibid., 82.
29. Ibid., 90.
30. Ibid., 91.

Anton LaVey and the invisible war

Anton LaVey loathed consumerism and conformism. The reasons concerned agency and freedom. Echoing a tradition from nineteenth-century occultism's discouragement against leaving one's will in the hand of others (e.g. mesmerists), he said that a Satanist "should not allow himself to be programmed by others".[31] Indeed, a true Satanist is a doer and "must be responsible for reaction and change",[32] rather than being the one who reacts to and is being changed by others. He abhorred "the masses", and presented conspiracy theory as myth-making for the masses. As myths they are necessary, "for they are essential to man's emotional needs".[33] That is, they are necessary to the kind of man who is not a born Satanist. Yet LaVey clearly involved himself in conspiracy theory.[34]

According to the ideology LaVey presents in *The Satanic Bible*, the strong rule by nature. So how did Christianity, which he deemed a religion of the weak, ascend to power in the Western world? How did the "herd" of weaklings pull down the strong, push them to the side, and make "slave morality" the law of society? Throughout his writings, but especially in *The Satanic Bible* and other early texts, we find religion in the role of subjugating humans. This comes complete with the conspiracy theorist's notion of deliberate, conscious agency behind the function. For instance, on the sinfulness of sex: "In order to insure the propagation of humanity, nature made lust the second most powerful instinct, the first being self-preservation. Realizing this, the Christian Church made fornication the 'Original Sin'."[35] This sorry state of affairs is the result of manipulation by priestcraft, a conspiracy by the Christian cabal: "The religionists have kept their followers in line by suppressing their egos."[36] This is why Satan is "the best friend the church has ever had".[37] The threat of damnation combined with suppression of natural tendencies manipulates their followers – and the result is the rule of the weak and the suppression of vital life.

This may look like any of a myriad of tales of a fight between powers of evil and good in history, with darkness and light inverted towards a preference for the material and self-related. It is that as well, but in a secularized version of esoteric discourse, the secular *text* was itself "Magus" LaVey's most powerful form of magic. It is also a conscious use of history as mythology of the evils of "spiritual" religion; LaVey's tale of the history of repression should also be read as an evocation, a call for a change of attitudes, for driving back harmful, life-denying influences and taking control of vital life. Thus also his continued use

---

31. LaVey, *The Devil's Notebook*, 63.
32. *Ibid.*
33. *Ibid.*, 108.
34. See Dyrendal, "Hidden Persuaders and Invisible Wars".
35. LaVey, *The Satanic Bible*, 47.
36. *Ibid.*, 94.
37. *Ibid.*, 25.

of "secret history", where LaVey marshals the rhetorical powers of simplistic Christianity and turns it on its head:

> [I]f the love of money is the root of all evil; then we must at least assume the most powerful men on earth to be the most Satanic. This applies to financiers, industrialists, popes, poets, dictators, and all assorted opinion-makers and field marshals of the world's activities.[38]

Satanism was a marginal, newly formed anti-religion, but he had it acquire a powerful legacy by route of this imaginative feat:

> Occasionally, through "leakages," one of the enigmatic men or women of earth will be found to have "dabbled" in the black arts. These, of course, are brought to light as the "mystery men" of history. Names like Rasputin, Zaharoff, Cagliostro, Rosenberg and their ilk are links – clues, so to speak, of the true legacy of Satan … a legacy which transcends ethnic, racial and economic differences and temporal ideologies, as well. The Satanist has always ruled the earth … and always will, by whatever name he is called.[39]

In constructing a "true" lineage of Satanism LaVey mirrors and reinvents conspiracy culture's lore: the powerful truly *are* Satanists.[40] That is, however, a *good* thing. Living life by satanic stratagems brings you success, and also makes life richer.

However, there is a dark side: If effective "black magic" works for Satanists, then it works for anyone. That includes those who create culture and religion for the masses. A true Satanist must avoid "the colorless existence of others",[41] but corporate interest and other forces are trying to mould everyone into mindless consumers and worse. This is "the invisible war":

> The skirmishes take place in the region of one's own mind. The less one is aware of the invisible war, the more receptive one is to its ongoing process of demoralization, for the insensate human is vulnerable, malleable and ripe for control.[42]

It is fought "with technologically advanced chemical and electromagnetic weapons, crowd control, weather control and misdirection to mask the entire

---

38. *Ibid.*, 104.
39. *Ibid.*
40. On this subject of "de facto Satanists", see Chapter 4 of the present volume.
41. LaVey, *Devil's Notebook*, 63.
42. LaVey, "The Invisible War", 163.

operation".[43] Subliminal messages and other hidden control measures attempt to deprive everyone of that "wondrous, unique experience"[44] life should be. Satanists should use their insight and "materialist magic" to make their own subliminals instead, thus avoiding unwanted influences.

This is no joke, but neither is it completely serious.[45] LaVey *plays* with the contents as well as the form of conspiracy theory, at times communicating a tongue-in-cheek attitude towards belief, mocking what he deems excesses. But LaVey's play with conspiracy theory may also be seen to follow quite logically from, and relate strongly to, his conceptions of magic and agency. His magical postulate that recipients of spells are most receptive while sleeping,[46] for instance, is mirrored by his arguments that "subliminals" work best while the recipient is asleep.[47]

How does LaVey know all this? Related to the element of play, we should not be at all certain that he *always* claims to know when he states something as fact. Some statements are mockery, some balance on the metaphorical. But largely – and although he frames Satanism as a religion demanding study, not worship, and the satanic mindset as one that asks questions – his style does not encourage doubt or deliberative reason. LaVey often leans toward the categorical statement or surprising observation, but tends to encourage little in the way of argument. We saw one example above, formulated as a seemingly argumentative "if-then" statement: "if the love of money is the root of all evil; then we must at least assume the most powerful men on earth to be the most Satanic".[48] In practice, this is a simple way of getting to a historically linked conclusion by way of common morality discourse instead of through historical research. LaVey rarely appeals directly to academic research. More often, he appeals in some way to his own, grounded, bodily experience. As noted by Jesper Petersen, LaVey may appeal to science and reason, but "[i]n essence, it is the experience of practical application or *experiential authority* that undergirds LaVeyan scientism – science is true because it resonates with satanic reasoning".[49] LaVey knows because it works: he, like Steiner, has *experienced* it. But often even this element of grounding is missing and we are left with the statement as revelation. The conspiracy against human agency may work along the principles of black magic, but the connection is not made explicit through argument.[50] He declares and concludes. Filling in the gaps is for the reader, who may, on closer reading, find seemingly simple statements to be ambiguous, playful and sardonic.

---

43. Barton, *The Secret Life of a Satanist*, 83.
44. LaVey, *Devil's Notebook*, 63.
45. See Dyrendal, "Hidden Persuaders".
46. LaVey, *The Satanic Bible*, 122.
47. LaVey, *Satan Speaks!*, 80.
48. LaVey, *The Satanic Bible*, 104.
49. Petersen, "'We Demand Bedrock Knowledge'", 85.
50. Most clearly in LaVey, "Invisible War".

"Seeing the fnords": conspiracy theory and guerrilla enlightenment in Discordianism

If LaVey indulged in play with conspiracy theory more or less tongue-in-cheek, Discordian play with conspiracy is both more and less serious. Less, because in Discordian writing anything and everything is doubtful and laughable; more, because conspiracy theory has for that very reason become an important part of Discordianism as a *religious* path.

Discordianism started as a mock religion around 1957, with *Principia Discordia* as an anarchic, mock scripture devoted to Eris, the goddess of chaos. It evolved in several stages, always keeping the anti-authoritarian elements of "humour, mockery and parody".[51] These are also important to the Discordian uses of conspiracy theory, which often cluster around secret societies, more particularly the mythology about the Bavarian Illuminati.

It starts already in the chaotic founding text, *Principia Discordia*, which includes an "advert" for the "Bavarian Illuminati":

> Founded by Hassan i Sabbah, 1090 AD (5090 AL, 4850 AM)
> Reformed by Adam Weishaupt, 1776 AD (5776 AL, 5536 AM)
>
> THE ANCIENT ILLUMINATED SEERS OF BAVARIA
>
> invite YOU to join
>
> The World's Oldest and Most Successful Conspiracy[52]

The chapter is, appropriately, called "The Epistle to the Paranoid", and the "advert" is a play on the style and content of similar advertisements for conspiracy literature. The mythological founding in the advert, pushing the foundation of the Illuminati back almost 700 years to Hassan i Sabbah, is quickly transcended on the following pages when we are thrown further back – to Atlantis and beyond.[53]

In the tradition of both esoteric societies' emic historiographies and conspiracy theories, the historical genealogy of the *true* Illuminati is unmasked as a chain through more of known (and unknown) history than most suspect. The "knowledge" presented is, however, as part of "nonsense as salvation"[54] partly contradicted, partly transcended by giving conflicting information. This strategy becomes even more central to Discordianism through the publication of Robert Shea and Robert Anton Wilson's *Illuminatus!* trilogy.[55] There we find the Illuminati to be all of, and anything but, what is generally assumed

---

51. Cusack, *Invented Religions*, 27.
52. Hill & Thornley, *Principia Discordia*, 70.
53. *Ibid.*, 72.
54. *Ibid.*, 74.
55. Shea & Wilson, *The Illuminatus! Trilogy*.

by historians, esoteric societies, and conspiracy theorists alike. The Illuminati *seems* the authoritarian, secret cabal behind the New World Order (NWO), but in reality "employs a totally different, laissez-faire (and Taoist) agenda."[56] In style with superconspiracies in general, *Illuminatus!* has the antagonists play both sides of an issue, infiltrating each other and making chaos. Of course, the Illuminati are made to have played their role in secret assassinations and plots that have shaped history. This includes "alternative" history, from Atlantis forward, but always with a twist, following a narrative style that consciously disorients the reader by frequently switching points of view, time, narrators, and what is presented as truthful.

The chaos is there to enlighten the reader. By creating confusion, casting doubt and uncertainty on everything, the reader is treated to a narrative "mindfuck" – a strategy for disrupting an established sense of reality related to "esoterrorism"[57] – forcing the reader to question what is real. This may allow the reader to glance the *fnords*, the hidden, fear-inducing words, topics, objects and so on that the authors tell us we are programmed to ignore. Through the right "initiation" we may, like the character George Dorn, become able to notice them:

> Then I saw the fnords.
> The feature story involved another of the endless squabbles between Russia and the U.S. in the UN General Assembly, and after each direct quote from the Russian delegate I read a quite distinct "Fnord!" The second lead was about a debate in Congress on getting the troops out of Costa Rica; every argument presented by Senator Bacon was followed by another "Fnord!" At the bottom of the page was a *Times* depth-type study of the growing pollution problem and the increasing use of gas masks among New Yorkers; the most distressing chemical facts were interpolated with more "Fnords."
> Suddenly I saw Hagbard's eyes burning into me and heard his voice: "Your heart will remain calm. Your adrenalin gland will remain calm. Calm, all-over calm. You will not panic. You will look at the fnord and see it. You will not evade it or black it out. You will stay calm and face it." And further back, way back: my first-grade teacher writing FNORD on the blackboard, while a wheel with a spiral design turned and turned on his desk, turned and turned, and his voice droned on,
> IF YOU DON'T SEE THE FNORD IT CAN'T EAT YOU, DON'T SEE THE FNORD, DON'T SEE THE FNORD …
> I looked back at the paper and still saw the fnords.[58]

---

56. LiBrizzi, "The Illuminatus! Trilogy", 340.
57. See Chapter 6 of this volume.
58. Shea & Wilson, *The Illuminatus! Trilogy*, 438.

Fnords are programmed to spread a low-grade fear making people eager to believe, and easy to control and manipulate. Fnords continue and develop the popular literary and political conspiracy theme of "brainwashing"[59] related to foreign power, government, and consumer society alike. Stealing people's autonomy with fear, the only avenue left for release is consumerism:

> Then I got a hunch, and turned quickly to the advertisements. It was as I expected: no fnords. That was part of the gimmick, too: only in consumption, endless consumption, could they escape the amorphous threat of the invisible fnords.[60]

Fnords hinder agency and promote mindless consumerism. But that is just a small countercultural element to the use of conspiracy theory in Discordianism. To some it may be important, but the confusing and complex plots, the humour and the mock academic elements are perhaps the more existentially essential element of how conspiracy theory is used: Through Discordian use, and particularly in the *Illuminatus!* trilogy, conspiracy theory functions as a deliberate "mind virus" to disrupt the reader's ordinary cognitive system. It becomes, in keeping with founder Kerry Thornley's vision of Discordianism as "an American form of Zen Buddhism",[61] a kind of absurd *koan*, taking rationality to extremes of paradox where every claim to knowledge collapses in on itself. In this way conspiracy theories become a form of "guerrilla enlightenment"-tactic, generating doubt to promote the laughter of sudden, sublime insight.[62]

CONSPIRACY CULTURE: DAVID ICKE AND JIM MARRS

The examples above show how some esoteric spokespersons have used conspiracy theory with regard to history, agency and knowledge. It works partly as a mythology of evil, making sense of history by revealing secrets about how the world works. The claims to knowledge have different qualities, from certain truth to complete doubt. Knowledge about the hidden conspiracy plays, in limited parallel to esoteric "gnosis", different roles in "salvation", but it is always a guide to action: from *understanding* the deeper issues and agents of our time, through purely personal protection, to deliberate chaos and the collapse of ontology as a way to enlightenment.

In the next section we shall have a look at some of the same issues with spokespersons for the most explicit part of conspiracy culture: conspiracy

---

59. E.g. Seed, *Brainwashing*.
60. Shea & Wilson, *The Illuminatus! Trilogy*, 439.
61. Cf. discussion in Cusack, *Invented Religions*.
62. *Ibid.*; cf. LiBrizzi, "The Illuminatus! Trilogy".

theorists making their living as such. As with the examples above, I have chosen from both the explicitly spiritual and the more secular side. While Jim Marrs starts from a basis of "event conspiracies" (the assassination of John F. Kennedy) and holds a more or less consistent secular basis for his thinking throughout his texts, David Icke is explicitly "spiritual" and anti-materialist in his mode of argument. There are reasons to consider both. The spiritual conspiracy theorists are numerous and we should not underplay the explicit connection. Considering the "secular" conspiracy theorists helps make sure that we are not merely comparing the same kind of apples.

David Icke and Babylonian reptiles from the fourth dimension

David Icke is one of the brightest stars on the occultural conspiracy scene, but controversial among some circles of conspiracy theorists, partly for his explicitly spiritual side, and partly for anchoring his conspiracy in shapeshifting reptiles. Sharing the general occultural critique of Christianity and organized religions, and framing the critique as a history of hidden plots, Icke favours an ontology with hidden "dimensions", levels of existence, materiality and spiritual existence beyond bodily death. Indeed, all of these general "New Age" topics are vital to his mode of argument when revealing the truth behind the "Babylonian Brotherhood".

Icke's books are crammed with alternative history, including alternative histories about religion. They serve as narrative critiques of politics and religion, grounding the criticism in a genealogy of the powerful: the secret societies, practices and ideas he criticizes are all attributed to a hybrid reptile–human bloodline from, among other places, "the lower fourth dimension".[63] These alien reptiles created religions like Christianity and Islam as tools for their own "Babylonian Brotherhood":

> Judaism, Christianity and Islam all base their beliefs on these same stories written by the Levites after their stay in Babylon. We are looking at a point in history which was to define and control the world from then until now. ... The Cabala is the esoteric stream of what is called Judaism, which is in fact a front for the Babylonian Brotherhood, as is the Vatican.[64]

This exemplifies a typical epistemological strategy: listing names combined with brief narratives of their hidden connections and their meaning, so that initiates may awaken to knowledge and be free. Here, esoteric societies and

---

63. E.g. Icke, *The Biggest Secret*, 26.
64. *Ibid.*, 84.

mainstream religions both carry the seal of the alien, draconian beasts. Icke effortlessly constructs correspondences (and substantive identity) between symbols and actors across time, culture, and political and religious identities. They all derive from the same source and have the same purpose: "casting a spell on the human mind and emotions" in order to destroy human understanding of "who we really are" – part of an energetic, divine whole with "no us and them, only we and ultimately 'I'".[65]

Even the reptilians are, in the final meaning, part of this "I", so why do they destroy this understanding? At the more limited level of being where separateness exists, they are obsessed with power:

> Humans who understand their true nature, power and worth would be impossible to manipulate … Only by delinking humanity from this knowledge has it been possible to orchestrate the reptilian-Brotherhood Agenda over thousands of years. The creation of religion and official "science" has been fundamental to that and … the same secret societies were responsible for establishing both.[66]

Fear is essential to how the reptilians control humans. This is part of the explanation, claims Icke, for the assassinations of John F. Kennedy, Princess Diana, and others.[67] It is also part of the explanation for war and crises. To create the strongest possible negative feelings associated with fear and guilt, so that it may dominate consciousness, "the Brotherhood use horrific Satanic rituals and sacrifice".[68] Initiates into their order are forced to participate in these rituals to ascertain their synchronization into "the reptilian wavelengths". More broadly, the construction of fear is said to stimulate the kind of society and behaviour the reptilians desire, and to do so through "vibrational patterns" leaving traces in our DNA. As if that was not sufficient, the reptilians are also claimed to work their mind control through technology, including "implants" of thought control devices.[69] These are, again, part of the plan to take control of human agency so that it is locked to a fearful existence on this plane of being. A preparation for this, recalling Steiner and his modern disciple, is the weakening of the mind–body through vaccines, which have been a tool of keeping mankind ill and functioning below par, and an important development in getting "access keys to the body-computer".[70] The function is similar to that promised by Steiner and his more anti-vaccine followers, in that it works both against bodily and spiritual health.

---

65. *Ibid.*, 472.
66. *Ibid.*, 472–3.
67. *Ibid.*, 478.
68. *Ibid.*, 474.
69. Icke, *The David Icke Guide*, 391–4.
70. *Ibid.*, 547.

Icke's style is declarative. He presents his claims to knowledge as statements of fact, and he uses the gamut of "New Age" validations of knowledge,[71] from personal experience and testimonials to science. He stresses the latter in the form of his own "research" with supportive testimonials as "independent confirmation", whether through others' research, channelling, or allegedly autobiographical information. Outside "research" is selected to support his own theses, and it is narrated within the story Icke wants to tell. Much of his writing consists of retelling other "rejected knowledge", repackaged to suit his own theories. In addition to strategies that at times parallel or serve as secularized versions of esoteric knowledge-strategies, Icke also employs "traditional" esoteric ones. "The Cabala", he writes, "is the secret knowledge hidden in codes within the Old Testament and other texts", and the sacred texts of "all the religions" are written in such code.[72] They all contain secret knowledge to be revealed. He goes on to reveal true names and "their true meaning". Similarly, he decodes the "true meaning" of colours, numbers and symbols, where similarity is made into identity across time and space. Everything concerns deeper truths and higher knowledge, hidden by esoteric elites and "hidden in the code of the mystery schools".[73]

Although standing in clear continuity with the broader "New Age" milieu, Icke is a critical member. He sees New Age as being ignorant of the dark, reptilian forces, calling it "spirituality as escapism".[74] Still, the solutions and the salvific messages are in line with the milieu: We may be programmed and controlled *intellectually*, but our emotions and intuition, as long as they are guided by love, not fear, will set us straight – and free:

> You think with your intellect and that is so vulnerable to programming through the eyes and ears by the daily diet of lies, suppression and misrepresentation in the media and by all those Brotherhood clones to which it offers a platform. But when we *feel*, we are tapping into our heart centre, our intuition, that connection with the cosmos.[75]

Intuition is a way to knowledge more certain than what the intellect can provide alone. When Icke states that "the truth shall make you free",[76] it is a truth where feeling and rationality are reintegrated and set to work by "healing" through love.[77] For this to happen, Icke's own texts and the conspiracy lore he presents are a necessary step.

---

71. See e.g. Hammer, *Claiming Knowledge*.
72. Icke, *The Biggest Secret*, 84.
73. *Ibid.*, 85.
74. *Ibid.*, 486.
75. *Ibid.*, 502.
76. E.g. Icke, *... And the Truth Shall Set you Free*.
77. Icke, *The Biggest Secret*, 504.

Jim Marrs and the rule of secrecy

Denial of accidents *in toto* is one of the traits often used for describing "grand conspiracy". Conspiracy lies at the heart of history and how one views it, writes Jim Marrs, now one of the veterans in conspiracy theory: "Here there are only two views: accidental or conspiratorial."[78]

Starting out from "event conspiracies" like the John F. Kennedy assassination, Marrs broadened out to "UFO cover-ups" and extraterrestrial presence, and more comprehensive theories encompassing the totality of history (and some prehistory). Literature theorist Samuel Chase Coale called his *Rule by Secrecy* "the quintessential text that reveals the ultimate vision of conspiracy of the era ... the Bible of conspiracy".[79] Although many other writers and texts vie for the title, Marrs does have prominence similar to Icke.

Marrs's texts belong to the secular side of conspiracy culture. Not in the sense of pressing an explicitly secular agenda, but in the sense that he, unlike many other writers of "grand conspiracy", does not present an explicitly religious agenda of his own. While he sometimes, and mostly in the "final perspective", includes extraterrestrials and "the alien agenda"[80] into the picture, what might have been explicitly religious overtones are secularized. Unlike with Icke, there is no talk about soul, spiritual development, or salvation from anything but an oppressive conspiracy and their evil plan. They may at times be called "satanic" or alleged to be Satanists, but he attributes no supernatural abilities to them. Nor are there explicit references to supernatural modes of acquiring knowledge, although such were employed by some of the "research" he relies on.

Marrs's main interest lies in the influence of "secret societies" on economics and politics.[81] These are the main areas where he sees the limitation of human freedom, and where the abuse of power by the conspiracy interferes deeply with the lives of people. They do so, for instance, through the production of wars and economic crises, both of which spread anxiety, fear and misery, leaving more control in the hands of the conspirators. Economic matters acquire a special importance for "thought control": not only are the media generally *owned* by the conspiracy, their revenues *controlled* by big business, but – by listing a set of prominent media figures as "members of" the Bilderberg group, Council on Foreign Relations, or the Trilateral Commission – he includes them as pawns of "NWO" or worse.[82] This is why "we" are not informed of the nefarious plans of these groups, and how "we" are kept passive. In addition

---

78. Marrs, *Rule by Secrecy*, 6.
79. Coale, *Paradigms of Paranoia*, 22.
80. Marrs, *Alien Agenda*.
81. Bankers are also presented as a secret society (Marrs, *Rule by Secrecy*, 77), and the economy likened to religion.
82. Marrs, *Rule by Secrecy*, 105.

there are other methods of more literal mind control, which Marrs relates to the heritage from Nazi scientists, through CIA experiments, and beyond. He mainly presents these techniques as being used on a few individuals rather than on whole populations,[83] but there is one exception ringing of Cold War fears. This is when he presents the fluoridation of water as part of the Nazi heritage of mind control, and alleges that "sodium fluoride was placed in the drinking water of Nazi concentration camps to keep inmates pacified and susceptible to external control".[84] Since he also alleges that fluoridation gives people cancer and other life-threatening diseases, it becomes a general threat.

While Marrs's main interest may lie with politics and economy as elements of limiting the free agency of the ordinary citizen, this does not preclude a very distinct interest in religion. Marrs, like Icke, devotes quite a lot of space to presenting alternative histories of religion. Like Icke, he follows "New Age" versions that repackage the Judaeo-Christian tradition as something quite different from how it is usually understood. But more than anything, he holds a continued interest in secret societies and, like Icke, sees a "Babylonian" heritage behind the current world conspiracy. This includes, as one might expect, the involvement of secret societies in greater and lesser event conspiracies. For instance, "World War II was largely the result of infighting between secret occult societies composed of wealthy businessmen on both sides of the Atlantic."[85] Although each event is traced to particular causes, they share a general trait: "The imprint of secret societies can be found in every war and conflict of the twentieth century."[86]

Like the Discordian pranksters, Marrs is enamoured with the Illuminati. So is an enormous amount of conspiracy culture, and like some of it, Marrs takes the "information" presented in the *Illuminatus!* trilogy at face value. He buys into their fake sources and historiography, for instance attributing to the historical Illuminati the prescience and/or influence to coin "flower power" (in the form "Ewige Blumenkraft") as slogan. When tracing their prehistory, however, he stops at a lineage back to "the infamous Muslim Assassins",[87] while its *present* history is connected to "the Round Tables of Mason Cecil Rhodes … the Royal Institute of International Affairs, Council of Foreign Relations, the Trilateral Commission"[88] – in short, all the usual suspects. As with Icke and other (il)luminaries of conspiracy culture, Marrs is interested in the "bloodlines" of this hidden elite, tracing their genealogical descent as well as their ideas and (abuse of) power through history. He finds that "[t]he world's deepest secrets all lead back to Sumer in Mesopotamia, the first known great

---

83. E.g. Marrs, *The Rise of the Fourth Reich*, 346–8.
84. *Ibid.*, 329.
85. *Ibid.*, 305.
86. Marrs, *Rule by Secrecy*, 200.
87. *Ibid.*, 237.
88. *Ibid.*, 109.

civilization".[89] Why them, why there? It was a prime, first site of extraterrestrial operations on earth, explains Marrs, seeking this space because it combined water, fuel and moderate weather.[90]

The historical narrative of *Rule by Secrecy* is jumbled. The origin with the extraterrestrial "Annunaki" is presented as a climax at the end of the book. Every chapter in itself deals with single strands of historical claims that may or may not be dealt with or linked to in other chapters. Continuity is underdeveloped. This may be the narrator's choice, but it also points towards the way his knowledge-claims are developed in the text. "There is no guarantee", he starts out with what seems a massive understatement, "that all of the information presented here is absolute ground truth."[91] With a powerful conspiracy trying to suppress knowledge and supply misleading evidence, anything is doubtful.[92] As is common to grand conspiracy, this is not a call for extra careful consideration of sources of information. Instead it serves to make the case for a liberal, more "esoteric" approach to the production of knowledge. The doubt and uncertainty presented at the outset is rarely seen again.

How then is knowledge produced? Two of the central strategies could be called innuendo and superficial resemblance. Coale comments that "Marrs weaves his web of guilt by association",[93] and all of the elements are important. Lists, names and connections produce hidden meanings. The links may be personal, or they may relate to ideas, with the latter being constructed as proof of personal contact. When important people need to be associated, the text may for instance delineate the possible links between degrees of separation. This results in a maze of small narratives about association. Similarity is often conferred on the basis of the conspiracy lore and alternative histories the theorist depends on. Such similarities may, as with Icke, be used to bridge even longer historical spans and conflate demonized enemies in conspiracy lore. A relatively short time span, with a useful gallery of persons, is bridged like this, for example:

> Marx's manifesto set forth the ten immediate steps to create an ideal communist state. They bear a striking similarity to the *Protocols of the Learned Elders of Zion*, suggesting some common origin. ... This list was also remarkably similar to the steps for creating an ideal society proposed by the Bavarian Illuminati, strongly indicating a close connection between the two.[94]

---

89. *Ibid.*, 374.
90. *Ibid.*, 381.
91. *Ibid.*, 17.
92. *Ibid.*
93. Coale, *Paradigms of Paranoia*, 23.
94. Marrs, *Rule by Secrecy*, 199.

Since the conspiracy is a web of relations, and everything is shrouded in secrets, the proof is in the linking. When the link may be made, it serves as proof. These forms of link may take the form of correspondences less intelligible to anyone versed in the requisite area of knowledge:

> The famous Egyptian Book of the dead, in a passage containing a confession to the "Lord of Righteousness", reveals a remarkable correlation to the Ten Commandments of the Old Testament.
>
> | Bible | Book of the Dead |
> |---|---|
> | Have no other gods before me | I do not temper with divine balance |
> | Make no idols | I stop not a god when he comes forth |
> | Do not misuse the name of God | I do not offend the god who is at the helm |
>
> ...
>
> This comparison provided compelling support for those who claim that the biblical Israelites drew heavily from the ancient Egyptian texts. The Egyptians, in turn, gained their knowledge and beliefs from the older cultures of Babylon and Sumer.[95]

Perceived similarities are proofs of contacts, influences and, finally, identity. If you cannot find the time to produce even the spurious similarities to "prove" the connections, you may, as we see exemplified in the final sentence, just postulate them.

All strategies of producing links and similarities have, however, another element tied to them. Like Icke, Marrs depends on the "research" of others not duped by the conspiracy; the research of someone in the same milieu. References to more mainstream academic endeavours are few and tied chiefly to results that may be fitted into the narrative being weaved. Although unnamed "researchers" abound, there are surprisingly few references to the common *topos* of mainstream scientists being shut up and having their results suppressed by the conspiracy. Still, the topic of the conspiratorial suppression of knowledge is always in place. Indeed, it plays a central role as what limits freedom and "salvation". Information ("the truth"), Marrs concludes, is what will set you free.[96]

---

95. *Ibid.*, 365.
96. *Ibid.*, 410.

DISCUSSION: CONSPIRACY THEORY AS ESOTERIC DISCOURSE?

When considering conspiracy theory in and about esoteric groups and discourses, questions of history, knowledge and agency are intertwined. Looking now at the merits of viewing conspiracy theory *as* esoteric discourse, I shall focus first on aspects of history and knowledge. Closing the discussion, I will consider the relation between knowledge and agency. The topics remain intertwined: in order to realize freedom, conspiracy theories maintain, one has to unveil hidden knowledge about secret plots and hidden power.

The unveiling of conspiracy tends to take the form of a historical narrative. The polemical content and narrative form serve conspiracy theories in their function as *mythologies of evil* revealing secret knowledge about the origins and nature of evils befalling humanity (and Nature). This goes especially for the more complex and wide-ranging theories about grand, systemic (up to, and including, cosmic) conspiracies we have looked at above. History gives meaning and shape to revelations about the hidden forces around us, how they have shaped past and current events, and where they are leading us.

In order to fulfil the role as *apokalypsis* of evil's roots and how its plan unfolds, a conspiracy theory must reveal secret knowledge about places of power. Besides, and allied with, the suspects in high finance, politics and the military, the historical "secret societies" are presented by both some esotericists and conspiracy theorists as important *loci* of hidden traditions wielding unknown power. This, as noted already by John Roberts,[97] is interesting also for its historic interrelation with older, self-mythologizing emic historiographies of esoteric societies. Two internally related elements seem important here. The first is related to secrecy as the two-faced coin of esoteric discourse. As discussed by Hugh Urban,[98] the very claim of possessing secret knowledge and hidden power may raise suspicion from outsiders. As Roberts noted for early anti-Masonry, initiatory knowledge as revealed through levels of esoteric insight quickly raises suspicion that lower levels are left in the dark, or actively misled. The second element is the esoteric discourse on "secret chiefs" or "ascended masters" as hidden leaders with *particularly* deep insight and power. Add the two, and we may see conspiracy theories involving secret societies as the outline of an esoteric movement-discourse, appropriated, filled in, and turned on its head: instead of guiding humanity in its progress, the secret chiefs of conspiracy mislead, corrupt and destroy, and the secrecy itself "proves" (as stated already in Roman conspiracy theories about early Christians) that suspicions are true.

Conspiratorial history may be seen as an inverted esoteric discourse on history, knowledge and agency. Alleged chains of transmission for the conspiracy

---

97. John M. Roberts, *The Mythology of the Secret Societies*.
98. See Chapter 9 of this volume.

are revealed, but the forebears of their own theories are often forgotten or under-communicated. In these cases conspiracy theory reacts to, parallels and partially inverts esoteric discourse in another manner as well: while partially adopting the content and form of esoteric discourse, it *reveals* secrets of history in order to *remove* secret power in the present. The soteriological aspect of conspiracy theory is served by removing the alleged veil of secrecy from esoteric knowledge, serving at the same time as "initiation" into this knowledge.

Conspiracy theories thus tend to reveal the least "ordinary"[99] aspects of occulture as destructive, while at the same time partaking in the same occulture they reveal as evil: The construction of history as conspiracy often ends up conflating other, equally marginalized competitors in occulture with a "demonic" mainstream. By identifying them with a hidden establishment of power, they are placed *outside* the subculture and made actors in a history of *power*. These revelations are made in order to remove the power of evil, but recalling Hammer's injunction to look at esotericism as/in specific social formations,[100] we should also take note of the power *constructed* by these revelations. In brief, the revelation of "secret knowledge" in conspiracy theory serves to delimit in-group from out-group, aiming in the same stroke to work as an "initiatory" experience regulating the possibility of salvation through disclosure: adopt, and awaken, or reject, and join the black brethren (or the sheeple).

The unveiling of hidden truth is in both conspiracy theory and esoteric discourse, to paraphrase von Stuckrad,[101] established contrary to the institutionalized academic interpretations of history. Conspiracy theory tends, however, to be characterized as "fundamentalist" rather than esoteric in its epistemology.[102] Indeed, it still holds true that conspiracy theories thrive in fundamentalist circles, and that they, as in several of the examples above, tend towards literalism in interpretation. They also tend to use biblical lore literally and have scant room for "higher criticism". But also like fundamentalist discourse, conspiracy discourse is more complex than etic simplification would have it. Literalism is but one aspect even of fundamentalist epistemology, and like modern prophecy literature, conspiracy theories go further in an "esoteric" direction. Like prophetic literature, they show a marked tendency to "semiotic arousal"[103] where the visible becomes transparent signs evidencing the invisible. Anything may become such a sign, and it is important to make note of everything pointing in the right direction. It is an oft-noted observation that conspiracy theories immunize themselves from critical inquiry (e.g. by the

---

99. See Chapter 6 of this volume.
100. Hammer, "Esotericism in New Religious Movements".
101. Von Stuckrad, *Western Esotericism*, 10.
102. E.g. Coale, *Paradigms of Paranoia*, 4, 24.
103. Landes, *Millennialism*.

stratagem that evidence to the contrary is manufactured by the conspiracy). Since evidence *against* any theory is rampant by reason of conspiracy and cover-up, evidence *for* the conspiracy theory is necessarily always hidden. But at the same time, conspiracy theory is driven by the narrative logic of suspense fiction;[104] the conspiracy *must* leave clues so that the detective may solve the case. This makes culture into a "Book of Nature" whereby the signature of its conspiratorial authors may be read.

We get a hermeneutic where the discerning eye can reveal the plot. The strategy may be simple inversions, as the "fact–fiction reversal" noted by Michael Barkun,[105] whereby *precisely* because something is marked as fiction, it may be deemed legitimate to view it as masked fact. Other strategies are more similar to the correspondences and analogies of traditional esoteric discourse. We have seen keys to interpretation ranging from Steiner's esoteric insight to revelations through secular "expertise" above.

Taking this epistemology seriously, one is caught in a web of contradictions and uncertainties: Nothing is certainly true, but anything *might* be true. This opens connections between different areas of occulture: stigmatized knowledge claims flow between different groups of interest, creating the improvised apocalyptics of dark occulture where all manner of conspiratorial claims fit. But it also opens up the arena for serious play with *uncertainty*: chaotic "ontological guerrilla" activity, esoteric initiations and self-initiations into deeper secrets of history, society, and self. We made note of the play with uncertainty in Discordian use of conspiracy theory and some elements of it as well with LaVey. In the other examples there were few real doubts and not much play. The claims to knowledge may be shrouded in a very limited uncertainty, but are nonetheless presented as fact.

The style in conspiracy discourse tends, as in cult archaeology and other types of alternative history, to appeal to the academic, and the prose may be dense with references to "research". It involves using phrases and terms from both academic and "rejected" science. The effect is a variation of "terminological scientism".[106] While many are explicitly "spiritual",[107] others adopt topics, storylines, and modes of argument that strip away references to the supernatural completely.[108] But even the first category tends to adopt an at least superficially secular rationality and a "scholarly" style that is completely absent from Steiner's explicit esoteric discourse, for example. An esotericist like Steiner is closer to "conventionally" religious conspiracy writers,[109] and his revelations may be more easily recognizable as the spiritual *gnosis* of the

---

104. See e.g. Wisnicki, *Conspiracy, Revolution, and Terrorism*.
105. Barkun, *A Culture of Conspiracy*.
106. Hammer, *Claiming Knowledge*, 236–9.
107. E.g. Icke, *The Biggest Secret*.
108. E.g. Marrs, *Rule by Secrecy*.
109. E.g. Des Griffin, *Fourth Reich of the Rich*.

mystically enlightened human. But all of the *apokalypses* considered above have a redemptive quality. Whether meant for the individual alone or for a larger collective, they serve to make sense and prepare for recovering agency from oppressive circumstances.

The relation between knowledge and agency is, then, in many ways the most important one as it holds the key to salvation. In order to break free one must be made aware of how one's agency is being subverted. This is, to paraphrase Partridge, occulture at its most ordinary: the attempts to subvert "brainwashing" by "mindfucks" or "esoterrorism" may be foregrounded by the esoteric avant-garde, but the fear of threats to agency through mainstream consumer culture is *itself* mainstream. It is a topic which brings into contact esoteric, conspiratorial, and mainstream discourses, and is mediated and written large through popular culture:[110] from mainstream thrillers to conspiracy lore, government and big business is portrayed as controlling the individual through powers both seen and unseen.

Still, the fear of agency loss grows when we move from the broader milieu to central spokespersons and their theories. This is when we may talk of agency *panic*:

> [I]ntense anxiety about an apparent loss of autonomy or self-control – the conviction that one's actions are being controlled by someone else, that one has been "constructed" by powerful external agents. ... This fear sometimes manifests itself in a belief that the world is full of "programmed" or "brainwashed" subjects, addicts or "mass-produced" persons.[111]

With the exception of Steiner's more specific fears of materialism vaccinating ("brainwashing") people against spiritual ideas, we have seen that the mass production of programmed subjects was a repeated concern of how conspiracy limits agency and commits evil. Indeed, in some of the theories, this, not the actions of murder and mayhem, is the epitome of the conspiracy's evil. This is one reason why knowledge is given soteriological status: it has the power to "break the programming". This also shows the *value* given to free agency and a free self. In line with modern assumptions generally, and self-spirituality specifically, the self as agent is functionally sacred. It is the last refuge of what should be protected from the onslaught of modernity and outside power, but which the lore of conspiracy culture tells us is under attack.

The underlying ideals and/or assumptions about agency and personhood tend towards idealization of a "diamantine" self with a core separated in essence from persuasion and influence. In mainstream culture the ideal tends

---

110. E.g. Melley, "Agency Panic"; Seed, *Brainwashing*.
111. *Ibid.*, 62.

towards "a rational, motivated agent with a protected interior core of beliefs, desires, and memories".[112] Notwithstanding its general lack of plausibility, this is a popular, normative idea of selfhood, generating a flood of recipes for how to *become* that diamantine, effective self. Popular esotericism – from *The Secret* and other positive thinking manuals to more complex introductions to magic(k) – thrives on this, but goes one level further: the diamantine self is a *higher* self, above the purely rational and interior. It tends to be both "supra-rational" and transpersonal, requiring "initiatory" knowledge in order to become self-aware. If we view the positive focus on strategies of "agency recovery" as the esoteric mainstream response to agency threats – an occultural positive psychology telling the prospective adherent that one may achieve "change according to Will" by personal change and use of specific techniques – the conspiracy response in dark occulture seems again an inverted image. It affirms personal agency, but, as brought to the fore by LaVey, through a different lens: The good news is that there exists effective, personal agency in the world, and that it uses recognizable techniques. The bad news is that the techniques are in use by evil forces so steeped in secrecy that they are almost impossible to reach. Exposing the conspiracy thus serves as key to "agency recovery" when conspiracy is brought into the picture. In both "light" and "dark" occulture, exposing hidden sources of power and agency leads to the recovery of agency.

Looking at conspiracy theory *in* esoteric discourse together with conspiracy theory *as* esoteric discourse primarily highlights similarities. It helps us notice the parallel ways in which knowledge, history and agency are constructed, their similar functions, and the internal connections between esoteric discourse and conspiracy discourse. Connecting anything with something else through hidden links, where everything is connected and identity is conferred on principles of "signatures", occult correspondences, and "as here, so there", conspiracy theory may take on the look of a modern esoteric discourse, preoccupied, perhaps, with social salvation rather than the divine. With the sacralization of the self, agency takes a central seat, and with secularization, hidden histories and "sciency" references take the place of more traditional mythical ones. Both esoteric discourse and conspiracy theories belong to occulture, and they seem to draw from the same *doxa*. Thus historiographies, topics, and concerns move between them, adding the dualistic, polemical edge to their response to a marginalizing mainstream. Conspiracy theory works to present hidden knowledge about evil, but it also cements an audience as "in-group" and attempts "transformation" of the passive individual to social mobilization through presenting the negative, where lighter occulture focuses on the positive. Conspiracy theory may thus be a natural, sociological side of esoteric

---

112. Melley, *Empire of Conspiracy*, 14.

discourse, as well as a logical extension of it in constructing an "Other" that does not recognize esoteric discourse and attendant movements as legitimate.

ACKNOWLEDGEMENT

This article has developed partly out of discussions with Egil Asprem, who has contributed numerous valuable ideas at different stages. The article would not have been possible without his contribution.

CHAPTER 11

DISCURSIVE TRANSFERS AND RECONFIGURATIONS

TRACING THE RELIGIOUS AND THE ESOTERIC IN SECULAR CULTURE

Kocku von Stuckrad

What is the place of esotericism in modern culture? The guiding question of this volume presents us with more than one theoretical problem. We have to answer subsets of questions, such as:

- What is esotericism?
- What is the West?
- What is modernity?

All three questions would merit a book-length discussion. In fact, the debate about what characterizes Western modernity – or, rather, modernities[1] – has become one of the major controversies in the social sciences and in the academic study of religion. The study of "Western esotericism" has only insufficiently taken notice of this debate.

In what follows I present the outline of an interpretational model that intends to add to our understanding of the place and function of religion and esotericism in the contemporary Western world. Put more precisely: I am proposing a model that locates the religious and the esoteric in contemporary European and North American fields of discourse. In doing so, I proceed from theoretical considerations that I have elaborated in earlier contributions.[2] My theoretical framework operates with the dynamic of a twofold pluralism that characterizes European history of religion – a pluralism of religious options

---

1. On the concept of multiple modernities see Eisenstadt, *Comparative Civilizations and Multiple Modernities*; Eisenstadt, *Multiple Modernities*. In my view, one should go a step further and identify multiple modernities not only in intercultural comparison but also within European culture itself.
2. For an earlier view on esotericism, see von Stuckrad, "Western Esotericism". Cf. this to von Stuckrad, *Locations of Knowledge*.

and a pluralism of societal systems and domains that interact with religious systems in manifold ways.[3] Within these pluralisms, discourses of perfect knowledge can be addressed as "esoteric discourse". The notion of esoteric discourse helps us to reconstruct the genealogies of modern identities in a pluralistic competition of knowledge.[4]

Building forth on this historical analysis, I am interested here in the discursive changes that have taken place since the rise of secularism. After a brief discussion of what is known as the secularization theory, I will present four perspectives on the reconfiguration of the religious fields of discourse that have also redefined the location of the esoteric in modern culture. In the final part of my contribution I will apply these analytical instruments to a case study, taken from contemporary science.

AFTER SECULARIZATION

Many books and thousands of articles have been devoted since the "long 1960s"[5] to the question of whether the process of secularization that started in western Europe in the eighteenth century would inevitably lead to the decline of religion in Europe or, more generally, in "the West". Because this is not the place to review the complex debate about the many different theories of secularization in any detail,[6] let me just point out a few general characteristics of what seems to be a broad scholarly consensus.

Scholars today usually agree that a general theory of secularization, with the expectation of an inevitable decline of religion in modern societies, has been falsified by actual developments in the twentieth century, with a powerful appearance of religion in the public sphere since the 1970s. When it comes to more nuanced variants of the secularization theory, the picture is different. The concept of secularization can be divided into many subcategories and phenomena: decreasing participation in activities of the Church; transference of Church institutions into the domain of the state; constitutional separation of Church and state; less power of institutionalized religion in modern societies; and religious indifference. It depends on our focus of analysis whether

---

3. Von Stuckrad, *Locations of Knowledge*, 7–23. See also Kippenberg *et al.*, *Europäische Religionsgeschichte*.
4. Von Stuckrad, *Locations of Knowledge*, 43–64. As a critical response to this approach, see Granholm, "Esoteric Currents as Discursive Complexes". Granholm correctly notes that the concept of discourse, even if limited to Michel Foucault's work, has to be defined more concretely. Instead of "esoteric discourse", Granholm suggests talking of "discourse on the esoteric".
5. On this notion see Callum G. Brown, *The Death of Christian Britain*.
6. On this discussion see Casanova, *Public Religions in the Modern World*; Herbert, *Religion and Civil Society*, 29–61; Swatos & Olson, *The Secularization Debate*. See also Kennet Granholm's contribution to the present volume.

we state a process of secularization and whether we diagnose such a process in all Western countries or only in a few of them.

Looking at the development of the secularization debate, it seems as if the very idea of secularization is more *explanandum* than *explanans*: Just like Kennet Granholm in his contribution to the present volume, I am convinced that the theory of secularization does not really explain the relationship between religion and modernization; rather, this theory is itself an integral part of the formation of modern Western identities and narratives.[7] In order to grasp this intricate relationship, it is fruitful to see the "formations of the secular"[8] directly linked to the "formations of the religious" in processes of religious change. In my terminology, I follow José Casanova who proposes a "basic analytical distinction between 'the secular' as a central modern epistemic category, 'secularization' as an analytical conceptualization of modern world-historical processes, and 'secularism' as a worldview".[9] Using the concept of secularism in this way, I argue that secularism has not brought the end of religion but that the cultural dynamics that brought forth secularism also determined the new place of religion in cultural discourse. In doing so, these dynamics established the religious in a new framework of meaning. Even in its more radical form of ideological atheism, secularism has fostered new modes of religious cultural expression, from deinstitutionalized religion to radical religious responses to what is perceived as "modernity".

In a similar vein, David Herbert notes that the religion–modernity relation should be framed in another way than what we have learned in secularization theories. To be sure, modernization "tends to weaken the power of traditional religious institutions because of the diversification of channels and forms of communication in modernity".[10] But the mediatization of modern communication does not necessarily lead to secularization.

> Rather, religion as discourse can become the central medium of public communication. And even in cases where religion does not become the dominant language of protest … religious discourses and practices can still thrive alongside advanced technology, mass literacy and urbanization. Thus, in both cases, and to borrow Foucault's … metaphor derived from the French Revolution, cutting off the head of the king does not destroy power but disperses

---

7. As a critical assessment see Bhambra, *Rethinking Modernity*.
8. Asad, *Formations of the Secular*. On Asad's important contribution to the discussion see also Scott & Hirschkind, *Powers of the Secular Modern*. On the formation of secularism see further Charles Taylor, *A Secular Age*. As most recent contributions to this open debate see Butler et al., *The Power of Religion in the Public Sphere*; Calhoun et al., *Rethinking Secularism*.
9. Casanova, "The Secular and Secularisms", 1049.
10. Herbert, *Religion and Civil Society*, 58.

it more widely through the system. Indeed, it may even intensify its disciplinary effects. So with religion, whose modern discursive power may even exceed its traditional institutionalized power.[11]

Regarding religion as discourse is an appropriate way to withstand the difficulties of the secularization theory. The concept of "discourse", together with the concepts of "field" and "communication", provides us with better analytical tools to study the complex and often dialectical processes of the formation of religion *and* the secular in modern societies.[12] This is why I prefer talking of *reconfigurations of religious fields of discourse*, when it comes to cultural and political changes since the rise of secularism in the eighteenth century, rather than addressing these developments as an unstoppable process of secularization.

The critique of common secularization theories has not yet led to alternative models of interpretation that really have gained currency in today's academic debate. While some scholars talk of a "return of religion" (assuming that "religion" had been gone for a while), others use the term "de-secularization" or "postsecular"[13] (assuming that secularization was a fact until recently) or describe the historical process with yet another vocabulary. It remains to be seen which theoretical model "after secularization" will gain the upper hand in the future. In the next section I will present a few considerations that follow from my assumption that "religion" actually has never been away; what we witness is a reconfiguration of the discursive field of religion. As I will make clear, this reconfiguration also affects the place of esotericism in contemporary culture.

RECONFIGURATIONS OF THE RELIGIOUS FIELDS OF DISCOURSE: FOUR PERSPECTIVES

If we consider religion as a constantly changing field of discourse, the dynamics of which have shaped the place and function of religion in the modern world, the question that follows is: how can we describe and analyse the reconfiguration of this field during the past three-hundred years? What are the conceptual tools that help us to operationalize the dynamics of this change? The approach that I am offering here addresses four "perspectives on religious change" which

---

11. *Ibid.*, 58–9.
12. For my understanding of a discursive study of religion, see von Stuckrad, "Discursive Study of Religion" and, more recently, "Reflections on the Limits of Reflection". This approach can easily be combined with an analysis of dispositives, on which see Bührmann & Schneider, *Vom Diskurs zum Dispositiv*; Jäger & Maier, "Theoretical and Methodological Aspects".
13. As a recent example see Molendijk *et al.*, *Exploring the Postsecular*. Again, see also Kennet Granholm's contribution to the present volume.

not only show the ways and modes of discursive transformation but also identify major cultural areas in which these changes become visible and where we find our data for such a change. I argue that the European religious landscape has been redesigned by (i) new forms of communitarization, (ii) the scientification of knowledge, (iii) new forms of aesthetic representations and (iv) the emergence of new public arenas that challenge the religious neutrality of the state in constitutional democracies. Put into conceptual language, the underlying processes can be called communitarization, scientification, aestheticization, and public activation. I will discuss these concepts separately and with reference to the changes of esoteric discourses in particular.

Communitarization

In order to better understand the relationship between the public and the private sphere in modern Western societies, we must have a closer look at the forms of community that have emerged here since the Enlightenment. I call this perspective *communitarization*. An influential differentiation in sociology is the distinction between primary and secondary groups. One of the first scholars who detailed this conceptual dichotomy was Ferdinand Tönnies.[14] He differentiated between *Gemeinschaft* on the one hand, which is compatible to primary group affiliation in pre-modern societies, and *Gesellschaft* on the other hand, which roughly corresponds to the forms of association found in impersonal groups reflecting the social formation of modern, urban societies. In 1890, Georg Simmel picked up this distinction and described two major types of groups: those in which personal attributes dominate relationships, such as friendship and kinship groups, and those in which an individual's official position dominates the relationship.[15] For Simmel, the first type was most common in religious association and socialization, while the latter was applicable to, for instance, the official role of a Catholic priest who dominates the relationship with his parishioners.

Max Weber further elaborated on these distinctions.[16] He defined the "formation of community" (*Vergemeinschaftung*) as "a social relationship if and to the extent that the orientation of social action – whether in the individual case, or average case, or as a pure type – rests upon subjectively *felt* (affectual or traditional) *mutual* belonging (*Zusammengehörigkeit*) of the participants". In contrast to this, Weber defined the "formation of association" (*Vergesellschaftung*) as "a social relationship if and to the extent that the orientation of social action rests upon the rationally motivated (either value-rational or

---

14. Tönnies, *Gemeinschaft und Gesellschaft*.
15. Simmel, "Über sociale Differenzierung".
16. Weber, *Wirtschaft und Gesellschaft*, 1–30.

instrumentally rational) *balancing* out of interests or upon similarly motivated linking of interests".[17]

In a parallel movement to the emergence of public spheres in modern societies, since the eighteenth century many new forms of *Vergemeinschaftung* have entered the social fields. Politically, one of the most important forms was the birth of the nation. Calling nationalism and "nation-ness" "cultural artefacts", Benedict Anderson argues

> that the creation of these artefacts towards the end of the eighteenth century was the spontaneous distillation of a complex "crossing" of discrete historical forces; but that, once created, they became "modular," capable of being transplanted, with varying degrees of self-consciousness, to a great variety of social terrains, to merge and be merged with a correspondingly wide variety of political and ideological constellations.[18]

This reshaping of the religious field during the nineteenth and twentieth centuries led to the emergence of national identities that create new forms of "mutual belonging" and emotional attachment. A civil identity was added to the religious group identities, which had impact on religious communities as well. And it had influence on political communities: For instance, the *völkisch* movements in Germany and the subsequent idealization of the nation as a "body of community" absorbed religious ideas and thus sacralized the political realm. Political theologies have been important not only for National Socialism, but are a characteristic of political discourse in modern Europe more generally.[19]

Another aspect of communitarization is linked to the processes of individualization that sociologists observe in modern Western societies. We are confronted here with a paradoxical situation. On the one hand, the common narrative has it that modernization has led to an increased individualization and a turn to the interior self as the source of religious experiences. Charles Taylor and Anthony Giddens call this the "disembedding" that characterizes modernization. In Giddens's definition, disembedding is "the 'lifting out' of social relations from local contexts of interaction and their restructuring across indefinite spans of time-space".[20] On the other hand, the narrative of individualization and disembedding is difficult to match with the thesis

---

17. I took this translation from Whimster, *The Essential Weber*, 343–4. On the importance that Weber attributed to the *sect* as a particularly successful form of community in the shaping of Western modernity, see Riesebrodt, "Religiöse Vergemeinschaftungen", 115–17.
18. Benedict Anderson, *Imagined Communities*, 4.
19. See the contributions in de Vries & Sullivan, *Political Theologies*.
20. Giddens, *The Consequences of Modernity*, 21. On the phenomenon of a "globalized" disembedding see Stahl, "Religious Opposition to Globalization", 345–6.

that religions have massively entered the modern public spheres.[21] Maybe we can find an answer to this seeming paradox by taking into account that disembedded religious identities are not necessarily private; that the notion of individualization is itself partly informed by a pessimistic narrative of "loss of community and meaning" in the modern age; and that on fields of discourse new agents can claim their place and their access to forms of capital, including agents that propagate individualism.

Often, and in a complex development, individualization has not led to solipsistic forms of religious experience. It has also led to an ideology of the individual, with new group identities as "being individual". Perhaps the best example of this is the so-called New Age movement: here, the religious quest is highly individualized and even expected from practitioners, but at the same time the textual and experiential arsenal available to the members is limited and almost canonized – something that Olav Hammer calls the "individualistic imperative".[22] Other forms of community that are available to the individual include communities of reading – from popularized science to the Harry Potter series[23] – and virtual communities that have emerged as part of the Internet revolution.[24]

Scientification

A second perspective on the reconfiguration of religious fields of discourse can be called *scientification*. This process has many different layers, all of them being linked to concepts of knowledge in one way or another. To begin with, the last two-hundred years have seen the institutionalization of the study of religion as an academic discipline. As a result, knowledge about religion has been professionalized and the ways of exploring religion have been discussed in disciplines such as anthropology, sociology, and non-confessional religious studies, or *Religionswissenschaft*. This also led to an enormous growth of religious texts and historical materials that have become available since the nineteenth century.[25]

---

21. As an influential essay that argues in such a way, see Casanova, *Public Religions in the Modern World*.
22. Hammer, "I Did It My Way?". On processes of communitarization in neopaganism see Pike, *Earthly Bodies, Magical Selves*.
23. Regarding the earlier history of these communities, see Colclough, *Consuming Texts*. On popularized science, which is a major influence on modern esotericism and New Age culture, see Bowler, *Science for All*; Gregory & Miller, *Science in Public*; Midgley, *Science as Salvation*; and particularly Leane, *Reading Popular Physics*.
24. See, among many other publications, Wu Song, *Virtual Communities*; Panteli, *Virtual Social Networks*; Sohn, *Social Network Structures and the Internet*; Aupers & Houtman, *Religions of Modernity*.
25. See Kippenberg, *Discovering Religious History in the Modern Age*.

As has been pointed out by Clifford Geertz, Hayden White and others, the scholar of religion is also an *author* whose writings influence his or her object of study.[26] In other words: The study of religion has lost its imagined role as mere observer and scholars have entered the fields of religious discourse as actors and stakeholders. Scholars standardize and publicize knowledge about religion to such an extent that in some instances they can even be considered the founders of new religions. This is particularly true with regard to Theosophy, witchcraft, neopaganism, modern Western shamanism, and various New Age milieus. All these movements were heavily influenced by academic theories about the history of religion and the place and continuation of non-Christian elements within this historical narrative.[27]

The process of scientification has yet another important dynamic. Since the eighteenth century a new episteme (in the Foucauldian sense) has emerged that considers the theories and methods of the natural sciences to be the only way to produce acknowledged and reliable knowledge of the world. In what I call a "polemical disjunction", branches of knowledge that still used to be regarded as united in the early modern period now were presented as entirely separated and even mutually exclusive: astrology versus astronomy, alchemy versus chemistry, or magic versus science. At the same time, religious and metaphysical elements of the "old sciences" are still present in metaphors of contemporary science, a fact that I call a "subcutaneous continuity".[28] As I will explain in more detail below, on religious fields of discourse natural scientists can act as interpreters of the essence of the world and can thus provide meaning beyond the limited system of scientific argumentation.

In the wake of this new episteme religious practitioners turned to scientific models of explanation in order to prove the truth of their claims. Again, the discursive field of esotericism is a particularly good example of this, from the Theosophical Society to the New Age.[29] But the scientific need of explanation is also felt in other religious contexts. The Roman Catholic Church itself is participating in this discourse, for instance with its attempt to prove scientifically that condoms do not protect against HIV/AIDS.[30] The Pontifical Academy of Sciences regularly hosts conferences that try to link scientific explanation and method to topics of religious interest. In 2009, a remarkable "Study Week on Astrobiology" was organized, with the brochure saying in its introduction:

---

26. Geertz, *Works and Lives*; Hayden White, *Metahistory*. See also Tenbruck, "Die Religion im Maelstrom der Reflexion". On the example of myth see Strenski, *Four Theories of Myth*.
27. On the example of shamanism see von Stuckrad, *Schamanismus und Esoterik*, 279–84; cf. Chapter 2 of this volume.
28. See von Stuckrad, *"Zo zijn we niet getrouwd"*.
29. As a contribution to this topic see Hammer, *Claiming Knowledge*, 201–330 ("Scientism as a Language of Faith"). See also Chapter 16 of the present volume.
30. See Benavides, "Western Religion and the Self-Canceling of Modernity", 104–5.

Astrobiology is the study of life's relationship to the rest of the cosmos: its major themes include the origin of life and its precursor materials, the evolution of life on Earth, its future prospects on and off the Earth, and the occurrence of life elsewhere. Behind each of these themes is a multidisciplinary set of questions involving physics, chemistry, biology, geology, astronomy, planetology, and other fields, each of which connects more or less strongly to the central questions of astrobiology.[31]

This example not only reveals the processes of scientification; it also makes clear that the fields of modern esoteric discourse – in this case "mystical astronomy" – are open and by no means populated by marginal actors only.

Aestheticization

A third perspective on religious change can be conceptualized as *aestheticization*. In the academic study of religion and culture, the notion of "aesthetics" has received remarkable new interest recently.[32] Scholars refer to Aristotle's understanding of *aisthesis* as our perception of the world through our five senses as an undivided whole. In De Anima, Aristotle argues that it is the capability of the human psyche to have a total sensorial experience of the world and to gain a sensuous knowledge of it. In Western intellectual discourse since the Enlightenment, such an understanding of the aesthetic dimension of knowledge and experience has gradually been substituted by a separation of the aesthetic and the bodily dimensions, or, rather, by privileging sensations received by the eye (and subsequently the visual metaphors of knowing). The influence of Immanuel Kant and later neo-Kantian aesthetic theory has been crucial in this regard. It is with Merleau-Ponty and his work on perception that the Aristotelian understanding of *aisthetic* experiences and forms of knowledge reappeared in cultural and philosophical interpretations.[33] The division between bodily sensation and knowledge of the mind was critically addressed, as was the division between "high art" (stored and exhibited at special places) and "low art" (often referred to as kitsch or mass-produced imagery and objects).

It can be argued that the modern episteme is not only built on rationality and reason, but equally on imagination and the mediated figurativeness of the

---

31. Pontifical Academy of Sciences, *A Study Week on Astrobiology*, 3.
32. Meyer & Verrips, "Aesthetics", provides a good overview.
33. Merleau-Ponty, *Phénoménologie de la Perception*. On the critical response to neo-Kantian aesthetics see also Plate, *Walter Benjamin, Religion, and Aesthetics*. In his reading of Wittgenstein, Richard Shusterman coined the term "somaesthetics", which was picked up by scholars of culture, as well; see Shusterman, "Wittgenstein's Somaesthetics".

new worldviews. Scholars have applied this analysis to the "aestheticization of everyday life",[34] to the realm of politics and power,[35] and to the creation of the modern self.[36] But the pivotal interrelations between religion and the aesthetic aspects of modernization are yet to be explored. In what has been called the "aesthetic turn" such a reorganization of the aesthetic dimensions of knowledge was picked up by scholars of religion and culture. Pushing the boundaries of visual culture, scholars now argue for a more contextualized, embodied understanding of (religious) aesthetics.[37] This is also a move beyond an artistic concept of aesthetics in addressing "aesthetic formations" within changing religious fields;[38] we can now ask how religious aesthetic forms meandered into areas of politics and art, popular culture, science, and the medial representation of knowledge; and we can scrutinize how religion itself was redefined in aesthetic terms (such as emotion and experience) as a response to the rationalization of religion in Enlightenment contexts.[39] "*Religious aesthetics*, in the current sense, refers to an embodied and embedded praxis through which subjects relate to other subjects and objects and which is grounded in and offers the ground for religious experience".[40] In addition to the importance of *praxis* – and, I would add, *communication* – in this understanding of aesthetics, it becomes clear that such an approach does not privilege the visual; rather, it addresses the human sensory apparatus in its entirety.[41]

In sum, the referential framework of religious aesthetics allows us to better understand the place of the religious in a secular environment. Today, art is not only a carrier of beauty, but a carrier of truth and meaning, and as such it has taken over functions that earlier had been associated with the religious domain. An excellent example of these discursive transfers and reconfigurations is the link between science, occultism, and the art of the Avant-Garde in the early twentieth century. Around 1900, scientific discoveries such as n-dimensionality, x-rays and electromagnetism entered the discourse of

---

34. Beck *et al.*, *Reflexive Modernization*.
35. Rancière, *The Politics of Aesthetics*.
36. Charles Taylor, *Sources of the Self*; Foucault, *Aesthetics, Method, and Epistemology*.
37. See e.g. Morgan, *Visual Piety*; Krüger & Nova, *Imagination und Wirklichkeit*; Lanwerd, *Religionsästhetik*; Meyer, *Aesthetic Formations*. Most recently, see the special issue of the *Journal of Religion in Europe* 4.1 (2011), devoted to "Relocating Religion(s) – Museality as a Critical Term for the Aesthetics of Religion" (guest editors are Jens Kugele and Katharina Wilkens).
38. Meyer, *Aesthetic Formations*.
39. On the importance of Friedrich Schleiermacher, see Korsch & Griffioen, *Interpreting Religion*.
40. Meyer & Verrips, "Aesthetics", 27 (emphasis original).
41. Mohr, "Perception/Sensory System". See also Charles Hirschkind's analysis of the cassette sermons in Islamic discourse and the importance of hearing, Hirschkind, *The Ethical Soundscape*, and Bruce Smith's analysis of the sound of early modern England, *The Acoustic World of Early Modern England*. See also Schulz, "Soundscape".

occultism and were subsequently reframed as the "occult fourth dimension", "clairvoyant x-ray vision", and "thought vibration".[42]

It is not simply the case that – as scholars of earlier generations have argued – religious experiences have been turned into experiences of art; rather, these scholarly interpretations are themselves part of the discursive change that the concept of aestheticization refers to. As soon as we overcome the conceptual barriers between art and aesthetics, and see aesthetics as a praxis and communication that includes all sensual perceptions, we will no longer talk of a decline of religious experiences or religious expressions in modern culture. To be sure, the institutionalized forms of religion have lost their interpretative hegemony in the field of religion, and their ability to control the discourse has decreased. But aesthetic dimensions of religion are everywhere in modern culture, and their influence has only increased in the twentieth century. To a large extent, religious discourse is controlled by (new) media and the visually and sensually communicated symbolic systems that populate the public sphere.

Public activation

Throughout the twentieth century, the notion of a "public sphere" has been a recurring issue in sociological and philosophical discussions. Ernst Mannheim, Reinhart Koselleck, Herbert Dieckmann and particularly Jürgen Habermas considered the eighteenth century as the birthplace of the public sphere in which democratic civil societies could flourish.[43] Charles Taylor, in his response to Habermas and Warner, describes

> the public sphere as a common space in which the members of society are deemed to meet through a variety of media: print, electronic, and also face-to-face encounters; to discuss matters of common interest; and thus to be able to form a common mind about these. I say "*a* common space", because although the media are multiple, as well as the exchanges which take place in them, these are deemed to be in principle intercommunicating. ... That's why we usually speak of the public sphere, in the singular.[44]

---

42. See Bauduin, "Science, Occultism and the Art of the Avant-Garde in the Early Twentieth Century". As a related topic see also Hahn & Schüttpelz, *Trancemedien und Neue Medien um 1900*. More examples are provided in Chapter 16 of this volume.
43. See the overview in Herbert, *Religion and Civil Society*, 96–103. Interestingly, from a perspective of esotericism, the same period saw the emergence of secret societies, a paradox that was addressed by Habermas and others, as well. See Simonis, *Die Kunst des Geheimen*, 9–45.
44. Charles Taylor, *A Secular Age*, 185. Taylor refers to Habermas's famous *Strukturwandel der Öffentlichkeit*, and to Warner, *The Letters of the Republic*.

Such an understanding of a *common* public sphere has been challenged by other scholars. David Herbert notes that "the concept of a unitary public sphere is no longer viable and needs to be replaced by an account of multiple, intersecting and contesting public spheres, whose inter-relation is problematic".[45] While the nature and characteristics of the public spheres that dominate modern societies – as well as their complex intersection and competition – are still in need of further research, there is no serious disagreement among scholars about the observation that during the last three-hundred years we have witnessed the emergence of a public space that is significantly different from earlier forms of public communication. This process I call *public activation*.

Recently, another aspect of religion and the public sphere has been put to the fore. The discourse on religion in constitutional democracies has tremendously changed during the past decades. While the role of the state used to be understood – almost mythically – as the neutral referee in religious matters, the secular state itself is now getting involved in religious debates. This has legal implications. Making use of Bourdieu's concept of "field", Astrid Reuter argues:

> Today's "new-type actors", who are competing with each other and the "old-type actors" at the borders of the religious field, consolidating these borders, breaking them up, and redefining them, are experts from the academic field, politicians, civil servants, journalists, and – last but not least – judges. For what has changed is not simply the areas of conflict, but also the forms in which they are being carried out: The religious-cultural climate of our days has increasingly become determined by judicial conflicts over religion, which often trigger significant public controversies. Courts have thus become the stages of a new mise-en-scène and controversial mobilization of religion in the public realm.[46]

With judges having to decide about definitions of religion, characteristics of religious communities, or the active role of the state in balancing the freedom of religion with the freedom of speech, the very basis of the separation of Church and state is at stake.[47] Again, we can conclude that secularism – arguably forming the ideological foundation of constitutional democracies – has not led to a control of religion, but to the reconfiguration of the religious fields of discourse.

The four perspectives on discursive change that I have discussed provide us with a referential framework that improves our understanding of the place

---

45. Herbert, *Religion and Civil Society*, 95.
46. Reuter, "Charting the Boundaries of the Religious Field", 1–2.
47. See Sullivan, "We Are All Religious Now. Again"; Kippenberg & Schuppert, *Die Verrechtlichte Religion*.

of religion in modern Western societies. In the last section I want to demonstrate how we can apply these methodological instruments to issues of esoteric discourse in contemporary Western culture. My example is by no means exhaustive. It simply illustrates how all four modes of discursive change can be operative together, and how discursive transfers between cultural systems work in practice. This should be read as a vision of and an invitation to future research into modern esoteric discourse.

AN EXAMPLE OF DISCURSIVE CHANGE: ESOTERIC INCLINATIONS IN CONTEMPORARY BIOLOGY

Questions pertaining to the "deep structure" of the cosmos have always been essential to esoteric quests. Subsets of such questions would look for the linguistic coding of the universe, the creative power of the divine, or the experiential dimensions of knowledge about nature. I have argued elsewhere that these debates have significantly shaped Western identities during the Middle Ages and the early modern period.[48] Major philosophical and scientific alternatives were formulated in these contexts.

Take, for instance, the emergence of nominalism in the Middle Ages, which can only be understood against the background of theological considerations. The question of whether the *nomina*, the names, of things, have an ontological status of their own and thus are carriers of *essentia* or *universalia*, is fraught with theological problems. For instance, when humans are studying the Book of Nature and ultimately decipher the secret structure of the cosmos, they arrive at a knowledge that was reserved for God alone. The medieval nominalists thus suggested that by studying the *nomina*, humans are not intermingling with the divine, because the names are not linked to any sort of transcendent or divine knowledge (in contrast to Platonism). This strategy led to what I call the tragedy of nominalism: although the manoeuvre enabled the emergence of free and rational science – because everything in nature can be studied without intermingling with divine realms – at the same time it was no longer possible to establish a rational and reliable knowledge of the "deep structure" of the revealed world, ranging from concepts of the divine to concepts of *natura naturans*. The idea that "science" is restricted to the revealed world or *natura naturata*, and that knowledge of nature is arbitrary and imperfect, while true knowledge of the divine world is impossible or derived from "belief", is part and parcel of Western concepts of scientific knowledge that fully emerged during the sixteenth and seventeenth centuries.

Esoteric discourses abound with alternatives to the nominalist protection of borders between the divine and the human. In fact, I regard the challenging

---

48. See von Stuckrad, *Locations of Knowledge*.

and transgressing of the borders between the divine and the human realms as characteristic of esoteric discourses, which rest on totalizing claims of knowledge. Examples would include the large field of magic (including, but not restricted to *magia naturalis*),[49] Jewish and Christian Kabbalah, or the notion of *natura naturans* in F. W. J. Schelling and other philosophers.[50] But this only forms the background of our discussion here. The question we have to answer is how these fields have been reconfigured in modern knowledge about nature and whether we can demonstrate transfers between religious, scientific, philosophical, political, and other systems in modern culture.

The life sciences of the twentieth and twenty-first centuries are excellent examples of such a process. From a cultural studies point of view, the modern life sciences – including the deciphering of the human genome – can be analysed as applications of literary tools of *reading* and *writing* in the Book of Nature.[51] Metaphors of coding and decoding have entered the public debate about the progress of the life sciences and the possibilities of creating life in the future. In this context we should not forget that – as has been shown by Philipp Sarasin who builds on Ludwik Fleck's sociology of knowledge – scientific metaphors are not "just metaphors" but clear indications of how a society structures what it regards as reality.[52] Let me illustrate this with two scientific incidents that have reached a wide audience after the turn of the twenty-first century.

On 26 June 2000, the White House organized a news conference to celebrate the finalization of the first phase of the Human Genome Project that resulted in the decipherment of the entire structure of the human genome. Speaking at this conference were US President Bill Clinton; the head of the Human Genome Project, Dr Francis S. Collins; and Dr J. Craig Venter, head of Celera Genomics, a company that also participated in the race to decipher the human genome. The British Prime Minister Tony Blair participated via satellite. Bill Clinton addressed the scientific breakthrough as follows:

> Today's announcement represents more than just an epoch-making triumph of science and reason. After all, when Galileo discovered he could use the tools of mathematics and mechanics to understand the motion of celestial bodies, he felt, in the words of one eminent researcher, that he had learned the language in which

---

49. As a comparison between early modern magic and the "disenchanted magic" of modernity, see Hanegraaff, "How Magic Survived the Disenchantment of the World".
50. For a more detailed discussion of these examples, I refer the reader again to my *Locations of Knowledge*; for Schelling's philosophy of nature, see also von Stuckrad, *Schamanismus und Esoterik*, 195–201.
51. See von Stuckrad, "Rewriting the Book of Nature"; Kay, "In the Beginning was the Word?"; Brandt, *Metapher und Experiment*.
52. See Sarasin, "Infizierte Körper, kontaminierte Sprachen". See also the classic study by Lakoff & Johnson, *Metaphors We Live By*.

> God created the universe. – Today we are learning the language in which God created life. We are gaining ever more awe for the complexity, the beauty, the wonder of God's most divine and sacred gift.[53]

Clinton, despite all his pathos, is aware of the transgressive potential of the Human Genome Project vis-à-vis theologically defined borders. Learning the language of God means that we can also write it. So he warns his audience:

> The third horizon that lies before us is one that science cannot approach alone. It is the horizon that represents the ethical, moral and spiritual dimension of the power we now possess. We must not shrink from exploring that far frontier of science. But as we consider how to use new discoveries, we must also not retreat from our oldest and most cherished human values.[54]

Francis S. Collins is also very much aware of the transgressive potential of his endeavour. In his speech at the same conference, he addresses this potential right away: "Alexander Pope wrote: 'Know then, thyself. Presume not God to scan. The proper study of mankind is man.' What more powerful form of study of mankind could there be than to read our own instruction book?"[55] It may be questioned whether Alexander Pope's prescription is a solution to the transgressive danger that Collins intends to avoid, but it clearly shows his concerns. Collins then proclaims: "Today we celebrate the revelation of the first draft of the human book of life." But again, he feels the need to put forward an ethical disclaimer:

> It is humbling for me and awe-inspiring to realize that we have caught the first glimpse of our own instruction book, previously known only to God. What a profound responsibility it is to do this work. Historians will consider this a turning point.[56]

They surely will! But the turning point is exactly what Collins plays down: what we witness is the most recent chapter in a long history of "scanning God", in Alexander Pope's poetic words.

I now come to a very recent event in the history of science. This event is closely related to J. Craig Venter who is a representative of the field of "synthetic biology". As we have seen already, Venter was involved with the Human Genome Project, though in a competitive research group. After 2000, Venter

---

53. Anon., "Reading the Book of Life".
54. *Ibid.*
55. *Ibid.*
56. *Ibid.*

took his career in various directions. Using US$100 million from Celera and other stock holdings, he started a non-profit organization, the J. Craig Venter Science Foundation. This organization freed him to do any kind of science he wanted without obligation to an academic review panel or other constraints. In 2002, the foundation launched the Institute for Biological Energy Alternatives in Rockville, Maryland. In May 2010, Venter's team succeeded in creating, for the first time, a fully synthetic new cell. In other words, a new life form. In *The New York Times* we read:

> At a press conference Thursday, Dr Venter described the converted cell as "the first self-replicating species we've had on the planet whose parent is a computer". "This is a philosophical advance as much as a technical advance," he said, suggesting that the "synthetic cell" raised new questions about the nature of life. ... "It's very powerful to be able to reconstruct and own every letter in a genome because that means you can put in different genes," said Gerald Joyce, a biologist at the Scripps Research Institute in La Jolla, Calif. In response to the scientific report, President Obama asked the White House bioethics commission on Thursday to complete a study of the issues raised by synthetic biology within six months and report back to him on its findings. He said the new development raised "genuine concerns," though he did not specify them further.[57]

There is even more fascinating material for our topic in this little story. When they synthesized their cell, Venter and his team introduced several distinctive markers into its genome. All of them were found in the synthetic cell when it was sequenced. These markers do not make any proteins, but they contain the names of 46 scientists that were involved with the project, as well as several quotations written out in a secret code. The markers also contain the key to the code. It is necessary to crack the code in order to read the messages. But Venter provided some hints as to the content of these quotations: "To live, to err, to fall, to triumph, to recreate life out of life", which is taken from James Joyce's *A Portrait of the Artist as a Young Man*; "See things not as they are but as they might be", which comes from *American Prometheus*, a biography of nuclear physicist Robert Oppenheimer; and the famous words by physicist Richard Feynman: "What I cannot build I cannot understand."[58]

Coding and decoding, reading and writing the book of nature and the book of life, the playing-God motive, the creation of a golem – with all its ethical challenges – all this has been part of Western intellectual, religious and

---

57. Wade, "Researchers Say They Created a 'Synthetic Cell'".
58. See Callaway, "Immaculate Creation".

scientific history. It is the heritage that Venter, Collins and others, consciously or unconsciously, are building on. Venter himself maintains that he has not created life. "We've created the first synthetic cell", he argues. "We definitely have not created life from scratch because we used a recipient cell to boot up the synthetic chromosome." In the *New Scientist*, we can read:

> Whether you agree or not is a philosophical question, not a scientific one as there is no biological difference between synthetic bacteria and the real thing, says Andy Ellington, a synthetic biologist at the University of Texas in Austin. "The bacteria didn't have a soul, and there wasn't some animistic property of the bacteria that changed," he says.[59]

Interestingly, now a vague concept of "soul" is invoked by the scientists to avoid their transgressive operation. Subsequently, they can leave the issue unresolved as "a philosophical question".

It would carry me too far into other topics if I were to follow this path here. Instead, I want to drive my argument home. The examples of contemporary life sciences and synthetic biology illustrate in a nutshell that the four dynamics of discursive change that I explained in this chapter can be operative together and in mutual dependency. These examples are not only clear evidence of scientification (in more than one way); they also reveal how scientific knowledge is aesthetically represented and communicated; and they take place in a public sphere that includes political actors, scientists, and a large audience that is interested in popularized forms of scientific claims. These truth claims by far transgress the borders of scientific thinking in immanent and empirically testable models. They stand in the line of esoteric quests to unlock the ultimate secrets of the cosmos and to reveal the hidden meaning of human history.

In their quest, J. Craig Venter and Francis S. Collins have embarked on the same journey as Stephen W. Hawking, the celebrated physicist, and an even more successful author of popularized science. Hawking, too, transgresses the borders of science and takes on the role of religious expert and esoteric teacher:

> Ever since the dawn of civilization, people have not been content to see events as unconnected and inexplicable. They have craved an understanding of the underlying order in the world. Today we still yearn to know why we are here and where we have come from. Humanity's deepest desire for knowledge is justification enough for our continuing quest. And our goal is nothing less then a complete description of the universe we live in.[60]

---

59. *Ibid.*
60. Hawking, *A Brief History of Time*, 15.

With such a claim, this scientist–saviour naturally deserves the last word in an essay on the place of the esoteric in contemporary culture: "A complete, consistent, unified theory is only the first step: our goal is a complete understanding of the events around us, and of our own existence".[61]

---

61. *Ibid.*, 187.

CHAPTER 12

RADICAL POLITICS AND POLITICAL ESOTERICISM
THE ADAPTATION OF ESOTERIC DISCOURSE WITHIN THE RADICAL RIGHT

Jacob Christiansen Senholt

What do esoteric phenomena such as Chaos Magick, runic symbolism, Tantric yoga and the mythical Atlantis have to do with radical right-wing politics? Not a lot, one would think, but as will be demonstrated in this chapter, the radical political right serves as an important example when talking about esoteric transfers, that is, the impact of esoteric currents and their discourse on "non-esoteric" social, cultural and ideological systems. There are numerous historical and contemporary examples of connections and overlaps between esoteric currents and right-wing political ideas. Beginning with the historical, a prominent example is the politicization of esotericism with the rise of the so-called *völkisch* movement in nineteenth-century Germany, emerging from the Romantic nationalism of Johann Gottlieb Fichte and Johann Gottfried von Herder. This movement combined nationalism, anti-liberalism, cultural pessimism and racism into a coherent ideological system.[1] In the early twentieth century these ideas mixed with Theosophical[2] notions and grew into Ariosophy, a doctrine of Aryan racist and occult ideas promoted by Jörg Lanz von Liebenfels, Guido von List and their followers.[3] In the wake of Ariosophy, numerous groups inspired by these ideas formed, from Theodor Fritsch's Germanenorden, Friedrich Marby's Rune Yoga and Liebenfels's Order of the New Templars (Ordo Novi Templi), to the Thule Society, which sponsored the burgeoning Nazi Party and included important party members such as Rudolf Hess and Dietrich Eckart. This *völkisch* awakening culminated during the Third Reich, although, quite ironically, most of these groups were banned

---

1. Goodrick-Clarke, *The Occult Roots of Nazism*, 2. For a general overview of the *völkisch* movement and related currents see Stern, *The Politics of Cultural Despair*; Mosse, *The Crisis of German Ideology*.
2. For a more detailed explanation of Theosophy in the tradition of Blavatsky see Godwin, *The Theosophical Enlightenment*; Bruce F. Campbell, *Ancient Wisdom Revived*.
3. Goodrick-Clarke, *The Occult Roots of Nazism*, 227.

and their members imprisoned. The notable exception was Himmler's own personal coterie, where Karl Maria von Wiligut acted as a personal adviser, or "Himmler's Rasputin", in matters of astrology and Ariosophy.[4]

A second historical example of overlaps between esotericism and radical politics is Traditionalism. Traditionalism, at times also referred to as "Integral Traditionalism" or the "Traditionalist School", is motivated by a religiously based opposition to modern Western society and its paradigmatic values of individualism, consumerism, and perpetual growth. It also upholds the idea of *perennialism*, the esoteric notion of the existence of universal, transcendent truths, which unite disparate religious traditions – an idea often found in other esoteric currents.[5] Key Traditionalist thinkers are René Guénon, Frithjof Schuon and Ananda Coomaraswamy.[6] More relevant for this article, however, is the more politicized, radical and controversial Traditionalism of Italian esotericist Julius Evola, who played a major role in conveying a radical political Traditionalism to anti-modern intellectuals. Initially this was attempted during the Fascist and Nazi regimes of Italy and Germany, with Evola forming ties to both the Fascist Party and the SS. After World War II Evola became indirectly and unwillingly involved as a right-wing ideologue in the "black terror" of the Italian "Years of Lead" from the late 1960s to the early 1980s, where left- and right-wing extremists were involved in numerous acts of terrorism against both each other and the state.[7] What makes Evola even more interesting when talking about esoteric transfers is the fact that he was involved in both political endeavours and various esoteric practices through his involvement with the esoteric fraternity Gruppo di Ur, co-founded by Evola, Arturo Reghini and Giovanni Colazza in 1927. The group provided Evola with numerous esoteric notions, which were also reflected in his political ideology.[8]

Going from the past to the present, it is apparent that the wide array of historical examples of overlaps between esotericism and the radical right are not unique, but instead part of a persistent trend which is still present in contemporary times.[9] Taking a cue from Traditionalism, in particular the politicized anti-modernism of Julius Evola, the radical right has adapted numerous

---

4. Flowers & Moynihan, *The Secret King*; Goodrick-Clarke, *The Occult Roots of Nazism*, 177.
5. Cf. Chapter 2 of this volume.
6. Sedgwick, *Against the Modern World*.
7. Evola's post-war political endeavours are described in Hansen, "Introduction"; Drake, "Julius Evola and the Ideological Origins of the Radical Right in Contemporary Italy", and the overall political situation and the "Years of Lead" in Ferraresi, *Threats to Democracy*; Merkl, *Political Violence and Terror*. Evola's own post-war political works are primarily Evola, *Orientamenti*; Evola, *Men among the Ruins*.
8. For more on Evola and his involvement with Gruppo di Ur see Hakl, "Die Magie bei Julius Evola und Ihre Philosophischen Voraussetzungen"; Evola, *Path of Cinnabar*, 88–95; Evola, *Introduction to Magic*.
9. For a more detailed overview of these phenomena and how they interrelate see Dahl, *Radikalare än Hitler?*; Arvidsson, *Aryan Idols*.

esoteric notions and quasi-esoteric symbolism into its ideology and visual expressions. A key concern for the radical right is religious and cultural preservation and resurrection. These ideas are often directly coupled to esoteric notions and politicized neopaganism, as well as attacks against Christianity, which is perceived as being the cause of the decline and degeneration of the modern age and the attendant promulgation of its values of liberalism, capitalism and egalitarianism.[10]

This chapter explores the origins and provides examples of transfers of esoteric notions within the political right, and examines explanations that might help us understand such transfers. This chapter is not the first to deal with examples of overlaps between esotericism and the right. The origins of the anti-modern movements from which right-wing esotericism springs can arguably be placed as far back as the so-called Counter-Enlightenment.[11] The contemporary movements of right-wing esotericism have already been explored by scholars such as Nicholas Goodrick-Clarke, Jocelyn Godwin and Mattias Gardell.[12] What is lacking in these studies, which primarily document the existence of these groups and describe the ideas they promote, are attempts to provide answers as to *why* we see such an overlap between esotericism and the right. The aim in this chapter is to do precisely that.

The first part of the chapter introduces contemporary anti-modern intellectuals, specifically the European New Right, Radical Traditionalism and Eurasianism. The second part looks at the historical relationship between radical politics and esotericism. It also presents examples of overlaps between esotericism and the radical right, and political adaptation of esoteric symbolism and ideological and mythical complexes, such as the Black Sun symbol and the idea of a primordial homeland, such as Thule or Atlantis. The third and final part of this chapter examines some of the more fundamental and theoretical questions and provides possible explanations. What kind of structural and ideological similarities exist between the radical right and esotericism? Is the radical right simply another form of countercultural cultic milieu, engaging in polemical discourses against the mainstream, and constructing its own "grand polemical narratives", or are there other and more deep-rooted reasons for such an overlap?

AN INTRODUCTION TO THE RADICAL RIGHT

Before going into a more detailed examination of contemporary bonds between esotericism and the radical right, let us first look at what the radical

---

10. A good example of Evola's anti-Christian viewpoints and his (neo)pagan alternative can be found in Evola, *Heathen Imperialism*.
11. Berlin, "The Counter-Enlightenment".
12. Goodrick-Clarke, *Black Sun*; Godwin, *Arktos*; Gardell, *Gods of the Blood*.

right is. The term "radical right" is in this article used as an overarching term denoting various groups that are all fundamentally in opposition to the current society, seeking a grand-scale societal transformation, and hence revolutionary in nature. We have already briefly mentioned historical examples such as the *völkisch* movement and the Traditionalist movement, but for the purpose of this article let us look in more detail at contemporary examples.

Radical Traditionalism is the newest iteration of the ideas present in Traditionalism and the New Right. The Radical Traditionalists are best known for their journal *Tyr*, edited and published by Joshua Buckley and Michael Moynihan, where the movement is described as a rejection of modern values and the materialist "reign of 'quantity over quality'".[13] They deplore what they consider a decline and absence of spiritual values, and the lack of true concern for the environment. Instead of modern progressivism they hail the re-emergence of homogeneous tribal societies as a (neo)pagan and antimodern alternative to contemporary society.[14] The Radical Traditionalists have successfully attracted interest and support from several scholars,[15] and achieved success in spreading Radical Traditionalism to a broader audience. However, the movement has existed for less than a decade and is still a minor constellation in the overall subculture of the radical right.

In order to understand the groups and ideas labelled the "New Right", it is necessary to first give some fundamental clarifications and definitions of terms. The necessity of this is made acute by the fact that more conventional connotations of the term "right", associated with a classical political left–right axis, do not properly fit the New Right groups. The left has historically been associated with the promotion of social equality through the promotion of collective rights, and it has been put in opposition to more individualistic, liberal ideas about the free market and private property. That the New Right actually promotes collective rights, albeit not egalitarianism, while at the same time opposing liberalism and capitalism makes the preconceived notions we might have of the left and right invalid.

Giving a clear-cut definition of the New Right is quite difficult as it incorporates heterogeneous groups and persons throughout Europe, such as the Nouvelle Droite in France whose main exponents are Alain de Benoist and Guillaume Faye, and the Neue Rechte in Germany with representatives such as Pierre Krebs and Karlheinz Weißmann. French commentator Pierre Vial has identified five distinct ideological elements that constitute main influences and strands of thought in the New Right, and Michael O'Meara has added a

---

13. See Tyr, "Tyr".
14. For a more detailed exposition of Radical Traditionalism see Senholt, "Radical Traditionalism and the New Right".
15. This includes contributions in the journal by scholars of Western esotericism such as Joscelyn Godwin and Christopher McIntosh. See also Senholt, "Radical Traditionalism and the New Right".

sixth to these. This list is a good starting point for a working definition. The six elements are:

1) The Anti-modern traditionalism of René Guénon and Julius Evola, influencing the Right since the early twentieth century
2) *Völkisch* and communitarian nationalism focusing on continental identity
3) Neopaganism as opposition to the Judaeo-Christian heritage, stressing the importance of "primordial European values"
4) Postmodernism, celebrating cultural pluralism as the new alternative after the breakdown of modernity's totalizing structures
5) Scientism, focusing on life sciences, genetics, eugenics, and their ideological implications
6) Geopolitics, such as the ideas of Eurasianism promulgated by Alexandr Dugin[16]

It is easy to gather from the diversity of the above ideological elements that the New Right is not a totalizing ideology that gives absolute ideological answers to all aspects of life, but a loosely structured ideological current that conveys a polyvalence of ideas, giving rise to a *Weltanschauung* with diverse and even divergent opinions. As such the European New Right should be considered a cultural and intellectual network presenting itself as working towards the preservation and rekindling of European culture, tradition and identity. It utilizes a metapolitical strategy aimed at inspiring a revolutionary change in the current cultural hegemony of the global liberal-democratic system, and works towards the establishment of new tribal communities. Over the last century, both the European New Right and the Traditionalists have succeeded in impacting intellectuals and scholars, as well as the political and cultural mainstream, securing their place within the field of radical politics and religion.

The final ideological constellation worth mentioning in this context is Eurasianism. Its contemporary variant, at times also referred to as neo-Eurasianism, can be considered a politicized variety of Traditionalism. Eurasianism has its origins in early twentieth-century Russian émigré circles and draws on classical theories of geopolitics, such as that of Halford Mackinder, who later became the first director of the London School of Economics. Eurasianism is a geopolitical theory which interprets the political situation through geographical factors rather than through cultural ones, and posits a Euro-Asian "heartland", with a continental axis centred in Greater Russia, in opposition to an Atlantic, US-dominated bloc.[17] Its most prominent contemporary spokesperson, Alexandr Dugin, began his political career

---

16. O'Meara, *New Culture, New Right*, 27.
17. Sedgwick, *Against the Modern World*, 226.

as a dissident opposing the Soviet system. He was, however, slowly alienated by the West during visits in the 1980s where he spoke at several New Right meetings in Belgium, France and Spain. He became convinced that the Soviet political model was a preferable alternative to Western democracies, right as the Soviet Union was about to fall. In 1993 he and Eduard Limonov founded the National Bolshevik Party, which utilized a strange mix of totalitarian symbolism and slogans from Stalinism and Nazism in its propaganda. Dugin left the party in 1998 after limited electoral success, moving towards the political mainstream. He became friends with Gennady Zyuganov, the leader of the CPRF (Communist Party of the Russian Federation), which was at that time still the leading party in the Duma.[18]

In 2001, Dugin founded the Eurasian Movement, which quickly became successful with several thousand members in Russia, and received economic support from several former KGB officers with ties to the Kremlin and Vladimir Putin.[19] Dugin's writings became increasingly prominent, and with his book *Geopolitical Foundations: The Geopolitical Future of Russia* (1997),[20] which was studied by both civilian and military analysts (and even used as a textbook in parts of the military), he became a highly recognized political theorist in Russia. The book argued for a Berlin–Moscow–Tokyo axis in opposition to an American–Atlantic one.[21] In 2008, his influence reached an even higher peak when he was appointed director and professor of a "Centre for Conservatism Studies" under the auspices of the Sociology Department at Moscow State University. There he teaches a curriculum of geopolitical Eurasianism, as well as Western philosophy, mysticism and Traditionalism. The purpose of the centre is to "stimulate research and the development of conservative theory" and to "overcome the negative factors that threaten Russian human sciences", such as "the imbalance towards Positivism in the Russian humanities" and the "lack of institutions that provide research on conservative social philosophy" in order to "develop and establish conservative ideology in Russia based on scientific research".[22] In addition to the centre in Moscow, six other branches are planned in major Russian cities, including St Petersburg and Novgorod. Dugin calls his own position "radical centrism", in the sense that he endorses a centralizing "father figure" like Putin while still maintaining radical (geo-) political stances with his opposition to liberal-capitalist American world hegemony. He is a good example of esoteric transfers within the political right, something which will be explained in further detail in the next section, where we will also expand on the overall relationship between the radical right and esotericism.

---

18. *Ibid.*, 229.
19. Mankoff, *Russian Foreign Policy*, 66–7.
20. Dugin, *Osnovy Geopolitiki*.
21. Sedgwick, *Against the Modern World*, 229–37.
22. Konservatizm.org, "About Center of Conservatism Studies".

ESOTERICISM AND THE RADICAL RIGHT

Before going into concrete examples of contemporary esoteric transfers, let us briefly reflect on how the relationship between esotericism and the right has remained a prominent underlying theme in both politics and popular culture. In politics, and in other places of power in society, esotericism has made a distinct mark. Frances Yates demonstrated an extensive esoteric impulse in Renaissance humanism, and in the intellectual culture of the Elizabethan era.[23] The spread of Freemasonry in higher tiers of society during the early modern period similarly established a foundation for the later emergence of esoteric freemasonry and initiatic orders. Two of the Founding Fathers of the United States, George Washington and Benjamin Franklin, were Freemasons, as were most kings of the Danish royal family since Frederick V (1723–66). There are many contemporary examples as well, such as former French president François Mitterrand, who openly showed interest in Freemasonry and esotericism, organizing the construction of the Louvre Pyramid, which later became important in Dan Brown's popular *The Da Vinci Code*. When it comes to the right more specifically and its relationship with esotericism, it is worth mentioning Umberto Eco and Theodor Adorno, who see esotericism as inherently connected to fascism and right-wing politics. Both see fascism as something esoteric, hidden and ever-present.[24] Eco even introduces the term "Ur-Fascism", describing it as a cult of tradition, which rejects modernism, and thus reverts to irrationalism and "action for action's sake". In *The New York Review of Books* Eco wrote:

> Ur-Fascism is still around us, sometimes in plainclothes. It would be so much easier, for us, if there appeared on the world scene somebody saying, "I want to reopen Auschwitz, I want the Black Shirts to parade again in the Italian squares." Life is not that simple. Ur-Fascism can come back under the most innocent of disguises. Our duty is to uncover it and to point our finger at any of its new instances – every day, in every part of the world.[25]

If not ever-present, there is at least evidence for a continuous line of esoteric right-wing thought after World War II, as documented by both Nicholas

---

23. E.g. Frances Yates, *Giordano Bruno and the Hermetic Tradition*; Frances Yates, *The Occult Philosophy in the Elizabethan Age*.
24. See Adorno, "Theses against Occultism", 172. Although both Eco and Adorno attack what they call "esotericism" and "the occult" respectively, it is worth noting that esotericism is here understood in a broad sense as irrationalism and the consummation of such irrationality in culture. An excellent academic examination of the phenomenon of "occulture" can be found in Partridge, *The Re-enchantment of the West*. Cf. Chapter 6 of this volume for a presentation of the concept of "occulture".
25. Eco, "Ur-Fascism", 12

Goodrick-Clarke and Joscelyn Godwin. It is worth mentioning the post-war activities of Savitri Devi, a woman of European origin who embraced both Hinduism and National Socialism, and Chilean diplomat and author Miguel Serrano, who provided the foundational texts for "esoteric Hitlerism" as it developed after the war.[26] The key idea for both is that Hitler is seen as guided by esoteric forces, and that he was not a mere human but instead an "avatar", an incarnation of a God. According to Devi and Serrano, Hitler was none other than Kalki, the last avatar of Vishnu, heralding the end of the current age of darkness, the *Kali Yuga*, which, following a period of cataclysmic destruction, will be followed by the golden age of *Satya Yuga*. Hitler's implementation of the Nuremberg race laws was, according to Savitri Devi, a first step towards a reimplementation of the Hindu caste system on a worldwide scale.[27] It was, however, not the esoteric Hitlerists who popularized the theme of esotericism and the right. Instead the influence came from Louis Pauwels and Jacques Bergier's *Le Matin des Magiciens* (1960), translated into English as *Morning of the Magicians*.[28] The book provides a fantastic account in which fiction is intermingled with fact, creating an esoteric mix similar to the later bestselling novels of Dan Brown. The book quickly became a success, was translated into numerous languages, and is still in print today. The success of the book led to the formation of a monthly magazine, *Planète* (in 1961), which within a few months reached a circulation of a hundred thousand copies, and was also translated into numerous other languages. Although the magazine faded in the 1970s, it had already made its mark, popularizing both esotericism in general as well as more marginal currents such as Traditionalism and Nazi occultism.[29] The book describes Hitler as having been possessed by a diabolical entity, and borrowed heavily from the writings of Hermann Rauschning, a former Nazi who, after emigrating from Germany in 1936, wrote several books denouncing the Nazi regime.[30] The popularization of negative occult characterizations of Hitler led to an increased interest in "Nazi mysteries" with numerous fictional and non-fictional books exploring this subject. The most well-known example is Trevor Ravenscroft's *The Spear of Destiny* (1972). Ravenscroft was a British soldier during World War II, and was interred as a prisoner of war in Germany between 1941 and 1945. He claims to have met a Viennese Jew, Walter Johannes Stein, who provided him with intimate

---

26. Goodrick-Clarke, *Black Sun*; Godwin, *Arktos*.
27. Devi, *The Lightning and the Sun*, 229–49; Goodrick-Clarke, *Black Sun*, 95–7. For a more general account of Savitri Devi and Miguel Serrano, see Goodrick-Clarke, *Hitler's Priestess*; Goodrick-Clarke, *Black Sun*, 173–92.
28. Pauwels has ties to the New Right, specifically to GRECE and Alain de Benoist, whom he offered the job as editor of *Le Figaro Magazine* in the late 1970s.
29. Sedgwick, *Against the Modern World*, 208.
30. Goodrick-Clarke, *Black Sun*, 108–11. One of Rauschning's books was *Hitler Speaks*, which was claimed to consist of transcripts of the author's personal conversations with Hitler and portrayed him as an unstable, fanatical, and diabolical character.

details of Hitler, whom Stein claims to have known, as well as Hitler's supposed interest in esotericism. More specifically, Ravenscroft details how Hitler since his early youth had been fascinated with the Grail mythos, inspired by the medieval novel *Parzival* and Wagner's *Parsifal* and *Lohengrin*, and that he already at an early age was set on acquiring the "Spear of Destiny", the spear of the Roman soldier Longinus that supposedly pierced the side of Jesus. According to legend, the wielder of the spear would be granted immense power and be able to control the world, and supposedly the spear has been in the hands of numerous successful military leaders including Constantine the Great. According to Ravenscroft, Hitler sought and acquired the spear in Vienna, where it had been stored in the Hofburg Palace's *Schatzkammer*, after Germany's *Anschluss* (annexation) with Austria in 1938.[31] Not only was Hitler determined to get the spear, but he was also initiated by two members of the Thule Society, Dietrich Eckart and Karl Haushofer, in order to "develop and open the centres in the astral body ... giving him [Hitler] the possibility of vision into the macrocosm and means of communication with the powers of darkness".[32] Such stories naturally sparked a renewed interest in right-wing esotericism, and numerous fictional and semi-fictional works were soon published on this topic,[33] providing at least part of the background for the contemporary examples of esotericism within the radical right to which we will now turn. As we shall see, in many instances right-wing esotericism borrows directly or indirectly from some of the many ideas postulated by speculative esoteric writings such as those of Pauwels, Bergier and Ravenscroft.

Broadly speaking, the use of esotericism within the radical right takes two different but related forms. On the one hand, we see the adaptation of occult and esoteric symbolism, often for superficial or aesthetic reasons, similar to the usage of such symbolism within certain music genres such as Black Metal and Neofolk.[34] On the other hand, we see a more far-reaching adaptation of not only symbols and aesthetics, but of radical rightist ideologies and mythologies as well. Starting with the latter, a recurrent theme within the radical right is the idea of a mythical "homeland", often conceived to be in the far north. This idea is far from new, and has its roots in the *völkisch* and Ariosophical currents described earlier.[35] In particular, the roots lie in the descriptions of researchers such as Hermann Wirth, leader of the National Socialist research institute Ahnenerbe, who, in his book *Der Aufgang der Menschheit* (1928), traces the prehistoric origins of Germanic civilization to an archaic civilization of

---

31. Ravenscroft, *The Spear of Destiny*, 47–88; Goodrick-Clarke, *Black Sun*, 118–20.
32. Ravenscroft, *The Spear of Destiny*, 230. Most of Ravenscroft's claims have since been debunked in Andersson, *Hitler and the Occult*.
33. For an extensive list of speculative non-fiction, see Goodrick-Clarke, *Black Sun*, 321n4.
34. See also Granholm, "'Sons of Northern Darkness'".
35. See Godwin, *Arktos*.

Nordic Atlanteans located in the arctic.[36] The idea of such a primordial homeland is conceived on the basis of sources from Antiquity, such as Plato's writing about the mythical continent Atlantis that rose and later sank in the Atlantic Ocean. Similarly, around 300 BCE Pytheas of Massilia makes references to a mysterious land called Thule which he described in the account of his travels to northern Europe.[37] These ancient tales have since gained a life of their own, reappearing in many variations, particularly in Theosophy, which made Atlantis a well-known subject within esoteric circles. The references to Thule and Atlantis appear throughout the radical right and beyond, being adapted into mainstream culture, such as in the comic book series and movie *Hellboy*. One example is New Right philosopher Alain de Benoist, who in his seminal book *Vu de Droite* devotes a whole section to Atlantis, claiming it to be the German island Helgoland.[38] Also, the name Thule occurs frequently among right-wing groups, most prominently in relation to the leading German group Thule-Seminar, led by Pierre Krebs. In addition to having adopted the name Thule for its group, presumably a reference both to the Thule Society and to the mythical geographical place in the north, the group also makes frequent use of various forms of occult-esoteric symbolism. One such symbol is the Black Sun,[39] a composite of twelve S-shaped runes that was embedded in the floor of Wewelsburg castle, often referred to as "Himmler's Camelot", which was to function as the Germanic Vatican of the thousand-year Reich. The symbol is used both on the cover of the Thule-Seminar's magazine *Metapo*, as well as on all the merchandise sold by the organization, including calendars, clothing, and even wrist-watches. In addition to the Black Sun, runic imagery abounds in their publications and in particular in their calendars, in which weekdays are named after the Germanic gods and the dates are written with runic numerals.[40]

Similar esoteric symbolism can also be found in connection with Alexandr Dugin, the leading contemporary thinker of Eurasianism mentioned earlier. Dugin is deeply indebted to Julius Evola's variant of Traditionalism, and Dugin himself translated and published Evola's *Heathen Imperialism* into Russian in 1981.[41] Several of Dugin's books deal not only with Traditionalism and its relation to Russian Orthodox Christianity, but also with various esoteric concepts. An example is the book *Hyperborean Theory*, which deals with the idea

---

36. Wirth, *Der Aufgang der Menschheit*; Goodrick-Clarke, *Black Sun*, 130. A few attempts at tracing the idea of an arctic-Atlantean *urheimat* have already been made, see Wegener, *Das Atlantidische Weltbild*; Godwin, *Arktos*.
37. Godwin, *Arktos*, 47–8.
38. De Benoist, *Vu de Droite*, 38–40.
39. The solar symbol supposedly originates from a medieval Merovingian design on brooches, but its architectural use by the Nazis has led to numerous post-war associations of the symbol with the occult. See Goodrick-Clarke, *Black Sun*, 148.
40. Thule-Seminar, "Inhalt".
41. Sedgwick, *Against the Modern World*, 222.

of a primordial *Urheimat* in the north and draws on *völkisch* theorists such as Hermann Wirth.[42] Dugin is thus linked both to the European New Right, directly through participating in conferences and indirectly by drawing on the same mythological complexes, and to one of the key historical influences on the radical right. A final example worth mentioning in relation to Dugin is the symbol chosen to represent the Eurasian Movement. Whenever the organization holds public demonstrations its members wave black banners portraying a classical symbol of chaos in bright yellow, an eight-pointed star, a symbol also used by the European New Right organization in the United Kingdom, as well as in Chaos Magick and role-playing games, such as Warhammer. Although this could be a coincidence, and no direct connection exists between Chaos Magick and the Eurasianism of Dugin, this confluent use is still interesting. Dugin is likewise aware of esoteric currents and personalities such as Aleister Crowley.[43] That is further evidence of interconnectedness between Dugin and esotericism.

The interest in *völkisch* occultism and runic magic is not limited to the Thule-Seminar, but is present among a broad range of radical right groups from all over the world. The American Radical Traditionalists of *Tyr* mentioned at the beginning of this article, most prominently Stephen Flowers and Michael Moynihan, have published numerous articles on *völkisch* occultists.[44] Flowers and Moynihan have even published a selection of writings by Karl Maria Wiligut, Himmler's personal adviser in occultism and Ariosophy, and creator of the Black Sun symbol in its contemporary form.[45] Flowers is also the head of the Rune Guild, a group practising rune magic, as well as a high-degree initiate in the Temple of Set.[46] During his active involvement with the Temple he was Grand Master of its Order of the Trapezoid, a group focused on various forms of Germanic/Nordic magic and grail mysticism.[47] Flowers and Moynihan are not the only rightists[48] with an interest in Ariosophy and *völkisch* occultism. Christian Bouchet, a leading voice in the French radical right and the publisher of the magazine *Résistance*, has recently published a whole book on Wiligut, through a publishing house, Avatar Éditions, that also features books by and about Savitri Devi (in which Bouchet is also a contributor).[49] In addition to France, Russia, the United States and Germany,

---

42. See the expanded version of this book, Dugin, "Znaki Velikogo Norda" ("Signs of the Great North").
43. See Dugin, "Uchenie Zverja" ("The Doctrine of the Beast").
44. For an overview of articles published in the journal so far, see Tyr, "Titles".
45. Flowers & Moynihan, *The Secret King*.
46. For more on the Rune Gild, see Granholm, "The Rune-Gild".
47. Order of the Trapezoid, "The Mysteries".
48. The "rightism" of Flowers and Moynihan is a reference to the ideological standpoints expressed in their writings, and their implications, rather than any active political engagement.
49. Bouchet, *Karl Maria Wiligut*; Avatar Éditions, "Website".

we find examples of the combination of right-wing philosophy, political Traditionalism, and occult–esoteric thought in other parts of the world. In Scandinavia, a radical expression of the right emerged with Allgermanische Heidnische Front (AHF) in the 1990s. This group was established in the wake of a sudden rise in anti-Christian sentiments among the youth, in particular in the burgeoning Norwegian Black Metal scene, which became infamous because of the numerous church arsons and even murders associated with it.[50] The AHF had regional websites in numerous European countries, with a focal point in Scandinavia, where the Swedish Heathen Front published the magazine *Budkavlen*, featuring articles on the previously mentioned *völkisch* occultists.[51] As recently as 2007, the Swedish right-wing metal band Fyrdung released their third album *Hyperborea*, which featured quotes from Savitri Devi and Evola, as well as a song entitled "Children of the Black Sun". In Italy we likewise find several groups involved in right-wing esotericism, the most prominent examples being the cultural crypto-Fascist group Raido and a group called Centro Studi la Runa which publishes the magazine *Algiza* on religion, mythology, and Indo-European tradition.[52] A final German example, in addition to the Thule-Seminar already mentioned, is the now defunct group Sonnenwacht, in the publications of which Ariosophy and *völkisch* nationalism, as well as the Black Sun symbol, were prominent topics.[53]

Having demonstrated the radical right's frequent use of esoteric notions and symbolism with numerous examples, let us now see if we can identify some common denominators and patterns. Are these examples of esoteric transfers part of a larger ideological constellation? It is my contention that nearly all of the above examples fall within one side of an established narrative and dichotomy. On the one hand, modern society with its values of egalitarianism and individualism, which according to the radical right are basically derived from secularized Christianity, and on the other hand, an anti-modern opposition to the establishment and its values, based on what is perceived as indigenous *pagan* values. I claim that the radical right constructs a grand narrative in which it places itself within a marginalized pagan opposition to a secularized Christian establishment. This narrative, construed in opposition to a similar anti-esoteric narrative within the mainstream, will be discussed in the final part of this article, but let us here look at how the radical right itself perceives and constructs the narrative, beginning with the radical right's view of Christianity as the cause of modernity.

According to the New Right the Reformation helped undermine the social authority of religion, resulting in the dissolution of society:

---

50. Søderlind & Moynihan, *Lords of Chaos*.
51. Svensk Hednisk Front, *Budkavlen*.
52. Centro Studi La Runa, "Info".
53. For a more detailed examination of the radical right in Germany and its use of the Black Sun and other esoteric symbols see Sünner, *Schwarze Sonne*.

> The secularizing forces it [Protestantism] unleashed shattered the old Biblical myths, dislodged transcendental references, and discredited Christianity among the European masses, most of whom today remain Christian in name only. This, though, marked not the end of Christian influence. Its most distinct beliefs have since been profaned and incorporated into the modernist project. Liberalism, for example, secularized the church's universalism, egalitarianism, and individualism, in the process reformulating Christian charity as humanitarianism, hope as progress, redemption as abundance.[54]

Thus Christian values survived in the liberal, modern society. The Enlightenment and liberalism are seen as the culmination and secularization of Christian values, and the fact that these are still embedded in modern society means that Christianity still constitutes a threat to European identity: "the *Entzauberung* [disenchantment] was not halted mid-route. In this regard, the rationalism of the 'Enlightenment', far from constituting the antithesis of biblical monotheism, represents rather its profane transposition and ineluctable culmination".[55]

The radical right unanimously, in one form or another, sees European pre-Christian traditions as the only real and credible alternative to Christianity, and as a form of spirituality that both acts as a bulwark against the "onslaught of modernity" and at the same time is a fulfilling tradition in line with basic European values. This does not necessarily imply practising pre-Christian religions *per se*, but rather to employ a "philosophical paganism" which provides people with a codex by which to live their everyday lives. According to the New Right, (neo)paganism is neither a cult phenomenon, involving religious practice, nor Christianity turned upside down. Rather, it has a positive and autonomous content. De Benoist stresses that the cultural focus should be on the pre-Christian origins of Europe.[56] The French organization GRECE (Groupement de recherche et d'études pour la civilisation européenne) contributed to this debate by publishing *Les Traditions d'Europe*; an attempt at an overview of all the different non-Christian European traditions. Another leading figure within the French New Right scene was Jean Haudry, a professor at the University of Lyon whose *Les Indo-Européenes* was translated into both English and German.[57] One of the reasons that Haudry is applauded by the New Right is that he supports the so-called "arctic hypothesis" of the Indo-European homeland.[58] From the beginning, Indo-European history and

---

54. O'Meara, *New Culture, New Right*, 96–7.
55. De Benoist, *On Being a Pagan*, 103.
56. *Ibid.*, 10.
57. Haudry, *Les Indo-Européens*.
58. The thesis of an "arctic" home of the Indo-Europeans was first put forth by the Indian nationalist Bal Gangadhar Tilak in his book *The Arctic Home in the Vedas* (1903). Tilak

language has been essential in the New Right project of defining European identity, understanding the Indo-Europeans as the indigenous tribes of Europe: "[L]a Nouvelle Droite postule, depuis sa fondation, l'idée selon laquelle les Indo-Européens, ethnie à l'origine de la majorité des langues européennes et élément important de la civilisation européenne, est le peuple indigène de l'Europe."[59] In tune with the New Right's project, one of the most interesting ideas of how paganism survived Christianity is set forward by cultural philosopher Sigrid Hunke in her book *Europas andere Religion* where she analyses the past 1500 years of European religious history. Hunke identifies certain ideological patterns which she claims are part of European consciousness, patterns which manifest as heresy during the time of Christianity; a heresy that, according to her, has tried to overcome the strong dualism imposed by Christianity throughout history.[60] She indentifies a number of mystics, self-taught geniuses and scientists, ranging from Antiquity up to the present day, who are representatives of "Europe's other religion" (i.e. "paganism").[61] Hunke thus attempts to add credibility to the New Right's idea of a "pagan" mentality that has survived the Christianization of Europe, as a *mythical* mentality in a world dominated by a rational *logos*. The basic distinction between Christianity and "paganism" in terms of a spiritual divide is thus the difference between *mythos* and *logos*:

> Logos – especially in its modern form – empties the world of those mythic truths that once constituted the essence of the European project. Against this "disenchantment", which leaves the European powerless before the great challenges threatening him, a revival of Europe's mythic heritage holds out the prospect that the true sources of his being might be recovered and the European project reborn.[62]

Rather than understanding myths as fantastical stories of the past, the radical right sees myths as models of behaviour, providing basic narratives of what a people and culture is and can be. Following Mircea Eliade they see myths as "creative and exemplary", generating "dimensions of truth inaccessible to rational experience" and providing a "normative framework that lends

---

argued that the Vedas could only have been composed in the arctic and later brought south by the Aryan invasion.
59. "[T]he New Right postulates, since its foundation, the idea that the Indo-Europeans, the ethnic origin of most European languages and an important part of European civilization, is the indigenous people of Europe". François, *Les Néo-paganismes et la Nouvelle Droite*, 53 (my translation).
60. See for example the use of Hunke in de Benoist, *On Being a Pagan*, 172, and Hunke, "Kampf um Europas Religiöse Identität", 75.
61. Hunke, *Europas Andere Religion*; Junginger, "Sigrid Hunke (1913–1999)", 151.
62. O'Meara, *New Culture, New Right*, 102.

coherence – meaning – to a people's activities, laws and world view".[63] The existence of a tradition, a common heritage of habits and beliefs, is seen as essential for the survival of a people, and thus the pre-Christian myths are needed in order to actualize a new renaissance in Europe. Indo-European prehistory is seen as indispensable, as it ascertains the common origins of the European peoples, and it is a common focal point among various radical right groups to focus on the Indo-European heritage. De Benoist states that a "spiritual" and "intuitive" familiarity with the Indo-Europeans is necessary in order to understand the underlying values that are also relevant to Europeans today.[64] Likewise, other New Right thinkers see the Indo-Europeans as the essential key to understand "our identity".[65] An example of how the "Indo-European heritage" is used as the ideal can be seen in the frequent references to the so-called *Männerbünde*, indigenous Indo-European "warrior-bands", in the New Right.[66] These are admired and viewed as worthy of emulation since they are said to have valued ideas such as honour, courage and loyalty, manifesting an order superior to clan and individual interests.[67]

Having now provided examples of esoteric transfers within the radical right, as well as having identified the clear dichotomy between modern Christian and anti-modern "pagan" worldviews that we can see here, we will now search for possible explanations to the frequent intermingling of esotericism with the right, and the dichotomy outlined above.

POLITICS AS ESOTERIC COUNTERCULTURE AND POLEMICAL NARRATIVE

The radical right utilizes esotericism, and in many instances takes part in a polemical discourse against "the establishment" which is similar to a mode of polemics found in esoteric sources. It thus makes sense to look at a few of the theories within the study of esotericism and consider to what extent these can also be applied to a political phenomenon such as that of the radical right. I am here in particular thinking of theories of polemical discourse, "othering", and the construction of "grand polemical narratives"; theories which may help explain the structural and ideological similarities present in the radical right

---

63. *Ibid.*, 103. On Eliade's connection to the construction of tradition, see Chapter 2 of this volume.
64. De Benoist, *On Being a Pagan*, 15.
65. Haudry, "Die Indoeuropäische Tradition als Wurzel unserer Identität", 107; Day, "In Quest of Our Linguistic Ancestors".
66. This topic is prominent in the writings of Day, Hunke and Haudry, and in Weissmann's *Männerbund*. See Wikander, *Der Arische Männerbund*, which presents the original theory of these warrior-bands, and Kershaw, *The One-Eyed God*; Brunotte, *Zwischen Eros und Krieg*, which represent the current state of research in this field.
67. O'Meara, *New Culture, New Right*, 70.

and esotericism.[68] I will argue that we find similar approaches to hegemonic thought both within the radical right and within esoteric currents influenced by anti-establishment and countercultural ideas.[69]

Starting with the structure of esotericism and the radical right, there are several obvious similarities, in particular as esotericism has been constructed since the 1960s as part of a countercultural trend, critical of modernity. Both the radical right and countercultural esotericism could be labelled "fringe movements"; they go "against the stream", acting as a counter-current, constructing their own polemical narratives against the establishment in the process.[70] Both can at least partially be explained by regarding the various marginal groups involved as forming a "cultic milieu". Historically, a similar, almost identical structure can be identified between the two. Esotericism experienced a popularization in the 1960s, protruding as part of the blossoming milieu of the 1960s counterculture, both in the United States and in Europe. The trends of the counterculture and the sexual revolution persisted, instead of vanishing in the 1970s like other fads of the time, becoming "a permanent feature of contemporary culture".[71] Similarly, the radical right, with the formation of the Nouvelle Droite (the New Right) in France in 1968, shortly before the student riots in Paris, became a permanent feature in modern European politics.[72] One might write off these historical instances of similarity as pure coincidence; however, they are not only structural, but also ideological. The New Right ideologically belongs to, or at least draws great inspiration from, what Hanegraaff calls the "religionist–counterculturalist" understanding of esotericism, which was primarily represented by the Eranos meetings in Ascona.[73] Being involved with the counterculturalist religionists of Eranos invites the same kind of issues that de Benoist and other proponents of the radical right encountered when

---

68. It is beyond the scope of this chapter to explain the theories of polemics within religion and esotericism in detail. For a volume exemplifying this approach, see Hammer & von Stuckrad, *Polemical Encounters*. The idea of Western esotericism constructed by a "Grand Polemical Narrative" is outlined in Hanegraaff, "Forbidden Knowledge".
69. It should be pointed out that, historically, esotericism has fluctuated in and out of respectability and mainstream culture. Here, however, I am talking about esotericism as it emerged as an essentialized construct in the twentieth century, especially related to the counterculture of the 1960s. For a more detailed examination of esotericism as variously mainstream, anti-establishment, and countercultural, see Hanegraaff, "Beyond the Yates Paradigm".
70. It is important here to note that esotericism for the countercultural movement is used as an oppositional construct against modernity, and that this construct is likewise projected back on history, in an attempt to present the "essence" of esotericism as something inherently anti-modern and anti-establishment.
71. Hanegraaff, "Beyond the Yates Paradigm", 18.
72. For an overview of the current constellation of right-wing parties in European parliaments, see Ignazi, *Extreme Right Parties in Europe*.
73. Hanegraaff, "Beyond the Yates Paradigm", 7.

professing their political views in public.[74] They were certain to evoke strong emotions, to inspire a combination of curiosity and repulsion, as well as the risk of stigmatization; in short, both were prone to accusations of acting simply as another type of counterculture. The counterculture of the 1960s was thus not only important for, and influential on, scholars of religion such as Mircea Eliade and Henry Corbin, new religious movements in general, and the New Age movement in particular; it was also, I will argue, a key influence on the development of the radical right. In this regard, the radical right could also be regarded as simply another form of counterculture.

Just as Eranos and the rise of new religious movements evinced a search and continued interest in religious alternatives to Christianity, so the radical right was dissatisfied with European spirituality under Christian "rule". According to Hanegraaff, a narrative of esotericism where "the Hermetic Tradition" is seen as a countercultural undercurrent battling Christianity on the one hand and rationalism and science on the other, was unwillingly established by Frances Yates through her influential *Giordano Bruno and the Hermetic Tradition*. It is this narrative, which posits a suppressed and traditional counterculture as "rebelling against forces of the establishment",[75] that is unconsciously adapted by the radical rightists. Polemics of late Antiquity were mostly Christian, directed towards "pagans and heretics", as well as deviant versions of Christianity, and the polemics of today are structurally very similar.[76] In both, a dichotomy between "us" and "them" is constructed. The only difference is that the current polemics are defined largely from the other side, with intellectuals from the radical right arguing against Christianity as a European heresy.

Sociologist Göran Dahl provides a crude (but nonetheless instructive) dichotomy, when trying to explain the New Right, acknowledging the power of attraction of a system of thought that offers alternative solutions to modern-day problems (Table 12.1). The table illustrates quite well a divide that was originally constructed as a monotheist polemic against "pagan idolatry". This dichotomy increased throughout history, from Christian Antiquity, which polemically posited a reified Gnosticism as its "other", to later Christian opposition to magic, occultism and "demon-worship".[77] On these grounds Hanegraaff argues that esotericism has been constructed by a "grand polemical narrative" within Western culture, a development that accelerated with the advent of Protestant and Enlightenment polemics.

---

74. See Ellwood, *The Politics of Myth*, which provides an overview of the political views implicit in the theories of three influential counterculturalists: Joseph Campbell, Mircea Eliade and C. G. Jung.
75. Hanegraaff, "Beyond the Yates Paradigm", 16–18.
76. Hammer & von Stuckrad, "Introduction", ix.
77. Hanegraaff, "Forbidden Knowledge", 225–39.

Table 12.1 Pagan–Christian dichotomy.[78]

Pagan/European	Jewish/Christian/American
Community*	Individualism
Idealism	Materialism
Belonging to a hierarchy	Egalitarianism
Polytheism	Monotheism
Respect for nature	Dominance of nature

* My translation. The Swedish word is "gemenskap", derived from the German *Gemeinschaft*, and has more connotations than the English word "community".

In opposition to this, "esotericists" responded to the polemical narrative by *inverting* it, and adapting it as their own:

> From the 18th century on and throughout the 19th, as a by-product of secularization and the disenchantment of the world, one sees them engaged in attempts at construing their own identity by means of the "invention of tradition": essentially adopting the Protestant and Enlightenment category of the rejected other, they sought to defend it as based upon a superior worldview with ancient roots, and opposed to religious dogmatism and narrow-minded rationalism. This process is part of a new kind of polemical discourse, in which self-styled "esotericists", "occultists", "magicians", and eventually "pagans" as well, self-consciously define themselves in opposition to religious and scientific orthodoxies.[79]

The adaptation and reversion of the Grand Polemical Narrative by self-defined "esotericists" and "pagans" is very similar to the narrative constructed within the radical right. As described earlier, both de Benoist and Hunke are good examples of how the radical right constructs a grand polemical narrative in its own right. When Hunke identifies certain ideological patterns manifesting as heresy during the reign of Christianity, and when she call all these "heretics" representatives of "Europe's other religion" and identifies them as bearers of a mythical mentality that has secretly survived a world dominated by *logos*, she is constructing a narrative almost identical to the one described by Hanegraaff. The "heretics" of Hanegraaff become Hunke's "pagan representatives of Europe's other religion". The devil-worshipping Knights Templar,[80] the heretic Cathars and the many witches burned by the Inquisition all become the true defenders of "pagan tradition" against a modernizing and non-European Judaeo-Christian one. In this way, the neopagan right can claim the European

---

78. The table is a translation of the one found in Dahl, *Radikalare än Hitler?*, 198n76.
79. *Ibid.*, 247.
80. The dissolution and trials of the Knights Templar, enacted by King Philip IV, resulted in accusations and confessions that the Templars had engaged in devil worship.

past of heresy and "otherness" as its own, and I believe that this, along with the structural similarities and the almost identical polemical narratives, helps explain why esotericism seems to be in so many instances interlinked with the radical right.[81] The polemical narrative of "the Hermetic Tradition" established by Yates thus assists the right in its battle against modernity and for spiritual reform:

> Yates' Hermetic Tradition was already congenial to religionism due to its emphasis on personal religious experience, the power of myths and symbols, and the religious imagination; and from a religionist–countercultural perspective it was natural to add the idea of "the sacred" as basic to a trans-denominational spirituality (easily combined with the esoteric concept of a *philosophia perennis*), and the ideological subtext of a battle against the values of the modern world in the name of spiritual reform.[82]

Where Giordano Bruno and Pico della Mirandola are cast as the martyrs of their time, the radical right perceives itself as being persecuted, proclaiming and praising their own martyrs such as Romanian Iron Guard leader Cornelia Codreanu,[83] Francis Parker Yockey[84] and Robert Jay Matthews.[85] Their "pagan" narrative is thus an attempt to combat the hegemonic discursive structures established by "mainstream" society and its science, knowledge and politics.[86] After almost two millennia of Christian hegemony in Europe,[87] where Christianity has been the main contributor to a grand narrative of European identity, the radical right has now attempted to deliver what they claim is a

---

81. For examples of such claims see Tyr, "Tyr"; Hunke, *Europas Eigene Religion*; de Benoist, *On Being a Pagan*; Wegener, *Alfred Schuler, der Letzte Deutsche Katharer*.
82. Hanegraaff, "Beyond the Yates Paradigm", 21.
83. Codreanu was at the end of his life imprisoned and later executed, together with fourteen other men, and subsequently dissolved in acid. See Norman Davies, *Europe*, 968; Codreanu, *The Prison Notes*. Although he was a Christian Traditionalist himself, Codreanu still fits well into the narrative of a dissident against the modern values present in non-Traditionalist Christianity.
84. Yockey is known for his neo-Spenglerian work *Imperium*. He was arrested by the FBI and died in 1960 by a supposed suicide in their custody. See Coogan, *Dreamer of the Day*.
85. Matthews was a leader of the white nationalist group The Order, burning to death in a shootout with the FBI in 1984. See Gardell, *Gods of the Blood*, 194.
86. For a more general description of the struggle over discursive hegemonies, see Skinner, *Visions of Politics*; Laclau & Mouffe, *Hegemony and Socialist Strategy*.
87. I am aware that Christianity is not monolithic, but instead displays significant internal pluralism, as has been documented in von Stuckrad, *Locations of Knowledge*. However, I still maintain an emphasis on Christianity's dominance in establishing European narratives of identity.

"postmodern"[88] alternative to the declining grand polemical narrative established by Christianity.[89] The radical right thus holds no illusions that their own narrative will be hegemonic and overarching, but that it at least will provide people with an alternative account viable in a postmodern setting: "if there is no single overarching narrative, and hence no single absolute truth, to explain history and justify the modernist project, then multiple developments, each with their own particularistic justification and local determination, are not only possible, but viable and desirable".[90]

The question then remains if the explanation of a "right-wing" essentialized inversion of the grand polemical narrative, and the identification of certain structural similarities, is enough to explain every aspect of the many instances of overlapping ideas and concepts between esotericism and the right. Although the idea of "copying" the narrative of esotericism might seem far-fetched, it seems clear to me that the right's penchant for paganism and the pre-Christian mythical and esoteric past is actually a logical part of a coherent worldview. Christianity is seen as the root-cause of the "malaise" of the modern world, and the primal origin behind concepts like capitalism, liberalism, egalitarianism and universalism, following Weber. It is these values that the right finds to be destructive to particularism and to the creation of a close-knit neo-tribal society based on uniformity in culture, tradition and identity. Being inspired by "pagan" and esoteric notions is thus not a free-standing disconnected trend, but ties well into the basic anti-modern and anti-Christian sentiments predominant in these groups and their worldview.

CONCLUSION

In the first part of the article we introduced several groups within the radical right, specifically the Radical Traditionalists, the European New Right, and the Eurasianists. Second, we looked at the many instances of esoteric transfers and the use of esoteric notions, symbolism, and counterculturalist ideology within the radical right, after which it was possible to identify a basic dichotomy in the radical right worldview; namely between "modern Christian

---

88. Postmodern should here be understood in two ways, both in a classical sense, where "postmodernism" equals the loss of grand truths, and the openness to relative and equally valid accounts of reality, and as "post modernity", a step *away* from modernity to a future based on archaic and pre-modern principles.
89. It would be interesting, but outside the scope of this article, to consider the difference between the neopagan radical rightists dealt with in this article and those who uphold Christian Tradition in order to evaluate where their narratives differ, and to what degree the New Right has provided a historically "correct" analysis. Christian Traditionalists probably still outnumber the neopagans.
90. O'Meara, *New Culture, New Right*, 22.

society" and the "traditional pagan" one. It became clear that the radical right does not view Christianity as a European phenomenon, despite its dominance in Europe for over a thousand years. The radical right looks at Christianity as something that is *das ganz Andere* ("the wholly other"), not in a metaphysical sense as originally implied by Rudolf Otto, but as something essentially different and foreign to European identity. Furthermore, Christianity is seen as one of the primary catalysts for the emergence of liberalism, egalitarianism, modernity, and the *"Entzauberung"* ("disenchantment") of the world – all of which are seen as detrimental to the European peoples. The strong dualism that Christianity entails was foreign to the European worldview, according to New Right thinkers such as de Benoist and Sigrid Hunke.

According to the New Right, the "European" alternative to Christianity is pre-Christian religion. This, however, does not imply that Europeans should return to the past and reinstate the worship of Zeus or Wotan, but rather that so-called pagan values and ideals should be adopted as the basis of postmodern society, constituting a form of *archeofuturism*[91] with the mix of antique ideals in a futuristic world. Thinkers like Hunke helped define this alternative to Christianity with her concept of a "pagan revival" in the Christian era, and Indo-European myths and societal constructions are seen not only as a description of the past, but also as an instruction for the future organization of small tribal communities and male warrior fraternities, the *Männerbunde*. The radical right thus weaves its own tale of Europe's pagan past, in which it construes itself as herald of a new age, unfettered by Christianity and its "children", egalitarianism, individualism, and liberal capitalism.

Despite the fact that "paganism" as a future ideal for Europe might seem utopian, if not outright absurd, the radical right does resonate with at least some Europeans that have been alienated from modern consumerist culture. The right has experienced a growing following of adolescents with a postmodern loss of identity, searching for a sense of belonging and believing, as a result of the loss of grand narratives. Followers of the radical right are Europeans in search of meaning and coherence in a world perceived full of arbitrary and capricious events, utilizing politics of identity as their means, and a revival of "pagan values" as their goal.

---

91. See Faye, *Archeofuturism*.

CHAPTER 13

NEW AGE SPIRITUALITY AND ISLAMIC JIHAD

PAULO COELHO'S *MANUAL OF THE WARRIOR OF LIGHT* AND SHAMIL BASAYEV'S *MANUAL OF THE MUJAHID*

Eduard ten Houten

> So fight in the cause of God; you are answerable only to yourself. And encourage the believers.[1]

On the face of it, New Age spirituality and post-9/11 violent Islam are irreconcilable forms of contemporary religiosity. Even as they may both announce the worldwide replacement of traditional religious authority by religious (hyper-)individualism, their doctrinal content seems to diverge too much to warrant an attempt at comparison. On the pedestrian level, as global phenomena, the contrast could indeed hardly be greater. New Age is seen as having brought comfort, self-worth and a sense of meaning to millions of ordinary people who struggle to find their identity in a world-system that increasingly marginalizes the genuine, the authentic and the sacred; whereas, it would seem, militant Islam has killed thousands and terrorizes millions in the name of a totalitarian religious ideology.

That there are affinities between New Age and Islamic jihad ideologies despite the seemingly unbridgeable differences can be shown in a concrete and very direct manner. In March 2004, the world-famous Chechen freedom fighting terrorist-cum-regional-jihad leader Shamil Basayev (1965–2006) appropriated, edited and redistributed under his own name a book written by one of the world's bestselling authors: the Brazilian New Age superstar Paulo Coelho (b. 1947).

In generous, deadpan and open fashion, Basayev acknowledged Coelho's primary authorship in the preamble to his version:

> In late March of this year [2004] I had two weeks of free time, when one day I found myself with Paulo Coelho's book *Manual of the Warrior of Light* and a computer. Wanting to derive benefits for

---

1. The Qur'an, 4: 84.

Mujahidin from this book, I rewrote a large part of it by removing some of the excesses and strengthening it all with ayat, hadith and stories from the lives of the Sahaba.[2]

Retitled *Kniga Mudzhakhida* (henceforth *Manual of the Mujahid*), the hybrid text was published on a trusted Chechen Islamist propaganda website in July 2004, where it has been promoted ever since as providing "the vital philosophy of the Mojahid, his character, experience, and a tactical and strategic idea … described in the art form and from position of the Islam [*sic*]."[3] Basayev, too, evidently intended his book to conform to "position of the Islam":

> Bismillah ir-Rahman ir-Rahim! Praise be to Allah, Lord of the Worlds, Who created us as Muslims and Who blessed us with Jihad on His Straight Path! Peace and Blessing be to the Prophet Muhammad, to his family, to his disciples and to all who follow the Straight Path until the Day of Judgment! *And then*: If something from what I wrote does not correspond with the Qur'an and the Sunna of the Prophet (peace be upon him), then I renounce it and ask Allah to forgive me my transgressions out of ignorance. … I have written it exclusively hoping for Allah's mercy and for Mujahidin to derive benefit from it for themselves and for the Jihad. There is neither might nor power except with Allah! Allahu Akbar![4]

Anyone cursorily acquainted with the tone of Coelho's inspirational novels and Basayev's capacity for astounding violence against the unarmed will wonder what possible benefit Basayev thought his mujahidin[5] could derive from a book like that; and, more generally, what Basayev appreciated in a book that, to western European eyes, so strongly emanates the cocooning, self-centred soft-focus spirituality of the awareness-minded middle classes.

This essay is not concerned with Coelho's popularity, however, nor with typologies of New Age and jihad ideology, or their development and origins. Much more limited in scope, it seeks to reconstruct the genesis of the *Manual of the Mujahid* through an exploration of the affinities and differences between the mentality, sentiments, beliefs and experiences captured by Paulo Coelho's *Manual of the Warrior of Light,* and the mentality, sentiments, beliefs and experiences of Shamil Basayev. It does so by discussing a number of more

---

2. Basayev, "Kniga Mudzhakhida".
3. *Kavkaz Tsentr*, "Book of Mujahiddeen".
4. Basayev, "Kniga Mudzhakhida"; cf. Qur'an 1: 1–7.
5. Throughout, when the word is capitalized, I refer to the "ideal" Mujahid of the Kniga; non-capitalized instances refer to Chechens fighting their jihad. In Basayev's statements the word is consistently capitalized.

or less concrete questions. How did Basayev live when he received the text and how did this influence his reading? What did he scrap, keep, or change and why? Why did he do anything at all with the text?

To answer these questions, we must not only zoom in on the two texts, but also consider a number of concrete preconditions, including the circumstances in which Shamil Basayev found himself when he picked up the *Manual* in early 2004; the kind of life he had led up to that time; some of the specifics of the struggle he was engaged in; and the cultural assumptions with which he approached the book. If we do this, we shall find that, odd as it may seem, the glorification of fighting in the cause of God (i.e. jihad) which informs the *Manual of the Mujahid* was not added by Basayev. It was already present, albeit in disguise.

Before we begin, a few final notes of a practical nature are in order. For considerations of space I have chosen not to include many Qur'anic references, even though I suspect that, to a Muslim eye, part of the *Manual*'s potential attraction lies in its use of prophetic rhetoric akin at times to that of the Qur'an. For identical considerations I have omitted completely Coelho's and force-marched through Basayev's career, presupposing on the side of the reader some general knowledge of the tenets and background of New Age,[6] as well as the history, complexity and brutality of the Chechen conflict.[7]

Our exploration will be guided by side-by-side comparisons of selected passages. To prevent the "Chinese whispers" effect produced by both books' translation routes – Portuguese to English and Portuguese to Russian to English, respectively – from obscuring the similarities, I have chosen to treat the English and Russian translations as if they are the same. That is to say, if my rendition of one of Basayev's originally Russian passages differs from the corresponding passage in HarperCollins's British edition of Coelho's *Manual*, this is, with one footnoted exception, always because Basayev made changes to the Russian translation.

---

6. Coelho's inclusion in the New Age galaxy may not be immediately apparent. Popular media call him an "inspirational" or "spiritual" author as often as a "New Age" one. So far no serious critical effort has been made to distil a consistent religious worldview and cosmology from his books and the statements he makes online and through other media. Any such effort would be hampered by the fact that he is first and foremost a fiction writer. As such, according to common twentieth-century practice, he cannot be held responsible for what his characters do, say, see, think or experience. This applies even if, as is often the case, the words of wisdom which they speak or think are literally identical to what Coelho offers elsewhere as his own convictions and views (and even if one considers that voices of "dissent" are rarely, if ever, present in Coelho's books). That said, the epilogue of his non-fictional *The Valkyries* contains explicit statements of his belief that the time of great transformations, personal and universal, has come. Writing in early 1992, he regarded the end of the Cold War as the beginning of another, simultaneously more violent and more spiritual æon.
7. Apart from those referred to below, notable English-language books on the Russian–Chechen wars include Baiev, *The Oath*; Hughes, *Chechnya*; Sakwa, *Chechnya*; Tishkov, *Chechnya*.

To facilitate further comparison between Basayev's original *Kniga Mudzhakhida* (кв) and Coelho's *Manual of the Warrior of Light* (мс), I have added references to *Kniga Voina Sveta* (кс), the 2002 Russian translation of the latter. All passages are cross-referenced, except of course if Basayev deleted something. Also, because there is no paginated print edition of the *Manual of the Mujahid*, references to it are to chapters, not page numbers.

PAULO COELHO, THE WARRIOR OF LIGHT AND SHAMIL BASAYEV

The notion of the Warrior of Light has been central to Coelho's spiritual arsenal from the beginning. It is mentioned in *The Alchemist* (1988), as well as in *The Pilgrimage* (1987) and *The Valkyries* (1992), two early books which, though they contain fictionalized elements, aspire to the autobiographical. Its importance is actually such that Coelho regards the *Manual of the Warrior of Light* (1997) as the "key book" to understanding "above all [his] ideological world"; in fact, as having "the same importance for him as the *Red Book* had for Mao or the *Green Book* for Gaddafi".[8] Warriors of the Light, he has said, are the "spiritual adventurers" of this world, those who actively try to realize their dream, regardless of what obstacles are placed in their way.[9] Fighting to the end for what they believe in, they know that winning or losing "doesn't matter, what counts is the struggle to bring something about".[10]

Structurally, the *Manual* is framed by a tale about a seaside encounter between a man and a mysterious veiled woman. "Write", she tells him as she gives the man a blue notebook and, before she begins to dictate, explains to him that the Warrior of Light is "someone capable of understanding the miracle of life, of fighting to the last for something he believes in", and that "everyone is capable of these things".[11] When she is finished, back at the beach in the single-page epilogue, he remarks that many of the things she has told him contradict each other. The woman, getting up to leave, does not deny this.

> [T]he Warrior of Light knows that everything around him – his victories, his defeats, his rapture, and his despair – form [*sic*] part of his Good Fight. And he will know which strategy to use when he needs it. A Warrior does not try to be coherent; he has learned to live with his contradictions.[12]

---

8. Morais, *A Warrior's Life*, 401.
9. Arias, *Paulo Coelho*, 21.
10. *Ibid.*, 26.
11. мс, xiii; вк, Preamble; кс, 13.
12. мс, 268; вк, 70 (with modifications); кс, 191.

The *Manual* proper consists of 133 single-page units about the amorphous Warrior of Light and the strategies and tactics he[13] needs, both militarily and psychologically, in order to fight the Good Fight, walk the Path and live his Personal Legend as part of his Spiritual Quest.[14] Essentially a manual to boost his morale by sanctioning "everything around him" as a necessary part of his destiny, the *Manual* mostly addresses in general, non-specific terms the Warrior's need for training and relaxation, rest and action, self-improvement and self-acceptance, etc., and outlines his strategy for overcoming the many negative emotions the difficulties of the Path inevitably bring him – doubt, fear, loneliness, disappointment, cowardice, anger, and so on. In the main, this strategy consists of either temporarily yielding to them or shrugging them off. Whether he does one or the other depends on what his heart or, because he is also capricious, his fancy tells him.

On whose recommendation Basayev first glanced at the *Manual* is unknown. Before filtering through to him, it had probably been circulating among his men for some time, probably as a printout of a text file originally downloaded from a Russian literary pirate website.[15] At the time, like among literate peoples the world over, Coelho was popular among young Chechens.[16] In *The Alchemist* they may have found temporary respite from the senseless deprivations of their lives. Or else they may have found encouragement to resist the tyranny under which they lived in its spiritual companion, the *Manual of the Warrior of Light*. Given his wide-ranging duties as coordinator of a regional jihad, it is doubtful that, even if he was fully aware of Coelho's currency among Chechen youth, Basayev had much if any grasp of Paulo Coelho's global influence, or that he was familiar with the latter's other work. This relative naïvety ensured that he approached the Warrior of Light with a certain freshness of vision.

In so far as the *Manual*'s emphasis on a struggle encompassing every aspect of one's life makes it suitable for guerrillas, nothing in it will have struck Basayev as strange. As a commander habituated to the unpredictable, chaotic, incoherent life of a guerrilla, he had learned that being flexible in the field was as important as being uncompromisingly determined in the pursuit of the "dreams" or "aim" he set for himself "at the beginning of his struggle" – which, in his case, was liberty and justice for the Chechen people.[17]

---

13. Although we are all Warriors of the Light and Coelho's protagonists are often women, for simplicity's sake I follow the *Manual*'s exclusive use of the masculine pronoun.
14. MC, *passim*.
15. Assuming that he received the *Manual* in digital form would lend support to his claim that he produced the book in only two weeks: he could have used the modern plagiarists' copy-and-paste method.
16. Anon., "What They're Reading", 88.
17. MC, 151; BK, 19; KC, 114.

On 1 September 1991, at the age of twenty-six, Shamil Basayev held a weapon in his hands for the first time.[18] Before that day he had led the life of an average young Chechen man. Born in 1965 in the mountain village Dyshne-Vedeno, he performed his military duties as a fireman and then travelled around as a seasonal labourer. In the mid-1980s he moved to Moscow, failed to enter the State University and went on to study at an agricultural institute. After having been expelled for absenteeism, he lived hand-to-mouth for some years, again working on construction sites, trading in computers on the black market, and doing other odd jobs of a (semi-)criminal nature.[19] Having been, in his own words, "an all-Soviet kid" who "overall ... really believed in the communist ideals" he was taught at school and elsewhere, his eyes were opened under perestroika.[20] With the disappearance of Soviet certainties, he later recalled, among all Soviet people "a lack of spirituality" had begun to make itself felt.[21] Basayev, too, began a search for his identity: "I found myself in the life of my people, in their aspirations".[22]

And so, on 1 September 1991, at the age of twenty-six, at a protest rally in support of an illegal Chechen National Congress in Chechnya's capital, Grozny, Shamil Basayev carried a weapon for the first time. It might be called the moment he found his personal legend, began to "walk the Path" and "fight the Good Fight", since from that moment on until his death in July 2006 he unflinchingly followed his own trajectory. In November 1991, when Soviet Russia introduced martial law in Chechnya, he co-hijacked a Russian airliner, diverted it to Turkey and demanded that they be allowed to speak to the press to protest against this move.[23] He saw his first combat in 1992 as a volunteer in the Georgian–Abkhaz war. He left the next year as the commander of the tightly knit Chechen Battalion (and, oddly enough, as Abkhazia's deputy minister of defence). In the spring of 1994, after briefly gaining further battle experience in Nagorno-Karabakh, the contested ethnic Armenian enclave in Azerbaijan, he and a number of his men travelled to Pakistan and Afghanistan seeking to receive more formal training in an Afghan training camp.[24] He returned to Chechnya in the summer of 1994 to prepare for an increasingly probable war with Russia. When it came in December that year, Basayev soon emerged as one of the most important commanders after the chief-of-staff and later president, Colonel Aslan Maskhadov (1951–2005).

---

18. Billingsley, *Immortal Fortress*.
19. Lieven, *Chechnya*, 36; Jagielski, *Torens van Steen*, 211–15.
20. Gall & de Waal, *Chechnya*, 260; Billingsley, *Immortal Fortress*.
21. Billingsley, *Immortal Fortress*.
22. *Ibid.*
23. Dunlop, *Russia Confronts Chechnya*, 121, 144; Liz Fuller, "The Rise of Russia's 'Terrorist No. 1'".
24. Blotsky, "Shamil Basaev". It might be noted that Al Khaldun, the camp in question, was managed and maintained by Pakistan's powerful intelligence agency, the ISI. Brian Glyn Williams, "Shattering The Al-Qaeda–Chechen Myth (Part II)".

In June 1995 Basayev entered the international stage. Weeks after a Russian airstrike on the family home of Basayev's uncle in Vedeno had killed around a dozen of his close kin, including several children, he gathered a volunteer force of some 130 to 150 trusted companions, told them to prepare for death and led them on a raid deep into Russia.[25] Their progress was halted in the southern Russian city of Budyonnovsk, where they herded up to 2000 civilians into a hospital and demanded an end to the war.[26] Personally leading the negotiations with Russia's Prime Minister Viktor Chernomyrdin, Basayev managed to obtain a temporary – and very welcome – ceasefire with Russia, as well as a safe passage out for him and his men, and the bodies of their dead.[27] The operation cost between 90 and 150 lives, mostly civilian.[28] In August 1996 he led the surprise retaking of Grozny that forced the Russians to negotiate and sign a peace agreement that halted the war.[29] In August 1999 he ignited another war when he crossed Chechnya's eastern border into the Republic of Dagestan with a force of some 1500–2000 mujahidin to assist some local Islamist friends who had declared an independent Islamic state.[30] In October 2002 he oversaw the organization of a second major hostage-taking operation, this time in the Russian capital and without his direct involvement in the field, to demand an end to the war and ask for renewed attention to Chechen suffering under Russian brutality; at least 129 of the 700–1000 hostages died when, as part of the rescue operation,

---

25. For the air raid, see e.g. Bennett, *Crying Wolf*, 425; Gall & de Waal, *Chechnya*, 259; Murphy, *The Wolves of Islam*, 20 (neglecting to identify its sources and using the dehumanizing blanket term "Wolves" to denote all militant Muslim Chechens, this book should be approached with caution). See also the film *Immortal Fortress*. For the estimated number of fighters, see e.g. Liz Fuller, "The Rise of Russia's 'Terrorist No. 1'"; Gall & de Waal, *Chechnya*, 257; Erlanger, "Moscow Accepts Chechnya Talks"; Murphy, *The Wolves of Islam*, 20; Sebastian Smith, *Allah's Mountains*, 200.
26. See e.g. Chadayev, "12th Anniversary of Basayev's Raid on Budyonnovsk"; Erlanger, "Russian Soldiers Storm a Hospital Seized by Rebels"; Murphy, *The Wolves of Islam*, 21; Liz Fuller, "The Rise of Russia's 'Terrorist No. 1'".
27. Liz Fuller, "The Rise of Russia's 'Terrorist No. 1'"; Jagielski, *Torens van Steen*, 228–9; Lieven, *Chechnya*, 124–5; Sebastian Smith, *Allah's Mountains*, 202; Specter, "TV Offers a Melodrama in Real Time".
28. See e.g. Erlanger, "Moscow Accepts Chechnya Talks"; Liz Fuller, "The Rise of Russia's 'Terrorist No. 1'"; Jagielski, *Torens van Steen*, 228; Lieven, *Chechnya*, 124; Murphy, *The Wolves of Islam*, 21; Sebastian Smith, *Allah's Mountains*, 203.
29. Liz Fuller, "The Rise of Russia's 'Terrorist No. 1'"; Gall & de Waal, *Chechnya*, 342; Bennett, *Crying Wolf*, 486; Faurby & Magnusson, "The Battle(s) of Grozny".
30. See e.g. Akhmadov & Lanskoy, *The Chechen Struggle*, 151–4; Evangelista, *The Chechen Wars*, 63 (Evangelista states that original reported estimates of the number of involved fighters "ranged from some 300 to over 2,000"); Hahn, *Russia's Islamic Threat*, 109; Murphy, *The Wolves of Islam*, 93, 98–102. Basayev himself stated in 2005: "There ... we sent a formation of 500 men. And further three separate groups of 150 men" (Babitsky, "Segodna Voyuet ves' Chechensky Narod!"). Assuming that Basayev means that these three groups consisted of 150 men each, the total number of fighters was 950.

Russian special forces pumped gas into the theatre building they were being held in.[31]

Even Basayev's enemies and those sympathetic to his cause, who nonetheless strongly rejected his resort to terrorist tactics, might retain respect for his fearlessness and skill. Few would in fact have denied that, though (co-)responsible for the deaths of hundreds of unarmed civilians, he was the most daring and charismatic commander of Chechen resistance to Russia.[32] In terms of fame and charisma, if not necessarily in experience and skill, he easily outshone his nearest rival and ally, President Maskhadov, whom he respected as a man and recognized as president, but to whose authority and opposition to terrorist tactics he would certainly not always listen.[33] Basayev had not only long repudiated many conventional rules and laws of war, but also developed a calm and composed determination to walk his narrow, isolated path chin-up and to let nothing and no one dissuade him from continuing the fight. It was under these circumstances that he first started reading Coelho's *Manual of the Warrior of Light*.

If he began at the beginning, he soon came across a very clear indication that, while the Warrior of Light may be a "warrior", he should not be thought of as a warrior like himself, not as the type capable of killing others for what he believes in. The eleventh passage gives us a single minute glimpse of the Warrior's, as it were, daily life when we are told that he "might dance down the

---

31. John Dunlop has offered perhaps the best dispassionate, factual, though not faultless, reconstruction of the crisis; see Dunlop, *The October 2002 Moscow Hostage-Taking Incident* (in three parts).
32. Responding to Basayev's death President Maskhadov's foreign-minister-in-exile, Akhmed Zakayev, commented that, though there was "simply no justification" for Basayev's attacks on civilians, he believed "that history will remember Shamil Basayev primarily … for his 15-year fight against Russian occupation" (Anon., "Rebels' Dilemma after Basayev Death"). In June 2004, three years before he was installed as Chechnya's pro-Moscow President, Ramzan Kadyrov told Novaya Gazeta: "He is a strong warrior. Knows how to fight. A good strategist. And a good Chechen. … As a warrior I respect Basayev, he is not a coward. I ask Allah that we shall meet with Basayev in open battle. [M]y dream is to fight against Basayev in the open field" (Politkovskaya, "Tsentrovoy iz Tsentoroya"). A more grudging expression of respect can be pried from Gordon M. Hahn's assessment of Basayev. A senior researcher at the Center for Terrorism and Intelligence Studies, Hahn views the Caucasian jihad fighters as such a threat to Western interests that he has in the past advocated "muting [the West's] public criticism of Moscow's frequently brutal prosecution of counterinsurgency operations"; nonetheless he called Basayev "one of the world's most ferocious and resourceful jihadi terrorists" (Hahn, "Anti-Americanism, Anti-Westernism, and Anti-Semitism among Russia's Muslims", 57, 5).
33. Maskhadov always called for and tried to practise adherence to the rules of war as laid down in international law. Basayev consistently rejected calls to abide by these rules unilaterally but, even though he called Maskhadov "an idealist", "a Don Quixote", respected his decision (Anon., "No-one Can Prevent Me from Doing what God Permits Me to Do"; Babitsky, "Segodna Voyuet ves' Chechensky Narod!").

street on his way to work".³⁴ This single passage shows that the whole of the book (also) suits the pedestrian, and strongly suggests that Coelho principally intended the book to be read by civilians. Basayev realized this because he scrapped the words.

Basayev was not put off by the Warrior's occasional inanity, however, because he found enough that he did like. In the book as a whole he detected a mentality bespeaking a true man of faith, whose understanding of the importance of courage, will power, and the capacity for overcoming inner (spiritual) as much as outer (physical) obstacles showed that he well understood the double-natured essence of his jihad. More importantly, the author showed an acute sensitivity to the need for obstinacy in the pursuit of fulfilling the task God had blessed him with. He recognized so much of himself and his attitude that, once he sat down for revision, he often did nothing to the text except substitute *Warrior of Light* with *Mujahid*.

[The Warrior] does not ask anyone else for permission to wield his sword; he simply takes it in his hands. Nor does he waste time explaining his actions; faithful to God's decisions, he gives his answer in what he does.	The Mujahid does not ask anyone else for permission to wield his sword; he simply takes it in his hands. Nor does he waste time explaining his actions; faithful to God's decisions, he gives his answer in what he does.³⁵

But it was not only that the book agreed with his appropriation of the absolute right to listen only to God for guidance on how to fight. It was also that one passage comes out strongly in favour of fighting unquestioningly for the liberty of one's people.

The Warrior of Light never falls into the trap of that word "freedom." When his people are oppressed, freedom is a very clear concept. At such times, using sword and shield, he fights as long as he has breath and life. When contrasted with oppression, freedom is easy to understand: it is the opposite of slavery. ...	The Mujahid never falls into the trap of that word "freedom." When his people are oppressed, freedom becomes a vital need. The Mujahid, using a weapon, fights for it to the death. In the face of oppression, freedom is easy to understand; it is the opposite of slavery. ... A Mujahid does not consider

---

34. MC, 23; KC, 28.
35. MC, 147; BK, 15; KC, 112.

> A Warrior of Light is always committed. He is the slave of his dream and free to act.
>
> himself free. He is free to act, yet he is a slave of Allah, Most Gracious and Most Merciful.[36]

Basayev's decision to make the Mujahid the slave of Allah rather than of his dream is justifiable in light of the rest of the book, which teaches that virtually all of the guidance the Warrior receives in life comes straight from God. Though He may use signs or the Warrior's guardian angel to speak, He usually speaks directly to the Warrior's heart. It is there, "in the silence of his heart", that the Warrior knows he will gain "an understanding of his responsibilities and of how he should behave accordingly", and where he will "hear an order that will guide him".[37] Though Basayev deleted these particular words, he retained others that are similarly inclined. The Warrior–Mujahid feels secure in the knowledge that he is "only an instrument of the Light/a slave of Allah", and hence bases his decisions "on inspiration and faith".[38] When he feels guilty at being blessed with his struggle while so much of mankind is miserable, his angel tells him to give it all up and the Warrior–Mujahid submits: He "kneels down and offers God/Allah his conquests/victories".[39] In fact, he is so committed to serving God that, when the divine order comes to move on, he breaks camp and abandons his companions without further ado since "he knows that his sword/weapon is sacred and that he must obey the orders of the One to Whom he offered up his struggle".[40]

The constancy of the Warrior's strict and steadfast subservience to God is counterbalanced by the overall incoherence of his quotidian existence. The *Manual* informs us now that the very moment that the Warrior begins to walk along the Path, he recognizes it, but also that he has not always known it, and at times strays or is forced from it.[41] That he is "never cowardly", yet that he is "often cowardly".[42] That he wears the "indestructible cloak of faith" even though he "often loses faith".[43] To allay the tension and confusion his life entails, the Warrior adopts a meta-strategy. He "adapts to the circumstances" and "treats each situation as if it were unique and never resorts to formulae, recipes or other people's opinions" and "has no 'certainties', he just has a path to follow, a path to which he adapts depending on the season", and therefore "no longer judges the world on the basis of 'right' and 'wrong', but on the basis of 'the most appropriate attitude for that particular moment'".[44]

---

36. MC, 155; BK, 37 (the Russian and English translations diverge too much here); KC, 117.
37. MC, 55; KC, 52.
38. MC, 139, 201; BK, 27, 42; KC, 106, 148.
39. MC, 151; BK, 19; KC, 114–15.
40. MC, 267; BK, 61; KC, 188.
41. MC, 33, 69, 43, 115; BK, 11, 14; KC, 36, 61, 44, 91.
42. MC, 79, 25, 169, 257; BK, 24, 10, 51; KC, 68, 30, 126, 183.
43. MC, 85, 101, 139; BK, 10, 32 (with modifications), 27; KC, 72, 82, 106–7.
44. MC, 67, 83, 225; BK, 5; KC, 60, 70, 162.

THE WARRIOR OF LIGHT BECOMES A CHECHEN

For Basayev all of this was no doubt familiar, what with his experience of mountain guerrilla, dynamic urban warfare and frontal combat, as well as every possible emotion from despair, hatred and sadness to elation, love and joy. More than that, he had actually held views quite similar to Coelho's long before he came across the *Manual*. Shortly after helping to reignite the Russian–Chechen conflict in the autumn of 1999, he was prompted by a journalist to talk about his spiritual development since the first war of 1994–6.

> The [first] war made me a true Muslim. We are all born *muslim*. You and I come into the world as children of the Almighty. But we can't find the right path from the start, we stumble, we struggle to find our way. Our leaders, our fathers, our religious guides and commanders stray. They often lead us astray in good faith. I too strayed for many years. My standards and values were false. During the last war I still fought under the banner "Liberty or death." Today, I also fight for my faith. I saw that the things in which I had believed are perishable illusions and that the only eternal value is faith in the Almighty, and only faith offers hope and peace. I didn't reach this conclusion in a day and a night. It ripened. Five years ago, when Russia attacked us, the Western world – guardian of all those sacred values like equality, freedom, justice, brotherhood and civil rights – turned away from Chechnya. The West betrayed us like a whore who goes with the highest bidder. This taught us, Chechens, a lot. We saw the untruthfulness of our own masters. We began to see that we could only count on ourselves and the mercy of Allah. That gave us immense strength. ... Today, we're approaching the war with Russia as completely different people. We are not just fighting for freedom, but also for the faith. Not only my Mujahidin, almost all Chechens turned to the Qur'an for answers on how to live. ... Many among us would like to introduce the Divine order overnight, because they don't understand that the people aren't ready for that. By the way, not just the people. Often those who are contemplating this haven't a clue about the Qur'an themselves, although they are convinced that they are in possession of the truth. As to me: I'm an enemy of both militant godlessness and militant ignorance. ... We all die once. The Almighty made us that way. The choice He gave us is not when we die, but how. We die when He wills it and there is nothing we can do about that, even if we hid in stone towers. The only choice is how we die. I have chosen to die as a warrior. What's so extremist about that?[45]

---

45. Jagielski, *Torens van Steen*, 265–6 (my translation).

Recorded in a country thousands of miles from Brazil, Coelho's country of birth, and distant not just geographically but also culturally, and years before Basayev could possibly have known the *Manual*, the sentiments, tendencies and vital philosophy his words express contain practically everything needed to begin to conclude the comparison between him and Coelho. Though not the most striking feature, his use of the first person plural is the most important. The man who spoke here spoke for himself as a human being and a Muslim, but he spoke first and foremost as a Chechen and in the name of the Chechens. This clear self-identification as a Chechen and as a Muslim not only influenced his reading of the *Manual* as much as it would have had he lived an average Western middle-class existence in which he felt trapped, but also led him to Chechenize and Islamize Coelho's Warrior. In doing so – and nothing in the *Manual* forbids him to identify himself or the Warrior as a Chechen Muslim, or to follow his dream of liberating the Chechens from Russia – the text acquires a wholly new urgency. It acquires weight. Words such as *freedom* and *oppression*, hitherto suspended in the near-vacuum of Coelho's rather amorphous warrior archetype, suddenly mean something when the qualifier *Chechen* is added. They suddenly refer to the Chechen people's lack of independence and unchecked Russian brutality against Chechnya's civilian population. The crucial difference between Coelho's New Age Warrior and Basayev's Chechen Mujahid is in fact to be found in this Chechen, that is communal or social aspect of Basayev's struggle.

Although Coelho legitimizes the non-committal self-interestedness of the Warrior by proclaiming that each of us ought to fulfil solely our own uniquely important destiny, it remains that in the *Manual*'s world the Warrior has no next of kin, no roots, no motherland or fatherland, no nationality, no religion, no ethnicity, no community function, no social responsibilities, nor even enduring social relations. To put it differently, the Warrior has nothing concrete for which to fight and no one with whom to fight. The Warrior, it is implied, rejects all such ties when he sets out on his Path towards his elusive dream. But in Basayev's case precisely his culture, his sense of kinship, rootedness, and community (as well as a fair dose of Chechen adventurism) had sent him on his collision course with Russian power in 1991.

Something else Basayev could little appreciate was that, unlike a mujahid with his need to act in accordance with the Qur'an and the Sharia, Coelho's Warrior has only a few communicable directions to abide by and is in principle not bound by anything except God's voice speaking infallibly to him in the silence of his heart. That is to say, even though Coelho clearly showed himself to be a believer, his Warrior fights in the path of God without any authoritative written spiritual guidance. Another disagreeable aspect must have been that, despite references to oppression and injustice, no attempt is made at a definition or delimitation of the Warrior's dream and, perhaps most importantly, his enemy is never identified. Within the world of the *Manual of the*

Warrior of Light neither can actually be imparted since the Warrior is "free to choose his desires" and even "chooses his enemies".[46]

While he must have picked up on Coelho's civilian side, Basayev chose to ignore it. He could even keep bits of passages which reveal the Warrior as the type of non-committal nonconformist who heeds no dogma and does what he wants regardless of other people's opinions.[47] He could also keep intact many segments that ring hollow when applied to civilian Warriors; having lost countless of his comrades in combat, for instance, Basayev had no problem being grateful to them "for their blood mingled with his on the battlefield".[48]

Because he grew up in a clannish, communal society that had inculcated him with a fighting ethos; because he was brought up in a culture of strong ancestor veneration; because his father had raised him and his brother on the tales of his ancestors, most of whom, according to Basayev family lore, had been "fighters, protecting their homeland against invaders" since at least the fourteenth century;[49] because Chechen cultural memory is filled with centuries of violent conflict with the Russians from Tsarist times onward; because his namesake was Imam Shamil, the great Caucasian leader of the long nineteenth-century war against the Russian Empire whose headquarters were near his birthplace; because his ancestors, most of whom, according to Basayev family lore, had been "fighters, protecting their homeland against invaders" from Tamerlane and General Yermolov to the Bolsheviks, since at least the fourteenth century;[50] because in light of all of this Basayev could convincingly claim that he and his Chechen comrades "have taken this baton from our forefathers, and this struggle has continued for centuries",[51] he had no difficulty in keeping a section such as this almost intact:

| Every blow of his sword carries with it centuries of wisdom and meditation. | His every blow against the enemy carries with it centuries of wisdom and reflection. |

---

46. MC, 5, 29; BK, 19; KC, 18, 33. Though this essay is not the place to discuss it, there is a strong case to be made for the idea that we never get to see and meet the Warrior's enemy face to face because, for Coelho, the enemy is precisely that which was so important for Basayev, namely rootedness in custom and tradition, i.e. having *limitations* (in Basayev's case: his being a Chechen). For Coelho, the social sphere itself, in its limiting entirety, seems to be the enemy. This could, I think, partly explain why Coelho's "message" resonates across cultures and creeds. It is not because it transcends and/or affirms them all, i.e. because it contains a positive universal element, but precisely because it *opposes* and *rejects* each culture and each creed as limiting. Its appeal is global not because he has found the words to speak something substantial that inheres within each, but because it is universally attractive to escape from limits set by culture and creed – and history.
47. See e.g. MC, 131; BK, 29; KC, 102.
48. MC, 3; BK, 1; KC, 17.
49. Gall & de Waal, *Chechnya*, 261.
50. *Ibid.*
51. Anon., "No-one Can Prevent Me from Doing what God Permits Me to Do".

Every blow needs to have the strength and skill of all the warriors of the past who, even today, continue to bless the struggle. Each movement during combat honours the movements that the previous generations tried to transmit through the Tradition.	Every blow needs to have the strength and skill of all the warriors of the past who, even today, continue to bless the struggle. Each movement during combat honours the movements that the previous generations tried to transmit through the Tradition.[52]

There are other segments that ring false if one thinks of the Warrior as a civilian and true when applied to a Chechen mujahid, when one takes into account that dignity, hospitality, and bravery are considered essential in Chechen culture and that Basayev was once described as "at his happiest when telling battle-stories, making his men around him laugh".[53]

The Warrior of Light sits around a fire with his companions. They talk about his conquests, and any strangers who join the group are made welcome because everyone is proud of his life and of his Good Fight. The Warrior speaks enthusiastically about the path ... When he tells stories, he invests his words with passion and romance. Sometimes he exaggerates a little. He remembers that at times his ancestors used to exaggerate too.	The Mujahid sits around a fire with his brothers. They talk about his conquests, and any ansar who join the group are made welcome because everyone is proud of his life and of his Good Fight. The Mujahid speaks enthusiastically about the path ... When he tells stories, he invests his words with passion and romance. Sometimes he exaggerates a little. He remembers that at times his ancestors used to exaggerate too.[54]

Anyone who has seen propaganda photographs or recruitment videos of Basayev and his mujahidin knows that they really sat around small campfires, drinking tea from dented tins as they waited for their clothes to dry. But the *Manual* grasps even more of the Chechen mujahidin's everyday world and the tough circumstances in which Basayev lived. The Warrior possesses little more than his sword and his shield, sleeps in a tent, is most often spotted out in the field, and "accepts without complaint that the stones along the

---

52. MC, 117; BK, 2; KC, 92.
53. Gall & de Waal, *Chechnya*, 262.
54. MC, 93; BK, 29; KC, 76.

path hinder his way across the mountains".[55] Russia's most wanted man and his companions probably spent a good many nights if not in tents pitched at the foot of a cliff, then in improvised quarters. A visiting journalist in 2005 felt he "was with a group of hunters camping in the woods", and described their living conditions as "very basic, extremely basic".[56] A final and easily overlooked correspondence between the *Manual*'s depiction of the Warrior's life and that of a Chechen mujahid is the small scale of their wars and the profound isolation in which they take place. Though in the case of the Chechens this was the result of mostly involuntary factors such as their ethnic isolation and lack of strong historical allies and, in the Warrior's case, of his disdain for swearing allegiance to other people, this fact resonated with the moral self-reliance to which Basayev had long ago accustomed himself. As early as 1995, following the Budyonnovsk operation, he had had a clear answer to those onlookers who condemned him for his tactics:

> You talk about terrorism forfeiting our moral superiority before world public opinion. Who cares about our moral position? Who from abroad has helped us, while Russia has brutally ignored every moral rule? If they can use such weapons and threats, then so can we.[57]

A decade later, in July 2005, he was downright scathing about outsiders who declared that he should abide by rules, conventions and laws that the Russians, too, so blatantly flouted in their conduct of the war:

> As long as the genocide of the Chechen nation continues, as long as this mess continues, anything can happen. Okay, I admit, I'm a bad guy. A bandit, a terrorist. Okay. So, I'm a terrorist. But what would you call them? If they are keepers of constitutional order, if they are anti-terrorists, then I spit on all these agreements and nice words. And I want to spit on the whole world if the whole world spits on me.[58]

In so far as the Warrior has set himself up as "the one who decides what he will do and what he will never do",[59] he evinces the same mentality that characterized Basayev until the end.

> We must not try to please either the West or the East. We must be ourselves, clench our teeth, and fight on, without looking to either

---

55. MC, 67; BK, 5; KC, 60.
56. Anon., "Reign of Terror".
57. Lieven, *Chechnya*, 33.
58. Anon., "Reign of Terror".
59. MC, 153; KC, 116.

side. As they say, "the path of evil is wide, and many people walk down it. But the path of good is narrow, and few walk down it".[60]

THE WARRIOR OF LIGHT TAKES SHAHADA

In the preamble to the *Manual of the Mujahid*, Basayev announced that he had added "ayat, hadith and stories from the lives of the Sahaba", and asked for God's Mercy if something should not correspond with the Qur'an and the Sunna. This very overt hope to have fully Islamized the text – each of the seventy short chapters of Basayev's text contains at least one aya and often a hadith – may be regarded as one of the results of his having failed to achieve either "Liberty or Death" earlier. Over time, struggling *itself* began to need a meaning, a meaning which he found in Islam.[61] But he also found it in the *Manual*. As a handbook for religious struggle that leaves the enemy's place vacant and the objective of the Good Fight to be defined by each individual, it possessed the negative requirements for an Islamizing revision. The most obvious example is naturally the substitution of "Warrior of Light" with "Mujahid". In other cases, a simple supplementation instantly solidified a passage that, to the non-Christian eye, may seem to lack in content.

He tries to establish what he can truly rely on. And he always checks that he carries three things with him: faith, hope and love.	He tries to establish what he can truly rely on. And he always checks that he carries three things with him: faith in Allah, hope for His mercy and love of Islam.[62]

Islamizing the Warrior was easy for another reason as well. Many key words from the *Manual* resonate with important Qur'anic concepts: "path";[63] "light";[64] "signs".[65] "The Good Fight" construed as a righteous struggle in which

---

60. Anon., "No-one Can Prevent Me from Doing what God Permits Me to Do".
61. Until the very end, however, his faith remained a secondary motive for fighting. When asked about this around a year before his death, his answer was clear: "For me, it's first and foremost a struggle for freedom. If I'm not a free man, I can't live in my faith. I need to be a free man. Freedom is primary. That's how I see it. Sharia comes second" (Anon, "Reign of Terror").
62. MC, 39; BK, 8; KC, 40–41.
63. E.g. "Guide us to the straight path, the path of those upon Whom your grace abounds" (Qur'an 1: 6–7).
64. E.g. "God is the Light of the heavens and earth. ... God guides whoever He will to His Light" (Qur'an 24: 35).
65. E.g. "Among His wonders is your sleep by day and night, and your pursuit of His bounty. In these are signs for a people who can hear" (Qur'an 30: 23ff; cf. MC, 91, 189; BK, 28, 33: KC, 75, 141).

winning or losing is less important than the righteous struggle itself can also be coupled with the Qur'an:

> To anyone who fights in God's way, whether killed or victorious, We shall give great reward. Why should you not fight in God's cause and for those oppressed men, women, and children who cry out, "Lord, rescue us from this town whose people are oppressors! By Your Grace, give us a protector and give us a helper!"?[66]

Only one section Basayev bluntly mutilated beyond recognition:

As the Warrior learns from his spiritual master, the light of faith shines in his eyes and he does not need to prove anything to anyone. He is not bothered by his opponent's aggressive arguments which say that God is a superstition, that miracles are just tricks, that believing in angels is running away from reality.	As the Mujahid learns from his brothers, the light of faith shines in his eyes and he does not need to prove anything to anyone. He is not bothered by the enemy's aggressive arguments which say that God is a superstition, that Jihad is terrorism, that Sharia is medieval and that one must bow to their military might.[67]

If these changes make the text look dangerously Salafist, it should be known that Basayev was unworried by the *Manual*'s various explicitly Christian references and very unorthodox, un-Islamic ideas. It opens with a motto lifted from the Gospel of Luke and dedicatory prayer to the Virgin Mary, and occasionally speaks of "Christ" instead of the more neutral "Jesus" – all of which are signs that outwardly place it in the (Roman Catholic) Christian camp. As to un-Islamic beliefs, several times the Warrior has some form of contact with the Soul of the World, an entity presented as separate from God – which comes perilously close to setting up a partner next to God, the gravest of Islamic sins according to the Qur'an, especially in the hardcore Salafist interpretation.[68]

THE BLUE BOOK

> Do they not ponder the Qur'an? Had it been from other than God, they would have found much inconsistency therein.[69]

---

66. Qur'an 4: 74–5.
67. мс, 173; вк, 25; кс, 129.
68. See e.g. Qur'an 27: 59–64.
69. Qur'an, 4: 82.

The immediate response to virtually all of the above might be that Basayev fatally misunderstood Paulo Coelho, who presumably never meant his text to be interpreted in this way. Though this objection is understandable, it does not address the fundamental question. Author's intentions mean little when the discourse of the text itself says something different. And what it says is that there are no boundaries between the material and spiritual. That is to say, Coelho's worldview is founded on a (conscious? semi-conscious?) blurring of the boundaries between warriors and "warriors", blood and "blood", swords and "swords", and between real and unreal or, to be more precise, between real and *make-believe*.

Having seen how well the contents of the Warrior's blue notebook grasped and could be harmonized with the lifeworld of a man who made no bones about summary executions and who, on top of that, gave the last full measure of devotion to his cause, one should like to ask Coelho whether he would concede that the Warrior of Light is not really a warrior. One should like to ask if he would concede that his invitation to take to heart that you do not have to ask anyone else for permission to wield your sword, nor waste time explaining your actions, implies an encouragement to dispose of all conventional (i.e. *communicable* and *negotiable*) criteria against which to measure behaviour. To appropriate the right to live according to a radically individual para-ethics comparable in aspiration (but only in aspiration) to that of Kierkegaard's Abraham. To declare war on everything that blocks your Path towards living the dream of total freedom from almost everything except the infallible inner guidance given by God? In sum, one would like to put the question to Coelho of whether the Warrior represents a warrior *with* spirit or *in* spirit – or potentially both? The glimpse of him dancing down the street strongly suggests that he only represents a warrior *in* spirit (i.e. a make-believe warrior). To deny this and assert that there are Warriors of Light on some immanent–worldly (as opposed to transcendent–astral) plane would open up the unpalatable possibility that Shamil Basayev's reading was indeed a justified one – in fact, that Basayev was a model Warrior of Light. A third option, presumably preferred by Coelho, would be to position the Warrior's *war* somewhere on the astral plane.[70] But that would raise the question of why a Warrior should be inclined to translate a divine calling into good works (i.e. "atheistic" action – and all social action is "atheistic", no matter how divinely inspired).[71]

In Coelho's intended meaning, I think it is safe to say, the *Manual* invites the reader to imagine being part of the adventure popularly associated with

---

70. Cf. Coelho, *The Valkyries*, 207.
71. Social relations exist only between humans on a plane on which God cannot *actively* and *directly* participate without destroying precisely what makes the social what it is. Therefore, social action – all action aimed at influencing the social realm directly – must without exception be regarded as "atheistic", that is, as though there were no God (ideally by the divinely inspired actors themselves as well).

the life of a real warrior without having to deal with any of the real inherent difficulties and dangers, for instance evading enemy mortar fire. Within the *Manual*'s world it is inconceivable that the Warrior finds death on the battlefield or ends up on the bottom of a pit behind enemy barracks. The enemy cannot kill him, defeat him, take him prisoner, torture him, nor abduct his kinsmen. The Good Fight in its intended meaning is therefore war without war, conflict without conflict against an enemy that does not really exist – *make-believe*.

Basayev was nevertheless neither naïve nor unreasonable when he interpreted Coelho's militant language of religious struggle not in its pedestrian and bloodless sense, but as speaking simultaneously of spiritual struggle against losing morale and of material struggle against an enemy. To support this point, here are three passages that together lay bare Coelho's seductive ontological sleight:

For the Warrior of Light, there are no abstractions. Everything is concrete and everything is meaningful. He does not sit comfortably in his tent, observing what is going on in the world; he accepts every challenge as an opportunity to transform himself. ... The Warrior ... transforms his thinking into action.	For the Mujahid, there are no abstractions. Everything is concrete and everything is meaningful. He does not sit comfortably in his tent, observing what is going on in the world; he accepts every challenge as an opportunity to transform himself. ... The Mujahid ... transforms his thinking into action.[72]
A Warrior of Light is never indifferent to injustice. He knows that all are one and that each individual action affects everyone on the planet. That is why, when confronted by the suffering of others, he uses his sword to restore order.	A Mujahid is never indifferent to injustice. He knows that all are one and that each individual action affects everyone on the planet. That is why, when confronted by the suffering of others, he uses his sword to restore order.[73]
Whenever the Warrior draws his sword, he uses it. ... The Warrior never makes threats. He can	Whenever a Mujahid bares his weapon, he uses it. On Chechen *kinzhals* [daggers] is written: "Do not unsheathe without need, do

---

72. MC, 69; BK, 14; KC, 61.
73. MC, 77; BK, 22; KC, 66.

attack, defend himself or flee; all of these attitudes form part of combat. It is not, however, part of combat to diminish the force of a blow by talking about it. ... The sword was not made to be used by the mouth.	not sheathe without deed." ... The Mujahid never makes threats. He can attack, defend himself or flee; all of these attitudes form part of combat. It is not, however, part of combat to diminish the force of a blow by talking about it. ... The weapon was not made to be used by the mouth.[74]

Which words in the first passage can be taken in a purely metaphorical, spiritual sense? Certainly, a Warrior with a mortgage will take the tent as a romantic adornment. Similarly, in the second passage the word that the pedestrian Warrior is inclined to read metaphorically is "sword". But what about the third passage? The make-believe Warrior is naturally pressed to interpret even this passage, including the unambiguous distinction between "swords" and "words", as referring, somehow, not to an actual, but to a spiritual sword. And this does more than diminish the force of its blows; it nullifies it.[75] For Basayev it was much easier to bring the text closer to his world. Fighting against a very real and very brutal enemy, he attained concretization just by replacing "sword" (*metch*) with "weapon" (*oruzhie*) and adding a Chechen *kinzhal* inscription. As regards the "astral sponsorship" of his lonely battle, he could rely on what the Qur'an teaches: "Prophet, urge the believers to fight: if there are twenty of you who are steadfast, they will overcome two hundred, and a hundred of you, if steadfast, will overcome a thousand of the disbelievers. ... God is with the steadfast".[76]

CONCLUSION

In the preceding pages we have seen the outlines of a variety of ways in which the book that Paulo Coelho regards as his most personal chimed with the spiritual and material life of Shamil Basayev. Since the *Manual of the Mujahid* is his main literary production, we may regard it as his spiritual testament as well. That both these books are so central to their authors may be their most peculiar characteristic. Had we, say, had only rumours that the great Chechen terrorist Shamil Basayev recreationally read a book by Paulo Coelho, we would have added him to the list of bloodstained men who appreciate Coelho's work

---

74. MC, 125; BK, 2; KC, 98.
75. It is superfluous to note that what Coelho is doing here and throughout the *Manual* is promote his belief in everyday magic.
76. Qur'an 8: 64–6.

– a list that includes General Augusto Pinochet, Russian President Vladimir Putin and Viktor Bout – and left it at that.[77]

But Basayev saw something in it that led him to improve on it and lend his name to it. And this leaves us with two guides to holy war written by two men whose public images could hardly be more opposed. Coelho was designated by the UN as a *Messenger of Peace* in 2007 and Basayev, by the same organization, designated an associate of Al-Qaeda in 2003. Coelho has never seen a day of real-life combat in his life and Basayev spent much of his adult life leading forces into battle. Placed side by side, they state in the starkest possible terms the problem of how to harmonize the gristle and grime of earthly war with the ethereal eternity of the divine Light. *Can you truly consider yourself to be a Warrior of Light if you have never considered the use of a grenade launcher? Is a headshot execution of a captured enemy ever* not *an atheistic act? What is better: to die or to kill for what you believe in? Or is just struggling to experience great feelings the best solution?* This problem is further complicated by the fact that Coelho is usually judged on his intentions and spiritual message, and Basayev on the concrete results and outcome of his actions. As we have seen, however, the distinction between the spiritual – about which we can speak only in terms transported by means of metaphor from the concrete so as to delimit and freeze it – and the concrete – about which we so often speak in terms transported by means of metaphor from the spiritual so as to animate and inspire it – has already been broken down.

Due to this, Basayev could approach Coelho and drag his Warrior down from the skies. In this respect, the *Manual*'s main weakness as a handbook for religious warriors was to his advantage. Had Coelho decided to offer positive, normative guidance on what is and what is not permissible to fight for, he would presumably have stuck to civilian, non-military dreams. But the book that is key to understanding Coelho's world, is founded on a faux ideology of *negative* freedom; the Warrior's dream appears to be nothing more and nothing less than to live in total freedom from all earthly, ethical, conventional, cultural and social constraints, all the while feeling that God is blessing you as you go along.

As a manual for the warrior without a cause, as a vacancy brimming with warrior spirit, however, it provided Basayev with the good, hard, lean battlefield liberation theology he needed but had no time to develop himself because he had a war to conduct. All that Coelho's religious fervour needed to give it direction and force was the temperance of a clear traditional mould. And once cast into the firm mould of Islamic jihad, Coelho's ideas were put to the test. His warrior attitude crystallized into military action. Suddenly inspiration drawn from wars fought in the days of the blade gushed back into the

---

77. Morais, *A Warrior's Life*, 413–14; Anon, "Putin Meets with Famous Brazilian Writer Paulo Coelho".

real world of blood-splattered snow, muddy boots, mutilated corpses, AK-47s and the charred ruins where houses once stood.

What followed the publication of the *Manual of the Mujahid*, finally, magnified Coelho's militant streak into shrill visibility. When Basayev revised the *Manual*, his bloodiest terrorist operation still lay six months in the future. On the morning of 1 September 2004, thirteen years to the day after he first held an assault rifle, a suicide squad of heavily armed mujahidin forced over 1100 children, parents and teachers into a school gymnasium in Beslan, North Ossetia, executed a dozen and a half or so of the strongest-looking adult male hostages, and demanded that the Russian army retreat from Chechen territory immediately. A few days later Russian troops, using excessive force, stormed the building in a badly controlled effort to end the stand-off. Many hundreds were wounded in the fighting and around 330 people lost their lives, including 186 children, scores of whom were crushed and burnt when the roof of the gymnasium caught fire and collapsed.[78]

To say that this operation in no way pertains to Paulo Coelho is not a circuitous way of stating that he is not responsible for any of Basayev's actions. It does not pertain to him because, as we have repeatedly seen, it is intrinsic to his "message" to refuse giving prescriptions or concrete advice on how to achieve a certain goal or how to decide upon a goal. Coelho is a partisan of a party of one. Therefore the Beslan attack pertains in no way to Coelho.

But it does pertain to the Warrior of Light. He lives according to the same divine para-ethics that led Basayev to say in connection with Beslan that, "No one can forbid me, while there is a war going on – I stress, while there is a war going on – from doing what God permits me to do."[79] But he will never be able to fight like Basayev: concretely, violently, cruelly and, above all else, *socially*. As much as he recognized the aggressively uncompromising and contrarian impetus of the *Manual* as his own, Basayev did not share the expansive solipsism of the Warrior and his prophet. He lived and died for the righteous community he was part of and which he believed in. "I am fighting not for my personal enrichment or still more my personal pleasure", he said in 2005. "I am fighting for my freedom and for the freedom of my people, to free ourselves once and for all from Russian oppression."[80] Only because he was a genuine partisan, only because he identified the enemy and himself (and simultaneously transformed the Warrior of Light into a Chechen mujahid), did he avoid the dirty little secret at the heart of Coelho's philosophy: the idea that I am only responsible for and answerable to myself, that I am the prophet of my life.

---

78. John Dunlop's reconstruction of events is very useful in showing that the above summary is more than a little simplistic; see Dunlop, "Beslan"; cf. Dunlop, "The September 2004 Beslan Terrorist Incident".
79. Anon., "No-one Can Prevent Me from Doing what God Permits Me to Do".
80. Anon., "Interview of Shamil Basayev to Channel 4 News".

CHAPTER 14

DEEP ECOLOGY AND THE STUDY OF WESTERN ESOTERICISM

Joseph Christian Greer

Deep Ecology's most enduring problem outside of the planetary ecological situation itself concerns its definition. In short, the multiplicity of competing interpretations of Deep Ecology has manifested a crippling amount of philosophical infighting, while at the same time providing its critics with the evidence needed to claim that the eco-philosophy is incoherent. Moreover, the dizzying array of interpretations has led astray scholars looking to account for Deep Ecology within overarching thematic rubrics like religion or esotericism. Scholars looking to place Deep Ecology within larger analytic categories more often than not fail to recognize the polyvalence of the term, and, thus, their usage of it is often superficial or distorted.[1] The intention of this chapter is not to solve this identity crisis; on the contrary, instead of validating any one interpretation of Deep Ecology, focus will be placed on unpacking the three most prominent interpretations of the eco-philosophy. In surveying these contents it shall become clear that, far from being a singular ideology, Deep Ecology is a hotly debated discursive field, and as such, lacks an essence beyond the assertions, polemics, practices and identities that compose it. That said, the analytic construct of "esotericism" shall orient the foregoing analysis for the simple reason that the three main interpretations of Deep Ecology all claim access to higher knowledge, despite their differences. As a point of orientation, the esoteric truth claims of each definition will be analysed in a manner

---

1. In his otherwise excellent two-volume work *The Re-enchantment of the West*, Christopher Partridge includes Deep Ecology within his "occulture" construct, describing the former as a singular orthodoxy that is composed of "the belief that all forms of life have intrinsic value, moral worth, and the right to 'self-realize'". As will be shown, two of the three most prominent interpretations of Deep Ecology regard it as neither a singular orthodoxy, nor directly linked to the "self-realization" ideal. Partridge, *The Re-enchantment of the West*, vol. 2, 58.

that illustrates the distinct and conflicting parameters each interpretation establishes for what is to be considered definitive for "Deep Ecology".

The considerable variance between the three main interpretations of Deep Ecology manifests in each possessing a different esoteric truth-claim. As a result, the problem that this chapter confronts concerns how the confusion over defining Deep Ecology extends into determining the place of esoteric elements in the milieu; esoteric discourses that are grounded in one particular definition are not seen as legitimate expressions of Deep Ecology according to the other definitions. Moreover, the esoteric discourses that have come to be embedded in the milieu, of which there are many, often draw upon the esoteric aspects of the three most prominent interpretations of Deep Ecology without acknowledging the significant differences between them. Accordingly, Deep Ecology must be understood as a number of divergent and overlapping claims, which, in turn, diverge from and overlap with esoteric and non-esoteric discourses alike. In order to underscore this crucial point, this chapter will use the graphical designation "DE" to refer not to a particular interpretation of Deep Ecology, but to the field of discourse that is referenced when the term Deep Ecology is used.[2] This is done so as to avoid unintentionally validating any interpretation of Deep Ecology above another and to stress the inherent plurality of such a field. Put differently, DE is the palimpsest formed by the various agents who assert their axiomatic claims on higher knowledge and the ways in which access to such knowledge create, organize, and perpetuate the social realities that compose DE as a discursive field. Betwixt and between, the esoteric elements in DE must be understood as idiosyncratic interpretations of particular definitions of Deep Ecology, that is to say, neither as odd pieces of esoteric flotsam nor wholly representative of the milieu.[3]

THE HISTORY OF DEEP ECOLOGY

The neologism "Deep Ecology" first appeared in a paper entitled "The Shallow and the Deep, Long Range Ecology Movement" delivered at the Third World Future Research Conference in Bucharest in 1972. In this groundbreaking paper, the celebrated Norwegian philosopher Arne Dekke Eide Naess proposed a polemical typology for environmentalism that posited a "deep ecology movement" over and against a "shallow ecology movement". While acknowledging that both sides were invested in stemming environmental destruction, Naess insisted that their vastly differing rationale, aims and conclusions constituted two separate movements, and thus necessitated a categorical division.

---

2. The concept of DE is largely informed by Colin Campbell's concept of the "cultic milieu". See Campbell, "The Cult, the Cultic Milieu and Secularization"; Bron Taylor, *Dark Green Religion*, 14.
3. Albanese, *Nature Religion in America*, 6.

In his paper, Naess dismissively summed up the entirety of the shallow ecology movement in two curt sentences: "Fight against pollution and resource depletion. Central objective: the health and affluence of people in the developed countries."[4] The two impulses that Naess identified at the heart of this approach were anthropocentrism and the drive to maintain the technological-industrial status quo. Similar to contemporary criticisms that refer to "green washing", Naess's typology made clear that any environmental ethic that put the needs of humans before those of non-human nature was not only shallow in terms of both its diagnosis and conclusions, but altogether insufficient. Being in favour of the deep approach, Naess used the platform afforded to him in Bucharest to enumerate seven "vague generalizations" that, to him, characterized the "long-range Deep Ecology movement".[5] Briefly stated, the seven generalizations were:

- an ontological worldview described as a "[r]ejection of the man-in-environment image in favour of the relational, total-field image";
- ecospherical egalitarianism which imprecisely became synonymous in DE with "nonanthropocentrism";
- diversitarianism;
- an anti-class posture;
- ending resource depletion and pollution by targeting their root causes and not "shallow quick-fixes";
- complexity understood in terms of a gestalt, and not in terms of a lack of such a unifying principle; and
- "local autonomy and decentralization".[6]

Naess concluded his paper by laying out three methodological points that governed his list of seven descriptive points. The first point was that the list was composed of normative values not derived from the science of ecology, but instead "suggested, inspired, and fortified by the ecological knowledge and the lifestyle of the ecological field-worker".[7] The second point reaffirmed the "forcefully normative" nature of the seven points, which he hoped would be "freely used and elaborated" to describe the Deep Ecology movement.[8] The last point stressed that the seven points he outlined represented a unified framework of ecological philosophy, which he termed an "ecosophy", and that by extension, the Deep Ecology movement was "long range" in that it served as an aggregate of numerous idiosyncratic ecosophies, with Aldo Leopold's

---

4. Naess, "The Shallow and the Deep, Long-Range Ecology Movements", 154.
5. *Ibid.*, 151.
6. *Ibid.*, 152.
7. *Ibid.*, 154.
8. *Ibid.*, 154.

biocentric "land ethic" and Rachel Carson's mystical "sea-ethic" standing as early exemplars.[9]

Naess's foundational paper provides a point of departure for tracking the ways in which supporters, critics and commentators would expand, reinterpret, and depart from the term's initial meaning and in so doing enlarge the discursive field of DE. In terms of historical context, DE's discursive expansion can be attributed to two American scholars, philosophy professor George Sessions and sociologist Bill Devall, who undertook a determined effort to use Naess's typology both in their work and in critiquing the eco-philosophies of others.[10] Along with disseminating and popularizing Naess's work in articles and the book they co-wrote entitled *Deep Ecology: Living as if Nature Mattered*, Sessions and Devall also developed the typology beyond its descriptive function by interpreting Deep Ecology as a solidified position largely based on the ontological propositions of Naess's own personal ecosophy as outlined in his Bucharest paper.[11] As Deep Ecology historian Warwick Fox notes, their efforts paid off, so much so that by February 1983 eco-philosopher John Passmore could confidently write, "it is now customary to divide the family of 'ecophilosophers' … into two genera, the 'shallow' and the 'deep'".[12] In 1985 Sessions and Naess co-authored and published the "Deep Ecology Manifesto", thereby adding another interpretive level to the seemingly distinct, yet increasingly complicated phenomenon.

The creation of a manifesto was a watershed in DE. Sessions and Devall – as well as a host of North American supporters, including Alan Drengson, the first editor of Deep Ecology's flagship journal *The Trumpeter* – were quick to refer to it, and not Naess's Bucharest paper, as the definitive statement on Deep Ecology. At the same time, a handful of scholars began to focus on how Naess's ontology ran like a red thread through the elaborations Sessions and Devall (as well as Drengson) made with regard to defining Deep Ecology. Critics including David Rothenberg, Andrew Light and Eric Katz all argued

---

9. Naess uses Rachel Carson's *Silent Spring* to date the beginnings of the international Deep Ecology movement, which is an overlooked but important link for the scholars who write Thoreau and Emerson, and American Transcendental in general, into Deep Ecology's history. For examples of this dating see Sessions, "Wildness, Cyborgs, and Our Ecological Future", 148; Fox, *Toward a Transpersonal Ecology*, 4; Naess, "Deepness of Questions and the Deep Ecology Movement", 208. For Carson's connection to Thoreau in particular see Brooks, *The House of Life*, 5–8.
10. Fox, *Toward a Transpersonal Ecology*, 43–77.
11. *Ibid.*, 233–6. Written in 1985 by Sessions and Devall, the first Deep Ecology book, entitled *Deep Ecology: Living as if Nature Mattered*, takes the seven points particular to Naess's ecosophy as normative in the philosophy of Deep Ecology. Due to the pressure of critics, they later recanted these philosophical associations and the text in general, describing the instances where they conflated Ecosophy T and Deep Ecology as "serious flaws". For explicit examples of these "flaws" see Devall & Sessions, *Deep Ecology*, 66–7, and for their retraction see Sessions, "Preface", xiv.
12. Passmore, quoted in Fox, *Toward a Transpersonal Ecology*, 69.

that Naess's Bucharest formulation, which later developed into Ecosophy T (named after Tvergastein, Naess's mountain hut), formed the ontological bedrock of DE theorizing, and further undergirded the claims made within the manifesto. DE's North American architects adamantly argued against conflating Naess's ecosophy with Deep Ecology and countered by stating that the *meaning* of Deep Ecology was to be found in the ecocentric, yet ontologically and "philosophically neutral" manifesto.[13]

Complicating matters further, Naess rejected all attempts to define Deep Ecology *qua* Deep Ecology. Instead, he insisted on his initial use of the term as a typological description of a pluralistic movement that could not be defined by any manifesto or distinct philosophical or religious worldview. Naess argued further that if Deep Ecology could be defined apart from the diverse movement, it was to refer to the formation of an ecosophy through a four-tier methodological system he called "normative derivation". As his interpretation of Deep Ecology regarded (as definitive) neither the authority of the manifesto, nor the claim that his own ecosophy articulated DE's ontology, Naess, along with critics and supporters, have continued to debate the question "what is Deep Ecology?" with scant conciliatory success. The endless and increasingly fruitless debate over this question has transformed DE into a ubiquitous, if not entirely ambiguous element in "radical environmentalism", leading one commentator to describe it as "a vague, formless, self-contradictory, invertebrate thing" and another to the conclusion that DE "has more interpretations than the Bible".[14]

DEEP ECOLOGY WITHIN THE STUDY OF WESTERN ESOTERICISM

Among a plethora of references to bioregionalism, Buddhism and Taoism, there is within DE an abundance of rituals, discourses and figures that belong to the field of Western esotericism. To name only a handful, "New Age science" luminaries Fritjof Capra and Ken Wilber both participate as agents in DE, the former as an outspoken proponent and the latter as a critical interlocutor.[15] Further, references to Lovelock's Gaia hypothesis and the "New Physics" of David Bohm are far from rare in the milieu. Moreover, the most prominent ritual in DE, Joanna Macy and John Seed's neoshamanic "Council of All Beings", consists of channelling intermediate beings, including nature spirits, spokes-entities for extinct animals, and Gaia herself, in order to elicit

---

13. Sessions, *Deep Ecology for the 21st Century*, 190.
14. Bookchin, "Social Ecology versus Deep Ecology"; Chase, "The Great Green Deep-Ecology Revolution", 166.
15. See Capra's contribution to *Deep Ecology for the 21st Century*, entitled "Deep Ecology: A New Paradigm", and Wilber, *A Brief History of Everything*, 39, 329; Wilber, *Sex, Ecology, and Spirituality*, 106.

higher knowledge for the participants involved.[16] Most tellingly, there is the work of the Church of Deep Ecology, which openly embraces a neopagan form of nature worship in their efforts to evangelize Sessions's interpretation of Deep Ecology. Add to this the neopagan lexicon employed in the work of Deep Ecology writer, Wiccan high priest and neoshamanic practitioner Gus diZerega, it should come as no surprise that a number of scholars have been led to categorize DE as either derivative of esotericism or as a new religious movement in itself.[17]

The aforementioned examples often act as red herrings for scholars looking to prove that Deep Ecology is a manifestation of Western esotericism. The problem with characterizing DE with regard to these esoteric elements relates back to the general trend of defining Deep Ecology in the singular and according to a selection of self-serving evidence. Describing Deep Ecology as definitively anything, but especially esoteric, glosses over the discrepancy between the interpretations and the truth-claims therein. The work of the prime movers in DE, like Sessions, illustrates this point perfectly, for he fortifies his interpretation of Deep Ecology – which scholars argue is the most widely accepted in the milieu[18] – with a wholehearted rejection of any claim that links Deep Ecology to the New Age movement or the occult; in point of fact, he likens the association to "cheap shots".[19] An accurate understanding of how the aforementioned esoteric elements fit into DE can only be formed when they are analysed in relation to how they covertly assume some aspect of the interpretations of Deep Ecology and disregard others. Analysis of this sort not only transforms what appears to be miscellaneous esoteric flotsam into specific articulations of particular interpretations of Deep Ecology, but more importantly, provides a more precise understanding of contemporary esoteric discourses.

Kocku von Stuckrad articulates the key methodological point for studying DE in light of both its interpretational plurality and the esoteric elements

---

16. See Seed *et al.*, *Thinking Like a Mountain*; Bron Taylor, "Earth and Nature-Based Spirituality (Part II)", 229.
17. Bron Taylor presents the strongest argument for understanding Deep Ecology *in toto* as a religion unto itself, or in his words, a "dark green religion". See Bron Taylor, "Ecological Resistance Movements"; Bron Taylor, *Dark Green Religion*, 293n45. In many ways anticipating Taylor's work, Catherine Albanese's work on "nature religion" similarly describes Deep Ecology as a religious worldview. Albanese, *Nature Religion*, 176.
18. Admittedly, the veracity of his claim is impossible to ascertain; however, there is a consensus among scholars which Harold Glasser articulates saying, "[s]upporters of the deep ecology movement are not united by a commitment to deep ecology as an academic ecophilosophy (which they may be familiar with or embrace), but with their willingness to endorse the eight-point deep ecology platform, prepared by Naess and Sessions in 1984". Glasser, "Series Editor's Introduction", xxxviii. See also Fox, *Toward a Transpersonal Ecology*, 114–118; Katz *et al.*, *Beneath the Surface*, x; Bron Taylor, "Deep Ecology and Its Social Philosophy", 269n28–29.
19. Sessions, "Deep Ecology and the New Age", 290.

within it. This point concerns the nature of Western esotericism itself: "'Esotericism' as object matter does not exist; 'esotericism' is a construction of scholars who order phenomena in a way that they find suitable to analyse processes of Western history of culture".[20] Accordingly, the study of contemporary esotericism is not confined to a tradition of esotericism that has survived, relatively intact, throughout the ages, nor is an attempt to trace a tradition as it continually undergoes radical reinvention. The reason for this is that no such tradition exists, etically speaking.[21] Without objective criteria that could be used to organize select historical currents under the rubric of esotericism, von Stuckrad rightly argues that the term is best understood as a structural element of Western culture that cuts across art, science and religion, and in so doing draws together similar discourses across cultural fields. Constructed to provide a framework for analysis and not a universal definition of esotericism, von Stuckrad's approach leads to the conclusion that "it is often better to talk about *the esoteric* rather than *esotericism*, because the esoteric is an element of cultural processes, while mention of esotericism suggests that there is a coherent doctrine or clearly identified body of tradition".[22] Hence, the question is not "is DE a form of contemporary Western esotericism?" but rather, "what part of which interpretations of Deep Ecology do the esoteric elements presume?"

Understood as a structural element of discourse, von Stuckrad describes the "esoteric" in terms of a claim of a higher form of knowledge, which additionally possesses the means of accessing it.[23] Elaborating on this quality, he states that such discourses frequently employ a "rhetoric of a hidden truth, which can be unveiled in a specific way and established contrary to other interpretations of the universe and history – often that of the institutional majority".[24] He adds that such a "claim to knowledge is often combined with an emphasis on individual *experience*, wherein a seeker attains higher knowledge through extraordinary states of consciousness", which usually function in conjunction with "a conception of the cosmos, which one can call *holistic* or *monistic*".[25] The concept of living nature and perennial philosophy are also singled out as common to esoteric worldviews. While disparate, the three most prominent interpretations of Deep Ecology do indeed intersect these criteria to varying degrees; however, that is not to say that they are all esoteric in the same way or even sufficiently esoteric to merit study as such.[26] Through

---

20. Von Stuckrad, "Western Esotericism", 88.
21. For a fuller engagement with the problem of "tradition" see von Stuckrad, *Locations of Knowledge*, 25–43; Hanegraaff, "Tradition"; Lewis & Hammer, *The Invention of Sacred Tradition*. Cf. Chapter 2 of the present volume.
22. Von Stuckrad, *Western Esotericism*, 10.
23. *Ibid.*, 9–11; von Stuckrad, "Western Esotericism", 88–93.
24. Von Stuckrad, *Western Esotericism*, 10.
25. *Ibid.*, 10–11.
26. As the most comprehensive scholarly index in the field, *The Dictionary of Gnosis and Western Esotericism* serves as a useful gauge to ascertain which currents and figures

analysing each interpretation according to the idiosyncratic relationship they have to these criteria, scholarship on DE will be able to move beyond the misleadingly wholesale characterization of the milieu as either esoteric or not.

Considering the foregoing framework for analysis, applying the analytical instrument of esotericism to DE produces two effects. The first effect is pragmatic, as Wouter Hanegraaff relates:

> [C]urrently accepted fields of study have failed to accommodate certain western discourses, and still tend either to exclude these from study altogether or reduce them to already existing but inappropriate categories. "Esotericism" is an appropriate label for characterising these traditions and making them available for research.[27]

While the field of environmental ethics is not an "inappropriate category" for the study of DE, the state of the art of academic research in the field remains marginal.[28] Correspondingly, the varying interpretations of Deep Ecology, as well as the esoteric and "spiritual" elements within them, position DE as neither philosophical enough to be considered philosophy (therefore garnering the descriptive and somewhat dubious title "eco-philosophy"), nor religious enough to be considered religion (likewise garnering similarly suspicious titles like "eco-spirituality" and "spiritual ecology"). As the interpretations of Deep Ecology intersect the criteria specified by von Stuckrad, studying them as esoteric discourses not only makes them available for research to a larger audience, but increases the panoramic understanding of esoteric discourses in the current Western episteme.

The second effect of analysing DE through esotericism is an extension of the last. The inherently interdisciplinary nature of the study of esotericism provides scholars studying DE the tools to recognize how particular interpretations of Deep Ecology reflect antecedents, overlaps and parallels in other discursive fields. Termed "discursive transfers", the processes of exchange that occur both inside and outside of DE stand as an essential area of study if one is to decipher exactly how the esoteric inhabits DE.

---

are conceived of as relevant to the academic study of Western esotericism. As such, the complete omission of entries on "ecology", "environmentalism" or "Deep Ecology" is telling, although the author of the entry on Gurdjieff states that Gurdjieff's "Ray of Creation" anticipates "Naess's Deep Ecology", which is described as a "Green holistic paradigm". See James Moore, "Gurdjieff", 448.

27. Hanegraaff, "Empirical Method in the Study of Esotericism", 109–10.
28. Inaugurated in 2003 and headed by environmental ethics scholar Bron Taylor, the University of Florida remains the only university to offer both MA and PhD degrees in "Religion and Nature" under the auspices of its religion department. Notably, the University of Hawai'i's anthropology department offers MA and PhD degrees in "Ecological Anthropology" with a special concentration in "Spiritual Ecology", which is the first of its kind in an anthropology department.

THE ESOTERIC IN DEEP ECOLOGY

Scholars interested in understanding DE have no choice but to adopt a polyfocal approach, and in so doing shift the search for Deep Ecology's *meaning* to the *meanings produced* by the conflicting interpretations. In mobilizing the polyfocal approach, the following descriptions of the leading interpretations of Deep Ecology will clarify the conflation that occurs when a scholar speaks of Deep Ecology in the singular. More than clarifying, using the polyfocal approach establishes a basis to determine the respective place of the esoteric in each interpretation as well as the developments that build on them. While the examples that opened the previous section indicate an overlap between esotericism and DE, they failed to indicate how esoteric discourses function in relation to the various interpretations of Deep Ecology. This section will make the status and place of the esoteric in these interpretations apparent.

The volume *Deep Ecology for the 21st Century*, edited by George Sessions, has become the de facto primer in DE. As such, it has come to be understood as offering what environmental ethics scholar Bron Taylor termed the "generic sense of Deep Ecology"[29] and similarly what Fox termed the "popular sense of Deep Ecology",[30] which is to say its most widely understood definition. Sessions introduces the volume by confronting the interpretational thicket that obscures what he felt to be the real definition of Deep Ecology.[31] He writes:

> One of the main purposes of this collection of papers is to attempt to clear up the misinterpretations and misunderstandings that have grown up recently around the Deep Ecology position, to respond to contemporary critics, and to lay out a contemporary version of the Deep Ecology position in a clear, easily accessible, but sophisticated manner.[32]

Indeed, Sessions goes on to lay out a clear and easily accessible definition in as far as he asserts that "[t]he philosophy of the Deep Ecology movement is characterized essentially by ecocentrism, as outlined in the 1984 Deep Ecology platform".[33] It is important to note why Sessions equates Deep Ecology with the "philosophically neutral general beliefs and attitudes" expounded in the

---

29. Bron Taylor, "Deep Ecology and Its Social Philosophy", 270.
30. Fox, *Toward a Transpersonal Ecology*, 114–18.
31. Proclaiming to "set the record straight" in terms of the definition of Deep Ecology has become a common rhetorical strategy in the literature. See Rothenberg, *Ecology, Community and Lifestyle*, 15; McLaughlin, "The Heart of Deep Ecology", 85; Katz et al., *Beneath the Surface*, ix–xxiv; Glasser, "Deep Ecology Clarified"; Drengson, "Editorial".
32. Sessions, "Preface", xiv.
33. *Ibid.*, xiii.

manifesto.[34] By defining Deep Ecology as an ecocentric movement based upon a philosophically neutral manifesto, it can, according to Sessions, "provide a universal unifying ecocentric prospective" for a diverse array of religious and philosophical beliefs.[35] Eric Katz sums Sessions's perspective up succinctly stating, "[t]o borrow a phrase from the Republican Party in the United States, deep ecology claims to be a 'big tent' within which many different fundamental philosophical perspectives can feel at home".[36]

Andrew McLaughlin's contribution to Sessions's volume offers both a concise re-articulation of this position and a telling example of its pervasive influence. As if to leave no room for misunderstanding, McLaughlin states, "[t]he heart of Deep Ecology is its platform, which consists of a number of inter-related factual and normative claims about humans and their relations with the rest of nature"[37] and later "the point of these principles is to define the Deep Ecology movement".[38] Thus, for Sessions and McLaughlin, as well as other North American architects like Devall and Drengson, Deep Ecology is (as opposed to Naess's original formulation) an ontologically neutral movement based on promoting ecocentrism through the following platforms:

- the wellbeing and flourishing of human and non-human life on earth have value in themselves (synonyms: intrinsic value, inherent value);
- richness and diversity of life forms contribute to the realization of these values and are also values in themselves;
- humans have no right to reduce this richness and diversity except to satisfy vital human needs;
- the flourishing of human life and cultures is compatible with a substantial decrease of the human population and the flourishing of non-human life requires such a decrease;
- present human interference with the non-human world is excessive, and the situation is rapidly worsening;

---

34. Sessions, *Deep Ecology for the 21st Century*, 4.
35. Sessions, "Postmodernism and Environmental Justice", 6. For the claim that the manifesto is "philosophically neutral" see Sessions, *Deep Ecology for the 21st Century*, 190; Sessions, "Wildness, Cyborgs, and Our Ecological Future", 165.
36. Eric Katz, "Against the Inevitability of Anthropocentrism", 19.
37. McLaughlin, "The Heart of Deep Ecology", 85–91. The phrase "heart of Deep Ecology" has appeared in a variety of the attempts to define DE, and is often used to reference one of the three interpretations discussed in this chapter. See Rothenberg, "Letter to the Editor from David Rothenberg", 25; Bron Taylor, "Evoking the Ecological Self", 266; Partridge, *The Re-enchantment of the West*, vol. 2, 58. As Glasser notes, reference to the "heart" of DE is ironic, at least from Naess's point of view, on account of the fact that Naess's ontology is based upon gestalts, which do not have hearts. Glasser, "On Warwick Fox's Assessment of Deep Ecology", 74n15.
38. McLaughlin, "The Heart of Deep Ecology", 91.

- policies must therefore be changed. These policies affect basic economic, technological, and ideological structures. The resulting state of affairs will be deeply different from the present;
- the ideological change is mainly that of appreciating life quality (dwelling in situations of inherent value) rather than adhering to an increasingly higher standard of living. There will be a profound awareness of the difference between big and great; and
- those who subscribe to the foregoing points have an obligation directly or indirectly to try to implement the necessary changes.[39]

Regardless of what Sessions states, the manifesto is saturated in philosophical implications;[40] yet, what is most noteworthy about Sessions's definition is how he conceptualizes the manifesto's collective meaning. As stated in the preface of *Deep Ecology for the 21st Century* as well as elsewhere, the manifesto, and by extension Deep Ecology, is intended to bring about "a major paradigm shift – a shift in perception, values, and lifestyles" which will facilitate the "move from anthropocentrism to ecocentrism".[41] The move to ecocentrism, as well as the notion of perennial philosophy which Sessions uses to validate this paradigm shift, are aspects of an esoteric discourse on higher knowledge; however, before relating why this is so, one vital caveat must be made. Following the argument made by Sessions, Devall, Drengson and McLaughlin, Deep Ecology is defined by the manifesto and not to be mistakenly defined by the contents of any particular ecosophy. This prohibition is repeatedly made and has become a benchmark in their writings. However, for the scholar studying the various interpretations of Deep Ecology, that is to say DE, *only the inverse is true*. At the risk of repetition, Deep Ecology does not exist outside of the discursive field that produces it. Accordingly, the claim that Deep Ecology is defined by its manifesto must be understood as merely an interpretive element that is shared by a number of theorists, the most significant of whom is Sessions, as he both co-authored the manifesto and stands as its foremost proponent. Therefore, the following section will not scrutinize the Deep Ecology-as-manifesto interpretation *per se* as much as it will focus on Sessions's interpretation in its entirety, in which paradigm shifts and perennial philosophy play a central role.[42]

---

39. *Ibid.*, 86–9.
40. See Glasser, "On Warwick Fox's Assessment of Deep Ecology"; Eric Katz, "Against the Inevitability of Anthropocentrism".
41. Sessions, *Deep Ecology for the 21st Century*, ix. See also Sessions, "Wildness, Cyborgs, and Our Ecological Future", 123.
42. This is not to say that Devall, Drengson and McLaughlin do not share Sessions's belief in paradigms shifts and perennial philosophy; they do; however, there are differences and their similar interpretations of Deep Ecology do not garner nearly as much attention as Sessions.

Drawing directly from Aldous Huxley's *The Perennial Philosophy*, Sessions conceptualizes Deep Ecology as the contemporary manifestation of a primordial metaphysic. Utilizing a form of green historicism, Sessions describes the history of human existence in terms of the conflict between an ecocentric perennial philosophy and the millennia-long "anthropocentric detour" that has marginalized it. In a section entitled "Ecocentrism and the Anthropocentric Detour: Why Deep Ecology Reemerged Late in Western History", which appeared in a longer essay that was reprinted in his volume, Sessions traces the roots of Deep Ecology's ecocentric perspective from the "most primal or hunting/gathering societies throughout the world" to the "Milesian philosophers", "Taoism and other Eastern religions [which] retained elements of the ancient shamanistic Nature religion", the Presocratics, and through to the thirteenth-century nature mystic St Francis of Assisi, the seventeenth-century "cosmic non-anthropocentric philosophy" of Spinoza, and "the Romantic Nature-oriented countercultural movement of the nineteenth century", the Transcendentalists, conservationists like Muir, to the ecological writings of Aldous Huxley, Rachel Carson and Aldo Leopold, to "the Zen Buddhism of Alan Watts, and Gary Snyder", and finally culminating in the work of Arne Naess and the Deep Ecology movement.[43] Over and against this perennial philosophy, Sessions, expanding on the Lynn White thesis, identifies an anthropocentric discourse that has "detoured" humanity from their primordial relationship with nature.[44] Originating with the advent of agriculture, Sessions claims that "the Western religious tradition [identified as 'Judaeo/Christian'] began to divorce itself from wild Nature" and with "the culmination of Athenian philosophy in Aristotle, an anthropocentric system of philosophy and science was set in place, which was to play a major role in Western thought until the seventeenth century".[45] Despite the "second opportunity for Western culture to abandon the anthropocentric detour" that Spinoza's philosophy afforded, Sessions maintains that anthropocentrism continued and indeed continues unabated as a result of the continued hegemony of the Abrahamic religions, Newtonian Science, and the anthropocentric humanism of modern and postmodern philosophy (with Marx and Dewey exemplifying the former, and Foucault, Derrida and Lyotard the latter).[46]

In placing Deep Ecology within an oppressed tradition of higher knowledge, Sessions's interpretation of Deep Ecology bears a striking resemblance

---

43. Sessions, "Ecocentrism and the Greens", 66–7; Sessions, "Preface", ix.
44. Made in 1967 in the pages of the renown journal *Science*, the Lynn White thesis refers to the historian Lynn White's article "The Historical Roots of Our Ecological Crisis", which argued that Christianity bore the heaviest burden for the environmental crisis as it was "the most anthropocentric religion the world has seen." White, "The Historical Roots of Our Ecological Crisis", 1205.
45. Sessions, "Ecocentrism and the Greens", 66–7.
46. *Ibid.*, 67; Sessions, "Postmodernism and Environmental Justice", 4; Devall & Sessions, *Deep Ecology*, 18–39, 41–9, 80–81.

to other esoteric discourses. Commenting on this strategy as it is often used by esoteric discourses to justify their access to higher knowledge, Olav Hammer notes that "emic historiography highlights only a few episodes in what is conceived as the spiritual development of mankind. It creates a (usually vague) chronology, from ancient civilizations ... and rapidly proceeds to the present age".[47] Hammer continues:

> these historical stations form a more or less fragmentary myth ... The oldest element [of the myth] is the meta-historical readiness to interpret history in terms of a movement from an ancient Golden Age, via a less-than-perfect present, up to a utopian future.[48]

In light of Hammer's analysis, Sessions's use of the term "anthropological detour" is thrown into sharp relief as the historiography of Deep Ecology conforms to the mythic trajectory Hammer describes. In fact, the Golden Age of this perennial philosophy not only persists on the margins of the mainstream, but historically speaking, casts a shadow over the present insofar as "99% of all humans who have ever lived on Earth have been hunter/gathers" leading Sessions to conclude "it is clear that ecocentrism has been the dominant human perspective throughout history".[49] Deviation from this perspective has, according to Sessions, landed man in an environmental crisis verging on the apocalyptic, and thus his reading of the present elevates the necessity of the ecocentric perspective to a matter of planetary life or death.[50] The present is so dire that nothing short of "the revival of the perennial philosophy tradition" wherein "metaphysics, psychology, theory of knowledge, ethics, and social and political theory" are united into a "coherent and integrated view of the world and meaning of human life" can ensure the ecosphere's continued existence.[51] A revival of this magnitude would constitute a planetary ecocentric paradigm shift, which Sessions describes as "a radically new understanding of reality; a 'conversion' to an ecological consciousness" that marks a clear break with the ecologically destructive *zeitgeist* of modern industrial society.[52] Vastly different from anthropocentrism, "the ecocentric perspective involves a biological, as well as a cultural, understanding of the human species resulting in a new

---

47. Hammer, *Claiming Knowledge*, 91–2.
48. Ibid., 92.
49. Sessions, "Ecocentrism and the Greens", 66.
50. It is important to note the mention of the "21st century" in the title of Sessions's text as it exemplifies his historiographic contextualization of the Deep Ecology movement, that is, as a contemporary manifestation of perennial wisdom. Additionally, the name reflects Sessions commitment to defining Deep Ecology as a solidified "here and now" movement, and is to be read as a response to an article Naess wrote three years previous entitled "Deep Ecology for the 22nd Century".
51. Devall & Sessions, *Deep Ecology*, 81.
52. Sessions, "Ecocentrism and the Greens", 66.

awareness of the place of humans in the ecological web and of the ecological limitations of humans in the Earth community".[53] Likening this paradigm to a new age of humanity, Sessions states, "The Age of Ecology involves a major 'paradigm shift' to an ecocentric mode of understanding the world".[54]

Given the unmistakable similarity between Sessions's "Age of Ecology" and the "Age of Aquarius", as well as the centrality of this seemingly utopian paradigm shift in all of his work,[55] it seems unreasonable for Sessions to define Deep Ecology as radically separate from the New Age movement. The problem here concerns the difficulty in defining the New Age movement and the complex way Sessions attributes higher knowledge to Deep Ecology. Following Kennet Granholm's comments on Wouter Hanegraaff's groundbreaking scholarship, it can be said that a short-lived New Age movement began in the 1970s and held as its central belief an expectation of a New Age of Aquarius before its general dissolution in the 1990s. Termed "New Age *sensu stricto*" by Hanegraaff, this relatively small movement is now understood by scholars as key in the popularization of esoteric discourses (including channelling, neopaganism, Transpersonal Psychology and holistic science), yet should not be conflated with these discourses directly.[56] Consequently, in the technical sense of the term, Sessions is right to differentiate between Deep Ecology and the New Age movement (even if he misinterprets the latter[57]); however, he is wrong in claiming that Deep Ecology exists apart from New Age understood as the popularization of esoteric discourses. Sharing both a temporal and geographical context,[58] DE and the popularized esoteric discourses fused in a number of highly innovative ways forming what von Stuckrad terms "discursive transfers".[59] Fritjof Capra's chapter in Sessions's volume, "Deep Ecology: A New Paradigm", and Sessions's general use of the term paradigm shift exemplify this type of transfer as both are marked by the appropriation of scientific discourses, namely physics and ecology, by esoteric vision of the cosmos.[60]

Sessions's historiography and his concept of an ecocentric paradigm shift form an esoteric basis that others have incorporated into their own expression of Deep Ecology, as Capra's work shows. The problem is that regardless of the degree of overlap between Sessions's interpretation of Deep Ecology and that of others, his interpretation does not permit any conflation between,

---

53. Ibid., 66.
54. Ibid., 66.
55. See Devall & Sessions, *Deep Ecology*; Sessions, "Ecological Consciousness and Paradigm Change"; Sessions, *Deep Ecology for the 21st Century*.
56. Granholm, "New Age or the Mass-popularization of Esoteric Discourse"; Hanegraaff, *New Age Religion and Western Culture*, 97.
57. Sessions, "Deep Ecology and the New Age Movement" 290–92.
58. Hanegraaff, *New Age Religion and Western Culture*, 97.
59. Von Stuckrad, "Western Esotericism", 88–94.
60. For a longer discussion of the New Age, Deep Ecology, and paradigm shifts see Zimmerman, *Contesting Earth's Future*, 57–90.

on the one hand, the formulation of ecocentrism outlined in the manifesto, and on the other, developments that stem from his historiography and use of the term paradigm shift. As far as Sessions' is concerned, esoteric, New Age, Wiccan and neopagan discourses can be a part of Deep Ecology, but Deep Ecology is not to be mistaken as inherently related to any of these discourses. So, despite the undeniable similarities between modern Western shamanism and Deep Ecology's ecocentrism, Sessions's definition prohibits reading anything from the former into a definition of the latter.[61] What has made defining Deep Ecology the most contentious aspect of DE is that Naess founded Deep Ecology (at least as it is nominally understood as a modern movement) on precisely a conflation of this sort. Recall that in his 1972 statement Naess described Deep Ecology as a reflection of holistic ontology. Sessions's claim, then, that the manifesto "superseded" the 1972 statement puts him in the peculiar position of imbuing Deep Ecology with esoteric knowledge, yet unable to endorse the outlooks that readily follow from it (and in many ways inspired it), such as ontological non-dualism or metaphysical holism.[62]

Sessions's impulse to, in the words of social ecologist John Clark, "conceive of deep ecology more as a completed theoretical edifice to be defended than a practical basis for cooperation between those with deep ecological concerns"[63] has fostered a noticeable amount of criticism from the movement's founder. Describing it as a "grave misinterpretation",[64] Naess has been vocal about his dissatisfaction with Sessions's movement-as-manifesto interpretation. In response to what had become the orthodox interpretation of Deep Ecology, Naess wrote:

> The Eight-Points are, of course, not intended to function as a definition of the deep ecology movement: neither as a rule-governed definition of the term, nor as a plain description of how the expression "deep ecology movement" is actually used, nor as an expression of the essence of the deep ecology movement. I do not know of any satisfactory definitions at the dictionary level.[65]

Illustrating the diplomatic tact that typifies Naess's writing, he followed his refutation by suggesting that the term "manifesto" should be replaced, stating "[a] longer name for the Eight Points is indispensable, for instance a set of fairly general and abstract statements that seem to be accepted by nearly all

---

61. For a brief summation of discursive transfer between neoshamanism and DE see von Stuckrad, "Reenchanting Nature", 782–4. Also of note with regard to the discursive transfer between Deep Ecology and the currents studied in the field of Western esotericism, see von Stuckrad, *Western Esotericism*, 143–4.
62. Sessions, "Wildness, Cyborgs, and Our Ecological Future", 149.
63. Clark, "How Wide is Deep Ecology?", 7.
64. Naess, "The Deep Ecology Eight-Points Revisited", 220.
65. *Ibid.*, 214.

supporters of the Deep Ecology movement".[66] Naess's hesitance to define the essence of Deep Ecology was pragmatic and mirrors the way in which he first used the term as descriptive and not proscriptive. According to Naess, Deep Ecology "is not a philosophy in any proper academic sense, nor is it institutionalized as a religion or ideology";[67] Rather, he claims that the closest one could come to a definition would include an index of all the diverse ecosophies in the movement in addition to describing the process by which ecosophies are created.[68] Therefore, these factors, in addition to his own Ecosophy T, must be examined if one is to map the complex and antagonistic relationship between the definitions of Deep Ecology, the esoteric truth claims which undergird them, and the esoteric elements that were developed from both. Also, it bears mention that Ecosophy T merits special attention as it is commonly conflated with the philosophy of Deep Ecology. Considering its influence, this conflation is the most problematic in terms of reconciling both the esoteric elaborations of Ecosophy T and the etic descriptions of Deep Ecology as esoteric with its most popular interpretation, namely the one posited by Sessions.

Describing Naess's Ecosophy T, Warwick Fox states, "the 'esoteric core' of deep ecology is bound up with the psychological–spiritual–metaphysical idea of what Naess refers to as *Self-realization*".[69] Though Fox's insinuation that DE is a unified eco-philosophy, and indeed has a "core", is to be dismissed, his use of the term "esoteric" is informative as it identifies the "psychological–spiritual–metaphysical" concept of Self-realization fittingly, as esoteric. Essentially, the transcendental state of Self-realization (inspired by Gandhi) and the framework by which it is achieved (inspired by Spinoza) is the higher knowledge Naess claims. Naess explains the context of this higher knowledge in the phenomenological lexicon of "gestalt ontology", the metaphysical framework he created for his ecosophy. The primary characteristic of gestalt ontology is ontological non-dualism, for, according to Naess, the universe contains "no completely separable objects, [and] therefore no separable ego or medium or organism [exists]".[70] Naess accounts for humanity's inclination towards dualist thinking by introducing the concept of a gestalt, which he describes as a unit of perception that takes as its object the "concrete contents" of reality, which in being perceived is separated into parts, objects and qualities by the ego.[71] Gestalt ontology organizes human development through a hierarchy of gestalts that range from the naïve realism perceived in normal states

---

66. *Ibid.*, 214.
67. Naess, "The Deep Ecology Movement", 266.
68. Glasser, "On Warwick Fox's Assessment of Deep Ecology", 83, with reference to an unpublished manuscript by Naess.
69. Fox, *Toward a Transpersonal Ecology*, 76.
70. *Ibid.*, 56–7.
71. Eric Katz, "Against the Inevitability of Anthropocentrism", 31.

of consciousness to the Self-realized state of holistic union with the cosmos. Therefore, starting from the bottom of the hierarchy, where one can only perceive the lesser gestalts that are defined by a myriad of abstractions, one can move upward to perceiving higher gestalts until Self-realization is achieved and all distinctions melt away in the awareness of the cosmos as one holistic gestalt. The transformation from the egotistical self to the larger ecospheric "Self" (with the capitalized "S" signalling identification with all the contents of the web of life) is nothing short of a "mystical" union with the totality of the cosmos.[72] Naess coined another neologism for this metaphysical self: the "ecological self".[73] The environmental ramifications of this are easy to guess, as lesser gestalts are linked solely to anthropocentrism and the higher ones are linked to increasing levels of ecocentrism.

Defined in terms of an epistemological break with the mechanist reductionism of Newtonian science, and in particular the "twisted and misused" notion of ecology or "ecologism", Naess argued that his ontology rectifies man's alienation from the natural world in ways that the scientific uses of ecology cannot.[74] This epistemological break is important as it allows Naess to characterize his ontological framework and the ecosophy derived from it as not only superior to the dominant scientific paradigm, but as a necessary succession of it.[75] Similar to the strategy employed in Sessions's historiographical account of Deep Ecology, Naess's ecosophy constituted a metaphysic that, unlike scientific empiricism, could prevent total ecospheric destruction. Hence, in addition to positing a holistic conception of reality, and being an individual path for merging with the totality of the cosmos, Naess's claim that gestalt ontology is superior to science mirrors von Stuckrad's criteria for esoteric discourse, which states:

> On the most general level of analysis we can describe esotericism as the claim of higher knowledge. Important here is not only the content of these systems but the claim to a wisdom that is superior to other interpretations of cosmos and history.[76]

---

72. For a longer discussion of what Fons Elders calls the "intimate connection" between Naess's ecosophy and mysticism see Elders, "Arne Naess, A philosopher and a Mystic", 45–9.
73. Naess, "Self-Realization", 226–7.
74. Naess, *Ecology Community and Lifestyle*, 39. Naess describes "ecologism" as the "excessive universalization or generalization of ecological concepts and theories". His position against ecologism relates to his theory of gestalt ontology insofar as the latter is meant as a corrective to what he sees as the deficiencies of scientific thought, namely, its inability to catalyse change: "Ecology as a science does not ask what kind of society would be the best for maintaining a particular ecosystem – that is considered a question for value theory, for politics, for ethics. As long as ecologists keep narrowly to their sciences they do not ask such questions" (as quoted in Glasser, "On Warwick Fox's Assessment of Deep Ecology", 166).
75. Naess, "Ecosophy and Gestalt Ontology", 245.
76. Von Stuckrad, "Western Esotericism", 88.

Underscoring the esoteric truth claim embedded in Naess's ecosophy is crucial because in presupposing ontological holism and the possibility of attaining a oneness with it, Ecosophy T provided a basis for similar esoteric truth-claims to manifest in DE. Going under a handful of names including "wide-identification", "deep identification" and, most revealingly, "the intuition of Deep Ecology", the non-dualism of Ecosophy T represents a lightning rod for esoteric elaborations on the esoteric elements of Sessions's and Naess's definitions of Deep Ecology. In fact, the ubiquity of ontological holism in DE theorizing led Warwick Fox to disregard the definitions of Deep Ecology posited by Naess and Sessions, and assert that Naess's ecosophy represented, definitively, what was unique about Deep Ecology. On account of its holistic basis, Fox argued that Deep Ecology would more properly be termed "Transpersonal Ecology", which simultaneously raised the ire of Naess and Sessions while adding another popularized esoteric discourse, specifically Transpersonal Psychology, to DE.[77]

The equation of Deep Ecology to Transpersonal Ecology marks a second discursive transfer between DE and a popularized esoteric discourse, which is somewhat similar to the discussion of paradigms though it marks an esoteric appropriation of a social science. However, the context of this discursive transfer is significantly dissimilar in its lasting and profound influence on critics and supporters. The fact that every analysis that states that Deep Ecology is esoteric is based on conflating (whether rightfully or not) Naess's ecosophy and Deep Ecology signals the extent of this influence. While the discussion will return to the allegation that Deep Ecology is rooted in Naess's ecosophy at the conclusion of this section, it is important to note how Transpersonal Ecology complicates accounting for the esoteric in DE. In positing an interpretation that violates both Naess's and Sessions's definitions of Deep Ecology, Transpersonal Ecology renegotiates how the esoteric elements of Ecosophy T and Sessions's definition (which may very well be read as his ecosophy) exist in DE. While previously distinct, Sessions's historiography and Naess's ontology are brought together in Fox's interpretation, thereby creating a new reference point for further conflations and discursive transfers to justify their inclusion in DE. Stated differently, those in DE who had previously held non-dualistic beliefs but kept them out of their scholarship on account of Sessions's and Naess's definitions could use Fox's thesis as a point of departure for developing more elaborate formulations of Deep Ecology, be they neopagan, Wiccan, or an amalgamation of esoteric discourses comparable with those going under the label "Eco-magick".[78]

---

77. Fox, *Toward a Transpersonal Ecology*, 197.
78. Growing from an activist "membership organization" to a decentralized network with conferences and a journal, the Dragon Environmental Network is the most salient hub for discursive transfers between DE and ritual magic, Kabbalah, rune magic, and Goddess Worship to name only a handful of discourses. See Dragon Environmental Network, "Eco-Magic".

Based on a polemic against "shallow ecology", Naess defined the Deep Ecology movement in terms of its "willingness to question and to appreciate the importance of questioning every economic and political policy in public".[79] Clarifying this statement, Naess asserted that the deepness of questioning that occurs in normative derivation was not "the kind found in graduate philosophy seminars", but is instead a "profound 'existential' undertaking" that brings individuals to their most deeply held belief, in the jargon of normative derivation, their "ultimate norm". Revisiting von Stuckrad's description of how esoteric discourse functions, we see that in addition to the claim on higher knowledge, esoteric discourse also emphasizes the individual experience in which an agent attains higher knowledge through an extraordinary realization.[80] This is precisely the function normative derivation serves. The underlying assumption behind normative derivation is that as a questioner answers progressively deeper questions, he or she comes closer to articulating sentiments that would normally remain obscured or otherwise impossible to access.[81] At the deepest level of normative derivation, the questioner comes face to face with their most profound truth, the single norm that orients their ecosophy, and more importantly, all the decisions regarding his or her life.[82] At the level of the ultimate norm, normative derivation shifts from a descriptive exercise to a proscriptive one, thereby leading Naess to claim that what is deep about Deep Ecology is not simply the level of questioning, but the premises reached and depth of change that they manifest.[83] Essentially, Naess claims that the deeper the questioning, the deeper the change. The transformative power of this system of "mental–phenomenological inquiry" is reflected in Naess's vision of Deep Ecology's aims, which he describes by stating: "The aim of supporters of the deep ecology movement is not a slight reform of our present society, but a *substantial reorientation of our whole civilization*."[84] Indeed, with comprehensive societal reorientation as its goal, there is little in DE that matches the personally transformative power of normative deviation.

In terms of conclusive findings, Ecosophy T, gestalt ontology, and normative derivation are all esoteric insofar as they make a claim on higher knowledge and provide access to it; however, there remains one key aspect of Naess's definition of Deep Ecology that defies the label "esoteric": the nature of all ecosophies in the Deep Ecology movement. Despite regularly writing as though every member of the Deep Ecology movement has an ecosophy created through normative derivation, Naess acknowledges that this simply is not the case.[85] This means that even though normative derivation is esoteric, it

---

79. Naess, "Deepness of Questions and the Deep Ecology Movement", 205.
80. Von Stuckrad, *Western Esotericism*, 10.
81. Naess, "Deepness of Questions and the Deep Ecology Movement", 207.
82. Katz *et al.*, "Introduction", xi.
83. Naess, "Deepness of Questions and the Deep Ecology Movement", 209.
84. Fox, "Deep Ecology", 158; Naess, *Ecology, Community and Lifestyle*, 45.
85. Naess, "Deepness of Questions and the Deep Ecology Movement", 205.

does not mean that the movement can comprehensively be labelled as such. This constitutes a difference between his interpretation and Sessions's. Yet this indeterminacy should be altogether expected from Naess as it remained a hallmark in his writing from early on in his career.[86] Keeping in mind what has been shown to be esoteric in Naess's definition, Katz's claim that all Deep Ecology theorizing, and by extension all ecosophies, rely on Naess's ontological framework makes the case that DE is in fact esoteric.

The third interpretation of Deep Ecology is echoed by a number of critics, but few accounts are as cogent as Eric Katz's "Against the Inevitability of Anthropocentrism". The pith of Katz's argument is the claim that Deep Ecology theorizing is based on Naess's worldview. Katz summarizes this position:

> It [Deep Ecology] is a philosophy that focuses on the fundamental ontological interrelatedness and identification of all life forms, natural objects, and ecosystems. The ethics and politics of deep ecology – those ideas most clearly expressed in its platform – are secondary; they are derived from the basic ontological commitments of a deep ecological worldview.[87]

Confronting Sessions's interpretation head-on, Katz's work demonstrates how the individual tenets of the manifesto, its composite statement of ecocentrism, and Naess's assumption that all normative derivation will lead to an ecocentric perspective rely on the ontological framework of Ecosophy T. The three aspects of this ontology, which Katz claims can be found in "virtually all discussions of deep ecology" as "core doctrines",[88] include the process of identification with the natural world, the goal of Self-realization and a relational holistic ontology.[89] Essential to Katz's argument is that Naess's belief in "the supremacy of environmental ontology and realism over environmental ethics"[90] carries with it the assumption that Deep Ecology is founded on gestalt ontology. While the specifics of Katz's argument do not concern us here, there is ample evidence that proves that, at one point in time, Sessions, Devall, McLaughlin and Naess all defined DE in terms of this ontological triumvirate.[91] When related back to Naess's and Sessions's definitions, the complications in working out who deems what a legitimate expression of Deep Ecology increases considerably.

---

86. See Naess, "Docta Ignorantia and the Application of General Guidelines".
87. Katz *et al.*, "Introduction", xiv.
88. Eric Katz "Against the Inevitability of Anthropocentrism", 25.
89. *Ibid.*, 18.
90. Naess, "Self-Realization", 236.
91. For a fuller treatment of the instances where these figures defined Deep Ecology in terms of Ecosophy T's ontology see Fox, *Toward a Transpersonal Ecology*, 225–42.

In order to clarify the complications which enshroud the esoteric elements in DE, the competing discourses on defining Deep Ecology can be laid out as follows: following Katz, DE should be labelled esoteric because the philosophy of Deep Ecology is based on Naess's esoteric ontology; therefore, all of the "pieces of esoteric flotsam" mentioned earlier in the text, including the Council of All Beings, Transpersonal Ecology, the ritual practice of eco-magick, and ecocentric paradigm shifts, should be understood as definitive expressions of Deep Ecology as they presume ontological holism and the possibility of Self-realization. Katz's conception of Deep Ecology dramatically differs from Arne Naess's interpretation, for what appear to be esoteric flotsams are actually ecosophical elaborations derived from an ultimate norm, which Naess "hypothesizes" will be ecocentric if sufficiently deep enough.[92] As the expression of an ecosophy, these esoteric elaborations are partially definitive of Deep Ecology, albeit non-exclusively, for Deep Ecology is both the process by which higher knowledge is achieved and the ecosophies which possess it.[93] In stark contrast to Katz and Naess, adopting Sessions's interpretation would lead one to conclude that the esoteric elements in DE are indeed flotsams that do not even remotely define Deep Ecology, but belong instead to personal ecosophical positions. The implications that follow from these perspectives play out in how Deep Ecology is reinterpreted beyond the writings of its foremost architects and its principal critique, and more importantly how scholars adjudicate these reinterpretations, or in other words, determine what can legitimately be ascribed to DE. Considering their drastic variation, it should come as no surprise that discussions concerning what Deep Ecology is and who belongs to it are going on their third decade.

CONCLUSION

The findings of the current study do not as much refute the claim that Deep Ecology is a form of contemporary esotericism, but rather revise what is inherently problematic in such a generalization. The revision can be summed up thus: the interpretations of Deep Ecology that act as a backbone for DE are esoteric in divergent ways. As has been shown, the variance between the three most prominent interpretations of Deep Ecology is reflected in the lack

---

92. *Ibid.*, 205.
93. Naess acknowledges that using normative derivation and arriving at one's ultimate norm is more suitable for "a small group of a movement's theorists" than a mass audience. Consequentially, he justifies his role in the manifesto as well as his advocacy for it in light of the fact that only a fraction of the people associated with DE have worked out ecosophies with the underlying assumption being that ecocentrism would be the ultimate norm arrived at if those who do not have ecosophies used normative derivation. Naess, "Deepness of Questions and the Deep Ecology Movement", 205.

of uniformity in how each interpretation is esoteric. Sessions's interpretation is esoteric on account of his portrayal of ecocentrism historiographically, that is, as a form of perennial wisdom. Working from different assumptions and towards different aims, Naess's definition was based on providing direct access to the esoteric knowledge Sessions historicized. Lastly, in locating the nondual ontology and potential for Self-realization of Ecosophy T in normative derivation and Sessions's concept of ecocentrism, Katz showed how all DE theorizing is essentially esoteric as it follows from ontological holism. Since the way Deep Ecology is defined determines the manner in which it is esoteric, the polyfocal approach presents the only way for scholars to adequately recognize the plurality of esoteric discourses in DE, and, further, which esoteric discourse is being utilized at any particular discursive junction.

Admittedly, the foregoing analysis focuses exclusively on highly specific academic interpretations of Deep Ecology. Little regard was afforded to the ethnographic data that explains how these theories are received outside of academia and even less regard was given to asking what these beliefs do to the people who hold them. While undoubtedly important, these questions belong to the field of sociology, and, more to the point, the sociology of esotericism.[94] However, a polyfocal understanding of DE permits both ethnographic researchers and scholars interested in the philosophy of DE a method of analysis that is able to organize expressions of Deep Ecology that borrow, obscure, conflate and disregard elements of the definitions which gave rise to the milieu. Moreover, in laying out the differences between the seminal definitions of Deep Ecology, scholars are better able to track how familiarity with particular definitions correlates to the inclusion or rejection of additional and alternative esoteric discourses. Going even further, in permitting scholars to discuss DE as a "semiotic" which Burkhard Gladigow describes as assembling "different religions and the constructions of meaning in parts of society like signs in a system of signs", the polyfocal approach draws into better detail the salient presence of channelling, neopaganism, Transpersonal Psychology, and New Physics in the milieu.[95] The discursive transfers between these fields signal more than the commingling of "fringe" influences with environmental concern; rather, their salient presence in the milieu testifies to an ongoing and dynamic process of popularization, innovation and appropriation that marks the existence of esoteric discourses in contemporary society.

---

94. See Granholm, "The Sociology of Esotericism".
95. Gladigow, quoted in von Stuckrad, "Western Esotericism", 87.

CHAPTER 15

THE SECULAR, THE POST-SECULAR AND THE ESOTERIC IN THE PUBLIC SPHERE

Kennet Granholm

From the very birth of sociology in the mid-nineteenth century, the eventual demise of religion was seen as inevitable. In recent times, however, increasing numbers of sociologists, social commentators and social theorists have come to describe the current state of Europe as "post-secular". What is suggested is not a straightforward "return of religion", but rather an awareness of the continued relevance of religion in secular societies, as well as changing perceptions of what actually counts as religion, what functions it may have and where it can be located. Quite naturally, the post-secular should be conceived of as having relevance for the esoteric as well. In fact, if looking at new arenas of religion (and I am thinking in particular of popular culture), we might even be witnessing a popularization of the esoteric that is unprecedented in Western religious history.

In this chapter I will be looking at secularization theory, and link it to recent discussions on the post-secular. I will then address, somewhat briefly and introductorily, potential transformations and further effects on the esoteric from both secularism and post-secularism. Finally, I will provide a few examples of the intersection of the secular, the post-secular and the esoteric on a particular genre of popular culture: science fiction film and television.

SECULARIZATION THEORY

The first thing to note when discussing secularization is that we are not dealing with a single theory. Rather, there are numerous distinct theories with different premises and focal points, and there has even been talk of a "secularization paradigm".[1] While it is difficult to untangle the complex that is the

---

1. Martin, *On Secularization*, 9; Bruce, *God is Dead*, 2.

secularization paradigm, Paul Heelas and Linda Woodhead's division into four main approaches to secularization is, while somewhat simplified, a good starting point.[2] The approaches are:

- the disappearance thesis;
- the differentiation thesis;
- the de-intensification thesis; and
- the coexistence thesis.

The meaning of the first and last of these approaches is more or less obvious, but the second and third may need some clarification. Somewhat simplified, the second approach indicates that religion, due to societal differentiation, becomes simply a subsystem among others, such as economy, science and education.[3] Due to this, religion loses cultural and societal significance. The third approach posits that religion might remain a societal factor, but in a less-intense and essentially powerless form. What is common to all approaches is that secularization lessens the overall societal impact of religion, and weakens its influence on other societal spheres.[4]

As already mentioned, the idea of the disappearance of religion was at the core of sociology from the very start of the discipline, with authors such as August Comte, Karl Marx, Émile Durkheim and Max Weber all working on the basis of this supposition. However, the unfortunate fate of religion was stated as a simple fact, and it was not until the second half of the twentieth century that systematic theories of secularization started to be developed.[5] According to Karel Dobbelaere, these theories were developed on the basis of Emile Durkheim's idea of societal differentiation, Max Weber's idea of rationalization, and Ferdinand Tönnies's distinction of *Gemeinschaft* (community) and *Gesellschaft* (society).[6] While it is correct to talk of a secularization paradigm, it would be erroneous to claim that the perspective was uncontested. The debate over the factuality of secularization has been ongoing since at least the 1960s,[7] and it has often taken fairly ugly dimensions with different factions regularly ridiculing each other in quite an unprofessional manner. The apparent resurgence of religion in the West in recent decades has lessened the overall appeal of secularization theories. For example, Peter Berger, who was

---

2. Woodhead & Heelas, "Secularization", 307–8.
3. Dobbelaere, "The Meaning and Scope of Secularization", 600–601.
4. Heelas, "The Spiritual Revolution", 375.
5. Dobbelaere, "The Meaning and Scope of Secularization", 599. For examples see Herberg, "Religion in a Secularized Society" (1962/3); Berger & Luckmann, "Secularization and Pluralism" (1966); Luckmann, *The Invisible Religion* (1967); Berger, *The Sacred Canopy* (1967).
6. Dobbelaere, "The Meaning and Scope of Secularization", 599.
7. For early critiques of secularization theories see e.g. Martin, "Towards Eliminating the Concept of Secularization"; Shiner, "The Concept of Secularization in Empirical Research".

one of the first to develop a systematic secularization thesis, has come to claim that we are now witnessing a "de-secularization".[8]

Current theories of secularization are very complex, something which opponents of secularization theory do not always acknowledge.[9] The theories often involve several layers of analysis. Dobbelaere points to three distinct, but connected, levels: "the societal or macro-level, the organizational or meso-level, and the individual or micro-level".[10] On a societal level we may be dealing with the separation of Church and state, which in turn encourages organizational differentiation where functions previously held by the Church organization are separated from it.[11] The result is the formation of secular institutions dealing with e.g. medicine and education, as well as the creation of a separate realm for the religious. An example of organizational adjustment to the new societal conditions produced by secularization is the ecumenical activities of many churches, implying a tolerance on the level of the religious institution.[12] On the individual level we see the individualization and compartmentalization of religion, where religious belief and activity become separated from both the public sphere and the individual's everyday life.[13] José Casanova similarly identifies several elements of secularization theory, where the notion of societal differentiation in modernity forms the core and, in Casanova's opinion, an unassailable fact.[14] The two sub-theories most often connected to this core are the decline and the privatization of religion.[15] Casanova sees these three theories as distinct, and the latter two as dubious.

Even with the diversity in the field, all secularization theory is united in the basic premise that "[t]o talk of secularization is to suppose that the present is less religious than the past".[16] Critics often argue that advocates of secularization theory overestimate the religiousness of the past, and there is some truth to this critique. Secularization theorists have at times based their estimates of the past on very scant empirical evidence. Peter Laslett, though a historian rather than a sociologist of religion, represents this in naming one of his books *The World We Have Lost*. Problematically, he asserts that:

---

8. Berger, *The Sacred Canopy*; cf. Berger, "Secularization and De-secularization", 292. On the other hand, there are scholars such as David Martin who criticized the concept of secularization already in the 1960s (see Martin, "Towards Eliminating the Concept of Secularization"), but who later developed a "general theory of secularization" (see Martin, *A General Theory of Secularization*; Martin, *On Secularization*).
9. Bruce, *God is Dead*, 4–29, is perhaps the best example of the complexity of secularization theory, and definitely too intricate to discuss in any detail in the present context.
10. Dobbelaere, "The Meaning and Scope of Secularization", 600.
11. *Ibid.*, 602–5.
12. *Ibid.*, 608.
13. *Ibid.*, 605–7.
14. It should be noted, however, that Casanova has more recently discussed "de-differentiation". See Casanova, "Rethinking Secularization".
15. Casanova, *Public Religions in the Modern World*, 19–20.
16. Bruce, *God is Dead*, 45.

> All our ancestors were literal believers, all of the time. Their beliefs were not only religious, of course, since they believed in witchcraft, evil and benign, and gave credence to many propositions and practices condemned by theologians as heathen survivals.[17]

Bruce is well aware of the critique and argues that "nothing in the secularization paradigm requires that the religious life of premodern Britain be a 'Golden Age of Faith'", but simply that "our ancestors were patently more religious than we are".[18] While he makes strong use of available statistical data to prove his point, such data is always problematic in being open to different and often conflicting interpretations.[19] Bruce is also clearer than some other theorists regarding the specific timeframe he investigates. In *Religion in the Modern World* Bruce sets this frame from 1517 (i.e. the year when Martin Luther presented his "ninety-five theses" and set in motion the Protestant Reformation) to the present day (i.e. the mid-1990s, when Bruce's book was published). The post-Reformation age is seen as a period of increase in popular religion (at the expense of popular magic), while it also produced a thorough individualization of religion which led to its eventual decline.[20] Still, at times Bruce does fall into a more simplistic argument, as when he states that "a world of rationality is less conducive to religion than a traditional society", and when he supports the conviction of "the bulk of the social-science community" that "modern societies are less religious than traditional ones".[21] This suggests a teleological understanding where societies become increasingly less religious as they modernize.

All this raises the question of what is encompassed by the term "religion" and what "being religious" signifies. The notion of secularization demands an explicit substantive definition of religion (i.e. focusing on its content rather than function), as it would otherwise be impossible to determine whether secularization is taking place or not.[22] Furthermore, most proponents of secularization theories seem to have various forms of Western Christianity and its institutions in mind.[23] Taken that the term "secular" and its derivates originated in a Catholic context, with secularization referring to "the legal (canonical) process whereby a 'religious' person left the cloister to return to the 'world' and its temptations, becoming thereby a 'secular' person",[24] and later

---

17. Laslett, *The World We Have Lost*, 71.
18. Bruce, *God is Dead*, 45.
19. See e.g. Hanson, "The Secularization Thesis".
20. Bruce, *Religion in the Modern World*, 3–4.
21. *Ibid.*, 48, 52. Cf. Chapter 2 of the present volume.
22. Dobbelaere, "The Meaning and Scope of Secularization", 600. See also Bruce, *God is Dead*, 2.
23. On secularization as a European rather than a global phenomenon see Davie, *Europe: The Exceptional Case*; Habermas, "Religion in the Public Sphere", 2.
24. Casanova, *Public Religions in the Modern World*, 13.

the post-Reformation seizure of Church holdings by secular states, it would perhaps be sensible to reserve the use of the term to official Christianity and its institutions.

Even with the preference for substantive definitions, however, Durkheimian understandings of the function of religion as the "glue holding a society together" can be discerned in the writings of many secularization theorists. This has the effect of most newer religious formations not being regarded as equal in importance to "conventional Christianity", as they do not have the same community-building potential as the latter. In defence of a theorist such as Bruce, it should be noted that he is very clear on his task being the examination of the *social* role of religion, and not more individualistic functions. In my opinion, however, this is a mistake. As society changes, so do forms of community, and therefore it is reasonable to assume that the social impact of religious formations arising under new conditions cannot be assessed by reference to old models. These problems are evident in most quantitative research and available data in that the questions asked rarely function well when trying to examine new functions and forms of religion. There is an apparent bias for conventional religiosities. As Kocku von Stuckrad has noted, it is useful (and indeed necessary) to distinguish between Christian doctrine and Christian culture, and the common failure to do so introduces many misunderstandings.[25] The difference here is between theological interpretations of a religion, and the ever-presence of it in visual and material culture. The problematic reliance on theological interpretations of "religion" is evident in the earlier quote from Laslett, and in Bruce's of the increase in popular religion at the expense of popular magic during the Reformation. The understanding of "magic" as referring to "folk beliefs" and assorted "superstitions" is based on early evolutionary models of religion, and is problematic both in according representative primacy to official religious institutions and religious professionals rather than to the large masses of religious people, and in its simplistic understanding of "magic".[26]

Another common ingredient of secularization theory is the idea that religious pluralism introduces a relativism, which makes adherence to particular religious worldviews less compelling.[27] One problem here is that this idea builds on the assumption that pluralism is a relatively recent phenomenon, and that people in earlier times would have been more or less unaware of the existence of competing worldviews.[28] While it is true that the Catholic Church

---

25. Von Stuckrad, *Locations of Knowledge in Medieval and Early Modern Europe*, 14.
26. For the inherent problems in the popularization of "evolutionary", cross-cultural understandings of magic see Lehrich, *The Language of Demons and Angels*, 3–11; Pasi, "Magic".
27. This is the central argument in Berger, *The Sacred Canopy*.
28. Pluralism can be understood in two different ways here. It can imply "the *organization of difference*", as discussed by Kocku von Stuckrad, *Locations of Knowledge in Medieval and Early Modern Europe*, 19, or as an ideology positing plurality as something positive. The

had a fairly solid ontological monopoly in medieval times, competitors such as Judaism, Islam and the various European pre-Christian religions were always a concern much addressed in Catholic discourse.[29] Furthermore, one should not forget the considerable internal pluralism of Christianity, even before the Reformation.

Another aspect of secularization theory, at times lost to some, is that processes of secularization affect society (the macro level), societal institutions – including religious ones (the meso level) – and sentiments of individuals (the micro level), but not religion directly. This is in line with the strict definition of religion contained in secularization theory itself, not an expression of essentializing understandings of "religion". Talk of "secularized religion" would be something of an oxymoron, as transformed religion would affect the definition of religion itself, and thus change the very outset of secularization theory.[30] *Expressions* of religion are, however, affected. As Wilson notes:

> Secularization affects religious bodies, not only marginalizing them within the social system, and by causing changes in religious commitment within a population, but also by making it likely that new religious expression will necessarily emerge in new forms and employ new language.[31]

The above discussion deals with the standard approaches to secularization. However, introducing a *discursive* approach brings in some additional interesting perspectives. While it may well be, as many scholars claim, that the internal structures of Christianity in themselves made secularization possible, I will focus on later developments; namely the Enlightenment and the ideals of secularism that gained ground here. The notion of secularization can be regarded a post-Enlightenment hegemonic discourse – informed by the ideology of secular*ism* – which helps create the situation it tries to describe. Sociology, of course, is in itself firmly embedded in the Enlightenment project of progress.[32] Thus, the secularization thesis can itself be regarded an expression of this discourse[33] of rationality, reason, and scientific progress – rather than an impartial description of what is/was occurring in the West.

---

former was certainly in effect in medieval Europe, whereas the latter is largely a modern phenomenon, or at least has accentuated in modernity.
29. See von Stuckrad, *Locations of Knowledge in Medieval and Early Modern Europe*, 19–23.
30. Note, however, that Wilson does call Scientology a "secularized religion". See Wilson, *The Social Dimensions of Sectarianism*, 267–88.
31. *Ibid.*, 275.
32. cf. Morozov, "Has the Postsecular Age Begun?", 40, on European secularism as a "social and anthropological project".
33. "Discourse" can here be understood as "a set of meanings, metaphors, representations, images, stories, statements and so on that in some way together produce a particular version of events" (Burr, *An Introduction to Social Constructionism*, 48).

This is a point noted by several other scholars involved in the secularization debate. For example, Martin notes that "[s]ociology itself emerged as part of the process of secularization", that secularization in turn can be seen as a guiding paradigm of the discipline, and that "[p]erhaps it [secularization theory] could be criticized as an ideological and philosophical imposition *on* history rather than an inference *from* history".[34] Similarly, Casanova concludes that "[w]e need to entertain seriously the proposition that secularization became a self-fulfilling prophecy in Europe" when enough people "accepted the basic premises of the theory of secularization".[35] In accordance with this, Bruce's claim that the motivations of specific scholars are inconsequential[36] cannot be accepted outright. As should be evident by this point, historiography (and other scholarly activities such as sociological analysis) is always subject to the bias of the researcher/interpreter. There is no truly objective analysis and the scholar always chooses his limited material from a much larger body of potential data.[37] Quantitative data, as used in much sociological research, is particularly precarious in this regard, as it builds on simplified categories from the start and thus does not take into account the inherent contradictions and uncertainties of human communication. Further, secularization theory and the secularist discourses it is bound to are problematic in their very conception and description of "religion". First, as made clear already, the focus is on conventional religious institutions and their theological understandings. This means that the actual lived religion and interpretations of others than religious professionals are accorded a secondary role. Second, and connected to the issue of theological understandings, on the individual level the focus is on "beliefs". Beliefs are simply not measurable. What *is* measurable are claims and statements concerning beliefs. This might seem a petty matter, but the implications are quite real. First, "belief" is a central factor in Christianity in ways that it simply is not in many other religions, and even in Christianity the primacy of belief could be claimed to be an issue of theological discourse. Orthopraxy would seem to be more common than orthodoxy in most religions.[38] Thus, measuring people's relation to beliefs targets Christianity specifically, rather than religion and religiosity in general. If people's understanding of religion is changing, then going by "old-school" approaches will not yield satisfactory results. People will respond to questionnaires according to dominant discourses, and including terms such as "belief", "God" and even "religion" will not do if discourses on religion themselves are changing.

---

34. Martin, *On Secularization*, 17, 19.
35. Casanova, "Religion, European Secular Identities, and European Integration", 84.
36. See Bruce, *Religion in the Modern World*, 52.
37. Von Stuckrad, *Locations of Knowledge in Medieval and Early Modern Europe*, 198–200.
38. This again demonstrates the theological bias in "old-school" approaches to religious studies. On this point, see Turner, "Religion in a Post-Secular Society", 658.

THE POST-SECULAR

"Post-secular" is fast becoming a key concept in the sociological study of religion. Just as with the concept of secularization – and possibly even more so – there are many different ways in which the term is understood. This is unfortunately compounded by the vague and unreflected use which is common, and there is thus a risk that "post-secular" will amount to little more than a new trend word with little actual theoretical content, much as was the case with the term "postmodern" in the 1980s and 1990s. There is in any case considerable need, as well as possibility, to develop and refine the concept.[39]

Tracing the origin and popularization of the term "post-secular" itself is made easy by using Google's new "Ngram Viewer", a database search engine that makes it possible to do keyword searches in a huge corpus of digitized books.[40] The graph drawn by the program clearly shows that there are no occurrences of the word until the early 1950s, and only occasional occurrences then and around 1970 and 1980.[41] Occurrences increase slowly in the 1990s, to go to a drastic upwards climb from 2005 onwards. This would appear to confirm Justin Beaumont's comments on 2007 as the year when discussion of the post-secular entered the social scientific mainstream. He explicitly mentions the publication of Charles Taylor's *A Secular Age*, a collection of articles dealing with "European postsecularism" in the online journal *Eurozine*,[42] and a special report on religion and public life published in *The Economist*.[43] Since then the academic discussion on the theme has intensified, evident in collected volumes such as *Exploring the Postsecular*.[44]

While the term post-secular saw some prior use in philosophy of religion and theology,[45] two thinkers in particular are regarded as the main inspiration

---

39. Cf. Moberg & Granholm, "The Concept of the Post-Secular".
40. See http://ngrams.googlelabs.com. A search on "postsecular" and "Postsecular", between the years 1900 and 2008 in the English-language corpus was done on 2 March 2011. The "post-secular/Post-secular" form was not included because Ngram searches do not accept hyphens. Of course, it should be noted that searches in the Ngram Viewer may not be perfectly reliable.
41. One of the first occurrences of "postsecular" would seem to be in 1956 in Jean Pierre Barricelli's *Dodecahedron: Collected Poems*. The earliest scholarly occurrence would seem to be in Martin E. Marty's *The New Shape of American Religion* from 1959.
42. Articles published in the journal from the mid-2000s dealing with "post-secular themes" include Reemtsma, "Must We Respect Religiosity?" (2005); Hervieu-Léger, "The Role of Religion in Establishing Social Cohesion" (2006); Eder & Bosetti, "Post-Secularism" (2006); Habermas, "Die Dialektik der Säkularisierung" (2008). The journal also has a "focal point" collection of articles dealing with the subject (see Eurozine, "Post-Secular Europe?").
43. Beaumont, "Transcending the Particular in Postsecular Cities", 5.
44. Molendijk et al., *Exploring the Postsecular*. It should be noted, however, that *Exploring the Postsecular* is still one of the few volumes explicitly dedicated to the subject.
45. E.g. Blond, *Post-Secular Philosophy*. For later works see e.g. Joas, *Do We Need Religion?*; Smith & Whistler, *After the Postsecular and the Postmodern*.

in social philosophy and the social sciences: Jürgen Habermas and Charles Taylor.[46] The inclusion of Taylor may seem odd considering that in his work most often referred to in this context, the nearly 900-page long *A Secular Age*, the term post-secular occurs only once. Concerning the post-secular, Taylor writes:

> I use this term not as designating an age in which the declines in belief and practice of the last century would have been reversed, because this doesn't seem likely, at least for the moment; I rather mean a time in which the hegemony of the mainstream master narrative of secularization will be more and more challenged. This I think is now happening.[47]

While this fits well with my own understanding of the term, I would be hard pressed to call Taylor a theoretician of the *term* post-secular itself. His inclusion is understandable, though, as he accords religion an important role in secular society. He could thus be termed a post-secular thinker.

Whereas Taylor's inclusion into the fold of theoreticians of the post-secular is dubious, there can be no question of Habermas's significance. For Habermas, a society being post-secular refers to "*a change in consciousness*" in relation to religion within it.[48] This change is due mainly to three reasons: the role religion plays in global conflicts, which essentially "undermines the secularistic belief in the *foreseeable disappearance* of religion and robs the secular understanding of the world of any triumphal zest"; the growing influence of religion in national public spheres, as religious actors continue to influence public opinion and participate in public debate; and the "*pluralism of ways of life*" introduced by increasing immigration from non-European localities.[49] A post-secular society is essentially a secularized one, but with an awareness that it "has to 'adjust itself to the continued existence of religious communities in an increasingly secularized environment'".[50] Habermas also limits the discussion to "the affluent countries of Europe or countries such as Canada, Australia and New Zealand", while explicitly leaving out the US as it has not experienced the same, earlier, lapse in religiosity.[51]

Commenting on Habermas's work, Austin Harrington notes that the post-secular does not really deal with religion "returned to a position of renewed

---

46. See Molendijk *et al.*, "Preface", ix. José Casanova is mentioned along with Habermas and Taylor.
47. Taylor, *A Secular Age*, 534–5.
48. Habermas, "Notes on Post-Secular Society", 20.
49. *Ibid.*, 20.
50. *Ibid.*, 21, 19.
51. *Ibid.*, 17. Leaving out the US is criticized by Dillon in "Can Post-Secular Society Tolerate Religious Differences?", 142.

public prominence", as the original decline proposed by secularization theorists has been put into question, but more with "a revision of a previously over-confidently secularist outlook".[52] Theorizing the post-secular thus deals with "the limits of the secularization thesis".[53] One could say that the post-secular relates more to changes in perceptions regarding religion, among scholars and laypeople alike, than to grand-scale societal transformations in themselves.[54] This relates directly to changes in Habermas's own views on religion and the societal role of it.[55] It was in what Harrington calls a third phase in Habermas's thinking, "anticipated in the book *Postmetaphysical Thinking* of 1988", that he turned from being a devoted secularist to appreciating the importance of religion.[56] Concerning the relations between the secular and the religious, Habermas writes:

> [T]he religious side must accept the authority of "natural" reason as the fallible results of the institutionalized sciences and the basic principles of universalistic egalitarianism in law and morality. Conversely, secular reason may not set itself up as the judge concerning truths of faith.[57]

Thus, both religious and secular actors need to acknowledge each others' rights to participate in societal and political life.[58] However, Habermas continues by noting that secular actors "can accept as reasonable only what it can translate into its own, in principle universally accessible, discourses".[59] Even though the secular state must allow a place for religion,[60] it is apparent here that the roles provided for religion and the secular are not equal. In effect, the religious is expected to speak with a secular voice and operate in the secular realm on the premises of the latter, and this betrays a secularist agenda

---

52. Harrington, "Habermas and the 'Post-Secular Society'", 547.
53. Beaumont, "Transcending the Particular in Postsecular Cities", 6.
54. These changes in perception of course change religion itself, as religious actors adapt to their new roles in the public sphere, see Knott, "Cutting Through the Postsecular City", 34.
55. As an example, Habermas has come to regularly engage in debate with religious representatives. See Ratzinger & Habermas, *The Dialectics of Secularization*; Habermas *et al.*, *An Awareness of What is Missing*. For more on this see Dillon, "Can Post-Secular Society Tolerate Religious Differences?", 144–5.
56. Harrington, "Habermas and the 'Post-Secular Society'", 544.
57. Habermas, "An Awareness of What is Missing", 16. Natural reason refers to "[t]he assumption of a common human reason" which makes a non-religious secular state feasible by relying on "public arguments to which supposedly *all* persons have *equal access*", Habermas, "Religion in the Public Sphere", 4 (cf. 9–10).
58. Habermas, "Notes on Post-Secular Society", 22–3; Habermas, "Religion in the Public Sphere", 4–6.
59. Habermas, "An Awareness of What is Missing", 16. Cf. Habermas, "Notes on Post-Secular Society", 28; Dillon, "Can Post-Secular Society Tolerate Religious Differences?", 146.
60. Habermas, "Religion in the Public Sphere", 7.

on the behalf of Habermas.[61] He drives the point further by saying that "the content of religion must open itself up to the normatively grounded expectation that it should recognize for reasons of its own the neutrality of the state towards worldviews, the equal freedom of all religious communities, and the independence of the institutionalized sciences".[62]

Habermas's (and subsequently others') discussion of religion involves similar problems as many secularization theories. For example, a thoroughly intellectualized understanding of religion is often involved,[63] with a focus on concepts such as "belief", "faith" and "convictions".[64] Habermas also makes what can be conceived as artificial distinctions between religious and secular citizens, where an individual can only be one or the other.[65] A second problem in Habermas's writing is that he, as a social philosopher, is not really describing an existing situation, but rather presenting *ideals* for the relation between the secular state and religious institutions. Connected to this is Habermas's hugely influential politicized understanding of "the public sphere". Religion in the public sphere thus implies the *political* importance of religion, primarily evident in the various religious fundamentalisms around the globe.[66] I feel that in order to grasp societal life more holistically – and as relating political life only to official political institutions is limited and artificial – the meaning of "public sphere" needs to be broadened to include at least mass media and popular culture.[67]

The post-secular is a central theme in the Åbo Akademi University Centre of Excellence research project Post-Secular Culture and a Changing Religious Landscape in Finland (PCCR).[68] In contrast to many other approaches to the post-secular, the aim in PCCR is to provide empirical examination, and to this effect a loose working definition has been developed. The four mutually dependent points of the definition mention changes in the understanding of the term "religion" itself, an increase in the awareness and public visibility of religion, changes in the power relations between religious and other

---

61. See Casanova, "Religion, European Secular Identities, and European Integration", 92n7; Dillon, "Can Post-Secular Society Tolerate Religious Differences?", 148.
62. Habermas, "An Awareness of What is Missing", 21.
63. Moberg & Granholm, "The Concept of the Post-Secular". See also Dillon, "Can Post-Secular Society Tolerate Religious Differences?", 146–7.
64. Habermas, "Religion in the Public Sphere", 8.
65. See Dillon, "Can Post-Secular Society Tolerate Religious Differences?", 148.
66. Habermas, "Religion in the Public Sphere", 1.
67. See Moberg & Granholm, "The Concept of the Post-Secular". It should be noted, however, that Habermas already in the 1960s discussed the "hijacking" of the public sphere by the mass media and the change of its meaning in this process; see Habermas, *The Structural Transformation of the Public Sphere*, 2.
68. The PCCR project started in 2010 and is led by Professor Peter Nynäs. The definition is discussed on the basis of an internal methodological document developed within the research group, of which I am a member.

institutions, and transformations in the environments of religion which in turn inform the shaping of new religious subjectivities. This is all set in the context of "profound macro-level transformations in the global political economy" since the 1980s, and the accompanying increase in "global interconnectedness of national societies with regard to economy, politics, culture, media, and populations". In this perspective, the post-secular does relate to large-scale transformations on both societal and organizational levels, but these transformations are intimately linked to and dependent on changing perceptions of religion.

Looking at the post-secular through discourse theory, and linking it to a discursive understanding of secularization, brings interesting new dimensions to the discussion. If secularization theory is bound in secularist discourses, then the post-secular can be regarded as discursive formations which signal the, at least partial, societal breaking up of the hegemony of secularism. These post-secular discourses are themselves heavily indebted to an awareness of the earlier hegemonic position of secularism. A discursive approach also brings to the front, as per the PCCR definition discussed above, the awareness that more religion is perceived at least in part due to the broadened understanding of the term religion itself. Just as secularization theories are dependent on secularist discourses and help bring into being what is described, so post-secular discourses are not simply neutral descriptions of "how things are". In seeing religion in new ways, and in according it new (or renewed) roles and functions, we are actively engaged in producing this new reality.

Scholars are not separated from this process in some way. In fact, we are on the forefront of it, just as the sociologists of a century or so ago were key actors in secularist discourse. This whole situation need not be a problem. At least to some degree, "finding what we are looking for" is an unavoidable aspect of scholarly inquiry, and thinking that it is not does not insulate from this fact. It does, however, mean that we as scholars should be aware of what we are doing when we are projecting "the post-secular condition". We should not just naïvely describe "the new post-secular reality" as a simple fact. The errors of the secularization paradigm need not be repeated.

While keeping this caveat in mind, the post-secular is very interesting from at least two standpoints. This emerging discourse is not limited to scholarly discussions, but does represent a broader societal phenomenon. This means that religion is indeed acquiring new and changed roles and functions, as well as a renewed visibility in the public sphere. We are thus witnessing some major transformations on the religious field of the West. Even with us scholars playing a part in producing this reality and these changes, the new perspectives provide us with new and interesting ways of advancing a field which has become somewhat stagnant. In short, it allows us to escape "old-school" ways of looking at religion where the conventional religious institution is more or less the only "right" arena for it, and where theological orthodoxy is awarded primacy when it comes to describing what a particular religion "really" is.

SECULARIZATION AND "THE POST-SECULAR CONDITION": IMPLICATIONS FOR THE ESOTERIC

Considering that most discussions on secularization and the post-secular relate to "religion" in fairly narrow and "old-school" ways, focusing on mainline religious institutions, "beliefs" and "convictions", and community-establishing functions, one may wonder if there is any relevance for something as apparently unorthodox as the esoteric. However one defines the esoteric, it can be conclusively determined that it does not fit into the conception of religion common to scholars such as Bruce and Habermas. A response could be to withdraw completely from these debates; but I believe that meaningful discussion is possible. However, in order to do so it is of considerable importance to delineate the esoteric and reassess previous theoretical descriptions and definitions. Obviously, common sociological interpretations of the esoteric and occult as dealing with secrecy and "deviant" knowledge claims are unusable if one is to discuss the subject in the public sphere. In most current scholarly accounts the esoteric is regarded not as a "tradition" consisting of distinct doctrines and practices and situated in clearly outlined institutions, but as specific approaches to knowledge that cross the borders of religious and secular identities.[69]

In short, esoteric approaches to knowledge may be religious, but are not necessarily so. This applies both to Hanegraaff's discussion of "gnosis" as a "third stream" in European cultural history, distinct from (but connected to) the streams of reason and faith,[70] and to von Stuckrad's description of the esoteric as relating to claims to higher knowledge and ways of accessing it.[71] Consequently, it might be possible to make a division into religious and non-religious esotericisms, and to conclude that secularization and the post-secular might then have a clear impact on the former but not the latter. Introducing such a divide would, however, compromise one of the most promising possibilities offered by the study of the esoteric: the examination of "that which lies in between", which problematizes the distinction of the secular and the religious in the first place. As clearly demonstrated by the examples of such figures as Paracelsus (1493–1541) and Sir Isaac Newton (1643–1727), and phenomena such as alchemy and astrology, reason and faith were in no way mutually exclusive in pre-Enlightenment times. Furthermore, as demonstrated by Kocku von Stuckrad in his contribution to this volume, contemporary science is not devoid of "trans-scientific" elements. This would, in turn, seem to suggest that the modern distinction between science (reason) and religion (faith) is, at least to some degree, an artificial construct. None of this, of course, implies that secularist and post-secularist discourses have no bearing on the esoteric.

---

69. See Chapter 2 of the present volume.
70. Hanegraaff, "Reason, Faith, and Gnosis".
71. Von Stuckrad, "Western Esotericism".

For a more detailed discussion of the esoteric in the secular I refer to von Stuckrad's chapter in the present volume. However, a more general discussion is in order here. Secularism and secularization have certainly affected esotericism, and the accounts in this regard provided by Hanegraaff and Hammer are spot on. Hanegraaff notes four principal changes in post-Enlightenment esotericism: an adaptation to the ideals of reason and rationality; the broadening of the scope of influence and source material to increasingly and more explicitly include non-Western cultures and non-Christian religions; the adoption of an evolutionary paradigm to spiritual development; and the introduction of psychologized interpretations of esoteric phenomena and teachings.[72] Hammer focuses on the appeal to science as one of three major legitimizing strategies in post-Enlightenment esotericism.[73] All these developments can be directly attributed to secularism and the effects of it on European societies in the form of secularization. Secularist discourses posited religion as something antiquated and belonging to more primitive stages of cultural development, and the effects were mostly directed towards the dominant religious institutions of society (i.e. various Christian Churches). Consequently, esoteric actors attempted to frame their teachings and vocabulary to more closely fit into the "new scientific worldview". A further effect of the relative "de-Christening" of Europe was that it became both possible and appealing to turn to non-Christian, "more authentic", religions for inspiration.[74]

However, even though Hanegraaff's description of post-Enlightenment esotericism as "all attempts by esotericists to come to terms with a disenchanted world"[75] is sound, his calling it *secularized* esotericism is not.[76] As discussed earlier, theories of secularization deal with changes in *society* and its institutions, which in turn may have indirect repercussions for religious doctrines, practices and "beliefs". It is not religion itself which is becoming secularized, but religious institutions, and the same could be said to apply to the esoteric. Hanegraaff's assertions that "the term 'secularisation' does not stand for a theory but for a historical fact" and entails "a profound *transformation* of religion" rather than a disappearance or a marginalization of it[77] is even more problematic.

So what about the post-secular? Some years ago I made a preliminary attempt to examine what "post-secular esotericism" could possibly be. While this attempt certainly had its flaws, the basic premise of the approach still

---

72. Hanegraaff, *New Age Religion and Western Culture*, 411–513; Hanegraaff, "How Magic Survived the Disenchantment of the World".
73. Hammer, *Claiming Knowledge*, 201–330.
74. For further discussion on these subjects see Granholm, "Locating the West".
75. Hanegraaff, *New Age Religion and Western Culture*, 422.
76. For a critique of Hanegraaff's use of the term "secularization" see Partridge, *The Re-enchantment of the West*, vol. 1, 40.
77. Hanegraaff, "How Magic Survived the Disenchantment of the World", 358.

holds. Building on Hanegraaff's comments on disenchantment involving a social pressure to discard spontaneous participation – understood as a tendency towards emotive, analogical, non-reasoning thought and action – in favour of instrumental causality,[78] I conceived of "post-secular esotericism ... as an active effort to acknowledge, embrace and seek affective and analogical thinking".[79] I also connected these changes to late modern societal transformations such as globalization, transnational networking, detraditionalization, and an overall intensification of developments set in motion in earlier phases of modernization. What could be added to this is the impact of modern communication media. As religion, just as the esoteric, is always mediated, it becomes relevant to look at how the media in question shapes it. The need is made further acute when looking at media as "sites where construction, negotiation, and reconstruction of cultural meaning takes place".[80] Written forms of communication work on a different set of parameters than oral ones, and both differ from the mass mediated forms of communication which dominate today. Examining the esoteric in contemporary times necessitates looking at the role played by modern electronic and digital communication media and popular culture. The term mediatization is useful here. It relates to "the process through which core elements of a social or cultural activity ... assume media form", implying that

> the activity is, to a greater or lesser degree, performed through interaction with a medium, and the symbolic content and the structure of the social and cultural activity are influenced by media environments and media logic, upon which they gradually become more dependent.[81]

While it is implicit in most discussions of mediatization, what is meant by "the media" are modern forms of mass communication and interactive media. Some effects of mediatization on the esoteric are when occult orders have their primary means of communication via the Internet, even to the extent where initiations need to be performed through this medium, and when a religion such as Wicca is informed by a popular television series such as *Charmed*.

I have discussed potential post-secular influences on the esoteric, but from a certain perspective the study of Western esotericism itself, and in particular the growing acceptance of it as a legitimate field of inquiry, could be regarded as an expression of post-secular trends. This is the case if the post-secular implies a broadening of academic sentiments regarding what is worthwhile

---

78. *Ibid.*, 377.
79. Granholm, "Post-Secular Esotericism?", 63. See also Granholm, "The Sociology of Esotericism", 795–6.
80. Horsfield, "Media", 113.
81. Hjarvard, "The Mediatization of Religion", 13.

to study in the world of religion, and indeed what can even be accepted under that very label. Still, scholars of esotericism have been curiously conservative in adopting some other aspects of "post-secular perspectives". What I am referring to here is the reluctance to examine non-traditional arenas such as popular culture,[82] or to even acknowledge it as a potentially worthwhile area of research.[83] This is odd, as esoteric influences are so dominant in popular culture that Christopher Partridge has even proposed that we are witnessing a shift from a Christian culture to one that is greatly informed by the esoteric and occult.[84] Popular culture is an arena in which requirements for the "seriousness of belief" and notions of religion as dealing with "ultimate concerns" must be abandoned, not necessarily due to them not being factors in popular cultural religiosity, but due to the arena itself demonstrating the artificiality of limiting religion to such functions. As scholars such as Gordon Lynch and Lynn Schofield Clarke have noted, popular culture both reflects and directs our cultural concerns, and it is thus doubly significant as an arena of examination.[85] Still, few scholars other than Christopher Partridge have done much in the way of actually connecting religious change and popular culture, and even fewer (Partridge is the exception again) have shown an interest in or recognition of the major role the esoteric plays in contemporary popular culture.[86]

In conjunction with this, and as discussed above, the Habermasian understanding of "the public sphere" must be broadened. It needs to include more than conventional religious institutions, and more than the (official) political sphere. "The public sphere" should encompass such phenomena as mass mediated communication and popular culture. In late modernity, and "post-secularity" we are witnessing an increasing erosion of the borders between the private and public spheres. Social networking sites such as Facebook, Myspace and Twitter are good examples in this regard. In regard to the esoteric and the public sphere we are then dealing with developments that increasingly take the esoteric "into the open", with numerous Facebook pages on esoteric/occult subjects demonstrating this. One of the results is a relative democratization of the esoteric.

---

82. In defence of scholars of esotericism it should be pointed out that scholars of media, popular culture, and religion have been equally slow in recognizing the esoteric as a valid subject of study.
83. This is a direct result of certain (still) dominating definitions and understandings of what esotericism "is". An example is Henrik Bogdan's discussion of the "[m]igration of esoteric ideas into nonesoteric materials", where popular culture is explicitly mentioned. Popular culture is not regarded to be as "properly" esoteric as more classic sources. See Bogdan, *Western Esotericism and Rituals of Initiation*, 20.
84. Partridge, *The Re-enchantment of the West*, vol. 1, 187. See also Partridge's chapter in the present volume.
85. Lynch, "Some Concluding Reflections", 158; Lynn Schofield Clark, "Religion, Twice Removed", 70.
86. Partridge, *The Re-enchantment of the West*.

SECULARIZATION AND "THE POST-SECULAR CONDITION": SCIENCE FICTION AND THE ESOTERIC

Science fiction is one of the best and most interesting cases to discuss when it comes to changes in the public perception of religion in contemporary times. While it is easy to regard science fiction as the ultimate fiction – it does after all deal with aliens, far-away worlds, the future and space travel – the genre does actually reflect very current and socially acute themes. The fantastic setting itself allows for dealing with subjects that might be too controversial to deal with in other forms of fiction. For example, in 1968 the television series *Star Trek* was groundbreaking in showing the first kiss between a white male and a black female on entertainment television.[87] In the present context it is interesting to note that religion has gone from being one of the most neglected themes in science fiction in the first half of the twentieth century, to becoming one of the most central themes in the latter half of the century. *Star Trek* is again a good example. Whereas the original series (1966–9) included some casual treatment of religion, mostly as representations of the superstitious and utterly pre-scientific past of humanity, the later show *Star Trek: Deep Space Nine* (1993–2001) has religion as a major theme and, more importantly, allows for ambiguous interpretations of it.

It is, however, not *Star Trek* but the *Stargate* franchise and the movie *Avatar* (2009) that I will look at in more detail here. The *Stargate* franchise got its start in 1994 with the movie *Stargate*. In the movie, an ancient artefact – a large circular portal – is found in Giza, Egypt. It is determined that the artefact is of alien origin and functions as a gateway to an alien world (named Abydos in the subsequent television series), to which a military team (along with a civilian archaeologist) is sent. We also find out that the old Egyptian god Ra was actually an alien who had possessed a human host body, subjugated humanity through advanced technology and the pretension of being a god, and was finally driven away from earth in a human uprising. Ra had, however, transported some humans to the new planet to be his slaves, and the movie focuses on the liberation of these people and the final defeat of Ra. The story was continued in the subsequent television series *Stargate SG-1* (1997–2007), *Stargate Atlantis* (2004–9), *Stargate Universe* (2009–11), the animated television series *Stargate Infinity* (2002–3), as well as several television movies, novels and comic books. Here we find out that Ra was just one representative of the parasitic "Goa'uld" species, other representatives of which having masqueraded as additional Egyptian gods and other mythological beings such as Ba'al, Cronus and Nirtti. One can definitely read a critique of religion into the series. However, we are also introduced to the benevolent alien species "the Asgard", who impersonate the Old Norse gods in order to protect humans

---

87. *Star Trek*, "Plato's Stepchildren".

from the Goa'uld, and who hide their true nature due to humans not yet being ready (i.e. advanced enough) for such information. Already in the basic premise of the franchise we find several themes which are, or have been, popular in esoteric circles. The central role of Egypt is one such theme, with the Stargate-object found in this country, the majority of the Goa'uld named after Egyptian deities, and the pyramids presented as landing platforms for alien spacecraft. A second example is the introduction of the lost city of Atlantis (actually an ancient alien city-ship) as the setting for one of the series in the franchise.

In the present context, the most interesting aspect of *Stargate* is the notion of "ascension". As described in the Stargate Wiki-page on the subject, "Ascension is a process that allows beings to be able to separate from their physical bodies and to live eternally as pure energy in a superior plane with greater amount of knowledge and power."[88] This process is made possible "once the brain achieves 90% synaptic activity", and the individual then focuses his/her brain activity and learns "how to convert their bodies into energy".[89] With ascension comes a number of preternatural abilities, such as control of the forces of nature, telekinesis and telepathy, manifestation of material objects at will, possession of non-ascended beings, the manipulation of the perceptions of others, and, perhaps most interestingly in the present context, the ability to evolve other beings to the level where they can ascend.[90] It is the role played by knowledge which is the most esoteric aspect of ascension in the *Stargate* franchise. Knowledge is both something gained when ascending, and something which is essential in making ascension possible in the first place. As the character Daniel Jackson says after ascending: "I see things, I understand things, in a way I never could have before".[91] This means that ascension fits neatly with von Stuckrad's conceptualization of the esoteric as dealing with "higher knowledge" and ways of gaining it. Ascension can be seen as a form of "gnosis", a spiritual insight that has the effect of transmuting a being. Initiatory processes are also involved. The initial process of achieving non-corporeal existence can be regarded as the first step, but it is not the endpoint of an individual's "enlightenment". Multiple levels of "higher existence" are posited, and each subsequent level comes with increased knowledge and extended powers. As Daniel Jackson comments, "Ascension doesn't make you all knowing or all powerful. It is just the beginning of the journey."[92] In borrowing from the

---

88. Stargate Wiki, "Ascension".
89. *Ibid.*
90. It should be noted that this list of abilities is almost a straight description of Siddhis (supernatural powers) in Tantra. In *Stargate*, ascended beings are also speculated to have provided the inspiration for Buddhism on Earth. By discussing ascension in *Stargate* in the context of the esoteric I am not disregarding this obvious Tantric/Buddhist influence, but simply shifting the focus of the analysis to the role accorded to "knowledge".
91. *Stargate SG-1*, "Abyss".
92. *Stargate SG-1*, "Full Circle".

common esoteric initiatory theme of "dying while still alive", Daniel Jackson needs to die in order to ascend.[93] Similarly, the character Rodney McKey needs to learn how to "let go", in essence implying a readiness to die, in order to ascend.[94] Another interesting feature is the inclusion of the standard esoteric trope of proper transmission, as an ascended being can "educate" a lower being in "enlightenment", not by providing "facts" but by stimulating the being in question to "evolve" him-/herself.

So it can be firmly established that the *Stargate* franchise cultivates an esoteric discourse. What makes it interesting in terms of the secular and the post-secular, however, is the explicit introduction of two distinct, but not diametrically opposed, ways of achieving ascension. Beings can achieve ascension through spiritual or evolutionary means. Spiritual ascension seems to be effected through meditation and the use of anecdotes reminiscent of Zen Buddhist *koans*,[95] but also by a higher being teaching a lower one,[96] as discussed above. Evolutionary ascension is reached when a being or a whole species advances to the level of "using more than 90% of their brain", again as discussed above. However, this evolutionary process need not be natural, as the series provides examples of beings and species having stimulated their brain activity by technological means, resequenced their DNA, "ascension machines" and so on, to the degree where they develop paranormal abilities and eventually ascension.[97] Even in technologically induced ascension, however, meditation and proper concentration are essential.[98] *Stargate*, and ascension in it, is a cultural phenomenon that portrays the marriage of technology and spirituality, in a way which puts neither in a privileged position.

The movie *Avatar* (2009) is, for several reasons, another interesting example of the intersection between the esoteric and popular culture, and the secular and post-secular. First, *Avatar* is the top-grossing movie of all time, with cinema revenue of nearly $2.8 billion and US DVD sales of nearly $200 million by early January 2011,[99] and it achieved its number one status in a very short amount of time. While not dismissing the impact of successful marketing, the popularity of the movie still means that it resonates with a considerable number of people, and it is thus reasonably safe to claim that it is a good reflection of concerns people today regard as being important. Second, the movie itself draws extensively from a number of key esoteric ideas. Combined with the first point, this strongly suggests that the esoteric has entered the mainstream, and that esoteric notions resonate with large numbers of

---

93. *Stargate SG-1*, "Meridian".
94. *Stargate Atlantis*, "Tao of Rodney".
95. *Stargate SG-1*, "Maternal Instinct".
96. *Stargate SG-1*, "Meridian".
97. See *Stargate SG-1*, "Prototype"; *Stargate Atlantis*, "Hide and Seek"; *Stargate Atlantis*, "Tao of Rodney".
98. *Stargate Atlantis*, "Tao of Rodney".
99. Numbers, "Avatar".

contemporary Westerners (and beyond). The esoteric notion most central to the movie is the ideas of a living, all-permeating nature, essentially in a modernized form as discussed by Hanegraaff.[100] All the animal and plant life on the moon Pandora, which the movie is set on, are connected in a "biobotanical neural network". The native Na'vi population, an alien humanoid species, can link with other life forms, and even the moon itself, by connecting a tentacle-like appendage to a similar one on the life-form in question. In connecting with the moon itself the Na'vi can commune with their ancestors, who have in death become part of the macro life form which consists of all life on the moon. That this macro life form is real and not just the result of religious imaginings of the Na'vi is confirmed at the climax of the movie, when it responds to a plea for help by amassing all animal life in the fight against the human oppressors who are set on destroying the way of life on Pandora. Potential secularist influences are demonstrated in the scientific rationale provided for the composition of Pandora. This confirms that the lifestyle of the Na'vi is not simply based on primitive superstitions, but is in fact based on scientifically objective reality. Potential post-secularist influences are demonstrated in the conflict between the technologically inclined humans and the holistic worldview of the Na'vi. While a scientific rationale is provided, it is made clear that science and technology are empty if not tempered by spirituality. Thus the Na'vi's victory over the humans is also the victory of a spiritually informed secularism over a purely capitalist–materialist one.

Third, and perhaps most interestingly, *Avatar* has garnered much discussion on spirituality and provided inspiration for esoteric actors. A video posted by YouTube user "MoonlitOpal" in January 2010 demonstrates the potential of *Avatar* to inspire to the esoteric. In discussing the essential interconnectedness of all life on Pandora, and her interpretation that this involves "to literally plug into their goddess", "MoonlitOpal" comments: "I know that it's all sci-fi but isn't that essentially what Wicca is?"[101] She goes on to say that she does not normally like science fiction, and that it was the spiritual dimension that compelled her. "MoonlitOpal" concludes: "I just connected it automatically to Wicca when I saw it".[102]

CONCLUSION

What I have tried to do in this chapter is to provide a broad account of secularization theory and the current discussions on post-secularity, combining this with some preliminary interpretations of what both might imply for the esoteric, and finally grounding these interpretations in a few case studies

---

100. Hanegraaff, *New Age Religion and Western Culture*, 407–9.
101. MoonlitOpal, "Avatar Through Pagan Eyes".
102. *Ibid.*

derived from science fiction film and television. There are still many issues to work out. Secularization theory is firmly grounded in "old-school" understandings of what religion is and does, and may not be suitable for discussions relating to much else than European institutional Christianity. Still, adopting a discursive understanding of processes and theories of secularization as being informed by secular*ism*, might open up new avenues for investigating transformations of the European religious landscape. When it comes to discussions of the post-secular, we are dealing both with relatively new scholarly developments and some unfortunate vagueness in the discussions thus far. We are also dealing with some of the same problems as can be found in secularization, such as an at times limited view of what religion can be. Here, as well, turning to discursive perspectives provide some interesting possibilities, and requires us to take a closer look at what we as scholars are doing when we are projecting specific societal scenarios. Something which is not always remembered in discussions of the post-secular, and which cannot be stressed enough, is that if discussions of the post-secular are to have any theoretical and analytical weight, they must *by necessity* be related to discussions of secularization. Finally, I want to highlight the need for scholars of esotericism, particularly of course in the investigation of contemporary expressions, to take popular culture seriously. Popular culture comprises one of the most, if not *the* most, significant arenas to explore in the study of religion today in contemporary society, and the esoteric has steadily increased in influence on this arena. In order to be able to seriously investigate the esoteric in conjuncture with popular culture, however, some changes in theory, method and overall perspectives might be required.

CHAPTER 16

PSYCHIC ENCHANTMENTS OF THE EDUCATED CLASSES

THE PARANORMAL AND THE AMBIGUITIES OF DISENCHANTMENT

Egil Asprem

Science will not remain mute on spiritual and ethical questions for long. Even now, we can see the first stirrings among psychologists and neuroscientists of what may one day become a genuinely rational approach to these matters – one that will bring even the most rarefied mystical experience within the purview of open, scientific inquiry. It is time we realized that we need not be unreasonable to suffuse our lives with love, compassion, ecstasy and awe; nor must we renounce all forms of spirituality or mysticism to be on good terms with reason.[1]

ACADEMICS AGAINST THE STREAM?

In his famous 1999 recantation of the strong secularization thesis, Peter Berger noted that there were really only two exceptions to what he called an ongoing and increasing *desecularization* of the world: European societies west of the old Iron Curtain, and "an international subculture composed of people with Western-type higher education".[2] Parallel to the inversion of secularization theory, scholars of new religious movements started reversing Max Weber's thesis of the disenchantment of the world as well (*Entzauberung der Welt*), arguing that a process of *re-enchantment* is sweeping through Western culture.[3] In 1918 Weber had proclaimed that all "mysterious incalculable forces"

---

1. Sam Harris, *The End of Faith*, 43.
2. Berger, "The Desecularization of the World", 10. For closer discussions of secularization and its related terms and theories, see Chapters 11 and 15 of this volume.
3. Weber, "Science as a Vocation", 155. The term "re-enchantment" appears to have entered academic discourse primarily through some early classics of postmodern criticisms of modern science in the 1980s, particularly Berman, *The Reenchantment of the World*, and

were being eradicated from the world by science and scientifically based technologies. *Entzauberung* – literally the disappearance of *magic* (*Zauber*)[4] – signified a new mentality in which modern people believed that anything around them could, in principle, be comprehended rationally, and that no offerings to capricious deities or magical manipulations of occult forces were needed to master the world.

"Magic", however, failed to disappear. Whether we are talking about self-designated modern magicians coming out of the various currents of occultism and neopaganism, or about that vague and poorly defined set of "occult" and "supernatural" beliefs and practices that somehow will not fit neat categories such as "religion" or "science", "magic", in fact, seems to thrive at the heart of high modernity.[5] Some have even connected the resilience of the "mysterious incalculable forces" to the secularization process itself; according to Christopher Partridge, for example,

> the deteriorating/secularized Christian culture is being replaced by a cultic milieu, which is not shaped like sectarian, denominational or ecclesiastical religion. Nor is it principally determined by that "international subculture" identified by Berger, which is "composed of people with a Western-type higher education". Increasingly, "official" definitions of reality are being challenged by a new subculture

---

David Ray Griffin, *The Reenchantment of Science*. From there it appears to have spread into the many fields of postmodern scholarship-cum-advocacy of the 1990s, including ecofeminism and deep ecology. For the more analytical use of re-enchantment in scholarship on modern and contemporary religion, see e.g. Heelas, *The New Age Movement*; Woodhead & Heelas, *Religion in Modern Times*; Partridge, *The Re-enchantment of the West*.

4. A caveat should be expressed at this point, as, in actuality, a distinction was beginning to be made between *Magie* and *Zauber* in German *Religionswissenschaft* in the early 1900s; "magic" would thus refer specifically to "occult" arts and techniques of controlling capricious forces – which made it more "scientific" and also more friendly to "community building", as an entry on "Magier, Magie" in the widely cited *Realencyklopädie für Protestantische Theologie und Kirche* stated it in 1900. Taken as a whole, Weber's late work (to which the thesis of *Entzauberung* truly belongs) displays some ambiguity when it comes to the actual relation between *Magie* and *Zauber* ("magic" and "enchantment"), but overall it seems clear that the process of transformation which he referred to as the "disenchantment of the world" did indeed include the disappearance of magical means of controlling the world and achieving salvation. For a discussion, see Breuer, "Magie, Zauber, Entzauberung", especially 119–20.

5. For the survival of various types of self-designated "Hermetic" ritual magic, drawing on pre- or early modern esoteric sources, see Hanegraaff, "How Magic Survived the Disenchantment of the World"; cf. Asprem, "Magic Naturalized?"; Asprem, *Arguing with Angels*, especially chapter 4. As has been made increasingly clear over the last decades, "magic" as an etic category in anthropology and the history of religion is deeply problematic, and based on little substance except an inheritance from centuries of identity politics and religious polemics. See e.g. Styers, *Making Magic*; Pasi, "Magic"; Hanegraaff, *Esotericism and the Academy*, chapter 3.

of *dissent* and *opposition*. In a sense, we are witnessing a return to a form of magical culture – what I will call "occulture".[6]

The observation that secularization was giving way to new forms of re-enchanted, magical culture was already made in the early 1970s, during what was perceived as a sudden and intense "occult revival".[7] As Partridge makes very clear in Chapter 6 of the present volume, his concept of occulture is much indebted to the "cultic milieu" model originally proposed by Colin Campbell, but with certain significant differences.[8] One of them is the question of *opposition* and *deviance*: whereas the cultic milieu was largely defined in terms of its opposition to "orthodox" science and religion, "occulture is ordinary". Even though particular groups, individuals, ideologies and belief systems may be described in terms of deviance from the mainstream, the broader occultural *environment*, as such, is becoming so ordinary as to *engulf* the mainstream. This is particularly emphasized by the place of popular culture in occultural production and dissemination; that is, the formation of a *popular* occulture manifesting itself in widely distributed products of literature, film and music.[9]

The inclusive definition of occultural re-enchantment notwithstanding, an oppositional trait still seems to be lingering when it comes to the question of the academy and higher education. Berger's observation that an international subculture of people with Western-style academic educations, a gobalized intellectual elite with largely secularist worldviews, is an exception to desecularization, is still implicated by current re-enchantment models. Occulture spreads largely through *popular* culture, and its ordinariness manifests primarily by reshaping the religious *vernacular*. Furthermore, we read that the return of this "form of magical culture" means that "'official' definitions of reality are being challenged"; the assumedly hegemonic, disenchanted worldview of the highly educated classes is being challenged by re-enchanted alternatives.[10]

According to Weber, the modern research university, as it arose during the nineteenth century, had been a driving force of the disenchantment of the world, especially through its extended influence on the engineers reshaping society's technological infrastructure and the government technocrats rationalizing and engineering its social structure. While new approaches to this domain of social theory emphasize instead the *sacralization* of technology

---

6. Partridge, *The Re-enchantment of the West*, vol. 1, 40.
7. An early reference in the sociological literature to this "occult revival" in the context of the youth culture born in the late 1960s, see Truzzi, "The Occult Revival as Popular Culture". For a more systematic discussion of these social phenomena in terms of secularization and typologies of religious organization, see Colin Campbell, "The Cult, the Cultic Milieu and Secularization"; Colin Campbell, "The Secret Religion of the Educated Classes".
8. Cf. Colin Campbell, "The Cult, the Cultic Milieu and Secularization"; Kaplan & Lööw, *The Cultic Milieu*.
9. Partridge, *The Re-enchantment of the West*, vol. 1, 119–84.
10. *Ibid.*, 40.

and the transformation of the patterns of religion and enchantment in society at large, we also notice that they have kept the black box closed when it comes to disenchantment's *engine*; at the heart of the machine, the wiring, the rising pistons, and spinning cogwheels are assumed to operate pretty much as before. The present chapter takes a peek into the box, to see if there may be ghosts hiding in the machine after all. Could it be that Berger's international subculture of the academically educated is itself touched by the occulture, or even to some extent implicated in its production?

Considered as a sociological term, occulture

> refers to the environment within which, and the social processes by which particular meanings relating, typically, to spiritual, esoteric, paranormal and conspiratorial ideas emerge, are disseminated, and become influential in societies and in the lives of individuals.[11]

Keeping this definition in mind, I will focus on the "paranormal" subset of occulture. Analysing the processes by which paranormal ideas "emerge, are disseminated, and become influential", one cannot avoid discussing certain of those highly educated subcultures which are often seen as agents of secularization and disenchantment. Following the traces of central paranormal concepts and themes, dissecting their discursive formation and tracing their dissemination, we find that occulture in fact has vital nerve centres inside universities and academic subcultures. This becomes particularly clear when viewed in a historical perspective, as we shall see. But there is also evidence that certain paranormal ideas remain part of a vital mode of re-enchantment among what may, perhaps, be seen as the highly educated echelons of contemporary occulture.

The rise in the early twenty-first century of an emphatically secularist "new atheism", which explicitly associates itself with a vision of science and critical thinking, may have widened the apparent chasm between educated subcultures and occulture. It is, however, intriguing to note that one of the "four horsemen of the apocalypse",[12] the neuroscientist Sam Harris, displays a very ambiguous position when we broaden the scope from classic theistic religion to the broader spectrum of occultural and "paracultural" re-enchantment. The author of such contemporary classics of atheism as *The End of Faith* (2004) and *Letter to a Christian Nation* (2006) also holds "mysticism" and "spirituality" to be compatible in practice with science and rationality, and has even gone so far as to validate parapsychology as a valuable source of scientific wonder:

> There also seems to be a body of data attesting to the reality of psychic phenomena, much of which has been ignored by mainstream

---

11. Partridge, page 116 of the present volume.
12. The other three being biologist Richard Dawkins, journalist Christopher Hitchens and philosopher Daniel Dennett.

science. The dictum that "extraordinary claims require extraordinary evidence" remains a reasonable guide in these areas, but this does not mean that the universe isn't far stranger than many of us suppose.[13]

While Harris has received severe criticism from fellow atheists, the position he occupies points towards something highly interesting.[14] It seems to suggest that scientism, secularism and atheism intersects in significant ways with *occulture*.

By reviewing the location of the paranormal within broader occulture, this chapter takes the opportunity to shed light on a number of relevant aspects of contemporary esotericism. The first of these, as we have hinted already, is to trace certain discursive transfers between academic and esoteric subcultures, and assess their importance. In terms of Kocku von Stuckrad's discursive approach, described elsewhere in this volume, we are interested in processes of the *scientification of knowledge*, as well as the influence of forms of *public activation*.[15] Second, analysing the formation of a "paranormal" discourse, and particularly its *parapsychological* subset, opens up intriguing questions about processes related to what has been called the "secularization of esotericism", the "disenchantment of magic" and the re-enchantment paradigm.[16] More to the point, I will suggest that the development of a *parapsychological discourse* in the twentieth century should be placed at the intersection of two parallel processes: the disenchantment of esoteric discourse on the one hand, and attempts to re-enchant science on the other. Before delving into these complex questions of interpretation, we should have a closer look at the place of paranormal beliefs among the educated public.

HOW DISENCHANTED ARE THE EDUCATED ELITES? SOME SOCIOLOGICAL ASPECTS OF "PARANORMAL BELIEF"

What the polls have to say

The religiosity of scientists is sometimes used as a way to gauge the effects of secularization and disenchantment. Polls typically show that self-reported

---

13. Harris, *The End of Faith*, 41.
14. For the controversy Harris elicited, see especially Gorenfeld & Harris, "Controversy over Sam Harris's Atheist Views".
15. See Chapter 11 of the present volume.
16. The secularization of esotericism and the disenchantment of magic are theoretical constructs that have been suggested by Wouter J. Hanegraaff. See Hanegraaff, *New Age Religion and Western Culture*, 411–513; Hanegraaff, "How Magic Survived the Disenchantment of the World".

religious belief and church attendance is significantly lower among scientists than the rest of the population. A recent poll by the Pew Research Center, for example, found that whereas 83 per cent of the general American public said they believed in a personal God, only 38 per cent of scientists said the same (with another 18 per cent subscribing to "a universal spirit or higher power").[17] With another 17 per cent of the scientists professing atheism, and 11 per cent styling themselves as agnostics – against only 2 per cent for each of these categories in the general population – there seem to be at the very least *something* to Berger's statement on the academic exception to desecularization.[18] Measured in traditional religious beliefs (pretty much on the model of Christian theism), scientists are significantly less "religious" than the rest of the population.[19]

The belief or disbelief in a theistic God, however, says nothing about re-enchantment and occulture. The academically trained may be low on this type of religiosity, but not necessarily on "paranormal beliefs". Judging from other available polls, some paranormal beliefs even seem to correspond *positively* with higher education. A Gallup poll conducted in 2001 indicated a general increase among the American public in paranormal beliefs since 1990. Among the types of belief polled for were ghosts, haunted houses, demonic possession, astrology and extraterrestrial visitors, but also typically parapsychological phenomena, namely extra-sensory perception (ESP), clairvoyance and telepathy. Excluding the more problematic category of "psychic or spiritual healing or the power of the human mind to heal the body", ESP was by far the most widespread paranormal belief in the American population in 2001, with a total of 50 per cent expressing belief, and another 20 per cent saying they were not sure (only 27 per cent rejected the possibility of ESP).[20] By comparison, belief

---

17. Pew Research Center, "Scientists and Belief".
18. We can also note that Berger qualified his statement by pointing out that it is particularly those with educations in the *humanities and social sciences* who tend to be more "secularized". This too is based on good evidence, as social scientists, particularly psychologists and anthropologists, consistently report less religious belief and more explicit rejection of religion than their colleagues in the natural sciences. This was one of the strong findings of the Carnegie Commission's important 1969 Survey of American Academics. See Stark *et al.*, "Religion, Science, and Rationality", 436.
19. Despite these findings, which are remarkably stable since the first such poll was carried out in 1914 by the psychologist James Leuba, certain fierce enemies of the secularization thesis have been able to turn these statistics into a case *against* secularization. This is particularly clear with Rodney Stark and his fellow supporters of rational choice theory, who seem to argue that the relatively stable 40 per cent of theistic scientists is much higher than what secularization theorists should be comfortable with. They also make much out of the fact that the "hard sciences" are more religious than the "soft" ones, turning the point into a rather tendentious correlation with what is the more "scientific" position. See e.g. Stark *et al.*, "Religion, Science, and Rationality", 436; Stark, "Secularization, RIP", 264–6.
20. I have chosen to leave out the data for belief in "psychic or spiritual healing", due to the extremely inclusive way in which this "power" was defined in the poll. Essentially, even the

in ghosts was expressed by 38 per cent, astrology by 28 per cent and reincarnation by 25 per cent of the total sample.[21]

As will be seen in the next section of this chapter, the term "extra-sensory perception" was coined by the founders of American experimental parapsychology in the 1930s, and it is, strictly speaking, an umbrella term for the parapsychological phenomena of anomalous perception. While there is no reason to suspect the general respondent of the Gallup polls to know all the niceties of parapsychological technical vocabulary, it is not surprising to find that both telepathy and clairvoyance score lower than general ESP, a class of which they are (technically speaking) subsets. Nevertheless, at 36 per cent (telepathy) and 32 per cent (clairvoyance) asserting belief in them, these are still very widespread paranormal beliefs on their own. A similar study from 2005 confirms this general picture: leaving out beliefs that are clearly rooted in "traditional" religious worldviews, ESP is the number one paranormal phenomenon Americans believe in.[22]

Non-denominational paranormal beliefs are in other words widespread; this much we would already expect from their being part of the pop-occultural mainstream. But the Gallup statistics from 2001 have the additional advantage of being broken down by demographical factors, including educational level. This gives us a way to assess one major question: just how disenchanted are the educated elites?

Keeping the polls of the religious beliefs of scientists cited above firmly in mind, one would expect beliefs clearly connected to traditional religious communities and mythological frameworks to decrease somewhat with educational level. Indeed the general tendency seems to be that less ambiguously "supernatural" beliefs, such as the belief in ghosts, haunted houses and communication with the dead, but also belief in astrology and extraterrestrial visits to Earth, generally decrease as the educational level increases from high school level towards college graduate and post-graduate level. Some interesting differences surface when we compare these generally quite heavily mythologized elements with less embedded parapsychological ones. Table 16.1 shows the distribution of belief in the three core parapsychological phenomena included in the poll (ESP, telepathy and clairvoyance), and one element more typically associated with traditional church religion ("that people on this earth are sometimes possessed by the devil"). I have also included the

---

medical doctor who, with basis in countless controlled medical trials considers the placebo effect to be a well-documented effect of self-healing would qualify as having a "paranormal belief". However, belief in the reality of placebos should hardly classify as paranormal in this context.

21. For all the numbers, see Newport & Strausberg, "Americans' Belief in Psychic and Paranormal Phenomena Is up Over Last Decade".
22. This means leaving out "demonic possession", which was more widespread than ESP in the 2005 poll (but, somewhat curiously, far from it in 2001). For the 2005 data, see David W. Moore, "Three in Four Americans Believe in Paranormal".

Table 16.1 Distribution of belief in three parapsychological beliefs and one "traditionally religious" belief over educational factors and self-reported importance of religion.

Belief	Education				Importance of religion			Total
	Post-graduate	College graduate only	Some college	High school or less	Very important	Fairly important	Not very important	
Possession	32	35	41	46	55	28	14	41
ESP	52	53	48	49	50	48	48	50
Telepathy	41	38	36	35	35	37	41	36
Clairvoyance	29	27	34	34	32	33	32	32

Data show percentage of respondents confirming belief.
Source: Newport & Strausberg, "Americans' Belief in Psychic and Paranormal Phenomena Is up Over Last Decade".

distribution over two demographical factors (namely educational level and the level of importance the respondent attributed to religion).

Belief in demonic possession has a clear negative correlation with higher education: whereas 46 per cent of those with only high school or less believed that the devil could sometimes possess human beings, the percentage decreases steadily as we move to demographical groups with college educations. One may perhaps still be surprised to find that *every third* American with post-graduate education believes in demonic possession; however, possession is a standard part of American evangelical Christianity, and is not uncommon among Catholics or mainline Protestants either.[23]

It seems that the "international subculture composed of people with Western-type higher education", also outside of the more restrictive class of "scientists", are increasingly less likely to entertain the "traditional" supernatural enchantments than the rest of the population is. What, then, about parapsychological beliefs? As we see in Table 16.1, belief in ESP is relatively stable around 50 per cent of the population for all educational groups, with the higher levels of education (college and post-graduate) actually scoring slightly *higher* than those with no education beyond high school. For telepathy, this tendency is even more marked, with a steady increase from 35 per cent of those with high school or less education, to a full 41 per cent of those with post-graduate educations expressing that telepathy is real. Belief in clairvoyance is also relatively stable, but more ambiguous in its relation to education; while college graduates generally are a few per cent less likely to believe than those with no college, post-graduates score higher than those with only graduate level college education.

Besides the question of education, the importance attributed to religion by these respondents also gives us some valuable pointers. With possession

---

23. See e.g. Cuneo, *American Exorcism*.

the correlation with religious belief seems to be essential, as only 14 per cent of those who do not think religion is important believe in it. This is not the case for parapsychological beliefs. For ESP and clairvoyance, the importance attached to religion does not seem to predict belief: people are about as likely to believe in ESP whether they find religion important or not. For telepathy (which also correlated positively with education) we even notice a *negative* correlation with the expressed importance of religion, with 41 per cent of those expressing little interest in religion believing in telepathy, against 36 per cent in the general population. Thus we note with some interest that two criteria tend to increase likelihood of belief in telepathy, namely a high education and an expressed low interest in "religion".

Interpretations and problems

These findings have not gone completely unnoticed by sociologists and psychologists interested in paranormal beliefs and religion. Paranormal beliefs are, as we have seen already, often subdivided into "religious" and "classic" types, where the first denotes elements that are "central to traditional Christian doctrine", whereas the latter are "commonly associated with the supernatural or the occult".[24] These two groups of paranormal belief correlate differently with social factors; while the "religious" type seems much more common among marginal groups and correlates with lower education and socio-economic status, the "classic" lacks any such pattern.[25] In short, while relative *deprivation* largely correlates with the religious type, it does not help predict "classic paranormal beliefs".

Related to the deprivation theory is the idea that belief in the paranormal and in "pseudosciences" is simply a matter of scientific illiteracy. If people know more about science, they will tend to believe less in the paranormal. Again, the data we have examined above do not support this interpretation. This has caused some concern for educationalists. For example, Massimo Pigliucci observed in the *McGill Journal of Education* in 2007 that

> scientists and science educators often assume that a major reason so many people believe in pseudoscience is that they do not know enough science. However, although the latter is an accurate empirical observation (most people do not know much about science), it does not follow that scientific illiteracy is the cause of widespread belief in all sorts of paranormal phenomena. If lack of scientific knowledge is not the root cause, then more science education will not necessarily solve, or even ameliorate, the problem.[26]

---

24. Rice, "Believe It Or Not", 96–7.
25. *Ibid.*, 96; cf. Goode, *Paranormal Beliefs*.
26. Pigliucci, "The Evolution–Creation Wars", 291.

Pigliucci also takes note of the difference between the "religious" and "non-religious" based types of paranormal belief, and the discrepancy in how they relate to science education, suggesting that "This means factors other than just the general degree of education are at play."[27] From an educational perspective, Pigliucci argues that the resilience of paranormal beliefs (he is particularly disturbed by the fact that "one in every four or five of the most educated people in the most prosperous country in the world" believes in demonic possession) among the educated classes means that something is wrong with the educational system itself. Based on his own surveys Pigliucci observes that science majors are much more likely to believe in paranormal phenomena than majors in psychology and philosophy, a difference which he attributes to differences in educational strategies. While philosophy and psychology majors "actually take courses on the scientific method and on critical thinking",

> science majors are seldom exposed to that sort of course, and spend most of their initial scientific education in large classrooms where a professor whom they can barely see from across a large lecture hall inundates them with a flood of disconnected facts that they are supposed to remember in order to pass the test.[28]

In short, could it be that the amount of science education says little about *critical thinking skills*, and that one should expect this ability rather than knowledge of "facts" to be the antidote of paranormal belief?

This is another empirical matter, but one that Pigliucci did not actually test. Sociologist Erich Goode, however, has designed and conducted some preliminary trials to check precisely this kind of correlation. Making the now familiar distinction between paranormal phenomena with a "religious lineage" and those with no such clear connection, Goode tested the correlation of belief in each category with science literacy (i.e. knowledge of "facts"), but also with proneness to use intuitive but rationally invalid cognitive heuristics, versus the use of scientifically valid reasoning.[29] Consistent with the earlier studies, believers in phenomena clearly embedded in religious history were likely to know less about science, and were also more prone to cognitive biases and invalid heuristics. In other words, "religious paranormal belief" corresponded with scientific illiteracy, and a poor understanding of how science (ideally) works. More intriguing, however, Goode could find no such correlation for the "non-religious" paranormal group. In fact, contrary to Pigliucci's prediction, Goode concluded that "non-religious paranormalists know about as much science, *and reason as scientifically*, as persons who reject the validity

---

27. *Ibid.*, 291.
28. *Ibid.*, 294.
29. Goode, "Education, Scientific Knowledge, and Belief in the Paranormal", 26–7.

of paranormal or extrascientific forces".[30] It would seem, then, that a decent understanding of scientific method and critical thinking is yet another factor which fails to predict the belief or disbelief in the paranormal.

While the prominence of paranormal ideas among highly educated people must be considered well-documented, there are as of yet no good, unambiguous social scientific explanations of why this is the case. In addition to the factors I have discussed above, psychologists have tried to find correlations between paranormal belief and personality factors. For example, schizotypy and fantasy proneness are among the personality factors that have been suggested as strong correlates for reporting paranormal experiences, and for the wider category who report *belief in* various paranormal phenomena and abilities.[31]

While factors such as these could help explain why one would expect paranormal beliefs of *one sort or another* to remain more or less constant in a population at large (given that personality types are more or less constant), they are less helpful for explaining the explicit *form* of beliefs that are held, and their distribution among different segments of a population. For these questions, social and cultural factors may be much more relevant. In the rest of this chapter I will situate the findings we have looked at in the context of broader historical and cultural processes. This means asking rather different questions than those considered in sociological and psychological studies. From looking at the distribution and correlations of "belief in ESP", we have to focus attention on the qualitative cultural *shape* of parapsychological beliefs. How were concepts such as telepathy and ESP formed in the first place? Could it be that the socio-cultural conditions of their formation shaped them in such a way as to be particularly well suited as articles of belief for the educated classes? What do the networks and channels of dissemination and cultural diffusion of parapsychological beliefs tell us? Asking these questions also gives opportunity to revisit some issues over disenchantment, re-enchantment and "secularized esotericism", and relate these historically to the emergence of occulture.

ACADEMICS AS CO-PRODUCERS OF OCCULTURAL KNOWLEDGE: PARAPSYCHOLOGY AND THE NATURALIZATION OF THE SUPERNATURAL

Psychical research and parapsychology: the professional dimension

The book *Extra-sensory Perception*, published in 1934, has been described as the foundational work for modern experimental parapsychology, and its

---

30. *Ibid.* (emphasis added).
31. See e.g. Parra, "'Seeing and Feeling Ghosts'"; Hergovich & Arandazi, "Scores for Schizotypy and Five Factor Model of a Sample of Distant Healers"; Wiseman & Watt, "Belief in Psychic Ability and the Misattribution Thesis".

author, Joseph Banks Rhine (1895–1980), as the father of the discipline.[32] Rhine was originally trained as a botanist; however, after encountering a whole series of questions that seemed to relate equally to religion as to science, he and his wife Louisa (also a botanist) decided to shift careers. Coming across the vitalistic philosophy of Henri Bergson (which was getting immensely popular in the US), and having their fascination with spiritualism sparked by one of its most famous missionaries, Arthur Conan Doyle, the couple turned to *psychical research* – the prospective scientific study of spiritualism and other (mental and physical) phenomena considered to be "supernormal". In 1927 Louisa and J. B. Rhine followed the British psychologist and former president of the American Society for Psychical Research, William McDougall (1871–1938), to Duke University. McDougall, who was himself well known for his vitalistic theories of life and mind, his attack on behaviourism, as well as his defence of Lamarckian evolution and eugenic policies (including racial ones), had been professor of psychology at Harvard University since 1920 (the chair previously held by another famous psychical researcher, William James). By relocating to Duke, McDougall became head of a new psychology department, and had the liberty to conduct research in his greatest areas of interest, including experimental psychical research. Rhine soon became his foremost research assistance in this area. Seven years later, Rhine's book made headlines in the United States and beyond: not only had the research team at Duke transformed psychical research to an experimental, laboratory-oriented discipline of research, but they also claimed to have found evidence for a number of technically named "psychic" abilities, going under the general heading of "ESP".

The contemporary notion of ESP and its related parapsychological phenomena can in the first instance be traced back to a cultural encounter in the 1920s and 1930s. On the one hand, occultism and spiritualism experienced a revival after World War I, bringing attention to a host of "paranormal" phenomena. On the other, a controversial scientific discourse was developing and spreading in psychology and biology, focusing on problems related to vitalism and organicism, as opposed to reductionistic materialism and mechanism. In the context of psychical research, these two impulses temporarily met over questions of *disenchantment*: is a worldview completely stripped of "mysterious incalculable forces" able to grasp all the phenomena of the world in which we live? Less of an unstoppable, irreversible *process* at the heart of modernity, disenchantment was rather a serious intellectual *problem* that scientists, philosophers and educated laymen were struggling with. As several historians of science have pointed out, fierce debates about reductionism, determinism/indeterminacy, vitalism and even causality raged across disciplines

---

32. See especially Mauskopf & McVaugh, *The Elusive Science*, 102–30. Cf. Asprem, "A Nice Arrangement of Heterodoxies".

from physics to biology during the inter-war period.[33] The professionalization of parapsychology not only coincided historically with these debates, but its main protagonists made explicit links to relevant concerns in these bordering disciplines.[34]

The problem of disenchantment has a longer history internally in psychical research. The first systematic, organized attempts to create a scientific discipline out of a field of knowledge typically associated with the occult and supernatural under this heading took place in late Victorian England.[35] The establishment of the Society for Psychical Research (SPR) in 1882 brought together a group of scientists, philosophers and other scholars, organized on the model of the scientific society or club, striving towards serious recognition by other scientific communities and professional societies.[36] The attempt to establish a discipline for this kind of research attests, on the one hand, to the presence of a whole range of esoteric religious practices in the Victorian "occult revival", especially spiritualism.[37] On the other hand, organized psychical research also bears testimony to the high authority of the scientific project around the turn of the nineteenth century. Psychical research was thus born from an encounter between the scientism of Victorian scientific naturalism, and the worldview, practices and rhetorical claims of spiritualists, occultists and some liberal Christian reformers.[38] This nexus gave rise to a discourse in which the invocation of scientific authority remained the primary legitimizing strategy, or, as Alex Owen writes concerning late-Victorian occultism in general, a discourse "undermining scientific naturalism as a worldview", while at the same time co-opting "the language of science" and staking "a strong claim to rationality".[39]

For the early psychical researchers, however, much more was at stake than merely claiming "the language of science". The organization itself consisted of some of the most reputed scientists of the day, including later Nobel laureates Lord Rayleigh, J. J. Thomson, and Charles Richet, later Prime Minister Arthur Balfour, and many other professors, journalists, editors and notables of British intellectual life. In other words, and this is important for our present concerns:

---

33. See e.g. Anne Harrington, *Reenchanted Science*; Forman, "Weimar Culture, Causality, and Quantum Theory, 1918–1927"; Allen, "Mechanism, Vitalism and Organicism in Late Nineteenth and Twentieth-Century Biology"; Wolffram, "Supernormal Biology".
34. See Asprem, "A Nice Arrangement of Heterodoxies", 135–9.
35. For some precursors and parallel developments in nineteenth-century Germany, see e.g. Treitel, *A Science for the Soul*; Wolffram, *The Stepchildren of Science*.
36. For the foundation and early history of the SPR, see Gauld, *The Founders of Psychical Research*; Oppenheim, *The Other World*; Frank Miller Turner, *Between Science and Religion*; cf. Luckhurst, *The Invention of Telepathy*.
37. The relation between spiritualism and psychical research is the main focus of Oppenheim, *The Other World*.
38. Cf. Frank Miller Turner, *Between Science and Religion*.
39. Owen, *The Place of Enchantment*, 13.

psychical research was, at the outset, *an elite phenomenon*. In fact, although it has become the habit among many contemporary esotericists, New Agers, and even parapsychologists to claim that paranormal phenomena would have been accepted as fact had it not been for the repression of "narrow-minded" academic elites, it is tempting to say that something of the opposite is true: at the turn of the nineteenth century it was precisely parts of the academic elite that elevated certain paranormal phenomena to a degree of acceptability among the public. The claim to scientific legitimacy for the paranormal was born in academic elite circles.

The latter is more than a trivial point. From a historical and scientific perspective, the question is not so much why "paranormal phenomena" have not become part of the scientific canon, but rather why the claim to scientific status of some of these phenomena has been as resilient as it has. Borrowing from actor-network theory and the sociology of science more broadly, it is tempting to make the case that the social and cultural resources the SPR pooled together were crucial for establishing credibility and legitimacy for its pursuit of psychical research.[40] Even if many of the biggest scientific celebrities of the society were less active members, and some surely belonged to its sceptical wing, sporting their names on the membership list provided the SPR with scientific–cultural legitimacy which made psychical research impossible to neglect for the educated public. Another social reason, or perhaps rather precondition, for the SPR's initial success was that it wielded a swift and efficient "boundary-work" towards spiritualist and occultist communities.[41] This made it possible to dissociate the "scientific" and "reputable" psychical research from "muddle-headed occultism", and claim the occult phenomena as part of legitimate science.

Finally, it is interesting to note that the kind of cultural legitimacy which psychical research had managed to establish largely disintegrated with the death of the leading members who had tied it all together, especially Henry Sidgwick, Frederic Myers and William James. This may be read as a collapse of the "actor-network" that the SPR had assembled; the ensuing generational shift also led to a reorientation of the society towards spiritualism, which may be read as a collapse of their boundary-work. As a result, SPR groups of the early twentieth century tended to break up over a pro-spiritualist/pro-science divide. Modern experimental parapsychology, in turn, grew out of the pro-science wing of the SPR milieu, of which William McDougall was a front figure.[42]

---

40. I have outlined this argument in somewhat more detail in Asprem, "Parapsychology"; Asprem, "A Nice Arrangement of Heterodoxies". A similar approach is developed in Luckhurst, *The Invention of Telepathy*.
41. For the concept of "boundary-work", see Gieryn, "Boundary-Work and the Demarcation of Science from Non-Science"; Gieryn, *Cultural Boundaries of Science*; cf. the broader approach developed in Hess, *Science in the New Age*, 145–6.
42. E.g. Asprem, "A Nice Arrangement of Heterodoxies".

To summarize the central point of this section: "paranormal" phenomena connected to extraordinary mental and perceptive abilities such as ESP, telepathy and clairvoyance, were lifted out of ("disembedded" from) occultism, spiritualism, and vernacular religiosity by a group of highly educated intellectuals, led by academics and scientists, in the name of "psychical research". Through the transition to parapsychology, the phenomena in question were repackaged and reformed, given technical designations, and supported with reference to experiment, evidence and philosophical arguments. Furthermore, attempts were made to connect them to central contemporary problems in reputable scientific disciplines, especially biology, psychology and physics. Reconnecting them to a discourse on religion and spirituality, parapsychological concepts were already packaged as standard elements of a prospective "scientific religion" for intellectuals. The hope that psychical research would help create a future scientific religion was indeed explicitly stated by one of the SPR's founders, Frederick Myers, and one finds similar traits in the popular and public writings of the pioneers of experimental parapsychology as well, including McDougall and Rhine.[43]

Disenchantment, re-enchantment, and the naturalization of the supernatural

In his important *New Age Religion and Western Culture* (1996), Wouter J. Hanegraaff described the post-war religious development of New Age as an expression of a broader "secularization of esotericism", a process that he linked to the Weberian notion of disenchantment: ideas that have been connected with the esoteric discourses of the Renaissance have gone through a reinterpretation in the light of a "disenchanted" culture that arose in the wake of the Enlightenment.[44] With reference to this process, Hanegraaff defined "occultism" as "all attempts by esotericists to come to terms with a disenchanted world or, alternatively, by people in general to make sense of esotericism from the perspective of a disenchanted secular world".[45] This definition

---

43. For Myers's views on psychical research, science, and religion, see Frank Miller Turner, *Between Science and Religion*, 104–133; for McDougall's linking of psychical research to religion, see Asprem, "A Nice Arrangement of Heterodoxies", 135–9; for parapsychology more generally, see Hess, *Science in the New Age*, 76–85.
44. For the whole argument, which is a lot more complex than can be shown from one sentence, see Hanegraaff, *New Age Religion and Western Culture*, 411–513. Also cf. Hanegraaff, "How Magic Survived the Disenchantment of the World".
45. Hanegraaff, *New Age Religion and Western Culture*, 422 (emphasis omitted). Note that this definition differs markedly from other common definitions of occultism in the literature. Essentially, for Hanegraaff occultism is a *type* of esoteric discourse under specific developmental conditions and encompasses a broad range of subjects, groups and currents. A more historically specific usage is also common, by which occultism refers to nineteenth-century attempts to revive Renaissance occult philosophy and magic, particularly in France, and later in England. For this usage, see e.g. Pasi, "Occultism".

carries within it an interesting distinction. The field of "occultism" consists *not only* of "disenchanted esotericists", but also of those interested outsiders who seek to make sense of claims that have been connected to the field of the esoteric, *in disenchanted terms*. This, in fact, gives a rationale for including all those academics and intellectuals, both the sympathetic and the sceptically minded, who sought to explain the phenomena of spiritualism with recourse to physical theories, or psychological models, as part of a broader discourse of "occultism".

What does it mean to make sense of the esoteric in disenchanted terms? Hanegraaff's analysis, which has focused on the reinterpretation of esoteric thought by self-professed esotericists, finds one crucial tendency to be that elements such as the supposition of a living nature, the mediation of higher knowledge, and the a-causal correspondences between things in the universe have been replaced by "disenchanted" alternatives where pseudo-mechanical and pseudo-materialistic interpretations have become the norm.[46] Where the Renaissance magus understood ritual efficacy in terms of interaction with the *anima mundi* or the intercession of spiritual entities of various kinds, the modern "disenchanted" magician would instead refer to "energies" or "forces" working through subtle but essentially causal principles (often in explicit analogy with electricity, magnetism and, increasingly in the twentieth century, quantum mechanics), or through "psychologized" understandings of mediating entities.[47] These tendencies belong to the first part of Hanegraaff's definition of occultism, namely the "attempts by esotericists to come to terms with a disenchanted world". If we go on to consider the second part, the attempts "by people in general to make sense of esotericism from the perspective of a disenchanted secular world", we open the door to a much wider range of interpretational strategies. One major difference is that while the esotericists will generally tend to take for granted that phenomena connected with the esoteric are actually *real*, in some significant and irreducible sense, the "general public" is not necessarily constrained by any such ontological presuppositions. Thus we might find fully and truly disenchanted perspectives, which flat out *deny* the mysterious incalculable forces which esotericists, through "terminological scientism" and "rhetorics of rationality", redefine in "disenchanted terms". Instead, the *claims* about such forces may be accounted for in terms of well-known, ordinary phenomena that may, at the most sceptical end of the spectrum at least, include illusions, psychopathology, trickery or lies.[48]

---

46. This difference is of course based on Antoine Faivre's description of the "esoteric form of thought" as consisting of four intrinsic characteristics plus two non-intrinsic ones. Faivre, *Access to Western Esotericism*, 10–15. See especially Hanegraaff, "How Magic Survived the Disenchantment of the World".
47. Hanegraaff, "How Magic Survived the Disenchantment of the World", 361–9; cf. Asprem, "Magic Naturalized?"; Asprem, *Arguing with Angels*, chapter 4.
48. For "terminological scientism", see Hammer, *Claiming Knowledge*.

The production of various disenchanted perspectives on esoteric discourse should be viewed in the context of a broader discourse on *the naturalization of the supernatural*.[49] An explicitly naturalistic stance grew popular during the professionalization of the natural sciences in the nineteenth century, and this development is indispensable to understanding some of the philosophical thrust behind psychical research.[50] Naturalism is, however, a flexible and broad concept, both philosophically and as a cultural–historical phenomenon.[51] In the closing decades of the nineteenth century, a debate over "scientific naturalism" and the place of the supernatural was at the heart of what was being perceived as a widening conflict between science and religion; this is well illustrated by the "agnosticism debate", of which Thomas Henry Huxley was the main protagonist and provocateur.[52]

The naturalization of the supernatural took a wide variety of forms. Although all are sceptical to traditional concepts of the "supernatural", their alternatives may differ radically.[53] On the sceptical wing, the psychiatrist Henry Maudsley's *Natural Causes and Supernatural Seemings* (1886) illustrates a completely disenchanted perspective. Maudsley concluded that claims about the supernatural could be accounted for by humans' inherent tendencies towards "malobservation and misinterpretation of nature", sometimes coupled with genuine psychological disturbances including hallucinations and hysteria.[54] Maudsley illustrates a point that was crucial to Huxley's notion of agnosticism, namely that one should always start to look for explanations of seemingly inexplicable occurrences (and claims of such) among mechanisms that we *do* know something about. In Maudsley's case, secure ground was found in our established knowledge of the human mind, particularly its weaknesses.

Psychical researchers were also part of this naturalizing tendency, but instead of reducing away the phenomena, they focused on finding room for them within a naturalistic worldview. Much of the intellectual effort to redefine the supernatural in the context of the SPR was carried out by Frederic W. H. Myers (1843–1901). Myers composed a whole regime of neologisms to

---

49. This term is borrowed from the title of an early first historical work on psychical research, written by a sceptical insider: Podmore, *The Naturalisation of the Supernatural*.
50. See e.g. Frank Miller Turner, *Between Science and Religion*, 8–37; Frank Miller Turner, *Contesting Cultural Authority*, 131–50, 171–200; Lightman, *The Origins of Agnosticism*.
51. For the cultural flexibility of naturalism in relation to "the supernatural" see e.g. Noakes, "Spiritualism, Science and the Supernatural in mid-Victorian Britain"; for reflections over the meaning of naturalism(s) as a position on science and metaphysics in modern philosophy, see e.g. De Caro & Macarthur, *Naturalism in Question*; Flanagan, "Varieties of Naturalism".
52. See e.g. Huxley et al., *Christianity and Agnosticism*; Ward, *Naturalism and Agnosticism*.
53. This point is made clear with regard to spiritualism by Noakes, "Spiritualism, Science and the Supernatural in mid-Victorian Britain".
54. Maudsley, *Natural Causes and Supernatural Seemings*, 354.

serve as technical terminology for the prospective discipline, most of which are listed in the glossary accompanying his posthumously published *Human Personality* (1903). Among the most enduring ones was the concept of "telepathy", designed as a technical term to replace the word "thought transference", which was associated with folk beliefs and sideshow tricks.[55]

Furthermore illustrating the naturalistic strategy of psychical research, Myers introduced the word "supernormal" to replace the problematic "supernatural". While the supernatural implied a contrariety with nature and natural law which was quite unacceptable for the scientifically minded, the supernormal referred merely to a deviance from "normality":

> The word supernatural is open to grave objections; it assumes that there is something outside nature, and it has become associated with arbitrary interference with law. Now there is no reason to suppose that the psychical phenomena with which we deal are less a part of nature, or less subject to fixed and definite law, than any other phenomena.[56]

This new scheme of definitions attempted to ground the many "supernormal" phenomena within a naturalistic discourse, making them capable in principle of being taken seriously by educated people and scientists. Telepathy, Myers's most successful neologism, was inscribed at the core of this project. After its first appearance in the 1880s, it saw a number of naturalistic and quasi-disenchanted interpretations, from an effect of "brainwaves" in electromagnetic fields (a theory first championed by the physicist Oliver Lodge, a pioneer of radio technology), to the exertion of obscure "metetherial" powers of the "subliminal self" (Myers's own later theory).[57] In general we could divide the naturalistic explanatory models of psychical research into three major types, on a continuum from the less to the more "disenchanted": some (notably Alfred Russel Wallace, co-inventor of the Darwinian selection theory of evolution) leaned towards spiritualism and wanted to open up naturalism to such a wide extent as to accommodate the actual, real existence of disembodied spirits; others, often termed "animists" (McDougall was a strong proponent of this position), did not believe in spirits, but instead attributed spiritualistic phenomena to capricious powers of the human organism, often connected to a theory of vitalistic, non-mechanistic biology; finally, a more disenchanted option was to focus on a few core "effects", such as telepathy, and look for mechanistic theories of them, usually in terms of electromagnetic fields or waves.[58]

---

55. Myers, *Human Personality*, vol. 1, xiii–xxii.
56. *Ibid.*, xxii.
57. For a discussion, see e.g. Asprem, "Parapsychology", 640–43; cf. Luckhurst, *The Invention of Telepathy*.
58. For a similar exploration of the varieties of naturalistic strategies to spiritualism, see Noakes, "Spiritualism, Science and the Supernatural in mid-Victorian Britain".

FROM LABORATORY TO MAINSTREAM: CONCLUSIONS ABOUT THE PARANORMAL IN OCCULTURE

I argue that psychical research and its professionalized daughter, parapsychology, have offered a uniquely naturalistic mode of enchantment. By moving certain of the claims and phenomena associated with religious and esoteric discourses into the laboratory, while at the same time taking them seriously and attempting to ground them within a worldview that is *naturalistic* but not necessarily *disenchanted*, parapsychology has engaged in what may be described, with an apt term borrowed from Roy Wallis, as a scientific *sanitization* of these claims.[59] The claims are dissociated from their "traditional" and mythological frameworks, and re-embedded in new, "rational" frames of reference and legitimizing structures. The result is a *scientistic detraditionalization*, along the lines of von Stuckrad's process of the *scientification of knowledge*. Meanwhile resisting the complete reduction of the phenomena to ordinary and well-understood mechanisms, such as psychopathology, trickery, cognitive biases and self-delusions, some of the mystery is still retained. This has made the detraditionalized and repackaged paranormal particularly well-suited for projects to re-enchant science itself, typically by insisting on a new "scientific revolution" or "paradigm shift".[60]

Having now argued that groups of academics, scientists and other highly educated persons have been at the heart of this process, it is time to turn again to the relation with a much broader and popular occulture. "Psychical" or parapsychological elements have been fed into the fledgling occulture about as far back as it makes sense to trace it. Partridge has been cautious with delineating the occulture historically, but as a re-enchanted mainstream, it arguably refers mainly to developments of the late twentieth century to the present. One might, however, identify a "proto-occulture" in the interface between, say, occultism, spiritualism, mesmerism, psychical research and popular culture already in the nineteenth century. Particularly towards the end of the century, psychic phenomena were stock elements of speculative fiction, including the late Victorian gothic and science fiction genres.[61] In the twentieth century the relation has renewed and intensified as the discourse on psychic abilities has changed and new media technologies come into use. With the popularity boom of spiritualism from World War I and into the 1920s, psychical research garnered much attention; the popular lecture tours of people like Oliver Lodge and Arthur Conan Doyle, and the popular writings of someone like Hereward

---

59. See Wallis, "Science and Pseudo-Science"; cf. Hess, *Science in the New Age*.
60. For an analysis of such calls as discursive strategies in a religio-scientific field, see Asprem, "Parapsychology", 656; cf. Hess, *Science in the New Age*, 79–81.
61. See e.g. Willis, *Mesmerists, Monsters, and Machines*, especially 28–62, 169–200; Luckhurst, *The Invention of Telepathy*, 181–213.

Carrington brought the sanitized discourse on psychic phenomena to a wider audience.[62] In the 1930s, Joseph Banks Rhine showed himself to be not only an innovative psychical researcher but also a very deft publicizer. Working with book clubs, his popular writings on ESP reached a broad public; in the early days of mass-media communication, he also made frequent appearances on radio shows, even featuring weekly ESP tests live from the studio.[63] The characteristic "Zener cards" used in his paradigmatic experiments published in *Extra-sensory Perception* were soon mass-produced and sold commercially. By the end of the decade, Rhine's new parapsychology was known all over the US, and his new terminology – ESP, psychokinesis, precognition – was gaining currency. The criticism and serious doubts about his results which were rapidly piling up in the psychological literature could do nothing to stop the growing notion in the public, advanced by the massive popularization of parapsychology, that this was scientifically legitimate knowledge.[64] In the years following World War II, the interest in what was increasingly being referred to as "psi" started to filter into new forms of popular culture, even giving rise to the "psi-fi" subgenre within pulp science fiction.[65]

This is where our story of the parapsychological naturalization of the supernatural comes together again with modern occulture. The sanitized discourse on the paranormal has made a significant impact on popular cultural productions of the late twentieth and early twenty-first centuries, especially in film and television. As such, they are inscribed centrally in a mode of knowledge transmission (linked with what von Stuckrad elsewhere in this volume defines as transformations in "public activation") which is entirely typical for contemporary occulture: the boundary between entertainment and religious expression and consumption gets blurred, and popular culture becomes a scene for re-enchantments.

The main point here is that ideas mediated through the paranormal subgenre of popular occulture – what David J. Hess has termed the "paraculture" – have their origin in the struggles of psychical researchers and parapsychologists to make such phenomena scientifically legitimate. This, I suggest, has given the ideas a cultural shape which make them particularly attractive to

---

62. Among Carrington's many and influential books in this field we might mention *The Coming Science*; *Personal Experiences in Spiritualism*; and his books about the medium Eusapia Palladino, e.g. *Eusapia Palladino and Her Phenomena*. The American author Upton Sinclair wrote another influential popular book on psychical research based on telepathic experiments with his wife in 1930, *Mental Radio*. This book has additional significance in that it came with a foreword by Albert Einstein.
63. Mauskopf & McVaugh, *The Elusive Science*, 160–63, 256. Rhine's first popular book on parapsychology and ESP was published in 1937. See Rhine, *New Frontiers of the Mind*.
64. For an overview of the critical responses, see e.g. Mauskopf & McVaugh, "The Controversy over Statistics in Parapsychology 1934–1938"; cf. Asprem, "Parapsychology", 654–5.
65. See e.g. Kripal, *Authors of the Impossible*; cf. Hess, *Science in the New Age*, 120–41.

people with higher education. As such, if the contemporary religious landscape is being formed into a broad occultural landscape, and if this occulture, furthermore, is connected with the withering away of "traditional" church religion, we should not be too surprised to find that the sanitized paranormal dimension of it is particularly popular among the more highly educated participants in occulture.

CHAPTER 17

THE NEW KIDS

INDIGO CHILDREN AND NEW AGE DISCOURSE

Daniel Kline

The New Age movement is a religious phenomenon that peaked in the 1980s and 1990s, a diverse conglomeration of disparate practices that are loosely bound by the concept of an imminent or present "new age" and by a critical reaction against rational materialistic explanations of the universe. Wouter Hanegraaff has painstakingly catalogued many of the practices and beliefs associated with this designation and many of the major New Age authors in *New Age Religion and Western Culture*.[1] While much ink has now been spent on describing this expansive phenomenon and its multiple manifestations, one area that remains largely untouched is the special role of *children* within New Age culture.[2]

In particular, I refer to the growth at the end of the twentieth century and beginning of the twenty-first of the discourse of the "Indigo Child", a gifted child who is the harbinger of the coming new age and possessor of special gifts. In a recent essay, Sarah Whedon submitted the first academic analysis of the Indigo Child discourse;[3] the present work will serve to complement and expand upon Whedon's analysis. Additionally, this chapter will address recent works on Indigo Children, including film and online media, and seek to contextualize both New Age authors and their sceptical opponents within this twentieth- and twenty-first-century discourse on childhood.

---

1. Hanegraaff, *New Age Religion and Western Culture*.
2. Among the many other authors who have written on New Age over the last two decades are Heelas, *The New Age Movement*; Steven J. Sutcliffe, *Children of the New Age*; Lewis & Melton, *Perspectives on the New Age*; Bochinger, *"New Age" und Moderne Religion*.
3. Whedon, "The Wisdom of Indigo Children", 60–76.

351

INTRODUCING THE "ESOTERIC CHILD"

Children are a topic of much concern in contemporary culture. The modern age has been marked by many changes to childhood, as well as a growing emphasis upon it. From compulsory education to the legal restriction of corporal punishment, emphasis on the wishes of the child in divorce cases and, most obviously, the widely ratified *Convention on the Rights of the Child* (1989), children's lives have become to a greater extent individualized, meaning that they are increasingly seen as individuals in their own right.[4] Since the 1960s, a growing scholarly interest has developed for studying the history of childhood. Philippe Aries's work *Centuries of Childhood* (1962), which highlights the diversity of historical attitudes toward children and childhood, has spearheaded this endeavour. I suggest that the Indigo Child discourse should be situated within this complex history of childhood and more particularly within the field of children in esoteric religious discourse and practice.

Before looking at the Indigo Child phenomenon, one should recognize that children have been participants and subjects in esoteric practices and theories since antiquity. In particular, I would draw attention to the role children have served as mediums and spirit contacts throughout history.[5] Each historical context has described different qualities that make children particularly suited to this role within esoteric practices. Currently, children's innocence is often seen as the defining trait that allows them special access to the spiritual, a shift in ideas about childhood that took place in the eighteenth century. Historically, this definitional shift represents a movement away from the parenting ideals of John Locke and toward the ideas of Jean-Jacques Rousseau and the Romantics.[6] This special relationship between children and the spiritual or unseen realms is an entrenched conception in modern culture, or more specifically, modern *occulture*.[7] Manifestations of this trend can be seen in films such as *The Sixth Sense* (1999) and *The Last Mimzy* (2007), and in books

---

4. James *et al.*, *Theorizing Childhood*, 7. Additionally, children are to a greater extent monitored and seen to exist in a "risk society" in which they must be protected from threats ranging from abduction to videogames and pornography. These two trends of individualization and separation exist in dichotomous tension within our society.
5. For examples, see Hamill, *The Rosicrucian Seer*; Kieckhefer, *Forbidden Rites*; or Fanger, "Virgin Territory".
6. John Locke, in his *Some Thoughts Concerning Education*, outlines a concept of childhood in which education is paramount. He envisions the newborn child as a *tabula rasa* that must be trained to rationalism. This perspective is contrasted with that of Jean-Jacque Rousseau, who believes that children should be left to nature, that children are innately good, and that they should learn through a painful process of trial and error. The Romantic poets have a third theory of childhood. Wordsworth and several other poets of his era described childhood as the best of times, saw the child as pure and untainted, especially close to nature and the divine, and believed childhood should be a time of freedom, play and natural beauty (Cunningham, *Children and Childhood*, 5, 59).
7. For a discussion of occulture, see Christopher Partridge's chapter in the current volume.

like John Wyndham's *The Chrysalids* (1955).[8] Indigo Children are rightly situated as a contemporary manifestation of this discourse of the "esoteric child".

The Indigo Child movement is a discourse of critique, revaluing children who are being diagnosed with attention deficit disorder (ADD), attention deficit with hyperactivity disorder (ADHD), or other conditions such as autism spectrum disorders.[9] A diagnosis like ADHD will mean that a child will probably receive pharmaceuticals such as Ritalin to calm them down; in the case of autism spectrum disorders, even stronger medication and constant therapy may be prescribed. These children will be pathologized and their identity will probably be partially defined by their mental illness diagnosis. The Indigo discourse recasts these children as spiritual healers and leaders specially sent to aid in the coming "new age". This recasting is a manifestation of New Age rejection of "materialist" pathologizing definitions and an attempt to re-envision "problem children". The Indigo Children movement has spawned a huge market, pumping out talk shows, books, seminars, music and educational programmes that employ thousands of specialists who refer to themselves variously as therapists, facilitators, psychics, healers or educators. These New Age voices hold a powerful counterposition in conflict with the medicalized identity offered by psychiatric authorities, both sides fighting to define the identities of these children. John Spalding, a critic of the Indigo Child movement, also joins the discursive battlefield expressing his vision of the movement as a manifestation of the failures of the "baby boomer" countercultural generation of the 1960s and 1970s. He characterizes this generation as unable to live up to their own ideals and argues that they are now projecting their hopes for saving the world upon their children.[10]

Although it began in America, the Indigo Child discourse can now be found in various European countries, parts of South America, Japan, and a growing number of other countries worldwide. It has become part of mass culture and the term "Indigo Child" has a growing meaning for people around the world.

---

8. Wyndham, *The Chrysalids*. Although there is no evidence of a direct link between Wyndham's *Chrysalids* and the later Indigo discourse, there is a striking similarity between the new breed of psychic kids in this novel and the concept of the Indigo Children. This is particularly relevant because *The Chrysalids* has often been used in school curriculums in North America in recent decades.

9. A definition of the scope of the field or domain of inquiry is needed. Indigo Children are defined in different ways by different authors, making a clear definition difficult. As we have said, it is often associated with ADD and ADHD. Additionally, certain authors (such as Meg Blackburn Losey) have outlined further groups of "special" children such as "the crystal children" and "the star kids" who are also associated with autism. In this chapter I will seek to analyse all of these diverse definitions and categories under the umbrella term of "Indigo Children", recognizing that they all share a similar discourse, and perceiving the crystal children and other innovations as expansions of the phenomenon, rather than separate phenomena unto themselves.

10. Spalding, "Brood Indigo".

ORIGINS OF THE INDIGO DISCOURSE

The Indigo Child phenomenon is relatively recent. Dating back to the mid-1980s, the first author to speak of Indigo children is Nancy Ann Tappe in *Understanding Your Life Thru Color* (1986). Lee Carroll and Jan Tober, the authors of *The Indigo Children* (and among the most influential figures in the Indigo movement), describe how Tappe "classified certain kinds of human behavior into color groups, and intuitively created a startlingly accurate and revealing system".[11] Tappe identifies herself as a synaesthete, in her case meaning that she is someone who can see colours around people that supposedly represent their emotional and psychological states. Tappe describes the various colours and their relation to aura colours and personality types, attributing each colour to the people born between certain years. She understands the concept of Indigo Children in relation to this greater colour-based typology. This differs from later authors who are only interested in the Indigos and not a greater context of personality through their relations to a specific colour. For Tappe, the Indigo children are contextualized within the more general concept of "Life Colours". These are understood as broad personality types that are divided into three categories: "physical",[12] "mental"[13] and "spiritual".[14] The colour indigo, however, is situated outside of these three, forming, along with "crystal", a final category, which Tappe designates as "floaters".[15] According to Tappe, the indigo Life Colour is indicative of "a new breed of children" whose "process is to show us tomorrow".[16]

Tappe explains that this new Life Colour first appeared about 16 or 17 years ago at the time of writing.[17] Indigos, according to Tappe, have "no lessons [to learn,] nor do they have an anxiety pocket"; they exist without suffering from guilt caused by external pressures and must be allowed to "do things their own way at times".[18] Tappe outlines several physical weaknesses associated with Indigo Children, such as allergies, difficulties related to the chest or bronchial area, and frequent sickness in the first four years of life. She advocates the benefits of a trained psychologist as an outside authority for the child should behavioural difficulties develop.[19] She also associates Indigos with the growth

---

11. Carroll & Tober, *The Indigo Children*, 5.
12. The physical colours according to Tappe are no colour, magenta, red, pink, orange, lavender and tan (which is also mental).
13. The mental colours are tan, yellow and green.
14. These are blue and violet.
15. Tappe, *Understanding your Life Thru Color*, 128.
16. *Ibid.*, 317.
17. *Ibid.* Since Tappe's book is published in 1986 this would indicate that Indigo Children started appearing in 1969 or 1970, which is much earlier than the date given by later Indigo theorists. Although this is interesting to consider, there is no literary record of the Indigo Child phenomenon before Tappe's book.
18. *Ibid.*
19. *Ibid.*, 318–21.

of science fiction-based toys and programmes, seeing this as connected with their "interstellar interests".[20] Sarah Whedon furthermore notes how Tappe initiates the association of Indigos with millennialism and 2012.[21]

Nancy Ann Tappe leaves few clues as to her potential influences and inspirations in creating her elaborate system of colours, or her more specific idea of a new group of specially gifted children that she names Indigos. She does have a bibliography, but it only contains two books, both of which are works by Faber Birren, a specialist in colour theory.[22] Birren's books appear to have influenced her ideas about colour, or perhaps simply confirmed her "synaesthetic" sense of them, but they contain nothing to specifically inspire favouritism for the colour indigo or to encourage the idea of a specially evolved new generation of children.

Other potential sources for Tappe's ideas, and thus the whole Indigo Child discourse, are the Spiritualist and Theosophical movements of the nineteenth and twentieth centuries. Theosophical ideas presage many New Age ideas, in particular the discussion of auras, spiritual colours and their connection to "spiritual evolution". The originator of the concept of auras and energy healing, as passed into the New Age, is the mesmerist and spiritualist Phineas Parkhurst Quimby (1802–66). He is also famous as the originator of the "New Thought" movement, based on the belief that the mind has the power to heal simply through believing one is healed.[23] It was in his works that the notion of a spiritual halo that can be perceived by a clairvoyant was first posited.[24] Although Quimby originated the idea of auras, it is the work of Charles Webster Leadbeater (1854–1934) that introduces the idea of the colour scheme of the aura. A key text for understanding his idea of the auric colour scheme is *Man Visible and Invisible*.[25] Leadbeater was one of the key figures in early twentieth-century Theosophy. He was an active occultist and psychic, using his clairvoyance to contact the Theosophical masters, explore distant times, discover the qualities of matter, and explicate past lives.[26] He spent much of his life searching for and training different boys in the hope that one of them would be the "world teacher", a boy who would be the next spiritual leader.[27]

---

20. *Ibid.*, 321–2.
21. Whedon, "The Wisdom of Indigo Children", 66. For an explication of the 2012 movement, see Defesche, "The 2012 Phenomenon".
22. The two entries are: Birren, *Color Psychology and Color Therapy*, and Birren, *New Horizons in Color*.
23. Hanegraaff, *New Age Religion and Western Culture*, 485.
24. *Ibid.*, 486.
25. Leadbeater, *Man Visible and Invisible*.
26. Tillet, *The Elder Brother*. See also the discussion of Leadbeater in Chapter 8 of this volume.
27. Leadbeater had a complex and rather problematic relationship with children and the spiritual. Throughout his life he sought out young boys who might prove to be the next spiritual master or "world teacher". He also was accused of pederasty in 1906 and chose to resign from the Theosophical Society for several years to avoid scandal. Furthermore he was

In *Man Visible and Invisible,* Leadbeater describes the qualities and appearance of the various spiritual or "astral" bodies. In his discussion of the meaning of various colours in an individual's aura Leadbeater makes no connection between indigo and spiritually developed children. Rather, indigo is described as one of the many derivations of the colour blue, which Leadbeater equates with the "religious feeling" in its various forms.[28] In comparing Leadbeater's scheme with Nancy Ann Tappe's it seems likely that the latter is to some extent inspired by the former. As interesting as this may be, Leadbeater's lack of emphasis upon the particular colour indigo, or its relation to children, leaves the conclusion that the concept of Indigo Children was not directly derived from Theosophy but was more likely to be an innovation of Tappe's. Thus it would seem that Tappe, influenced by colour theory from Theosophy and other sources, has laid the foundations from which other authors expanded the ideas into what has become the Indigo Child phenomenon, wherein children are seen as sources of hope, religious teaching and ultimately the salvation of an endangered planet.

WHAT IS AN INDIGO CHILD?

According to Jan Tober and Lee Carroll, "an Indigo Child is one who displays a new and unusual set of psychological attributes and shows a pattern of behaviour generally undocumented before".[29] To clarify this description, almost every book in the literature on Indigo Children contains a checklist for determining whether your child or you yourself are in fact an Indigo. These checklists range from extremely vague to quite specific in their criteria. Here are two examples, the first taken from Lee Carroll and Jan Tober's book *The Indigo Children*:

> Ten of the most common traits of Indigo Children:
>
> 1. They come into the world with a feeling of royalty (and often act like it).
> 2. They have a feeling of "deserving to be here," and are surprised when others don't share that.
> 3. Self worth is not a big issue. They often tell the parents "who they are."
> 4. They have difficulty with absolute authority (authority without explanation or choice).

---

reported to have a teenage boy companion who slept with him in his room. See Lutyens, *Krishnamurti*, 203. For more on the biography of Leadbeater see Tillet, *The Elder Brother*.
28. Leadbeater, *Man Visible and Invisible*, 71.
29. Carroll & Tober, *The Indigo Children*, 1.

5. They simply will not do certain things; for example, waiting in line is difficult for them.
6. They get frustrated with systems that are ritual-oriented and don't require creative thought.
7. They often see better ways of doing things, both at home and in school, which makes them seem like "system busters" (non-conforming to any system).
8. They are antisocial unless they are with their own kind. If there are no others of like consciousness around them, they often turn inward, feeling like no other human understands them. School is often extremely difficult for them socially.
9. They will not respond to "guilt" discipline ("Wait till your father gets home and finds out what you did").
10. They are not shy in letting you know what they need.[30]

Another extensive list, which is more embedded in New Age culture, comes from Doreen Virtue's book *The Care and Feeding of Indigo Children*:

- Strong willed
- Born in 1978 or later
- Headstrong
- Creative, with an artistic flair for music, jewellery making, poetry, etc.
- Prone to addictions
- An "old soul" as if they're 13, going on 43
- Intuitive or psychic, possibly with a history of seeing angels or deceased people
- An Isolationist, either through aggressive acting-out, or through fragile introversion
- Independent and proud, even if they're constantly asking you for money
- Possesses a deep desire to help the world in a big way
- Wavers between low self-esteem and grandiosity
- Bores easily
- Has probably been diagnosed as having ADD or ADHD
- Prone to insomnia, restless sleep, nightmares, or difficulty/fear of falling asleep
- Has a history of depression, or even suicidal thoughts or attempts
- Looks for real, deep, and lasting friendships
- Easily bonds with plants or animals[31]

---

30. *Ibid.*, 1–2.
31. Virtue, *The Care and Feeding of Indigo Children*, 19–20.

With reference to Virtue's list, she states that

> if your children responded positively to 14 or more of the above characteristics, then they're most likely Indigos. If they related to between 11 and 13 of the above characteristics, they're probably "Indigos in training", or those who are just developing their "little lightworker" traits.[32]

These two checklists are typical of the Indigo discourse. Indigos are characterized by individualism, independence, alternate learning styles, and a special spiritual or metaphysical openness or giftedness. Doreen Virtue succinctly describes an Indigo Child as "someone who is highly sensitive with a warrior personality".[33] Another of Virtue's definitions of Indigos derives from *The Care and Feeding of Indigo Children*, in which she states that:

> Children who were born in the mid-1970s through the present day are often called Indigo Children because they are, literally, "Children of the indigo ray." They are highly psychic, and they take their psychic visions and knowingness for granted. Their Spiritual gifts are so highly attuned that they're often gifted (although they may think of it as cursed) in other life areas as well.[34]

Virtue suggests that these gifts may be artistic, musical or emotional, and that the gifts will often manifest in an unorthodox manner, often working outside the established system. She gives an example of children who "may flunk music classes because they can't memorize musical scales, but after school, they might compose the most beautiful music at home on their musical instruments, using their inner senses".[35] In addition to their spiritual gifts, Indigos are described by Virtue as "sensitive to a fault" and exceptionally sensitive to two things in particular: truth and toxins. She describes Indigos as possessing a "spiritual B.S. detector"[36] and indicates that this is part of their "remarkable psychic abilities and is a huge part of their Life Purpose".[37] When lied to or treated with insincerity Indigos become aggressive or isolated. The second Indigo sensitivity according to Virtue, and the subject for a large portion of her book, is their difficulty in dealing with "environmental toxins".[38]

---

32. *Ibid.*, 20.
33. Doreen Virtue in *Indigo Evolution*.
34. Virtue, *The Care and Feeding of Indigo Children*, 10.
35. *Ibid.*
36. *Ibid.*, 11; Virtue did not originate this term but rather cites it as derived from the work of Sam Keen.
37. *Ibid.*
38. *Ibid.*, 12.

Virtue says that Indigo Children are "natural children in an unnatural world" and that many of them are "experiencing their first lifetime on planet Earth, and their immune systems (physically and emotionally) aren't able to assimilate the earthly toxins in food, water, air, toiletries, cleaning supplies, artificial lighting and relationships".[39] Here Virtue seems to suggest that immunology is related to the incarnation cycle, and that souls become familiar with "environmental toxins" and become more able to deal with them in the next life.

Tappe, the first person to identify the Indigos, outlines a potential dark side to these children. She says that they have the potential for great evil and to become dangerous, and that "These young children – every one of them I've seen thus far who kill their schoolmates or parents – have been Indigos."[40] This outlines an area of the Indigo Child discourse not commonly emphasized: the potential for the Indigos to become a danger to society rather than solely a source of its salvation. Another important aspect of the Indigo discourse is the connection with ADHD and the revaluing of these children who are marked as problem children by the educational system.

INDIGOS AND ATTENTION DEFICIT WITH HYPERACTIVITY DISORDER

The discourse of the Indigo Child is almost universally associated with children who have been diagnosed with ADD or ADHD. This is an integral aspect to the phenomenon and represents a "recasting" of a socially stigmatized trait into an indicator for spiritual election. Whedon describes this process as "a restoration of the value of special children through a proactive inversion of meaning".[41] She describes how in the 1990s certain children were "turned into monsters or the incurably ill" by the dual factors of school violence and the rising diagnoses of ADD.[42] The Indigo Child discourse of the late 1990s is an inversion of this trend towards pathologizing children. It is estimated from recent surveys conducted by the American National Center for Health Statistics that 8.4 per cent of children aged 5–17 were diagnosed with ADHD in 2006.[43] In response to these statistics it seems safe to say that children being diagnosed with ADHD is a relatively common experience in American culture, and perhaps global culture.[44] The child is often first acknowledged as potentially ADHD in the classroom. They are perceived to be a "problem

---

39. *Ibid.*
40. Carroll & Tober, *Indigo Children*, 9.
41. Whedon, "The Wisdom of Indigo Children", 61.
42. *Ibid.*, 62.
43. Pastor & Reuben, "Diagnosed Attention Deficit Hyperactivity Disorder and Learning Disability".
44. Statistics for global prevalence of ADHD can be found in Polanczyk *et al.*, "The Worldwide Prevalence of ADHD".

child", one who has difficulty paying attention, requires special treatment and may need disciplinary action. This classroom assessment leads to psychiatric consultation and a large portion of the children diagnosed with ADHD end up being treated with pharmaceuticals, in particular with Ritalin. In addition to this, the stigma of a mental illness diagnosis becomes part of their identity and these diagnoses are rarely reassessed; ADHD treatment is often life-long and as with many mental disorders it is rarely deemed to be "cured".[45]

Within New Age discourse there is a rejection of the "Western scientific" model of medicine and its associated reliance upon pharmaceuticals.[46] This rejection of "materialist" answers is typified in the Indigo Child discourse wherein diagnosis as attention deficit becomes an indicator of the child's special status as an Indigo. Thus a parent or friend of the child can cease to view the child as a problem, a child with a disadvantage, and instead view them as special or gifted and simply in need of unique training. There is also, within the Indigo Child discourse, a critique of the Western educational system with its inability to provide the individual care needed to help these children or teach them in the way they need to be taught.[47] In this way, Indigo Children, in addition to their role in New Age discourse, are part of a larger anti-medical discourse, opposing the psychiatric and medical establishment in its diagnosing and medication of children.[48] Sandra Sedgbeer provides an excellent example of this cultural critique in her interview for the documentary film *Indigo Evolution* (which will be discussed in more detail later in this chapter), in which she describes the reason for labelling children as Indigo: "If we don't label them, other people will. They are already being labelled dyslexic, autistic, disruptive, troublesome, ADD, ADHD, problem children and I think that if we don't create a different kind of label for them then mainstream society will."[49] Sedgbeer is describing exactly this process of recasting, of creating a new role for these "problem children".

In the interview, Sedgebeer is responding to a discourse around the problem of labelling children as Indigos. Primarily, the discussion consists of an acknowledgement of the pressures put upon children by the label of Indigo. More generally this discussion is participating in a discourse of critique in which labelling is perceived as inherently negative and part of the mainstream scientific approach, thus even the label Indigo is seen as negative. The mainstream scientific approach is portrayed as in conflict with the "holistic" approach that is championed by New Age enthusiasts.[50]

---

45. Baren, "Multimodal treatment for ADHD".
46. Hanegraaff, *New Age Religion and Western Culture*, 43–4.
47. Carroll & Tober, *Indigo Children*, 95.
48. Other examples of this discourse are books such as Caplan, *They Say You're Crazy*.
49. *Indigo Evolution*.
50. For a discussion of the concept of holism within New Age discourse see Hanegraaff, *New Age Religion and Western Culture*, 119.

A second example of the inversion or recasting of problem children comes from Doreen Virtue. Her recasting is literal, as well as value-based, in that she reinterprets the acronym ADHD as "Attention Dialed in to a Higher Dimension".[51]

KEY FIGURES IN THE INDIGO DISCOURSE

The key voices championing the Indigo discourse are all expanding upon the ideas of Nancy Ann Tappe. A general history of these core sources and voices is central to understanding what the Indigo Child phenomenon is about. The first ones to write a book entirely devoted to the Indigo Children were Lee Carroll and Jan Tober. Their aforementioned book *The Indigo Children*, with the catchphrase "the new kids have arrived", was written in 1998 and became the core text of the Indigo discourse. Their ideas followed Tappe's closely and interviews with her were included as part of the book. Lee Carroll is a practitioner of channelling, and discovered his abilities in this regard later in life after a successful career in business. He began channelling Kryon,[52] an entity that he identifies as an archangel similar to Michael, in 1991, and continues to this day. The majority of Carroll's channelling sessions take place before large audiences and he has even appeared multiple times at the United Nations building in New York before their recreational *Society for Enlightenment and Transformation*. Carroll has authored several books of his channelling with Kryon and has co-authored three books on Indigo Children: *The Indigo Children* (1999), *Indigo Celebration* (2001) and *The Indigo Children: 10 Years Later* (2009). Jan Tober, Carroll's co-author, is a jazz singer and local television show host who became involved with Carroll's Kryon Channelling sessions.[53] She gives her own workshops on sound and colour at many of the Kryon events. It was the "spiritual partnership" of these two New Age celebrity figures that initially popularized the Indigo Child concept and as a result their book, *The Indigo Children*, quickly became a bestseller. It should be noted that the book is largely the writing of other people, edited, compiled and commented upon by Tober and Carroll. *The Indigo Children* is quite different from some other books on Indigos in that it seeks to avoid alienating an audience that is unaccustomed to New Age ideas. Carroll and Tober keep the "spiritual aspects of Indigos" segregated within their own chapter in the book, and this chapter begins with a disclaimer:

---

51. *Indigo Evolution*.
52. Kryon, "Lee Carroll Bio". Channelling "refers to the conviction of psychic mediums that they are able, under certain circumstances, to act as a channel for information from sources other than their normal selves. Most typically, these sources are identified as discarnate 'entities' living on higher levels of being" (Hanegraaff, *New Age Religion and Western Culture*, 23).
53. Tober, "Bio".

> Please note: If you are at all offended by New Age metaphysics or spiritual talk in general, then please skip this chapter. We don't want the information contained here to bias your feelings about this book, or the principles being presented in the other chapters.
>
> For some, the subject is foolishness and goes against common spiritual teachings in the Western world. The perception might be that it contains information that goes against doctrinal issues taught from birth about God and established religion. Therefore, it might cause you to question your acceptance of the quality information coming in subsequent chapters.
>
> Yet for others, it is the Holy Grail of the whole message![54]

This attempt to separate the concept of the Indigo Children from New Age teachings is probably part of the reason why the book, and by virtue of that the whole Indigo Children discourse, has been so influential. Even this part of the book makes no mention of Kryon or channelling in any form, rather the book is limited to hinting at reincarnation, karma, reiki energy healing and a few other staples of New Age culture. In comparison with other authors writing on the subject, the Indigos are portrayed in a relatively mundane fashion, as gifted children who want to be treated as equals and not powerful psychics here to save the world. Their next book, *Indigo Celebration*, was published in 2001 and contained more stories and personal anecdotes from parents, educators, New Age authors and several self-identifying Indigo Children.

Doreen Virtue is another figure of immense influence and importance for the Indigo Child movement. Virtue has a PhD in Counselling and has worked extensively with abused women.[55] She also identifies herself as a medium and gives this testimony from her life:

> As a child, Doreen was a natural clairvoyant, seeing and conversing with what many people call "invisible friends". But this natural gift and ability was little understood by the young Doreen and her family, and was the cause of teasing by her friends. Consequently, Doreen learned to deny her abilities, effectively shutting them down before she was mature enough to fully appreciate them. But on July 15, 1995, Doreen's personal life and her career, marked by exemplary but conventional success, would be irrevocably altered by an incident that is nothing short of miraculous.[56]

---

54. Carroll & Tober, *Indigo Children*, 109.
55. There is some uncertainty over where Doreen Virtue received her PhD and whether it is an accredited institution. This information is derived from various "Sceptic" sites on the web. Like so many other figures in the Indigo Children discourse (or New Age in general) Virtue's whole life has become a battlefield between New Age enthusiasts and self-identified sceptics.
56. Virtue, "About Doreen Virtue".

Virtue's miracle came in the form of angelic communications, which she describes as saving her from an attempted mugging and carjacking. The majority of Virtue's work has been on the subject of angelic communications, mediumship and their use in healing. Doreen Virtue has also written books on Indigos, "crystal children" and "rainbow children", including her aforementioned *The Care and Feeding of Indigo Children*. She has appeared on many talk shows, gives seminars, and edits and writes for several magazines. Doreen Virtue also appeared in the documentary film on Indigo Children, entitled *Indigo Evolution*, which serves as the next step in this survey of sources for the Indigo Child movement.

Indigo Evolution is a documentary film made in 2005 about the Indigo Child phenomenon. It was directed and produced by James Twyman and Kent Romney, and featured interviews with authors, educators, ADHD specialists, parents and several self-professed Indigo Children. The film does not attempt to give a unified vision of what the Indigo Children are or why they are here. At several points throughout the film it becomes clear that the term "Indigo Child" means radically different things to different people. The film portrays this pluralistic vision of the discursive landscape, which ranges from Virtue and those who advocate "psychic children", to medical professionals who are focused solely on the difficulties of educating a new generation, to those who say that every child is an Indigo Child. The film also contains interviews with several self-identified Indigo Children who demonstrate their artistic and creative genius. Finally, a good portion of the film is devoted to the personal stories of parents who have received messages or spiritual insights from their Indigo Children. The film presents an overview of many of the core figures and issues in the Indigo Child discourse and led to greater public exposure for the Indigo phenomenon.

Twyman also produced a previous film, *Indigo*, in 2003, which starred Neale Donald Walsch, the author of *Conversations with God*, a bestselling New Age title.[57] *Indigo* tells the story of an Indigo Child who performs various spiritual feats, such as mediumship, healing, telepathy and other psychic abilities, as she travels with her grandfather (played by Walsch) and brings her estranged family back together. Carroll and Tober assert that "The storyline never specifically revealed that the protagonist was an Indigo Child, but the marketing and the title were obviously meant to take advantage of the growing awareness of Indigo kids."[58] Twyman, in the description of the film, states that: "Indigo children and their ability to communicate in unique ways with each other, heal, and even foresee events, are well documented. This inspirational film ... serves as an affirmation of spiritual principles universal to all mankind."[59] Twyman, through these films, has employed two forms of this powerful medium: dramatic

---

57. *Indigo*.
58. Carroll & Tober, *The Indigo Children 10 Years Later*, 4.
59. Twyman, "Movies".

fiction and documentary. Through film his work is able to expand the potential audience for his message about these children and their place in our society. His films, especially *Indigo Evolution*, have become an important part of the ongoing discourse of the Indigos.

Indigo Child is not the only term used within the Indigo discourse to describe New Age children that are perceived as somehow "different", or "special". Meg Blackburn Losey's book *The Children of Now* serves as an excellent example of this trend as it is not in fact about Indigo Children. *The Children of Now* is about the children who come after the Indigos. Losey says that these special children "are *not* all Indigos!" and that these others "are generally younger" and "have evolved far beyond the Indigo Children".[60] She explains that the "Children of Now fall into several distinct categories, and [her] research has shown that there are overlapping attributes that make it nearly impossible to pigeonhole these amazing beings into neat little boxes".[61] Her categories for these new children are the "Crystalline Children", the "Star Kids", the "Earth Angels" and the "Transitional Children". Unsurprisingly, she has long checklists for each of these to determine if your child is one of her "children of now". The first of these, the Crystal Children, are obviously derived conceptually from Tappe's other "floater" life colour. The other names are the product of the growing discourse of Indigo Children fuelled by channelling, angelic communication, aura reading, intuition and personal observation. It is unclear whether any of these names originate with Losey. *The Children of Now* describes new types of children who are similar to the Indigos but without the warrior, violent aspect. They are often highly sensitive and physically frail, suffering from allergies, ADD, and other difficulties. Losey, in one part of her book, even expands the typical recasting of problem children to include those with severe mental or physical disabilities. She describes a subgroup within her Children of Now, made up from among both the "Crystalline" and "Children of the Stars", that she refers to as "Our Beautiful Silent Ones". She says that these are

> amazing children who, at a glance, appear to be considerably less than perfect, in fact nonfunctional – at least on the outside. But on the inside these kids carry beauty that is often overwhelming in its message, and heart expanding in its truth.[62]

These children with severe autism and mental disabilities are seen in a radically positive and hopeful light. Losey tells us that she "came to the conclusion that these children are the forerunners of the new evolution of humanity. They

---

60. Losey, *The Children of Now*, 22.
61. *Ibid.*, 21.
62. *Ibid.*, 148.

have moved into nearly pure conscious existence while remaining present in our physical world, albeit with apparent dysfunction."[63] These children are often unable to speak but instead "they communicate telepathically and with ease".[64] Losey's book contains many more examples of divergence within the Indigo discourse. Her book is an example of a growing field in the Indigo discourse that postulates other groups of special children, often children considered by medical science to be severely disadvantaged, who actually represent further steps on humanity's evolutionary path.

In reaction to divergence within the Indigo discourse, Carroll and Tober published a third book entitled *The Indigo Children 10 Years Later*. The authors intend the book to advance the Indigo discussion into the realm of Indigo teenagers and to describe how Indigos fare in school and in the work force. This is an attempt to respond to media attention, derision for the Indigo Child movement, and the growing divergence that people like Losey represent. The authors state that

> if you've read any articles on the subject or have seen the television specials about this "Indigo explosion," you might think that Indigo Children are *special, gifted, superpsychic kids from space with dark blue auras who are going to save the world*. This particular message is wrong on *all* counts.[65]

This statement clearly contravenes the writings of other authors, and in my estimation *The Indigo Children 10 Years Later* is a direct attempt to regain control of the Indigo discourse and to direct it along the path envisioned by its creators. Carroll and Tober are seeking to distance the Indigo discourse from certain New Age ideas and reaffirm it as a mainstream phenomenon. The primary blame for the misinformation is not put upon other authors but rather upon bad coverage in the media. They claim that "the American media has biased the public toward this entire subject in a way that might take years to correct – at the expense of the kids".[66] They suggest that niche markets will treat the subject better and they urge other authors, speakers, or film makers not to "throw it to the wolves of the mainstream media".[67]

The book seeks to demonstrate how the aforementioned perceptions about the Indigo Children are wrong. In an interview with Nancy Ann Tappe they ask her about Indigos and their auras, and come to the conclusion that Tappe does not see auras and that her synaesthesia is something entirely

---

63. *Ibid.*
64. *Ibid.*, 149.
65. Carroll & Tober, *The Indigo Children 10 Years Later*, 3 (emphasis original).
66. *Ibid.*, 5.
67. *Ibid.*

unrelated.[68] "The colour has nothing to do with auras or being psychic" says Tappe. Furthermore, Tappe affirms that through her synaesthesia she "is firm in her statement that there are 'no new colors'", meaning that the various new types described by Losey and many others are all to be subsumed under the heading of Indigos.[69] In the interview, Tappe is asked specifically about Crystal and Golden Children, and she replies that she doesn't know anything about those colours and that she "only sees Indigo". "Early on", she says, "I sensed that there would be two colors, but so far I've only seen the one."[70] Carroll and Tober turn to Tappe as their authority, as both the originator of the idea and as an authority on what colours exist "according to the definition stemming from her synesthesia".[71] All this restriction is tempered somewhat by the statement that they "openly welcome those who have named these children other things and who have separated themselves from the 'Indigo' label".[72]

The rest of the book continues in the vein of their other two books, seeking to legitimize the Indigo Child discourse by having various business, medical and educational professionals write small pieces about subjects to do with the Indigo Children and teens. All the professionals clearly emphasize their degrees and position to promote the idea that they are authorities on the subject matter. The descriptions of Indigos in the work force are particularly entertaining as they describe how Indigo teenagers reject the customer service model and make poor employees in hospitality or other service industries.[73] This book demonstrates how different the various agendas are and the variety of techniques that spokespersons employ in their quest for legitimacy for, and control of, the discourse.

INDIGOS AND THE MARKETPLACE

One might ask why it is so important to control the discourse on Indigo Children. It is obvious that the authors of most of these books are sincerely interested in promoting a happier and healthier life for children. They are deeply concerned that certain contemporary children are perceived to be "monsters" and "incurably ill", and seek ways to explain these seemingly unchildlike behaviours. Despite all of these altruistic motives one must also recognize that there is a lot of money to be made off Indigo Children and their

---

68. Carroll & Tober, *The Indigo Children 10 Years Later*, 11–12. This is rather ironic because the back cover of *Understanding Your Life Thru Color* clearly states that the book is about auras and Tappe refers to auras throughout the work.
69. Ibid., 13.
70. Ibid., 17.
71. Ibid., 13.
72. Ibid.
73. Ibid., 114–15.

concerned, well-meaning parents. The Indigo Child discourse has grown into a global discourse, a part of mass culture. As such it has created a huge international market for books, seminars, films, and even specialized schools to train Indigo Children and their parents. Eager parents are more than willing to pay for their special child to get special training, a special diet and play special educational games tailored to their Indigo needs.

An example of this trend towards consumer products can be found in the form of CosmiKids, a corporation that offers products and classes tailored to help children "achieve the clarity necessary to recognize the path they were meant to follow".[74] CosmiKids is a business, with local storefront outlets, which is intended to supplement the regular teaching that children receive in school and through extracurricular activities. It was started by the current CEO, Judy Julin, in 2003. Inspiration "came out of necessity" while working at the Chopra Centre, where a practice developed.[75] All children are welcome and a special focus is given to their ability to work with children with learning difficulties and mental or physical disabilities. Children and parents can go to the CosmiKids location for seminars, after-school play sessions, summer camps, or to arrange a private session at their own home for a special event. CosmiKids products are focused on "self-exploration" as the company sees this as an essential part of a child's development process. Their goal is to:

> encourage children to explore who they truly are in mind, body and spirit – their likes and dislikes, their greatest joys and deepest fears, how they relate to the world and the people in it. We help them learn to trust their intuition and how to tell the difference between what is real and authentic and what is unnecessary noise. With each new revelation a child's sense of confidence is strengthened, forming a solid foundation of self-esteem that will exist no matter the situation because it's pure, true and organic, not fashioned by peer pressure or socially imposed guidelines.[76]

A child who attends CosmiKids seminars or playtimes can be expected to gain a "more mindful and conscious attitude about themselves and the world around them" and there might be an increase in the quantity of "smiles, hugs, life questions, thank yous and pleases" from the child. In addition there "have been reports of increasing incidences involving the words 'I love you.'"[77] The store front offers specialized magazines, books, games, party packages, and educational toys for "inspired parenting". There are also numerous events such as special parenting seminars; support networks for homeschooling parents;

---

74. CosmiKids, "About Us".
75. *Ibid.*
76. *Ibid.*
77. *Ibid.*

workshops for kids on numerous subjects to express creativity, learn about themselves, experience the joy of giving and receiving, and "Angel Bear Yoga".

CosmiKids is offering a form of language very familiar to New Age parents. This is the discursive style of the wellness magazine, self-help book or self-actualization guide. There is a market for the CosmiKids style of "inspired parenting". Parents in the late twentieth and early twenty-first centuries have become increasingly concerned with the activities and lives of their children. In addition, New Age and wellbeing culture have raised serious concerns about the types of play and the types of food that children are consuming. Furthermore, these parents seek to instil their progeny with similar values, and so may feel that they need the cultural trappings and commodities to accomplish this. Finally, the Indigo Child discourse underlies the whole CosmiKids business model although Indigo Children are not explicitly mentioned on their website. CosmiKids was featured in the film *Indigo Evolution*. It is one of the many companies to capitalize upon the growing market for New Age products targeted at children. There are numerous books, seminars, workshops and other opportunities available to participate in the Indigo discourse.[78]

A self-professed sceptic, Lorie Anderson has written an online paper entitled "Indigo: The Color of Money" in which she notes, with some derision and disdain, the large amount of money that is being made by Indigo Child-based New Age authors and speakers.[79] In particular Anderson attacks the work of James Twyman, the man behind the aforementioned movies *Indigo* and *Indigo Evolution*. She seeks to discredit his work by pointing out the lack of scientific support for his various claims, the danger of encouraging children with various behavioural problems, mental illness, or mental disabilities to believe that they are psychic, and has accused Twyman of collecting donations for fraudulent purposes. Anderson offers a "cautionary commentary to my community, Ashland, Oregon (and to the world)", seeing herself as protecting people from fraudulent beliefs and superstition.

Her critique is typical of the sceptics' movement, which often positions itself against New Age beliefs and alternative medicine.[80] Often, sceptics are not professionals in the fields that they criticize, but rely upon the scientific work of others. Olav Hammer defines sceptics as those "who are thoroughly un-sceptical of the foundations of the modern, scientific worldview" and are thus "sceptical of particular sets of propositions because they are problematic when viewed from the perspective of these normative methods".[81] In particular they tend to target suppositions that are "prevalent in popular culture" such as urban legends and paranormal experiences.[82] The New Age movement

---

78. See e.g. Roseberry New Age Centre, "Kids"; Aquarian Dreams, "Aquarian Dreams".
79. Lorie Anderson, "Indigo".
80. Hammer, "New Age Religion and the Sceptics".
81. *Ibid.*, 382.
82. *Ibid.*

has been a particular target. Sceptics often see New Age practice as dangerous and fraudulent, an abuse of science, and so seek to prove the New Agers wrong and liberate the truth.[83] It is clear that some of the sceptics are more involved in (or knowledgeable about) the actual practice of scientific experimentation and reasoning than their New Age antagonists, but both sides often utilize the same rhetoric and both assert that scientific evidence is on their side. Ironically, both groups make similar claims to scientific proof for their arguments. They see the opposition as irrational and dogmatic in their adherence to their beliefs despite the evidence.[84] Both views are clearly ideological standpoints. Both sceptics and proponents of New Age thinking utilize the rhetoric of science to legitimize their claims within the greater Indigo Child discourse.

CHILDREN OF THE BABY BOOMERS

Another figure who weighs in on the sceptic side in the Indigo Child discourse is self-identified Christian columnist John D. Spalding. His online essay, entitled "Brood Indigo", describes the relationship between Indigo Children and the ideals of the "baby boomer" generation. Spalding claims that the Indigos are a projection of the failed ideals of their parents' generation. He says that "it doesn't take a metaphysicist to explain that the offspring of Baby Boomers, raised on the vocabulary of self-help and New Age thinking, might speak a spiritual language earlier generations didn't".[85] Spalding unfortunately does not enter into an analytical criticism of the Indigo phenomenon in comparison to "baby boomer" values. He does highlight the baby boomer idealization of "what Rousseau called the 'vigor of youth'" and notes that the "Indigo Children are supposed to save the world – just like their Boomer parents set out to do." The rest of his article consists of his personal inquiry into the phenomenon including discussions with major figures including Doreen Virtue. She, in her own book, seems to mirror his thoughts on the baby boomers, stating that:

> In the 1960s, many of the first Indigos (often referred to as "hippies") were given the assignment to bring integrity to our government and other systems. But they got distracted by heavy drug usage, became disheartened by the Vietnam War and Watergate, and later got sidetracked by mainstream responsibilities.[86]

Spalding quotes a moderator at a seminar who states that Indigos are:

---

83. Ibid., 396.
84. Hess, Science in the New Age, 15.
85. Spalding, "Brood Indigo".
86. Virtue, The Care and Feeding of Indigo Children, 41.

the Children of New Age Parents ... and they're smarter, more gifted, and more confident than any previous generation. I know the Indigo Children and they're far more spiritually aware and eloquent than my generation was at their age. They will save the planet.

This illustrates Spalding's core thesis: that the Indigo discourse exists to ease the conscience of the idealistic baby boomer generation. Spalding perceives the Indigos as wishful thinking on the part of the baby boomers, who see the Indigos as here to fix all the problems of the world, many of which the baby boomers feel were their own responsibility. He highlights the passivity within certain New Age discourses in which emphasis is placed upon an impending salvation; in this case "there is no need to worry about the problems of the world because the Indigo Children will save us". Spalding's response to the Indigo discourse is largely articulated through ridicule and an attempt to point out the absurdity of Indigo Child advocates. He states that "it is tempting to counter all this talk of transcendence with the observation that a generation deeply wowed by Christina Aguilera is unlikely to change the world".[87]

Spalding outlines a huge divide between the will of the parents and the actions of the children, between ideals and actualities. Following the line of Spalding's argument, I would argue that Indigo Children do, in part, represent an element of wish fulfilment on the part of New Age parents but that the discourse represents something more. Indigo Children represent a new valuing of children and children's insights. They reflect a growing trend toward engaging with the opinions of children and seeing them in a more democratized fashion.

INDIGO CHILDREN AND EMPOWERED CHILDHOOD

The Indigo discourse may be seen as a very visible manifestation of the empowerment of children. Indigo Children are described as being here with a message and a mission. They represent a role reversal in which the parent is expected to speak to them respectfully, as if they were adults, and to listen to what the Indigos have to say. The parent is even encouraged to "take notes" of what their child is saying, as if they were a disciple of their child, since the Indigo could be sharing special teachings from higher sources.[88] The Indigo Children are claimed to remember past lives, see the dead, communicate with spirits, and in general have access to a world of experience that parents are denied. As mentioned, Indigo Children are part of a long-lived

---

87. Spalding, "Brood Indigo".
88. *Indigo Evolution.*

discourse about children and their spiritual powers. The discourse of Indigo Children takes its place as the most recent manifestation of esoteric conceptions of childhood.

The Indigo Child movement is in line with the growing emphasis on children and children's welfare in our society. Despite the fears of certain sceptics, many of the suggestions of the Indigo movement seem to be in line with contemporary parenting advice. The parents of the Indigo Children are encouraged to stop feeding them junk food, to listen, and be respectful of their children. The largest fears of the sceptics are the potential for withholding medical or psychological help from those who need it, and the possibility of spoilt children with overblown egos. The discourse of the Indigo Children is about revaluing children who are seen, by their parents and other adherents to New Age ideas, to have been delegitimized by modern culture and the mental health system. The sources for the Indigo Children are embedded in the twentieth-century New Age movement and the roots of that movement in nineteenth-century Theosophy and New Thought. Through the work of Tappe, Carroll, Tober, Virtue and many others, this discourse has grown to global proportions. These children of the New Age form an integral part of the complex religious landscape of the twenty-first century.

CHAPTER 18

A SMALL-TOWN HEALTH CENTRE IN SWEDEN

PERSPECTIVES ON THE WESTERN ESOTERICISM DEBATE

Liselotte Frisk

In this chapter I intend to discuss some features prominent on the contemporary spiritual (or post-secular) scene in Sweden in the context of the Western esotericism debate, as well as to relate parts of the research on Western esotericism to selected research about new religious movements and contemporary expressions of religion.

The concept of Western esotericism has been used in a number of different ways. In this chapter various themes are discussed from several of these perspectives, (sometimes in relation to each other): the dynamics of religious change, the relationship between Western esotericism and mainstream/established churches, and individual inner experience. These and related themes are also important in two theoretical perspectives about new religious movements and contemporary expressions of religion discussed in this chapter: Stark and Bainbridge's theory of religion, and Riis and Woodhead's approach to the sociology of emotion. These themes form the central discussion in the present chapter.

The empirical material used for this study derives from a local mapping project of religion and worldviews that I have been conducting in Sweden since 2008.[1] Dalarna is a local area in Sweden, situated around 250 km northwest of Stockholm, with about 270,000 inhabitants. All groups with religious social activities or meetings with some kind of religious connotation in a broad sense (with two or more participants present) have been mapped, with special focus on activities outside traditional Christianity. In this study, I make use of a semi-structured interview with Anette Hansson, a life yoga teacher and stress therapist.

---

1. I am conducting this study together with Peter Åkerbäck, Stockholm University, with financial support from The Swedish Research Council (Vetenskapsrådet).

First, I will give a very short summary of the Western esotericism debate. After that, I will sum up the perspectives of Stark and Bainbridge, and Riis and Woodhead. Then follows a description of the health centre in Dalarna, leading up to a discussion where the different perspectives are related to the contemporary situation, focusing on the three themes mentioned above.

Three main arguments will be advanced in the chapter:

- that instead of contemporary spirituality being conceived of as a "part of" Western esotericism, esotericism in the historical sense should be seen as one among several sources of influence on contemporary spirituality;
- that the focus on *gnosis* and experience in attaining "higher knowledge" in some of the typological and discursive approaches to esotericism should be linked to a broader discussion of "religious experience" that is currently taking shape in the study of religion; and
- that a focus on deviance, margin–mainstream conflicts and rejected knowledge as a structural feature in esotericism should be brought into a broader discussion of tension between religious groups and mainstream society, and, increasingly in the contemporary scene, should be questioned and nuanced.

The final conclusion is that Western esotericism as a field of research could benefit from, and contribute to, select sociological research from other fields.

THE WESTERN ESOTERICISM DEBATE

The recent debate about theory, definition and delimitation in the study of esotericism has revealed that the term itself is being employed in a number of different and sometimes conflicting ways. Olav Hammer has noted that two usages of the concept of esotericism dominate in scholarly literature.[2] The first and most central one defines Western esotericism in historical and geographic terms as a specific set of historically related currents in the West. This usage originates with Antoine Faivre's well-known definition of Western esotericism as a form of thought, identifiable by the presence of six fundamental characteristics or components. The first four are "intrinsic", meaning that they must all be present for a given material to be classified under the rubric of esotericism. These are: correspondences, living nature, imagination and mediations, and experience of transmutation. To those characteristics two more components are added, which are not seen as fundamental, but are nevertheless often present: "the praxis of the concordance" and special forms of "transmission".[3]

---

2. Hammer, "Esotericism in New Religious Movements", 445–6.
3. Faivre, *Access to Western Esotericism*, 10–15.

Faivre has been criticized for selecting his criteria on an arbitrary basis.[4] Kocku von Stuckrad says that Faivre also includes currents not fitting all his characteristics, and excludes currents matching, but falling outside, his scope of interest. He further claims that Faivre marginalizes Jewish, Muslim and pagan identities, which all have influenced European esotericism, and concludes that Faivre's approach may be best suited to Christian esotericism in the early modern period.[5]

Wouter Hanegraaff has expanded on several perspectives on esotericism, one of them being the historical definition. In his classic study of the New Age movement Hanegraaff observed that there is a historical continuity between Western esotericism and New Age, but that there is also a continually ongoing process of reinterpretation.[6] Ideas change according to the cultural context in which they are located.[7] While Western esotericism in the historical sense is clearly based on pre-Enlightenment worldviews, Hanegraaff considers the New Age movement to be a characteristically post-Enlightenment phenomenon, which at the same time rejects and is influenced by Enlightenment norms and values. Whenever New Age practitioners borrow "traditional" esoteric concepts, they interpret them from a twentieth-century, secularized perspective. Hanegraaff calls this tendency "the secularization of Western esotericism", and identifies five modern developmental traits that have been of crucial importance for the emergence of New Age reinterpretations of the esoteric: the emergence of *occultism* from the late eighteenth century, the importance of *Oriental influences*, the impact of *evolutionism*, a trend towards *psychologization* and (increasingly in the late twentieth century) the influence of *the market economy*.[8] These have all shaped the reception of historical esotericism, according to Hanegraaff, and I will return to them later.

A second usage of the concept of esotericism (usually *without* the "Western" label) is typological, and is used to denote and analyse currents and religions that have certain structural features in common. This kind of usage describes esotericism in ahistorical and cross-cultural ways.[9] It has often centred on the etymological meaning of the word, with "eso" meaning "inner" as contrasted with "exo" meaning "outer". In this sense, "esoteric" implies teachings that are intended for, or understood by, only a chosen few, for example an inner group

---

4. Asprem, "På Epleslang i Kunnskapens Tre", 11.
5. Von Stuckrad, "Western Esotericism", 83.
6. Hanegraaff, *New Age Religion and Western Culture*. While "New Age" and "New Age movement" are problematic concepts, they will not be discussed here. For a further discussion, see e.g. Frisk, "Globalization". The client cults at Hälsogränden, which are analysed below, could be classified as belonging to the New Age environment.
7. Hanegraaff, "The New Age Movement and Western Esotericism", 26.
8. *Ibid.*, 42–8.
9. Asprem, "På Epleslang i Kunnskapens Tre", 7–8.

of disciples or initiates.[10] By contrast, many of the teachings traditionally included in *historical* esotericism were never concealed in this sense.[11]

Other typologies also exist. Besides his historically oriented work, Hanegraaff has also elaborated on a typological model originally introduced by Gilles Quispel. Here he distinguishes between three basic types of knowledge, referred to as *reason, faith* and *gnosis*.[12] This division is meant as an analytical tool that may help to distinguish different kinds of knowledge referred to by both esotericists and non-esotericists. Mainstream Christianity, as represented by the established churches, could, according to Hanegraaff, be seen as based for the most part on faith in divine revelation through scripture and/or tradition. "Reason" is typified by the rational inquiry of ancient Greek philosophy, culminating in an intellectual tradition which supported the emergence of modern science. Lastly, "gnosis" is characterized by valuing special, private experience (of God and the Self), over and beyond reason and faith.[13] While all three kinds can be found in Christian Churches, philosophy, science and Western esotericism, the degree of emphasis on each type tends to differ between these systems. Thus gnosis, or the (claim to) direct apprehension of ineffable metaphysical truth, is often preceded by philosophic teachings, the truth of which first has to be understood by reason and then accepted as true on the authority of the teacher. Hanegraaff says that special trance-like "altered states of consciousness" could be involved, and calls for taking the experiential dimension seriously.[14] Meanwhile, nothing is said about the *content* of such gnosis. He implies that the culture criticism of the New Age movement is based on gnosis, which has been rejected as unacceptable from the perspectives of faith and reason, and thus has become a reservoir for all ideas being incompatible with the dominant trends of Western culture.[15]

A third type of usage of the term "esotericism" is classified by Egil Asprem as "discursive approaches".[16] While von Stuckrad has developed the most self-consciously discursive approach to esotericism, discussed below, Hanegraaff has lately developed a perspective that moves in this direction as well, claiming that what we call esotericism today is the result of a specific *polemical discourse*, spanning centuries of Western history. Esotericism, in this perspective, is an umbrella term for more or less all currents or phenomena which have been seen as problematic (heretical, irrational, evil, ridiculous) from the

---

10. Hammer, "Esotericism in New Religious Movements", 445–6.
11. Von Stuckrad, "Western Esotericism", 81.
12. Hanegraaff, "Reason, Faith, and Gnosis", 138–41.
13. Hanegraaff, "The New Age Movement and Western Esotericism", 40–41.
14. Hanegraaff, "Reason, Faith, and Gnosis", 138–41.
15. Hanegraaff, "The New Age Movement and Western Esotericism", 40–41.
16. Asprem, "På Epleslang i Kunnskapens Tre", 8. Asprem also notes that several authors are somewhat ambivalent in their reliance on the three approaches, and that some have relied on different approaches at different times (*Ibid.*, 13).

perspectives of established religion and science. The concept of esotericism, while not necessarily picking out something tangible "out there", has rather come to comprise a large variety of such "negative others" internal to Western culture.[17] It has become a polemically construed waste-basket of "rejected knowledge".

A different discursive approach has been proposed by von Stuckrad, who wants to use "the esoteric" as a discourse analytical instrument, a model to recognize and analyse esoteric discourses rather than focus strictly on a few specific historical currents.[18] Von Stuckrad wants to use the concept of the esoteric to gain insights into the dynamics of Western history.[19] He identifies two dimensions of esoteric discourse: claims of higher knowledge and ways of accessing this truth. What is more important than the *content* is the *claim* to wisdom, or a vision of truth as a master key for answering all questions of humankind. Esoteric claims are, according to von Stuckrad, absolutist, and closely linked to a discourse of secrecy. Claims of this sort are present in many kinds of religion and philosophy, but also in science.[20] Although they can be part of established and well-accepted cultural domains, they at times challenge the truth claims of institutionalized religious traditions. As soon as a majority is established, various deviant minorities enter the stage, both through strategies of exclusion by the majority and through the conscious decision of spokespersons to espouse alternative systems of meaning. The minority's claim to provide an individual way to true knowledge has further fuelled the underlying conflicts. Further, von Stuckrad identifies two typical ways to gain higher knowledge in esoteric discourse: *mediation* and *individual experience.* The mediators – gods, angels, spirits, and so on – are also present in mainstream Christianities, but their ability to provide deep metaphysical knowledge to the individual is usually constrained by theology. Similarly, individual experience as an important mode of gaining access to secret or higher knowledge can also be a threat to institutionalized forms of religion.

To these dimensions for gaining knowledge von Stuckrad adds certain worldviews that are typically found in esoteric discourses. The prime example is ontological monism – a necessary precondition for doctrines of correspondences and magical rituals or ideas about living nature – although esoteric discourses have often wrestled with the problem of dualism as well. While those currents that are usually addressed as esoteric show all these dimensions and worldviews, it is also possible to approach other currents or phenomena with this model of interpretation.[21] von Stuckrad also refers to the

---

17. *Ibid.,* 15–16.
18. *Ibid.,* 18.
19. Von Stuckrad, "Western Esotericism", 80.
20. Cf. Chapter 11 of the present volume, where von Stuckrad analyses an esoteric dimension of modern life sciences.
21. Von Stuckrad, "Western Esotericism", 88–93.

notion that esotericism came to be understood as something different from Christianity in the nineteenth and twentieth centuries, and was then seen as a subculture that had formulated alternatives to the Christian mainstream from the Renaissance onwards. Esoteric currents were regarded as having been suppressed as heretical by orthodox Christianity.[22] Von Stuckrad questions this understanding of esotericism, and calls for an emphasis on the internal *pluralism* of Christianity, and the need to pay attention to the neglect of non-Christian traditions in Western culture. He maintains that European history is characterized by transfers of meaning between different religious and other systems like philosophical, philological and juridical systems, as well as art and literature. Identities, not only in the modern age, were constructed along the lines of fields of discourse, biographical narratives, and a tension between inner and outer perception. For example, in early modern times many Christians could easily pick up pantheistic thoughts or practices that officially were regarded as heretical. In the history of Western esotericism we find many personalities that can be described as junctions for the transfer of religions and traditions.[23]

Summarily, we might identify three themes that keep coming back in different kinds of perspectives on Western esotericism: *dynamics of religious change*, the relationship between Western esotericism and *mainstream/established churches* (or gnosis versus reason and faith), and *inner experiences* as leading to gnosis or special esoteric knowledge (experience of transmutation, experience of God and self, trance-like altered states of consciousness, etc.). I will discuss these three themes further below, bringing them into discussion with perspectives on contemporary religion more broadly.

STARK AND BAINBRIDGE'S THEORY OF RELIGION

Rodney Stark and William Sims Bainbridge have presented their general theory of religion in several books and articles, the main ones being *The Future of Religion* (1985) and *A Theory of Religion* (1987). Their theory highlights some important issues concerning religion, religious change, and new religious movements. In line with the points raised concerning the esotericism debate above, I will especially focus on the parts of Stark and Bainbridge's theory that concern *dynamics of religious change* and *tension with mainstream society*. The third theme of this chapter, *inner experience leading to gnosis*, will be discussed in the next section, in relation to Riis and Woodhead's recent work on religion and emotion.

Stark and Bainbridge argue that secularization is a process found in parts of all societies, together with a countervailing *intensification* of religion. The

---

22. *Ibid.*, 80.
23. *Ibid.*, 84–6.

dominant religious organizations in any society become progressively more "worldly" or more secularized. Secularization is, however, only one of three fundamental and interrelated processes. One of the other two is religious *revival*, as a demand for less worldly religion produces breakaway sect movements. The second process is religious *innovation*, or the formation of new religious traditions.[24] Stark and Bainbridge call the schismatic movements, which result from revivals within established religious organizations, *sects*. The non-schismatic, deviant groups that represent either cultural *innovation* or cultural *importation* they call *cults*. In the case of imported cults, the group represents (or claims to represent) a well-established tradition from another culture.[25] But both sects and cults are deviant religious bodies – they are in a state of relatively high tension with their surrounding socio-cultural environment. Stark and Bainbridge define tension with the surrounding socio-cultural environment as "subcultural deviance", marked by difference, antagonism and separation.[26]

Cults are classified into three categories according to, among other criteria, their degree of tension with the surrounding socio-cultural environment.[27] The category of *client cult* is particularly relevant in connection to my case study, Hälsogränden in Hedemora, and is therefore the only one discussed in detail here.[28] As I intend to make clear, it is also relevant for certain developmental traits of contemporary esotericism. Client cults are, according to Stark and Bainbridge, characterized by "therapist–patient" or "consultant–client" relationships, in place of "priest–congregation" or other types of social organization more typical of religion. Client involvement is partial and non-exclusive: the clients often retain an active commitment to another religious movement or institution, or to other client cults.[29] Client cults often compete with medical and psychiatric services, and offer cures for specific physical and emotional problems.[30] Tension with the surrounding socio-cultural environment does not, according to Stark and Bainbridge, get really high until the engagement is more intense than it can be in a client cult. The more radical the movement, the more total the opposition.[31]

---

24. Stark & Bainbridge, *The Future of Religion*, 2.
25. The differentiation of sect and cult by Stark and Bainbridge has several differences compared to the most common ways to define these terms. See for example McGuire, *Religion*.
26. I do not go further into these concepts here, which, in the terminology of Stark and Bainbridge, basically deal with interpersonal competition for scarce rewards. See Stark & Bainbridge, *A Theory of Religion*, 139–42.
27. Stark & Bainbridge, *The Future of Religion*, 24–5.
28. The other two are "audience cults" and "cult movements". The degree of organization and the degree of tension with society is seen as lower in the audience cult than in the client cult, and higher in the cult movement.
29. Stark & Bainbridge, *The Future of Religion*, 26–8.
30. *Ibid.*, 209.
31. *Ibid.*, 36.

Stark and Bainbridge locate one possible reason for the innovation of cults in inner experiences or visions. However, they seem to consider all kinds of religious experiences as originating in psychopathology and being hallucinations produced by either a sick mind or drugs.[32] In order to get a better view of the role of experience, I shall now turn to Riis and Woodhead's recent "sociology of religious emotion".

RIIS AND WOODHEAD'S SOCIOLOGY OF EMOTION

In a recent book, Ole Riis and Linda Woodhead propose a perspective of sociology of emotion.[33] Although the multidimensional nature of religion has often been noted,[34] Riis and Woodhead argue that there has nevertheless been an enduring bias towards the text- and belief-based approaches to religion. They observe that the neglect of the *emotional* dimension reflects class, ethnic and gender biases, and note that emotional labour often lies in the hands of the least privileged in society.[35] Emotion may thus help to produce, resist and reproduce inequalities of power and status.[36]

Riis and Woodhead claim that there are significant variations in the degree to which different forms of religion are emotionally expressive,[37] and also which kinds of emotions are encouraged.[38] At one extreme there are those kinds of religion, including contemporary spirituality, that have as their aim emotional improvement and transformation. The teachings and rituals of these religious formations may be explicitly directed to specific emotional ends,[39] while they authorize and sacralize subjective life.[40] At the opposite extreme are forms of religion that make little reference to emotions, and that downplay emotional expression. Some of these may be strongly practice-based – what matters is doing rather than feeling – whereas others are more oriented to scholarly study and interpretation.[41] For the contemporary religious landscape, Riis and Woodhead refer to several studies concluding that religious groups emphasizing emotions are the most popular ones.[42] They observe a general trend whereby religion becomes more explicitly focused upon the

---

32. *Ibid.*, 173–5.
33. Riis & Woodhead, *A Sociology of Religous Emotion*.
34. See e.g. Smart, *Dimensions of the Sacred*.
35. Riis & Woodhead, *A Sociology of Religious Emotion*, 3–4.
36. *Ibid.*, 19.
37. *Ibid.*, 13.
38. *Ibid.*, 163.
39. *Ibid.*, 13.
40. *Ibid.*, 162.
41. *Ibid.*, 13.
42. *Ibid.*, 1.

emotional demands of its "users", and takes steps to ensure that its emotional programme is appropriate to those it wishes to recruit or retain.[43] Religion in late modern society has a range of possibilities open with different emotional consequences. Denominations that have adapted to religious pluralism generally follow a strategy of offering those parts of the emotional scale for which there is a societal demand. Religious reform movements may in a more direct way confront the social and cultural sources of emotional dissonance, offer critique, and propose social reform. Alternative forms of spirituality often deal directly and explicitly with the emotional states and requirements of individuals, and may offer either more encompassing emotional regimes, or more limited therapeutic interventions. Some sects and minority religions may encapsulate themselves to provide an internally consistent and encompassing emotional regime that offers a sharp alternative to the emotional orderings of wider society.[44]

Riis and Woodhead reject reducing emotions to something private, personal and subjective, and instead favour an analysis of emotion as constructed in the interplay between social agents and structures. They argue that emotion is both personal and relational, private and social, biological and cultural, active and passive.[45] Emotions are shaped not just by interpersonal relations, but by relations with complexes of cultural symbols and material settings as well. Our emotional life is shaped by encounters not only with living beings, but also with imagined, transcendent, inanimate and dead ones. The significance of culture, material objects, memories, places and symbols has to be taken into account. Emotion is generated in these interactions between self and society, self and symbol, and symbol and society.[46] Religious emotion is further expressed through ritual, music, art and architecture.[47]

Riis and Woodhead also note the relation between emotion and charisma, in connection with Max Weber's notion of charismatic authority. They observe that the charismatic individual appears emotionally charged, catches the attention of his followers, and provokes strong feelings.[48] This point easily connects to the contemporary spiritual scene, where close relations between "consultant" and "client" are common. These connections will become clear in the following section, where we shall look at the case study of Hälsogränden in Hedemora.

---

43. *Ibid.*, 203.
44. *Ibid.*, 205–6.
45. *Ibid.*, 5.
46. *Ibid.*, 7.
47. *Ibid.*, 13.
48. *Ibid.*, 164.

HÄLSOGRÄNDEN IN HEDEMORA

Hälsogränden is a health centre situated in central Hedemora, a small Swedish town with medieval roots and around 7300 inhabitants (2005). In November 2009 five different therapists shared premises at this health centre.[49] Anette Hansson, who is the initiator of Hälsogränden, conducts classes in "life yoga", which is a local development of the kundalini yoga of Yogi Bhajan.[50] She is also a stress therapist.[51] The second therapist at Hälsogränden works with mindfulness, light therapy, Rosen therapy, essential movement and classic massage. She also sells African cotton clothes – produced in a small factory where the employees enjoy relatively fair wages, free health care and certain other material advantages. Rosen therapy is a massage technique with mental and emotional connotations, aimed at contacting unconscious emotions and memories locked into the body. Essential movement is a body movement therapy, developed from Rosen therapy, where dance, music and voice are used to get in touch with one's own creativity, expressiveness and inner confidence.[52] Essential movement is also concerned with reconnecting with the body as a source of aliveness, creativity and wisdom.[53] The third therapist at Hälsogränden is a dietician, works with physical exercise and sells dietary supplements. The fourth one is a hairdresser, whose team, besides the ordinary hairdressing procedures, also does "aura haircuts", explained as a kind of "hair balancing" where acupuncture energy is stimulated, the chakras are balanced and support is provided so that imbalances inside the body may be healed. The hair is seen as antennae, receiving energy from the aura.[54] The hairdressing team can also give reiki healing in connection with head massage. The fifth therapist works with psychotherapy on a psychodynamic basis.[55]

---

49. At the time of writing this article, in September 2010, some changes as to which therapists share the premises have occurred. It is still, however, a mixture of mainstream and alternative health care, as it was in November 2009. The spiritual scene is quite flexible, and such changes are common.
50. The parent organization of Yogi Bhajan's kundalini yoga is 3HO (Healthy, Happy, Holy Organization), which was founded in USA in 1969. This form of yoga was introduced to Sweden during the 1990s by Tomas Frankell, a well-known spokesperson for new religions and alternative spirituality. He has chosen to stay outside the organization of 3HO and has distanced himself from Yogi Bhajan, nowadays calling his approach "life yoga", considering it a Western adaptation of yoga. For further information, see Frisk, *Nyreligiositet i Sverige*; Livsyoga, "Livsyogan".
51. As a stress therapist, Anette Hansson works with breathing, relaxation, body awareness, thought awareness, affirmations, visualization and dialogue/coaching (interview by author, Hedemora, Sweden, 11 November 2009).
52. Hälsogränden, "Hälsogränden".
53. Essential Motion, "Essential Motion".
54. Hälsogränden, "Hälsogränden".
55. Hansson, interview by author, Hedemora, Sweden, 11 November 2009.

According to Anette Hansson, the purpose of Hälsogränden is to be a kind of oasis, where people can freely select among different kinds of treatments. The therapists active at Hälsogränden often recommend each other to their customers, and Hansson thinks that there is something for everyone at the centre. She says that someone might come in for a simple haircut, and eventually leave with a spiritual experience. Hansson feels that there is really not much difference between yoga and psychotherapy, and says that the psychotherapist at Hälsogränden works with the inner part of the person exactly as in yoga.

The key concept of Hälsogränden is "health",[56] which Anette Hansson interprets as having both an external and an internal meaning. Internal and external health are, according to her understanding, connected, and exist in a dialectal relationship. On the one hand, if you are in contact with your inner space, you will also want to take care of your external part. Hansson likes to conceive of the body as a temple to be taken care of like a holy space. On the other hand, when you feel better by taking care of your external part, you will also want to take care of your inside. Thus, health could well be connected to, for example, a haircut, with the purpose of taking care of your body, but also to spirituality. For Hansson, spirituality is another term for internal health. She explains spirituality as making contact with your own inner space which, in turn, is in contact with a higher intelligence. According to Hansson, there is a great need in society for people to listen inwards and to be in touch with their feelings. Anette Hansson thinks that to practise spirituality means to be in contact with the internal space, to be love itself, not to judge, and to be in one's own heart. For her, yoga is the gateway to spirituality in this sense. When she started practising yoga, she felt that the dimension of spirituality was present only during yoga classes – now, however, she says that this feeling has expanded to be present in her life all the time. Besides her ordinary yoga classes, Hansson also conducts one class a week in cooperation with the Swedish social insurance administration and the employment office, for people on long-term sick leave and long-term unemployment. She says that she experiences a big change in how spiritual teachings are perceived today compared with a few years ago – there is much more acceptance now than there used to be.[57]

In my interview, Anette Hansson was asked if she recognizes the components of Faivre's concept of Western esotericism in life yoga. Although this approach could be taken to misrepresent Faivre's original intentions, as he suggested a historical perspective and not a typological definition of universal application, Hansson's answer to this question is still relevant in the context of this chapter as it illustrates the presence or absence of affinities with "historical esotericism".[58] Hansson says that the first criterion, "correspondences", exists

---

56. As indicated by the name: "Hälso" means "health", and "gränden" means "small street".
57. Interview by author, Hedemora, Sweden, 11 November 2009.
58. As noted above, Faivre meant to describe certain European historical currents, from which yoga of course is excluded. As we saw, there has however been criticism expressed towards

in traditional yoga, for example in the kind of numerology expressed by the habit of repeating a yogic body movement a certain number of times. Mudras, a group of physical practices with symbolic meaning, could traditionally be seen as linked to the planets, which also illustrates a doctrine of correspondences. However, although correspondences might be present in traditional yoga, Hansson says that it is not at all prominent in the life yoga that she practises. In her yoga classes she hardly uses them at all. The second component, "living nature", is, however, important both in traditional yoga and in life yoga. Hansson says that she considers the world to be permeated by a spiritual force, and that yoga is a way to absorb *prana*: life force, or higher intelligence. As to imagination and mediations, Hansson recognizes visualization and mantra chanting as ways to contact one's own higher self or spiritual guide. The experience of transmutation, she says, is certainly the goal of yoga, to experience the contact with the higher self, intuition or enlightenment. But Hansson wants to emphasize that this is only one part of the goal. We are also humans living in the ordinary world, with the need to see and understand our fears and patterns connected to this world. Furthermore, Hansson believes that different religious traditions have the same essence, confirming what Faivre calls the "praxis of concordance", or the tendency to establish common denominators between different or all traditions (e.g. assuming the existence of a *philosophia perennis*). There are, however, no transmissions from master to disciple in life yoga, and no initiations.[59] Still, Hansson considers "keeping the energy in the class" to be her task as a teacher, as the function of the yoga teacher is to be an open channel through which higher intelligence can flow to the yoga students.[60] Furthermore, in terms of Stark and Bainbridge's model of the client cult, one might theorize that consultant–client relations may in some cases be the contemporary counterpart of master–disciple relations. This sociological difference correlates with late modern implications of buying and selling consultation services, an increased therapeutic orientation and partial commitment, while the personal relationship remains very central and retains some elements of spiritual transmission, albeit in new forms.

DISCUSSION

Below I will first discuss the activities at Hälsogränden as a product of the dynamics of religious change, focusing on different ways to describe and interpret contemporary spirituality. Next, I will discuss the concept of mainstream/

Faivre as these concepts seem arbitrarily chosen and may fit in other contexts as well. My motivation to ask these questions was to test these concepts in a cultural context different from that of Renaissance Europe.
59. As is well known, however, there are initiations in many other yogic traditions.
60. Interview by author, Hedemora, Sweden, 11 November 2009.

established religion, the role it occupies in the different theories of Western esotericism and theories of religious change, and the relevance for the contemporary situation. After that, individual experience and emotion is discussed, in relation to contemporary spirituality and the selected perspectives that have been introduced. Finally, Faivre's six criteria are discussed in relation to the main activity at Hälsogränden: life yoga.

Hälsogränden as a product of the dynamics of religious change

Centres like Hälsogränden have become common in Sweden during the first decade of the twenty-first century. During our research in Dalarna, we have come across several such places, typically situated in small towns, being operated cooperatively by women, focusing on health and spirituality, and offering different kinds of activities, depending on the momentary orientations of the producers. Structurally, small businesses like this have been economically encouraged by the employment office in Sweden, as a way of getting people out of unemployment, which may also be one reason for the growth of such places.

What are the historical backgrounds of the activities at Hälsogränden, and how could these activities be described from the perspective of dynamics of religious change? The first activity, life yoga, has a background in Indian culture, but has been locally adapted and changed according to Swedish circumstances by the founder Tomas Frankell. The yoga teacher Anette Hansson is also active as a stress therapist, which is an innovative title with no support in mainstream society through acknowledged educational programmes, for example, or certified titles.

Mindfulness, which is one of the activities of the second therapist at Hälsogränden, also has a non-Western background. Originating as a Buddhist practice, mindfulness has during the last few years accumulated more psychological connotations in Western culture, becoming part of cognitive–behavioural therapy.[61] Rosen therapy, essential movement and massage originate in the American human potential movement of the 1960s, with roots in humanistic psychology.[62] Important characteristics in the human potential movement, most of which are also prominent in Rosen therapy, essential movement, and massage, are the focus on inner human potential and on expressing emotions through body therapies, a focus on the here and now, or group therapy. A certain syncretism aiming at bridging the boundaries between East–West,

---

61. Frisk, "The Human Potential Movement". For more information about the historical conditions that made an increasing assimilation of Buddhist ideas into Western psychology and psychotherapy possible, see Dryden & Still, "Historical Aspects of Mindfulness".
62. Classical massage, as this therapist advertises, also originates in the Swedish health movement in the twentieth century.

inner–outer and science–religion is also characteristic.[63] Concerning hair therapy, it is a bit more difficult to trace the historical roots, as it uses elements from a variety of sources. There is a degree of creativity or innovation, combined with possibly Theosophical elements (Theosophy in turn being subject to early inspiration from Indian religions) as the use of concepts such as "aura" and "chakra" suggests. Reiki healing originates in Japan, but is rather innovative also in Japanese culture, while different kinds of healing have older roots in Japanese religions. The hairdressing team also refers to acupuncture, originating in China, where it is a well-established healing system. However, the concrete connection to acupuncture in hair therapy remains quite unclear. The mixture of elements from different sources, both imported and innovative, is characteristic of hair therapy, and a procedure that in itself is a form of innovation through synthesis.

Several of the authors discussed in previous sections aim to say something about the dynamics of religious change. Hanegraaff describes New Age as being in a historical continuity with Western esotericism, reinterpreted through the five developmental traits discussed earlier. His approach implies that cultural and structural changes in society are important factors influencing religious change. Hanegraaff also implies that the New Age movement emphasizes "gnosis", which is rejected as unacceptable from the more conventional perspectives of "faith" and "reason", and thus connected with a reservoir of ideas regarded incompatible with the dominant trends of Western culture. Thus a turn towards gnosis – or the individual experience of self or God – has, in the view of Hanegraaff, been an important feature in the dynamics of religious change.

Concerning the therapies at Hälsogränden, few of them have historical roots in what we could call historical or geographical esotericism. We find no astrology, no alchemy, no initiatory orders and no magic (in the esoteric sense) in the activities of Hälsogränden. Only the hairdressing company, using concepts originating in the Theosophical tradition, could be seen as having some kind of direct connection to historical esotericism. The other activities at Hälsogränden could rather be said to have roots in the human potential movement, psychology and Eastern traditions. The only way to relate these phenomena to Western esotericism in a historical sense would be in terms of the reinterpretation in the modern context that Hanegraaff has suggested, and in a radical way. The question then arises of whether it is fruitful to use the label "Western esotericism" for this contemporary environment (and, if so, why). The historical roots of the specific orientations and practices lie mainly elsewhere. Regarding contemporary influences on the New Age environment, Hanegraaff is precisely to the point in formulating the five developmental traits discussed previously. However, I would suggest reconsidering the role

---

63. See also Walter Truett Anderson, *The Upstart Spring*.

of Western esotericism in this account of religious change. Rather than being a label for the whole field, a historical class to which "New Age" belongs, it could be considered one of many historical preconditions for its formation. In short, taken in a historical sense Western esotericism could be added as a sixth trait, and seen as another important historical influence on contemporary spirituality.

If the role of historical esotericism can be reconsidered, so can the typological and discursive constructs. For example, several of the authors discussed agree that individual experience is crucial for religious change. Hanegraaff notes the connection between "gnosis" and New Age religion, and von Stuckrad discusses experience as an epistemic dimension of esoteric discourse (although with a shift from private mental events to "discourse"). Stark and Bainbridge locate an important reason for the innovation of cults in inner experiences or visions, while Riis and Woodhead note the strong relation between emotion and charisma, and point to different ways of handling emotion in religious organizations, some of them intentionally aiming at religious and social change. Finally, in the empirical material a major focus in several if not all of the activities at Hälsogränden is precisely individual and emotional experience.

Von Stuckrad calls attention to the presence of non-Christian traditions in Western culture, and transfers of meaning between different religious and non-religious systems. While this is fruitful for historical perspectives, it is also very relevant for analysing contemporary spirituality. Migration (in several senses), cultural transfers and individuals who function as junctions for the transfer of religions and traditions are all abundant today. Related to globalization, they are crucial factors for the contemporary dynamics of religious change. Stark and Bainbridge's concepts of innovation and importation might prove analytically useful in this context, and could be fruitfully employed both for analysing the historical developments of Western esotericism and for contemporary religion.[64] Individual experience is one of the crucial elements of religious change through *innovation*, while migration (of individuals or cultural products) is one of the crucial elements of religious change through *import*. Today, globalization has intensified the processes of migration and importation.[65] This is reflected at Hälsogränden, where a conglomerate of elements from different parts of the world is evident. The activities at Hälsogränden discussed so far also express the characteristics of the client cult in the sense of Stark and Bainbridge: partial involvement, consumer structure

---

64. These concepts also need to be problematized, as is evident from the discussion of pluralism and the meaning of "mainstream" below. For example, there are constant transfers between different environments, and the problems with defining the borders of a culture are notorious. There will always be problems of this kind with ideal-types, which, however, do not disqualify them as starting points for discussions.
65. See Frisk, "Globalization".

(influence of the market economy, in the scheme of Hanegraaff), and ambivalence between religion and therapy ("psychologization").

The mainstream perspective

There are, however, also other activities at Hälsogränden, which cannot be described as "cultic" in the sense of Stark and Bainbridge, as they are part of the dominant socio-cultural environment rather than being in tension with it. This concerns the therapist working with dietary issues and physical exercise, the psychotherapist, and also the hairdressing team, who basically conduct ordinary hair procedures like haircuts and hair colouring, with healing procedures being merely optional.

The relationship between esoteric currents and the mainstream has been discussed by several authors in the Western esotericism debate. Esotericism has sometimes been understood as being different from Christianity, or presenting alternatives to mainstream interpretations of it. Most important in this context is Hanegraaff's model of the "grand polemical narrative", where esotericism is understood as an umbrella term for currents or phenomena that have at some point been seen as problematic by established religion and cultural institutions.[66] Other authors, like von Stuckrad, point to a more ambiguous relationship between esotericism and the mainstream. While claims of higher knowledge may at times challenge the truth claims of institutionalized religious traditions, they may also be part of established and well-accepted cultural domains.

Focusing on discourses of gnosis or discourses of rejected knowledge has, in my opinion, the potential for interesting analyses, and may provide a bridge from the historical currents of Western esotericism to the contemporary environment of new religious movements and spirituality. The ambivalence to the mainstream noted by von Stuckrad also holds for the contemporary environment. Complicating the matter, there are several different kinds of religious phenomena with different kinds of relationships to the mainstream. The theory of Stark and Bainbridge may contribute to this discussion by its emphasis on the possibility for religious groups to be in different *degrees* of tension with the mainstream, and for different reasons. Thus the discussion of esotericism in terms of tension with the mainstream, including polemics, deviance and opposition, could be inscribed in a larger scholarly discourse encompassing *all* kinds of religious and cultural systems with a problematic relationship to the mainstream.

The degree of tension with the surrounding socio-cultural environment is a crucial factor in the theory of Stark and Bainbridge.[67] Some phenomena are

---

66. Hanegraaff, "Forbidden Knowledge".
67. Other interpretations of the definition of tension to society and the world at large exist. For a more detailed discussion, see Frisk, *Nya Religiösa Rörelser i Sverige*.

considered part of the dominant tradition, while other phenomena are in different degrees of tension with it. This holds true for other cultural sectors than religion as well. In the medical sector, conventional medicine would be seen as representing the dominant socio-cultural tradition, building its prestige largely on appeals to science and the results of clinical trials. The same is valid for the psychological branch of the health care sector, where, taking Hälsogränden in Hedemora as an example, psychotherapy belongs to the tax-subsidized mainstream of the Swedish health sector, while Rosen therapy does not.

This border between mainstream and "holistic" therapies is not, however, cut in stone. Some therapies, which have at some point been in tension with the socio-cultural mainstream, could later move towards less tension with mainstream society, or even to full social acceptance. If a therapeutic practice is deemed effective through controlled scientific testing it becomes part of the mainstream.[68] One such example is acupuncture, which originally, in the terminology of Stark and Bainbridge, could be considered to be an imported client cult, building on supernatural and magical visions of energies in the physical body. In Sweden acupuncture for pain relief has received mainstream status in ordinary health care since several years back. It is used in childbirth for pain relief, as well as in the ordinary health care clinics concerning other kinds of pain problems.[69]

Recently, however, additional therapies from the holistic environment seem to be crossing the border to, or at least decreasing the tension with, the mainstream socio-cultural environment. The most evident example is mindfulness meditation, which is today routinely used in cognitive–behavioural therapy with, so it seems, good results.[70] In the Dalarna mapping project, we had examples of courses in mindfulness being conducted for people working in mainstream health care, funded by the employer. Yoga also seems to be moving towards greater societal acceptance. Anette Hansson and her life yoga is an example of this, as she conducts yoga classes in cooperation with the Swedish social insurance administration and the employment office. Yoga is also used in other places in Dalarna for employees in mainstream health care. Hansson says that, in her experience, yoga is much more accepted today than it was only a few years ago.

Hälsogränden in Hedemora is thus an example of another trend in Swedish society as well: the increasingly blurred borders between the medical mainstream and complementary and alternative therapies. In the context of increased globalization and cultural pluralism, a concept such as the "dominant socio-cultural environment" loses its meaning. Taking the religious

---

68. For a further discussion on deviance and rejected knowledge as it applies to science, see e.g. Wallis, *On the Margins of Science*.
69. However, other uses of acupuncture would still be considered client cults, as they are not accepted in conventional medicine.
70. Nilsonne, *Mindfulness i Hjärnan*.

sector as an example, Christianity was in many respects much more of a dominant religious tradition in Western societies as late as a few decades ago than it is today. In the 1980s when Stark and Bainbridge developed their theory of religion it still made sense to keep the typologies of "sect" and "cult" based on tension with traditional mainstream religion, and explain phenomena outside it in terms of schisms, import or innovation. Today, however, innovative and imported characteristics have intermingled and mixed with elements that earlier were considered traditional, creating new and changing traditions. Still, none of these are as dominant as the Christian culture used to be. With increased individualism, old boundaries have broken down and are today continually and habitually crossed over, creating and recreating new cultural phenomena. In this context, the notion of a tension with the socio-cultural environment becomes much more problematic. Which socio-cultural environment are we measuring against in a society increasingly marked by pluralism? At Hälsogränden, mainstream and complementary therapies exist side by side, and, as for the hairdressing company, as different possibilities within the same activity, as well as intermingled with mainstream institutions. For the individual who receives dietary advice, haircuts, yoga and Rosen therapy, any kind of borders would probably be experienced as constructed and artificial.

CONCLUSIONS

Historical perspectives on Western esotericism have been useful and fruitful for the study of contemporary religiosity. There are historical connections and relations between different phenomena which ought to be acknowledged. However, I would call for a further discussion about different kinds of criteria which could be used in this context, and welcome a more inclusive dialogue with other approaches in religious studies. Thus, the possibility of combining research on "esotericism" (itself a scholarly construct that has been used and developed in several different and conflicting ways) with other theoretical perspectives about new religious movements and contemporary expressions of religion has been the main agenda of this chapter. By using relevant parts of the perspectives of Stark and Bainbridge, and Riis and Woodhead, the themes of dynamics of religious change, relationships with the mainstream, and the place of individual inner experience, important in several of the perspectives on Western esotericism, could be developed further. This could lead to insights which would be especially useful and applicable in relation to the contemporary spiritual scene.

Structural, cultural and individual factors all influence religious change. As Hanegraaff noted with regard to the reinterpretations of esotericism in New Age religion, the market economy, psychologization and Oriental influences are among the factors that shape the contemporary spiritual environment. To these, I suggest, one might add Western esotericism in a historical and cultural sense, as one current among several others influencing and fuelling the contemporary spiritual environment. An important aspect of this is that the general effects of migration and globalization may be reconstrued so that they are not limited to influences from foreign cultures. Writing about Western esotericism, von Stuckrad has suggested that greater attention should be given to non-Christian traditions and alternatives *within* Western culture, and their importance for the dynamics of religion in Europe. Stark and Bainbridge's concepts of innovation and importation may prove useful in developing this point, and as a tool for understanding religious change both historically and in contemporary times.

The role of individual religious experience similarly seems a promising starting point for further research on the dynamics of religious change. The individual religious experience, conceptualized as *gnosis*, is essential in several of the scholarly conceptions of esotericism, but, as we have seen, its characteristics are not analysed much further. The notion of gnosis in esotericism research has to be further discussed, problematized and positioned against other possible kinds of religious experience. For this, further research on religious emotion in different contexts is needed, also with attention to, for example, symbols and artistic expressions. The approach of Riis and Woodhead to the sociology of religious emotion may start to show the way in this matter.

I have also argued that a focus on discourses of gnosis and discourses of "rejected knowledge" has potential for interesting analyses and discussions. Stark and Bainbridge's perspective on different kinds of relationship to the mainstream and different degrees of tension with society may be helpful to develop the discussion further. From this perspective, both historical and contemporary phenomena outside the mainstream could be discussed. The discussion ought, however, to be conducted against the whole range of religious groups, including both sects and cults in the sense of Stark and Bainbridge. As was argued earlier, contemporary spirituality maintains a problematic and ambivalent relation to the mainstream – as has also been the case for esoteric currents in the historical sense – which may call for special attention to processes specific to contemporary society. The effects of globalization and individualization challenge all kinds of traditionally conceived borders. Imported and innovative features mix with traditional ones, creating new syntheses and traditions, both organizationally and individually. In an increasingly pluralistic society, it becomes more and more problematic to conceive of a dominant socio-cultural environment, and therefore also more problematic to discuss, for example, degrees of tension to "it". Hälsogränden in Hedemora represents a new social space where these border transgressions are particularly clear. Mainstream and "holistic" or complementary therapies are practised on the same premises, with a focus on the concepts of internal and external health. The focus on health is also an expression of the contemporary trend towards individualism combined with the sometimes more or less religious overtones of self-sacralization. Also, the border between the secular and sacred is blurred, as it is up to the individual to attribute "secular" or "religious" meanings to the activities they participate in at Hälsogränden. Tentative data from the study of Dalarna indicate that there is a great span as to how individuals think about their own engagement, if they conceptualize their engagement in any specific terms at all.

Concepts and definitions become what we make them; they do not possess an essential meaning cut in stone. My suggestion in this chapter has been that the different approaches that have been proposed to Western esotericism could be developed further by joining them with perspectives from other research areas, especially sociologically oriented research on religious change and the contemporary religious landscape.

CHAPTER 19

ENTHEOGENIC ESOTERICISM

Wouter J. Hanegraaff

The title of this chapter was not chosen lightly. It brings two highly controversial terms together in a novel combination and, in so doing, attempts to call attention to a specific phenomenon in contemporary religion, namely the religious use of psychoactive substances as means of access to spiritual insights about the true nature of reality. The question of why, and in what sense(s), this type of religion should be understood as a form of "esotericism" will be addressed below; but something must be said at the outset about the adjective "entheogenic" and its implications. The substantive *entheogen* was coined in 1979 by a group of ethnobotanists and scholars of mythology who were concerned with finding a terminology that would acknowledge the ritual use of psychoactive plants reported from a variety of traditional religious contexts, while avoiding the questionable meanings and connotations of current terms, notably "hallucinogens" and "psychedelics".[1] As suggested by its roots in Greek etymology (ἔνθεος), natural or artificial substances can be called *entheogens* (adjective: *entheogenic*) if they generate, or bring about, unusual states of consciousness in which those who use them are believed to be "filled", "possessed" or "inspired" by some kind of divine entity, presence or force.[2] While the altered states in question are pharmacologically induced, such religious interpretations of them are obviously products of culture.

Although the terms "entheogen" and "entheogenic" were invented with specific reference to the religious use of psychoactive substances, it is important to point out – although this broadens current understandings of the term – that the notion of "entheogenic religion", if taken literally, does not strictly imply such substances: after all, there are many other factors that may trigger

---

1. Ruck *et al.*, "Entheogens".
2. On the rich vocabulary for such states of consciousness in classic antiquity, see the exhaustive overview in Pfister, "Ekstase", especially 955–7.

or facilitate a state of ἐνθουσιασμός ("enthusiasm"), such as specific breathing techniques, rhythmic drumming, ritual prayer and incantations, meditation, and so on. This was already the case in antiquity, and remains so today. It will therefore be useful to distinguish between entheogenic religion in a *narrow* and in a *wide* sense: with respect to the wider category, one could think of such cases as the ritual practices known as "theurgy", described for instance by the third/fourth-century neoplatonic philosopher Iamblichus,[3] the complicated techniques known as "ecstatic kabbalah", developed by the Jewish mystic Abraham Abulafia in the thirteenth century,[4] or even the experience of being "filled by the Holy Spirit" in contemporary Pentecostalism. The historical evidence in Western culture for entheogenic religion in a *narrow* sense (that is, involving the use of psychoactive substances) is a contentious issue to say the least, and discussing it seriously would require a book-length treatment; but in order to establish that we are not pursuing a chimaera it suffices, for now, to point out that the existence of such kinds of religion in indigenous cultures is well documented, particularly in the Latin American context.[5] The present chapter will focus exclusively on one particular trend of contemporary entheogenic religion – in a narrow sense – which may be defined as a form of Western esotericism and has not yet received the attention it deserves.

ENTHEOGENS AND RELIGION: CONCEPTUAL PITFALLS AND PREJUDICES

That entheogens might have a legitimate place in religion at all is controversial among scholars, but for reasons that have less to do with factual evidence than with certain ingrained prejudices rooted in Western intellectual culture. First, on the crypto-Protestant assumption that "religion" implies an attitude in which human beings are dependent on the divine initiative to receive grace or salvation, the use of entheogens is bound to suggest a "magical" and therefore not "truly religious" attitude in which human beings themselves dare to take the initiative and claim to have the key of access to divinity. Such a distinction (in which the former option is coded positively and the latter negatively) makes intuitive sense to us because modern intellectual culture since the Enlightenment has internalized specific Protestant assumptions to an extent where they appear wholly natural and obvious: in Clifford Geertz's

---

3. See e.g. Shaw, "Theurgy"; Luck, "Theurgy and Forms of Worship". Luck suggests that Neoplatonic theurgy may in fact have been entheogenic religion in the narrow sense as well, but the evidence does not allow us to establish this as a fact.
4. Scholem, *Major Trends in Jewish Mysticism*, 146–55; Idel, *Mystical Experience in Abraham Abulafia*, 13–52.
5. See for example the ritual use of *ayahuasca* (*aka yage, hoasca, daime*) in a variety of Latin American religions (Labate & Jungaberle, *The Internationalization of Ayahuasca*), or peyote religion in the USA.

famous formulation, the dominant symbolic system clothes them with such an "aura of factuality" that the "moods and motivations" connected to them seem "uniquely realistic".[6] These assumptions are, however, culture-specific and highly problematic. The underlying opposition of "religion" versus "magic" (along with "science") as reified universals has been thoroughly deconstructed, in recent decades, as artificial and ethnocentric to the core: it depends on normative modernist ideologies and implicit hegemonic claims of Western superiority that are rooted in heresiological, missionary and colonialist mentalities but cannot claim universal or even scholarly validity. Ultimately based upon the theological battle against "paganism", the "magic versus religion" assumption, including its "manipulative" versus "receptive" connotations, is a distorting mirror that fails to account for the complexity of beliefs and practices on *both* sides of the conceptual divide.[7]

A second cause of controversy has to do with certain idealist frameworks or assumptions that seem so natural to Western scholars that they are seldom reflected upon. Religion is generally supposed to be about spiritual realities, not material ones, and therefore the claim that modifying brain activity by chemical means might be a religious pursuit seems counterintuitive. It comes across as a purely technical and quasi-materialist trick that cheats practitioners into believing they are having a "genuine" religious experience. However, such objections are extremely problematic. First, they wrongly assume that there are scholarly procedures for distinguishing genuine from fake religion. Second, they ignore the fact that *any* activity associated with mind or spirit is inseparable from neurological activity and brain chemistry. In our experience as human beings we know of no such thing as "pure" spiritual activity (or, for that matter, any other mental activity) unconnected with the body and the brain: if it did exist, we would be incapable of experiencing its effects![8] Since all forms of experience, including "experiences deemed religious",[9] are bodily phenomena by definition, it is arbitrary to exclude entheogenic religion merely because of the particular method it uses to influence the brain.

A final cause of controversy is, of course, the well-known rhetoric employed in the "war on drugs" since the end of the 1960s. Here the polemical use of reified universal categories is once again decisive: rather than carefully differentiating between the enormous variety of psychoactive substances and their effects, the monolithic category of "drugs" suggests that all of them are

---

6. Geertz, "Religion as a Cultural System".
7. See detailed discussion in Hanegraaff, *Esotericism and the Academy*, chapter 3, with special reference to Styers, *Making Magic*.
8. Some critics might point to out-of-body experiences as counter-evidence, but any account of such experiences is communicated to us *after* the fact, that is, after the subject has purportedly "returned" to his or her body. Therefore all we have is *memories* in the minds of embodied persons, indirectly communicated to us in the form of verbal accounts.
9. Taves, *Religious Experience Reconsidered*, 8–9 and *passim*.

dangerous and addictive. Although the medical and pharmacological evidence does not support this assumption, politics and the media have been singularly successful in promoting the reified category; and as a result, the notion that entheogens might have a normal and legitimate function in some religious contexts is bound to sound bizarre to the general public. Scholars who insist on differentiating between different kinds of "drugs", pointing out that some of them are harmless and might even be beneficial,[10] therefore find themselves in a defensive position by default: it is always easy for critics to suggest that their scholarly arguments are just a front for some personal agenda of pro-psychedelic apologetics.

The bottom line is that, for all these reasons, the very notion of entheogenic religion as a category in scholarly research finds itself at a strategic disadvantage from the outset. It is simply very difficult for us to look at the relevant religious beliefs and practices from a neutral and non-judgemental point of view, for in the very act of being observed – that is, even prior to any conscious attempt on our part to apply any theoretical perspective – they *already* appear to us pre-categorized in the terms of our own cultural conditioning. Almost inevitably, they are perceived as pertaining to a negative "waste-basket category" of otherness associated with a strange assortment of "magical", "pagan", "superstitious" or "irrational" beliefs; and as such, they are automatically seen as different from "genuine" or "serious" forms of religion. The "drugs" category further causes them to be associated with hedonistic, manipulative, irresponsible, or downright criminal attitudes, so that claims of religious legitimacy are weakened even further.

In this chapter an attempt will nevertheless be made to treat entheogenic esotericism as just another form of contemporary religion that requires our serious attention. A first reason for doing so is strictly empirical: if it is true that entheogenic esotericism happens to exist as a significant development in post-World War II religion and in contemporary society, then it is simply our business as scholars to investigate it. A second reason is more theoretical in nature: both the "esoteric" and the "entheogenic" dimension of this topic challenges some of our most deeply ingrained assumptions about religion and rationality, and studying their combination may therefore be particularly helpful in making us aware of our blind spots as intellectuals and scholars.

---

10. See for example the clinical research presented in the special issue "Ayahuasca Use in Cross-Cultural Perspective", *Journal of Psychoactive Drugs* 37.2 (2005), edited by Marlene Dobkin de Rios and Charles S. Grob. Obviously, and confusingly, the "harmless or even beneficial" category is often referred to by the same term "drugs" (as in "prescription drugs"). That substances such as ayahuasca could be understood as "drugs" in such a sense is widely experienced as counterintuitive because of its hallucinogenic properties (associated with the recreational or hedonistic practice of "tripping"); but that such properties are incompatible with beneficial medical or psychiatric effects is an *a priori* assumption rather than an established fact.

ENTHEOGENS AND THE NEW AGE

The wider context in which entheogenic esotericism has appeared is usually referred to as the New Age. In my 1996 study *New Age Religion and Western Culture: Esotericism in the Mirror of Secular Thought*, I wrote the following:

> One of the most characteristic elements of the counterculture was the widespread use of psychedelic drugs. It has often been noted that most of the New Religious Movements which enjoyed their heyday in the wake of the counterculture (late 1960s and early 1970s) strongly discouraged or flatly forbade the use of drugs. Instead, they emphasized meditation and other spiritual techniques as alternative means of expanding consciousness. This same approach has become typical for the New Age movement of the 1980s, which no longer encourages the use of psychedelic drugs as part of its religious practices.[11]

Rereading this passage fifteen years later, I must confess that I find it rather naïve. In my book I analysed the beliefs and ideas of the New Age on the basis of a representative sample of primary sources, and found almost no evidence for the relevance of psychedelics. However, I should have been more sensitive to the social and discursive necessity for New Age authors to be discreet or secretive about the role that psychoactives might have played in their life and work, particularly after LSD and other psychedelic substances were criminalized during the second half of the 1960s. A good example is the famous case of Fritjof Capra. His bestseller *The Tao of Physics* (1975) begins with an oft-quoted description of the experience that had set him on the course towards writing his book. Capra described how, one late summer afternoon in 1969, he was sitting by the ocean and suddenly became aware of his whole environment as "being engaged in a gigantic cosmic dance":

> I "saw" cascades of energy coming down from outer space, in which particles were created and destroyed in rhythmic pulses; I "saw" the atoms of the elements and those of my body participating in this cosmic dance of energy; I felt its rhythm and I "heard" its sound, and at that moment I *knew* that this was the Dance of Shiva, the Lord of Dancers worshipped by the Hindus.[12]

Capra may have found it preferable to have his readers assume that this experience happened to him "just like that"; but the description is of such a nature that, especially coming from the pen of a typical representative of the hippie

---

11. Hanegraaff, *New Age Religion and Western Culture*, 11.
12. Capra, *Tao of Physics*, 11.

generation, we may safely assume that it occurred under the influence of LSD or some other psychedelic substance.[13] It revealed to Capra that spirit and matter were not radically separate, and eventually led him to explore the parallels and mutual interpenetration of modern physics and Eastern mysticism.

In going through my sample of New Age sources, I came across countless other descriptions of impressive "mystical" or visionary experiences. Many authors described them as crucial turning points in their spiritual development, and emphasized (like Capra) that they had provided them with essential *knowledge* about the true nature of reality. The case of Jane Roberts, author of the bestselling Seth books and arguably the most influential source of basic New Age metaphysics,[14] may be used here as one more representative example. According to her own account, published in 1970, her first exposure to "spiritual" reality occurred out of the blue on the afternoon of 9 September 1963, when she was quietly sitting at the dinner table:

> Between one normal minute and the next, a fantastic avalanche of radical, new ideas burst into my head with tremendous force, as if my skull were some sort of receiving station, turned up to unbearable volume. Not only ideas came through this channel, but sensations, intensified and pulsating ... It was as if the physical world were suddenly tissue-paper thin, hiding infinite dimensions of reality, and I was suddenly flung through the tissue paper with a huge ripping sound. My body sat at the table, my hands furiously scribbling down the words and ideas that flashed through my head. Yet I seemed to be somewhere else, at the same time, traveling through things. I went plummeting through a leaf, to find a whole universe open up; and then out again, drawn into new perspectives.
>
> I felt as if knowledge was being implanted in the very cells of my body so that I couldn't forget it – a gut knowing, a biological spirituality. It was feeling and knowing, rather than intellectual knowledge ... When I came to, I found myself scrawling what was obviously meant as the title of that odd batch of notes: The Physical Universe as Idea Construction. Later the Seth Material would develop those ideas, but I didn't know that at the time.[15]

Everything in this description suggests a psychedelic experience, yet nowhere in her published writings does Jane Roberts mention any instances of experimentation with LSD, mescalin, DMT or other substances that were available

---

13. Capra does not mention LSD, but does refer to the powerful impact of his experiences with unspecified "power plants" (see *Ibid.*, 12).
14. Hanegraaff, "Roberts, Dorothy Jane", 999, with reference to my extensive analyses of her writings in Hanegraaff, *New Age Religion and Western Culture*.
15. Jane Roberts, *The Seth Material*, 11–12.

and widely publicized at the time. Her official account should be compared with the notes in her unpublished journal, now at Yale University. Just two weeks before, on 23 August 1963, she noted that she and her husband had "both become very interested in ESP and parapsychology", and for 9 September we read only this: "Strange, try to be cautious – but seem to have hit upon new thought-system. My definition of time is original – I think will have a lot of work to do on it". One month later, on 10 October, she noted: "'Physical World as IDEA construction' began today".[16] These scanty notes seem to suggest that this manuscript was not in fact the result of automatic writing, but a deliberate writing project started a month after the breakthrough experience.

As suggested by the cases of Capra and Roberts, it would be naïve to simply believe the authors of influential New Age publications at their word when they write that such experiences happened to them "just like that", especially after the start of criminalization. It is obvious that neither they nor their publishers had anything to gain from acknowledging the role that psychoactives may have played in their spiritual development: if you wish to convince a general readership that the universe revealed its true nature to you, that you found yourself communicating with superior spiritual entities on other planes of reality, or saw spectacular visions of other worlds, it just does not help your credibility to tell them that it all happened while you were tripping on acid! Nevertheless, most scholars of New Age – with the notable exception of Christopher Partridge (see below) – seem to have made the same assumptions that I made in 1996. J. Gordon Melton's *New Age Encyclopedia* from 1990 and Christoph Bochinger's 700-page monograph on the New Age (1994) made no reference at all to "drugs" or "psychedelics"; Paul Heelas's study of 1996 mentioned them only in passing; and they are entirely absent from Daren Kemp and James R. Lewis's recent multi-author *Handbook of New Age* (2007). In the pioneering volume *Perspectives on the New Age*, edited by Melton together with James R. Lewis, only one author said at least something about it: in her research on the Ananda World Brotherhood Village, Susan Love Brown noted that many of its members had evolved from an initial use of drugs towards an emphasis on drugless techniques such as meditation.[17] Michael York's *Emerging Network* (1995) emphasized the same point, quoting Marilyn Ferguson's 1980 bestseller: "The annals of the Aquarian Conspiracy are full of accounts of passage: LSD to Zen, LSD to India, psilocybin to Psychosynthesis".[18] Evincing a

---

16. Jane Roberts, "Journal". Note that Roberts's notes about the murder of President Kennedy, later that year, are much longer and evince much more bewilderment and emotion.
17. Susan Love Brown, "Baby Boomers, American Character, and the New Age", 89, 94–5.
18. York, *The Emerging Network*, 50; see also 111 and 181 about the neopagans Starhawk and Margot Adler. In Adler's 1985 questionnaire among pagans, fifty-six respondents are quoted as responding "never, never, ever, ever use drugs" (certainly not a formulation used identically by all of them), but 76% of her sample responded that it was a matter of personal choice because such substances were "occasionally very valuable", and thirteen respondents saw them as "a powerful tool" if used in a sacred context.

similar pattern, a monograph by Sarah M. Pike and an overview for the general public by Nevill Drury (both 2004) referred to psychedelics only in discussing the 1960s counterculture, implying that it ceased to be a factor after that period.[19]

That a widespread shift from drugs to meditation occurred during the 1970s is not in doubt, and it is easy to understand that for organized groups (spiritual communities, new religious movements) it became a practical necessity to regulate or prohibit drug-use among their membership. However, this should not make us overlook the other side of the coin: the fact that putting an emphasis on their development from hedonistic drug use to more respectable and safe alternatives was simply quite convenient for erstwhile counterculturalists. As they were losing popular credit due to the excesses of the psychedelic era and the criminalization of psychoactives, it was in their best interest to emphasize the pursuit of "spirituality" as a healthy and socially responsible way of life rather than advertise the use of drugs. As a result, we cannot determine with any degree of certainty how many of the experiences highlighted by New Age authors were in fact linked to clandestine experimentation with psychoactives, and how many of them somehow occurred spontaneously, resulted from specific drugless techniques, or were simply invented or exaggerated. But absence of evidence is no evidence of absence, and the *argumentum ex silentio* is rightly classed among the logical fallacies. In a society where psychoactives were the talk of the town and widely available, it stretches credulity to assume that the entire 1960s generation that created the foundations of New Age religion would suddenly have become so obedient to authority as to have stopped using them privately as a means to explore spiritual realities. It is more reasonable to assume that while many replaced drugs by meditation, others continued using psychoactives but just stopped talking about it. This makes it relevant to be attentive to passing hints such as this one by the holistic healer William Bloom in 1993: "At the very least you should know about [psychedelic drugs], for they are – albeit secretly – a portal of change and illumination for many people."[20]

In short, my suggestion is that after its sensational and exhibitionistic public phase during the 1960s, the use of psychedelics in a spiritual context evolved after 1970 into a private and discreet, individualist practice, which continued to have a considerable impact on New Age religion because of the types of religious experiences and visions that it produced or facilitated. This makes it into an aspect of "esotericism" in the specific dictionary sense of secrecy and concealment – but *not* of the well-known discursive practice of secrecy as "skilled revelation of skilled concealment" (as elegantly formulated by Michael

---

19. Pike, *New Age and Neopagan Religions in America*, 83–5; Drury, *The New Age*, 73–4, 76–96.
20. Bloom, *First Steps*, 65, as quoted in Steven J. Sutcliffe, *Children of the New Age*, 235n9.

Taussig[21]), where secrets are forms of social capital that impart power to those who are in a position to hide or reveal them. Instead, we are dealing with practices of secrecy and concealment born simply out of social or legal necessity. The obvious difficulties of finding hard data under such conditions are not a sufficient reason to ignore this dimension of New Age, for at least two reasons. First, simply by being more attentive to it, evidence relevant to entheogenic esotericism may be noted and recognized that would otherwise be overlooked: authors and practitioners do make references to it, but often just in passing and by means of coded language (e.g. "power plants" and "psychotechnologies" rather than "drugs" or "psychedelics"). Second, even where there is no strict empirical proof of entheogenic esotericism, it may still be the most plausible explanation in specific cases, such as those discussed above. The assumption that spectacular experiences as reported by Capra and Roberts happened "just like that" (because we cannot think of anything better), are unsatisfactory and in fact rather lazy from an intellectual point of view: until somebody comes up with a better explanation, it seems much more reasonable to attribute them, at least provisionally, to the use of substances that are known from clinical research to have exactly these kinds of effects.

ENTHEOGENIC SHAMANISM

The only scholar who has given systematic attention to the role of entheogens in what he calls contemporary "occulture" is Christopher Partridge. In a very well-documented overview, he distinguished between three phases in the "modern spiritual psychedelic revolution":

1. from Albert Hofmann's discovery of LSD in 1938 to the end of the 1950s, with Aldous Huxley as the central figure;
2. the psychedelic era from the 1960s to 1976, with Timothy Leary at the centre; and
3. the development of rave culture since the mid-1980s.[22]

Publishing his book in 2005, Partridge sketched the emergence of a fourth phase dominated by cyberculture as well. While such a periodization makes perfect sense, I will be emphasizing an element of *continuity* from the 1960s to the present (with roots in the 1950s), concerning a specific current or subculture that is usually discussed in terms of (neo)shamanism. It is in this context that we find the clearest examples of what I propose to call *entheogenic esotericism*.

---

21. Taussig, "Viscerality, Faith, and Skepticism", 273.
22. Partridge, *The Re-enchantment of the West*, vol. 2, 82–134; see also parts of the chapter on "Cyberspirituality" (135–64).

Neoshamanism has attracted much attention from scholars in recent years, but even in some of the best research we find, once again, strange blind spots that have more to do with the intellectual preoccupations of academics than with the subjects they are studying. The evidence shows beyond a shred of doubt that what is now known as neoshamanism emerged during the 1960s as a movement dominated by enthusiasm for natural psychoactives (peyote, ayahuasca, psilocybin mushrooms and various other less well-known species), but many scholars of the phenomenon seem remarkably blind to the evidence in that regard. For example, all specialists of neoshamanism acknowledge the books by Carlos Castaneda as a major catalyst (Kocku von Stuckrad even calls Castaneda's *Teachings of Don Juan* the "foundational document of modern Western Shamanism"[23]), but, amazingly, they tend not to mention, even in passing, that his spectacular "shamanic" experiences were described, in explicit detail, as being induced by psychoactive "power plants".[24] No general reader of Castaneda misses this fact, and it accounts in no small measure for his bestselling success; so how could it have escaped the academics? Similarly, the anthropologist Michael Harner is rightly highlighted as seminal to the development of neoshamanism since the 1970s, but, again, the fact that he was initiated into shamanism by drinking ayahuasca in the Ecuadorian Amazon forest, and discussed it as almost inseparable from hallucinogens in his earlier work,[25] is usually treated as irrelevant or marginal at best.[26]

The basic flaw in these analyses of neoshamanism is that they automatically equate the legally enforced turn away from public entheogenic practice with a freely developed preference for drugless techniques. For example, Andrei Znamenski notes that Harner "purposely moved away from replicating [hallucinogenic] experiences in Western settings", searching instead for alternatives "by experimenting with drugless techniques from native North American, Siberian, and Sámi traditions".[27] Strictly speaking, these statements are correct, but they fail to mention the most decisive factor: the simple fact that, after 1970, Harner had no other choice if he wanted to organize anything public and stay out of jail. In a very similar way, the closely related movement of transpersonal psychotherapy pioneered by Stanislav Grof was forced to abandon the use of LSD and develop "holotropic breathing" as a legal alternative.[28] In both cases, there is no reason to doubt that workshop leaders would have continued using psychedelics (albeit perhaps more cautiously and with more

---

23. Von Stuckrad, *Schamanismus und Esoterik*, 155.
24. E.g. Hutton, *Shamans*, 156–9; von Stuckrad, *Schamanismus und Esoterik*, 153–5.
25. Harner, *Hallucinogens and Shamanism*; Harner, "Sound of Rushing Water"; Harner, *The Way of the Shaman*, 1–19.
26. It is not mentioned at all by Hutton, *Shamans*, 156–61. Von Stuckrad, *Schamanismus und Esoterik*, 157–8, and Znamenski, *Beauty of the Primitive*, 233, discuss it as merely a preparation for the development of his "core shamanism".
27. Znamenski, *Beauty of the Primitive*, 233.
28. Grof, *Beyond the Brain*; Grof, *LSD Psychotherapy*.

safeguards than during the wild 1960s) if only the law had allowed it. For these reasons, applying the post-1970 model of Harnerian "core shamanism" as a model for describing the nature of neoshamanism as a historical phenomenon is anachronistic and misleading: it reduces the phenomenon to only its sanitized and politically correct dimension intended for the general public. Much more than as an example of the literary and popular reception of Siberian and Native American spirituality – a sophisticated etic focus congenial to academic interests, and certainly fascinating in itself, but rather remote from the emic concerns of practitioners "on the ground" – neoshamanism should be seen, first of all, as a form of modern entheogenic religion. Having been born from experimentation with natural psychoactives (entheogenic in the narrow sense), it branched off into two directions after 1970: a "safe", legal and therefore publicly visible ritual and psychotherapeutic practice (entheogenic in the wider sense), and a clandestine underground culture that continued to work with psychoactives.

The main outlines of the pre-prohibition phase are reasonably clear,[29] although more critical research from outsiders would certainly be welcome. The most crucial pioneer was the investment banker R. Gordon Wasson, who developed a fascination with the cultural significance of mushrooms since 1927 and, in the summer of 1955, participated in mushroom ceremonies with the Mexican Mezatec shamaness Maria Sabina. Two years later, in 1957, a lavishly illustrated account of these sessions in *Life* magazine[30] made Wasson and Sabina into instant celebrities. The article in question, "Seeking the Magic Mushroom", inspired Timothy Leary to follow in Wasson's footsteps and travel to Mexico, where he set up the Harvard Psilocybin Project; later in the 1960s, Maria Sabina's residence Huautla was overrun by hippie tourists. A parallel and converging development emerged from William Burroughs's participation in ayahuasca ceremonies in the Amazon in 1953, and similar explorations by his friend Allen Ginsberg in 1960, resulting in a classic of the psychedelic counterculture known as *The Yage Letters* (1963).[31] Riding the wave of growing popular excitement about these indigenous entheogenic traditions, anthropologists like Carlos Castaneda and Michael J. Harner began exploring Mexican and Amazon traditions; and it is on this basis that they eventually became literary and practical founding figures of what was to become known as "neoshamanism".

After the prohibition of psychoactive drugs, this original form of neoshamanic practice somehow continued as an underground tradition through the 1970s and into the 1980s. How this happened exactly and on what scale, which personal networks were involved, how they developed, and how its participants communicated and exchanged information, remains largely

---

29. For a short overview, see e.g. Znamenski, *Beauty of the Primitive*, 121–64.
30. Wasson, "Seeking the Magic Mushroom".
31. Burroughs & Ginsberg, *Yage Letters Redux*.

unknown at present. Since many participants and sympathizers are still alive and potentially available for interviews, one can only hope that somebody will pick up the question and try to write the history of this lineage, particularly for the period of the 1970s and the early 1980s. There is no doubt that with the emergence of rave culture by the mid-1980s and the spread of the Internet, entheogenic neoshamanism (in the narrow sense) re-emerged in public view. It became accessible and attractive to a new generation, and because the Internet makes discussion of potentially illegal practices so much safer and easier, the number of online sources relevant to entheogens and shamanism has exploded exponentially. At present, it is simply overwhelming.

ENTHEOGENIC ESOTERICISM

In this short programmatic article I cannot do more than try to illustrate the nature of contemporary entheogenic shamanism as exemplified by a few representative figures. Arguably its central figurehead was the American prophet of an "archaic revival", Terence McKenna (1946–2000). Elsewhere I have described how his intense entheogenic experiences in the Colombian Amazon forest in 1971, together with his brother Dennis and some friends, inspired him to develop a radical spiritual worldview that stands at the very origin of contemporary millenarian fascination with the year 2012.[32] Several books published by McKenna in the early 1990s have become classics of the new underground scene of entheogenic shamanism;[33] and McKenna himself has attained an iconic status as "public intellectual" in that context, not least due to a series of audio and video recordings of his lectures that are now easily accessible online. His charismatic status rests upon the unique combination of a sharp intellect, a high level of erudition, a delightful self-relativizing sense of humour and excellent communication skills (his books are extremely well written, and his unmistakable nasal voice and hypnotic style of delivery has even been sampled in trance music recordings online) – all in the service of expounding one of the weirdest worldviews imaginable.

McKenna's mature work is a 1990s upgrade of the radical countercultural ideals of the 1960s, and appeals to a new generation that sympathizes with the hippie culture of that period, but does not share its anti-technological bias.[34] At the heart of this "cultic milieu" we find a profound sense of cultural crisis: Western society, built upon the life-denying and totalitarian dogmatisms

---

32. Hanegraaff, "And End History". On McKenna's worldview, see also Kripal, *Esalen*, 369–375. In spite of its remarkable popularity, 2012 millenarianism is another aspect of contemporary esotericism that seems to be neglected almost completely by academic research.
33. McKenna & McKenna, *Invisible Landscape*; McKenna, *Archaic Revival*; McKenna, *Food of the Gods*; McKenna, *True Hallucinations*.
34. Zandbergen, "Silicon Valley New Age", 161.

of traditional Christianity and materialist science, is spiritually bankrupt and heading for military and ecological disaster. In a deliberately utopian search for how humanity might find a way "back to the garden", McKenna is referring first of all to indigenous cultures that are still in touch with nature and with the "archaic" roots of humanity. But underneath this most immediately obvious emphasis on "shamanic" cultures, there is an intellectual discourse grounded in assumptions proper to Western esotericism. While references to it can be found throughout his work, this background is nowhere more explicit than in a series of unpublished "Lectures on Alchemy" delivered at Esalen, California, around 1990, available online as an unedited transcript.[35]

These lectures show the enormous impact of what I would like to refer to as *Eranos religionism*. Religionism means the exploration of historical developments in view of eternal truths or realities that transcend history and change.[36] Characterized by a valuation of myth and symbolism over doctrine and discursive rationality, this inherently paradoxical but intellectually fascinating project was central to the famous Eranos meetings organized since 1933 in Ascona, Switzerland;[37] and largely due to the financial support of the Bollingen foundation, it became enormously successful in the United States after World War II. Many of the central scholars associated with Eranos – notably Carl Gustav Jung, Mircea Eliade, Gershom Scholem, D. T. Suzuki, James Hillman and Joseph Campbell – achieved an iconic status in the American popular (counter)culture, and their ideas have become essential to post-war understandings of "esotericism".[38] It is only since the "empirical turn" in the study of Western esotericism since the early 1990s that this religionist perspective has come to be perceived, at least in the academic world, as primarily an object *of* research – a sophisticated form of post-war esotericism – rather than as an appropriate methodology *for* research.[39]

McKenna's understanding of "alchemy" and "hermeticism" turns out to be a typical example of Eranos religionism, with Jung and Eliade as central figures. From this perspective, he was making a valiant effort to introduce his audience to Frances Yates's classic *Giordano Bruno and the Hermetic Tradition* (1964), her ideas about the Rosicrucian Enlightenment, and even a wide collection of original hermetic and alchemical texts, next to some of his favourite philosophers such as Plato, Plotinus, Bruno, Bergson and Whitehead. During

---

35. McKenna, "Lectures on Alchemy". The transcript available online would deserve some thorough editing, particular as regards the many spectacular misspelling of titles and names of authors that were clearly unknown to the transcriber but can still be identified (although sometimes barely) by specialists.
36. For extensive discussion of religionism and its various manifestations, see Hanegraaff, *Esotericism and the Academy*, especially chapters 2 and 4.
37. On Eranos and its cultural impact, see *Ibid.*, chapter 4, and the standard history by Hakl, *Verborgene Geist von Eranos*.
38. Hanegraaff, *Esotericism and the Academy*, chapter 4.
39. *Ibid.*

the course of his lectures he read and discussed long passages from the *Corpus Hermeticum*, the *Asclepius*, and the *Theatrum Chemicum Britannicum*. In short, he was giving his audience a crash course in the main currents of early modern esotericism, presented as the epitome of a traditional enchanted worldview radically different from the wasteland of modernity and contemporary society. A good example of how McKenna combined his considerable knowledge of alchemical literature with a creative form of "esoteric hermeneutics" is his discussion of mercury:

> You all know what mercury looks like – at room temperature it's a silvery liquid that flows, it's like a mirror. For the alchemists, and this is just a very short exercise in alchemical thinking, for the alchemists mercury was mind itself, in a sense, and by tracing through the steps by which they reached that conclusion you can have a taste of what alchemical thinking was about. Mercury takes the form of its container. If I pour mercury into a cup, it takes the shape of the cup, if I pour it into a test tube, it takes the shape of the test tube. This taking the shape of its container is a quality of mind and yet here it is present in a flowing, silvery metal. The other thing is, mercury is a reflecting surface. You never see mercury, what you see is the world which surrounds it, which is perfectly reflected in its surface like a moving mirror, you see. And then if you've ever – as a child, I mean, I have no idea how toxic this process is, but I spent a lot of time as a child hounding my grandfather for his hearing aid batteries which I would then smash with a hammer and get the mercury out and collect it in little bottles and carry it around with me. Well, the wonderful thing about mercury is when you pour it out on a surface and it beads up, then each bead of mercury becomes a little microcosm of the world. And yet the mercury flows back together into a unity. Well, as a child I had not yet imbibed the assumptions and the ontology of science. I was functioning as an alchemist. For me, mercury was this fascinating magical substance onto which I could project the contents of my mind. And a child playing with mercury is an alchemist hard at work, no doubt about it.[40]

In this passage it is easy to recognize a whole range of basic esoteric assumptions central to McKenna's thinking: the interconnectedness of mind and matter, the notion of microcosmos/macrocosmos, the idea of individual minds being ultimately part of a universal Mind, and the idea of the human mind as the "mirror of nature" (and the reverse). Interestingly, he pointed out that as

---

40. McKenna, "Lectures on Alchemy", lecture 1.

far as he was concerned, the occultist currents since the nineteenth century were of little interest, since they had already been infected by modernizing and secularizing trends. McKenna was pointing towards *pre*-Enlightenment hermeticism – flourishing, as he emphasized, first in late antiquity and then in the Renaissance, both periods of "crisis" similar to our own – for models of a "magical" and enchanted revival that was still in touch with the symbolic and mythopoeic thinking in analogies and correspondences proper to "archaic" cultures. As I have explained elsewhere, it was precisely from such a perspective that the counterculture had been reading Frances Yates's narrative of "the Hermetic Tradition".[41] Authors like McKenna perceived it as a tradition dominated by magic, personal religious experience, and the powers of the imagination; it promoted a world-affirming mysticism consonant with an "enchanted" and holistic science that looked at nature as a living, organic whole, permeated by invisible forces and energies; and it reflected a confident, optimistic, forward-looking perspective that emphasized humanity's potential to operate on the world and create a better, more harmonious, more beautiful society. To all this, McKenna added a direct avenue towards the attainment of *gnosis*: the use of entheogenic substances.

Few participants in the contemporary subculture of entheogenic neoshamanism are as well read in alchemical and hermetic literature as McKenna was, but they do share his basic worldview. Elsewhere I have argued that the various currents and ideas that may be constructed as "esotericism" have ultimately emerged from the encounter in Western culture between biblical monotheism and hellenistic paganism.[42] First, they share a rejection of the doctrine of *creatio ex nihilo*, emphasizing instead that the world is co-eternal with God. This basic principle may lead to an extreme "gnostic" dualism or to radical pantheism, but most commonly it has taken the shape of a "cosmotheism" in which the divine is present in the visible world of creation without being identical with it. From this first principle there emerged a second one: the belief that as human beings, we are able to attain direct experiential knowledge of our own divine nature. We are not dependent on God revealing himself to us (as in classic monotheism, where the creature is dependent on the Creator's initiative), nor is our capacity for knowledge limited to the bodily senses and natural reason (as in science and rational philosophy), but the very nature of our souls allows us direct access to the supreme, eternal substance of Being. Such direct experiential knowledge, or gnosis, is believed to be attained through "ecstatic" states of mind. Seen from this perspective, contemporary neoshamanism as represented by a central author like McKenna is, indeed, a typical form of entheogenic esotericism in the narrow sense of the word. McKenna's "archaic revival" means a revival of *cosmotheism* against the

---

41. Hanegraaff, *Esotericism and the Academy*, chapter 4 (section on Frances Yates).
42. *Ibid.*, conclusion.

worldviews of classic monotheism and rationalist science; and he highlights entheogenic substances as providing a direct doorway to *gnosis*.

McKenna died of brain cancer in 2000, but remains alive on the Internet. His most prominent successor in recent years is another American, Daniel Pinchbeck, who has inherited a somewhat similar "neoshamanic" worldview, including a millenarian focus on 2012.[43] They represent two different generations, but have much in common. McKenna often contrasted his mature worldview against the "intellectual despair" of post-war existentialism that was dominant during his childhood:

> I grew up reading those people and it made my adolescence much harder than it needed to be. I mean, my god, there wasn't an iota of hope to be found anywhere. That's why, for me, psychedelics broke over that intellectual world like a tidal wave of revelation. I quoted to you last night Jean Paul Sartre's statement that nature is mute. Now I see this as an obscenity almost, an intellectual crime against reason and intuition. It's the absolute antithesis of the logos.[44]

Pinchbeck, for his part, actually converted from existentialist despair to entheogenic esotericism. The typical case of a "jaded Manhattan journalist", he had fallen into a deep spiritual crisis: "Wandering the streets of the East Village, I spent so much time contemplating the meaninglessness of existence that I sometimes felt like a ghost. *Perhaps I am already dead*, I thought to myself."[45] He experimented with psychedelics, but without much result, until he made the radical step of travelling to the African country Gabon to participate in a ritual with the Bwiti people, who used a famous psychoactive substance known as Iboga. This was the beginning of what he describes, in his *Breaking Open the Head* (2002), as an initiation into shamanism that cured him of existential ennui and despair.

Pinchbeck now stands at the centre of a new movement that has been referred to by various terms, including "cyber-spirituality", "techno-shamanism", or "new edge". As explained by Dorien Zandbergen in a recent analysis:

> The rise and popularization of digital technologies such as Virtual Reality and the Internet in [the 1990s] was accompanied by the hopeful expectation of spiritual seekers that these would make permanently available the utopian worlds and the altered states of consciousness sought after by a previous generation of hippies. ... Because of the supposed inherent disembodied nature of

---

43. Pinchbeck, *Breaking Open the Head*; Pinchbeck, *2012*; Pinchbeck, *Notes from the Edge Times* (based on columns for his website www.realitysandwich.com).
44. McKenna, "Lectures on Alchemy", lecture 2, part 2.
45. Pinchbeck, *Breaking Open the Head*, 14.

cyberspace, some scholars argued in the 1990s that cyberspace has become the "Platonic new home for the mind and the heart", a "new Jerusalem", or a "paradise".[46]

In the decade after 9/11, the high-tech hippie utopianism of this New Edge movement (visible not just as an online community but also in very popular annual festivals such as Burning Man in Nevada's Black Rock Desert) has taken on progressively darker and apocalyptic shades. In its stronger versions, global capitalist consumer society is perceived as a huge, impersonal, demonic system of dominance and control, with politicians and the media hypnotizing the population into tacit submission and enslavement to "the matrix".[47] In that context, Native American cultures and their shamanic spirituality are seen as preservers of a traditional wisdom that Western society has tragically lost: they belong to the "Forces of Light" set against the powers of darkness that seek to enslave and dominate the planet. Entheogenic sacraments are credited with the capacity of breaking mainstream society's spell of mental domination and restoring us from blind and passive consumers unconsciously manipulated by "the system" to our original state of free and autonomous spiritual beings: quite like Morpheus's "pill" in *The Matrix*, they open participants' eyes, causing them to wake up to the true nature of the collective deception passed on as "reality" ("the world that has been pulled over your eyes to blind you from the truth"[48]), and introduce them to a wider, meaningful universe of spiritual truth, love and light. In short, they are seen as providing gnosis in a "gnostic–dualistic" rather than a "hermetic" sense: a salvational knowledge of the true nature of one's self and of the universe, which does not just open the individual's spiritual eyes, but liberates him from dominion by the cosmic system.

CONCLUDING REMARKS

It is, of course, impossible to predict how these contemporary manifestations of entheogenic esotericism will develop in the future. But that they already represent a significant phenomenon in contemporary culture is clear, and scholars of religion have an obligation to study them closely and find ways to place them in their proper historical, social and cultural contexts. The gist of this chapter is that in order to do so, scholars will need to take the phenomenon of

---

46. Zandbergen, "Silicon Valley New Age", 161, 163.
47. The reference is, of course, to the famous 1999 movie by the Wachowski brothers. On the gnostic nature of *The Matrix* series, see e.g. Flannery-Dailey & Wagner, "Wake Up!"; Bowman, "The Gnostic Illusion".
48. Formulation by Morpheus during his first meeting with Neo in *The Matrix*. This dialogue amounts to a short catechism of neo-gnosticism.

"entheogenic religion" much more seriously than they have been doing so far. Whether we like it or not, we are dealing here with a vital and vibrant dimension of popular Western spirituality that has been with us for more than half a century now, and shows no signs of disappearing. It challenges traditional assumptions about what religion is all about, and its radical focus on ecstatic gnosis within a cosmotheistic context makes it particularly interesting from the perspective of the study of Western esotericism. Specialists in the field of contemporary religion should become aware of their inherited blind spots regarding the role that entheogens have been playing in these contexts for half a century. That role is not marginal, but central, and requires serious study. Scholars may have agendas and preoccupations of their own, but these cannot be an excuse for refusing to take notice of what is happening right in front of our eyes.

CHAPTER 20

A DELICIOUSLY TROUBLING DUO

GENDER AND ESOTERICISM

Jay Johnston

The definitions, boundaries and constituents signified by the terms "gender" and "esotericism" are necessarily troubling and dynamic. As is evidenced throughout this volume, the academic study of esotericism has included rigorous and ongoing debates about the field and its "objects" of study. Similarly – but with amplification – the academic study of gender is an ever-expanding labyrinth of contested definitions, discourses and practices. To draw these two lively areas together can only create more trouble; trouble for conceptual categories, for binary logics, and for dominant discursive practices. Such trouble is both inspiring and imperative.

This chapter aims to canvas not only some of the valuable work already achieved in the study of contemporary esotericism and gender, but also to identify enduring tribulations and places of silence. No doubt some of these are over-ripe for analysis; however, not every dilemma is in need of resolution. In fact, withholding the desire to resolve and represent in favour of teasing out difficulties and sitting with the politics their difference engenders is often as academically valuable as the proposition of a synthesized logic or resolution. The aim therefore is not a definitive or exhaustive overview, but an opening out of discussion, a re-evaluation of relations and a celebration of the problematic. How could it be otherwise when both key terms remain contested and nebulous?

In order to commence, the "necessary evil" of providing some definitional ground remains requisite. The accounts of terminology detailed below are necessarily provisional and most valuable for the way in which they incorporate and accommodate conceptual change and multiplicity. Turning first to esotericism, the dynamic debates about its definition and field (and, as the editors of this volume so clearly articulate, its increasing status as an "object") are encountered elsewhere in this volume and there is certainly no need to supplement that erudite analysis. It is instructive to note that in thinking through gender *and* esotericism in the contemporary world, Kocku von Stuckrad's proposition of esotericism as an "element of discourse"[1] is most salient and applicable. The necessarily interdisciplinary nature of the study of esotericism is accommodated in von Stuckrad's figuring, as is the deeply contextual mode of critical analysis it advocates. Such methodologies – especially those associated with the projects of Michel Foucault and Pierre Bourdieu, and their troubling of the "subject" and the "field" – have figured prominently in the critical approaches deployed in gender and cultural studies. Taken as an "element of discourse" esotericism is an aspect of deeply complex forms of intersectionality, implicit with discourses of gender, race, power and class (to name a few). To this end, this chapter focuses its examination on esotericism's interrelation with the critical category of gender.

Deployed in numerous ways over the past one hundred years or so, "gender" has signalled everything from specifically women's subjectivity, reproductive biology, sexual orientation and subject positions. The once clear-cut analytic distinction between the terms "sex" (biology) and "gender" (cultural and social roles) has been thoroughly destabilized.[2] The normative categorization of dimorphic gender (that is, that only two gender positions are available: female and male) has been the focus of sustained critical scrutiny, leading to conceptualizations of gender as a spectrum of possible subject positions. Accompanying this work, biological essentialism (biological determinist) and social constructivism as the only two options available for the ontological conception of gender have similarly been critiqued: their mutual imbrication now a feature of many contemporary approaches. Thus in summary, critical theory and post-structural approaches have thoroughly undermined the binary logic upon which much gender thinking had been established, and in so doing identified the "centrality", endurance and potentiality of the non-normative, deviant and unstable subject.

Regarding this vexing "gender" term, Morny Joy's overview of its interpretation and application within the field of religious studies is instructive for the consideration of its use vis-à-vis Western esotericism. Joy acknowledges, but does not step into, the essentialist and/or constructivist gender debates (or the degree of the mutual imbrication of these positions); rather, she focuses on the diverse ways in which the term has been deployed in the academic study of religion.[3] Summarizing the outcome of this diversity, Joy notes:

> As a consequence, "gender," insofar as it is an integral element of all religion, has been disentangled from its former assumed function as a natural element of sexuality to a recognized means of imposing idealized expectations, if not obligations. As such, "gender," as a simplistic coding can never be taken for granted again.[4]

---

1. Von Stuckrad, *Western Esotericism*, 10.
2. See Butler, *Gender Trouble*; Haraway, *Simians, Cyborgs and Women*.
3. Joy, "The Impact of Gender on Religious Studies".
4. *Ibid.*, 101.

From a term initially employed to signal "woman" to a marker of strategy for "subversive disturbance" of normativity, many of these modes of use are to be found within contemporary analysis of esotericism, some of which are detailed below. The subversive potential of contemporary gender theory will also be considered, especially in relation to what is generally assumed (as a popular and enduring trope) to be the inherent subversive nature of esoteric discourses *per se*. The prescription of subversion – the discursive positioning of esotericism – itself is the result of normative logic and dominant cultural expectation.

AREAS, APPROACHES AND ARGUMENTS

In this section the major themes and strategies for thinking gender in the field of Western esotericism are examined. It is not intended to provide a comprehensive survey but rather to highlight the diverse nature of their intersection and to provide instructive examples of scholarly approaches and analysis. The subheadings below designate dominant themes and broad areas of inquiry; however they are not presented as fixed categories, and, as will become apparent, many of the examples cited can be placed in more than one simultaneously. It must be noted that the vast majority of these studies are quite contemporary; for far too long the discipline of Western esotericism – alongside other humanities disciplines – has reproduced the use of "man" in some type of gender "neutral" sense (although it is far from clear how such neutrality can be conceptualized) when "human" might have been a more salient choice. Indeed, this is not only a historical blindness, and accounts exist in which the history of Western esotericism can be presented as a series of charismatic individuals and the movements they founded; the vast majority of which are men (with a few notorious exceptions). The question as to whether this is a historically accurate reflection of the tradition(s), or an outcome of the biases of dominant reportage, remains. Indeed, what is most troubling is that it seems that the question has yet to even be adequately asked. The potential answers to such questions would be complex, multiple, partial but so important for both the history which they "present" but also the reflections on research methodology and the process of historicity they would necessarily produce.

Sacred sexuality

The often implicit sexualization of esoteric discourses is the "elephant in the essay" in any consideration of the relation of gender discourses to the discipline. That gender is not equivalent to sex, nor can the two terms be considered to exist in any clear-cut relation to one another, or to any specific aspect of embodied existence, has been explored above; nonetheless, the binary logic through which esotericism is placed as the dominant discourses' "other" as deviant evokes associations with the transgressive. Therefore, this – to an extent – both feminizes and sexualizes the discursive field (a point that will be considered in more detail in the discussion of epistemology below). This positioning is coupled with content that addresses sex, desire and the erotic in a multiplicity of ways, and hence the libidinous associations with the field remain. This conceptual association is well illustrated in volumes such as Hanegraaff and Kripal's *Hidden Intercourse: Eros and Sexuality in the History of Western Esotericism*:

> Indeed, what is so striking about so many of the figures treated in these essays is their conviction that in the depths of human sexuality lies hidden *the* secret of religion, occultism, magical power, spirituality, transcendence, life, God, Being itself. This astonishing connection, such figures would insist, is not metaphorical, or rhetorical, or symbolic, as some would prefer to have it. It is fundamental, cosmic, ontological, religious.[5]

Here, in this introductory statement, is an example of the deeply intersectional nature of esoteric and gender discourse. Both are being positioned as implicit in a concept of subjectivity, and sexuality – or I would argue, more specifically *desire* – is identified as an element of esoteric discourse which signals an ontological, spiritual formation. Foucauldian approaches to the topic would stress the relatively recent "invention" of an individual's sex/gender orientation as *the* marker of identity/individuality. That is, that sexualities' implicit interrelation with ontology, with concepts of the self and identity are the result of very specific socio-cultural contexts and therefore that one's sexual orientation has not always been laden with the expectation that it reveals the essence of self-identity or indeed the nature of life, the cosmos, or the divine itself.

Nonetheless, the intertwining of sexual orientation and practices with ontological, religious beliefs is most certainly a feature of contemporary esoteric practices. Hugh Urban's *Magia Sexualis: Sex, Magic and Liberation in Modern Western Esotericism* provides a particularly erudite account of the positioning of sexuality in occult thought from the nineteenth-century sex magic of Paschal Beverly Randolph to contemporary Chaos Magick. The text investigates the most significant cultural "moments" of this intertwining of discourses, including Western tantra, neopaganism and the notorious Aleister Crowley. Urban's exploration clearly places these sex magic discourses and their accompanying concepts of gender and subjectivity, as articulating very precise social, political and religious debates and anxieties. Indeed, Urban

---

5. Kripal & Hanegraaff, "Introduction", xiv.

identifies the discourses on sex magic as significant elements in the nineteenth century's proliferating discourses on sexuality:

> the Victorian era was by no means simply an era of prudish repression and denial of sexuality; on the contrary, the nineteenth century witnessed an unprecedented explosion of discourse about sex, which was now categorized, classified, debated, and discussed in endless titillating detail. A key part of this discourse on sexuality, I would suggest, was the new literature on sexual magic, which spread throughout the United States, England, and Western Europe from the mid-nineteenth century onward.[6]

In one of the most significant essays on this topic, Joy Dixon maps how the development – and pathologization – of non-normative sexual identities correlates and intersects with the development of new religious movements, especially Theosophy and Spiritualism. "Sexology and the Occult: Sexuality and Subjectivity in Theosophy's New Age" traces not only the trope of equating homosexuality with heresy, but its ambiguous position in the thinking of the early sexologists Havelock Ellis and Edward Carpenter. Indeed, she argues that there was a marginalization of individual claims about spiritual belief in early sexology's case studies.[7] Further, Dixon's analysis identifies the particular way that Theosophical concepts of reincarnation questioned the application of a fixed gender identity to an "authentic subjectivity". Therefore, from the perspective of occult science (rather than the science of sexology), "it is perhaps not surprising that a female theosophist might prefer to think of herself not as a neurotic, hysterical, or deviant woman but as a Viking warrior who had only recently taken up residence in a woman's body".[8] That is, Theosophical propositions regarding the capacity for a gender orientation from a past life to influence current gender identity, and indeed be implicit to spiritual development provided counter-narratives to the articulation of normative subjectivities and fixed gender identities espoused by sexologists of the era. It would seem with this example that the correlation of alternative spiritual beliefs with non-normative gender identities worked to undermine rather than to reinforce dominant binary logic. However, conservative approaches to gender roles also remain evident. For example the heteronormative gender roles attributed to spirit guides and their relation to the medium which "hosts" their spirit recorded by Michael Brown in American New Age channelling culture. This practice will often feature a female host and a male spirit entity: hence the feminine is the body that "houses" the "wise" male spirit/consciousness. The dimorphic gender attribution may be deployed in an effort to express

---

6. Urban, *Magia Sexualis*, 1.
7. Dixon, "Sexology and the Occult", 289, 292.
8. *Ibid.*, 304.

harmonious gender relations, as Brown also illustrates that the Theosophical ideal for sacred androgyny remained vital in channelling culture, however, its ascription in many cases continued to carry gender-normative stereotypes.[9]

Although only two examples of contemporary academic work on the relation between sexuality and esoteric traditions, Urban and Dixon artfully illustrate what Joy would delineate as gender as a "critical tool" that she (following Joan Scott) summarizes as "that there can be no ahistorical let alone 'essential' definitions, particularly on matters of sex and gender".[10] It is certainly true, as Hanegraaff and Kripal claim, that the esoteric furnishes many examples of beliefs and practices that position sexuality and the erotic at the ontological heart of self and the divine, but it is equally true as Dixon's work demonstrates, that esoteric discourses have also challenged normative accounts of the fixed sexual subject or the centrality of sex/gender to identity.

Gender in discourse and practice

The consideration of gender in the field of Western esotericism has also focused upon highlighting the roles of marginalized subjects through a rereading and rewriting of dominant historical narrative, inclusive of uncovering and redressing scholarly bias and the deployment of "gender" to mean women and/or non-normative sexualities. There are ample examples of this genre, which has been particularly active in the area of Theosophy, spiritualism, New Age religion, and neopaganism. For example, Alex Owen's *The Darkened Room: Women, Power and Spiritualism in Late Victorian England* (1990); Cynthia Eller's *Living in the Lap of the Goddess* (1993), and Margot Adler's *Drawing Down the Moon* (1979). Such works discuss the significant role that individuals and gender discourses played in the development of particular esoteric practices, often highlighting the influence of socio-political circumstances on their articulation.

This approach is also inclusive of texts like Jeffrey J. Kripal's *Roads of Excess, Palaces of Wisdom: Eroticism and Reflexivity in the Study of Mysticism*, which took as its remit not only gendered interpretations of esoteric literature but also the gender orientations (and ambiguities) of the scholars who undertook the studies. In particular Kripal considers the way in which an understanding of the authors' own subjectivities impacted upon their scholarship. Kripal's prime concern is the erotic or mystical experiences of the authors themselves, highlighting "that mystical communities and literatures have offered some of the most successful, if still ethically ambiguous, venues in which alternative sexualities and genders have expressed themselves".[11] Here, then, is the identification of mystical discourse as a site of subversion.

---

9. Michael F. Brown, *The Channeling Zone*, 93–114.
10. Joy, "The Impact of Gender on Religious Studies", 99.
11. Kripal, *Roads of Excess, Palaces of Wisdom*, 17.

The association of mysticism with sexuality has a long and complex heritage, which lies largely outside the bounds of this chapter; however, works like Kripal's do tie the consideration of such literature more closely to the academic study of esotericism. It should also be noted that the work of Elliot R. Wolfson and Moshe Idel present particularly erudite analyses of the central role of concepts of masculinity and femininity in Kabbalistic discourses and the subversive potential of such texts for understanding mystical experience and religious subjectivity.[12]

Secret societies and initiation-based organizations, including Masonic lodges, are all taken as "core" objects of study for contemporary esotericism, and these include the production of studies specifically focused on the issue of gender. Masonic traditions in particular as a bastion of men-only clubs have come under sustained scrutiny both for the concepts of masculinity they utilize and develop[13] and for women's roles in their institutions.[14] Máire Fedelma Cross's edited volume on *Gender and Fraternal Orders* contributes to this topic while placing considerations of Freemasonry in a broader context of social guilds and monastic communities.[15] Also found in this topic area is Mary K. Greer's historical account of *Women of the Golden Dawn* which is noteworthy as a historical volume as well as an astrological analysis (a work *of* esotericism itself).[16]

As already mentioned, a strong focus for the investigation of gender and esotericism has been placed upon movements in which women have played a leading role, including Theosophy, spiritualism, New Age religion and neopaganism. The latter in particular has accrued numerous studies, which is unsurprising given the centrality of embodied experience to conceptualizations of the divine (e.g. Goddess and God) in its various belief systems and in particular groups that have consciously identified with specific gender identities, for example Dianic Wicca or the Radical Faeries. Examples are readily found of groups which challenge normative dimorphic concepts of gender as well as those that reinforce dominant (and essentialist) concepts of masculinity = culture = rationality and femininity = nature = intuition. Indeed, the assumption that magicians are only men and witches are only women is disappointingly common. This is no doubt furnished by long-held popular images of wicked female witches and diabolical male magicians from Faustus to Witchy-Poo (of the *H. R. Pufnstuf* television series, 1969). Such stereotypes persist in the public imagination despite the central role of, for example, Gerald Gardner and Alex Sanders in the development of popular forms of contemporary Wicca.

---

12. See e.g. Wolfson, *Language, Eros, Being*; Idel, *Kabbalah and Eros*.
13. E.g. William D. Moore, *Masonic Temples*.
14. As exemplified by Heidle & Snoek, *Women's Agency and Rituals in Mixed and Female Masonic Orders*.
15. Cross, *Gender and Fraternal Orders in Europe, 1300–2000*.
16. Greer, *Women of the Golden Dawn*.

The "femininity = nature = intuition" logic was (and continues to be) actively used by practitioners like Diane Stein, whose biography for *Women's Psychic Lives* (1995) presents her as: "healer, psychic, witch and priestess of the Goddess. An activist in anti-war movements, women's rights, gay rights and rights of the disabled".[17] In this text psychic skills and intuition are presented as particularly feminine traits that have been "submerged" by patriarchal culture. While she acknowledges that men can be psychic too, as an extra-sensory skill it is understood by Stein to be specifically women's knowledge: "women are psychic, and the experiences of virtually every woman prove this".[18] It is, she contends, intimately interwoven with female reproductive and sexual anatomy:

> From the place of creation, the womb and the vulva of the Great Mother Goddess of a thousand names and all cultures, comes the psychic lives and psychic wisdom of women. The woman who knows her womb power, her psychic life and claims it, stroked the python.[19]

Such a universal concept of "woman" has been critiqued – especially by post-colonial theorists – not only for its deployment in the field of contemporary spiritualities, but also for its use by feminist philosophers (such as Luce Irigaray) who have argued for specifically feminine forms of epistemology and aligned them with a generic category "woman", that is actually based upon the experience of Euro-centric white women, to the exclusion of other types of difference, for example racial and class difference.[20] However, the construction of a feminine universal subject is not the only form of gender essentialism to be found in neopagan cultures.

It is clear in Michael F. Strmiska and Baldur A. Sigurvinsson's study of Icelandic and American Ásatrú that normative gender essentialism features in contemporary Nordic neopagan practices.[21] These subject positions – prescriptions of warrior men and hearth-tending women – are defined and maintained through reference to contemporary interpretations of gender relations in saga literature. It should be noted, as Strmiska points out in his discussion of Icelandic Ásatrú, that regional and cultural location play a significant role in the beliefs and practices of different Ásatrú communities: "All Ásatrú groups are united in attempting to reconstruct and reinterpret for modern times the myths, beliefs, and folklore of pre-Christian Scandinavia ... they differ widely in the types of knowledge and assumptions which they bring to

---

17. Stein, *Women's Psychic Lives*.
18. *Ibid.*, 5.
19. *Ibid.*, xvniii.
20. See for example, Moreton-Robinson, *Talkin' Up to the White Woman*.
21. Strmiska & Sigurvinsson, "Asatru".

this enterprise".[22] These assumptions include the degree to which contemporary gender stereotypes are taken up and reproduced by group members. The strong membership of current and ex-military personnel in American Ásatrú, for example, has engendered very active masculine roles and groups like the Brotherhood of the Sacred Hunt, while Icelandic Ásatrú is figured more prominently as an aspect of national cultural heritage that underlies the lived reality of day-to-day life.[23] As such, although normative gender roles still feature, the degree of retrospective, "romantic" stereotyping does not seem as acute.[24] In both cases it seems clear that the dominant socio-cultural and historical context of the specific groups directly affect their interpretation of gender, as well as the degree to which the group defines itself either in defiance or in support of the dominant cultural tropes.

In further contradistinction, Jenny Blain identifies (in the same root tradition) forms of subversive gender identities. She provides an innovative application of queer theory (elucidated in more detail below) to present a reading of *seidr* (magic) practitioners as inhabiting unstable and queer gender identities.[25]

It is the "shamanic" associations with *seidr* practices that underpin the fluidity of subjectivity that Blain proposes. Indeed, the general assumption that shamanic practice involves the capacity for embodied transformation across gender-binary and species (human–non-human) is most certainly a platform for destabilizing gender and human-centric identity. This feature is clearly evident in contemporary Otherkin discourse, where for some practitioners part of the appeal is the potential for gender ambiguity that their non-human self imparts (be it animal, spiritual being, elf, faery, mystical beast, etc.). Therian (animal–human) Lupa demonstrates a strong awareness of contemporary gender theory and debates in hir *Field Guide to Otherkin* where she/he argues that with an Otherkin identity dimorphic gender distinction become increasingly nebulous and inept: hence the use of non-specific pronouns like "hir" and "she/he".[26]

Otherkin is an umbrella term, and the individuals and groups it is employed to signify do not necessarily approve of, or use it. Nonetheless, the term itself signifies the challenge to dominate concepts of the human that the multiplicitous subcultures embrace. Indeed, when Lupa writes of the reasons why she/he employs gender ambiguous pronouns it is because: "they are very useful in a day and age where the ideas of sex and gender are becoming less like a dichotomy and more like a continuum".[27] As already noted, the "reading" of sexual orientation as the "essence" of self is a core feature of contemporary

---

22. Strmiska, "Ásatrú in Iceland", 108.
23. Strmiska & Sigurvinsson, "Asatru", 152–3, 174–5.
24. My thanks to Egil Asprem for discussion on these issues.
25. Blain, *Nine Worlds of Seid-Magic*, 111–41.
26. Lupa, *A Field Guide to Otherkin*, 26.
27. *Ibid.*

concepts of subjectivity. The denial of clear identity labels – or their confusion by the incorporation of the non-human in an individual's identity – disrupts these narratives upon which concepts of the human subject are built. This is especially acute when the non-human element is a metaphysical being or beast with ambiguous or unstable gender attribution – the "sexing" of angels for example. Indeed, even Therian gender identities sit uneasily in dimorphic schemes. As Myra J. Hird's work on animal trans has argued, the gender identity and sexual behaviour of many animal species are "much more plastic and diverse than human culture allows".[28] Given such, an Otherkin animal–human "hybrid" subjectivity has the strong potential to trouble – in very useful and significant ways – the assumed interrelation of stable gender identity and subjectivity.

Conceptions of nature in esoteric discourses and traditions are implicitly intertwined with gender tropes, whether these are academically acknowledged or not. As the next section will endeavour to illustrate, certain types of knowledge and phenomena are in dominant Western culture gendered in quite specific ways. The tight coupling of the feminine with nature has been deployed to argue for female subservience, for dimorphic gender difference, for women's "natural" affinity with the environment. Thus it has been positioned as having had *both* positive and negative roles in the construction of femininity and its socio-cultural articulation. Richard Roberts, Susan Greenwood and Elizabeth Puttick all contribute to the critical analysis of assumed relations between nature and women (usefully found in the same volume) in an appraisal of contemporary nature religions.[29] This is a conceptual coupling that while relatively well investigated in neopagan and neoshamanic practices, can also usefully be applied to hermeneutic approaches found in the discipline, theories of "living nature" for example. In particular, analysis could investigate Marsilio Ficino's system of correspondences, not only identifying implicit gender ascriptions of plant, stone, planet, and so on (and the way such gendering has carried forth into contemporary beliefs and practices), but also considering the way in which such a "natural" magic might (or might not) challenge and subvert gender conventions of the period (including the degree to which certain forms of education were unevenly available to subjects of gender, social, and racial difference). Such analysis would also necessarily need to question the nature–culture divide. That is, the degree to which such practices and ideologies were part of a larger cultural framework that masked the specifically cultural construction of the very concept of "nature", which in turn enabled the positioning of the human as the mediator or interpreter of a divine material, "natural" language. Can "natural magic" be read (as other narratives about "nature" have been by feminist philosophers) as discourses that tie the feminine to the

---

28. Hird, "Animal Trans", 235.
29. Roberts & Samuel, *Nature Religion Today*.

physical world, and thereby, by extension, undermine any ascription of reason (in its broadest sense), consciousness and enlightenment to a female gender? The forms of knowledge used by contemporary animal oracles, and animal and nature psychics, could also be investigated in the same manner.[30] Central to the questions to be asked – even if absolute answers are necessarily elusive – are to what degree in contemporary esoteric discourses on nature are gender normative prescriptions reproduced, and to what degree are they challenged? Where are potential sites of slippage? How has nature as a "trope" for the pure, the uncivilized, the feminine, even the divine, been central to the construction of esoteric discourses of magical mastery and power?

The aforementioned accounts of previous work take as their object of study either the representation of gender, the attribution of gender roles and subsequent practices, or the interface of practitioner/scholar gender identity and the interpretation of esoteric discourse. In many ways these are the dominant modes with which the intersectionality of gender and the academic study of esotericism have thus far been analysed.

As detailed above, the methodological approaches to gender have been diverse. There are accounts that consider gender in a specific cultural formation without critiquing the definitions or prescriptions of the discourse. This is what Joy refers to as "gender as essentialism",[31] an approach which while recognizing a specific socio-cultural positioning – even those that are marginalized – does not critique the symbolic logic of dominant values that construct and maintain gender positions. The other main approach employs the term gender to signal a concern for deviant or marginalized positions which may or may not include a critique of discourse formation, what Joy would term "gender as a mode of subversive disturbance".[32]

It is certain that significant work in the area has been and continues to be undertaken. However, as previously noted, this is a relatively recent phenomena and the deployment of a neutral (masculine) subject characterizes much early work in the discipline. It may be that Theosophists referred to the "spiritual bodies of man" for example, as a supposedly "neutral" concept of subjectivity (something feminist philosopher Luce Irigaray would argue is not possible),[33] but that is no reason not to note the informing gender bias, if not explore its socio-cultural foundations. There are enormously rich possibilities for the application of gender theory to further studies of Western esoteric practices both in the "recovering" of marginalized figures and practices – who has been written out of "esoteric" history and why – and in the critical investigation of the valuation and creation of a spectrum of gender positions

---

30. As I hope to do in a forthcoming publication with Paul, the (now deceased) octopus who predicted the results of World Cup football matches.
31. Joy, "The Impact of Gender on Religious Studies", 95.
32. *Ibid.*, 97.
33. Irigaray, *Speculum of the Other Women*.

with esoteric discourse. That is, are there "already" spectrums of gender in esoteric discourses that have been overlooked because the dominant conceptual regime is to "sort" subjectivity (of any species, human or non-human) into male, female, androgynous? Can the implicit taint of the "devious" that accompanies esoteric traditions be critically embraced to produce "new" subjectivities? Donna Haraway's work on "emergent" subjectivities could perhaps provide a useful paradigm with which to commence any such task.[34] As I have attempted to demonstrate elsewhere, her challenges to the boundaries of human and non-human, nature and culture, can have strong resonance with esoteric concepts of the subtle body.[35]

To summarize, in the above overview of approaches it is also evident that certain esoteric groups and practices have garnered more interest than others in gender investigation: Theosophy, spiritualism, some sex magic traditions (especially Crowley), mysticism, New Age religion and neopaganism. This interest can be understood as stemming from either a clear association with sex acts and practices and/or traditions in which female figures held dominant organizational roles or featured strongly in the public consciousness, and/or groups (for example the Radical Faeries) that clearly privileged non-normative gender identities, including (but not exclusively) lesbian and gay.

Gender and esoteric epistemologies

Sitting in a sometimes conscious, sometimes unconscious relation to this selection of "objects" of study is the issue of the way in which the epistemologies valorized and utilized by esoteric traditions are gendered. This is a multi-layered consideration, which takes into account the gendering of esoteric discourses in relation to dominant modes of rationality, as well as the way in which, within the dynamic corpus of Western esotericism, certain knowledges and practices are clearly feminized and masculinized. As alternate epistemologies (creative imagination, symbolic and ontological correspondences, intuition, higher perception, etc.) are a core feature of esoteric discourse, consideration of the gendering of these epistemologies (within both dominant and esoteric discourse) should be requisite for the field. Such studies would not be about "gender in" esotericism but rather "gender as foundational/formative" to Western esotericism.

Given this central placement of creative practice, active imaginative and correspondent logic in Western esotericism (including in Faivre's oft-cited "tenets")[36] it is not surprising that part of the traditions' "deviant" aura results from the non-normative epistemologies valorized in their discourse and

---

34. Haraway, *Simians, Cyborgs and Women*.
35. Johnston, "Cyborgs and Chakras".
36. Faivre, *Access to Western Esotericism*, 10–12.

employed in their practices. These are implicit in the socio-cultural "othering" of esotericism in a general sense, and with regard to contemporary "occulture"[37] they are part of their popular appeal.

Over the last few decades cultural studies and feminist philosophy have contributed significantly to thinking through both the gendering of knowledge and of the senses (see for example the work of Genevieve Lloyd, David Howes and Constance Classen).[38] This work uncovered implicit bias in the valuation and regard of certain types of knowledge, which are conceptually linked to normative prescriptions of gender identity. Thus women were presented as "naturally" (a troubling word if ever there was one) more emotional, which at best resulted in heightened perception but much more commonly carried associations of emotional liability and in increased innate risk to hysteria or nefarious "spirit possession". Without recounting these arguments in detail, it is enough to note in this context that such binaries (reason–emotion) and privileging of the "masculinized" sense of vision over the "feminized" touch have also been critiqued in their application in contemporary "wellbeing spirituality" and healing practices associated with New Age religion,[39] but this remit could be most usefully broadened.

Therefore, on one level esoteric practices challenge the dominance of a certain type of scientific reason privileged by dominant discourse. This is in part their appeal. On the other hand, normative gender associations continue to be reproduced in esoteric discourses and practices. The most obvious generalization aligns male subjectivity with ritual magic or the "occult" *sciences* and female subjectivity with "intuitive" knowledge (with the caveat that in Theosophical discourse intuition is highly masculinized and the feminine is associated with unruly emotional, "astral" states) and with a multiplicity of forms of nature spirituality. This is the "men do magic/occult and women are witches/mediums" trope. There are of course exceptions to this (a bit) naughty generalization, but it does broadly seem that this dimorphic association features not only as an element of the object of study – movement, discourse, epistemology, practice, belief, ritual etc. – but is also reproduced in academic analysis.

QUEERING THE ESOTERIC: FLUID SUBJECTS FOR FLUID OBJECTS

This final section turns to discuss possibly the most vibrant and contentious application of gender theory to esoteric subject matter (including esoteric

---

37. On "occulture" see Partridge, *The Re-enchantment of the West*. Also cf. Chapter 6 of the present volume.
38. See Lloyd, *The Man of Reason*; Howes, *The Sixth Sense Reader*; Classen, *The Colour of Angels*.
39. See Barcan, *Complementary and Alternative Medicine*.

epistemologies): that of queer theory. As with the term gender itself, the term queer is encircled by debates as to its application and whether its deployment – now thoroughly part of academic gender discourse – has made the use of "queer" itself redundant.

Emerging out of critical gender studies, queer signals unstable genders and sexualities and is most often associated with a desire to trouble gender identity politics. As Annamarie Jagose recounts: "Queer theory's debunking of stable sexes, genders and sexualities develops out of a specifically lesbian and gay reworking of the poststructuralist figuring of identity as a constellation of multiple and unstable positions."[40] It therefore carries within it a deliciously fluid and open notion of subjectivity, gender and sexuality that inherently undermines not only dualist logic, but (crucially) the construction of any type of stable gender identity (normative or non-normative). Indeed, Jagose argues that queer's applicability "to any number of discussions" is the result of its disassociation from "specific identity categories".[41]

The process of "queering" has been taking place in numerous academic disciplines, and, as noted before, Jenny Blain takes up the queer "approach" in her consideration of *seidr*. In regard to modern esotericism, it has been applied to movements like Spiritualism (which are more commonly read vis-à-vis discourses on women's emancipation and the crisis of faith in late Victorian society). Molly McGarry unfurls queer in this context as follows:

> From a twenty-first century standpoint, Spiritualism seems rather queer in at least three ways: as gender deviance and resistance to gender binarism, as sexual deviance both in the form of free love, which defied the regulatory structure of heterosexual marriage, and in corporeal same-sex connections that belie easy division between the homo-social and the homosexual; and as a language of gendered practice and erotic attachment that directly influenced the seemingly secular consolidation of these categories in the name of sexological science.[42]

This is a great diagnostic for not only *what* queer might usefully do/challenge, but also clearly illustrates that the queer project itself is not a monolith, and embraces many strategies, concerns, differing objects of focus and applications.

Queer, then, has a myriad of potential applications within the study of contemporary Western esotericism. It can be employed to disrupt normative epistemological binaries (exoteric–esoteric; male–female; homo–hetero,

---

40. Jagose, *Queer Theory*, 3.
41. *Ibid.*, 2.
42. McGarry, *Ghosts of Futures Past*, 159.

etc.) and, in so doing, open out multiplicitous subject positions.[43] However, to queer esotericism is not only to mark fluid subject positions and analyse their critical positioning, it is also to ask questions of the discipline's own investment in stable identities and positioning. What is it to queer esotericism's status as "other" to dominant discourse? Can queer refigure the discipline's own discursive identities? That is, can we trouble the set of conceptual dualisms that position esotericism as either personal spiritual practice and academic field of study? Thinking through the division drawn in the academy between theory and practice is one such avenue for "queering" the study of esotericism. What presumptions of subjectivity, scholarship and validity rest upon aligning oneself too closely with either of these dichotomous terms? What spectrum of relations are we missing by employing the theory–practice dualism at all? Is it as "simple" as identifying an inherited conceptual Cartesian bias between the physical–doing (feminine) and the conceptual–thinking (masculine)? Surely not. Wrapped up in such distinctions between practitioners and scholars are the very foundations of academic identity as detached mastery of subject; mastery of discourse. Identities of course troubled no-end by poststructural critiques of the objective author. As Fowden has argued about the division of the *Hermetica* into "technical" and "philosophical" works, a commitment to such categorical imperatives can make invisible their shared characteristics and import a division that made no conceptual sense at the time of their creation.[44]

Indeed, at a superficial level it may seem that the study of esotericism as an academic endeavour is by nature queer with regard to its former (and current?) academic marginalization and its multiple conceptual lineages that privilege qualities and ontologies of fluidity, multiplicity, as well as its emphasis – in practice and theory – on relations. As Jagose notes, queer's "definitional indeterminacy, its elasticity, is one of its constituent characteristics",[45] and the field of Western esotericism is nothing if not elastic and mercurial.

However, not only is it apparent that gender identity markers – implicitly or explicitly – remain resolutely normative/deviant and fixed in much scholarship on gender and contemporary esotericism, but also that the field's own identity-as-other, its assumed "innate" deviance and sexualization is itself a fixed identity that may usefully prosper in as yet unknown ways if not only its objects of study are queered but also its disciplinary formation. Such a project is conceptually slippery terrain, and while some academics would seek to highlight esotericism's deviance as part of its identity, others desire to mark its normalcy and integral place within the academy. Both are strategically valid and exceptionally useful positions. But to "queer" is to upset the dialogic. At

---

43. For an example, see Chapter 6 of the present volume, in which Christopher Partridge discusses Genesis P-Orridge's body-transforming art and queering of gender.
44. Fowden, *The Egyptian Hermes*.
45. Jagose, *Queer Theory*, 1.

the heart of both such positions is the negotiation of "otherness": an otherness that is made stable if celebrated or erased if integrated. Is an otherness so mastered still an otherness? Are these the only two options? It will surprise none that I do not have an answer to the question: I do however suspect that esotericism's mercurial heritage and contemporary diversity might signal more confounding possibilities for the thinking of disciplinary identities and boundaries. So, even though, perhaps inherently unanswerable I will keep asking the question as the range of possibilities will continue to trouble at least my own conceptual predispositions.

This last section, while introducing an increasingly prominent aspect of gender analysis in esoteric discourse, ventured a little further afield in discussing disciplinary identity. This itself is an application of gender as a critical category of inquiry wherein not only the gender of one's specific objects of study are considered, but also the gendered position of knowledges and disciplines. The saucy taint of deviance remains an enduring marker of esoteric discourses (both in general public discourse and academically). Perhaps it is time to trouble – in deliciously unresolved ways – that condiment's staple ingredients.

BIBLIOGRAPHY, DISCOGRAPHY AND FILMOGRAPHY

BIBLIOGRAPHY

Adorno, Theodor W. "Theses against Occultism". In his *The Stars Down to Earth and Other Essays on the Irrational in Culture*, 128–34. London: Routledge, 1994.

Afrika, Llaila O. *Nutricide: The Nutritional Destruction of the Black Race*. New York: A & B Publishers, 2000.

Akhmadov, Ilyas & Miriam Lanskoy. *The Chechen Struggle: Independence Won and Lost*. New York: Palgrave Macmillan, 2010.

Albanese, Catherine. *Nature Religion in America: Algonkian Indians to the New Age*. Chicago, IL: University of Chicago Press, 1991.

Alexa. "About the Alexa Traffic Rankings". www.alexa.com/help/traffic-learn-more (accessed 24 November 2010).

Alexa. "Sites Linking In – but I have more than that!". www.alexa.com/faqs/?p=91 (accessed 23 May 2012).

Alisauskiene, Milda. "The Peculiarities of Lithuanian Satanism: Between Crime and Atheism in Cyberspace". In Petersen, *Contemporary Religious Satanism*, 121–29.

Allen, Garland E. "Mechanism, Vitalism and Organicism in Late Nineteenth and Twentieth-Century Biology: The Importance of Historical Context". *Studies in the History and Philosophy of Biological and Biomedical Science* 36 (2005): 261–83.

Aloi, Peg. "Rooted in the Occult Revival: Neo-Paganism's Evolving Relationship with Popular Media". In Murphy Pizza & James R. Lewis (eds), *Handbook of Contemporary Paganism*, 539–74. Leiden: Brill, 2009.

Anderson, Benedict. *Imagined Communities: Reflection on the Origin and Spread of Nationalism*. Revised edition. New York: Verso, 2006 [1983].

Anderson, Lorie. "Indigo: The Color of Money", 2003. www.selectsmart.com/twyman.html (accessed 6 June 2009).

Anderson, Walter Truett. *The Upstart Spring. Esalen and the Human Potential Movement: The First Twenty Years*. Lincoln, NE: iUniverse, 2004.

Andersson, Ken. *Hitler and the Occult*. New York: Prometheus Books, 2005.

Anon. "Interview of Shamil Basayev to Channel 4 News". *Kavkaz Tsentr*, 4 February 2005. www.kavkazcenter.com/eng/content/2005/02/04/3500.shtml (accessed 16 May 2012).

Anon. "No-one Can Prevent Me from Doing what God Permits Me to Do". *Kavkaz Tsentr*, 24 March 2005. www.kavkazcenter.com/eng/content/2005/03/24/3640_print.html (accessed 16 May 2012).

Anon. "Putin Meets with Famous Brazilian Writer Paulo Coelho". *RIA Novosti*, 1 June 2006. http://en.rian.ru/russia/20060601/48934990.html.

Anon. "Reading the Book of Life; White House Remarks On Decoding of Genome". *The New York Times online*, 27 June 2000. www.nytimes.com/2000/06/27/science/reading-the-book-of-life-white-house-remarks-on-decoding-of-genome.html?pagewanted=all (accessed 16 May 2012).

Anon. "Rebels' Dilemma after Basayev Death". *BBC News*, 12 July 2006. http://news.bbc.co.uk/2/hi/europe/5168984.stm (accessed 16 May 2012).

Anon. "Reign of Terror". *ABC Nightline*, 28 July 2005. Transcript available at http://web.archive.org/web/20060131105425/http://mkazmin.com/pages/ntl50728.doc (accessed 9 June 2012).

Anon. "What They're Reading: Chechnya's Literary Pyre". *Foreign Policy* 141, March/April 2004.

"Anonymous" (hacker group). "Message to Scientology". *Wikisource.org*, 2008. http://en.wikisource.org/wiki/Message_to_Scientology (accessed 20 December 2010).

Antes, Peter, Armin W. Geertz & Randi R. Warne (eds). *New Approaches to the Study of Religion. Volume 1: Regional, Critical and Historical Approaches*. Berlin: Walter De Gruyter, 2004.

Appadurai, Arjun. *Modernity at Large: Cultural Dimensions of Globalization*. Minneapolis, MN: University of Minneapolis Press, 1996.

Appiah, Kwame Anthony. "Europe Upside Down: Fallacies of the New Afrocentrism". In Richard Roy Grinker & Christopher B. Steiner (eds), *Perspectives on Africa*, 728–31. Oxford: Blackwell, 1997.

Aquarian Dreams. 2003. "Aquarian Dreams". www.aquariandreams.com/shop/viewCategories.asp (accessed 1 March 2011).

Aquino, Michael A. *The Church of Satan*. 6th edition. San Francisco, CA: Temple of Set, 2009. www.xeper.org/maquino/nm/COS.pdf (accessed 16 May 2012).

Arias, Juan. *Paulo Coelho: Confessions of a Pilgrim*. London: Harper, 2001.

Aries, Philippe. *Centuries of Childhood: A Social History of Family Life*. New York: Vintage, 1962.

Arvidsson, Stefan. *Aryan Idols: Indo-European Mythology as Ideology and Science*. Chicago, IL: University of Chicago Press, 2006.

Asad, Talal. *Formations of the Secular: Christianity, Islam, Modernity*. Stanford, CA: Stanford University Press, 2003.

Asante, Molefi Kete. *An Afrocentric Manifesto*. Cambridge: Polity Press, 2007.

Asante, Molefi Kete. *Afrocentricity: A Theory for Social Change*. Chicago, IL: African American Images, 2003.

Asante, Molefi Kete. *The Egyptian Philosophers: Ancient African Voices from Imhotep to Akhenaten*. Chicago, IL: African American Images, 2000.

Asante, Molefi Kete. "A Quick Reading of Rhetorical Jingoism: Anthony Appiah and his Fallacies". www.asante.net/articles/11/a-quick-reading-of-rhetorical-jingoism-anthony-appiah-and-his-fallacies (accessed 3 November 2010).

Ashby, Muata. *Egyptian Yoga: The Philosophy of Enlightenment*. Miami, FL: Sema Institute, 2005.

Asprem, Egil. *Arguing with Angels: Enochian Magic and Modern Occulture*. Albany, NY: SUNY Press, 2012.

Asprem, Egil. "Heathens up North: Politics, Polemics, and Contemporary Paganism in Norway". *The Pomegranate* 10.1 (2008): 42–69.

Asprem, Egil. "*Kabbalah Recreata*: Reception and Adaptation of Kabbalah in Modern Occultism". *The Pomegranate* 9.2 (2007): 132–53.

Asprem, Egil. "Magic Naturalized? Negotiating Science and Occult Experience in Aleister Crowley's 'Scientific Illuminism'". *Aries* 8.2 (2008): 139–65.

Asprem, Egil. "A Nice Arrangement of Heterodoxies: William McDougall and the Professionalization of Psychical Research". *Journal of the History of the Behavioral Sciences* 46.2 (2010): 123–43.

Asprem, Egil. "På Epleslang i Kunnskapens Tre: En Kritisk Drøfting av Teori i Nyere Esoterismeforskning". *Din* 1–2 (2009): 5–27.

Asprem, Egil. "Parapsychology: The Naturalization of the Supernatural, the Re-enchantment of Science". In Lewis & Hammer, *Handbook of Religion and the Authority of Science*, 633–70.

Atack, Jon. *A Piece of Blue Sky: Scientology, Dianetics and L. Ron Hubbard Exposed*. New York: Carol Publishing Group, 1990.

Aupers, Stef. "'Where the Zeros Meet the Ones': Exploring the Affinity between Magic and Computer Technology". In Aupers & Houtman, *Religions of Modernity*, 219–38.

Aupers, Stef & Dick Houtman (eds). *Religions of Modernity: Relocating the Sacred to the Self and the Digital.* Leiden: Brill, 2010.

Ausar Auset Society. "Florida Study Group". www.aasorlando.org (accessed 3 November 2010).

Austin, Algernon. *Achieving Blackness: Race, Black Nationalism, and Afrocentrism in the Twentieth Century.* New York: New York University Press, 2006.

Avatar Éditions. "Website". www.avatareditions.com (accessed 15 October 2010).

Babitsky, Andrey. "Segodna Voyuet ves' Chechensky Narod!" *Chechenpress*, 17 August 2005. http://web.archive.org/web/20070927205354/www.chechenpress.info/events/2005/08/17/06.shtml (accessed 16 May 2012).

Baddeley, Gavin. *Lucifer Rising: Sin, Devil Worship and Rock 'n' Roll.* London: Plexus, 2000.

Baiev, Khassan (with Ruth & Nicholas Daniloff). *The Oath: A Surgeon Under Fire.* New York: Walker & Co., 2004.

Baigent, Michael, Richard Leigh, & Henry Lincoln. *Holy Blood, Holy Grail.* London: Dell, 1982.

Bainbridge, William S. "Expanding the Use of the Internet in Religious Research". *Review of Religious Research* 49.1 (2007): 7–20.

Bainbridge, William S. *Satan's Power: A Deviant Psychotherapy Cult.* Berkeley, CA: University of California Press, 1978.

Barber, Malcolm. *The New Knighthood: A History of the Order of the Temple.* Cambridge: Cambridge University Press, 1994.

Barcan, Ruth. *Complementary and Alternative Medicine: Bodies, Therapies, Senses.* Oxford: Berg, 2011.

Baren, Martin. "Multimodal treatment for ADHD". *Patient Care* 29.20 (1995): 77–94.

Barkun, Michael. *A Culture of Conspiracy: Apocalyptic Visions in Contemporary America.* Berkeley, CA: University of California Press, 2003.

Barkun, Michael. "Religion and Secrecy after September 11". *Journal of the American Academy of Religion* 74.2 (2006): 275–301.

Barkun, Michael. *Religion and the Racist Right.* Chapel Hill, NC: North Carolina University Press, 1994.

Barnes, Carol. *Melanin: The Chemical Key to Black Greatness.* Chicago, IL: Lushena Books, 2001.

Barrett, David V. "Chaos Magick". In Peter B. Clarke (ed.), *Encyclopedia of New Religious Movements*, 105–6. New York: Routledge, 2006.

Barrett, David V. *Sects, "Cults" and Alternative Religions: A World Survey and Sourcebook.* London: Blandford, 1996.

Barton, Blanche. *The Church of Satan.* New York: Hell's Kitchen Productions, 1990.

Barton, Blanche. *The Secret Life of a Satanist: The Authorized Biography of Anton LaVey.* Los Angeles, CA: Feral House, 1990.

Basayev, Shamil. "Kniga Mudzhakhida", 2004. www.kavkazcenter.com/russ/islam/kniga_mudjahida (accessed 20 October 2010).

Bauduin, Tessel M. "Science, Occultism and the Art of the Avant-Garde in the Early Twentieth Century". *Journal of Religion in Europe* 5.1 (2012): 23–55.

BBC. "Anonymous Hacktivists Say Wikileaks War to Continue". *BBC News*, 9 December 2010. www.bbc.co.uk/news/technology-11935539 (accessed 16 May 2012).

BBC. "*Da Vinci Code* Wins Top Book Award". *BBC News*, 20 April 2005. http://news.bbc.co.uk/1/hi/entertainment/arts/4466933.stm (accessed 17 May 2012).

Beaumont, Justin. "Transcending the Particular in Postsecular Cities". In Molendijk et al., *Exploring the Postsecular*, 3–17.

Beck, Ulrich, Anthony Giddens & Scott Lash. *Reflexive Modernization: Politics, Tradition and Aesthetics in the Modern Social Order.* Cambridge: Polity Press, 1994.

Behar, Richard. "The Thriving Cult of Greed and Power". *Time*, 6 May 1991, 50–57.

Benavides, Gustavo. "Western Religion and the Self-Canceling of Modernity". *Journal of Religion in Europe* 1.1 (2008): 85–115.

Benjamin, Richard M. "The Bizarre Classroom of Dr Leonard Jefferies". *The Journal of Blacks in Higher Education* 2 (1993–4): 91–6.

Bennett, Vanora. *Crying Wolf: The Return of War to Chechnya.* London: Picador, 1998.

Berger, Helen, & Douglas Ezzy. *Teenage Witches: Magical Youth and the Search for Self.* New Brunswick, NJ: Rutgers University Press, 2007.

Berger, Peter L. "The Desecularization of the World: A Global Overview". In his *The Desecularization of the World: Resurgent Religion and World Politics*, 1–18. Grand Rapids, MI: Eerdmans Publishing Company, 1999.
Berger, Peter L. *The Sacred Canopy: Elements of a Sociological Theory of Religion*. New York: Doubleday, 1967.
Berger, Peter L. "Secularization and De-secularization". In Woodhead *et al.*, *Religions in the Modern World*, 291–8.
Berger, Peter L. & Thomas Luckmann. "Secularization and Pluralism". In *International Yearbook for the Sociology of Religion* 2 (1966): 73–84.
Berlin, Isaiah. "The Counter-Enlightenment". In his *The Proper Study of Mankind: An Anthology of Essays*, 243–68. New York: Farrar, Straus & Giroux, 2000.
Berman, Morris. *The Reenchantment of the World*. Ithaca, NY: Cornell University Press, 1981.
Bernal, Martin. *Black Athena: The Afroasiatic Roots of Classical Civilization*. Piscataway, NJ: Rutgers University Press, 1987.
Beyer, Peter & Lori Beaman (eds). *Religion, Globalization and Culture*. Leiden: Brill, 2007.
Bhambra, Gurminder K. *Rethinking Modernity: Postcolonialism and the Sociological Imagination*. Basingstoke: Palgrave Macmillan, 2007.
Binder, Amy J. *Contentious Curricula: Afrocentrism and Creationism in American Public Schools*. Princeton, NJ: Princeton University Press, 2003.
Biroco, Joel. *KAOS 14*. London: The Kaos-Babalon Press, 2002. www.biroco.com/kaos/kaos.pdf (accessed 16 May 2012).
Birren, Faber. *Color Psychology and Color Therapy: A Factual Study of the Influence of Color on Human Life*. New Hyde Park, NY: University Books, 1961.
Birren, Faber. *New Horizons in Color*. New York: Reinhold Publishing Corporation, 1955.
Blain, Jenny. *Nine Worlds of Seid-Magic: Ecstasy and Neo-Shamanism in North European Paganism*. London: Routledge, 2002.
Blavatsky, Helena P. *The Secret Doctrine*. 2 vols. London: The Theosophical Publishing Company, 1888.
Blond, Phillip (ed.). *Post-Secular Philosophy: Between Philosophy and Theology*. London: Routledge, 1998.
Bloom, William. *First Steps: An Introduction to Spiritual Practice*. Forres: Findhorn Press, 1993.
Blotsky, Oleg. "Shamil Basaev". 28 September 2006 [3 December 1996]. http://zhurnal.lib.ru/b/blockij_o_m/shamilxbasaew.shtml (accessed 17 May 2012).
Bly, John. *Iron John: A Book About Men*. Reading, MA: Addison-Wesley, 1990.
Bochinger, Christoph. *"New Age" und Moderne Religion: Religionswissenschaftliche Untersuchungen*. Gütersloh: Kaiser, 1994.
Bogdan, Henrik. "The Sociology of the Construct of Tradition and Import of Legitimacy in Freemasonry". In Kilcher, *Constructing Tradition*, 239–52.
Bogdan, Henrik. *Western Esotericism and Rituals of Initiation*. Albany, NY: SUNY Press, 2007.
Bookchin, Murray, "Social Ecology versus Deep Ecology: A Challenge for the Ecology Movement". *Green Perspectives: Newsletter of the Green Program Project* 4.5 (1987). http://libcom.org/library/social-versus-deep-ecology-bookchin (accessed 17 May 2012).
Bouchet, Christian. *Karl Maria Wiligut: Le Raspoutine D'Himmler*. Paris: Avatar Éditions, 2007.
Bourdieu, Pierre. "The Forms of Capital". In John G. Richardson (ed.), *Handbook of Theory and Research for the Sociology of Education*, 241–58. New York: Greenwood Press, 1986.
Bowler, Peter J. *Science for All: The Popularization of Science in Early Twentieth-Century Britain*. Chicago, IL: University of Chicago Press, 2009.
Bowman, Donna. "The Gnostic Illusion: Problematic Realized Eschatology in *The Matrix Reloaded*". *Journal of Religion and Popular Culture* 4 (2003). www.usask.ca/relst/jrpc/art4-matrixreloaded-print.html (accessed 16 May 2012).
Bradley, Michael. "Official Homepage". www.michaelbradley.info (accessed 3 November 2010).
Brandt, Christina. *Metapher und Experiment: Von der Virusforschung zum Genetischen Code*. Göttingen: Wallstein, 2004.
Breckenridge, Jr, Paul G. "Decision". *Church of Scientology of California v. Gerald Armstrong*, Superior Court of the State of California, No. C421053, 22 June 1984.
Breuer, Stefan. "Magie, Zauber, Entzauberung". In Hans G. Kippenberg & Martin Riesebrodt (eds), *Max Webers 'Religionssystematik'*, 119–30. Tübingen: J. C. B. Mohr (Paul Siebeck), 2001.

Brierley, Peter. *Pulling Out of the Nosedive: A Contemporary Picture of Churchgoing*. London: Christian Research, 2006.
Brierley, Peter. "Religion". In Albert H. Halsey & Josephine Webb (eds), *Twentieth-Century British Social Trends*, 650–74. Basingstoke: Macmillan, 2000.
Brill, Ann & Ashley Packard. "Silencing Scientology's Critics on the Internet: A Mission Impossible?" *Communications and the Law* 19.4 (1997): 1–23.
Brooks, Paul. *The House of Life: Rachel Carson at Work*. Boston, MA: Houghton Mifflin, 1972.
Brown, Callum G. *The Death of Christian Britain*. London: Routledge, 2001.
Brown, Dan. *Angels and Demons*. New York: Pocket Books, 2000.
Brown, Dan. *The Da Vinci Code*. London: Corgi Books, 2004.
Brown, Michael F. *The Channeling Zone: American Spirituality in an Anxious Age*. Cambridge, MA: Harvard University Press, 1997.
Brown, Scot. *Fighting for US: Maulana Karenga, the US Organization, and Black Cultural Nationalism*. New York: New York University Press, 2003.
Brown, Susan Love. "Baby Boomers, American Character, and the New Age: A Synthesis". In Lewis & Melton, *Perspectives on the New Age*, 87–96.
Bruce, Steve. *God is Dead: Secularization in the West*. Oxford: Blackwell, 2002.
Bruce, Steve. *Religion in the Modern World: From Cathedrals to Cults*. Oxford: Oxford University Press, 1996.
Brunotte, Ulrike. *Zwischen Eros und Krieg: Männerbund und Ritual in der Moderne*. Berlin: Klaus Wagenbach Verlag, 2004.
Bührmann, Andrea D. & Werner Schneider. *Vom Diskurs zum Dispositiv*. Bielefeld: transcript, 2008.
Burr, Vivien. *An Introduction to Social Constructionism*. London: Routledge, 1995.
Burroughs, William S. *Ali's Smile: Naked Scientology*. Bonn: Expanded Mind Editions, 1991.
Burroughs, William S. *The Ticket That Exploded*. New York: Grove Press, 1992.
Burroughs, William S. & Allen Ginsberg. *The Yage Letters Redux*. Edited by Oliver Harris. San Francisco, CA: City Lights Books, 2006.
Burroughs, William S. & Brion Gysin. *The Third Mind*. New York: Viking Press, 1978.
Butler, Judith. *Gender Trouble: Feminism and the Subversion of Identity*. New York: Routledge, 2006 [1999].
Butler, Judith, Jürgen Habermas, Charles Taylor & Cornel West. *The Power of Religion in the Public Sphere*. Edited by Eduardo Mendieta & Jonathan van Antwerpen. New York: Columbia University Press, 2011.
Calhoun, Craig, Mark Juergensmeyer & Jonathan van Antwerpen (eds). *Rethinking Secularism*. Oxford: Oxford University Press, 2011.
Callaway, Ewen. "Immaculate Creation: Birth of the First Synthetic Cell". *New Scientist*, 20 May 2010. www.newscientist.com/article/dn18942-immaculate-creation-birth-of-the-first-synthetic-cell.html (accessed 16 May 2012).
Calleja, Gordon. "Virtual Worlds Today: Gaming and Online Sociality". *Online: Heidelberg Journal of Religions on the Internet* 3.1 (2008): 7–42. http://archiv.ub.uni-heidelberg.de/volltextserver/volltexte/2008/8288/pdf/calleja.pdf (accessed 17 May 2012).
Campbell, Bruce F. *Ancient Wisdom Revived: A History of the Theosophical Movement*. Berkeley, CA: University of California Press, 1980.
Campbell, Colin. "The Cult, the Cultic Milieu and Secularization". *A Sociological Yearbook of Religion in Britain* 5 (1972): 119–36.
Campbell, Colin. *The Easternization of the West: A Thematic Account of Cultural Change in the Modern Era*. Boulder, CO: Paradigm Publishers, 2008.
Campbell, Colin. "The Secret Religion of the Educated Classes". *Sociological Analysis* 39.2 (1978): 146–56.
Campbell, Colin & Shirley McIver. "Cultural Sources of Support for Contemporary Occultism". *Social Compass* 34.1 (1987): 41–60.
Campbell, Heidi. *Exploring Religious Community Online: We are One in the Network*. New York: Peter Lang, 2005.
Campbell, Heidi. "Who's Got the Power? Religious Authority and the Internet". *Journal of Computer-Mediated Communication* 12.3 (2007). http://jcmc.indiana.edu/vol12/issue3/campbell.html (accessed 17 May 2012).

Caplan, Paula J. *They Say You're Crazy: How the World's Most Powerful Psychiatrists Decide Who's Normal*. Cambridge, MA: Da Capo Press, 1996.
Capra, Fritjof. "Deep Ecology: A New Paradigm". In Sessions, *Deep Ecology for the 21st Century*, 19–25.
Capra, Fritjof. *The Tao of Physics: An Exploration of the Parallels between Modern Physics and Eastern Mysticism*. Glasgow: Fontana, 1983 [1975].
Capra, Fritjof. *The Turning Point: Science, Society and the Rising Culture*. London: Flamingo, 1983.
Carducci, Giosuè. "Inno a Satana". In Gerhard Zacharias, *The Satanic Cult*, 1326–31. London: George Allen & Unwin.
Carrington, Hereward. *The Coming Science*. With an introduction by J. H. Hyslop. Boston, MA: Small, Maynard & Co., 1908.
Carrington, Hereward. *Eusapia Palladino and Her Phenomena*. London: T. Werner Laurie, Clifford's Inn, 1909.
Carrington, Hereward. *Personal Experiences in Spiritualism (Including the Official Account and Record of the American Palladino Séances)*. London: T. W. Laurie, 1913.
Carrington, Hereward. *The Psychic World*. London: Methuen/Dutton & Co, 1938.
Carroll, Peter. *Liber Null and Psychonaut: An Introduction to Chaos Magic*. San Francisco, CA: Red Wheel/Weiser, 1987 [originally published as two separate volumes by Morton Press, Yorkshire: *Liber Null*, 1978, and *Psychonaut*, 1981].
Carroll, Lee & Jan Tober. *The Indigo Children*. Carlsbad, CA: Hay House, 1999.
Carroll, Lee & Jan Tober. *The Indigo Children 10 Years Later*. Carlsbad, CA: Hay House, 2009.
Carson, Rachel. *Silent Spring*. Boston, MA: Houghton Mifflin.
Carter, John. *Sex and Rockets: The Occult World of Jack Parsons*. Los Angeles, CA: Feral House, 1999.
Casanova, José. *Europas Angst vor der Religion*. Berlin: Berlin University Press, 2009.
Casanova, José. *Public Religions in the Modern World*. Chicago, IL: University of Chicago Press, 1994.
Casanova, José. "Religion, European Secular Identities, and European Integration". In Timothy A. Byrnes & Peter J. Katzenstein (eds), *Religion in an Expanding Europe*, 65–92. Cambridge: Cambridge University Press, 2006.
Casanova, José. "Rethinking Secularization: A Global Comparative Perspective". In Beyer & Beaman, *Religion, Globalization and Culture*, 7–22.
Casanova, José. "The Secular and Secularisms". *Social Research* 76.4 (2009): 1049–66.
Castaneda, Carlos. *Journey to Ixtlan*. New York: Simon & Schuster, 1972.
Castaneda, Carlos. *Tales of Power*. New York: Simon & Schuster, 1974.
Castaneda, Carlos. *The Teachings of Don Juan: A Yaqui Way of Knowledge*. Berkeley, CA: University of California Press, 1968.
Castells, Manuel. *The Rise of the Network Society*. 2nd edition. Oxford: Blackwell, 2000 [1996].
Centro Studi La Runa. "Info". www.centrostudilaruna.it/info (accessed 15 October 2010).
Chadayev, Umalt. "12th Anniversary of Basayev's Raid on Budyonnovsk". *Prague Watchdog*, 15 June 2007. www.watchdog.cz/?show=000000-000005-000004-000144&lang=1 (accessed 16 May 2012).
Chase, Alston. "The Great Green Deep-Ecology Revolution". *Rolling Stone* 498, 29 April 1987.
Childs, Joe & Frank C. Tobin. "Scientology: The Truth Rundown". *St Petersburg Times*, 29 June 2009. www.tampabay.com/specials/2009/reports/project (accessed 20 December 2010).
Christensen, Dorthe Refslund. "Inventing L. Ron Hubbard: On the Construction and Maintenance of the Hagiographic Mythology of Scientology's Founder". In James R. Lewis & Jesper A. Petersen (eds), *Controversial New Religions*, 227–58. New York: Oxford University Press, 2005.
Church of Satan. "Satanic Bunco Sheet". www.churchofsatan.com/Pages/Bunco.html (accessed 5 November 2010).
Church of Scientology. "Letter". *The Sunday Times*, 28 December 1969.
Clark, John. "How Wide is Deep Ecology?". In Katz *et al.*, *Beneath the Surface*, 3–16.
Clark, Lynn Schofield. *From Angels to Aliens: Teenagers, the Media, and the Supernatural*. New York: Oxford University Press, 2003.

Clark, Lynn Schofield. "Religion, Twice Removed: Exploring the Role of Media in Religious Understandings among 'Secular' Young People". In Nancy Ammerman (ed.), *Everyday Religion: Observing Modern Religious Lives*, 69–81. New York: Oxford University Press, 2007.

Clark, Lynn Schofield, Stewart M. Hoover & Lee Rainie (eds). *Faith Online*. Washington, DC: Pew Internet & American Life Project, 2004. http://pewinternet.org/~/media//Files/Reports/2004/PIP_Faith_Online_2004.pdf.pdf (accessed 17 May 2012).

Clarke, Peter B. *New Religions in Global Perspective: A Study of Religious Change in the Modern World*. London: Routledge, 2006.

Clarke, Peter B. (ed.). *The Oxford Handbook of the Sociology of Religion*. Oxford: Oxford University Press, 2009.

Classen, Constance. *The Colour of Angels: Cosmology, Gender and the Aesthetic Imagination*. London: Routledge, 1998.

Coale, Samuel Chase. *Paradigms of Paranoia: The Culture of Conspiracy in Contemporary American Fiction*. Tuscaloosa, AB: University of Alabama Press, 2005.

Codreanu, Corneliu. *The Prison Notes*. London: Arktos Media, 2011.

Coelho, Paulo. *The Alchemist*. London: Harper, 2002.

Coelho, Paulo. *Kniga Voina Sveta*. Moscow: AST/Astrel, 2010.

Coelho, Paulo. *Manual of the Warrior of Light*. London: Harper, 2003.

Coelho, Paulo. *The Pilgrimage*. London: Harper, 2005.

Coelho, Paulo. *The Valkyries*. London: Harper, 2007.

Colclough, Stephen. *Consuming Texts: Readers and Reading Communities, 1695–1860*. Basingstoke: Palgrave Macmillan, 2007.

Cole, David & James X. Dempsey. *Terrorism and the Constitution: Sacrificing Civil Liberties in the Name of National Security*. New York: The New Press, 2002.

Collins, Patricia Hill. *From Black Power to Hip Hop: Racism, Nationalism, and Feminism*. Philadelphia, PA: Temple University Press, 2006.

Connery, Brian A. "IMHO: Authority and Egalitarian Rhetoric in the Virtual Coffeehouse". In Porter, *Internet Culture*, 161–80.

Coogan, Kevin. *Dreamer of the Day: Francis Parker Yockey and the Postwar Fascist International*. Brooklyn, NY: Autonomedia, 1999.

Cook, John. "Cult Friction". *Radar*, April 2008. www.anti-scientologie.ch/cult-friction.htm (accessed 17 May 2012).

Corradi-Musi, Carla. "Supernatural Heroes in Finno-Ugric Shamanism". In Hoppál & Pentikäinen, *Northern Religions and Shamanism*, 127–33.

Corrigan, John. *Business of the Heart: Religion and Emotion in the Nineteenth Century*. Berkeley, CA: University of California Press, 2002.

Corrigan, John (ed.). *Religion and Emotion: Approaches and Interpretations*. Oxford: Oxford University Press, 2004.

CosmiKids. "CosmiKids – Open Minds. Pure Potential". www.cosmikids.org (accessed 23 June 2009).

Cowan, Douglas E. "Contested Spaces: Movement, Countermovement and E-Space Propaganda". In Dawson & Cowan, *Religion Online*, 233–49.

Cowan, Douglas E. *Cyberhenge: Modern Pagans on the Internet*. New York: Routledge, 2005.

Cowan, Douglas E. "Researching Scientology: Perceptions, Premises and Problematics". In Lewis, *Scientology*, 53–79.

Crabtree, Vexen. "The Descriptions, Philosophies and Justification of Satanism". www.dpjs.co.uk (accessed 5 November 2010).

Cross, Máire Fedelma (ed.). *Gender and Fraternal Orders in Europe, 1300–2000*. Basingstoke: Palgrave Macmillan, 2010.

Crowley, Aleister. *Magick in Theory and Practice*. Edison, NJ: Castle Books, 1991.

Crowley, Aleister. "Magick in Theory and Practice". In Aleister Crowley with Mary Desti & Leila Waddell, *Magick: Liber ABA*, 119–290. San Francisco, CA: Weiser Books, 1997.

Crowley, Aleister. "The Vision and the Voice". *The Equinox* 1.5 (1911): 1–176.

Cuneo, Michael W. *American Exorcism: Expelling Demons in the Land of Plenty*. New York: Broadway Books, 2002.

Cunningham, Hugh. *Children and Childhood in Western Society Since 1500*. Harlow: Pearson, 2005.

Cunningham, Hugh. *The Invention of Childhood*. London: BBC Books, 2006.
Curry, Richard. *Freedom at Risk: Secrecy, Censorship and Repression in the 1980s*. Philadelphia, PA: Temple University Press, 1988.
Cusack, Carole M. *Invented Religions: Imagination, Fiction and Faith*. Farnham: Ashgate, 2010.
Cusack, Carole M. & Christopher Hartney (eds). *Religion and Retributive Logic: Essays in Honour of Professor Garry W. Trompf*. Leiden: Brill, 2010.
Dahl, Göran. *Radikalare än Hitler? De Esoteriska och Gröna Nazisterna. Inspirationskällor. Pionjärer. Förvaltare. Ättlingar*. Stockholm: Atlantis, 2006.
Davidsen, Markus. "What is Wrong with Pagan Studies? A Review Essay on the *Handbook of Contemporary Paganism*". *Method and Theory in the Study of Religion* 24 (2012): 183–99.
Davie, Grace. *Europe: The Exceptional Case: Parameters of Faith in the Modern World*. London: Darton, Longman & Todd, 2002.
Davies, Norman. *Europe: A History*. New York: HarperCollins, 2007.
Davies, Owen. *Grimoires: A History of Magic Books*. Oxford: Oxford University Press, 2009.
Davis, Erik. *Techgnosis: Myth, Magic and Mysticism in the Age of Information*. New York: Three Rivers Press, 1998.
Davis, Erik. "Technopagans: May the Astral Plane be Reborn in Cyberspace". *Wired* 3.07 (1995). www.wired.com/wired/archive/3.07/technopagans.html (accessed 16 May 2012).
Davis, Philip G. *Goddess Unmasked: The Rise of Neopagan Feminist Spirituality*. Dallas, TX: Spence Publishing, 1998.
Dawson, Lorne L. "The Mediation of Religious Experience in Cyberspace". In Højsgaard & Warburg, *Religion and Cyberspace*, 15–37.
Dawson, Lorne L. "Religion and the Internet: Presence, Problems, and Prospects". In Antes *et al.*, *New Approaches to the Study of Religion*, 385–405.
Dawson, Lorne L. "Religion and the Quest for Virtual Community". In Dawson & Cowan, *Religion Online*, 75–89.
Dawson, Lorne L. & Douglas E. Cowan (eds). *Religion Online: Finding Faith on the Internet*. New York: Routledge, 2004.
Day, John V. "In Quest of Our Linguistic Ancestors: The Elusive Origins of the Indo-Europeans". *The Occidental Quarterly* 2.3 (2002). www.scribd.com/doc/46512347/John-v-Day-In-Quest-of-Our-Linguistic-Ancestors-The-Elusive-Origins-of-the-Indo-Europeans (accessed 17 May 2012).
de Benoist, Alain. *On Being a Pagan*. Atlanta, GA: Ultra, 2004.
de Benoist, Alain. *Vu de Droite: Anthologie critique des idées contemporaines*. Paris: Le Labyrinthe, 2001.
De Caro, Mario & David Macarthur (eds). *Naturalism in Question*. Cambridge, MA: Harvard University Press, 2004.
Dede, Chris. "Immersive Interfaces for Engagement and Learning". *Science* 323 (2009): 66–9.
Defesche, Sacha. "The 2012 Phenomenon: A Historical and Typological Approach to a Modern Apocalyptic Mythology". *Skepsis* 2008. http://skepsis.no/?p=599 (accessed 17 May 2012).
Delany, Martin Robison. "Origin and Objects of Ancient Freemasonry". In Martin R. Delany (ed.), *A Documentary Reader*, 46–67. Chapel Hill, NC: The University of North Carolina Press, 2003.
De Montellano, Bernard Ortiz. "Melanin, Afrocentricity and Pseudoscience". *Yearbook of Physical Anthropology* 36 (1993): 33–58.
De Montellano, Bernard Ortiz. "Multicultural Pseudoscience: Spreading Scientific Illiteracy Among Minorities". *Skeptical Inquirer* 16.1 (1991): 46–50.
DeNora, Tia. "Aesthetic Agency and Musical Practice: New Directions in the Sociology of Music". In Patrik N. Juslin & John A. Sloboda (eds), *Music and Emotion: Theory and Research*, 161–80. Oxford: Oxford University Press, 2001.
DeNora, Tia. *Music in Everyday Life*. Cambridge: Cambridge University Press, 2000.
Denselow, Robin. *When the Music's Over: The Story of Political Pop*. London: Faber & Faber, 1989.
Denzin, Norman K. "Cybertalk and the Method of Instances". In Steve Jones (ed.), *Doing Internet Research*, 97–126. Thousand Oaks, CA: Sage, 1999.
de Rios, Marlene Dobkin & Charles S. Grob (eds). "Ayahuasca Use in Cross-Cultural Perspective". Special issue, *Journal of Psychoactive Drugs* 37.2 (2005).
Devall, Bill & George Sessions. *Deep Ecology: Living as if Nature Mattered*. Layton, UT: Gibbs Smith, 1985.

Deveney, John Patrick. *Astral Projection or Liberation of the Double and the Work of the Early Theosophical Society*. Fullerton, CA: Theosophical History, 1997.
Deveney, John Patrick. "An Unpublished Lecture by W. Q. Judge in 1876 on His Magical Progress in the Theosophical Society". *Theosophical History* 9.3 (2003): 12–20.
Devi, Savitri. *The Lightning and the Sun*. New York: Samisdat Publishers, 1979.
de Vries, Hent & Lawrence E. Sullivan (eds). *Political Theologies: Public Religions in a Post-Secular World*. New York: Fordham University Press, 2006.
Dillon, Michele. "Can Post-Secular Society Tolerate Religious Differences". *Sociology of Religion* 71.2 (2010): 139–56.
Dixon, Joy. "Sexology and the Occult: Sexuality and Subjectivity in Theosophy's New Age". In Elizabeth A. Castelli (ed.), *Women, Gender, Religion*, 288–309. New York: Palgrave, 2001.
Dobbelaere, Karel. "The Meaning and Scope of Secularization". In Clarke, *The Oxford Handbook of the Sociology of Religion*, 599–615.
Dragon Environmental Network. "Eco-Magic – Heady Mix of Paganism and Environmentalism". www.dragonnetwork.org (accessed 12 September 2010).
Drake, Richard H. "Julius Evola and the Ideological Origins of the Radical Right in Contemporary Italy". In Merkl, *Political Violence and Terror*, 61–89.
Drengson, Alan. "Editorial: Terminology of the Deep Ecology Movement". *The Trumpeter: Journal of Ecosophy* 13.3 (1996). http://trumpeter.athabascau.ca/index.php/trumpet/article/view/256/377 (accessed 17 May 2012).
Droge, Arthur J. *Homer or Moses? Early Christian Interpretations of the History of Culture*. Tübingen: J. C. B. Mohr, 1989.
Drury, Nevill S. *The New Age: The History of a Movement*. London: Thames & Hudson, 2004.
Drury, Nevill S. *Rosaleen Norton's Contribution to the Western Esoteric Tradition*. PhD thesis, School of Humanities and Social Science, University of Newcastle, Australia, 2008.
Dryden, Windy & Arthur Still. "Historical Aspects of Mindfulness and Self-Acceptance in Psychotherapy". *Journal of Rational-Emotive and Cognitive-Behavior Therapy* 24.1 (2006): 3–28.
Du Bois, William E. B. *The Souls of Black Folk*. New York: Cosmo Classics, 2007.
Dugin, Alexandr. *Osnovy Geopolitiki: Geopoliticheskoe Budushchee Rossii*. Moscow: Arktogeia, 1997.
Dugin, Alexandr. "Uchenie Zverja". www.angel.org.ru/3/crowley.html (accessed 28 March 2011)
Dugin, Alexandr. *Znaki Velikogo Norda*. Moscow: Veče, 2008.
Dunlop, John. "Beslan: Russia's 9/11?" Washington, DC: Jamestown Foundation, 2005.
Dunlop, John. "The October 2002 Moscow Hostage-Taking Incident (Part 1)". *Radio Free Europe/Radio Liberty*, 18 December 2003. www.rferl.org/articleprintview/1342392.html (accessed 16 May 2012).
Dunlop, John. "The October 2002 Moscow Hostage-Taking Incident (Part 2)". *Radio Free Europe/Radio Liberty*, 8 January 2004. www.rferl.org/articleprintview/1342329.html (accessed 16 May 2012).
Dunlop, John. "The October 2002 Moscow Hostage-Taking Incident (Part 3)". *Radio Free Europe/Radio Liberty*, 15 January 2004. www.rferl.org/articleprintview/1342330.html (accessed 16 May 2012).
Dunlop, John. *Russia Confronts Chechnya: Roots of a Separatist Conflict*. Cambridge: Cambridge University Press, 1998.
Dunlop, John. "The September 2004 Beslan Terrorist Incident: New Findings". *Center on Democracy, Development, and The Rule of Law*, CDDRL Working Paper 115 (July 2009).
Dyrendal, Asbjørn. "Devilish Consumption: Popular Culture in Satanic Socialization". *Numen* 55.1 (2008): 68–98.
Dyrendal, Asbjørn. "Hidden Persuaders and Invisible Wars: Anton LaVey and Conspiracy Culture". In Faxneld & Petersen, *The Devil's Party*, 123–39.
Dyrendal, Asbjørn. "Sykdomsindustrien. Moderne Medisin i Alternativkulturens Demonologi". *DIN: Tidsskrift for Religion og Kultur* 1–2 (2010): 141–60.
Eco, Umberto. "Ur-Fascism". *The New York Review of Books* 42.11 (1995): 12–15.
Eder, Klaus & Giancarlo Bosetti. "Post-Secularism: A Return to the Public Sphere". *Eurozine*, 17 August 2006. www.eurozine.com/articles/2006-08-17-eder-en.html (accessed 16 May 2012).

Edighoffer, Roland. "Rosicrucianism I: First Half of the 17th Century". In Hanegraaff *et al.*, *Dictionary of Gnosis and Western Esotericism*, 1009–14.
Edsman, Carl-Martin (ed.). *Studies in Shamanism*. Stockholm: Almqvist & Wiksell, 1967.
Einstein, Mara. *Brands of Faith: Marketing Religion in a Commercial Age*. New York: Routledge, 2008.
Eisenstadt, Shmuel N. *Comparative Civilizations and Multiple Modernities*. 2 vols. Leiden: Brill, 2003.
Eisenstadt, Shmuel N. (ed.). *Multiple Modernities*. New Brunswick, NJ: Transaction Publishers, 2002.
Elders, Fons. "Arne Naess, a Philosopher and a Mystic: A Commentary on the Dialogue between Alfred Ayer and Arne Naess". In Witoszek & Brennan, *Philosophical Dialogues*, 45–49.
Eliade, Mircea. *The Myth of the Eternal Return: or, Cosmos and History*. London: Arkana, 1989 [1954; original French edition 1949].
Eliade, Mircea. "Shamanism: An Overview [First Edition]". In Jones, *Encyclopedia of Religion*, 8269–74.
Eliade, Mircea. *Shamanism: Archaic Techniques of Ecstasy*. London: Arkana, 1989 [1964; original French edition 1951].
Ellwood, Robert. *The Politics of Myth: A study of C. G. Jung, Mircea Eliade and Joseph Campbell*. Albany, NY: SUNY Press, 1999.
Erlanger, Steven. "Moscow Accepts Chechnya Talks". *New York Times*, 19 June 1995. www.nytimes.com/1995/06/19/world/moscow-accepts-chechnya-talks.html?pagewanted=all&src=pm (accessed 16 May 2012).
Erlanger, Steven. "Russian Soldiers Storm a Hospital Seized by Rebels" *New York Times*, 17 June 1995. www.nytimes.com/1995/06/17/world/russian-soldiers-storm-a-hospital-seized-by-rebels.html (accessed 16 May 2012).
Ernst, Edzard. "Anthroposophy: A Risk Factor for Noncompliance with Measles Immunization". *The Pediatric Infectious Disease Journal* 30.3 (2011): 187–9.
Essential Motion, "Essential Motion". www.essential-motion.com (accessed 15 September 2010).
Eurozine. "Post-Secular Europe?" www.eurozine.com/comp/focalpoints/postseceurope.html (accessed 1 March 2011).
Evangelista, Matthew. *The Chechen Wars: Will Russia Go the Way of the Soviet Union?* Washington, DC: Brookings Institution Press, 2002.
Evans, Dave. *The History of British Magic After Crowley: Kenneth Grant, Amado Crowley, Chaos Magic, Lovecraft, The Left Hand Path, Blasphemy and Magical Morality*. London: Hidden Publishing, 2007.
Evola, Julius. *Heathen Imperialism*. France: Thompkins & Cariou, 2007.
Evola, Julius. *Introduction to Magic: Rituals and Practical Techniques for the Magus*. Rochester, VT: Inner Traditions, 2000.
Evola, Julius. *Men Among the Ruins: Postwar Reflections of a Radical Traditionalist*. Rochester, VT: Inner Traditions, 2002 [originally published in Italian as *Gli Uomini e le Rovine* in 1953].
Evola, Julius. *Orientamenti: Undici Punti*. Rome: Imperium, 1950.
Evola, Julius. *The Path of Cinnabar: An Intellectual Autobiography*. London: Integral Tradition Publishing, 2009.
Ezzy, Douglas. "The Commodification of Witchcraft". *Australian Religious Studies Review* 14.1 (2001): 31–44.
Ezzy, Douglas. "New Age Witchcraft? Popular Spell Books and the Re-enchantment of Everyday Life". *Culture and Religion* 4.1 (2003): 47–65.
Ezzy, Douglas. "White Witches and Black Magic: Ethics and Consumerism in Contemporary Witchcraft". *Journal of Contemporary Religion* 21.1 (2006): 15–31.
Faivre, Antoine. *Access to Western Esotericism*. Albany, NY: SUNY Press, 1994.
Faivre, Antoine. "Borrowings and Misreadings: Edgar Allen Poes's 'Mesmeric' Tales and the Strange Case of their Reception". *Aries* 7.1 (2007): 21–62.
Faivre, Antoine. *The Eternal Hermes*. Grand Rapids, MI: Phanes Press, 1995.
Faivre, Antoine. "Introduction I". In Antoine Faivre & Jacob Needleman (eds), *Modern Esoteric Spirituality*, xi–xxii. London: SCM, 1993.

Faivre, Antoine. "Note sur la Transmission des Traditions dans le Contexte des Courants Ésotériques Occidentaux Modernes". In Kilcher, *Constructing Tradition*, 31–46.
Fanger, Claire. "Virgin Territory: Purity and Divine Knowledge in Late Medieval Catoptromantic Texts". *Aries* 5.2 (2005): 200–24.
Farrar, Janet & Stewart Farrar. *A Witches Bible: A Complete Witches Handbook*. 3rd edition. Custer, WA: Phoenix Publishing, 1996.
Faurby, Ib & Märta-Lisa Magnusson. "The Battle(s) of Grozny". *Baltic Defence Review* 2 (1999). http://web.archive.org/web/20110310161558/http://www.caucasus.dk/publication1.htm (accessed 9 June 2012).
Fava, Sergio. "'When Rome Falls, Falls the World': *Current 93* and Apocalyptic Folk". In Christopher Partridge (ed.), *Anthems of Apocalypse: Popular Music and Apocalyptic Thought*, 72–89. Sheffield: Phoenix Press, 2012.
Faxneld, Per. "The Devil is Red: Socialist Satanism in Nineteenth and Early Twentieth Century Europe". *Numen*, forthcoming.
Faxneld, Per. *Mörkrets Apostlar: Satanism i Äldre Tid*. Sundbyberg: Ouroboros Produktion, 2006.
Faxneld, Per. "The Strange Case of Ben Kadosh: A Luciferian Pamphlet from 1906 and its Current Renaissance". *Aries* 11.1 (2011): 1–22.
Faxneld, Per. "Witches, Nihilist Anarchism and Social Darwinism: Przybyszewski's Satanism and the Demonic Feminine". In Faxneld & Petersen, *The Devil's Party*, 53–77.
Faxneld, Per & Jesper A. Petersen (eds). *The Devil's Party: Satanism in Modernity*, Oxford: Oxford University Press, 2012.
Faye, Guillaume. *Archeofuturism: European Visions of the Post-Catastrophic Age*. London: Arktos Media, 2010.
Fazekas, Jenö. "Hungarian Shamanism, Material and History of Research". In Edsman, *Studies in Shamanism*, 97–119.
Fenster, Mark. *Conspiracy Theories: Secrecy and Power in American Culture*. Minneapolis, MN: University of Minnesota Press, 1999.
Ferguson, Marilyn. *The Aquarian Conspiracy: Personal and Social Transformation in Our Time*. London: Paladin, 1982 [1980].
Ferraresi, Franco. *Threats to Democracy: The Radical Right in Italy after the War*. Princeton, NJ: Princeton University Press, 1996.
Flanagan, Owen. "Varieties of Naturalism". In Philip Clayton & Zachary Simpson (eds), *Oxford Handbook of Religion and Science*, 430–52. Oxford: Oxford University Press, 2006.
Flannery-Dailey, Frances & Rachel Wagner. "Wake Up! Gnosticism & Buddhism in *The Matrix*". *Journal of Religion and Film* 5.2 (2001). www.unomaha.edu/jrf/gnostic.htm (accessed 16 May 2012).
Flowers, Stephen E. & Michael Moynihan. *The Secret King: The Myth and Reality of Nazi Occultism*. Port Townsend, WA: Feral House, 2007.
Ford, Simon. *Wreckers of Civilisation: The Story of Coum Transmissions and Throbbing Gristle*. London: Black Dog Publishing, 1999.
Forman, Paul. "Weimar Culture, Causality, and Quantum Theory: Adaptation by German Physicists and Mathematicians to a Hostile Environment". *Historical Studies in the Physical Sciences* 3 (1971): 1–115.
Foster, Derek. "Community and Identity in the Electronic Village". In Porter, *Internet Culture*, 23–38.
Foucault, Michel. *Aesthetics, Method, and Epistemology*. Essential Works of Foucault, 1954–1984, vol. 2. London: Penguin Books, 2000.
Foucault, Michel. *The History of Sexuality. Volume One: An Introduction*. Harmondsworth: Penguin, 1990 [1976].
Foucault, Michel. *The Order of Things: An Archaeology of the Human Sciences*. London: Routledge, 1989 [1966].
Fowden, Garth. *The Egyptian Hermes: A Historical Approach to the Late Pagan Mind*. Princeton, NJ: Princeton University Press, 1986.
Fox, Warwick. "Deep Ecology: A New Philosophy of our Time". In Witoszek & Brennan, *Philosophical Dialogues*, 153–65.

Fox, Warwick. *Toward a Transpersonal Ecology: Developing New Foundations for Environmentalism*. Boston, MA: Shambhala, 1990.
François, Stephane. *Les Néo-paganismes et la Nouvelle Driote (1980–2006): Pour une Autre Approche*. Milan: Archè, 2008.
Friends of Ron. *L. Ron Hubbard: A Profile*. Los Angeles, CA: Bridge Publications, 1995.
Frisk, Liselotte. "Globalization: A Key Factor in Contemporary Religious Change". *Journal for Alternative Spiritualities and New Age Studies* 5 (2009–11). www.open.ac.uk/Arts/jasanas (accessed 16 May 2012).
Frisk, Liselotte. "The Human Potential Movement in the Nordic Countries". In Olav Hammer & Henrik Bogdan (eds), *Western Esotericism in Scandinavia*. Leiden: Brill, forthcoming.
Frisk, Liselotte. "New Age-utövare i Sverige: Bakgrund, trosföreställningar, engagemang och 'omvändelse'". In Carl-Gustav Carlsson & Liselotte Frisk (eds), *Gudars och Gudinnors Återkomst: Studier i Nyreligiositet*, 52–90. Umeå: Institutionen för Religionsvetenskap, 2000.
Frisk, Liselotte. *Nya Religiösa Rörelser i Sverige: Relation till Samhället/Världen, Anslutning och Engagemang*. Åbo: Åbo Akademi, 1993.
Frisk, Liselotte. *Nyreligiositet i Sverige: Ett Religionsvetenskapligt Perspektiv*. Nora: Nya Doxa, 1998.
Frisk, Liselotte. "Religion och Medicin inom Nyreligiositeten: Deepak Chopra och Stephen Levine som två Företrädare". *Chakra* 2 (2004): 33–46.
Frisk, Liselotte. "Some Problematic New Age Related Aspects of the Stark & Bainbridge Theory of Religion: A Case of an Old Style Paradigm of Constructing Religion". In Steven Sutcliffe & Ingvild Gilhus (eds), *New Age, The New Spirituality and Theories of Religion*. Durham: Acumen, forthcoming.
Fuller, Liz. "The Rise of Russia's 'Terrorist No. 1'". *Radio Free Europe/Radio Liberty*, 28 June 2006. www.rferl.org/content/article/1069537.html (accessed 16 May 2012).
Fuller, Neeley. *Textbook for Victims of White Supremacy*. Washington, DC: Library of Congress, 1969.
Furedi, Frank. *Therapy Culture: Cultivating Vulnerability in an Uncertain Age*. London: Routledge, 2004.
Gall, Carlotta & Thomas de Waal. *Chechnya: Calamity in the Caucasus*. New York: New York University Press, 1998.
Gallagher, Eugene. "Sources, Sects and Scripture: The 'Book of Satan' in *The Satanic Bible*". In Faxneld & Petersen, *The Devil's Party*, 103–22.
Gardell, Mattias. *Gods of the Blood: The Pagan Revival and White Separatism*. Durham, NC: Duke University Press, 2003.
Gauld, Alan. *The Founders of Psychical Research*. London: Routledge & Kegan Paul, 1968.
Geertz, Clifford. "Religion as a Cultural System". In Michael Banton (ed.), *Anthropological Approaches to the Study of Religion*, 1–46. London: Tavistock, 1966.
Geertz, Clifford. *Works and Lives: The Anthropologist as Author*. Cambridge: Polity Press, 1989.
Gibbons, Brian J. *Spirituality and the Occult: From the Renaissance to the Modern Age*. London: Routledge, 2001.
Giddens, Anthony. *The Consequences of Modernity*. Cambridge: Polity Press, 1990.
Gieryn, Thomas F. "Boundary-Work and the Demarcation of Science from Non-Science: Strains and Interests in Professional Ideologies of Scientists". *American Sociological Review* 48 (1983): 781–95.
Gieryn, Thomas F. *Cultural Boundaries of Science: Credibility on the Line*. Chicago, IL: University of Chicago Press, 1999.
Gilbert, Alan D. *The Making of Post-Christian Britain: A History of the Secularization of Modern Society*. London: Longman, 1980.
Gilbert, Robert A. *A. E. Waite: Magician of Many Parts*. Wellingborough: Crucible, 1987.
Gilmore, Peter H. "A Map for the Misdirected". 2006 [1999]. www.churchofsatan.com/Pages/Map.html (accessed 13 October 2010).
Gilmore, Peter H. *The Satanic Scriptures*. Baltimore, MD: Scapegoat Publishing, 2007.
Gilroy, Paul. *The Black Atlantic: Modernity and Double Consciousness*. Cambridge, MA: Harvard University Press, 1993.

Glasser, Harold. "Deep Ecology Clarified: A Few Fallacies and Misconceptions". *The Trumpeter: Journal of Ecosophy* 12.3 (1995). http://trumpeter.athabascau.ca/index.php/trumpet/article/view/312/471 (accessed 17 May 2012).

Glasser, Harold. "On Warwick Fox's Assessment of Deep Ecology". *Environmental Ethics* 19 (1997): 69–85.

Glasser, Harold (ed.). *Selected Works of Arne Naess*. Vol. X. Dordrecht: Springer, 2005.

Glasser, Harold. "Series Editor's Introduction". In his *Selected Works of Arne Naess*, xvii–lxii.

Godwin, Joscelyn. *Arktos: The Polar Myth in Science, Symbolism and Nazi Survival*. London: Thames & Hudson, 1993.

Godwin, Joscelyn. *The Theosopical Enlightenment*. Albany, NY: SUNY Press, 1994.

Goode, Erich. "Education, Scientific Knowledge, and Belief in the Paranormal". *Skeptical Inquirer* 26.1 (2002): 24–6.

Goode, Erich. *Paranormal Beliefs: A Sociological Introduction*. Prospect Heights, IL: Waveland Press Inc, 2000.

Goodrick-Clarke, Nicholas. *Black Sun: Aryan Cults, Esoteric Nazism and the Politics of Identity*. New York: New York University Press, 2002.

Goodrick-Clarke, Nicholas. *Hitler's Priestess: Savitri Devi, the Hindu-Aryan Myth, and Neo-Nazism*. New York: New York University Press, 2000.

Goodrick-Clarke, Nicholas. *The Occult Roots of Nazism*. New York: New York University Press, 1992.

Goodrick-Clarke, Nicholas. *The Western Esoteric Traditions: A Historical Introduction*. Oxford: Oxford University Press, 2008.

Gorenfeld, John & Sam Harris. "Controversy over Sam Harris's Atheist Views". *Skeptical Investigations*. www.skepticalinvestigations.org/Debates/Gorenfeld_Harris.html (accessed 13 March 2011).

Granholm, Kennet. "Dragon Rouge: Left-Hand Path Magic with a Neopagan Flavour". *Aries* 12.1 (2012): 131–56.

Granholm, Kennet. "Embracing Others Than Satan: The Multiple Princes of Darkness in the Left-Hand Path Milieu". In Petersen, *Contemporary Religious Satanism*, 85–103.

Granholm, Kennet. "Esoteric Currents as Discursive Complexes". *Religion* Special Issue on Discourse Analysis in the Study of Religion (2013).

Granholm, Kennet. "The Left-Hand Path and Post-Satanism: The Temple of Set and the Evolution of Satanism". In Faxneld & Petersen, *The Devil's Party*, 209–28.

Granholm, Kennet. "Locating the West: Problematizing the *Western* in Western Esotericism and Occultism". In Henrik Bogdan & Gordan Djurdjevic (eds), *Occultism in Global Perspective*. Durham: Acumen, forthcoming.

Granholm, Kennet. "*New Age* or the Mass-Popularization of Esoteric Discourse: Some Preliminary Reflections on the Reconceptualization of the New Age". Torino: CESNUR, 2008. www.cesnur.org/2008/london_granholm.htm (accessed 16 May 2012).

Granholm, Kennet. "Post-Secular Esotericism? Some Reflections on the Transformation of Esotericism". In Tore Ahlbäck (ed.), *Western Esotericism: Scripta Instituti Donneriani Aboensis 20*, 50–67. Åbo/Stockholm: Donner Institute for Research in Religious and Cultural History, 2008.

Granholm, Kennet. "'The Prince of Darkness on the Move': Transnationality and Translocality in Left-Hand Path Magic". Torino: CESNUR, 2007. www.cesnur.org/2007/bord_granholm.htm (accessed 16 May 2012).

Granholm, Kennet. "The Rune-Gild: Heathenism, Traditionalism, and the Left-Hand Path". *International Journal for the Study of New Religions* 1.1 (2010): 95–115.

Granholm, Kennet. "The Sociology of Esotericism". In Clarke, *The Oxford Handbook of the Sociology of Religion*, 783–800.

Granholm, Kennet. "'Sons of Northern Darkness': Heathen Influences in Black Metal and Neofolk Music". *Numen* 58.4 (2011): 514–44.

Gray, David. *Inside Prince Hall*. Lancaster: Anchor Communications, 2004.

Greer, Mary K. *Women of the Golden Dawn: Rebels and Priestesses*. Rochester, VT: Park St. Press, 1995.

Gregorius, Fredrik. *Modern Asatro: Att Konstruera Etnisk och Kulturell Identitet*. Lund: Lunds Universitet, 2009.
Gregory, Jane & Steve Miller. *Science in Public: Communication, Culture, and Credibility*. London: Plenum Press, 1998.
Gremillion, Zachary P. *African Origins of Freemansonry: The True History of Free Masonry in Africa and Its Resurrection among Africans in the Diaspora*. Bloomington, IN: Author House, 2005.
Griffin, David Ray. *The Reenchantment of Science: Postmodern Proposals*. Albany, NY: SUNY Press, 1988.
Griffin, Des. *Fourth Reich of the Rich*. South Pasadena, CA: Emissary Publications, 1976.
Grof, Stanislav. *Beyond the Brain: Birth, Death and Transcendence in Psychotherapy*. Albany, NY: SUNY Press, 1985.
Grof, Stanislav. *LSD Psychotherapy*. Sarasota, FL: Multidisciplinary Association for Psychedelic Studies, 1980.
Haag, Michael, & Veronica Haag. *The Rough Guide to The Da Vinci Code*. London: Penguin/Rough Guides, 2004.
Habermas, Jürgen. "An Awareness of What is Missing". In Habermas *et al.*, *An Awareness of What is Missing*, 15–23.
Habermas, Jürgen. "Die Dialektik der Säkularisierung". *Eurozine*, 15 April 2008. www.eurozine.com/articles/2008-04-15-habermas-de.html (accessed 16 May 2012).
Habermas, Jürgen. "Notes on Post-Secular Society". *New Perspectives Quarterly* 25.4 (2008): 17–29.
Habermas, Jürgen. "Religion in the Public Sphere". *European Journal of Philosophy* 14.1 (2006): 1–25.
Habermas, Jürgen. *The Structural Transformation of the Public Sphere: An Inquiry into a Category of Bourgeois Society*. Cambridge, MA: The MIT Press, 1989 [1962].
Habermas, Jürgen. *Strukturwandel der Öffentlichkeit*. Neuwied: Luchterhand, 1962.
Habermas, Jürgen. *The Theory of Communicative Action: A Critique of Functionalist Reason*. Vol. 2. Trans. Thomas McCarthy. London: Polity Press, 1987.
Habermas, Jürgen *et al. An Awareness of What is Missing: Faith and Reason in a Post-Secular Age*. Cambridge: Polity Press, 2010.
Hacking, Ian. *Historical Ontology*. Cambridge, MA: Harvard University Press, 2002.
Hadden, Jeffrey K. & Douglas E. Cowan. "Virtually Religious: New Religious Movements and the World Wide Web". In Lewis, *The Oxford Handbook of New Religious Movements*, 119–40.
Hahn, Gordon. "Anti-Americanism, Anti-Westernism, and Anti-Semitism among Russia's Muslims". *Demokratizatsia* 16.1 (2008): 49–60.
Hahn, Gordon. *Russia's Islamic Threat*. New Haven, CT: Yale University Press, 2007.
Hahn, Marcus & Erhard Schüttpelz (eds). *Trancemedien und Neue Medien um 1900: Ein anderer Blick auf die Moderne*. Bielefeld: transcript, 2009.
Håkansson, Håkan. *Seeing the Word: John Dee and Renaissance Occultism*. Lund: Department of Intellectual History, Lund University, 2001.
Hakl, Hans Thomas. "Die Magie Bei Julius Evola und Ihre Philosophischen Voraussetzungen". In Richard Caron, Joscelyn Godwin, Wouter J. Hanegraaff & Jean-Louis Vieillard-Baron (eds), *Ésotérisme, Gnoses & Imaginaire Symbolique*, 415–36. Leuven: Peeters, 2001.
Hakl, Hans Thomas. "The Theory and Practice of Sexual Magic, Exemplified by Four Magical Groups in the Early Twentieth Century". In Hanegraaff & Kripal, *Hidden Intercourse*, 445–78.
Hakl, Hans Thomas. *Verborgene Geist von Eranos: Unbekannte Begegnungen von Wissenschaft und Esoterik. Eine alternative Geistesgeschichte des 20. Jahrhunderts*. Bretten: Scientia Nova, 2001.
Hall, Julie. "The Saptaparna: The Meaning and Origins of the Theosophical Septenary Constitution of Man". *Theosophical History* 13.4 (2007): 5–38.
Hälsogränden, "Hälsogränden". www.halsogranden.se (accessed 15 September 2010).
Hamill, John. *The Rosicrucian Seer*. London: Aquarian Press, 1986.
Hammer, Olav. *Claiming Knowledge: Strategies of Epistemology from Theosophy to the New Age*. Leiden: Brill, 2001.
Hammer, Olav. "Contested Diviners". In Hammer & von Stuckrad, *Polemical Encounters*, 227–52.

Hammer, Olav. "Esotericism in New Religious Movements". In Lewis, *The Oxford Handbook of New Religious Movements*, 445–65.
Hammer, Olav. "I Did It My Way? Individual Choice and Social Conformity in New Age Religion". In Aupers & Houtman, *Religions of Modernity*, 49–67.
Hammer, Olav. "New Age Religion and the Sceptics". In Kemp & Lewis, *Handbook of New Age*, 207–29.
Hammer, Olav & James R. Lewis . "Introduction". In Lewis & Hammer, *The Invention of Sacred Tradition*, 1–17.
Hammer, Olav & Kocku von Stuckrad. "Introduction". In their *Polemical Encounters*, vi–xxii.
Hammer, Olav & Kocku von Stuckrad (eds). *Polemical Encounters: Esoteric Discourse and Its Others*. Leiden: Brill, 2007.
Hanegraaff, Wouter J. "'And End History. And Go to the Stars': Terence McKenna and 2012". In Cusack & Hartney, *Religion and Retributive Logic*, 291–312.
Hanegraaff, Wouter J. "Beyond the Yates Paradigm: The Study of Western Esotericism between Counterculture and New Complexity". *Aries* 1.1 (2001): 5–37.
Hanegraaff, Wouter J. "The Birth of Esotericism from the Spirit of Protestantism". *Aries* 10.2 (2010): 197–216.
Hanegraaff, Wouter J. "Empirical Method in the Study of Esotericism". *Method and Theory in the Study of Religion* 7.2 (1995): 99–129.
Hanegraaff, Wouter J. *Esotericism and the Academy: Rejected Knowledge in Western Culture*. Cambridge: Cambridge University Press, 2012.
Hanegraaff, Wouter J. "Forbidden Knowledge: Anti-Esoteric Polemics and Academic Research". *Aries* 5.2 (2005): 225–54.
Hanegraaff, Wouter J. "How Magic Survived the Disenchantment of the World". *Religion* 33.4 (2003): 357–80.
Hanegraaff, Wouter J. "The New Age Movement and Western Esotericism". In Kemp & Lewis, *Handbook of New Age*, 25–50.
Hanegraaff, Wouter J. *New Age Religion and Western Culture: Esotericism in the Mirror of Secular Thought*. Leiden: Brill, 1996.
Hanegraaff, Wouter J. "On the Construction of 'Esoteric Traditions'". In Antoine Faivre & Wouter J. Hanegraaff (eds), *Western Esotericism and the Science of Religion*, 11–62. Leuven: Peeters, 1998.
Hanegraaff, Wouter J. "Reason, Faith, and Gnosis: Potentials and Problematics of a Typological Construct". In Peter Meusburger, Michael Welker & Edgar Wunder (eds), *Clashes of Knowledge: Orthodoxies and Heterodoxies in Science and Religion*, 133–44. Dordrecht: Springer Science & Business Media, 2008.
Hanegraaff, Wouter J. "Roberts, Dorothy Jane". In Hanegraaff *et al.*, *Dictionary of Gnosis and Western Esotericism*, 997–1000.
Hanegraaff, Wouter J. "The Study of Western Esotericism: New Approaches to Christian and Secular Culture". In Antes *et al.*, *New Approaches to the Study of Religion*, 489–519.
Hanegraaff, Wouter J. "Sympathy or the Devil: Renaissance Magic and the Ambivalence of Idols". *Esoterica* 2 (2000): 1–44. www.esoteric.msu.edu/printable/SympdevilFastprintable.html (accessed 16 May 2012).
Hanegraaff, Wouter J. "Tradition". In Hanegraaff *et al.*, *Dictionary of Gnosis and Western Esotericism*, 1125–35.
Hanegraaff, Wouter J. "The Trouble with Images: Anti-Image Polemics and Western Esotericism". In Hammer & von Stuckrad, *Polemical Encounters*, 107–36.
Hanegraaff, Wouter J. & Jeffrey J. Kripal (eds). *Hidden Intercourse: Eros and Sexuality in the History of Western Esotericism*. Leiden: Brill, 2008.
Hanegraaff, Wouter J., with Antoine Faivre, Roelof van den Broek & Jean-Pierre Brach (eds). *Dictionary of Gnosis and Western Esotericism*. Leiden: Brill, 2005.
Hansen, Hans T. "Introduction: Julius Evola's Political Endeavors". In Julius Evola, *Men Among the Ruins*, 1–104. Rochester, VT: Inner Traditions, 2002.
Hanson, Sharon. "The Secularization Thesis: Talking at Cross Purposes". *Journal of Contemporary Religion* 12.2 (1997): 159–79.
Haraway, Donna. *Simians, Cyborgs and Women: The Reinvention of Nature*. London: Free Association Books, 1991.

Harkness, Deborah. *John Dee's Conversations with Angels: Cabala, Alchemy, and the End of Nature*. New York: Cambridge University Press, 1999.
Harner, Michael (ed.). *Hallucinogens and Shamanism*. Oxford: Oxford University Press, 1973.
Harner, Michael. "The Sound of Rushing Water". In his *Hallucinogens and Shamanism*, 15–27 (originally published in *Natural History* 77.6 [1968]).
Harner, Michael. *The Way of the Shaman: A Guide to Power and Healing*. New York: Bantam Books, 1982 [1980].
Harrington, Anne. *Reenchanted Science: Holism in German Culture from Wilhelm II to Hitler*. Princeton, NJ: Princeton University Press, 1996.
Harrington, Austin. "Habermas and the 'Post-Secular Society'". *European Journal of Social Theory* 10.4 (2007): 543–60.
Harrington, Melissa. "Paganism and the New Age". In Kemp & Lewis, *Handbook of New Age*, 435–52.
Harris, Sam. *The End of Faith: Religion, Terror, and the Future of Reason*. New York: W. W. Norton, 2004.
Harris, Sam. *Letter to a Christian Nation*. New York: Random House, Inc., 2006.
Harvey, Graham. "Inventing Paganisms: Making Nature". In Lewis & Hammer, *The Invention of Sacred Tradition*, 277–90.
Haudry, Jean. "Die Indoeuropäische Tradition als Wurzel unserer Identität". In Krebs, *Mut Zur Identität*, 105–44.
Haudry, Jean. *Les Indo-Européens*. Paris: Presses Universitaires de France, 1981.
Hawking, Stephen W. *A Brief History of Time: From the Big Bang to Black Holes*. London: Bantam Press, 1988.
Heelas, Paul. "Introduction: Detraditionalization and its Rivals". In Heelas *et al.*, *Detraditionalization*, 1–20.
Heelas, Paul. *The New Age Movement: The Celebration of the Self and the Sacralization of Modernity*. Oxford: Blackwell, 1996.
Heelas, Paul. *Spiritualities of Life: New Age Romanticism and Consumptive Capitalism*. Oxford: Blackwell, 2008.
Heelas, Paul. "The Spiritual Revolution: From 'Religion' to 'Spirituality'". In Woodhead *et al.*, *Religions in the Modern World*, 357–77.
Heelas, Paul, Scott Lash & Paul Morris (eds). *Detraditionalization: Critical Reflections on Authority and Identity*. Oxford: Blackwell, 1996.
Hegarty, Paul. *Noise/Music: A History*. London: Continuum, 2007.
Heidle, Alexandra & Jan A. M. Snoek (eds). *Women's Agency and Rituals in Mixed and Female Masonic Orders*. Leiden: Brill, 2008.
Heldal-Lund, Andreas. "What is Scientology?". *Operation Clambake*. www.xenu.net/roland-intro.html (accessed 20 December 2010).
Helland, Chris. "Online-Religion/Religion-Online and Virtual Communitas". In Jeffrey K. Hadden & Douglas E. Cowan (eds), *Religion on the Internet: Research Prospects and Promises*, 205–23. London: JAI Press, 2000.
Helland, Chris. "Surfing for Salvation". *Religion* 32.4 (2002): 293–302.
Herberg, Will. "Religion in a Secularized Society". Part 1, *Review of Religious Research* 3.4 (1962): 145–58; part 2, *Review of Religious Research* 4.1 (1963): 33–45.
Herbert, David. *Religion and Civil Society: Rethinking Public Religion in the Contemporary World*. Aldershot: Ashgate, 2003.
Hergovich, Andreas & Martin Arendasy. "Scores for Schizotypy and Five Factor Model of a Sample of Distant Healers". *Perceptual and Motor Skills* 105 (2007): 197–203.
Hervieu-Léger, Danièle. "The Role of Religion in Establishing Social Cohesion". *Eurozine*, 17 August 2006. www.eurozine.com/articles/2006-08-17-hervieuleger-en.html (accessed 16 May 2012).
Hervieu-Léger, Danièle. "In Search of Certainties: The Paradoxes of Religiosity in Societies of High Modernity". *Hedgehog Review* 8 (2006): 59–68.
Hess, David J. *Science in the New Age: The Paranormal, its Defenders and Debunkers, and American Culture*. Madison, WI: University of Wisconsin Press, 1993.
Hill, Ciaran Scott. "Developing Psychomotor Skills the Wii Way". *Science* 323 (2009): 1169.

Hill, Gregory ("Malaclypse the Younger") & Kerry Thornley ("Omar Khayyam Ravenhurst"). *Principia Discordia*. 5th edition. San Francisco, CA: Loompanics Unlimited, 1979 [1957].
Hill, J. Arthur. *Spiritualism: Its History, Phenomena and Doctrine*. London: Cassell & Co., 1918.
Hine, Christine. *Virtual Ethnography*. London, Sage, 2000.
Hine, Christine. *Virtual Methods: Issues in Social Research on the Internet*. New York: Berg, 2005.
Hine, Phil. *Oven-Ready Chaos*. www.philhine.org.uk/writings/pdfs/orchaos.pdf (accessed 3 December 2010) [originally published as *Condensed Chaos* by Chaos International Publications, London, 1992].
Hine, Phil. *Techniques of Modern Shamanism*. Vol. I. www.philhine.org.uk/writings/pdfs/wbtw01.pdf (accessed 3 December 2010) [originally published by Pagan News Publications, Leeds, 1989–1990].
Hine, Phil. *Techniques of Modern Shamanism*. Vol. II. www.philhine.org.uk/writings/pdfs/2worlds.pdf (accessed 3 December 2010) [originally published by Pagan News Publications, Leeds, 1989–1990].
Hine, Phil. *Techniques of Modern Shamanism*. Vol. III. www.philhine.org.uk/writings/pdfs/tbfv1.pdf (accessed 3 December 2010) [originally published by Pagan News Publications, Leeds, 1989–1990].
Hird, Myra J. "Animal Trans". In Norren Giffney & Myra J. Hird (eds), *Queering the Non-Human*, 227–47. Aldershot: Ashgate, 2008.
Hirschkind, Charles. *The Ethical Soundscape: Cassette Sermons and Islamic Counterpublics*. New York: Columbia University Press, 2006.
Hjarvard, Stig. "From Bricks to Bytes: The Mediatization of a Global Toy Industry". In Ib Bondebjerg & Peter Golding (eds), *European Culture and the Media*, 43–63. Bristol: Intellect Books, 2004.
Hjarvard, Stig. "The Mediatization of Religion: A Theory of Media as Agents of Religious Change". *Northern Lights* 6 (2008): 9–26.
Hobsbawm, Eric. "Introduction: Inventing Traditions". In Hobsbawm & Ranger, *The Invention of Tradition*, 1–14.
Hobsbawm, Eric. "Mass-Producing Traditions: Europe, 1870–1914". In Hobsbawm & Ranger, *The Invention of Tradition*, 263–308.
Hobsbawm, Eric, & Terence Ranger (eds). *The Invention of Tradition*. Cambridge: Cambridge University Press, 1983.
Hoggendorf, Hedvig, A. Mankertz, R. Kundt & M. Roggendorf. "Spotlight on Measles 2010: Measles Outbreak in a Mainly Unvaccinated Community in Essen, Germany". *Euro Surveillance* 15.26 (2010). www.eurosurveillance.org/ViewArticle.aspx?ArticleId=19609 (accessed 16 May 2012).
Højsgaard, Morten T. & Margit Warburg. "Introduction: Waves of Research". In their *Religion and Cyberspace*, 1–13.
Højsgaard, Morten T. & Margit Warburg (eds). *Religion and Cyberspace*. London: Routledge, 2005.
Holman, John. *The Return of the Perennial Philosophy: The Supreme Wisdom of Western Esotericism*. London: Watkins.
Holtved, Erik. "Eskimo Shamanism". In Edsman, *Studies in Shamanism*, 23–31.
Hoppál, Mihály & Juha Pentikäinen (eds). *Northern Religions and Shamanism*. Helsinki: Finnish Literature Society, 1992.
Horsfield, Peter. "Media". In Morgan, *Keywords in Religion, Media and Culture*, 111–22.
Houston, Siobhán. "Chaos Magic: A Peek into this Irreverent and Anarchic Recasting of the Magical Tradition". *Gnosis* 36 (1995): 55–9.
Houtman, Dick & Stef Aupers. "The Spiritual Turn and the Decline of Tradition: The Spread of Post-Christian Spirituality in Fourteen Western Countries, 1981–2000". *Journal for the Scientific Study of Religion* 46 (2007): 305–20.
Howe, Stephen. *Afrocentrism: Mythical Pasts and Imagined Homes*. New York: Verso, 1999.
Howes, David (ed.). *The Sixth Sense Reader*. Oxford: Berg, 2009.
Hubbard, L. Ron. "Auditor's Security Check". *HCO Policy Letter*, 7 July 1961.
Hubbard, L. Ron. *Dianetics 55*. Los Angeles, CA: Bridge Publications, 2007.
Hubbard, L. Ron. "Dianetics: The Evolution of a Science". *Astounding Science Fiction* 45.3 (1950): 43–87.

Hubbard, L. Ron. *Dianetics: The Modern Science of Mental Health*. Los Angeles, CA: Bridge Publications, 2007.
Hubbard, L. Ron. *Have You Lived Before This Life? A Scientific Survey*. Los Angeles, CA: Church of Scientology of California, 1977.
Hubbard, L. Ron. "HGC Pre-processing Security Check". *HCO Policy Letter*, 23 October 1961.
Hubbard, L. Ron. "The Only Valid Security Check". *HCO Policy Letter*, 22 May 1961.
Hubbard, L. Ron. "Penalties for Lower Conditions". *HCO Policy Letter*, 18 October 1967.
Hubbard, L. Ron. *The Philadelphia Doctorate Course*. Los Angeles, CA: Golden Era Publications, 2001.
Hubbard, L. Ron. *Ron's Journal 67*. Los Angeles, CA: Golden Era Productions, 1983.
Hubbard, L. Ron. *Scientology: The Fundamentals of Thought*. Los Angeles, CA: Bridge Publications, 1997.
Hubbard, Jr, L. Ron. "Penthouse Interview". *Penthouse*, June 1983, 111–13, 166, 170–75.
Hughes, James. *Chechnya: From Nationalism to Jihad*. Philadelphia, PA: University of Philadelphia Press, 2007.
Hultkrantz, Åke. "Aspects of Saami (Lapp) Shamanism". In Hoppál & Pentikäinen, *Northern Religions and Shamanism*, 138–45.
Hultkrantz, Åke. "Spirit Lodge, a North American Shamanistic Séance". In Edsman, *Studies in Shamanism*, 32–68.
Hunke, Sigrid. *Europas Andere Religion: Die Überwindung der religiösen Krise*. Düsseldorf: Eco Verlag, 1969.
Hunke, Sigrid. *Europas Eigene Religion*. Tübingen: Grabert Verlag, 1997.
Hunke, Sigrid. "Kampf um Europas religiöse Identität". In Krebs, *Mut Zur Identität*, 75–104.
Hutton, Ronald. *Shamans: Siberian Spirituality and the Western Imagination*. London: Hambledon Continuum, 2001.
Huxley, Thomas H., Henry Wace, W. C. Magee, W. H. Mallock & Humphry Ward. *Christianity and Agnosticism: A Controversy*. New York: The Humboldt Publishing Company, 1889.
Huysmans, Joris-Karl. *The Damned (Là-Bas)*. London: Penguin Books, 2001.
Icke, David. *... And the Truth Shall Set You Free*. Isle of Wight: David Icke Books, 1995.
Icke, David. *The Biggest Secret*. Isle of Wight: David Icke Books, 1999.
Icke, David. *The David Icke Guide to the Global Conspiracy (and How to End It)*. Isle of Wight: David Icke Books, 2007.
Idel, Moshe. *Kabbalah and Eros*. New Haven, CT: Yale University Press, 2005.
Idel, Moshe. *The Mystical Experience in Abraham Abulafia*. Albany, NY: SUNY Press, 1988.
Idinopulos, Thomas A. & Edward A. Yonan (eds). *Religion and Reductionism: Essays on Eliade, Segal, and the Challenge of the Social Sciences for the Study of Religion*. Leiden: Brill, 1994.
Ignazi, Piero. *Extreme Right Parties in Europe*. Oxford: Oxford University Press, 2006.
Incao, Philip. "Report on Vaccination". *Gateways* 34 (1998). www.waldorflibrary.org/index.php?option=com_content&view=article&id=334:spring-1998-issue-34-report-on-vaccination&catid=15:gateways&Itemid=10 (accessed 9 June 2012).
Ingalls, Margaret. "The Evolution of Maat Magick: From Cornfields to Cyberspace". *Starfire* 2.3 (2008): 175–89.
Inglehart, Ronald. *Culture Shift in Advanced Industrial Society*. Princeton, NJ: Princeton University Press, 1988.
Inglehart, Ronald & Paul R. Abramson. "Measuring Postmaterialism". *American Political Science Review* 93 (1999): 665–77.
Irigaray, Luce. *Speculum of the Other Women*. Ithaca, NY: Cornell University Press, 1989 [1974].
Jackson, Peter. "Apparitions and Apparatuses: On the Framing and Staging of Religious Events". *Method and Theory in the Study of Religion*, forthcoming.
Jäger, Siegfried & Florentine Maier. "Theoretical and Methodological Aspects of Foucauldian Critical Discourse Analysis and Dispositive Analysis". In Ruth Wodak & Michael Meyer (eds), *Methods of Critical Discourse Analysis*, 2nd edition, 34–61. London: Sage, 2010.
Jagielski, Wojciech. *Torens van Steen: Reportages uit Tsjetsjenië*. Breda: De Geus, 2008.
Jagose, Annamarie. *Queer Theory: An Introduction*. New York: New York University Press, 1996.
James, George G. M. *Stolen Legacy: The Greek Philosophy is a Stolen Egyptian Philosophy*. Charlotte, NC: KHA Books, 2008.

James, Allison, Chris Jenks & Alan Prout. *Theorizing Childhood*. Cambridge: Polity Press, 1998.
Jayakar, Pupul. *Krishnamurti: A Biography*. Cambridge, MA: Harper & Row, 1986.
Jenkins, Simon. "Rituals and Pixels: Experiments in Online Church". *Online: Heidelberg Journal of Religions on the Internet* 3.1 (2008). http://archiv.ub.uni-heidelberg.de/volltextserver/volltexte/2008/8291/pdf/jenkins.pdf (accessed 17 May 2012).
Joas, Hans. *Do We Need Religion? On the Experience of Self-Transcendence*. Boulder, CO: Paradigm Publishers, 2008.
Johnston, Jay. *Angels of Desire: Esoteric Bodies, Aesthetics and Ethics*. London: Equinox, 2008.
Johnston, Jay. "Cyborgs and Chakras: Intersubjectivity in Scientific and Spiritual Somatechnics". In Cusack & Hartney, *Religion and Retributive Logic*, 313–22.
Jolly, Karen L. *Popular Religion in Late Saxon England: Elf Charms in Context*. Chapel Hill, NC: University of North Carolina Press, 1996.
Jones, Lindsay (ed.). *Encyclopedia of Religion*. 2nd edition. Detroit, MI: Macmillan Reference, 2005 (1st edition 1987).
Jones, Prudence & Nigel Pennick. *A History of Pagan Europe*. London: Routledge, 1995.
Jorgensen, Danny L. *The Esoteric Scene, Cultic Milieu, and Occult Tarot*. New York: Garland, 1992.
JoS. "Joy of Satan". www.joyofsatan.org (accessed 5 November 2010).
Joy, Morny. "The Impact of Gender on Religious Studies". *Diogenes* 225 (2010): 93–102.
Junginger, Horst. "Sigrid Hunke (1913–1999) – Europe's New Religion and its Old Stereotypes". In Hubert Cancik & Uwe Puschner (eds), *Antisemitismus, Paganismus, Völkische Religion*, 151–62. Munich: K. G. Saur, 2004.
Kaczynski, Richard. *Perdurabo: The Life of Aleister Crowley, the Definitive Biography of the Founder of Modern Magick*. Berkeley, CA: North Atlantic Books, 2010.
Kapelrud, Arvid S. "Shamanistic features in the Old Testament". In Edsman, *Studies in Shamanism*, 90–96.
Kaplan, Jeffrey, & Heléne Lööw (eds). *The Cultic Milieu: Oppositional Subcultures in an Age of Globalization*. Walnut Creek, CA: Alta Mira Press, 2002.
Karaflogka, Anastasia. *E-religion: A Critical Appraisal of Religious Discourse on the World Wide Web*. London: Equinox, 2006.
Karenga, Maulana. *Afro-American Nationalism: Social Strategy and Struggle for Community*. PhD dissertation, United States International University, San Diego, CA, 1976.
Karenga, Maulana. *Introduction to Black Studies*. Los Angeles, CA: Kawaida Publications, 1983.
Karenga, Maulana. *Kwanzaa: A Celebration of Family, Community and Culture*. Los Angeles, CA: University of Sankore Press, 1998.
Karenga, Maulana. *Maat, the Moral Ideal in Ancient Egypt: A Study in Classical African Ethics*. PhD dissertation, University of Southern California, Los Angeles, CA, 1994.
Karjala, Matti Y. "Aspects of the Other World in Irish Folk Tradition". In Hoppál & Pentikäinen, *Northern Religions and Shamanism*, 176–80.
Karlsson, Thomas. "Esoterism and the Left-Hand Path". Internal Dragon Rouge document, undated. www.scribd.com/doc/6540392/Esoterism-and-the-Left-Hand-Path# (accessed 25 April 2011).
Karlsson, Thomas. *Götisk Kabbala och Runisk Alkemi: Johannes Bureus och den Götiska Esoterismen*. Stockholm: Stockholm University, 2010.
Katz, David S. *The Occult Tradition: From the Renaissance to the Present Day*. London: Jonathan Cape, 2005.
Katz, Eric. "Against the Inevitability of Anthropocentrism". In Katz *et al.*, *Beneath the Surface*, 17–42.
Katz, Eric, Andrew Light & David Rothenberg (eds). *Beneath the Surface: Critical Essays in the Philosophy of Deep Ecology*. Cambridge, MA: MIT Press, 2000.
Katz, Eric, Andrew Light & David Rothenberg. "Introduction: Deep Ecology as Philosophy". In their *Beneath the Surface*, ix–xxiv.
Kavkaz Tsentr. "Book of Mujahiddeen". www.kavkazcenter.com/eng/help/ebook.shtml (accessed 20 October 2010).
Kay, Lily E. "In the Beginning was the Word? The Genetic Code and the Book of Life". In Mario Biagioli (ed.), *The Science Study Reader*, 224–33. London: Routledge, 1999.
Keenan, David. "Childhood's End: Current 93". *The Wire* 163 (1997): 34–7.

Kemp, Arthur. *March of the Titans: A History of the White Race.* Washington, DC: Ostara Publications, 2006.
Kemp, Daren & James R. Lewis (eds). *Handbook of New Age.* Leiden: Brill, 2007.
Kendall, Lori. "Recontextualizing 'Cyberspace': Methodological Considerations for On-line Research". In Steve Jones (ed.), *Doing Internet Research*, 57–74. Thousand Oaks, CA: Sage, 1999.
Kent, Stephen. "Scientology – Is this a Religion?" *Marburg Journal of Religion* 4.1 (1999). www.uni-marburg.de/fb03/ivk/mjr/pdfs/1999/articles/kent1999.pdf (accessed 16 May 2012).
Kershaw, Kris. *The One-Eyed God: Odin and the (Indo-)Germanic Männerbünde.* Austin, TX: Institute for the Study of Man, 2000.
Keyworth, David. "Occultism and the Contemporary Vampire Subculture". *KHTHÓNIOS: A Journal for the Study of Religion* 1.1 (2003): 5–13.
Keyworth, David. "The Socio-Religious Beliefs and Nature of the Contemporary Vampire Subculture". *Journal of Contemporary Religion* 17 (2002): 335–70.
Kieckhefer, Richard. *Forbidden Rites: A Necromancer's Manual of the Fifteenth Century.* University Park, PA: Pennsylvania State University Press, 1998.
Kieckhefer, Richard. *Magic in the Middle Ages.* Cambridge: Cambridge University Press, 1989.
Kilcher, Andreas (ed.). *Constructing Tradition: Means and Myths of Transmission in Western Esotericism.* Leiden: Brill, 2010.
Kilcher, Andreas. "Introduction: Constructing Tradition in Western Esotericism". In his *Constructing Tradition*, ix–xv.
King, Francis (ed.). *Astral Projections, Ritual Magic, and Alchemy: Golden Dawn Material by S. L. MacGregor Mathers and Others.* Rochester, VT: Destiny Books, 1987.
Kippenberg, Hans G. *Discovering Religious History in the Modern Age.* Princeton, NJ: Princeton University Press, 2002.
Kippenberg, Hans G. & Gunnar Folke Schuppert (eds). *Die Verrechtlichte Religion: Der Öffentlichkeitsstatus von Religionsgemeinschaften.* Tübingen: Mohr-Siebeck, 2005.
Kippenberg, Hans G., Jörg Rüpke & Kocku von Stuckrad (eds). *Europäische Religionsgeschichte: Ein mehrfacher Pluralismus.* 2 vols. Göttingen: Vandenhoeck & Ruprecht, 2009.
Klim, George. *Stanislaw Przybyszewski: Leben, Werk und Weltanschauung im Rahmen der deutschen Literatur der Jahrhundertwende.* Paderborn: Igel Verlag, 1992.
Knight, Peter. *Conspiracy Culture: From Kennedy to the X-Files.* London: Routledge, 2000.
Knight, Peter (ed.). *Conspiracy Nation: The Politics of Paranoia in Postwar America.* New York: New York University Press, 2002.
Knott, Kim. "Cutting Through the Postsecular City: A Spatial Interrogation". In Molendijk et al., *Exploring the Postsecular*, 19–38.
Konservatizm.org. "About Center of Conservatism Studies". 2008. http://konservatizm.org/about.xhtml (accessed 15 October 2010).
Korsch, Dietrich & Amber L. Griffioen (eds). *Interpreting Religion: The Significance of Friedrich Schleiermacher's "Reden über die Religion" for Religious Studies and Theology.* Tübingen: Mohr Siebeck, 2011.
Krebs, Pierre (ed.). *Mut Zur Identität – Alternativen zum Prinzip der Gleichheit.* Stuckum: Verlag für ganzheitliche Forschung und Kultur (Thule Seminar), 1988.
Kripal, Jeffrey J. *Authors of the Impossible: The Paranormal and the Sacred.* Chicago, IL: University of Chicago Press, 2010.
Kripal, Jeffrey J. *Esalen: America and the Religion of No Religion.* Chicago, IL: University of Chicago Press, 2007.
Kripal, Jeffrey J. *Roads of Excess, Palaces of Wisdom: Eroticism and Reflexivity in the Study of Mysticism.* Chicago, IL: University of Chicago Press, 2001.
Kripal, Jeffrey J. & Wouter J. Hanegraaff. "Introduction: Things We Do Not Talk About". In Hanegraaff & Kripal, *Hidden Intercourse*, ix–xxi.
Kristiansen, Roald E. "Satan in Cyberspace: A Study of Satanism on the Internet in the 1990s". 1995. www.love.is/roald/satanism.html (accessed 3 November 2010).
Krüger, Klaus & Alessandro Nova (eds). *Imagination und Wirklichkeit: Zum Verhältnis von Mentalen und Realen Bildern in der Frühen Neuzeit.* Mainz: Philipp von Zabern, 2000.
Kryon. "Lee Carroll Bio". www.kryon.com/Leebio.html (accessed 27 January 2011).

Labate, Bia & Henrik Jungaberle (eds). *The Internationalization of Ayahuasca*. Göttingen: Hogrefe, 2011.
Laclau, Ernesto & Chantal Mouffe. *Hegemony and Socialist Strategy: Towards a Radical Democratic Politics*. London: Verso, 2001.
Lakoff, George & Mark Johnson. *Metaphors We Live By*. Updated 2nd edition (1st edition 1980). Chicago, IL: University of Chicago Press, 2003.
Landers, Chris. "Serious Business". *Baltimore City Paper*, 2 April 2008. www.citypaper.com/news/story.asp?id=15543 (accessed 16 May 2012).
Landes, Richard. "Millennialism". In Lewis, *The Oxford Handbook of New Religious Movements*, 333–58.
Lanwerd, Susanne. *Religionsästhetik: Studien zum Verhältnis von Symbol und Sinnlichkeit*. Würzburg: Königshausen & Neumann, 2002.
Lap, Amina & O. Wolf. "Satanismens Danske Rødder – i Dag". *Satanisk Bulletin* 9.1 (2003): 11–18.
Larsen, Elena (ed.). *CyberFaith: How Americans Pursue Religion Online*. Washington, DC: Pew Internet & American Life Project, 2001. http://pewinternet.org/~/media//Files/Reports/2001/PIP_CyberFaith_Report.pdf.pdf (accessed 17 May 2012).
Laslett, Peter. *The World We Have Lost – Further Explored*. 3rd edition. London: Methuen & Co., 1983 [1965].
LaVey, Anton Szandor. *The Devil's Notebook*. Los Angeles, CA: Feral House, 1992.
LaVey, Anton Szandor. "The Invisible War". In Adam Parfrey (ed.), *Apocalypse Culture*, 193–5. Portland, OR: Feral House, 1990.
LaVey, Anton Szandor. *The Satanic Bible*. New York: Avon Books, 1969.
LaVey, Anton Szandor. *The Satanic Rituals*. New York: Avon Books, 1972.
LaVey, Anton Szandor. *Satan Speaks!* Venice, CA: Feral House, 1998.
Laycock, Joseph. *Vampires Today: The Truth About Modern Vampirism*. Westport, CT: Praeger, 2009.
Leadbeater, Charles W. *The Astral Plane*. Adyar: The Theosophical Publishing House, 1970 [1895].
Leadbeater, Charles W. *Man Visible and Invisible*. Madras: Theosophical Publishing House, 1964 [1902].
Leadbeater, Charles W. & Annie Besant. *The Beginnings of the Sixth Root Race*. Adyar, India: Theosophical Publishing House, 1931.
Leane, Elizabeth. *Reading Popular Physics: Disciplinary Skirmishes and Textual Strategies*. Aldershot: Ashgate Publishing, 2007.
Lefkowitz, Mary. *Not Out of Africa: How "Afrocentrism" Became an Excuse to Teach Myth as History*. New York: Basic Books, 1996.
Lehrich, Christopher, I. *The Language of Demons and Angels: Cornelius Agrippa's Occult Philosophy*. Leiden: Brill, 2003.
Lévi, Éliphas. *Secrets de la Magie: Dogme et Rituel de la Haute Magie; Histoire de la Magie; La Clef des Grands Mystères*. Edited by Francis Lacassin. Paris: Robert Laffont, 2000.
Lewis, James R. (ed.). *Encyclopedic Sourcebook of UFO Religions*. Amherst, NY: Prometheus Books, 2003.
Lewis, James R. "Fit for the Devil: Toward an Understanding of 'Conversion' to Satanism". *International Journal for the Study of New Religions* 1.1 (2010): 117–38.
Lewis, James R. "Infernal Legitimacy". In Petersen, *Contemporary Religious Satanism*, 41–59 [original 2002].
Lewis, James R. *Legitimating New Religions*. New Brunswick, NJ: Rutgers University Press, 2003.
Lewis, James R. (ed.). *The Oxford Handbook of New Religious Movements*. Oxford: Oxford University Press, 2004
Lewis, James R. (ed.). *Scientology*. New York: Oxford University Press, 2009.
Lewis, James R. "Who Serves Satan? A Demographic and Ideological Profile". *Marburg Journal of Religious Studies* 6.2 (2001). http://archiv.ub.uni-marburg.de/mjr/lewis2.html (accessed 17 May 2012).
Lewis, James R. & Olav Hammer (eds). *Handbook of Religion and the Authority of Science*. Leiden: Brill, 2011.
Lewis, James R. & Olav Hammer (eds). *The Invention of Sacred Tradition*. Cambridge: Cambridge University Press, 2007.

Lewis, James R. & J. Gordon Melton (eds). *Perspectives on the New Age*. Albany, NY: SUNY Press, 1992.
LiBrizzi, Marcus. "The Illuminatus! Trilogy". In Peter Knight (ed.), *Conspiracy Theories in American History*, 339–41. Oxford: ABC-Clio, 2003.
Lieven, Anatol. *Chechnya: Tombstone of Russian Power*. New Haven, CT: Yale University Press, 1998.
Lightman, Bernard. *The Origins of Agnosticism: Victorian Unbelief and the Limits of Knowledge*. Baltimore, MD: John Hopkins University Press, 1987.
Lincoln, Bruce. *Authority: Construction and Corrosion*. Chicago, IL: University of Chicago Press, 1994.
Lincoln, Bruce. *Discourse and the Construction of Society: Comparative Studies of Myth, Ritual, and Classification*. New York: Oxford University Press, 1989.
Lincoln, Bruce. "Theses on Method". *Method and Theory in the Study of Religion* 8.3 (1996): 225–7.
Livsyoga, "Livsyogan: Ny gren växer fram på yogans stora träd". www.livsyoga.nu/livsyoga2.html (accessed 27 September 2010).
Lloyd, Genevieve. *The Man of Reason: "Male" and "Female" in Western Philosophy*. London: Routledge, 1993 [1984].
Locke, John. *Some Thoughts Concerning Education*. London: A. and J. Churchill, 1693.
Losey, Meg Blackburn. *The Children of Now: Crystalline Children, Indigo Children, Star Kids, Angels on Earth, and the Phenomenon of Transitional Children*. Franklin Lakes, NJ: New Page, 2007.
Louv, Jason. *Generation Hex*. New York: Disinformation Company, 2006.
Luck, Georg. "Theurgy and Forms of Worship in Neoplatonism". In his *Ancient Pathways and Hidden Pursuits: Religions, Morals, and Magic in the Ancient World*, 111–52. Ann Arbor, MI: University of Michigan Press, 2000.
Luckhurst, Roger. *The Invention of Telepathy 1870–1901*. Oxford: Oxford University Press, 2002.
Luckmann, Thomas. *The Invisible Religion: The Problem of Religion in Modern Society*. New York: Macmillan, 1967.
Lupa. *A Field Guide to Otherkin*. Stafford: Megalithica Books, 2007.
Lutyens, Mary. *Krishnamurti: The Years of Fulfilment*. New York: Avon Books, 1983.
Lynch, Frederick R. "'Occult Establishment' or 'Deviant Religion'? The Rise and Fall of a Modern Church of Magic". *Journal for the Scientific Study of Religion* 18.3 (1979): 281–98.
Lynch, Gordon. "The Role of Popular Music in the Construction of Alternative Spiritual Identities and Ideologies". *Journal for the Scientific Study of Religion* 45.4 (2006): 481–8.
Lynch, Gordon. "Some Concluding Reflections". In his *Between Sacred and Profane: Researching Religion and Popular Culture*, 157–63. London: I. B. Tauris, 2007.
Lynch, Gordon. *Understanding Theology and Popular Culture*. Oxford: Blackwell, 2005.
Lyon, David. *Jesus in Disneyland: Religion in Postmodern Times*. Cambridge: Polity Press, 2000.
MacKenzie, Angus. *Secrets: The CIA's War at Home*. Berkeley, CA: University of California Press, 1997.
Macpherson, James. *The Poems of Ossian; To which Are Prefixed a Preliminary Discourse and Dissertation on the Æra and Poems of Ossian*. Boston, MA: Phillips, Sampson & Company, 1851 [reprint of 1773 edition].
MacWilliams, Mark. "Digital Waco: Branch Davidian Virtual Communities after the Waco Tragedy". In Højsgaard & Warburg, *Religion and Cyberspace*, 180–99.
Mankoff, Jeffrey. *Russian Foreign Policy: The Return of Great Power Politics*. Lanham, MD: Rowman & Littlefield, 2009.
Markham, Annette N. "The Internet as a Research Context". In Clive Seale, Giampietro Gobo, Jaber F. Gubrium & David Silverman (eds), *Qualitative Research Practice*, 358–74. London: Sage, 2004.
Markham, Annette N. & Nancy K. Baym. *Internet Inquiry: Conversations about Method*. Thousand Oaks, CA: Sage, 2009.
Marrs, Jim. *Alien Agenda: Investigating the Extraterrestrial Presence Among Us*. New York: HarperPaperbacks, 1998.
Marrs, Jim. *The Rise of the Fourth Reich: The Secret Societies that Threaten to Take Over America*. New York: Harper Lux, 2008.

Marrs, Jim. *Rule by Secrecy: The Hidden History that Connects the Trilateral Commission, the Freemasons, and the Great Pyramid.* New York: HarperCollins, 2001.
Martin, David. *A General Theory of Secularization.* Oxford: Basil Blackwell, 1978.
Martin, David. *On Secularization: Towards a Revised General Theory.* Aldershot: Ashgate, 2005.
Martin, David. "Towards Eliminating the Concept of Secularization". In Julius Gould (ed.), *The Penguin Survey of the Social Sciences,* 169–82. London: Penguin, 1965.
Mathews, Chris. *Modern Satanism: Anatomy of a Radical Subculture.* Westport, CN: Praeger, 2009.
Maudsley, Henry. *Natural Causes and Supernatural Seemings.* London: Kegan Paul, Trench & Co, 1886.
Mauskopf, Seymour H. & Michael R. McVaugh. "The Controversy over Statistics in Parapsychology 1934–1938". In Seymour H. Mauskopf (ed.), *The Reception of Unconventional Science,* 105–24. Boulder, CO: Westview Press, 1979.
Mauskopf, Seymour H. & Michael R. McVaugh. *The Elusive Science: Origins of Experimental Psychical Research.* Baltimore, MD: Johns Hopkins University Press, 1980.
McGarry, Molly. *Ghosts of Futures Past: Spiritualism and the Cultural Politics of Nineteenth-Century America.* Berkeley, CA: University of California Press, 2008.
McGuire, Meredith. *Religion: The Social Context.* 5th edition. Belmont, CA: Wadsworth Thomson Learning, 2002.
McIntosh, Christopher. *The Rose Cross and the Age of Reason: Eighteenth-Century Rosicrucianism in Central Europe and Its Relationship to the Enlightenment.* Leiden: Brill, 1997.
McKee, Gabriel. "Taking it to the Streets". *Religion Dispatches,* 11 June 2008. www.religion dispatches.org/archive/culture/294/taking_it_to_the_streets%3A_anonymous_vs._scientology (accessed 16 May 2012).
McKenna, Terence. *The Archaic Revival: Speculations on Psychedelic Mushrooms, the Amazon, Virtual Reality, UFOs, Evolution, Shamanism, the Rebirth of the Goddess, and the End of History.* San Francisco, CA: Harper, 1991.
McKenna, Terence. *Food of the Gods: The Search for the Original Tree of Knowledge. A Radical History of Plants, Drugs, and Human Evolution.* New York: Bantam Books, 1992.
McKenna, Terence. "Lectures on Alchemy". www.well.com/user/davidu/tmalchemy.html (accessed 29 April 2011).
McKenna, Terence. *True Hallucinations: Being an Account of the Author's Extraordinary Adventures in the Devil's Paradise.* San Francisco, CA: Harper, 1993.
McKenna, Terence & Dennis McKenna. *The Invisible Landscape: Mind, Hallucinogens, and the I Ching.* New York: The Seabury Press, 1975.
McLaughlin Andrew. "The Heart of Deep Ecology". In Sessions, *Deep Ecology for the 21st Century,* 85–94.
McNeil, Legs & Gillian McCain. *Please Kill Me: The Uncensored Oral History of Punk.* New York: Grove Press, 1996.
Melley, Timothy. "Agency Panic and the Culture of Conspiracy". In Knight, *Conspiracy Nation,* 57–81.
Melley, Timothy. *Empire of Conspiracy: The Culture of Paranoia in Postwar America.* Ithaca, NY: Cornell University Press, 2000.
Melton, J. Gordon (ed.). *New Age Encyclopedia.* Detroit, MI: Gale Research, 1990.
Melton, J. Gordon. *The Church of Scientology.* Salt Lake City, UT: Signature Books, 2000.
Meningall, Deanne. *The Melanin Diet.* Indianapolis, IN: Wordclay, 2009.
Merciless, R. "Giosuè Carducci: 19th Century Poet, Statesman and Satanist". 2000. www.churchofsatan.com/Pages/RMCarducci.html (accessed 13 April 2011).
Merkl, Peter H. (ed.). *Political Violence and Terror: Motifs and Motivations.* Berkeley, CA: University of California Press, 1986.
Merleau-Ponty, Maurice. *Phénoménologie de la Perception.* Paris: Gallimard, 1945.
Meyer, Birgit (ed.). *Aesthetic Formations: Media, Religion, and the Senses.* New York: Palgrave Macmillan, 2009.
Meyer, Birgit. *Religious Sensations: Why Media, Aesthetics and Power Matter in the Study of Contemporary Religion.* Amsterdam: Faculteit der Sociale Wetenschappen, Vrije Universiteit, 2006.

Meyer, Birgit & Annelies Moors (eds). *Religion, Media, and the Public Sphere*. Bloomington, IN: Indiana University Press, 2006.
Meyer, Birgit & Jojada Verrips. "Aesthetics". In Morgan, *Keywords in Religion, Media and Culture*, 20–30.
Midgley, Mary. *Science as Salvation: A Modern Myth and its Meaning*. London: Routledge, 1992.
Miller, Russell. *Bare-Faced Messiah: The True Story of L. Ron Hubbard*. New York: H. Holt, 1988.
Mitchell, Alexander. "Scientology: Revealed for the First Time". *Sunday Times*, 5 October 1969. www.lermanet.com/scientologynews/crowley-hubbard-666.htm (accessed 9 June 2012).
Moberg, Marcus & Kennet Granholm. "The Concept of the Post-Secular and the Contemporary Nexus of Religion, Media, Popular Culture, and Consumer Culture". In Peter Nynäs, Mika Lassander & Terhi Utriainen (eds), *Post-Secular Society*, 95–127. New Brunswick, NJ: Transaction Publishers.
Mohr, Hubert. "Perception/Sensory System". In von Stuckrad, *The Brill Dictionary of Religion*, 1435–48.
Molendijk, Arie, Justin Beaumont & Christoph Jedan (eds). *Exploring the Postsecular: The Religious, the Political, and the Urban*. Leiden: Brill, 2010.
Molendijk, Arie, Justin Beaumont & Christoph Jedan. "Preface". In their *Exploring the Postsecular*, ix–xii.
Moliné, Keith. "The Road to Salvation: Current 93". *The Wire* 269 (2006): 28–33.
Mollenauer, Lynn W. *Strange Revelations: Magic, Poison and Sacrilege in Louis XIV's France*. University Park, PA: Pennsylvania State University Press, 2007.
Moody, Edward J. "Magical Therapy: An Anthropological Investigation of Contemporary Satanism". In Irving I. Zaretsky & Mark Leone (eds), *Religious Movements in Contemporary America*, 355–82. Princeton, NJ: Princeton University Press, 1974.
MoonlitOpal. "Avatar Through Pagan Eyes". 17 January 2010. www.youtube.com/watch?v=gBLHwIiupqg (accessed 5 March 2011).
Moore, David W. "Three in Four Americans Believe in Paranormal". *Gallup*, 16 June 2005. www.gallup.com/poll/16915/three-four-americans-believe-paranormal.aspx#1 (accessed 16 May 2012).
Moore, James. "Gurdjieff, George Ivanovitch". In Hanegraaff et al., *Dictionary of Gnosis and Western Esotericism*, 445–50.
Moore, William D. *Masonic Temples: Freemasonry, Ritual Architecture and Masculine Archetypes*. Knoxville, TN: University of Tennessee Press, 2006.
Morais, Fernando. *A Warrior's Life: A Biography of Paulo Coelho*. London: HarperCollins, 2009.
Moreton-Robinson, Aileen. *Talkin' Up to the White Woman*. St Lucia: University of Queensland Press, 2000.
Morgan, David. *Visual Piety: A History and Theory of Popular Religious Images*. Berkeley, CA: University of California Press, 1998.
Morgan, David (ed.). *Keywords in Religion, Media and Culture*. London: Routledge, 2008.
Morozov, Aleksandr. "Has the Postsecular Age Begun?" *Religion, State & Society* 36.1 (2008): 39–44.
Morrison, Grant. *The Invisibles*. 3 vols, 59 issues. New York: DC Comics, 1994–2000.
Morrison, Grant. "Pop Magic!". In Richard Metzger (ed.), *Book of Lies: The Disinformation Guide to Magick and the Occult*, 16–25. New York: The Disinformation Company, 2003.
Moses, Wilson Jeremiah. *Afrotopia: The Roots of African American Popular History*. Cambridge: Cambridge University Press, 1998.
Mosse, George L. *The Crisis of German Ideology: Intellectual Origins of the Third Reich*. New York: Howart Fertig, 1999.
Muraskin, William A. *Middle-Class Blacks in a White Society: Prince Hall Freemasonry in America*. Berkeley, CA: University of California Press, 1975.
Murphy, Paul J. *The Wolves of Islam: Russia and the Faces of Chechen Terror*. Washington, DC: Brassey's Inc., 2004.
Murray, Craig D. & Judith Sixsmith. "The Corporeal Body in Virtual Reality". *Ethos* 27.3 (1999): 315–43.
Myers, Frederick W. H. *Human Personality and Its Survival of Bodily Death*. 2 vols. New York: Longmans, Green & Co, 1903.

Naess, Arne. "The Deep Ecological Movement: Some Philosophical Aspects". In Andrew Light & Holmes Rolston III (eds), *Environmental Ethics: An Anthology*, 262–74. Malden, MA: Blackwell, 2003.

Naess, Arne. "The Deep Ecology Eight-Points Revisited". In Sessions, *Deep Ecology for the 21st Century*, 213–21.

Naess, Arne. "Deepness of Questions and the Deep Ecology Movement". In Sessions, *Deep Ecology for the 21st Century*, 204–12.

Naess, Arne. "Docta Ignorantia and the Application of General Guidelines". In Glasser, *The Selected Works of Arne Naess*, 2810–15.

Naess, Arne. *Ecology, Community and Lifestyle: Outline of an Ecosophy*. Cambridge: Cambridge University Press, 1993.

Naess, Arne. "Ecosophy and Gestalt Ontology". In Sessions, *Deep Ecology for the 21st Century*, 240–45.

Naess, Arne. "Self-Realization: An Ecological Approach to Being in the World". In Sessions, *Deep Ecology for the 21st Century*, 225–39.

Naess, Arne. "The Shallow and the Deep, Long-Range Ecology Movements". In Sessions, *Deep Ecology for the 21st Century*, 151–5.

Neugebauer-Wölk, Monika. "Der Esoteriker und die Esoterik: Wie das Esoterische im 18. Jahrhundert zum Begriff wird und seinen Weg in die Moderne findet". *Aries* 10.2 (2010): 217–32.

Newport, Frank & Maura Strausberg. "Americans' Belief in Psychic and Paranormal Phenomena Is up Over Last Decade". *Gallup*, 8 June 2001. www.gallup.com/poll/4483/Americans-Belief-Psychic-Paranormal-Phenomena-Over-Last-Decade.aspx (accessed 16 May 2012).

Nilsonne, Åsa. *Mindfulness i Hjärnan*. Stockholm: Natur och Kultur, 2009.

Noakes, Richard. "Spiritualism, Science and the Supernatural in mid-Victorian Britain". In Nicola Brown, Carolyn Burdett & Pamela Thurschwell (eds), *The Victorian Supernatural*, 23–43. Cambridge: Cambridge University Press, 2004.

Nocturnum, Corvis. *Embracing the Darkness: Understanding Dark Subcultures*. Fort Wayne, IN: Dark Moon Press, 2005.

Numbers, The. "Avatar". www.the-numbers.com/movies/2009/AVATR.php (accessed 6 March 2011).

Olsson, Tord. "Verbal Representation of Religious Beliefs: A Dilemma in the Phenomenology of Religion". In Erik R. Sand & Jørgen Podemann Sørensen (eds), *Comparative Studies in History of Religions*, 75–92. Copenhagen: Museum Tusculanum Press, 1999.

O'Meara, Michael. *New Culture, New Right: Anti-Liberalism in Postmodern Europe*. Bloomington, IN: 1stBooks, 2004.

Oppenheim, Janet. *The Other World: Spiritualism and Psychical Research in England, 1850–1914*. Cambridge: Cambridge University Press, 1985.

Order of the Trapezoid. "The Mysteries". www.trapezoid.org/mission/mysteries.html (accessed 15 October 2010).

OTO. "Library". http://oto-usa.org/library.html (accessed 30 September 2010).

Owen, Alex. *The Darkened Room: Women, Power, and Spiritualism in Late Victorian England*. Chicago, IL: University of Chicago Press, 1990.

Owen, Alex. *The Place of Enchantment: British Occultism and the Culture of the Modern*. Chicago, IL: University of Chicago Press, 2004.

Panteli, Niki (ed.). *Virtual Social Networks: Mediated, Massive and Multiplayer Sites*. Basingstoke: Palgrave Macmillan, 2009.

Paradise, Matt. *Bearing the Devil's Mark*. Burlington, VT: Purging Talon, 2007.

Parra, Alejandro. "'Seeing and Feeling Ghosts': Absorption, Fantasy Proneness, and Healthy Schizotypy as Predictors of Crisis Apparition Experiences". *The Journal of Parapsychology* 70.2 (2006): 357–72.

Parsons, Jack. *Book of BABALON*. Berkeley, CA: Ordo Templi Orientis, 1982.

Partner, Peter. *The Murdered Magicians: The Templars and Their Myth*. New York: Barnes & Noble Books, 1993.

Partridge, Christopher. "Alternative Spiritualities, New Religions, and the Reenchantment of the West". In Lewis, *The Oxford Handbook of New Religious Movements*, 39–67.

Partridge, Christopher. *Dub in Babylon: Understanding the Evolution and Significance of Dub Reggae in Jamaica and Britain from King Tubby to Post-Punk*. London: Equinox, 2010.

Partridge, Christopher. "King Tubby Meets the Upsetter at the Grass Roots of Dub: Some Thoughts on the Early History and Influence of Dub Reggae". *Popular Music History* 2 (2007): 309–31.

Partridge, Christopher. "Lost Horizon: H. P. Blavatsky's Theosophical Orientalism". In Olav Hammer & Mikael Rothstein (eds), *Handbook of the Theosophical Current*. Leiden: Brill, forthcoming.

Partridge, Christopher. "The Occultural Significance of *The Da Vinci Code*". *Northern Lights* 6 (2008): 107–26.

Partridge, Christopher. "Popular Music, Affective Space, and Meaning". In Gordon Lynch (ed.), *Religion, Popular Culture and Everyday Life*, 182–93. London: Routledge, 2012.

Partridge, Christopher. *The Re-enchantment of the West: Alternative Spiritualities, Sacralization, Popular Culture and Occulture*. 2 vols. London: T. & T. Clark International, 2004/5.

Partridge, Christopher. "Religion and Popular Culture". In Linda Woodhead, Hiroko Kawanami & Christopher Partridge (eds), *Religions in the Modern World: Traditions and Transformations*, 489–521. London: Routledge, 2009.

Partridge, Christopher (ed.). *UFO Religions*. London: Routledge, 2003.

Partridge, Christopher & Eric Christianson (eds). *The Lure of the Dark Side: Satan and Western Demonology in Popular Culture*. London: Equinox, 2009.

Pasi, Marco. "Magic". In von Stuckrad, *The Brill Dictionary of Religion*, 1134–9.

Pasi, Marco. "The Neverendingly Told Story". *Aries* 3.2 (2003): 224–45.

Pasi, Marco. "Occultism". In von Stuckrad, *The Brill Dictionary of Religion*, 1364–8.

Pastor, Patricia & Cynthia Reuben. "Diagnosed Attention Deficit Hyperactivity Disorder and Learning Disability: United States, 2004–2006". *Vital and Health Statistics* 10.237 (2008). www.cdc.gov/nchs/data/series/sr_10/Sr10_237.pdf (accessed 16 May 2012).

Pauwels, Louis & Jacques Bergier. *Le Matin des Magiciens*. Paris: Gallimard, 1960.

Pendle, George. *Strange Angel: The Otherworldly Life of John Whiteside Parsons*. Orlando, FL: Harcourt, 2005.

Petersen, Jesper A. "Binary Satanism: The Construction of Community in a Digital World". In James R. Lewis & Jesper A. Petersen (eds), *The Encyclopedic Sourcebook of Satanism*, 593–610. Amherst, NY: Prometheus Books, 2008.

Petersen, Jesper A. (ed.). *Contemporary Religious Satanism: A Critical Anthology*. Farnham: Ashgate, 2009.

Petersen, Jesper A. "Introduction: Embracing Satan". In his *Contemporary Religious Satanism*, 1–24.

Petersen, Jesper A. "Satanists and Nuts: The Role of Schisms in Modern Satanism". In James R. Lewis & Sarah M. Lewis (eds), *Sacred Schisms: How Religions Divide*, 218–48. Cambridge: Cambridge University Press, 2009.

Petersen, Jesper A. "The Seeds of Satan: Conceptions of Magic in Contemporary Satanism". *Aries* 12.1 (2012): 91–129.

Petersen, Jesper A. "'Smite Him Hip and Thigh': Satanism, Violence, and Transgression". In James R. Lewis (ed.), *Violence and New Religious Movements*, 351–76. Oxford: Oxford University Press, 2011.

Petersen, Jesper A. "'We Demand Bedrock Knowledge': Modern Satanism between Secularized Esotericism and 'Esotericized' Secularism". In Lewis & Hammer, *Handbook of Religion and the Authority of Science*, 67–114.

Petros, George. *Art that Kills: A Panoramic Portrait of Aesthetic Terrorism 1984–2001*. London: Creation.

Pew Research Center for the Public and the Press. "Scientists and Belief". *The Pew Forum on Religion and Public Life*, 5 November 2009. http://pewforum.org/Science-and-Bioethics/Scientists-and-Belief.aspx (accessed 17 May 2012).

Pfister, Friedrich. "Ekstase". In his *Reallexikon für Antike und Christentum*, 944–87. 2nd edition. Stuttgart: Hiersemann, 1970.

Picknett, Lynn & Clive Prince. *The Stargate Conspiracy: Revealing the Truth Behind Extraterrestrial Contact, Military Intelligence, and the Mysteries of Ancient Egypt*. London: Little, Brown & Company, 1999.

Piff, David & Margit Warburg, "Seeking for Truth: Plausibility Alignment on a Baha'i Email List". In Højsgaard & Warburg, *Religion and Cyberspace*, 86–101.

Pigliucci, Massimo. "The Evolution–Creation Wars: Why Teaching More Science Just is Not Enough". *McGill Journal of Education* 42.2 (2007): 258–306.

Pike, Sarah M. *Earthly Bodies, Magical Selves: Contemporary Pagans and the Search for Community*. Berkeley, CA: University of California Press, 2001.

Pike, Sarah M. *New Age and Neopagan Religions in America*. New York: Columbia University Press, 2004.

Pinchbeck, Daniel. *2012: The Return of Quetzalcoatl*. New York: Jeremy Tarcher/Penguin, 2006.

Pinchbeck, Daniel. *Breaking Open the Head: A Psychedelic Journey into the Heart of Contemporary Shamanism*. New York: Broadway Books, 2002.

Pinchbeck, Daniel. *Notes from the Edge Times*. New York: Jeremy Tarcher/Penguin, 2010.

Plate, S. Brent. *Walter Benjamin, Religion, and Aesthetics: Rethinking Religion through the Arts*. New York: Routledge, 2005.

Podmore, Frank. *The Naturalisation of the Supernatural*. New York: G. P. Putnam's Sons, 1908.

Polanczyk, Guilherme, M. S. de Lima, B. L. Horta, J. Biederman & L. A. Rohde. "The Worldwide Prevalence of ADHD: A Systematic Review and Metaregression Analysis". *American Journal of Psychiatry* 164.6 (June 2007): 942–8.

Politkovskaya, Anna. "Tsentrovoy iz Tsentoroya: Interv'yu s Ramzanom Kadyrovym". *Novaya Gazeta*, 21 June 2004. www.novayagazeta.ru/data/2004/43/22.html (accessed 16 May 2012).

Pontifical Academy of Sciences. *Study Week on Astrobiology, 6–10 November 2009, Casino Pio IV*. Vatican City: The Pontifical Academy of Sciences, 2009. www.vatican.va/roman_curia/pontifical_academies/acdscien/2009/booklet_astrobiology_17.pdf (accessed 2 October 2010).

P-Orridge, Genesis. *Esoterrorist: Selected Essays 1980–1988*. London: OV Press, 1988. www.scribd.com/doc/21064820/Genesis-P-Orridge-Esoterrorist (accessed 16 May 2012).

P-Orridge, Genesis. "Eyes Wide Shut". *The Guardian*, 15 November 2003. www.guardian.co.uk/books/2003/nov/15/art.classics (accessed 22 May 2012).

P-Orridge, Genesis. *Painful but Fabulous: The Lives and Art of Genesis P-Orridge*. New York: Soft Skull Press, 2002.

P-Orridge, Genesis. "The Process is the Product: The Processean Influence on Thee Temple Ov Psychick Youth". In Timothy Wyllie, *Love, Sex, Fear, Death: The Inside Story of the Process Church of the Final Judgment*, 173–84. Edited by Adam Parfray. Port Townsend, WA: Feral House, 2009.

P-Orridge, Genesis. *Thee Psychick Bible: Thee Apocryphal Scriptures of Genesis P-Orridge and Thee Third MIND ov Psychic TV*. Edited by Jason Louv. Port Townsend, WA: Feral House, 1994.

Porter, David (ed.). *Internet Culture*. New York: Routledge, 1997.

Porter, Roy. "Witchcraft and Magic in Enlightenment, Romantic and Liberal Thought". In Bengt Ankarloo & Stuart Clark (eds), *Witchcraft and Magic in Europe: The Eighteenth and Nineteenth Centuries*, 191–274. Philadelphia, PA: University of Pennsylvania Press, 1999.

Prendergast, Alan. "Stalking the Net". *Denver Westword News*, 4 October 1995. www.westword.com/1995-10-04/news/stalking-the-net (accessed 9 June 2012).

Prensky, Marc. "Digital Natives, Digital Immigrants, Part II: Do They Really *Think* Differently?" *On the Horizon* 9.6 (2001). www.marcprensky.com/writing/Prensky%20-%20Digital%20Natives,%20Digital%20Immigrants%20-%20Part2.pdf (accessed 16 May 2012).

Puttick, Elizabeth. "The Rise of Mind–Body–Spirit Publishing: Reflecting or Creating Spiritual Trends?" *Journal of Alternative Spiritualities and New Age Studies* 1 (2005): 129–49.

Qur'an (trans. Tarif Khalidi). London: Penguin, 2009.

Radde-Antweiler, Kerstin. "'Virtual Religion': An Approach to a Religious and Ritual Typology of Second Life". *Online: Heidelberg Journal of Religions on the Internet* 3.1 (2008). http://archiv.ub.uni-heidelberg.de/volltextserver/volltexte/2008/8294/pdf/Radde.pdf (accessed 17 May 2012).

Raine, Susan. "Surveillance in a New Religious Movement: Scientology as a Test Case". *Religious Studies and Theology* 28.1 (2009): 63–94.

Rancière, Jacques. *The Politics of Aesthetics: The Distribution of the Sensible*. London: Continuum, 2004.

Ratzinger, Joseph & Jürgen Habermas. *The Dialectics of Secularization: On Reason and Religion*. San Francisco, CA: Ignatius Press, 2006.

Rauschning, Hermann. *Hitler Speaks: A Series of Political Conversations with Adolf Hitler on His Real Aims*. Whitefish, MT: Kessinger Publishing, 2006.

Ravenscroft, Trevor. *The Spear of Destiny: The Occult Power behind the Spear Which Pierced the Side of Christ*. London: Neville Spearman, 1972.

Redden, Guy. "The New Age: Towards a Market Model". *Journal of Contemporary Religion* 20.2 (2005): 231–46.

Reemtsma, Jan Philipp. "Must We Respect Religiosity? On Questions of Faith and the Pride of the Secular Society". *Eurozine*, 2 December 2005. www.eurozine.com/articles/2005-12-02-reemtsma-en.html (accessed 16 May 2012).

Reitman, Janet. "Inside Scientology". *Rolling Stone* 994 (23 February 2006). www.rollingstone.com/culture/news/inside-scientology-20110208 (accessed 9 June 2012).

Religious Technology Center. "Mr David Miscavige". 2008. www.rtc.org/david-miscavige.htm (accessed 20 December 2010).

Religious Technology Center. "Protecting the Advanced Technology". 2008. www.rtc.org/guarant/pg003.html (accessed 20 December 2010).

Rennie, Bryan. "Eliade, Mircea". In von Stuckrad, *The Brill Dictionary of Religion*, 573–7.

Reuter, Astrid. "Charting the Boundaries of the Religious Field: Legal Conflicts over Religion as Struggles over Blurring Borders". *Journal of Religion in Europe* 2.1 (2009): 1–20.

Reynolds, Simon. *Rip It Up and Start Again: Post-Punk 1978–1984*. London: Faber & Faber, 2005.

Rhine, Joseph B. *Extra-Sensory Perception*. Boston, MA: Boston Society for Psychic Research, 1934.

Rhine, Joseph B. *New Frontiers of the Mind: The Story of the Duke Experiments*. New York: Farrar & Rhinehart, 1937.

Rhodes, H. T. F. *The Satanic Mass: A Criminological Study*. London: Jarrolds, 1968 [1954].

Rice, Tom. "Believe It Or Not: Religious and Other Paranormal Beliefs in the United States". *Journal for the Scientific Study of Religion* 42.1 (2003): 95–106.

Riesebrodt, Martin. "Religiöse Vergemeinschaftungen". In Hans G. Kippenberg & Martin Riesebrodt (eds), *Max Webers "Religionssystematik"*, 101–17. Tübingen: Mohr Siebeck, 2001.

Riis, Ole & Linda Woodhead. *A Sociology of Religious Emotion*. Oxford: Oxford University Press, 2010.

Ringvee, Ringo. "Satanism in Estonia". In Petersen, *Contemporary Religious Satanism*, 129–40.

Roberts, Jane. "Journal". Jane Roberts Papers, Yale University Manuscript and Archives, Box 1, Folder 1–6.

Roberts, Jane. *The Seth Material*. Toronto: Bantam Books, 1970.

Roberts, John M. *The Mythology of the Secret Societies*. London: Watkins Publishing, 2008 [1972].

Roberts, Richard H. "Body". In Robert A. Segal (ed.), *The Blackwell Companion to the Study of Religion*, 213–28. Oxford: Blackwell, 2006.

Roberts, Richard. H. & Geoffrey Samuel (eds). *Nature Religion Today: Paganism in the Modern World*. Edinburgh: Edinburgh University Press, 1998.

Robertson, Robert. *Globalization: Social Theory and Global Culture*. London: Sage, 1992.

Robinson, Timothy S. "Scientology Raid Yielded Alleged Burglary Tools". *Washington Post*, 14 July 1977: A13.

Roof, Wade Clark. *A Generation of Seekers: The Spiritual Journey of the Baby Boom Generation*. New York: HarperCollins, 1993.

Rose, Elliot. *A Razor for a Goat: A Discussion of Certain Problems in the History of Witchcraft and Diabolism*. Toronto: University of Toronto Press, 1989 [1962].

Roseberry New Age Centre. "Kids". www.roseberrythailand.com/products/kids-range (accessed 16 May 2012).

Rosén, Anne-Sofie & Liselotte Frisk. "Varieties of Intense Experience of Female and Male Members of New Religious Movements and Comparison Groups". Paper presented at *Religious Experience in Women and Men: 6th Symposium for Psychology of Religion*. 19–22 June 1994. Lund University, Lund, Sweden.

Rothenberg, David (ed.). *Ecology, Community, Lifestyle: Outline of an Ecosophy*. Cambridge: Cambridge University Press, 1993.

Rothenberg, David. "Letter to the Editor from David Rothenberg". *International Society for Environmental Ethics Newsletter* 18.3 (2007): 25.

Rothstein, Mikael. "'His Name was Xenu. He Used Renegades ...': Aspects of Scientology's Founding Myth". In Lewis, *Scientology*, 365–87.

Ruck, Carl A.P., Jeremy Bigwood, Danny Staples, Jonathan Ott & R. Gordon Wasson. "Entheogens". *Journal of Psychedelic Drugs* 11.1–2 (1979): 145–6.

Russett, Cynthia Eagle. *Sexual Science: The Victorian Construction of Womanhood*. Cambridge, MA: Harvard University Press, 1989.

Sakwa, Richard (ed.). *Chechnya: From Past to Future*. London: Anthem Press, 2005.

Sandford, Christopher. *Bowie: Loving the Alien*. New York: Da Capo Press, 1998.

Sappel, Joel & Robert W. Welkos. "Scientologists Block Access to Secret Documents: 1500 Crowd into Courthouse to Protect Materials on Fundamental Beliefs". *Los Angeles Times*, 5 November 1985. http://pqasb.pqarchiver.com/latimes/access/64568420.html?dids=64568420:64568420&FMT=ABS&FMTS=ABS:FT (accessed 9 June 2012).

Sarasin, Philipp, "Infizierte Körper, Kontaminierte Sprachen. Metaphern als Gegenstand der Wissenschaftsgeschichte". In his *Geschichtswissenschaft und Diskursanalyse*, 191–230. Frankfurt: Suhrkamp, 2003.

Sarno, David. "Anonymous Hacker Pleads Guilty to 2008 Attack on Scientology Sites". *Los Angeles Times*, 11 May 2009. http://latimesblogs.latimes.com/technology/2009/05/perpeterator-of-2008-cyberattack-on-scientology-pleads-guilty.html (accessed 17 May 2012).

Satanas, Venus. "The Foundations of Satanism". 2009. www.spiritualsatanist.com/articles/satan/theism.html (accessed 27 September 2010).

Satanas, Venus. "Welcome to Spiritualsatanist.com". www.spiritualsatanist.com (accessed 5 November 2010).

Satanic Reds. "Member Sites". www.satanicreds.org/satanicreds/sr-orgs.html (accessed 30 November 2010).

Satanic Reds. "The Roots of the Satanic Reds". www.satanicreds.org/satanicreds/sr-roots.html (accessed 27 November 2010).

Schmitt, Carl. "*Prisca Theologia* e *Philosophia Perennis*: Due Temi del Rinascimento Italiano e la Loro Fortuna". In Giovannangiola Tarugi (ed.), *Il Pensiero Italiano del Rinascimento e il Tempo Nostro*. Florence: Leo S. Olschki, 1970.

Schock, Peter A. *Romantic Satanism: Myth and the Historical Moment in Blake, Shelley, and Byron*. Basingstoke: Palgrave Macmillan, 2003.

Scholem, Gershom G. *Major Trends in Jewish Mysticism*. New York: Schocken, 1961.

Schulz, Dorothea E. "Soundscape". In Morgan, *Keywords in Religion, Media and Culture*, 172–86.

Scientology.org. "L. Ron Hubbard: a Chronicle". 2009. http://mediaresources.lronhubbard.org/chronicle/page01.htm (accessed 9 June 2012).

Scientology.org. "What has been the Church's Role in Protecting Free Speech?". 2009. www.scientologynews.org/faq/what-has-been-the-church-role-in-protecting-internet-free-speech.html (accessed 9 June 2012).

Scott, David & Charles Hirschkind (eds). *Powers of the Secular Modern: Talal Asad and His Interlocutors*. Stanford, CA: Stanford University Press, 2006.

Sedgwick, Mark. *Against the Modern World: Traditionalism and the Secret Intellectual History of the Twentieth Century*. Oxford: Oxford University Press, 2004.

Seed, David. *Brainwashing: The Fictions of Mind Control*. Kent, OH: Kent State University Press, 2004.

Seed, John, Joanna Macy, Pat Fleming & Arne Naess. *Thinking Like a Mountain: Towards a Counsel of All Beings*. San Bruno, CA: Catalyst Books, 2007.

Segal, Robert A. "In Defense of Reductionism". *Journal of the American Academy of Religion* 51.1 (1983): 97–124.

Senholt, Jacob C. "Radical Traditionalism and the New Right: An Examination of Political Esotericism in America". In Arthur Versluis, Lee Irwin & Melinda Phillips (eds), *Esotericism, Religion, and Politics*. Minneapolis, MN: North American Academic Press, 2012.

Senholt, Jacob C. "Secret Identities in the Sinister Tradition: Political Esotericism and the Convergence of Radical Islam, Satanism and National Socialism in the Order of the Nine Angles". In Faxneld & Petersen, *The Devil's Party*, 250–74.

Sentencing Memorandum. *United States of America v. Jane Kember*, 487 F. Supp. 1340 (D.D.C. 1980). N. 78–401 (2) & (3).
Sessions, George. "Deep Ecology and the New Age Movement". In his *Deep Ecology for the 21st Century*, 290–310.
Sessions, George (ed.). *Deep Ecology for the 21st Century: Readings on the Philosophy and Practice of the New Environmentalism*. Boston, MA: Shambhala, 1995.
Sessions, George. "Ecocentrism and the Greens: Deep Ecology and the Environmental Task". *The Trumpeter: Journal of Ecosophy* 5.2 (1988): 65–9.
Sessions, George. "Ecological Consciousness and Paradigm Change". In Michael Tobias (ed.), *Deep Ecology*, 28–44. San Diego, CA: Avant Books, 1984.
Sessions, George. "Postmodernism and Environmental Justice: The Demise of the Ecology Movement?" *The Trumpeter: Journal of Ecosophy* 12.3 (1995). http://trumpeter.athabascau.ca/index.php/trumpet/article/view/305/456 (accessed 17 May 2012).
Sessions, George. "Preface". In his *Deep Ecology for the 21st Century*, ix–xxviii.
Sessions, George. "Wildness, Cyborgs, and Our Ecology Future: Reassessing the Deep Ecology Movement". *The Trumpeter: Journal of Ecosophy* 22.2 (2006). http://trumpeter.athabascau.ca/index.php/trumpet/article/view/906/1338 (accessed 17 May 2012).
SFO. "En Anmodning til Brugerne" ["A Request to the Users"]. 2004. http://forum.sataniskforum.dk/viewtopic.php?f=2&t=724&p=4728&hilit=en+anmodning#p4728 (accessed 30 November 2010).
SFO. "Hvad Indenbære Satanismen ..." ["What does Satanism Entail?"]. 2006. http://forum.sataniskforum.dk/viewtopic.php?f=2&t=1482&hilit=laveys+sataniske+ritualer (accessed 30 November 2010).
SFO. "LaVey's Sataniske Ritualer" ["LaVey's Satanic Rituals"]. 2004. http://forum.sataniskforum.dk/viewtopic.php?f=3&t=886&hilit=laveys+sataniske+ritualer (accessed 30 November 2010).
SFO. "Ritual=Styrke" ["Ritual=Strength"]. 2005. http://forum.sataniskforum.dk/viewtopic.php?f=3&t=1185&p=8138&hilit=ritual%3Dstyrke#p8138 (accessed 30 November 2010).
SFO. "Vedtægter for Satanisk Forum" ["Bylaws for the Satanic Forum"]. 2006. www.sataniskforum.dk/content/view/240/64 (accessed 30 November 2010).
Shankbone, David. "Satanism: An Interview with Church of Satan High Priest Peter Gilmore". 2007. http://en.wikinews.org/wiki/Satanism:_An_interview_with_Church_of_Satan_High_Priest_Peter_Gilmore (accessed 13 October 2010).
Shaw, Gregory. "Theurgy: Rituals of Unification in the Neoplatonism of Iamblichus". *Traditio* 41 (1985): 1–28.
Shea, Robert & Robert Anton Wilson. *The Illuminatus! Trilogy*. London: Constable & Robinson, 1998 [1975].
Sherman, Chris. "Google Airs Scientology Infringement Demand". *Internetnews.com*, 15 April 2002. www.internetnews.com/bus-news/article.php/1009321/Google+Airs+Scientology+Infringement+Demand.htm (accessed 16 May 2012).
Sherwin, Ray. *The Book of Results*. Morrisville, NC: Lulu Press, 2005 [originally published by Morton Press, Yorkshire, 1978].
Sherwin, Ray. *The Theatre of Magick*. Morrisville, NC: Baphomet Publishing/Lulu Press, 2006 [originally published by Sorcerer's Apprentice Press, Leeds, 1982].
Shils, Edward. *Tradition*. London: Faber & Faber, 1981.
Shiner, Larry. "The Concept of Secularization in Empirical Research". *Journal for the Scientific Study of Religion* 5.2 (1967): 207–20.
Shiva, Frater. *Inside Solar Lodge/Outside the Law: True Tales of Initiation and High Adventure*. York Beach, ME: Teitan Press, 2007.
Shusterman, Richard. "Wittgenstein's Somaesthetics: Body Feeling in Philosophy of Mind, Art, and Ethics". *Revue Internationale de Philosophie* 219 (2002), 91–108.
Sidky, Homayun. "On the Antiquity of Shamanism and its Role in Human Religiosity". *Method and Theory in the Study of Religion* 22.1 (2010): 68–92.
Sieg, George. "Angular Momentum: From Traditional to Progressive Satanism in the Order of the Nine Angles". Unpublished article.
Simmel, Georg. "The Secret and the Secret Society". In Kurt Wolff (ed.), *The Sociology of Georg Simmel*, 305–76. New York: Free Press, 1950.

Simmel, Georg. "Über Sociale Differenzierung". In his *Gesamtausgabe*, vol. 2. Edited by Heinz-Jürgen Dahme. Frankfurt: Suhrkamp, 1989.
Simonis, Linda. *Die Kunst des Geheimen: Esoterische Kommunikation und Ästhetische Darstellung im 18. Jahrhundert*. Heidelberg: C. Winter, 2002.
Sinclair, Upton. *Mental Radio*. Introduction by W. MacDougall, preface by Albert Einstein. Monrovia, CA: self-published, 1930.
Singel, Ryan. "Wikipedia Bans Church of Scientology". *Wired*, 29 May 2009. www.wired.com/epicenter/2009/05/wikipedia-bans-church-of-scientology (accessed 16 May 2012).
Skinner, Quentin. *Visions of Politics: Regarding Method*. Vol. 1. Cambridge: Cambridge University Press, 2002.
Smart, Ninian. *Dimensions of the Sacred: An Anatomy of the World's Beliefs*. Berkeley, CA: University of California Press, 1998.
Smith, Bruce. *The Acoustic World of Early Modern England*. Chicago, IL: University of Chicago Press, 1999.
Smith, Sebastian. *Allah's Mountains: The Battle for Chechnya*. London: Tauris Parke Paperbacks, 2009.
Smith, Anthony Paul & Daniel Whistler (eds). *After the Postsecular and the Postmodern: New Essays in Continental Philosophy of Religion*. Newcastle upon Tyne: Cambridge Scholars Publishing, 2010.
Smoczynski, Rafal. "Cyber-Satanism and Imagined Satanism: Dark Symptoms of Late Modernity". In Petersen, *Contemporary Religious Satanism*, 141–53.
Søderlind, Didrik & Michael Moynihan. *Lords of Chaos: The Bloody Rise of the Satanic Metal Underground*. Venice, CA: Feral House, 1998.
Sohn, Dongyoung. *Social Network Structures and the Internet: Collective Dynamics in Virtual Communities*. Amherst, MA: Cambria Press, 2008.
Sørensen, Øystein. *Den Store Sammensvergelsen*. Oslo: Aschehoug, 2007.
Spaink, Karen. "The Fishman Affidavit". 1995. www.xs4all.nl/~kspaink/fishman/ot8b.html (accessed 20 December 2010).
Spalding, John. "Brood Indigo". 2003. www.beliefnet.com/Entertainment/Books/2003/03/Brood-Indigo.aspx (accessed 27 February 2011).
Specter, Michael. "TV Offers a Melodrama in Real Time". *New York Times*, 20 June 1995. www.nytimes.com/1995/06/20/world/tv-offers-a-melodrama-in-real-time.html?pagewanted=print&src=pm (accessed 9 June 2012).
Stahl, William A. "Religious Opposition to Globalization". In Beyer & Beaman, *Religion, Globalization, and Culture*, 335–53.
Stargate Wiki. "Ascension". http://stargate.wikia.com/wiki/Ascension (accessed 2 March 2011).
Stark, Rodney. "Secularization, RIP". *Sociology of Religion* 60.3 (1999): 249–73.
Stark, Rodney & William S. Bainbridge. *The Future of Religion: Secularization, Revival, and Cult Formation*. Berkeley, CA: University of California Press, 1985.
Stark, Rodney & William S. Bainbridge. *A Theory of Religion*. New Brunswick, NJ: Rutgers University Press, 1996.
Stark, Rodney, Laurence Iannaccone & Roger Finke. "Religion, Science, and Rationality". *The American Economic Review* 86.2 (1996): 433–7.
Starr, Martin. "Chaos from Order: Cohesion and Conflict in the Post-Crowley Occult Continuum". *The Pomegranate* 8.1 (2006): 84–117.
Stein, Diane. *Women's Psychic Lives*. St Paul, MN: Llewellyn, 1995.
Steiner, Rudolf. "Fall of the Spirits of Darkness, Lecture 13: The Fallen Spirits' Influence in the World". 1917. http://wn.rsarchive.org/Lectures/GA177/English/RSP1993/19171027p01.html (accessed 17 May 2012).
Steiner, Rudolf. *Secret Brotherhoods and the Mystery of the Human Double*. London: Rudolf Steiner Press, 2004.
Stern, Fritz R. *The Politics of Cultural Despair: A Study in the Rise of Germanic Ideology*. Berkeley, CA: University of California Press, 1974.
Steuco, Agostino. *De Perenni Philosophia Libri X*. Basle: Nicolaus Bryling & Sebastianus Francken, 1542 [1540].

Strenski, Ivan. *Four Theories of Myth in Twentieth-Century History: Cassirer, Eliade, Lévi-Strauss and Malinowski*. Basingstoke: Macmillan, 1987.

Strmiska, Michael. "Ásatrú in Iceland: The Rebirth of Nordic Paganism". *Nova Religio* 4.1 (2000): 106–32.

Strmiska, Michael F. & Baldur A. Sigurvinsson. "Asatru: Nordic Paganism in Iceland and America". In Michael F. Strmiska (ed.), *Modern Pagans in World Cultures: Comparative Perspectives*, 127–79. Santa Barbara, CA: ABC-CLIO, 2005.

Stubbs, David. "Clearing the Wreckage: Throbbing Gristle". *The Wire* 281 (2007): 30–37.

Styers, Randall. *Making Magic: Religion, Magic, and Science in the Modern World*. Oxford: Oxford University Press, 2004.

Subrahmanyam, Kaveri & Patricia Greenfield. "Online Communication and Adolescent Relationships". *The Future of Children* 18.1 (2008): 119–46.

Sullivan, Winnifred Fallers. "We Are All Religious Now. Again". *Social Research* 76.4 (2009): 1181–98.

Sünner, Rüdiger. *Schwarze Sonne: Entfesselung und Missbrauch der Mythen in Nationalsozialismus und Rechter Esoterik*. Freiburg: Herder, 2003.

Sutcliffe, Richard. "Left-Hand Path Ritual Magick: An Historical and Philosophical Overview". In Graham Harvey & Charlotte Hardman (eds), *Paganism Today. Wiccans, Druids, the Goddess and Ancient Earth: Traditions for the Twenty-First Century*, 109–37. London: Thorsons, 1996.

Sutcliffe, Steven J. *Children of the New Age: A History of Spiritual Practices*. London: Routledge, 2003.

Sutcliffe, Steven J. & Marion Bowman. "Introduction". In their *Beyond the New Age: Exploring Alternative Spirituality*, 1–13. Edinburgh: Edinburgh University Press, 2000.

Sutin, Lawrence. *Do What Thou Wilt: A Life of Aleister Crowley*. New York: St. Martin's Press, 2000.

Svanberg, Jan. *Schamantropologi: I Gränslandet Mellan Forskning och Praktik. En Studie av Förhållandet Mellan Schamanismforskning och Neoschamanism*. Åbo: Åbo Akademi University, 2003.

Svensk Hednisk Front. *Budkavlen* 1–5 (2001–2003).

Swatos, Jr., William H. & Daniel V. A. Olson (eds). *The Secularization Debate*. Lanham, MD: Rowman & Littlefield, 2000.

Symonds, John. *King of the Shadow Realm: Aleister Crowley, His Life and Magic*. London: Duckworth, 1989.

Tappe, Nancy Anne. *Understanding Your Life Thru Color: Metaphysical Concepts in Color and Aura*. Costa Mesa, CA: Starling Publishing, 1986.

Taussig, Michael. "Viscerality, Faith, and Skepticism: Another Theory of Magic". In Birgit Meyer & Peter Pels (eds), *Magic and Modernity: Interfaces of Revelation and Concealment*, 272–306. Stanford, CA: Stanford University Press, 2003.

Taves, Ann. *Religious Experience Reconsidered: A Building-Block Approach to the Study of Religion and Other Special Things*. Princeton, NJ: Princeton University Press, 2009.

Taylor, Bron. *Dark Green Religion: Nature Spirituality and the Planetary Future*. Ewing, CA: University of California Press, 2009.

Taylor, Bron. "Deep Ecology and Its Social Philosophy: A Critique". In Katz *et al.*, *Beneath the Surface*, 269–99.

Taylor, Bron. "Earth and Nature-Based Spirituality (Part II): From Earth First! And Bioregionalism to Scientific Paganism and the New Age". *Religion* 31.3 (2001): 225–45.

Taylor, Bron. "Ecological Resistance Movements: Not Always Deep But if Deep, Religious". *The Trumpeter: Journal of Ecosophy* 13.2 (1996). http://trumpeter.athabascau.ca/index.php/trumpet/article/view/261/387 (accessed 17 May 2012).

Taylor, Bron. "Evoking the Ecological Self". *Peace Review: The International Quarterly of World Peace* 5.2 (1993): 225–30.

Taylor, Charles. *A Secular Age*. Cambridge, MA: The Belknap Press of Harvard University Press, 2007.

Taylor, Charles. *Sources of the Self: The Making of Modern Identity*. Cambridge, MA: Harvard University Press, 1989.

Tefft, Stanton. *The Dialectics of Secret Society Power in States*. Atlanta, GA: Humanities Press, 1992.
Temple, Robert K. G. *The Sirius Mystery*. New York: St Martin's Press, 1975.
Tenbruck, Friedrich H. "Die Religion im Maelstrom der Reflexion". *Religion und Kultur: Sonderheft der Kölner Zeitschrift für Soziologie und Sozialpsychologie* 33 (1993): 31–67.
Thilman, Börje. "Suvuista ja Nimistä". In his *Suomalaisia Sukuja ja Sukunimiä: Joka Perheen Sukunimi- ja Sukututkimusopas*, 7–39. Kauniainen: Taidevakka, 1968. Excerpt at www.genealogia.fi/nimet/nimi98s.htm (accessed 12 April 2011).
Thomas, Keith. *Religion and the Decline of Magic: Studies in Popular Beliefs in Sixteenth and Seventeenth Century England*. Harmondsworth: Penguin, 1973.
Thompson, John B. "Tradition and Self in a Mediated World". In Heelas *et al.*, *Detraditionalization*, 89–108.
Thorson, Edred (Stephen Flowers). *Rune Might*. St Paul, MN: Llewellyn Publications, 1994.
Thule-Seminar. "Inhalt". www.thule-seminar.org/inhalt_referenz.htm (accessed 15 October 2010).
Tilak, Bal Gangadhar. *The Arctic Home in the Vedas: Being Also a New Key to the Interpretation of many Vedic Texts and Legends*. Poona City: Tilak Bros, 1903.
Tillet, Gregory. *The Elder Brother*. London: Routledge, 1982.
Tiryakian, Edward A. (ed.). *On the Margins of the Visible: Sociology, the Esoteric, and the Occult*. New York: John Wiley & Sons, 1974.
Tiryakian, Edward A. "Preliminary Considerations". In his *On the Margin of the Visible*, 1–15.
Tiryakian, Edward A. "Toward the Sociology of Esoteric Culture". In his *On the Margin of the Visible*, 257–80.
Tishkov, Valery. *Chechnya: Life in a War-Torn Society*. Berkeley, CA: University of California Press, 2004.
Tober, Jan. "Bio". www.jantober.com (accessed 15 February 2011).
Toffoletti, Kim. *Cyborgs and Barbie Dolls: Feminism, Popular Culture and the Posthuman Body*. London: I. B. Tauris, 2007.
Tomasi, Luigi (ed.). *Alternative Religions Among European Youth*. Aldershot: Ashgate, 1999.
Tönnies, Ferdinand. *Gemeinschaft und Gesellschaft*. Leipzig: Fues's Verlag, 1887.
TOPY. *Thee Grey Book*. www.kondole.com/theegreybook/greycover.htm (accessed 5 October 2010).
ToS. "Temple of Set". www.xeper.org (accessed 5 November 2010).
Trafton, Scott. *Egypt Land: Race and Nineteenth-Century American Egyptomania*. Durham, NC: Duke University Press, 2004.
Treitel, Corinna. *A Science for the Soul: Occultism and the Genesis of the German Modern*. Baltimore, MD: Johns Hopkins University Press, 2004.
Truzzi, Marcello. "Definitions and Dimensions of the Occult: Towards a Sociological Perspective". In Tiryakian, *On the Margin of the Visible*, 243–55.
Truzzi, Marcello. "The Occult Revival as Popular Culture: Some Random Observations on the Old and the Nouveau Witch". *The Sociological Quarterly* 13 (1972): 16–36.
Turner, Bryan S. "Religion in a Post-Secular Society". In Bryan S. Turner (ed.), *The New Blackwell Companion to the Sociology of Religion*, 649–67. Chichester: Blackwell, 2010.
Turner, Frank Miller. *Between Science and Religion: the Reaction to Scientific Naturalism in Late Victorian England*. New Haven, CT: Yale University Press, 1974.
Turner, Frank Miller. *Contesting Cultural Authority: Essays in Victorian Intellectual Life*. Cambridge: Cambridge University Press, 1993.
Twyman, James. "Movies". 2009. www.jamestwyman.com/Movies_Indigo.html (accessed 24 June 2009).
Tyr. "Titles". www.radicaltraditionalist.com/titles.htm (accessed 15 October 2010).
Tyr. "Tyr". www.radicaltraditionalist.com/tyr.htm (accessed 15 October 2010).
Urban, Hugh B. *The Church of Scientology: A History of the World's Most Controversial New Religion*. Princeton, NJ: Princeton University Press, 2011.
Urban, Hugh B. "Fair Game: Secrecy, Security and the Church of Scientology in Cold War America". *Journal of the American Academy of Religion* 74.2 (2006): 356–89.
Urban, Hugh B. *Magia Sexualis: Sex, Magic, and Liberation in Modern Western Esotericism*. Los Angeles, CA: University of California Press, 2006.

Urban, Hugh B. "The Occult Roots of Scientology? L. Ron Hubbard, Aleister Crowley, the Origins of a Controversial New Religion". *Nova Religio* 15.3 (2012): 91–116.
Urban, Hugh B. "Secrecy in New Religious Movements: Concealment, Secrecy and Privacy in a New Age of Information". *Religion Compass* 2.1 (2008): 66–83.
Urban, Hugh B. *Tantra: Sex, Secrecy, Politics, and Power in the Study of Religion*. Los Angeles, CA: University of California Press, 2003.
Vail, Charles H. *The Ancient Mysteries and Modern Masonry*. New York: Macoy Publishing & Masonic Supply Co., 1909.
Vale, V. (ed.). *RE/Search 4/5: William S. Burroughs, Brion Gysin and Throbbing Gristle*. San Francisco, CA: RE/Search Publications, 2007.
Valliere, Paul. "Tradition". In Jones, *Encyclopedia of Religion*, 9267–81.
Vásquez, Manuel A. *More than Belief: A Materialist Theory of Religion*. New York: Oxford University Press, 2011.
Vera, Diane. "Theistic Satanism: The New Satanisms of the Era of the Internet". http://theisticsatanism.com (accessed 27 November 2010).
Versluis, Arthur. *Magic and Mysticism: An Introduction to Western Esotericism*. Lanham, MD: Rowman & Littlefield, 2007.
Virtue, Doreen. "About Doreen Virtue". www.angeltherapy.com/about.php (accessed 16 February 2011).
Virtue, Doreen. *The Care and Feeding of Indigo Children*. Carlsbad, CA: Hay House, 2001.
von Stuckrad, Kocku (ed.). *The Brill Dictionary of Religion*. Leiden: Brill, 2005.
von Stuckrad, Kocku. "Constructions, Normativities, Identities: Recent Studies on Shamanism and Neo-Shamanism". *Religious Studies Review* 31.3–4 (2005): 123–8.
von Stuckrad, Kocku. "Discursive Study of Religion: From States of the Mind to Communication and Action". *Method and Theory in the Study of Religion* 15.3 (2003): 255–71.
von Stuckrad, Kocku. *Locations of Knowledge in Medieval and Early Modern Europe: Esoteric Discourse and Western Identities*. Leiden: Brill, 2010.
von Stuckrad, Kocku. "Reenchanting Nature: Modern Western Shamanism and Nineteenth-Century Thought". *Journal of the American Academy of Religion* 70.4 (2002): 771–99.
von Stuckrad, Kocku. "Reflections on the Limits of Reflection: An Invitation to Discursive Study of Religion". *Method and Theory in the Study of Religion* 22.2–3 (2010): 156–69.
von Stuckrad, Kocku. "Rewriting the Book of Nature: Kabbalah and the Metaphors of Contemporary Life-Sciences". *Journal for the Study of Religion, Nature, and Culture* 2.4 (2008): 419–42.
von Stuckrad, Kocku. *Schamanismus und Esoterik: Kultur- und Wissenschaftsgeschichtliche Betrachtungen*. Leuven: Peeters, 2003.
von Stuckrad, Kocku. "Secrecy as Social Capital". In Kilcher, *Constructing Tradition*, 239–52.
von Stuckrad, Kocku. *Western Esotericism: A Brief History of Secret Knowledge*. London: Equinox, 2005.
von Stuckrad, Kocku. "Western Esotericism: Towards an Integrative Model of Interpretation". *Religion* 35.2 (2005): 78–97.
von Stuckrad, Kocku. *"Zo zijn we niet Getrouwd": Religie, Natuurwetenschap en de Radicalisering van de Moderniteit*. Inaugural Lecture for the Chair of Religious Studies, University of Groningen. Groningen: Faculteit Godgeleerdheid en Godsdienstwetenschap, 2010.
Wade, Nicholas. "Researchers Say They Created a 'Synthetic Cell'". *The New York Times*, 20 May 2010. www.nytimes.com/2010/05/21/science/21cell.html?ref=science (accessed 16 May 2012).
Waite, A. E. *Shadows of Life and Thought: A Retrospective Review in the Form of Memoires, etc.* London: Selwyn & Blount, 1938.
Wallis, Roy (ed.). *On the Margins of Science: The Social Construction of Rejected Knowledge*. Keele: University of Keele, 1979.
Wallis, Roy. *The Road to Total Freedom: A Sociological Analysis of Scientology*. New York: Columbia University Press, 1976.
Wallis, Roy. "Science and Pseudo-Science". *Social Science Information* 24.3 (1985): 585–601.
Ward, James. *Naturalism and Agnosticism*. 2 vols. London: Adam & Charles Black, 1906 [1899].
Warner, Michael. *The Letters of the Republic*. Cambridge, MA: Harvard University Press, 1990.

Wasserstrom, Steven M. *Religion After Religion: Gershom Scholem, Mircea Eliade, and Henry Corbin at Eranos*. Princeton, NJ: Princeton University Press, 1999.
Wasson, R. Gordon. "Seeking the Magic Mushroom". *Life*, 13 May 1957.
Watson, Don. "Beyond Evil: Genesis P-Orridge". *The Wire* 182 (1999): 30–35.
Webb, James. *The Occult Establishment*. La Salle, IL: Open Court Publishing Company, 1976.
Webb, James. *The Occult Underground*. La Salle, IL: Open Court Publishing Company, 1974.
Weber, Max. "Science as a Vocation". In H. H. Gerth & Charles Wright Mills (eds), *From Max Weber: Essays in Sociology*, 129–56. New York: Oxford University Press, 1946.
Weber, Max. *Wirtschaft und Gesellschaft*. 5th ed. Edited by Johannes Winckelmann. Tübingen: J. C. B. Mohr (Paul Siebeck), 1972.
Wegener, Franz. *Alfred Schuler, der Letzte Deutsche Katharer*. Gladbeck: KFVR, 2003.
Wegener, Franz. *Das Atlantidische Weltbild: Nationalsozialismus und Neue Rechte auf der Suche Nach der Versunkenen Atlantis*. Gladbeck: KFVR, 2003.
Weissmann, Karlheinz. *Männerbund*. Schnellroda: Edition Antaios, 2004.
Welsing, Frances Cress. "Interviews with Dr Cress Welsing". www.africawithin.com/welsing/welsing_interview.htm (accessed 3 November 2010).
Welsing, Frances Cress. *The Isis Papers: The Keys to the Colors*. Chicago, IL: CW Publishing, 1991.
Whedon, Sarah. "The Wisdom of Indigo Children". *Nova Religio* 12.3 (2009): 60–76.
Whimster, Sam (ed.). *The Essential Weber: A Reader*. London: Routledge, 2004.
White, Hayden. *Metahistory: The Historical Imagination in Nineteenth-Century Europe*. Baltimore, MD: Johns Hopkins University Press, 1973.
White, Lynn Townsend Jr. "The Historical Roots of Our Ecological Crisis". *Science* 155.3767 (1967): 1203–7.
Whitehead, Harriet. *Renunciation and Reformulation: A Study of Conversion in an American Sect*. Ithaca, NY: Cornell University Press, 1987.
Wikander, Stig. *Der Arische Männerbund: Studien zur Indo-Iranischen Sprach- und Religionsgeschichte*. Lund: Håkan Ohlssons Buchdruckerei, 1938.
Wilber, Ken. "The Atman Project". In William Bloom (ed.), *Holistic Revolution: The Essential New Age Reader*, 77–83. Harmondsworth: Allen Lane, 2000.
Wilber, Ken. *A Brief History of Everything*. Boston, MA: Shambhala, 2001.
Wilber, Ken. *Sex, Ecology, and Spirituality: The Spirit of Evolution*. Boston, MA: Shambhala, 2001.
Wilde, Julian. *The Grimoire of Chaos Magick*. http://into-thedarkness.tripod.com/sitebuilder content/sitebuilderfiles/thegrimoireofchaosmagick.pdf (accessed 7 December 2010) [originally published by Sorcerer's Apprentice Press, Leeds, 1986].
Williams, Brian Glyn. "Shattering The Al-Qaeda–Chechen Myth (Part II)". *Chechnya Weekly*, 4.40 (2003). www.brianglynwilliams.com/shattered_ll.pdf (accessed 9 June 2012).
Williams, Loretta J. *Black Freemasonry and Middle-Class Realities*. Columbia, MO: University of Missouri Press, 1980.
Williams, Raymond. "Culture is Ordinary". In Jim McGuigan & Ann Gray (eds), *Studying Culture: An Introductory Reader*, 5–14. London: Arnold, 1993.
Willis, Martin. *Mesmerists, Monsters, and Machines: Science Fiction and the Cultures of Science in the Nineteenth Century*. Kent, OH: Kent State University Press, 2006.
Wilson, Bryan. *The Social Dimensions of Sectarianism: Sects and New Religious Movements in Contemporary Society*. Oxford: Clarendon Press, 1990.
Wind, Edgar, *Pagan Mysteries in the Renaissance*. New York: W. W. Norton, 1958.
Winkelman, Michael. "Shamanism: An Overview [Further Considerations]". In Jones, *Encyclopedia of Religion*, 8274–80.
Wirth, Herman. *Der Aufgang der Menschheit: Untersuchungen zur Geschichte der Religion, Symbolik und Schrift der Atlantisch-Nordischen Rasse*. Jena: E. Diederichs, 1928.
Wiseman, Richard & Caroline Watt. "Belief in Psychic Ability and the Misattribution Thesis". *British Journal of Psychology* 12.5 (2006): 1–17.
Wisnicki, Adrian S. *Conspiracy, Revolution, and Terrorism from Victorian Fiction to the Modern Novel*. London: Routledge, 2008.
Witoszek, Nina & Andrew Brennan (eds). *Philosophical Dialogues: Arne Naess and the Progress of Ecophilosophy*. Lanham, MD: Rowman & Littlefield, 1999.

Wolf. "Danskproblemer" ["Language Problems"]. 2007. http://forum.sataniskforum.dk/viewtopic.php?f=15&t=1573&hilit=danskproblemer (accessed 30 November 2010).
Wolf. "Nye Retningslinjer" ["New Guidelines"]. 2005. http://forum.sataniskforum.dk/viewtopic.php?f=15&t=1225 (accessed 30 November 2010).
Wolffram, Heather. *The Stepchildren of Science: Psychical Research and Parapsychology in Germany, c. 1870–1939*. Amsterdam: Editions Rodopi, 2009.
Wolffram, Heather. "Supernormal Biology: Vitalism, Parapsychology and the German Crisis of Modernity, c. 1890–1933". *The European Legacy* 8.2 (2003): 149–63.
Wolfson, Elliot R. *Language, Eros, Being: Kabbalistic Hermeneutics and Poetic Imagination*. New York: Fordham University Press, 2005.
Wood, Earnest. *Clairvoyant Investigations by C. W. Leadbeater and 'The Lives of Alcyone' (J. Krishnamurti): Some Facts Described*. Adyar: Theosophical Publishing House, 1947.
Woodhead, Linda & Paul Heelas. "Detraditionalization: Introduction". In their *Religion in Modern Times*, 342–46.
Woodhead, Linda & Paul Heelas (eds). *Religion in Modern Times: An Interpretative Anthology*. Oxford: Blackwell, 2000.
Woodhead, Linda & Paul Heelas. "Secularization: Introduction". In their *Religion in Modern Times*, 307–8.
Woodhead, Linda & Paul Heelas. *The Spiritual Revolution: Why Religion is Giving Way to Spirituality*. Oxford: Blackwell, 2005.
Woodhead, Linda, Paul Fletcher, Hiroko Kawanami & Paul Smith (eds). *Religions in the Modern World: Traditions and Transformations*. London: Routledge, 2002.
Wu Song, Felicia. *Virtual Communities: Bowling Alone, Online Together*. New York: Peter Lang, 2009.
Wyllie, Timothy. *Love, Sex, Fear, Death: The Inside Story of the Process Church of the Final Judgment*. Edited by Adam Parfray. Port Townsend, WA: Feral House, 2009.
Wyndham, John. *The Chrysalids*. London: Michael Joseph, 1955.
Yates, Frances. *Giordano Bruno and the Hermetic Tradition*. London: Routledge & Kegan Paul, 1964.
Yates, Frances. *The Occult Philosophy in the Elizabethan Age*. London: Ark, 1983.
Yates, Simeon J. "Researching Internet Interaction: Sociolinguistics and Corpus Analysis". In Margaret Wetherell, Stephanie Taylor & Simeon J. Yates (eds), *Discourse as Data: A Guide for Analysis*, 93–146. London: Sage, 2001.
Yockey, Francis Parker. *Imperium: The Philosophy of History and Politics*. Newport Beach, CA: Noontide Press, 2000.
York, Michael. *The Emerging Network: A Sociology of the New Age and Neo-Pagan Movements*. London: Rowman & Littlefield, 1995.
Zandbergen, Dorien. "Silicon Valley New Age: The Co-constitution of the Digital and the Sacred". In Aupers & Houtman, *Religions of Modernity*, 161–85.
Zander, Helmut. *Anthroposophie in Deutschland: Theosophische Weltanschauung und gesellschafliche Praxis 1884–1945*. Göttingen: Vandenhoek & Ruprecht, 2007.
Zimmerman, Michael E. *Contesting Earth's Future: Radical Ecology and Postmodernity*. Berkeley, CA: University of California Press, 1994.
Znamenski, Andrei A. *The Beauty of the Primitive: Shamanism and the Western Imagination*. Oxford: Oxford University Press, 2007.

DISCOGRAPHY

Fyrdung. *Hyperborea*. Nordiska Förlaget, 2007.
Marilyn Manson. *Mechanical Animals*. Interscope, 1998.
Nas. *God's Son*. Ill Will Records, 2002.
Richard Hell and the Voidoids. *Blank Generation*. Sire, 1977.
Throbbing Gristle. *In the Shadow of the Sun*. Illuminate Records, 1984.

FILMOGRAPHY

500 Years Later. Directed by Owen 'Alik Shahadah. Codeblack Entertainment, 2005.
Angel Heart. Directed by Alan Parker. TriStar Pictures, 1987.
Avatar. Directed by James Cameron. 20th Century Fox, 2009.
Baby Boy. Directed by John Singleton. Columbia Pictures, 2001.
Charmed. 178 episodes. Spelling Television, 1998–2006.
Contact. Directed by Robert Zemeckis. Warner Bros, 1997.
Da Vinci Code, The. Directed by Ron Howard. Columbia Pictures, 2006.
H. R. Pufnstuf. 17 episodes, NBC, 1969.
Immortal Fortress: A Look Inside Chechnya's Warrior Culture. Directed by Dodge Billingsley. Combat Films & Research, 2005.
In the Shadow of the Sun. Directed by Derek Jarman. Dark Pictures, 1980.
Indigo. Directed by Stephen Simon. Monterey Studio, 2005.
Indigo Evolution. Directed by Kent Romney & James Twyman. Emmisary Productions, 2006.
Last Mimzy, The. Directed by Robert Shaye. New Line Cinema, 2007.
Matrix, The. Directed by Andy Wachowski & Larry Wachowski. Warner Bros, 1999.
Ninth Gate, The. Directed by Roman Polanski. Artisan Entertainment, 1999.
Paranormal Activity. Directed by Oren Peli. Paramount Pictures, 2007.
Rosemary's Baby. Directed by Roman Polanski. Paramount Pictures, 1968.
Sixth Sense, The. Directed by M. Night Shyamalan. Hollywood Pictures, 1999.
South Park. "Trapped in the Closet". Series 9, episode 12. Comedy Central, 2005.
Stargate. Directed by Roland Emmerich. Metro-Goldwyn-Mayer, 1994.
Stargate Atlantis. "Hide and Seek". Series 1, episode 3. Metro-Goldwyn-Mayer, 2004.
Stargate Atlantis. "Tao of Rodney". Series 3, episode 14. Metro-Goldwyn-Mayer, 2006.
Stargate SG-1. "Abyss". Series 6, episode 6. Metro-Goldwyn-Mayer, 2002.
Stargate SG-1. "Full Circle". Series 6, episode 22. Metro-Goldwyn-Mayer, 2003.
Stargate SG-1. "Maternal Instinct". Series 3, episode 20. Metro-Goldwyn-Mayer, 2000.
Stargate SG-1. "Meridian". Series 5, episode 21. Metro-Goldwyn-Mayer, 2002.
Stargate SG-1. "Prototype". Series 9, episode 9. Metro-Goldwyn-Mayer, 2005.
Star Trek (original series). "Plato's Stepchildren". Series 3, episode 10 (production no. 67). Paramount Television, 1968.
Star Trek: Deep Space Nine. 176 episodes. Paramount Television, 1993–1999.
Wicker Man, The. Directed by Robin Hardy. British Lion Films, 1973.

INDEX

2012 (millenarianism) 355, 403, 407
9/11 199, 265, 408

Abrahamsson, C. 131
ADHD/ADD (diagnoses) 19, 353, 357, 359–61, 363
Adorno, T. 250
aestheticization 15, 234
Afrocentrism 8, 51–2, 61
 and esoteric theories of race 65–9
agency 10, 14, 172, 201–7, 209, 212, 214, 217, 220
 agency panic 223–4
 agency recovery 224
Agrippa, H. C. 35, 79
Ahnenerbe 252
Albanese, C. 292n
alchemy 14, 37, 104, 121, 233, 321, 404
Alexa Web Information Database 144, 146–7
Altered States of Consciousness (ASC) 168–9, 375, 375, 392, 407
Ancient Mystical Order Rosae Crucis (AMORC) 31, 46, 57
Anderson, B. 149, 231
Anderson, Lorie 368
Andreae, Johann Valentin 5, 45
Angel Heart (film) 116
Annunaki 218
Anonymous (hacker group) 13, 195–7
anthropocentrism 289, 297–9, 303
Anthroposophy 201, 203–4
Aquino, Michael 73, 87n, 137, 142
archaic revival 403, 406
Ariosophy 244–5, 254–5
Asante, Molefi Kente 8, 59, 61–3, 67, 69–70
Asclepius 405

astral plane 12–3, 160–64, 166, 168, 171, 178, 180, 282
astral travel 159, 164–9, 176, 179–80
 cyberastral travel 160–61, 168, 176, 178–80
 geo-temporal and symbolic types 164–7
astrology 14, 37, 121, 233, 245, 321, 335–6, 385
atheism 18, 21, 53, 228, 333–5
 "new atheism" 18, 333–4
Atlantis 15, 57, 210–1, 244, 246, 253, 326
Augustine 34
Aupers, S. 115, 170, 178–9
auras 19, 354–6, 364–6, 381, 385
Avatar (movie) 18, 325, 327–328

Babalon Working, the 184–5
baby boomers (generation) 19, 115, 353, 369–70
Bainbridge, William Sims 102, 372–3, 377–9, 383, 386–90
Barkun, Michael 199, 202, 222
Barton, Blanche 73, 81–2, 84, 86
Basayev, Shamil 16, 265–86
Baudelaire, Charles 86
Benoist, Alain de 247, 251n, 253, 256, 258–9, 261, 264
Berger, Helen 116
Berger, Peter L. 310, 330–3, 335
Bergson, Henri 341, 404
Beslan school hostage crisis 16, 286
Bilderberg group 216
Black Mass 76, 83, 86
Blavatsky, Helena Petrovna 57, 74, 85, 164–5, 184
Bloom, William 399

463

Bogart, Raymond   75n
Bohm, David   291
boundary-work   138, 343
Bowie, David   127n
Bowman, Marion   17
brainwashing   194, 212, 223
Breaking Open the Head (book)   407
Breyer, Jacqueline   128–9
Brotherhood of Satan   88
Brown, Dan   123, 250–51
Brown, Michael F.   170–71, 414–15
Bruno, Giordano   5, 262, 404
Buddhism   29, 47, 168, 176, 183, 194, 212, 291, 298, 326n, 327, 384
Bulwer-Lytton, Edward   46, 89
Burning Man   408
Burroughs, William S.   95, 125, 127, 129, 197–8, 402

Cagliostro, Alessandro di (Giuseppe Balsamo)   79, 83, 208
Calleja, Gordon   172
Campbell, Colin   11, 102, 117–9, 122, 132, 134, 203, 332
Campbell, Heidi   154
Campbell, Joseph   42, 46, 260n, 404
capitalism   29, 122, 246–7, 263–4
Capra, Fritjof   17, 291, 300, 396–8, 400
Carducci, Giosuè   86
Carrington, Hereward   349
Carroll, Lee   354, 356, 361–3, 365–6, 371
Carroll, Peter   91, 94n, 95–6, 98, 100, 102–105
Carson, Rachel   290, 298
Castaneda, Carlos   40–41, 401–2
Castren, Matias Aleksanteri   40
Catholicism   16, 34, 118, 230, 233, 281, 312, 313–14, 337
Cayce, Edgar   160
Charmed (TV series)   323
Chechen Wars   16, 267n, 27n
Church of Deep Ecology   292
Church of Satan   8, 76–6, 78, 80–90, 136–7, 139–46, 152, 157, 203
   Church of Satan, The (book)   82
CIA   182, 217
Coale, Samuel Chase   216, 218
Codreanu, Corneliu   262
Coelho, Paulo   16, 265–9, 272–3, 275–7, 282–6
Cold War   13, 182, 187–8, 192, 217, 267n
commodity fetishism   48
communitarization   15, 230–32
community, imagined   101
computer programming   13, 179
Conan Doyle, Arthur   341, 348

conspiracy culture   200–03, 208, 212, 216–17, 223
conspiracy theory   14, 81, 200–04, 207, 209–10, 212, 216
   as esoteric discourse   220–25
Contact (film)   116
Corbin, Henry   42–3, 260
core shamanism   41, 402
Corpus Hermeticum   405
Corrigan, John   164
CosmiKids   367–8
cosmotheism   406, 409
Council of All Beings   17, 291, 307
Council on Foreign Relations   216
Covenstead   176, 179
cover-up   216, 222
Cowan, Douglas   170–71
critical thinking   77, 333, 339–40
Crowley, Aleister   78, 87n, 91, 94–6, 102, 103–4, 106, 109–11, 130–31, 160, 168–9, 254
Cruise, Tom   181, 195–6
Crystalline Children   19, 364
Cthonian orientation   138
cultic milieu   11, 117–22, 203, 246, 259, 231–2, 403
Current 93   130
Cusack, Carol   203n
cut-up method   127–30, 133
cybercovens   13, 170–71, 176–8
cyber-ritual   177–8
cyberspace   10, 139, 160–61, 170–71, 173, 177, 180, 182, 192–8, 408

Dashwood, Francis   81
Da Vinci Code, The (book and film)   117, 123, 250
Davis, Erik   160, 171, 180
Dawson, Lorne L.   170
de Naglowska, Maria   75
Dede, Chris   174
Dee, John   5, 79, 87n, 104, 162
Deep Ecology   16–17, 287–308, 331n
Deep Ecology for the 21st Century (book)   295, 297
Deep Ecology Manifesto/Eight Points   290–91, 301
Deep Ecology Movement   288–9, 290n, 291, 302, 305
Deep Ecology: Living as if Nature Mattered (book)   290
Denzin, Norman   151
Descartes, René   163
desecularization *see* secularization
de-territorialization / re-territorialization   135, 137, 141, 149

detraditionalization 25, 28–30, 323, 348
Devall, Bill 290, 296–7
Devi, Savitri 251, 254–5
deviance 11, 20–21, 117, 138, 260, 321, 332, 376, 378, 387, 411
    and "the occult" 5
    and mainstreaming 17, 332, 373
Devil's Notebook, The (book) 73
Dianetics 187–8
Die Elektrischen Vorspiele 80
Discordianism 14, 95–6, 201, 203
    and conspiracy theory 210–12, 217, 222
discussion boards/forums 150–51, 171–2
disenchantment 18–19, 92, 239*n*, 256–7, 261, 264, 322–3, 330
    and the academy 332–5, 348–50
    as intellectual problem 341–2
    and re-enchantment 330–34, 344–8
Dixon, Joy 414–5
diZerega, Gus 17, 292
DMT (psychoactive substance) 397
Dogon 66–7
double-self / astral double 164
Dragon Rouge 44, 85*n*
Drengson, Alan 290, 296–7
Drury, Nevill 138, 399
dualism (Cartesian) 163, 178, 376
dualism (cosmological) 257, 264, 406
    and monism/holism 301–2, 304
Dugin, Alexandr 248–9, 253–4

Earth Angels 19, 364
easternization 114, 117
Eco, Umberto 250
ecocentrism 291, 295–301, 303, 306–8
eco-philosophy 287, 290, 294, 302
ecosophy 289–90, 297, 302, 307
    Ecosophy T (Naess) 291, 302–305
Egypt (as imagined orient) 8, 31, 84, 319, 325–6
Eliade, Mircea 4, 39*n*, 40–3, 105, 257, 260, 404
embodiment 164, 171, 179–80, 184
Emery, Florence Farr 166
emotion, sociology of religious 20, 379–81, 384, 386, 390
Enlightenment, the 15–16, 18, 23, 35–6, 92–4, 121, 230, 234–5, 256, 260–61, 314, 321–2, 344, 361, 393, 404
Enochian (angelic language) 79, 87
entheogens 20, 392–408
epistemology 213, 303, 413
    of conspiracy theory 221–2
    and gender 417, 421–3
Eranos circle 38*n*, 39*n*, 42–3, 46, 259–60, 404
Esalen 404
esoteric Hitlerism 251

esoteric, popularization of the 11, 29, 309
esoterrorism 124–5, 129–31, 133, 203*n*, 211, 223
Eurasianism / Eurasian Movement 16, 246, 248–9, 253–4, 263
European Society for the Study of Western Esotericism (ESSWE) 32, 44, 113
Evola, Julius 42, 245–6, 248, 253, 255
Extra-sensory Perception (book) 340, 349
Extra-sensory perception (ESP) 335–8, 340–41, 344, 349, 398
Ezzy, Douglas 116

Facebook 137, 139, 144–5, 158, 196, 324
Faivre, Antoine 2*n*, 5, 10–1, 23, 43–4, 79, 98–9, 345*n*, 373–4, 382–4, 421
Farr, Florence *see* Emery, Florence Farr
Farrar, Janet and Stewart 168
Faye, Guillaume 247
FBI 13, 182, 188, 190–2, 262*n*
femininity 21, 416–17, 419
Fichte, Johann Gottlieb 244
Ficino, Marsilio 5, 33, 35, 99
Fight Against Coerce Tactics Network (FACTNet) 193
Flowers, Stephen 137, 143, 147, 254
fluoridation 217
fnords 210–12
Fort, Charles 82
Fortean Society 82
Foster, Derek 149
Fox, Warwick 290, 295, 302
Franklin, Benjamin 81, 250
Fraternitas Saturni 75
freemasonry 8, 35–6, 46, 50, 52, 56–7, 59, 70, 104, 182, 250
    esoteric freemasonry 35, 169
    Prince Hall Masonry 53–5, 69

Gaia Hypothesis 17, 291
Galilei, Galileo 82, 83*n*, 239
Gardner, Gerald B. 88, 168, 416
gender 20–21, 162, 172–3, 180, 379, 411–25
    as critical category 411–12
    esoteric gender essentialism 416–18
    identities 21, 128, 414, 416–24
    and sex magic 413–14, 421
Generation X 115
Generation Y 115
gestalt ontology 302–3, 305–6
Gibbons, B. J. 121
Gilbert, Alan D. 120
Gilmore, Peter H. 73, 87, 140–42, 148
Ginsberg, Allen 402
Glasser, Harold 292*n*, 296*n*
globalization 114, 323, 386, 388, 390

465

gnosis 13, 20, 115, 182, 198, 212, 222, 321, 326, 373, 375, 377, 385–7, 390, 406–9
  see also higher knowledge
Goode, Erich 339
Goodrick-Clarke, Nicholas 3–4, 37–8, 121, 246, 251
Google 137, 195, 197, 316
gothic fiction 118, 121, 348
Grand Polemical Narrative 16, 201–2, 246, 258–61, 263, 387
Granholm, Kennet 101, 228, 300
green historicism 298
Grey Book, Thee 95, 126
Grof, Stanislav 401
Gruppo di Ur 245
Guardian of the Threshold 89
Guénon, René 42, 99, 245, 248
Gysin, Brion 95, 127–9

Habermas, Jürgen 118n, 149n, 236, 317–19, 321, 324
hacktivism 13, 197
Hall, Julie 163
Hammer, Olav 6n, 25, 31, 72, 84, 90, 92, 97–8, 158, 221, 232, 299, 322, 368, 373
Hanegraaff, Wouter J. 5, 16, 26, 33n, 34–5, 38, 43–4, 92, 94, 98–9, 101, 163, 168, 203, 259–61, 294, 300, 321–3, 328, 334n, 344–5, 351, 374–5, 385–7, 389, 413, 415
Hardinge Britten, Emma 46
Harner, Michael 41, 401–2
Harris, Sam 18, 21, 333–4
Harva-Holmberg, Uno 40
Harvey, Graham 88–9
Heelas, Paul 28–30, 310, 398
Hegarty, Diane 73
Hell-Fire Club 81
Herder, Johann Gottfried von 244
Hermes 31, 33, 35
Hermetic Order of the Golden Dawn 31, 37, 46, 80, 93, 104, 109–10, 126, 159–60, 162, 164, 166, 168–9, 182, 416
Hermeticism 37, 104
hieros gamos 123
higher knowledge 20, 31, 35, 111, 205, 215, 287, 292, 297–8, 300, 302, 305, 307, 321, 326, 345, 373, 376, 387
Hill, Ciaran Scott 174
Hine, Phil 95, 102–7
Hjarvard, Stig 123
Hobsbawm, Eric 25, 30–31, 39
Hofmann, Albert 400
holotropic breathing 401
Hörbiger, Hans 79n
House of Kheperu 130
Houtman, Dick 115

Hubbard, L. Ron 31, 46, 182–9, 191–2, 194, 198
Human Genome Project 15, 239–40
human sacrifice 78, 214
Hunke, Sigrid 257, 261–2, 264
Huxley, Aldous 17, 34n, 87, 99, 298, 400
Huxley, Thomas Henry 346
Huysmans, J.-K. 86
hybrid texts 135, 150–51, 153, 156–8, 266
hypertext 143, 150

Iamblichus 393
I Ching 77
Icke, David 14, 212–19
Iconoclasm 98–100, 102, 111, 112
Illuminati (as conspiracy theme) 14, 79–80, 86–7, 104, 200, 210–11, 217–18
Illuminatus! Trilogy, The (books) 203, 210–12, 217
Indigo children 19, 21, 351–71
Ingalls, Margaret 159, 176
Inglehart, Ronald 114
invisible war 207–8
Islam 27, 62, 70–71, 109, 116, 213, 235n, 265–6, 280–81
  Islamism 16, 265–6, 271, 285
Issue Crawler 145

Jagose, Annamarie 423–4
James, George G. M. 8, 55–9, 70
James, William 341, 343
Jarman, Derek 125n, 126
Jediism 46
Jenkins, Simon 175–6
Jolly, Karen L. 120
Joy of Satan 137, 142, 144–6
Joy, Morny 415, 420
Jubilee (film) 126
Judge, William Quan 164–5
Jung, Carl Gustav 42, 50, 63, 106, 260n, 404

Kabbalah 37, 64, 163, 239, 314n, 393
  Christian Kabbalah 29, 239
  and occultism 37, 64
Kadosh, Ben (Carl William Hansen) 75
Kalevala 40
Kaplan, Jeffrey 11, 117–19, 122
Karenga, Maulana 8, 59–67
Karlsson, Thomas 44
Katz, Eric 290, 296, 306–8
Kennedy, John F. 213–14, 216, 398n
Knights Templar 76, 78, 80, 84, 104, 244, 261
Krebs, Pierre 247, 253
Kripal, Jeffrey 415
Krishnamurti, Jiddu 165
Kryon 361–2

Là-Bas (Huysmans) 86
LaVey, Anton Szandor 8–9, 14, 72–90, 136–42, 152–4, 203, 207–10, 222, 224
La Voisin (Catherine Monvoisin) 81
Leadbeater, Charles Webster 159, 162, 164–6, 180, 355–6
Leary, Timothy 400, 402
Left-Hand Path 84, 89, 91*n*, 138–9, 142, 144–7
Leonardo (da Vinci) 82
Leopold, Aldo 289, 298
Lévi, Eliphas 37, 106
Lewis, James R. 25, 31, 72, 90, 398
Liebenfels, Jorg Lanz von 244
Life Colours 354, 364
lifeworld 118*n*
Light, Andrew 290
Lincoln, Bruce 32
List, Guido von 8, 244
Lodge, Oliver 347–8
Lönnrot, Elias 40
Lööw, H. 11, 117–19, 122
Losey, Meg Blackburn 353*n*, 364–6
Louv, Jason 131
Lovecraft, H. P. 46, 80*n*, 87–8
LSD 76, 396–8, 400–01
Lucas, George 46
Lynch, Frederick R. 169, 324

MacWilliams, Mark 157
Macy, Joanna 17, 291
magic 2–3, 5*n*, 9, 21–2, 35, 37, 44, 76–7, 93–5, 100, 102–13, 117, 128, 165, 182, 184, 187, 224, 233, 260, 331, 394, 406, 418–19, 422
  black magic 186, 208–9
  in cyberspace 169–70, 177–8
  psychologisation of 94, 106
  in the Renaissance 2, 120–21, 162, 239, 313
  rune magic 254
  sex magic 413–14, 421
Magnus, A. 79
Männerbünde 258, 264
Manson, Charles 118
Manson, Marilyn 128
Manual of the Warrior of Light (book) 16, 265–6, 268–9, 272–4, 277–8, 280, 282–3, 285–6
Markham, Annette 134
Marrs, Jim 14, 212–13, 216–19
masculinity 21, 54, 416, 418, 420–22, 424
Mathews, Chris 141
Matrix, The (film) 46–7, 408
Matrixism 46–7
Matthews, Robert Jay 262
Maudsley, Henry 346

McCain, G. 126*n*
McDougall, William 341, 343–4, 347
McKenna, Terence 403–7
McNeil, L. 126*n*
McSherry, Lisa 171
mediatization 11–12, 18, 123, 135, 228, 323
melanin 8
Melton, J. Gordon 186, 398
Merciless, R. 86
mescalin 397
mind control 131, 214, 217
mindfuck 211, 223
Mirandola, Pico della 79, 262
mock religion 203, 210
Moonbase Temple 159, 178
Morrison, Grant 9
Moses 31, 33, 35, 54–5
Moynihan, Michael 247, 254
Murray, Craig D. 172–3, 177, 179
Myers, Frederic 343–4, 346–7
mysticism 37, 101, 116, 249, 303*n*, 330, 333, 397, 406, 415–16, 421

Naess, Arne 288–91, 296, 301–8
Naglowska, Maria de 75
Nation of Islam 59–60
native Americans 31, 42, 162*n*, 402, 408
naturalization 340, 344, 346, 349
nature 21, 207, 222, 238–41, 261, 290–93, 296, 298, 326, 346–7, 404, 406–7, 416–7, 419–422
Nazism, Nazis 118, 217, 244–5, 249, 251, 253*n*
Necronomicon (fictional book) 87
Nema, Sorror *see* Ingalls, Margaret
neopaganism 1*n*, 3, 8, 13, 22, 41*n*, 88–9, 116, 160, 168, 176, 184, 203, 233, 292, 300–01, 304, 308, 331, 413, 415–16, 421
  Germanic 39
  and right-wing politics 246, 248, 255–8, 261–3
Neoplatonism 161, 163, 393
neurology 107, 174, 398
New Age 1, 5, 16–7, 19–20, 70, 84–5, 99, 101, 153, 160, 168–70, 176, 191–2, 199, 232–3, 260, 264, 300–01, 343, 374–5, 385–6, 389
  and anti-psychiatry 360
  and children 351–3, 355–7, 360–70
  and conspiracy theory 213–15, 217
  and entheogens 396–409
  and jihad 265–9, 276–9
  and radical environmentalism 291–2, 300–01
New Age Religion and Western Culture (book) 344, 351, 396

467

New Right (movement) 16, 246–9, 253–60, 264
New Thought Movement 355, 371, 398
Newton, Isaac 14, 298, 303, 321
New World Order, NWO 211, 216
Nintendo Wii 174
Ninth Gate, The (film) 123
NocTifer 139, 142, 145, 147
Nocturnum, Corvis 139–41, 148
normative derivation 291, 307*n*

occult revival 113, 168, 332, 342
occult science 93, 414, 422
occultism 9, 31, 36–7, 46, 91–97, 99, 102–12, 117, 123–4, 132–4, 159–60, 168, 180, 182, 207, 235–6, 251, 254, 260, 331, 341–5, 348, 374, 413
  and Scientology 184–8, 194
occulture 11, 14, 19, 101–2, 139, 141, 148, 202–3, 221–4, 250*n*, 287*n*, 352, 400, 422
  ordinaryness of 113–33
Olcott, Henry 89
Olsson, Tord 150
O'Meara, Michael 247
ontological guerrilla 222
Operating Thetan (OT) 188–90, 192–5, 197–8
Order of the Golden Dawn *see* Hermetic Order of the Golden Dawn
Order of the Nine Angles 88
Order of the Vampyre 130
Ordo Templi Orientis 79–80, 104, 131, 148, 168–9, 184, 188, 200
Orwell, George 87
Otherkin 418–19
Our Beautiful Silent Ones 364
Our Lady of Endor Coven 75*n*
Owen, Alex 342, 415

pagan studies 1, 4, 22
Pandrogyny Project 128–9
Paracelsus (Philippus Aureolus Theophrastus Bombastus von Hohenheim) 5, 79, 163, 321
paraculture 333, 349
paradigm shift 297, 299–300, 307, 348
Paranormal Activity (film) 116
paranormal 18–19, 116, 327, 330, 333–41, 343–4, 348–50, 368
parapsychology (discipline) 18–19, 21, 333–8, 340–44, 347–9, 398
Parsons, John Whiteside 184–8
Partridge, Christopher 11, 17, 23–4, 45, 95, 101–2, 169, 202–3, 223, 287*n*, 324, 331–2, 348, 398, 400
Pauwels, Louis 251

PCCR (Post-Secular Culture and Changing Religious Landscape in Finland, research project) 319–20
Pentecostalism 85, 393
perennial philosophy / *philosophia perennis* 7, 9, 17, 26, 33–8, 43–4, 50, 83–5, 93, 98–102, 104, 109–12, 245, 293, 297–9, 383
Perennial Philosophy, The (book; A. Huxley) 17, 99, 298
performance speech 151
Pesce, Mark 160, 171–2
Petersen, Jesper Aagaard 12, 209
phenomenology 4, 42, 173, 302, 305
Pigliucci, Massimo 338–9
Pinchbeck, Daniel 407
Plethon, Gemistos 33
Plotinus 404
Polanski, Roman 123
popular culture 6, 8–12, 14–19, 22–3, 26, 45–7, 67, 115–17, 122–4, 130, 133, 136, 139, 181, 223, 232, 235, 250, 309, 323–4, 327–9, 332, 348–9
P-Orridge, Genesis 11, 95, 124–33, 424*n*
Porter, Roy 121
possession 121, 336*n*, 337, 339, 422
post-secular 18, 21, 309, 316–20, 321, 372
post-secular esotericism 322–3
Prensky, Marc 174
Principia Discordia (pamphlet) 96, 203, 210
prisca theologia 33–5, 38, 98–9
Process Church of the Final Judgment 75, 130
professionalization 1–2, 15, 232, 340–42, 346–8
Project Chanology 196
Protestantism 20, 24, 35, 256, 260–61, 312, 337, 393
Protocols of the Learned Elders of Zion 218
Przybyszewski, Stanislaw 74
pseudoscience 338
psilocybin 398, 401–2
psychedelics 76, 392, 396–401, 407
psychical research 340–49
Psychick Bible, Thee 131
Psychic TV (band) 95, 124, 130–31, 133
psychodrama 78, 81, 90
psychologization 94, 106–7, 322, 345, 374, 387, 389
psychotechnologies 400
public activation 15, 230, 233, 236–7, 334, 349
public sphere 197*n*, 227, 231–2, 236–7, 242, 311, 317, 319–21, 324
Puttick, Elizabeth 123, 419

queer theory 21, 418, 422–4
Quimby, Phineas Parkhurst 355

Rabelais, François 82
race / racialism 8, 29, 39, 51–3, 60, 65–9, 71,
    118, 126, 162, 173, 180, 244, 251, 341,
    411, 417, 419
Radde-Antweiler, Kerstin 175–6
Raelian Movement 130
Ranger, Terence 30
Rasputin, Grigori Yefimovich 83, 208, 245
rave culture 400, 403
Ravenscroft, Trevor 251–2
Redbeard, Ragnar 73
Reformation (Protestant) 23, 34–6, 45, 255,
    312–14
Reghini, Arturo 245
reiki 90, 139, 362, 381, 385
rejected knowledge 20, 23, 35, 44, 118, 134,
    203, 215, 373, 376, 387–8, 390
reptilians (aliens) 214–15
Rhine, Joseph Banks 341, 344, 349
Riis, Ole 372–3, 377, 379–80, 386, 389–90
rising on the planes *see* astral travel
Roberts, Jane 397–8, 400, 419
Romanticism 39, 114, 121
Rosemary's Baby (film) 116
Rosicrucianism 5, 31–2, 35, 37, 45–6, 50,
    56–7, 79, 104, 404
    Rosenkreutz, Christian 45–6
    Rosicrucian manifestos 5, 32, 45–6
Rothenberg, David 290
Rubin, Rick 128*n*
Rule by Secrecy (book) 216, 218
Rune Guild 254

Sabina, Maria 402
sacralization 19, 21, 116, 224, 231, 332, 379, 390
Satanas, Venus 139–41, 143, 145–6, 148, 158
Satanic Bible, the (LaVey) 73, 77, 79–80, 86,
    137, 153, 207
Satanisk Forum 142, 147, 151–2, 154–7
Satanism (modern religion) 8–9, 74–90, 134,
    201, 208–9
    esoteric Satanism(s) 75, 138, 152
    rationalist Satanism(s) 138, 152
    reactive Satanism(s) 138
    satanic milieu 136–58
Satan Speaks! (LaVey) 73, 81
Schreck, Nikolas and Zeena 89
science fiction 18, 46, 184, 187, 309, 325–9,
    348, 349, 355
scientification 15, 230, 232–4, 242, 334, 348
scientific naturalism 342, 346
scientism (discursive strategy) 209, 222, 345
scientism (ideology) 248, 334, 342
Scientology 13, 46, 144, 147, 181–99, 314*n*
    Church of Scientology 13, 181–3, 185–7,
    190–92, 194–8

Second Life (virtual reality) 13, 160–1, 172–3,
    175–80
secrecy 13, 14, 36, 56, 104, 111, 182–3,
    187–90, 192, 194, 197–9, 220–22, 224,
    321, 376, 399–400
    and conspiracy theory 198, 217, 220
*Secret Brotherhoods and the Mystery of the
    Human Double* (book) 205
Secret Doctrine, The (book) 57, 74
Secret Life of a Satanist, The (book) 73, 81
secularism (ideology) 18, 227–9, 237, 309,
    314, 320, 334
Secularization (theory) 15, 18, 27*n*, 28, 92,
    116, 224, 261, 309–15, 377–8
    critique of secularization theory 227–9, 315
    desecularization 311, 330–32, 335
    on different levels 311, 314
    as disappearance of religion 310, 311–12
    and disenchantment 334
    and individualization 311, 312
    secularized esotericism 92–3, 203, 322,
    334, 340, 344, 374
    secularization paradigm 15, 18, 309–10
    as social differentiation 310
Sedgbeer, Sandra 360
Seed, John 17, 291
self-realization 287*n*, 302–3, 305–6, 308
semiotic arousal 221
Serrano, Miguel 251
Sessions, George 17, 290, 292, 295–301,
    304–8
Set (Egyptian god) 89, 138, 397
sexuality / sexualisation 121, 126, 411–16, 423
shamanism 7, 20, 26–7, 96, 100, 102–5, 108,
    110, 233, 301
    construction of 38–43
    and entheogens 400–3, 406–7
Shea, Robert 210
Sherwin, Ray 91, 93–6, 102–4
Siberia 40, 401–2
Sidgwick, Henry 343
sigils 9, 95, 103, 107, 159
    Sigil of Baphomet 80, 187*n*
Simmel, Georg 14, 183, 189, 198, 230
Simpson, Elaine 166
Sixsmith, Judith 172–3, 177, 179
Sixth Sense, The (film) 116, 352
Sloane, Herbert 75*n*
Smith, Joseph 85, 184
Smith, Patti 127*n*
Societé des Luciferiens 86
Society for Psychical Research (SPR) 342–4,
    346
    American SPR (ASPR) 341
Solar Lodge 169
South Park (TV series) 189, 197

Spalding, John 353, 369–70
Spare, Austin Osman 91, 94–6, 103–4, 106–7
Spiritualism (movement) 92*n*, 162–3, 341–9, 414–16, 421, 423
Stargate (movie and TV series) 18, 325–7
Star Kids 19, 353*n*, 364
Star Trek (TV series) 88, 325
Stark, Rodney 102, 335*n*, 372–3, 377–9, 383, 386–90
Steiner, Rudolf 14, 89, 203–6, 209, 214, 222
Steuco, Agostino 34
Stuckrad, Kocku von 3, 15, 23–4, 100, 111, 221, 292–4, 300, 313, 321, 349, 374–7, 386–7, 390, 401
subjectivization 99, 115
supernatural beliefs 5, 331, 336
Sutcliffe, Steven 17
Suzuki, D. T. 404
Swedenborg, Emmanuel 162

Tappe, Nancy Ann 19, 354–6, 361, 364–6, 371
tarot 77, 123, 166–7, 187*n*
Taylor, Bron 294*n*, 295
Taylor, Charles 231, 236, 316–17
Teachings of Don Juan (book) 41, 401
telepathy 19, 326, 335–8, 340, 344, 347, 363
Temple of Set 85*n*, 130, 137, 142–6, 254
Temple ov Psychick Youth (TOPY) 95, 126, 130–33
Thee Majesty 124
Thelema (religion) 97, 82, 110–11, 139, 158
Theosophy 50, 75, 79, 101, 116, 169, 233, 253, 355–6, 371, 385, 414–16, 421
    Theosophical Society 37, 74–5, 109, 159, 163–4, 168–9, 233, 355*n*
theurgy 393
Thomas, Keith 120
Thornley, Kerry 96, 212
thought control 214, 216
Throbbing Gristle 124
Thule Society 8, 244, 252–3
Tibet 31, 84
Tibet, David 130
Tober, Jan 354, 356, 361, 363, 365–6, 371
tradition (construction of) 7–9, 25–48, 72–6, 88–91, 92–102, 111–12, 261–3
    role of scholars 38–45
Traditionalism 42, 245, 248–9, 251
    Radical Traditionalism 16, 246–7
Travolta, John 181
Trilateral Commission 216–17
Truzzi, Marcello 5, 44
Twyman, James 363, 368
Tyr (journal) 247, 254

UFO 130, 169, 216
Unarius 130
Ur-Fascism 250

vaccines/anti-vaccination 204–6, 214, 223
Vera, Diane 137, 142, 145–6, 148
Vial, Pierre 247
Virtual Reality Modeling Language (VRML) 171
virtual reality 135, 149, 160, 172–3, 180, 407
Virtue, Doreen 358–9, 361–3, 369, 371
vitalism 341, 347
völkisch movement 231, 244, 247–8, 252, 254–5

Waite, Arthur Edward 37
Wallis, Roy 186, 188, 348
war on drugs 20, 394
Wasson, R. Gordon 402
Watson, Don 125
Weber, Max 230, 263, 310, 330–32, 344, 380
Weißmann, Karlheinz 247
Wells, H.G. 87
Welsing, Frances Cress 8, 65–8
Whedon, Sarah 351, 355, 359
White, Lynn 298
Wicca 17, 88, 116, 123, 168, 292, 301, 304, 323, 328, 416
Wicker Man, The (film) 116
Wikileaks 13, 197*n*
Wilber, Ken 17, 291
Wiligut, Karl Maria von 245, 254
Williams, Raymond 119, 121–3, 132
Wilson, Robert Anton 210
Wirth, Hermann 252, 254
Wood, Earnest 166
Woodhead, Linda 28, 310, 372–3, 377, 379–80, 386, 389–90
World of Warcraft (computer game) 172

Xenu 189, 193–4, 197

Yage Letters (book) 402
Yates, Frances 36, 250, 260, 262, 404, 406
Yeats, Willam Butler 87
Yezidi 78, 84–5
Yockey, Francis Parker 262
YouTube 14, 139, 144, 147, 195–7, 328
Yronwode, Nagasiva *see* NocTifer

Zandbergen, Dorien 407
Zanoni (novel) 46
Zener cards 349
Znamenski, Andrei 41, 401
Zoroaster 31, 33, 35